International Handbooks on Information Systems

Series Editors

Peter Bernus, Jacek Błażewicz, Günter Schmidt, Michael Shaw

Titles in the Series

T.C. Edwin Cheng • Tsan-Ming Choi (Eds.)

Innovative Quick Response Programs in Logistics and Supply Chain Management

 Springer

Editors

Professor T.C. Edwin Cheng
The Hong Kong Polytechnic University
Department of Logistics
and Maritime Studies
Hung Hom, Kowloon
Hong Kong SAR
edwin.cheng@inet.polyu.edu.hk

Professor Tsan-Ming Choi
The Hong Kong Polytechnic University
Business Division
Institute of Textiles and Clothing
Faculty of Applied Science and Textiles
Hung Hom, Kowloon
Hong Kong SAR
jason.choi@inet.polyu.edu.hk

ISBN 978-3-642-04312-3   e-ISBN 978-3-642-04313-0
DOI: 10.1007/978-3-642-04313-0
Springer Heidelberg Dordrecht London New York

Library of Congress Control Number: 2010920283

Cover design: SPi Publisher Services

Printed on acid-free paper

Springer is part of Springer Science+Business Media (www.springer.com)

Preface

Quick response (QR) policy is a market-driven business strategy under which supply chain channel members work together to react to volatile market demand. Traditionally, QR involves the use of information technologies such as EDI and bar-coding systems. The fundamental tenet of QR is to respond quickly to market changes and cut ordering lead times. QR was first established in the 1980s in the apparel industry in USA. In the 1990s, with advances in technology and the development of many supply chain theories (such as the Bullwhip Effect and the importance of information), QR became a very hot topic. Nowadays, with further advances in information technologies (such as RFID and ERP systems) and other scientific areas (such as 3D body scanning technologies and material sciences), challenges and opportunities arise for the application of QR. As a result, we believe that it is crucial and timely that QR be extensively and deeply explored with a view of discovering innovative QR measures that can help tackle the observed and emerging challenges.

With the aforementioned view, we have co-edited this Springer handbook. This handbook contains four parts that cover introductory materials to innovative QR, modelling and analysis of QR programmes, enabling technologies for innovative QR programmes, and applications and case studies. The specific topics covered include the following:
- The evolution of QR
- Impacts of information systems on QR
- Fast fashion as a means for achieving global QR
- Procurement flexibility under price uncertainty
- The value of information in QR supply chains
- Improving revenue management via a real option approach
- Supply chain scheduling under QR
- Dynamic pricing of seasonal product
- Supplier selection in make-to-order manufacturing supply chain
- Enhancing responsiveness for mass customization strategies
- Innovative process in e-commerce fashion supply chains
- The next generation demand network in QR systems
- RFID's applications in QR
- ERP systems for the textiles and clothing industry
- Simulation-based optimization of inventory model with products substitution

– Methods for quantifying benefits for fast fashion
– A case study on hybrid assemble-to-order/make-to-order electronics manufacturing
– QR practices in the Hong Kong apparel industry
– Cases in China on efficient response systems with RFID technology
– Fast fashion business model for Chinese fabric manufacturers
– Innovative mass customization in the fashion industry
– A case study on improving inventory allocation under QR

We are pleased to see that this handbook contains new analytical and empirical results with valuable insights, which will not only help supply chain agents to better understand the latest applications of QR in business, but also help practitioners and researchers to know how to improve the effectiveness of QR based on innovative methods. This is especially meaningful to industries such as fashion apparels, in which many companies have not fully understood the critical features of QR, and there is a lack of innovative ideas to cope with the associated challenges.

We take this opportunity to thank Dr. Werner A. Mueller for his support and advice throughout the course of this project. We are grateful to all the authors who have contributed their interesting research to this handbook. We are indebted to the reviewers who reviewed the submitted papers and provided us with timely comments. We also acknowledge the funding support of The Hong Kong Polytechnic University under grant number of J-BB6U. Last but not least, we are grateful to our families, colleagues, and students, who have been graciously supporting us during the development of this handbook.

The Hong Kong Polytechnic University   *T.C.E. Cheng, Tsan-Ming Choi*

Contents

Part III   Enabling Technologies for QR Programmes

Part IV   Applications and Case Studies

Contributors

Jeff Barker School of Information Technology, Bond University, Gold Coast, QLD 4229, Australia, jbarker@bond.edu.au

Margaret Bruce Marketing, International Business and Strategy Division, Manchester Business School, Booth Street West, Manchester, M15 6PB, UK, margaret.bruce@mbs.ac.uk

Jimmy Chang Institute of Textiles and Clothing, The Hong Kong Polytechnic University, Hunghom, Kowloon, Hong Kong, tcchangj@inet.polyu.edu.hk

Bintong Chen Department of Civil and Environmental Engineering, University of Delaware, Newark, DE 19716, USA, bchen@udel.edu

Frank Y. Chen Department of SEEM, The Chinese University of Hong Kong, Shatin, N.T., Hong Kong, yhchen@se.cuhk.edu.hk

Shuang Chen Institute of Systems Engineering, Huazhong University of Science and Technology, Wuhan 430074, P.R. China, chenshuang@smail.hust.edu.cn

T.C.E. Cheng Department of Logistics and Maritime Studies, Faculty of Business, The Hong Kong Polytechnic University, Hung Hom, Kowloon, Hong Kong, lgtcheng@polyu.edu.hk

Wai-Ki Ching The Advanced Modeling and Applied Computing Laboratory and Department of Mathematics, The University of Hong Kong, Pokfulam Road, Hong Kong, wching@hkusua.hku.hk

Chun-Hung Chiu Business Division, Institute of Textiles and Clothing, Faculty of Applied Science and Textiles, The Hong Kong Polytechnic University, Hung Hom, Kowloon, Hong Kong, chchiu2000@gmail.com

Tsan-Ming Choi Business Division, Institute of Textiles and Clothing, Faculty of Applied Science and Textiles, The Hong Kong Polytechnic University, Hung Hom, Kowloon, Hong Kong, tcjason@inet.polyu.edu.hk

Pui-Sze Chow Business Division, Institute of Textiles and Clothing, Faculty of Applied Science and Textiles, The Hong Kong Polytechnic University, Hung Hom, Kowloon, Hong Kong, linda.chow@polyu.edu.hk

Lucy Daly Centre for Engagement, Manchester Business School, Booth Street West, Manchester, M15 6PB, UK, ldaly@mbs.ac.uk

Tej S. Dhakar Department of Quantitative Studies and Operations Management, School of Business, Southern New Hampshire University, 2500 North River Road, Manchester, NH 03106-1045, USA, t.dhakar@snhu.edu

Qing Ding Lee Kong Chian School of Business, Singapore Management University, Singapore 178899, Singapore, dingqing@smu.edu.sg

Matthew J. Drake Palumbo-Donahue Schools of Business, Duquesne University, 925 Rockwell Hall, 600 Forbes Avenue, Pittsburgh, PA 15282-0180, USA, drake987@duq.edu

Daniel Eyers Innovative Manufacturing Research Centre, Cardiff University, Aberconway Building, Cardiff CF10 3EU, Wales, UK, eyersdr@cf.ac.uk

Cheng Cheng Fan School of Economics and Management, Beihang University, 37 Xueyuan Road, Haidian District, Beijing 100191, China

Qi Feng McCombs School of Business, The University of Texas at Austin, Austin, TX, USA, annabelle.feng@mccombs.utexas.edu

Gavin Finnie School of Information Technology, Bond University, Gold Coast, QLD 4229, Australia, gfinnie@bond.edu.au

Warren H. Hausman Department of Management Science and Engineering, Stanford University, Stanford, CA 94305, USA, hausman@stanford.edu

Di Huang School of Economics and Management, Beihang University, 37 Xueyuan Road, Haidian District, Beijing 100191, China

Patrick C.L. Hui Institute of Textiles and Clothing, Faculty of Applied Science and Textiles, The Hong Kong Polytechnic University, Hung Hom, Kowloon, Hong Kong, tchuip@inet.polyu.edu.hk

P.G.S.A Jayarathne Nottingham University Business School, The University of Nottingham, Jubilee Campus, Nottingham, NG8 1BB, UK, lixpgj@nottingham.ac.uk

Kenneth Kong SUGA International Holding Ltd, Units 1904-1907, 19/F, Chevalier Commercial Centre, 8 Wang Hoi Road, Kowloon Bay, Kowloon, Hong Kong

Carl A. Lawrence Institute for Material Research, The University of Leeds, Clarendon Road, Leeds, West Yorkshire, LS2 9JT, UK, c.a.lawrence@leeds.ac.uk

Mark Lee Department of SEEM, The Chinese University of Hong Kong, Shatin, N.T., Hong Kong

Xiang Li Research Center of Logistics, College of Economic and Social Development, Nankai University, Tianjin 300071, P.R. China, xiangli@mail.nankai.edu.cn

Xun Li Department of Applied Mathematics, The Hong Kong Polytechnic University, Kowloon, Hong Kong, malixun@inet.polyu.edu.hk

Yongjian Li Business School, Nankai University, Tianjin 300071, P.R. China, liyongjian@nankai.edu.cn

Na Liu Institute of Textiles and Clothing, Faculty of Applied Science and Textiles, The Hong Kong Polytechnic University, Hung Hom, Kowloon, Hong Kong, 08900900r@polyu.edu.hk

Shuk-Ching Liu Business Division, Institute of Textiles and Clothing, Faculty of Applied Science and Textiles, The Hong Kong Polytechnic University, Hung Hom, Kowloon, Hong Kong, ching_0608@hotmail.com

Bart L. MacCarthy Nottingham University Business School, The University of Nottingham, Jubilee Campus, Nottingham, NG8 1BB, UK, bart.maccarthy@nottingham.ac.uk

Kathryn A. Marley Palumbo-Donahue Schools of Business, Duquesne University, 470 Rockwell Hall, 600 Forbes Avenue, Pittsburgh, PA 15282-0180, USA, marleyk@duq.edu

David M. Miller Department of Information Systems, Statistics, and Management Science, Culverhouse College of Commerce, University of Alabama, Tuscaloosa, Al 35487-0223, USA, dmiller@cba.ua.edu

Samar K. Mukhopadhyay SungKyunKwan University – GSB, Jongno gu, Seoul 110-745, Korea, samar@skku.edu

Chi Ho Ng SUGA International Holding Ltd, Units 1904-1907, 19/F, Chevalier Commercial Centre, 8 Wang Hoi Road, Kowloon Bay, Kowloon, Hong Kong

Jennie Hope Peterson Institute of Textiles and Clothing, The Hong Kong Polytechnic University, Hunghom, Kowloon, Hong Kong, jhopepeterson@yahoo.com

Charles P. Schmidt Department of Information Systems, Statistics, and Management Science, Culverhouse College of Commerce, University of Alabama, Tuscaloosa, AL 35487-0223, USA, cschmidt@cba.ua.edu

Robert Setaputra John L. Grove College of Business, Shippensburg University, 1871 Old Main Drive, Shippensburg, PA 17257, USA, rsseta@ship.edu

Suresh P. Sethi School of Management, The University of Texas at Dallas, Richardson, TX, USA, sethi@utexas.edu

Tak Kuen Siu Department of Mathematics and Statistics, Curtin University of Technology, Perth, W.A. 6845, Australia, T.Siu@curtin.edu.au

John S. Thorbeck Chainge Capital, 15060 NW Dominion Drive, Portland, OR 97229, USA

Zhongjun Tian School of International Business Administration, Shanghai University of Finance and Economics, 777 Guoding Road, Shanghai 200433, China, tian.zhongjun@mail.shufe.edu.cn

Thuhang Tran Department of Management and Marketing, Jennings Jones College of Business, Middle Tennessee State University, MTSU Box 449, Murfreesboro, TN 37132, USA, ttran@mtsu.edu

Kidith Tse Institute of Textiles and Clothing, Faculty of Applied Science and Textiles, The Hong Kong Polytechnic University, Hung Hom, Kowloon, Hong Kong, kidith.tse@gmail.com

Hajnalka Vaagen Molde University College, P.O. Box 2110, NO-6402 Molde, Norway, hajnalka.vaagen@himolde.no

Stein W. Wallace Department of Management Science, Lancaster University Management School, Lancaster University, Lancaster, LA1 4YX, UK, Stein.W. Wallace@lancaster.ac.uk

Hongwei Wang Institute of Systems Engineering, Huazhong University of Science and Technology, Wuhan 430074, P.R. China, hwwang@mail.hust.edu.cn

Ying Wei Université catholique de Louvain, CORE, Voie du Roman Pays 34, 1348 Louvain-la-Neuve, Belgium and Department of SEEM, The Chinese University of Hong Kong, Shatin, N.T., Hong Kong, ying.wei@uclouvain.be

Hartanto Wong Innovative Manufacturing Research Centre, Cardiff University, Aberconway Building, Cardiff CF10 3EU, Wales, UK, wongh@Cardiff.ac.uk

Yiu-Hing Wong Institute of Textiles and Clothing, The Hong Kong Polytechnic University, Hunghom, Kowloon, Hong Kong, msyhwong@inet.polyu.edu.hk

Zhenyu Wu Department of Finance and Management Science, N. Murray Edwards School of Business, University of Saskatchewan, Saskatoon, Saskatchewan, SK, Canada S7N 5A7, wu@edwards.usask.ca

Yu Xia Department of Management and Marketing, Jennings Jones College of Business, Middle Tennessee State University, MTSU Box 441, Murfreesboro, TN 37132, USA, axia@mtsu.edu

Yong Xie Institute of Systems Engineering, Huazhong University of Science and Technology, Wuhan 430074, PR China

Houmin Yan Department of SEEM, The Chinese University of Hong Kong, Shatin, N.T., Hong Kong, yan@se.cuhk.edu.hk

Dongqing Yao Department of E-Business and Technology Management, Towson University, 8000 York Road, Towson, MD 21252, USA, dyao@towson.edu

Ho-Ting Yeung Business Division, Institute of Textiles and Clothing, Faculty of Applied Science and Textiles, The Hong Kong Polytechnic University, Hung Hom, Kowloon, Hong Kong, tina_yeung@ymail.com

Jinfeng Yue Department of Management and Marketing, Jennings Jones College of Business, Middle Tennessee State University, MTSU Box 75, Murfreesboro, TN 37132, USA, jyue@mtsu.edu

Xiaohang Yue Shelbon B. Lubar School of Business, University of Wisconsin – Milwaukee, P.O. Box 742, Milwaukee, WI 53201, USA, xyue@uwm.edu

Qiu Hong Zhao School of Economics and Management, Beihang University, 37 Xueyuan Road, Haidian District, Beijing 100191, China, qhzhao@buaa.edu.cn

Xiaowei Zhu College of Business and Public Affairs, West Chester University of Pennsylvania, West Chester, PA 19383, USA, xzhu@wcupa.edu

Part I
Introduction

The Evolution of Quick Response Programs

Matthew J. Drake and Kathryn A. Marley

Abstract In companies' constant quest to find ways to maintain or improve customer service levels while simultaneously reducing their investment in inventory, apparel companies in the mid-1980s focused on the problem of long lead times between product design and availability in retail stores. They developed the strategy of quick response (QR) to shorten this lead time and to create a supply chain that was more responsive to customers' demand for fashion items. In this chapter we define QR programs, discuss the origins of these programs in the apparel industry, and compare QR with subsequently developed methods of inventory control widely used across industries.

Keywords History of Quick Response · lead time reduction · apparel industry

1 Introduction

The Toyota Production System and the broader lean philosophy that has grown out of it since its introduction to the Western business world are widely recognized as pillars of world-class operations. Both of these programs emphasize the elimination of all forms of waste in internal operations as well as in the supply chain to allow the system to match supply with customer demand, giving them the moniker of "just-in-time" systems. Without such a system in place, many companies use inventory to manage the supply–demand mismatch. In addition to being a costly use of company funds, inventory has potentially the more harmful negative consequence of masking the source of a firm's operational problems. By addressing these sources of waste, firms and supply chains in general are able to maintain or even improve product availability for customers with lower inventory levels. Attempts to

M.J. Drake (✉)
Palumbo and Donahue Schools of Business, Duquesne University, Pittsburgh
PA 15282-0180, USA
e-mail: drake987@duq.edu

T.C. Edwin Cheng and T.-M. Choi (eds.), *Innovative Quick Response Programs in Logistics and Supply Chain Management*, International Handbooks on Information Systems, DOI 10.1007/978-3-642-04313-0_1,

implement a just-in-time system without first removing or reducing the sources of waste can be disastrous.

One of the major forms of waste that induces many firms to maintain excess inventory levels is supply chain lead time, also known as *cumulative lead time* (Comber 2008). Cumulative lead time includes the value-added production time where components are made and assembled into finished goods, the waiting time within the process where these components must wait for resources to work on them, and the transportation and storage time between company-owned and external locations within the supply chain. For many products, the transportation time can actually be the most significant component of cumulative lead time. This is especially true for companies in the United States or Europe who source products or components from suppliers in China and Southeast Asia. Without the use of high-cost air transportation, which may not even be feasible for all types of products and materials, the minimum time to receive a shipment of goods from a foreign supplier is about three weeks via an ocean-going vessel. Depending on the destination of the shipment relative to the domestic port, internal transit of the shipment by a rail or trucking carrier can add another ten days to the lead time.

Consider the example of Leed's, a medium-sized firm located in western Pennsylvania that provides business products such as pens, portfolios, bags, and mugs customized with company or organization logos and slogans. Leed's imports most of its blank products (e.g., pens, portfolios, etc.) from foreign suppliers all over Asia, yet the company is committed to providing its customers with short lead times for the customized orders. In fact, approximately one-third of the catalog products are eligible for next-day shipment; if the logo design is received by a certain time, the customized shipment is guaranteed to ship during the next business day. The rest of the items in the catalog can be customized and shipped within three or four days.

Obviously, Leed's does not have the ability to wait until customers place their orders to acquire the blank products from its foreign vendors. The long lead time requires Leed's to import large quantities of blanks far in advance of demand and store them in a warehouse for several months until they are requested by customers.[1] This process allows the company to maintain extremely high customer service levels and customer satisfaction, but it comes with the cost of holding and storing large amounts of inventory far in advance of demand. As networks of suppliers and customers have expanded around the world in the past three decades, more and more companies have looked for innovative ways to manage these long lead times effectively.

In the mid-1980s the textile and apparel industry in the United States, beset by extreme foreign competition, hired consulting firm Kurt Salmon Associates to analyze its industry supply chain and identify opportunities for firms to improve their competitive position. This study illuminated the extremely long cumulative lead

---

[1] In fact, Leed's operates a bonded warehouse so that it can avoid paying the import duties on the blank products all at once at the time of import. The bonded warehouse allows Leed's to incur the duty expense at the time at which the individual items are extracted from the facility to fill a customer's order.

time that existed in apparel supply chains and led to the development of the strategy of quick response (QR). Fisher and Raman (1996) describe QR as a general strategy designed to reduce manufacturing and distribution lead times of apparel goods. They acknowledge that a vast array of methods exist to reduce these lead times, including the deployment of information technology, improved logistics operations, and advanced manufacturing techniques. Under a QR program, suppliers, manufacturers, and retailers work together to improve the responsiveness of the entire system to the ultimate needs of the customer (Lummus and Vokurka 1999). In the subsequent two-plus decades, the principles of QR that lead to supply chain integration and lead time reduction have been implemented in other industries and have become the cornerstones of other innovative supply chain coordination programs and activities. The remainder of this chapter discusses the origins of QR in the apparel industry, the underlying principles of the strategy, and the evolution of QR into similar programs with more far-reaching goals and objectives.

2 The Development of QR in the Apparel Industry

The Kurt Salmon Associates study of the apparel supply chain led to the development of the QR strategy in the mid-1980s. Several specific characteristics of the apparel industry suggested that these firms could benefit the most from a reduction in the cumulative lead time for providing goods for customers. The apparel supply chain is largely fragmented with various layers of fiber producers, raw textile manufacturers, apparel manufacturers, and retailers; each of these members of the channel has important activities to perform in the production of a seasonal apparel assortment, and materials must pass sequentially from the upstream members downstream for processing. All of these processing and transportation operations can take a great deal of time. The Salmon study estimated the length of the average supply chain for apparel to be 66 weeks, of which only 6–17% represented actual production time. Opportunities existed across this fragmented supply chain to reduce the flow time from the raw textile to the retail level (Hammond 1990).

A 66-week lead time means that retailers must plan their apparel assortment approximately one and a quarter years before the items are expected to appear in a store. Regardless of the nature of the product, demand forecasts produced for time periods so far into the future are subject to large errors because the opportunity exists for a number of exogenous variables to affect the demand process. Forecasts produced for time periods in the near future are likely more accurate because there is less of an opportunity for the demand process to be affected by these exogenous variables.

Of course, the same phenomenon holds true in industries other than apparel. Leed's, for instance, struggles with the same issues of forecast inaccuracy and is willing to compensate for this difficulty by carrying extra inventory. Leed's blank products, however, have a reasonably long shelf life because portfolio, mug, and pen styles do not change significantly from season to season or even from year to year. So other than the cost of carrying the excess inventory, Leed's does not necessarily realize a large cost of inventory obsolescence from carrying the extra units to accommodate the long supply lead time.

The apparel industry, on the other hand, has several defined sales seasons throughout the year, and these seasons vary greatly from year to year. Because of this fast clockspeed of products in the apparel industry, the framework of a traditional apparel supply chain with its long cumulative lead time affords retailers and manufacturers only one opportunity to make stocking decisions within a given selling season. As a result, many researchers have used the newsvendor framework to model stocking decisions in this industry (e.g., Gallego and Moon 1993; Lee 2007). The optimal decision in the newsvendor framework balances two competing costs in this single-period stocking problem. If the retail firm orders too many units, there is a chance that a significant number of leftover units must be liquidated at a discounted price at the end of the selling season. As opposed to items that are stocked on a regular basis throughout the year or multiple years and can be carried over in inventory from period to period, these leftover units have a lower residual value due to the short life cycle of fashion apparel products. On the other hand, an order quantity that is too small causes the firm to lose out on potential demand and also results in fewer customers being able to purchase the goods that they want.

The premise behind QR programs is that the entire apparel supply chain can benefit from the added flexibility and responsiveness that comes with reducing the cumulative lead time. One of the ways that these programs reduce the lead time is by enabling retailers to place or adjust their merchandise orders closer to the selling season. This additional time allows retailers to collect additional market demand information about their fashion apparel products to develop more accurate forecasts of demand during the selling season. For example, Blackburn (1991) reports a case study where a reduction of the forecast horizon from six to four months yielded a change in forecast error rate from 40 to 20%. Improving forecast accuracy helps the supply chain improve product availability for consumers while simultaneously reducing the number of overstocked units that must be marked down.

3 Implementation of QR

It is not coincidental that the development and formulation of the first supply chain collaboration programs (including QR) occurred in the mid-1980s at the same time as the proliferation of business-to-business communication technology such as electronic data interchange (EDI) and point-of-sale (POS) terminals in retail stores. Any attempts at truly managing the extended supply chain necessarily involve the use of advanced information systems to collect and transmit data both upstream and downstream in the channel. In addition to the large capital cost of these information systems, supply chains may also experience an incentive problem, in that the benefits of QR programs are not necessarily realized equally (or at all) by all parties in the system without incentive realignment efforts.

3.1 Use of Technology in QR

QR programs start at the store level with the retailer's ability to collect real-time sales data using POS terminals. To facilitate the collection of this data using the POS systems, the apparel industry widely adopted the universal product code (UPC) symbology that was popular in the grocery industry (Larson and Lusch 1990). It is not enough to simply collect the demand data; it must be shared with upstream supply chain partners so that they can utilize this information in their operations. In the mid-1980s most companies used EDI to transmit this information to their upstream partners; while EDI is still used, this information can now be relayed over secure internet connections. This sharing of end-customer demand data can also reduce the impact of the bullwhip effect in serial supply chains and distribution networks because each entity in the channel is able to base its production and inventory decisions on the actual end-user demand and not on the more-variable orders observed from immediate customers in the channel (Lee et al. 1997; Yu et al. 2001).[2]

The benefits of collecting real-time inventory information are not limited to the utility gained by sharing this information with supply chain partners. These barcode scanning and radio frequency identification (RFID) systems can also yield improvements for internal operations within a distribution center by reducing material handling and order picking costs. Distribution centers also stand to increase their inventory accuracy to levels approaching that of six-sigma quality (99.9997% accuracy) (Yao and Carlson 1999).

The implementation of this technology, especially EDI systems, does not come without a significant cost to the companies in the supply chain. In a study assessing the impact of a decade of QR activities, Hunter and Valentino (1995) report that retailers experienced data errors in approximately 70% of their EDI transactions, including the data stored in barcodes. They traced the problem to many vendors' failure to comply with UPC data standards, and retailers even went so far as to establish monetary penalties for vendors' non-compliance. Even by the mid-1990s, enterprise technology systems were overwhelmed by the amount of POS sales data being collected through QR and similar programs; they did not have enough processing speed and memory to store and manipulate the data, effectively reducing the utility of the program.

Many companies that wanted to implement QR were not using EDI and POS technology at the time. Therefore, they had to purchase and install these systems, as well as acquire the human resource intelligence to use and support the technology. This capital expenditure can be significant, especially for small companies. A study by Sullivan and Kang (1999) examined the differences between companies that had adopted QR and those that had not; they found that smaller companies were

---

[2] Interestingly, experiments by Steckel et al. (2004) show that the performance of systems with particular demand patterns may actually degrade through the sharing of POS sales data because the orders placed by downstream customers are more relevant to inventory decisions in these certain environments.

significantly less likely to implement a QR program, at least in part because of the capital investment involved.

Firms looking to establish a QR program do not, however, have to set up the technology or collaborative processes all at once. They can take an incremental strategy toward implementing the program that can allow them to postpone their commitment of future funds and resources until they have realized measurable results from the current stage of the system; this is a recommended strategy for the implementation of many different types of technology programs and applications (Chopra and Meindl 2007). A study by Fiorito et al. (1995) found that firms used this sort of incremental approach to implement the various technologies and collaborative processes that support QR. Palmer and Markus (2000) suggest the following four levels of implementing QR processes and technologies, each of which requires additional technology resources and a greater amount of collaboration between supply chain partners:

- *QR Level 1:* Collect POS data by using barcodes and UPC product labeling; enable automatic price lookup and other in-store customer service elements; transmit purchase orders to vendors via EDI.
- *QR Level 2:* Establish automated inventory replacement based on POS sales data to pull inventory downstream; create joint sales and inventory forecasts; expand use of EDI to transmit invoices, order status reports, and advanced shipping notices.
- *QR Level 3:* Integrate POS information and joint forecasts into planning process; improve distribution process through advanced container tracking and cross-docking operations.
- *QR Level 4:* Allocate inventory responsibility to suppliers, including yield targets and shelf space management; move toward "seasonless retailing" where all products can be available throughout the year and retailers do not have to plan only for specific fashion seasons many months in advance.

Birtwistle et al. (2003) provide a similar series of steps that are required to implement a complete QR system within a fashion supply chain. Their stages are divided up by the level at which the activities must be performed. From a technological perspective, stage one involves POS equipment being used to scan UPC barcodes, enabling the transformation of real-time information to supply chain partners via EDI or an internet-based platform. At the second stage, the retailer undergoes a redesign of its stocking processes to support cross-docking and automatic inventory replenishment systems. In addition, retailers begin to order smaller lots to reduce overall inventory levels. At the strategic level of the supply chain, firms work together to measure the success of their QR efforts as an integrated supply chain and collaborate in the functions of planning, forecasting, and product development. Supply chains that can successfully implement these QR processes can expect to realize reduced product cycle times, increased margins and sales, quicker inventory turns, and overall improved customer service.

3.2 Aligning Operations to Support QR

While information technology is an essential element for a successful QR program, these systems by themselves are not enough to guarantee success. In fact, a study by Rabinovich et al. (2003) found that improvements to operational processes had more of an impact on a firm's inventory performance than the implementation of enterprise-wide information systems does. Firms can undertake specific actions that ensure that their operations can support the overall goal of QR: reducing cumulative lead time. In short, any process improvement that reduces any part of the product's flow through the supply chain will increase the system's ability to meet customer demand with lower levels of inventory.

Opportunities abound up and down the channel to improve the product flow time. In the apparel industry the product design process is responsible for a large portion of the total flow time and is part of the reason why traditional fashion seasons had to be planned so far in advance. Forza and Vinelli (1996) describe several strategies for reducing the length of the design phase, including rationalization of the variety of fabric designs that can be used in the production of the final product and utilizing computer-aided-design (CAD) technology to reduce the time it takes for designers to evaluate the look of different colors and styles on models.

Within each of the manufacturing operations, traditional process improvement methods can aid a firm's attempt to participate in a QR system. These efforts should focus on the bottleneck activities in the production process because these are the activities that restrict flow through a facility. Successful improvement efforts will allow a facility to attain a certain level of throughput with lower levels of inventory and lower process flow time than before. Moreover, attempts to improve non-bottleneck activities will *not* affect the throughput and flow time and, thus, are wasted efforts toward that goal.[3] Efforts to improve initial product quality can also decrease cumulative flow time because it reduces the need for rework on defective items and can reduce the need to conduct as many (or any) product inspections either before the units are shipped or once they reach the downstream customer (Comber 2008).

It is also possible in some instances to adjust production operations explicitly to support QR goals. Fisher and Raman (1996) analyze the value of a fashion-apparel manufacturer's ability to update the production schedule with demand information after initial orders are received. They test their model with data from Sport Obermeyer, a ski-wear provider, and estimate that the extra flexibility reduces stockout cost by about 8.5% of sales. (See Sect. 4.1 for a more detailed discussion of Sport Obermeyer's QR practices.) Choi (2007) presents a similar multistage stocking problem with information updating close to the selling season that also considers

---

[3] Of course, process improvements that lead to higher levels of product or service quality can be valuable even for non-bottleneck activities. Thus, it is important that managers do not ignore the impact of these non-bottleneck activities completely. As the flow time for the bottleneck activities decreases, other activities will inevitably become new bottlenecks and will deserve the attention of flow time reduction efforts.

the optimal pricing policy for the product. Johnson and Scudder (1999) develop a production scheduling rule to maximize product availability in a QR environment that seeks to keep only small amounts of finished goods inventory to handle demand uncertainty. Unlike many production scheduling environments, traditional measures of job completion flow times are not relevant to this scheduling decision because demand is fulfilled from the small amount of finished goods inventory held for each item. They compared their scheduling rule, which focused on maximizing the minimum days of inventory held for each item, to several well-known policies in a series of experiments with independent and correlated demand and found that their rule performed well relative to the other policies. Their method had the additional benefits that it is computationally simple and provides a realistic daily production schedule that does not require much human modification.

3.3 Supply Chain Incentives Induced by QR

While it is clear that the principles and activities involved in a QR program *should* improve a supply chain's ability to satisfy its end-users' demand with lower amounts of inventory and supply risk, all levels of the supply chain have not been wholly enthusiastic about becoming involved in QR programs. This is especially true for some manufacturers of fashion products whose demand has a high degree of uncertainty with respect to the color, pattern, and style popularity (Hammond 1990). One would think that these manufacturers stood to reap significant benefits from participating in a QR system. Some manufacturers, though, still view their relationships with their retailers as adversarial in nature, contributing to their hesitation and skepticism about retailers' efforts to develop a QR system with them (Birtwistle et al. 2006).

The results of some QR implementations have also been lackluster from the perspective of the retailers. One particularly discouraging recent study measured the performance of 11 QR-adopting firms compared with 16 similarly sized nonadopting companies on a host of financial metrics related to profitability, cost efficiency, and inventory turnover. The researchers could find no difference in the performance of these two groups of firms on *any* of the measures that they studied (Brown and Buttross 2008). While the scope of this study was limited, it does highlight the chance that certain parties (and perhaps all parties) in the supply chain may not realize tangible benefits from practical implementations of QR programs. It re-emphasizes the importance of implementing these kinds of systems slowly and measuring the value created before continuing the investment of company resources.

The overall goal of collaborative supply chain initiatives such as QR is to improve the competitive position of the entire channel of supply. Individual firms are sometimes asked to sacrifice short-term performance levels to secure the long-term success of the channel. It is clear, however, that the incentives must be aligned in such a way that each firm will benefit from its involvement in the system in the long run, or else the company will eventually drop out of the relationship. All parties in the channel must ensure that participation in a program such as QR will be *Pareto* improving, meaning that each firm is no worse off for its participation in the system (and hopefully some if not all of the firms will be strictly better off due to their participation); otherwise, the collaborative program will not be sustainable for the foreseeable future.

Unfortunately, many of the benefits of a QR program, such as the reduction in markdown pricing at the end of the selling season and the lower level of stockouts during the selling season, are captured by the retailer. Ko et al. (2000) found that a manufacturer's perceived benefits are a major determinant of whether or not that firm adopts QR technology, and so it is in the retailer's interest to make it clear to the manufacturer how it will benefit from the program. To make the system *Pareto* improving for the manufacturer, the retailer must sometimes provide certain guarantees to the manufacturer to absorb some of the risk of inventory obsolescence. Iyer and Bergen (1997) and Choi et al. (2006) examine these supply chain incentives in several different QR channel structures.

Iyer and Bergen found that QR systems are inherently *Pareto* improving when the optimal channel service level (i.e., the probability of satisfying all demand in a selling season with the given stocking level) is less than one half. These low service levels are not likely to be found in practice because they can generate frustration on the part of customers, which can spill over to their feelings about the retailer's other products as well. When the optimal service level is one half or larger, QR systems do increase the total supply chain profit, but the retailer captures these gains at the expense of the manufacturer. The authors recommend the use of either service level commitments or volume commitments by the retailer to absorb some of the supply risk from the manufacturer and generate sufficient expected profit to satisfy the manufacturer's individual-rationality constraint.[4]

These economic models of QR supply chains discussed above admittedly take simplified views of the benefits realized by each of the parties as a result of their involvement in the relationship. Vendors, in particular, can receive additional benefits from the program, whose value are difficult to assess. These benefits include reduced levels of paperwork, more integration with customers through EDI (and now internet) links, better forecasts, and increased sales volume with QR retailers. The value of these positive by-products of the relationship may be enough to induce the vendors to participate in the program even if expected profit as computed in the above studies is a little less than the *status quo* business environment (Giunipero et al. 2001).

Of course, another way to address the issue of individual company incentives being misaligned with the goals of the overall supply chain is simply to eliminate the individual incentives by creating a vertically integrated channel. In this system the manufacturing process and the retailing process are both a part of the same

---

[4] The individual-rationality constraint, also known as the participation constraint, ensures that each party realizes at least a minimum required benefit from participating in a given activity (Tirole 1988). In this case, the minimum required benefit is the manufacturer's expected profit from a traditional channel that does not utilize a QR strategy.

company and should be acting to maximize the performance of the parent company. Richardson (1996) considers the issues involved in implementing a QR program in a vertically integrated channel and provides several examples of companies that have used this strategy effectively. Many channels, however, have chosen to integrate "virtually" through supply chain collaboration efforts instead of becoming part of the same company. Effective collaboration relationships can achieve similar levels of performance without the added challenge of owning and managing such a far-reaching extended enterprise as a single entity.

4 Examples of QR in the Apparel Industry

In the quarter of a century since Kurt Salmon Associates proposed the concept of QR to improve the responsiveness of the apparel supply chain, many apparel companies have implemented these programs with great success. In this section we discuss some successful and particularly innovative examples of QR programs developed by apparel supply chains.

4.1 QR at Sport Obermeyer

Sport Obermeyer, a manufacturer of skiwear located in Aspen, Colorado, is a classic example of a QR strategy applied in the apparel industry. Faced with the decision each year of what styles and quantities of skiwear items that they should manufacture, Sport Obermeyer contemplated the potential consequences of these decisions. Because the environment had high demand uncertainty, the firm faced the risks of either ordering not enough of certain items, leading to stockouts, or ordering too much of other items, resulting in excess inventory at the end of the season that would need to be discounted. To address this issue, Sport Obermeyer adopted the following three strategies of addressing uncertainty: reducing it, avoiding it, and hedging against it. Reducing uncertainty involved soliciting early orders from the best customers and using that data to predict demand across various product lines. The company avoided uncertainty by finding ways to shorten cumulative lead times day-by-day. Finally, the company hedged against uncertainty by combining forecasts produced by individual team members of a committee to develop one forecast that could be used to predict what styles to produce. The results of these measures led to a 60% increase in profits and greater than 99% availability of products (Fisher 1997; Hammond and Raman 2006).

4.2 QR at Zara

International clothing brand, Zara, has achieved remarkable success due to its proficiency in implementing its QR program. Zara was founded in 1974 in La Coruna,

Spain, and by 2008 the company operated 1,058 stores in 69 different countries. Despite the fact that the retailing industry is known for long lead times, overproduction, and excess inventory, Zara has "pioneered the concept of customized retailing" with a cumulative lead time from design to delivery of a garment of less than 3 weeks (Indu and Govind 2008). It is important to recognize, however, that Zara operates a vertically integrated channel, controlling the product design, manufacturing, distribution, and retailing operations. Traditional retailers who must work with external vendors may find this lofty performance difficult to emulate (although they do not have the managerial headache that comes with managing so many different parts of the supply chain process).

The QR process for Zara involves three steps: design, production, and distribution. In the design phase, employees develop ideas for new designs and constantly update the home office with details about new trends worldwide. Store managers place orders frequently and designers create new styles based on outlines delivered by specialists. After assessing relevant costs, prototypes are available hours later. Because the fabric is already available, the garments are created quickly within Zara's facilities. Bar codes are placed on cut fabric, which is then shipped to sewing facilities across Spain and Portugal. Armed with sewing instructions, garments are completed and ready for distribution within one week (Indu and Govind 2008; Indu and Gupta 2006).

Distribution takes place in Zara's distribution centers located in Arteizo and Zaragoza. Optical reading devices scan the garments prior to the merchandise being labeled and they are sorted according to their destination. The goods that are to be distributed within Europe are received within 24–36 hours, while non-European retailers receive the garments within 2 days. (Indu and Govind 2008).

One of the keys to Zara's success in implementing QR is the simplicity of the company's offerings. For most garments Zara keeps its variety limited to three colors and sizes. In addition, Zara differs from most clothing companies in the timing of its commitment to production. At the beginning of the season, the firm manufactures only 50–60% of its items, with 15–25% committed prior to the season's start and the remainder developed during the season. Because inventory is refreshed so frequently within its stores, customers are more accustomed to making purchases at Zara stores because they are uncertain that items will be available in the future. This changes the management's perspective of stockouts from a negative indicator to a positive indicator, as it provides customers with evidence of the uniqueness of Zara's offering (Kumar and Linguri 2006).

4.3   QR at Hennes and Mauritz (H&M)

Clothing pioneer Hennes and Mauritz (H&M) was founded in 1947 in Vasteras, Sweden, and the company had grown to 1,000 stores worldwide by 2004. Similar to Zara, H&M's design, production, and distribution functions work seamlessly to deliver a good to the shelf within 21 days. The design stage involves centralization of the planning activities through cooperation with buyers and designers. Emphasizing "fashion, quality, and price," H&M presents two major collections per year that highlight previous successes and upcoming trends. In production, H&M operates within two distinct supply chains located in Asia and Europe. The Asian supply chain focuses on manufacturing methods to increase profits and decrease costs, while the European supply chain uses "rapid reaction" for the unpredictable fashion items. Distribution is centralized through the company's single major warehouse in Hamburg, Germany. A separate distribution center was established in all countries that have H&M operations, and merchandise is shipped daily to stores from these local DCs. Stores are restocked daily to increase the turnover of individual items. Although the lead time for H&M is slightly longer than that of its competitor, Zara, H&M's prices are an average of 40% less expensive, giving them a significant cost advantage over their rival (Indu and Govind 2008).

4.4 QR at Benetton

Over the past several decades, Italian clothing company Benetton has established a competitive edge in the clothing market because of their efficient manufacturing process. The traditional garment manufacturing process involved first dying yarn in specified colors and then knitting it into final products. However, in 1964, Benetton devised a new process that involved delaying the dyeing of sweaters until the demand was determined. This involved building an inventory of standard garments and postponing completion until customer orders were received. Despite this model's early success through the 1990s, Benetton was unable to adapt to the changing demands of its customers. In addition, Benetton was requiring its stores to place their orders several months in advance, before store managers were confident of the trends of the upcoming seasons. This limited Benetton to bringing out two collections a year compared to its competitors who were able to bring out several.

As a result, in 2004, Benetton began to implement a dual supply chain model to adapt to the changing demands of its customers. This revised supply chain now included two components: a sequential and an integrated supply chain. In the sequential dual supply chain, goods were pushed into production based on forecasted demand, while the integrated supply chain operated by pull-based production off of customer sales and inputs. The new model enabled Benetton to present five collections within a season with varying lead times from 6 to 8 months prior to the season, to its "Evergreen" collection brought out in as short as 1 week. Orders for the Evergreen collection were placed online to ensure that the finished goods arrived to the stores within these quick lead times (Indu and Govind 2008).

4.5 QR at Adidas

The sports shoe market is one that is characterized by innovative design and development as well as a wide assortment of products to meet individual customer needs.

In addition, increasingly wealthy customers prefer to purchase customized products to express their individual personalities. In the mid 1990s, Adidas Salomon AG (Adidas) recognized this trend and invested in the option of producing a portion of their footwear in a make-to-order strategy instead of relying solely on make-to-stock manufacturing. As a result, in 2001, Adidas implemented the innovative QR program, *mi Adidas*, targeted at serious athletes interested in high-performance, customized athletic footwear (Berger and Piller 2003). The *mi Adidas* program requires customers to proceed through three steps within an Adidas store or mobile units to create their shoes. Customers first provide sales personnel with information with respect to their sports interests and fit or comfort level. At a scanning station customers' feet are measured and analyzed, and customers have the option of trying on different shoes to see which model(s) they prefer. Lastly, customers can choose the style and color of the shoes from a wide assortment of variations at a price approximately 50% higher than a standard option. The time required for this process is 30 min, and the shoes are typically delivered to the customer within 21 days (Tait 2004). This program is currently available in New York and San Francisco Adidas stores with plans to expand to Chicago stores in the future (Anonymous 2008). In addition, customized shoes produced in the same way with the exception of the foot-scanning step can be purchased online at the company's website. (Adidas 2008).

Adidas has achieved significant benefits as a result of implementing this program. In a traditional make-to-stock environment, the firm makes the product and then it is sold to the customer. However, because the final production of the footwear is delayed until the order is completed, Adidas is able to achieve a negative cash flow. In addition, there is a reduced forecasting and obsolescence risk, along with an increase in flexibility enabling them to adapt more rapidly to a changing market. Involving customers in the design of footwear also provides Adidas with a wealth of customer preference data that can lead to greater innovation for both their mass produced and mass customized product lines (Berger and Piller 2003).

4.6 QR at Hilton Hosiery

Hilton Hosiery is an Australian producer of hosiery goods with a sales volume of 65 million pairs per year. With a wide assortment of brand names and a distribution network that supplies 1,500 customers, Hilton spent the late 1980s attempting to reduce inventory levels within its warehouses and decrease the number of manufacturing plants. Despite the fact that the company used forecasts to control the production schedule and resource needs, customer service at Hilton was struggling. By 1991, management decided to implement a QR system dubbed "QUIRK" to improve the inventory mix within their facilities. (Perry and Sohal 2000).

The QUIRK system involves several innovative features that have enabled Hilton to achieve significant benefits in the areas of cost and efficiency. Forecasts for individual hosiery styles are translated to the requirement for each SKU by computers using the past 60 days of sales data and making assumptions on the duration of the mix. Data from retailers are also used to determine the forecasts for each SKU. For higher volume items, the length of forecasts is shortened and the system gives planners the option of changing model parameters at any time. For each plant, a "daily knit report" is created by QUIRK that shows the previous day quantities and the current day requirements, as well as an adjustment for seasonal fluctuation. Within the facilities, batch sizes have significantly decreased, which has created an emphasis for managers to find ways to increase changeovers to move production through the finishing area more quickly. EDI is used to increase the efficiency in order entry and updating. In addition, Hilton attempts to be flexible downstream by cross-training employees and using temporary workers during demand peaks. For Hilton Hosiery, the benefits of their QUIRK system include improved customer service, a 50% reduction in inventory levels within 1 year, and a 50% increase in stock-mix efficiencies (Perry and Sohal 2000).

4.7 QR at Patrizia Pepe

Fashion producer Patrizia Pepe attempts to differentiate its products from those of competitors Zara and H&M by offering quality merchandise with a distinctive style. To generate a consistent consumer buzz about the product assortment, the company develops 40 quasi-weekly apparel collections each year followed by "mini-collections" offered on a weekly basis. Retailers make decisions on which items to carry weekly based on visits that they make to Patrizia Pepe showrooms. By having retailers make small purchases regularly, Patrizia Pepe is able to continuously renew its fashions and establish partnerships with retailers. Lead time to the stores ranges from 1–3 weeks for garments, and goods flow through the network of 50–70 suppliers working on a "continuous flow" system of production. By communicating weekly with retailers, information sharing has become a valuable resource to gather details on customer requests and fashion trends. This has enabled Patrizia Pepe to distribute its goods to over 100 stores across the world by 2004 (Corbellini 2006).

4.8 QR at New Look

Apparel company New Look competes as the third largest woman's apparel brand in the UK. Proponents of the "fast-fashion" supply chain approach, New Look strives to respond rapidly to trends and changes in the fashion market to meet the needs of its growing customer base by being "able to transform a fashion idea into clothing in about 8–12 weeks, although there is the constant drive to shorten this even further." To achieve this success, New Look has had to overcome several challenges to be "demand-driven" when sourcing products in different marketplaces throughout the world.

They adopted a QR approach to this challenge through several strategies. They opened up consolidation centers in Singapore and Turkey to aid in distributing their products faster and more efficiently. Some of their suppliers ship products directly to consolidation centers in specific regions to shorten lead times and reduce markdowns. Another key to the company's strategy is its product design-supply chain interface, which focuses on mitigating the risk inherent in streamlined supply chains. They have consolidated 25 designers in one location to provide over 50% of their total designs with the goal creating a fashionable, quality product at an affordable price. They also utilize a CAD system to communicate with offshore suppliers during the design phase. This technology "enables designers or production developers to map out the individual parts for a garment on layer of fabric to minimize fabric waste and they link this to technology with their suppliers so that they can share data and compress time from design to manufacture, hence, reducing lead time" (Khan 2008).

4.9 QR at World Company

World Company, a fashion retailer headquartered in Japan, has significantly shortened lead times and reduced inventory investment through a QR approach to supply chain management characterized by several key strategies. To improve and predict the accuracy of their forecasts, a group of employees at company headquarters takes on the personas of their set of target customers and provides opinions on the success of different products. Collaboration with supply chain partners begins before orders are placed to achieve shorter response times. In addition, they hold high levels of raw material inventory because they feel they can develop more accurate forecasts for these items than for finished goods. They have "debug areas" within the factories where designers and employees can work jointly to solve problems and enable more efficient manufacturing. Employees at World are empowered to make decisions when doing so can avoid costly and lengthy delays. This responsiveness enables them to speed along the design, pricing, and procurement processes significantly compared to other retailers (Fisher et al. 2000).

5 Further Development of QR

With the advent of more robust (and cheaper) information systems over the subsequent 25 years since QR was initially developed, the program's major principles and goals have been adopted by industries outside of apparel. Efforts to reduce cumulative lead time and provide greater visibility of production and inventory levels throughout the supply chain have developed into closely related automated replenishment systems and formal methods of collaborative planning. We conclude this chapter of a discussion of QR's application to new industries as well as its relationship to these other methods of inventory control.

5.1 QR Beyond the Apparel Industry

The majority of the practical examples of QR implementation are centered in volatile, fast-paced industries where there is a desire to bring items from design to delivery faster to capture the most current customer buying trends and desires. The grocery industry differs remarkably from that description; however, there has been success in implementing this type of program in grocery supply chains to improve flows and decrease lead times. In the grocery industry this kind of system falls under the classification of Efficient Consumer Response (ECR), and it expands the purview of QR process improvement to ensuring more efficient space management within warehouses and inducing customers to stop forward buying activities. The overall goal of ECR is to realize improved efficiency for retailers (Fernie 1994).

According to the Joint Industry Project for ECR (1994), the major areas where ECR can improve efficiency for retailers are by the following:

1. "Optimizing store assortments and space allocations to increase category sales per square foot and inventory turnover
2. Streamlining the distribution of goods from the point of manufacture to the retail shelf
3. Reducing the cost of trade and consumer promotion
4. Reducing the cost of developing and introducing new products"

Hoffman and Mehra (2000) examined five different firms in the grocery industry to assess the level of adoption of the retailers and to draw conclusions on the essential steps for implementation. Their recommendations included the establishment of early involvement between customers and vendors to enhance the quality of these relationships and improved clarity of the established priorities between supply chain partners. In addition, they suggested that supply chain members utilize process mapping tools to pinpoint the location of value-added and non-value-added activities in their processes, as well as enhanced understanding of the technology needs of all of the supply chain partners.

At the UK's leading grocery retailer, Tesco, the ECR process suggested that products be routed through Regional Distribution Centers (RDC) to enable daily deliveries and lead times of under 24 hours for many products. Tesco also supported the consolidation of deliveries to stores through the construction of temperature-controlled units with these RDCs. The firm adjusted the storage space in the facility and installed various kinds of technology to improve the order picking process and allow for the desired amount of lead time reduction. As in a QR system, Tesco established EDI links with its suppliers to manage purchasing activities (Fernie 1994). It is noted by Whiteoak (1993), however, that it is essential that these quick response ideas be accompanied by increased information sharing within supply chain partners in the grocery industry to lead to more accurate planning and scheduling.

The frozen food industry specifically handles a variety of different products well-suited for a QR program. This is due to the high level of variability in demand for frozen food items, which is affected mostly by seasonality. Since almost all frozen food travels through RDCs before being sold to customers, the lead time of these items is dependent on the time that it spends in storage before being picked and delivered. To reduce costs, retailers could potentially decrease the size of the frozen shipments and increase the frequency of delivery by implementing cross-docking. Instead of frozen food items sitting on shelves in RDCs for up to 10 days prior to being picked for shipments, cross-docking would enable retailers to receive, sort, and ship these items in an 8–10 hour time period. In addition, implementation of QR through cross-docking could save suppliers from having to pick orders by store, thereby decreasing the time it takes to fill orders and reduce the time that items would be in storage prior to being distributed (McKinnon and Campbell 1998).

Despite the success that many have had in developing QR and its related programs, significant barriers to implementation still exist in many parts of the world. For example, the proximity of El Salvador to the United States would make it a strong candidate for supply chain collaboration with retailers interested in QR. However, there are several drawbacks of operating in this region. Specifically, these include the lack of raw materials and financing to properly develop business. As relationships between US and Asian facilities grow exponentially, Central American countries are struggling with the lack of commitment that US-based firms have to invest in the region. In addition, many of these countries do not have the logistics infrastructure in place to handle the transportation of goods a consistent, timely manner.

These challenges do not, however, necessarily exclude these countries from being hopeful that future collaboration in the area of design and product innovation may seek the attention of US firms. An example of this is the El Salvador company, Parthex, which manufactures athletic apparel for Nike, Reebok, and Adidas. The success of this firm is rooted in the principles of lean management that have improved the efficiency of operations and eliminated the need for warehouses to store finished goods. The firm, instead, focuses on production that matches the pattern of customer demand (Speer 2004).

5.2   QR and Other Methods of Supply Chain Collaboration

Both the trade and academic press are littered with acronyms that refer to collaborative methods of inventory control (e.g., QR, ECR, CRP, VMI, etc.). This "alphabet soup" of inventory control is made even thicker by the fact that many writers use these terms interchangeably (or sometimes inappropriately). Sabath et al. (2001) seem to provide the clearest distinction between these related programs. QR and ECR are industry-specific methods that use real-time sales data to pull inventory through the physical distribution network. This is also the case under Continuous Replenishment Programs (CRP) and Vendor Managed Inventory (VMI). The difference is that the buyer (usually the retailer) makes decisions about target inventory levels and restocking policies in CRP, while this responsibility is delegated completely to the supplier in a VMI system. All these systems require significant collaboration between vendors and retailers and are expected to increase inventory velocity, decrease cumulative lead times, improve customer service levels, and result in fewer end-of-season markdowns.

In addition, within the literature there are similarities drawn between the strategy of mass customization and QR programs. Mass customization describes an operations strategy that runs contrary to the traditional idea that supporting high volumes requires firms to produce standardized products or services. Instead, in mass customization firms develop the capabilities to provide customized products at high volumes and low cost through development of flexible processes and use of technology (Squire et al. 2006). Levi Strauss was considered the first large apparel company to offer mass customized production through their "Original Spin" program. In this program, customers could have their jeans tailored to their exact measurements within the store and then the finished products were mailed to their home when completed. Since then, mass customization in retailing has expanded. Today, mass customization in retailing is facilitated through the technology inherent in QR programs and involves either the option of "body scanning for a better fitting product or co-design for a unique aesthetic design" (Fiore et al. 2004).

In Sect. 3.1 we described the different levels of QR implementation. One of these stages included joint forecasting between the buyer and the supplier. The scope of this specific activity has been expanded to a formal business process known as Collaborative Planning, Forecasting, and Replenishment (CPFR). The CPFR process was developed and is maintained by the Voluntary Interindustry Commerce Standards (VICS) Association. It was initially conceived of as a sequence of nine connected processes, but many now prefer to view the activities as a wheel on which companies can start anywhere. The goal of CPFR is to link sales and marketing plans with supply chain plans among several entities within the supply chain to improve product availability while reducing total logistics costs (including inventory).

There are many successful CPFR case studies that highlight the power and potential of the process. The most famous case study is probably that of West Marine, a large retailer of boating supplies. After piloting a CPFR program with a few choice suppliers, West Marine extended it to approximately 200 suppliers accounting for 20,000 different items and representing about 90% of the firm's catalog. Weekly stocking levels consistently achieve their goal of 96%, even in the peak sales season, and the company has been able to improve its forecast accuracy to 85% (Smith 2006).

The CPFR process, like the CRP and VMI systems described above, represents the next major milestone on the path of improved inventory control, a trail blazed initially by the QR programs developed in the mid-1980s.

References

Adidas (2008) Company Website. www.adidas.com. Accessed 7 Nov 2008

Anonymous (2008) Mi adidas—customized shoes. Gear Patrol. http://www.gearpatrol.com/blog/2008/06/20/mi-adidas-customized-shoes. Accessed 7 Nov 2008

Berger C, Piller F (2003) Customers as Co-Designers. IEE Manuf Eng 82(4):42–45

Birtwistle G, Moore CM, Fiorito SS (2006) Apparel quick response systems: The manufacturer perspective. Int J Logist Res Appl 9(2):157–168

Birtwistle G, Siddiqui N, Fiorito, SS (2003) Quick response: Perceptions of UK fashion retailers. Int J Retail Distrib Manag 31(2):118–128

Blackburn JD (1991) Time Based Competition: The Next Battleground in American Manufacturing. Business One Irwin, Homewood, IL

Brown T, ButtrossTE (2008) An empirical analysis of the financial impact of quick response. Int J Retail Distrib Manag 36(8):607–626

Choi TM (2007) Pre-season stocking and pricing decisions for fashion retailers with multiple information updating. Int J Prod Econ 106:146–170

Choi TM, Li D, Yan H (2006) Quick response policy with Bayesian information updates. Eur J Oper Res 170:788–808

Chopra S, Meindl P (2007) Supply Chain Management: Strategy, Planning, & Operation, Third Edition. Pearson Prentice Hall, Upper Saddle River, NJ

Comber DB (2008) Streamlining lead time. APICS—The Performance Advantage 18(7):38–41

Corbellini E (2006) Patrizia Pepe: Advanced quick fashion. Bocconi School of Management Case 306–475–1

Fernie J (1994) Quick response: An international perspective. Int J Phys Distrib Logist Manag 24(6):38–46

Fiore AM, Lee S, Kunz G (2004) Individual difference, motivations, and willingness to use a mass customization option for fashion products. Eur J Market 38(7):835–849

Fiorito SS, May EG, Straughn K (1995) Quick response in retailing: Components and implementation. Int J Retail Distrib Manag 23(5):12–21

Fisher ML (1997) What is the right supply chain for your product? Harv Bus Rev 75(2):105–116

Fisher ML, Raman A (1996) Reducing the cost of demand uncertainty through accurate response to early sales. Oper Res 44(1):87–99

Fisher ML, Raman A, McClelland AS (2000) Rocket science retailing is almost here – Are you ready? Har Bus Rev 78(4):115–124

Forza C, Vinelli A (1996) An analytical scheme for the change of the apparel design process towards quick response. Int J Clothing Science & Technology 8(4):28–43

Gallego G, Moon I (1993) The distribution free newsboy problem: Review and extensions. J Oper Res Soc 44:825–834

Giunipero LC, Fiorito SS, Pearcy DH, Dandeo L (2001) The impact of vendor incentives on quick response. Int Rev Retail Distrib Consum Res 11(4):359–376

Hammond JH (1990) Quick response in the apparel industry. Harvard Business School Press. Case 9–690–038

Hammond JH Raman A (2006) Sport Obermeyer, Ltd. Harvard Business School Press. Case 9–695–022

Hoffman JM, Mehra S (2000) Efficient consumer response as a supply chain strategy for grocery businesses. Int J Serv Ind Manag 11(4):63–373

Hunter NA, Valentino P (1995) Quick response—ten years later. Int J Cloth Sci Tech 7(4):30–40

Indu P, Govind S (2008) Supply chain practices of three European apparel companies. ICFAI Center for Management Research. Case 608–020–1

Indu P, Gupta V (2006) Zara's supply chain management practices. ICFAI Center for Management Research. Case 606–021–1

Iyer AV, Bergen ME (1997) Quick response in manufacturer-retailer channels. Manag Sci 43(4):559–570

Johnson ME, Scudder G (1999) Supporting quick response through scheduling of make-to-stock production/inventory systems. Decis Sci J 30(2):441–467

Joint Industry Project on Efficient Consumer Response (1994). An ECR best practices report. Washington, DC: Grocery Manufacturers of America

Khan O (2008) New Look – Competing through the design-supply chain interface. Cranfield School of Management. Case 608–016

Ko E, Kincade D, Brown JR (2000) Impact of business type upon the adoption of quick response technologies. Int J Oper Prod Manag 20(9):1093–1111

Kumar N, Linguri S (2006) Fashion sense. Bus Strat Rev 17(2):80–84

Larson PD, Lusch RF (1990) Quick response retail technology: Integration and performance measurement. Int Rev Retail Distrib Consum Res 1(1):17–35

Lee CH (2007) Coordination on stocking and progressive pricing policies for a supply chain. Int J Prod Econ 106:307–319

Lee HL, Padmanabhan V, Whang S (1997) The bullwhip effect in supply chains. Sloan Manag Rev 38(3):93–102

Lim H, Istook CL, Cassill NL (2009) Advanced mass customization in apparel. J Textile and Apparel Tech Manag 6(1):1–16

Lummus RR, Vokurka RJ (1999) Defining supply chain management: A historical perspective and practical guidelines. Ind Manag Data Syst 99(1):11–17

McKinnon AC, Campbell JB (1998) Quick-response in the frozen food supply chain: The manufacturers' perspective. Christian Salvesen Logistics Research Paper No 2. Heriot-Watt University School of Management, Edinburgh, Scotland

Palmer JW, Markus ML (2000) The performance impacts of quick response and strategic alignment in specialty retailing. Inform Syst Res 11(3):241–259

Perry M, Sohal AS (2000) Quick response practices and technologies in developing supply chains. Int J Phys Distrib Logist Manag 30(7/8):627–639

Rabinovich E, Dresner ME, Evers PT (2003) Assessing the effects of operational processes and information systems on inventory performance. J Oper Manag 21:63–80

Richardson J (1996) Vertical integration and rapid response in fashion apparel. Organ Sci 7(4): 400–412

Sabath RE, Autry CW, Daugherty PJ (2001) Automatic replenishment programs: The impact of organizational structure. J Bus Logist 22(1):91–105

Smith L (2006) West Marine: A CPFR success story. Supply Chain Manag Rev 10(2):29–36

Speer J (2004) On the scene: El Salvador building the CAFTA brand. Apparel Mag 46(2):50–56

Squire B, Brown S, Readman J, Bessant J (2006) The impact of mass customization on manufacturing trade-offs. Prod Oper Manag 15(1):10–21

Steckel JH, Gupta S, Banerji A (2004) Supply chain decision making: Will shorter cycle times and shared point-of-sale information necessarily help? Manag Sci 50(4):458–464

Sullivan P, Kang J (1999) Quick response adoption in the apparel manufacturing industry: Competitive advantage of innovation. J Small Bus Manag 37(1):1–13

Tait N (2004) How 'mi adidas' provides personalized style, fit. Apparel Mag 45(5):10–13

Tirole J (1988) The Theory of Industrial Organization. MIT Press, Cambridge, MA

Whiteoak P (1993). The realities of quick response in the grocery sector – a supplier viewpoint. Int J Retail Distrib Manag 21(8):3–11

Yao AC, Carlson JG (1999) The impact of real-time data communication on inventory management. Int J Prod Econ 59:213–219

Yu Z, Yan H, Cheng TCE (2001) Benefits of information sharing within supply chain partnerships. Ind Manag Data Syst 101(3):114–119

Impact of Information Systems on Quick Response Programs

Robert Setaputra, Xiaohang Yue, and Dongqing Yao

Abstract A quick response (QR) program is a proven system to deal with the ever changing customer's demand and requirements. Effective information system is one of the backbones to have a successful QR program. This paper discusses how each of the recent technological developments in information technology (IT) has impacted QR program. This paper also discusses the steps that companies need to take in order to take complete advantage of these IT developments, as well as the directions of where IT and QR are heading.

Keywords Information systems · Information technology developments · Quick response

1 Introduction

Rapid technological developments, shorter product life cycles, and increased customer expectations have reshaped how business operates. To survive, it is essential for the firms nowadays to be able to meet the ever changing business situations. Companies need to collaborate with the lower and upper echelons in the supply chain to be able to compete since they have exhausted most of the opportunities to improve internally. With the ever more fragmented customers, companies also need to be able to react quickly to customer's demand and changes. Supply chains simply must be more efficient and effective so that goods, funds, and information can travel fast. Handfield and Nichols (1998) estimated that the costs of the flow of materials through the supply chain are approximately 75% of the total cost.

Companies have for long been relying on quick response (QR) program to deal with various customer's demand and changes. Inefficiencies in the supply chain

R. Setaputra (✉)
John L. Grove College of Business, Shippensburg University, Shippensburg PA, USA
e-mail: rsseta@ship.edu

T.C. Edwin Cheng and T.-M. Choi (eds.), *Innovative Quick Response Programs in Logistics and Supply Chain Management*, International Handbooks on Information Systems, DOI 10.1007/978-3-642-04313-0_2,

could lead to extra inventories and unnecessary production and long delivery lead times, which may result in lower profit margins and customer satisfactions. QR program is aimed to minimize production and delivery lead times. QR is based on a combination of the just-in-time (JIT) and Information Technology (IT) systems (Birtwistle et al. 2006). Unlike lean concept, which is suitable when demand is relatively stable and customer requirements are more uniform, QR concept is suited well when demand is volatile and customer requirements are more varied (Christopher and Towill 2001). The impact of successful QR in certain industry such as apparel industry could be substantial (Choi et al. 2006).

Mohr and Nevin (1990) described communication as the glue that holds together a channel of distribution. To manage communication flows effectively and efficiently, we need to successfully identify, analyze, and coordinate the interactions among the entities. A study done by the National Institute of Standards and Technology (NIST) found that poor data integration in the supply chain is costing manufacturers billions of dollars each year (NIST 2004). It is clear that an effective coordination throughout the entire supply chain will significantly increase the firm's capability to compete in the market place. SCM systems should be able to facilitate the synchronization of the entire supply chain as they can assist a firm in integrating internal business processes within the corporate boundary so that all internal function areas can operate in synchronization (Tarn et al. 2002).

On these fronts, IT has been a godsend for supply chain management. Schnetzler and Schonsleben (2007) showed that information management has an impact on all target areas of SCM, that is, quality, delivery, reliability, delivery lead times, flexibility, assets, and costs. Hitt and Brynjolfsson (1996) estimated that 40% of the new capital equipment investment in the US is allocated to technology. A survey by Gartner/Dataquest indicates that about 40% of the surveyed companies would increase their spending this year than last year on supply-chain software (Violino 2004). According to ARC Advisory Group, the quest for efficient supply chains led companies worldwide to spend more than $5 billion on supply-chain-management technology last year, which expected to grow to more than $7 billion by 2008. Even during global economic crisis, IT spending is still expected to grow at 2.3% in 2009 (Campbell 2008). Recent developments in IT have significantly reshaped the supply chain behaviors in the last two decades. For example, Sarbanes-Oakley Act introduced in 2002 was affecting the way the firms formulate their supply chain's information technology strategies (Tirschwell 2004).

Much of the current interest in linking information technology to supply chain management research is motivated by the possibilities that are introduced by the abundance of data and the savings inherent in the sophisticated analysis of these data (Sridharan et al. 2005). Information is crucial to the performance of a supply chain because it provides the basis on which decisions are made. The same goes for QR program. QR strategies are dependent on building long-term relationships, sharing information and investment in technology and facilities with suppliers (Birtwistle et al. 2006). A successful QR system has to quickly catch the information from day-to-day transactions, and hence needs to consider IT and non-IT solutions and procedures to improve knowledge sharing, storage, delivery, and application

(Lo et al. 2008). Therefore, IT strategy plays two important components in QR program, namely to facilitate and maintain efficient and timely information sharing across the supply chain. Supply chain's success would then be dependent on the accuracy and velocity of the information provided by the supply chain members.

Effective information systems allow not only the collection of data across the supply chain, but also the analysis of decisions that maximize supply chain profitability. Gunasekaran and Ngai (2004) argued that it is not possible to achieve an effective supply chain without IT, as it enables the management and exchange of information as well as the integration of the trading partners along the supply chain. The primary function of information technology in the supply chain is to seamlessly link the points of procurement, production, and delivery. This gives a significant benefit to the firm by greatly easing the ability to share information (such as point-of-sale data, inventory, forecast data, order change, and sales trends) in a relatively quick and inexpensive manner. For example, with the adoption of EDI, web service, service-oriented architecture (SOA), RFID, etc., the supply chain partners can communicate and conduct business with downstream and upstream partners electronically, and thus realize zero information latency and full supply chain visibility. This also allows planning, tracking, and estimating lead times based on real-time data. By improving their information systems, Longs Drug Stores' inventory at its distribution centers has decreased to 65% since 1997, which translates to $36 million annual savings (Lee 2004). These improvements in turn help upstream partners to respond to the downstream partner's requirements quickly and enhance value-adding services to customers (Au and Ho 2002). All these efforts are expected to streamline, integrate, and speed up the business processes from production to delivery.

In this paper, we wish to accomplish two main objectives. First, we would like to detail how each of the recent technological developments in IT have impacted QR. Second, we would like to review the steps that companies must take in order to take complete advantage of these IT developments. This will also raise some important issues that we feel researchers should address. We will conclude this paper by discussing the directions in which the interaction between IT and QR is heading.

2 Recent IT Developments and Their Impacts on QR

Popular information systems that have had a significant impact on the day-to-day supply chain operations include electronic data interchange (EDI) and point of sales (POS), RFID (radio frequency identification), enterprise resource planning (ERP), customer relationship management (CRM), and collaborative planning, forecasting, and replenishment (CPFR). The following subsections detail on how each of these developments has affected QR performance.

2.1 Electronic Data Interchange and Point of Sales

Electronic data interchange (EDI) software is designed to automate inter-organizational communication and thus improve the effectiveness of QR program. EDI is the use of standard electronic formats for the creation, transmission, and storage of documents, such as requisition, quotation, purchase orders, and invoices (Owens and Levary 2002). According to Giga Research, 88% of larger enterprises used EDI for supply chain communications because of the fewer errors and lower cost per transaction over manual processing methods (Brockmann 2003). Boyson et al. (2003) argued that electronic information exchange leads to reduction of errors and increased efficiency of processes. EDI connects the databases of different companies. For example, order placed by a company is transmitted directly from the company's system to its supplier's system. Supplier's system then transmits the billing information directly to the ordering company's system.

In its early use, EDI allowed companies to utilize material requirements planning (MRP) to inform suppliers of the upcoming orders by providing them with access to the database of planned orders. Although this approach was innovative at that time, it still represented only a limited sharing of information between the supply chains. In supply chain management, EDI is a means of sharing information among all members of a supply chain. Additionally, shared databases can ensure that all supply chain members have access to the same information, providing visibility to everyone and avoiding problems such as the bullwhip effect. Moreover, EDI system contributes to cutting lead times by reducing the portion of the lead time that is linked to order processing, paperwork, stock picking, transportation delays, and so on.

Cash and Konsynski (1984) discussed the impact of electronic links such as EDI to the inter-organizational system. They argued that electronic links, in addition to improving efficiency, would change the power balance between supplier and buyer relationship, and in most instances, shift the competitive position of intra-industry competitors. Clemons and Row (1993) studied the impact of EDI on manufacturer and retailer relationship in the consumer packaged goods industry. They concluded that resistance by the expected adopters limits the potential strategic benefits of EDI. Dearing (1990) studied the strategic benefits of EDI in the supply chain. He classified the benefits into three major categories, namely direct, indirect, and strategic benefits. Mukhopadhyay et al. (1995) studied the cost effectiveness of implementing EDI at Chrysler Corporation. They found that Chrysler successfully lowered the operating costs associated with carrying inventories, obsolescence, and transportation. They estimated that by implementing EDI, Chrysler saved $220 million annually. Chatfield and Yetton (2000) examined the strategic payoff of EDI. They argued that EDI impact on strategic performance depends on the level of EDI embeddedness by moderating the impact of EDI adopter use on initiator strategic benefits.

POS, on the other hand, is an integral part of EDI system. POS data transfer system provides a distributor/manufacturer with real-time information on what is selling at the retailers. Weber and Kantamneni (2002) examined the benefits and barriers of adopting POS and EDI in retailing business. They concluded that the retail managers see the adoption of POS technology as an operational and tactical decisions, while the adoption of EDI technology as a strategic decision. Retailers, on average, carry 2 months of inventory of their suppliers' products (Aiyer and Ledesma 2004). At that rate, companies must look at more accurate and efficient ways to create reliable forecasts and manage inventory in the system. POS data are viewed by many as the answer. The major benefit of using POS data is that it reflects the true sales. This leads to a more efficient inventory replenishment, which ultimately leads to customer-driven replenishment (CDR). POS also allows companies to employ more responsive and real-time pricing strategy. The Beer Store, for example, is using POS data to automatically alert their system to modify their pricing for in-stock brand or package configuration of beers when particular item is out of stock (Gentry 2004). Ko and Kincade (1997) studied the impacts of various QR technologies on time/availability, store environment, and value-added service for apparel retailers. They found that POS improves the retailer's performance although the effect is being moderated by the size and type of the store.

The effect of sharing POS data among supply chain members is, however, not clear. Lee et al. (2000) study the effect of information sharing when the demand is nonstationary AR(1). They showed that the manufacturer will benefit significantly when retailer shares their POS data. Using an experimental study, Croson and Donahue (2003) investigate whether sharing POS data among supply chain members reduce the bullwhip effect when the demand distribution is known. They showed that when demand is stationary and stable, sharing POS data can help reduce the bullwhip effect by helping upstream suppliers to better anticipate the customer's demand. When the demand is nonstationary and unknown, in contrast to Lee et al. (2000), they showed that sharing POS data can bias upstream player's demand forecast. This finding is also consistent with that of Raghunathan (2001). He found that the parameters of the demand are known, and sharing POS data is insignificant since the manufacturer can utilize available order history to forecast the demand.

EDI implementation is expensive and complicated; therefore, it typically is applicable for larger companies with huge initial investment. Nowadays, many companies along a supply chain have adopted SOA, which allows for widespread sharing of services (e.g., real-time information) among trading partners. SOA can be implemented by the internet-based languages and protocols such as extensible markup language (XML), universal description, discovery, and integration (UDDI), web services description language (WSDL), and simple object access protocol (SOAP).

2.2 Radio Frequency Identification

One technology that will increase a firm' supply chain visibility is radio-frequency identification (RFID). RFID is a wireless technology that identifies objects without having either contact or sight of them (Levary and Mathieu 2004). RFID is basically a chip bearing a unique serial number affixed to, for example, a container, a pallet. The reader receives a signal from RFID tag carrying the item's serial number, which logs the item's location and time in an online database, creating a detailed history of each item's movement. The data obtained from RFID could be fed directly into ERP system, allowing company to track and operate on a real time basis. The tag of RFID can be active, passive, or semipassive. Active tag broadcasts information and require a power source, while passive tag just responds to queries without power source. SAP and PeopleSoft (now Oracle) had made a significant investment to modify their existing system software for RFID to prepare applications for collecting more data more frequently (Bacheldor 2004).

Firms are expecting RFID to bring improvements on inventory status, tracking and management of assets, and responsiveness and customer service. The technology is deemed to be so important that some large retailers require their vendors to employ RFID. In 2003, chain store giant, Wal-Mart, decreed that its 100 leading suppliers should all be RFID equipped by January 2005 (Holland 2004). Bednarz (2004) reported that United Parcel Service (UPS) is under the gun to begin tagging cases and pallets with RFID labels to comply with mandates from Wal-Mart, Target, Albertsons, Best Buy, and other retailers. The number of firms that are using the technology is also increasing. Aberdeen survey revealed that 5% of the companies – primarily in the consumer goods sector – planned to deploy RFID by June, 11% within 6 months, 34% within 12 months, and 39% within 2 years (Violino 2004). RFID has also been adopted in the apparel industry. Jones Apparel Group is pioneering a program to assess the benefits of applying passive RFID technology (O'Connor 2008). Chow et al. (2007) reported an integrated logistics information management system case study among supply chain players. They found that by integrating RFID and IT companies can significantly improve their logistics functions performance. They showed that companies can reduce their average inventory by 27%, out-of-stock frequency by 68%, and average delivery time by 32%. de Kok et al. (2008) studied the impacts of RFID implementation in the situation where inventory is sensitive shrinkage. They found that break even prices of the RFID implementation are highly related to item's value, shrinkage percentage, and remaining shrinkage. With the implementation of RFID technology, the visibility and velocity of a supply chain can be dramatically improved; furthermore, with the combination of RFID and POS data, the true demand information can be determined since the retailer can estimate the lost sale (Simichi-Levi et al. 2008).

2.3   Enterprise Resource Planning

An enterprise resource planning (ERP) system is a broadly used industrial term to describe the multi-module application software for managing an enterprise's suppliers, customers, and functional activities. ERP software systems are designed to link and integrate the various business processes of enterprises. An ERP system uses a single database and a common software infrastructure to provide a broader scope and up-to-date information. This allows the ERP system to integrate all aspects of the company, such as financial, production, supply, and customer order information. Companies can keep track of materials, orders, and financial status efficiently and coordinate manufacturing and inventory across different locations and business units. The industry views ERP system as a tool that enables them to have higher efficiency by enabling them to move financial and other data speedily from one department to another department (Holt 1999). ERP software can also be used to integrate internal business activities of a multi-facility organization, or enterprise, to ensure that it was operating under the same information system to achieve better coordination across the supply chain. Furthermore, ERP software can also support operations functions such as production scheduling to enable company to quickly respond to customers' demand, high quality of product, reliable delivery, etc. (Metaxiotis et al. 2003). For example, Microsoft Window's client-based and object-oriented QR tool was designed to "augment ERP applications with more precise and constraint-based scheduling of both materials and resources" (Hickey 1999).

Although the system promises significant benefits, this, however, comes with big costs and risks. ERP implementation requires flexibility and risk tampering as the project cannot be completed within a short period of time; in fact, it is an ongoing process. ERP systems are complex, and implementing the system can be a difficult, time-consuming, and expensive project for companies. Implementation can take many years to complete and cost tens to hundreds of millions of dollars. Moreover, even with significant investments in time and money, there is still no guarantee of the outcome. Cliffe (1999) quoted that 65% of executives believe that ERP systems have at least a moderate chance of hurting their businesses because of the potential for implementation problems, which may disrupt the day-to-day operations. Davenport (1998) argued that ERP system is difficult to implement and expensive. He also argued that most ERP system projects fail during the implementation stage. Umble and Umble (2002) discussed ten factors that may lead to implementation failure. In the survey that they quoted, 77% of respondents believe that poor planning and management are major contributors for the implementation failure. It then follows by change of business goals during the project (75%) and lack of business management support (73%). Umble et al. (2003) presented empirical findings on the implementation and critical success factors of ERP projects. Barker and Frolick (2003) examined the failure of ERP implementation at a soft drink bottler company. They argued that this company undermined the importance of involving, supervising, recognizing, and retaining those who work or will work with the system. O'Leary (2002) offered a discussion on when is it appropriate to use heterogeneous expert opinion as a basis for research on ERP systems.

ERP systems have continued to evolve in the twenty-first century. ERP systems are also designed to take advantage of Internet technology, and users are able to share information and communicate via the Internet. By the second generation of ERP (ERP II), vendors had learned to create Web-centric systems by consolidating data and allowing dynamic access from various clients. One of the latest developments is the integration of e-business capabilities to use the internet to conduct business transactions, such as sales, purchasing, inventory management, and customer service. ERP systems provide vast amounts of data for analysis. Software vendors have developed powerful new analytic tools and applications that capitalize on ERP's central repository of data. Examples of such software systems are customer relationship management (CRM), supplier relationship management (SRM), advanced planning and optimizer (APO), and collaborative commerce (CPC). Capgemini's recent survey revealed that the top five investments in supply chain technology for 2005 were CRM (38%), demand planning (35%), warehouse management system (33%), supplier integration (32%), and ERP (31%), indicating a slight shift away from traditional transaction data systems towards those that link supply and demand more closely (Capgemini 2004)

ERP aims to improve internal efficiency by integrating the different parts in the organization. The proliferation of ERP systems forces companies to provide communication and information flow between supply chain agents, overcoming natural boundaries (Tarn et al. 2002). Therefore, integration of ERP and QR is a natural and necessary process as their successes rely on a very similar framework that is the accuracy and velocity of the information flow. Actually, ERP systems help support a variety of QR manufacturing by providing real-time information access, improving responsiveness and shortening lead time along a supply chain. The future of ERP is to improve the supply chain and foster greater collaborating across many different locations and business units, and hence more responsive QR. For example, coordinated with other components such as product lifecycle management, CRM, procurement, SCM, the Oracle ERP system has become an integral part of Oracle E-business suite.

2.4 Customer Relationship Management

Customer relationship management (CRM) plays a very important role in QR program as it connects company with its customers. CRM is software that plans and executes business processes that involve customer interaction, such as sales, marketing, fulfillment, and customer service. CRM allows real-time order submissions, which results in an improved customer service. As soon as a customer places the order, the system confirms adequate inventory, verifies order receipt, and goes immediately to the warehouse for delivery. CRM changes the focus from managing products to managing customers. In CRM, all data go into a data warehouse, where it is analyzed for hidden patterns (called data mining) and from which predictions of future behavior are made. For example, in apparel and footwear industry, it was found that 34% of men purchasing shoes were republicans (Jordan 2004). MedicalDispatch adopted Sendia's WorkSpace CRM wireless software to shorten the company's sales cycle by around 50% (from 61 days to the average of 31), which leads to the company's QR to the market (Beasty 2006). CRM allows firms to integrate database marketing strategy to their organizations to achieve better customer segmentation (Weinberger 2004). In addition to collecting and analyzing data,

CRM provides decision support for forecasting demand, demand management, pricing products and services, quoting order delivery dates, and planning for customer service needs. The apparel retailers can use data mining to analyze POS data, and then to forecast size, color, and consumer's purchasing habits (Suzette 1998).

2.5 Collaborative Planning, Forecasting, and Replenishment

Collaborative forecasting and replenishment (CPFR) is a web-based standard that empowers vendor-managed inventory and continuous replenishment by making joint forecasting (Simchi-Levi et al. 2007). It enables firms in the supply chain to plan, forecast, and replenish inventories in a collaborative manner. With CPFR, parties exchange electronically sales trends, scheduled promotions, and forecast. This allows the participants to coordinate joint forecasts by working on their forecast differences. Sharing forecasts with other partners can result in a significant decrease in forecast errors and inventory levels. As a result, CPFR could take QR to the next level (Margulis 1999).

Latest CPFR model comprises four major iterative collaborative activities: strategy and planning, demand and supply management, execution, and analysis. Each activity also includes two tasks. The CPFR model is applicable to different scenarios. For example, collaborative assortment planning, one of the CPFR scenarios, is suitable for apparel and seasonal goods. Internet-based CPFR can coordinate the requirements planning prices among upstream and downstream supply chain partners for demand creation and order fulfillment activities, and thus to shorten the lead time (Bowersox et al. 2010).

3   How Should Companies Respond to Advances in IT?

It is not an exaggeration to say that QR has not fully exploited to the changes in information technology. By using the available information in a superficial manner, the companies are not taking full advantage of the information available to them. The main reasons for such an incomplete use of information are as follows:

Supply chain design: The strategic design of a supply chain (e.g., location and number of facilities, operating policies) has been determined long before the information was available. Now that the information is available, to make the best use of it, it may be necessary for the supply chain to be redesigned. Many companies have failed to recognize this need for redesign and have instead decided to stay with the old design while trying to make the best use of the available information. As a result, QR captured only a fraction of the IT benefits.

Decision making process: It is reasonable to say that most of the decision making in the current supply chains is very much manual as well as subjective, and makes very little use of a rigorous and automated decision making process. As a result of this manual interaction, the voluminous data that has recently become available cannot be analyzed, interpreted, and incorporated into the decision making process. This in turns hinders a speedy decision making on new customer's demand and requests.

Existence of supply chain metrics: One of the major issues associated with any supply chain collaboration project is the manner in which the benefits will be shared among the participants. To achieve a mutually agreeable sharing of the benefits, one must be able to exactly compute the benefits associated with a particular strategy. In the current state of affairs, the financial picture at most companies is so muddled (with significant time lag) that it is almost impossible to determine the improvements realized from a supply chain collaboration endeavor. If the information-based collaboration is to proceed, the issues associated with QR and SCM metrics must be adequately addressed.

Based on the observations detailed above, it is imperative that companies address some or all of these issues before we can say that the IT-based revolution is complete. In the presence of information, it is necessary for companies to change the design and management of their supply chain to better support the QR program. As such they should obtain the ability to evaluate alternative supply chain strategies available, pick the one that is most information compatible. The companies must also develop a user-friendly, automated, rigorous decision making process with as little human or subjective involvement as possible. Such an approach will be better able to handle the voluminous data that is being transmitted across the supply chain. The in-built algorithms should be able to automatically incorporate the information and produce the appropriate decisions. In addition, they must be in a position to accurately and in a timely manner calculate their financial position.

4 The Existing Problems and Direction for Potential Future Research

Although the aforementioned information systems have been widely implemented, there is a significant disagreement over the actual benefit they have provided. It has been reported that a large percentage of QR and supply chain IT projects have failed to recoup their investments. To understand why it is so, it is necessary to look at how supply chains are managed in the presence of information. In addition, one needs to be able to compute the benefits of such endeavors and be in a position to estimate an ROI. A lot of work has already been done in this direction and more needs to be done.

The ability to access information across the supply chain and use it in real time provides various opportunities. Inventory requirements for buffer stocks are likely to be lower, because the uncertainty in forecasts and demand can be reduced across the supply chain. Allocation of inventory to different retail outlets or customers as part of order fulfillment can be done more effectively when there is visibility about the number and type of inventory located at the different sites in the supply chain.

As more supply chain execution information becomes available, firms can plan for future operations using advanced planning and optimization (APO) tools. The ability to share information creates an opportunity for firms to have collaborative planning and design, which removes the inefficiencies in these processes.

A number of papers have dealt with this type of information flow in the QR and supply chain and the effect of that on its performance. Palmer and Markus (2000) studied the relationship among business process change, degree of new information technology, and firm performance. They found that QR technology adoption at a minimal level is associated with higher performance. Cachon and Fisher (2000) showed that timely information sharing helps speed up decision making and often results in shorter lead times and smaller batch sizes. Russell and Hoag (2004) argued that the most significant challenge in implementing IT is not the technical portion but the human portion. A number of social and organizational factors, such as user perceptions, culture, communication, and leadership, affect the success of an implementation. Sparks and Wagner (2003) compared four retailing concepts that promote supply chain efficiencies: QR, ECR, CPFR, and Retail Exchange. They overviewed the fundamental IT differences between the four concepts. Brown and Buttross (2008) studied the financial impact of a QR program. They found that QR adopters did not benefit as expected in terms of their profitability, cost efficiency, and inventory level performances.

A lot more needs to be done before one can rest be assured that supply chains are making the best use of information systems. Here we list three of them: (1) The information systems are usually imposed on the existing supply chain setups. If one wants to maximize the impact of the information systems, there needs to be a significant redesign of the supply chain structure or operational policies; (2) It is necessary to capture the strategic/competitive behavior of the participants. If the gaming tendencies of the participants are ignored, the policies developed could result in inferior performance; (3) Information in the real world is often inaccurate and this has to be incorporated into the analysis. To have the most impact, it is necessary for the QR researchers to incorporate these complexities in the models they study. For example, supply chain partners can adopt recent IT technology standards such as RosettaNet or ebXML to manage their business process. Furthermore, enterprises have to rely on business analytics to improve their decision making process (Davenport 2006).

5 Conclusions

It is fair to say that this is the start of a fruitful relationship between IT and QR, and the interaction could be mutually beneficial for a long time. To improve demand predictability and supply chain coordination in more volatile environments, it is more cost efficient to invest in IT than in manufacturing flexibility (Khouja and Kumar 2002).There will be new developments in information technology, and QR programs will evolve to incorporate these developments and improve their operation. On the other hand, QR could demonstrate a need, and an appropriate technology will be developed to address it. Thus the interaction should be a bi-directional one. In recognition of the mutual benefit, it behooves that the researchers in IT and QR work collaboratively on these issues.

References

Aiyer S, Ledesma G (2004) Waste not, want not. Logist Today 45(4):35–37

Au KF, Ho DCK (2002) Electronic commerce and supply chain management: value-adding service for clothing manufacture. Integrated Manuf Syst 13(4):247–255

Barker T, Frolick MN (2003) ERP implementation study: a case study. Inform Syst Manag 20(4):43–49

Beasty C(2006). A wireless emergency. Customer Relationship Manag 10(3):42

Bednarz A (2004) RFID joins wireless lineup at UPS. Netw World 21(38):8

Birtwistle G, Moore CM, Fiorito SS (2006) Apparel quick response systems: the manufacturer perspective. Int J Logist Res Appl 9(2):157–168

Bowersox D, Closs D, Cooper B (2010) Supply chain logistics management. McGraw-Hill, NY

Boyson S, Corsi T, Verbraeck A (2003) The e-supply chain portal: A core business model. Transport Res E 39(2):175–195

Brockmann P (2003) EDI and XML. World Trade 16(9):68

Brown T, Buttross TE (2008) An empirical analysis of the financial impact of quick response. Int J Retail Distrib Manag 36(8):607–626

Cachon G, Fisher M (2000) Supply chain inventory management and the value of shared information. Manag Sci 46(8):1032–1048

Campbell S (2008) Gartner lowers 2009 IT spending outlook, CRN. http://: www.crn.com. Accessed 13 Oct 2008

Capgemini (2004) Connectivity in supply chains key to operational excellence, according to the new study. http://www.us.capgemini.com. Accessed 6 Oct 2004

Cash JI, Konsynski BR (1984) IS redraws competitive boundaries Harv Bus Rev 63(2):134–142

Chatfield AT, Yetton P (2000) Strategic payoff from EDI as a function of EDI embeddedness. J Manag Inform Syst 16(4):195–224

Choi TM, Li D, Yan H (2006) Quick response policy with Bayesian information updates. Eur J Oper Res 170(1):788–808

Chow HKH, Choy KL, Lee WB, Chan FTS (2007) Integration of web-based and RFID technologu in visualizing logistics operations – a case study. Supply Chain Manag Int J 12(3):221–234

Clemons EK, Row MC (1993) Limits to interfirm coordination through technology: result from a field study in consumer packaged good distribution. J Manag Inform Syst 10(1):73–95

Cliffe S (1999) ERP Implementation. Harv Bus Rev 77(1):16–17

Croson R, Donahue K (2003) Impact of POS data sharing on supply chain management: an experimental study. Prod Oper Manag 50(4):458–464

Davenport T (1998) Putting enterprise into the enterprise system. Harv Bus Rev 76(4):121–131

Davenport T (2006) Competing on analytics. Har Bus Rev 84(1):99–107

de Kok AG, van Donselaar KH, van Woensel T (2008) A break even analysis of RFID technology for inventory sensitive to shrinkage. Int J Prod Econ 112(2):521–531

Dearing B (1990) The strategic benefits of EDI. J Bus Strat 11(1):4–6

Gentry CR (2004) 99 bottles of beer. Chain Store Age 80(3):62–63

Gunasekaran A, Ngai EWT (2004) Information systems in supply chain integration and management. Eur J Oper Res 159(2):269–295

Handfield RB, Nichols EL Jr (1998) Introduction to supply chain management, 1st edn. Prentice Hall, NJ

Hickey K (1999) Product roundup. J Commerce, 37

Hill S (1998) Crystal ball gazing becomes a science. Apparel Industry Magazine 59(5):18–23

Hitt L, Brynjolfsson E (1996) Productivity, business profitability, and consumer surplus: Three different measures of information technology value. MIS Quarterly 20(2):121–142

Holland T (2004) Shopping cart spy chips. Far E Econ Rev 167(36):36–39

Holt L (1999) Competition heats up in ERP. InfoWorld 21(6):65

Khouja M, Kumar RL (2002) Information technology investments and volume-flexibility in production systems. Int J Prod Res 40(1):205–221

Ko E, Kincade DH (1997) The impact of quick response technologies on retail store attributes. Int J Retail Distrib Manag 25(2):90–98

Lee H (2004) Simple theories for complex logistics. Optimize 42–47

Lee HL, So KC, Tang CS (2000) The value of information sharing in a two level supply chain. Manag Sci 46(5):626–664

Levary RR, Mathieu R (2004) Supply chain's emerging trends. Ind Manag 46(4):22–27

Lo WS, Hong TP, Jeng R (2008) A framework of –SCM multi-agent systems in the fashion industry. Int J Prod Econ 114(2):594–614

Margulis R (1999) CPFR takes quick response to next level, ID. http://www.allbusiness.com/services/business-services-mailing-reproduction/4439837–1.html. Accessed 1 Aug 1999

Metaxiotis KS, Psarras JE, Ergazakis KA (2003) Production scheduling in ERP systems: An AI-based approach to face the gap. Bus Process Manag J 9(2):221–247

Mohr J, Nevin JR (1990) Communication strategies in marketing channels: A theoretical perspective. J Market 54(4):36–51

Mukhopadhyay T, Kekre S, Kalathur S (1995) Business value of information technology: a study of electronic data interchange. MIS Quarterly 19(2):137–156

NIST (2004) Lack of data standardization costs industry billions. Frontline Solutions 5(9):11–12

O'Connor MC (2008) Jones apparel group plans RFID pilot in Nine West Stores, RFID J. http://www.rfidjournal.com/article/articleview/4264/. Accessed 15 August 2008

O'Leary DE (2002) Discussion of information system assurance for enterprise resource planning systems: unique risk considerations. J Inform Syst 16(1):115–126

Owens SF, Levary RR (2002) Evaluating the impact of electronic data interchange on the ingredient supply chain of a food processing company. Supply Chain Manag Int J 7(4):200–211

Palmer JW, Markus ML (2000) The performance impacts of quick response and strategic alignment in specialty retailing. Inform Syst Res 11(3):241–259

Raghunathan S (2001) Information sharing in a supply chain: a note on its value when demand is nonstationary. Manag Sci 47(4):605–610

Russell DM, Hoag AM (2004) People and information technology in the supply chain. Int J Phys Distrib Logist Manage 34(2):102–122

Schnetzler MJ, Schonsleben P (2007) The contribution and role of information management in supply chains: a decomposition-based approach. Prod Plann Contr 18(6):497–513

Simchi-Levi D, Kaminsky P, Simchi-Levi E (2007) Designing and managing the supply chain, 3rd edn. McGraw-Hill, NY

Sparks L, Wagner BA (2003) Retail exchanges: a research agenda. Supply Chain Manag Int J 8(3):201–208

Speer JK (2004) Digging deep: extreme data mining. Apparel 45(12):1

Sridharan UV, Caines WR, Patterson CC (2005) Implementation of supply chain management and its impact on the value of firms. Supply Chain Manag Int J 10(4):313–318

Tarn JM, Yen DC, Beaumont M (2002) Exploring the rationales for ERP and SCM integration. Ind Manag Data Syst 102(1–2):26–34

Tirschwell P (2004) Why Sarbanes-Oxley matters in logistics. J Commerce 1

Umble EJ, Umble MM (2002) Avoiding ERP implementation failure. Ind Manag 44(1):25–33

Umble EJ, Haft RR, Umble MM (2003) Enterprise resource planning: implementation procedure and critical success factors. Eur J Oper Res 146(2):241–257

Violino B (2004) RFID, Sarbox spurs supply chain spending. Optimize 77
Weber MM, Kantamneni SP (2002) POS and EDI in retailing: an examination of underlying benefits and barriers. Supply Chain Manag Int J 7(5):311–317
Weinberger J (2004) Database marketers mine for perfect customer segmentation. Customer Relationship Manag 8(10):19

Fast Fashion: Achieving Global Quick Response (GQR) in the Internationally Dispersed Clothing Industry

Bart L. MacCarthy and P.G.S.A. Jayarathne

Abstract The clothing industry is one of the most mobile industries in the world. Global supply poses significant challenges in ensuring the right volume and mix of products within retail stores. Here we define a new concept – Global quick response (GQR) – which strives to combine the cost and scale efficiencies arising from sourcing globally with quick and accurate response to market requirements. GQR is based on lead time compression, effective information management, dynamic planning, and strong logistics. We examine GQR in the context of the new garment development process, the initial volume order process, and the repeat order process, and discuss its requirements with respect to market intelligence, rapid new product introduction, network structure, network planning, and network capability. The importance of staged planning postponement is noted, where commitments to precise mix requirements are delayed as late as possible in the supply process. Different operational approaches for achieving GQR are possible, from fully integrated, centrally controlled systems to response based on contractual relationships. Two contrasting examples from practice – Zara and Primark – are noted. GQR offers significant opportunities for further research both in the clothing sector and more widely.

Keywords Clothing industry · Fast fashion · Global quick response · Order fulfilment · Postponement · Quick response · Supply chain management

1 Introduction

The textile and clothing sectors are fundamental to the world economy. International trade in the combined sector has increased 60-fold during the past 40 years, a period characterized by major increases in the globalization of business, deregulation, and

B.L. MacCarthy (✉)
Nottingham University Business School, The University of Nottingham, Nottingham
NG8 1BB, UK
e-mail: bart.maccarthy@nottingham.ac.uk

T.C. Edwin Cheng and T.-M. Choi (eds.), *Innovative Quick Response Programs in Logistics and Supply Chain Management*, International Handbooks on Information Systems, DOI 10.1007/978-3-642-04313-0_3,
© Springer-Verlag Berlin Heidelberg 2010

gradual removal of quotas (UNCTAD 2005). The textile sector covers the production and processing of the primary textile materials – the natural and synthetic fibers, yarns, and fabrics used in a wide variety of industrial, medical, household furnishings, and clothing applications. Here we are concerned with the clothing industry, which is "fed" by the textile industry, primarily by textile fabric producers but in some categories by yarn producers as well.

International export trade in clothing increased by approximately 118% in the period 1990–2003 (UNCTAD 2005). The clothing industry is also one of the most mobile industries in the world (Martin 2007). Over the last two decades, complex global supply networks have emerged to supply clothing to world markets. The nature of these global networks poses significant challenges for quick and accurate response in the clothing sector. Ensuring the right product volume and mix within retail stores from a globally dispersed supply network requires innovative operational strategies and practices.

Quick response (QR) has been a dominant theme in the clothing sector for almost two decades (Hunter 1990; Cooper et al. 1997; Al-Zubaidi and Tyler 2004; Holweg 2005; Birtwistle et al. 2006). QR is premised on understanding precise market demands and on compressing key components of lead time to supply those demands quickly and accurately. However, much of the emphasis in QR initiatives has been on internal production systems. When the value chain is geographically dispersed with diverse forms of supply chain relationships and ownership patterns, QR requires a global perspective.

Here we define a new concept, *Global quick response (GQR)*, which has emerged in buyer-driven global supply networks in the internationally dispersed clothing sector. GQR strives to combine cost and scale efficiencies by sourcing globally with quick and accurate response to specific market requirements. We examine how GQR affects the major operational processes in clothing design, manufacture, and distribution. We discuss its requirements with respect to market intelligence and rapid new product introduction; network planning and staged postponement; and network capability. Different approaches to GQR are possible and two contrasting examples are discussed briefly.

2 Globalization in the Clothing Industry

2.1 Globalization and Mobility in the Clothing Industry

In the last three decades, clothing manufacture has migrated substantially from the developed to the less well developed economies. The major clothing producing nations in 2005 were China, India, Indonesia, Bangladesh, and Pakistan (Audet 2007). The growth in Chinese as well as Indian clothing production has been substantial in the last two decades. In 2002, over 70% of the Japanese and over 77% of the Australian apparel markets originated from China (Nordas 2004). Chinese manufactured clothing entering the US and the EU apparel markets grew by 43%

and 47%, respectively, in the period 2004–2005 (Audet 2007). India has also shown considerable growth of 30% and 25% in the EU and the US apparel markets, respectively, in the period 2004–2005 (Audet 2007). The tremendous growth of China and India in these sectors has been heavily influenced by the complete elimination of the existing restrictions in the Multi Fiber Agreement (MFA) at the end of 2004 (Audet 2007). This growth has had a major impact on the global clothing industry (Nordas 2004; UNCTAD 2005; Abernathy et al. 2006; Audet 2007).

There have also been significant movement in parts of the clothing sector across the newly industrialized, developing, and under-developed economies, influenced by changing patterns of international trade, as well as regulatory and quota changes (Nordas 2004; UNCTAD 2005; Abernathy et al. 2006; Audet 2007). This has affected countries that supply the major global markets at any one time. For instance, the top five suppliers of clothing to the US market in 1990 were Hong Kong (16%), China (15%), South Korea (12%), Taiwan (10%), and the Philippines (4%). In 2000, the rankings were Mexico (15%), China (11%), Hong Kong (7%), Dominican Republic (4%), and Honduras (48%). In 2006, this had changed to China (29%), Mexico (7%), India (5%), Indonesia (4%), and Bangladesh (3%) (US Department of Commerce, Office of Textile and Apparel – cited from Martin 2007).

Deregulation and the abolition of quotas in the sector have had a major effect in some countries. The Sri Lankan garment industry declined from 71% of that country's total industrial exports in 2004 to 44% in 2006 with the abolition of the MFA (CBARSL 2005, 2007). Mexico and Turkey lost some of their share in major apparel markets, with Mexico experiencing a 7% drop in the US in 2004–2005 and Turkey's growth in the EU in 2004–2005 being only 4% (Audet 2007).

Although textiles and clothing production has migrated substantially from the developed to less well-developed economies, it is still a significant industry in some Western countries. In 2006, there were over two million people employed in the combined textile and clothing industry across the EU. Although there was a 5% drop over a 1 year period (2005–2006), this still represents a substantial employment sector (Euratex 2006 – cited from EMCC 2008). In the US, the sector employed approximately 1.9 million workers in November 2008 (The US Department of Labour – www.bls.gov). Importantly, most of the major international retailers and brand owners are based in Western countries.

All these phenomena are important in understanding current and emerging supply chain structures in the clothing sector that are based on global supply but often supplemented by local supply where desirable. Marks and Spencer (M&S), the major UK retailer with a retailing presence also in a number of other countries, sourced substantially from a core UK supply base up until the late 1990s, but now makes full use of a global sourcing strategy (Tokatli et al. 2008).

2.2 Buyer-Driven Supply Networks in Clothing

Clothing may be categorized in different ways. The US Department of Trade (www.osha.gov) identify a number of categories, including men's and boy's wear (SIC 231 and SIC 232), women's wear (SIC 233 and SIC 234), hats, caps, and millinery (SIC 235), children and infant wear (SIC 236), fur goods (SIC 237), and miscellaneous apparel and accessories (SIC 238). Some of these categories would traditionally have been classed as volume or commodity products. However, both product variety and the rate of new product introduction have been accelerating across all apparel categories (Sen 2008). Many volume and commodity categories have developed a strong fashion element, with significant changes from season to season (Tokatli 2007; Sen 2008).

The traditional fashion markets, characterized by two fixed seasons per year, have also been affected by the need for more rapid refreshing of ranges, styles, and colors. Demanding consumers and competitive retailing have generated pressures to respond with multiple refreshes per season. The focus is on replenishment of the specific styles, designs, and colors that are selling well, while reducing, changing, or abandoning those that turn out to be less popular than forecast. This reduces the problem of marking down the price of less popular clothing that fails to sell in the forecasted volumes (Ferdows et al. 2004; Tokatli 2007). This trend, when taken to the extreme of compressing design times, multiple refreshes, coupled with very quick response from the supply base, and all done at low cost, describes the so-called *Fast Fashion* market (Tokatli 2007).

Irrespective of the category, clothing products can take a circuitous route from fabric production, through garment production and distribution, to eventually reach an individual retail customer (Wadhwa et al. 2008). Figure 1 illustrates the generic high-level structure of globally dispersed clothing supply chains. The textile producers supply the clothing plants, which in turn feed into distribution and logistics systems to enable garments produced in dispersed global networks to meet anticipated demand in specific retail chains and stores. In Fig. 1, the solid line crossing the regional distribution network (RDC) is highlighting conceptually that the balance of what is globally and locally dispersed, as well as ownership and control patterns, can vary significantly, depending on the specific supply chain considered. Thus a major brand owner that sources globally and supplies major retailers will have to manage the interface between its distribution network and that of each of the retailers it supplies in their national markets.

In reality, any specific clothing supply configuration will resemble more a supply network than a "linear" supply chain. Much of the material flow complexity occurs around the clothing plants and in the distribution and logistics parts of the system. However, describing just the physical configuration and the material flow is insufficient to understand and analyze the operation and performance of any specific system. The high-level view illustrated in Fig. 1 is limited in displaying the diverse sets of entities that can play a part in any particular supply network. As well as fabric producers, garment manufacturing plants, and retailers, a global supply network will include designers, buyers and merchandisers, distribution, logistics, and warehousing companies, and may include additional finishers that ensure products are ready for display and sale in any particular market.

Key issues that need to be understood include the different participants within the network; the nature of their relationships; ownership, power, and control structures;

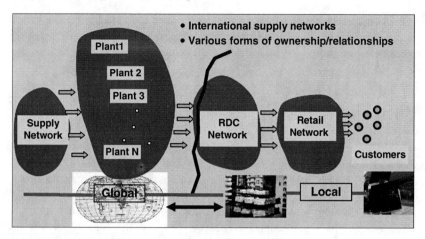

Fig. 1 Generic high-level structure of the global apparel supply chain

how the network is managed, coordinated, and controlled; and how information flows in the network (Lambert and Cooper 2000; Hunter et al. 2002).

Gereffi (1999) and Tyler et al. (2006) highlight how today's clothing supply networks are driven by the buying entities – major retailers, brand owners, and branded manufacturers. Buyer-driven chains are controlled by these powerful players through their ability to stimulate and shape demand via strong brand names and extensive retailing outlets or presence within retail outlets (e.g., M&S, Primark, Zara, Levi's). Such buyer-driven supply networks are different from the producer-driven supply networks common in some sectors such as the auto-industry. Producer-driven supply networks are characterized by large and powerful multinational manufacturers (e.g., Toyota) controlling tightly coupled networks of supply, production, and distribution. Profits are derived from the scale and volume of operations and technological advances in both products and process (Gereffi 1999). Gereffi (1999) notes that technology rent (e.g., the use of unique technology) and organizational rents in the form of intra-organizational processes (e.g., employing JIT and TQM) act as barriers to entry in producer-driven supply networks, and that relational rent (interfirm relationships), trade rent (tariffs and quotas), and brand name rent (established brands) act as barriers to entry in buyer-driven supply networks.

In contrast to producer-driven supply networks, buyer-driven networks in clothing are often characterized by looser and more dynamic couplings linking production principally in developing countries to demand for fashion in developed countries. They rely on global sourcing strategies to meet demand. Profits and margins in buyer-driven supply networks are generated from design, sales, marketing, and services that link globally dispersed factories with consumer markets (Tyler et al. 2006).

This more complex view of globally dispersed clothing supply networks incorporating multiple entities, a powerful control entity and various forms of relationships, must be considered when evaluating the capabilities and capacity of any system, how it performs, and how it could be improved. Given the buyer-driven, globally dispersed clothing supply network, how is QR achieved?

3 Global Quick Response

Responsiveness in operations management has been defined in different ways (Kritchanchi and MacCarthy 1999; Reichhart and Holweg 2007). Common elements typically highlighted for responsive operational systems include information management, partnerships between supply chain members, manufacturing flexibility, effective inventory management, and strong logistics systems. The importance of QR strategies has been emphasized in the clothing and apparel sectors since the late 1980s and a number of QR initiatives have been undertaken in the sector (e.g. Hunter 1990; Perry and Sohal 2001; Hunter et al. 2002; Al-Zubaidi and Tyler 2004; Barnes and Lea-Greenwood 2006). The study of QR was initiated by Kurt Salmon Associates (KSA) in the US apparel industry in 1986 (Barnes and Lea-Greenwood 2006) and has spread widely in the apparel industry since 1990 (Al-Zubaidi and Tyler 2004).

QR in the clothing sector has been defined in different ways and from different perspectives. Lowson et al. (1999) define QR as *a state of responsiveness and flexibility in which an organization seeks to provide a highly diverse range of products and services to a customer/consumer in the exact quantity, variety, and quality, and at the right time, place, and price as dictated by real-time customer/consumer demand.* Forza and Vinelli (2000) define QR as *modifying the current organizational system of the chain and speeding up the physical and information flows, in both directions, between all the phases of the value operative chain system.*

The potential benefits of QR initiatives have been noted by a number of researchers – increased sales volumes, reduced markdowns, reduced stock-outs, reduced costs and prices, greater price validity in retail stores, and improved financial performance and increased competitiveness (Hunter 1990; Hunter et al. 2002; Al-Zubaidi and Tyler 2004; Hayes and Jones 2006). Retailers improve the profitability of their business by using rotation of stock as leverage (replenishment of orders), which helps to minimize forced markdowns and discounts and ensure that more sales take place at the normal retail price (Hunter et al. 2002). However, such responsiveness may result in a reduction in order sizes, higher ordering frequency, and a requirement for shorter lead times than in conventional supply systems.

As highlighted in the preceding sections, the clothing industry now operates with global supply networks, presenting greater challenges for QR. Here we label this as GQR and define it as follows:

GQR is a strategy that seeks to achieve accurate, rapid, and cost-effective response to specific markets dynamically by leveraging the potential of dispersed global supply and production resources through lead time compression, effective real time information management, flexible pipeline management, and optimal logistics and distribution systems.

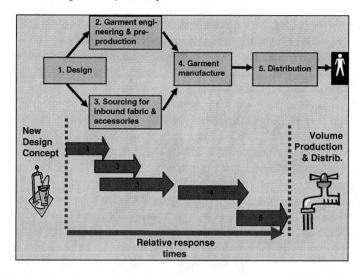

Fig. 2 Generic process for garment design, development, production, and distribution

GQR strives to combine cost and scale efficiencies by sourcing globally with quick and accurate response to specific market requirements derived from information management, dynamic planning, and strong logistics. GQR requires that the complexities, risks, and additional coordination inherent in managing international supply routes with multiple linkages are absorbed if sales opportunities are to be maximized and the risks of supplying the wrong products minimized. What does GQR require and how is it done?

4 Achieving GQR

4.1 From Sample to Volume

Figure 2 illustrates a generic garment development, sourcing, production, and distribution process. The process is initiated by a new garment design that is produced in a sample form in very small quantities. If the design (typically a set of related garment styles in various combinations of colors and sizes) is successful in the marketplace with buyers, merchandisers, or retailers, then volume orders are placed.

The process must be capable of "ramping up" to volume production if a substantial volume order is placed. The flow of garments may then be sustained for a period of time by repeat orders that will typically vary in mix during the period, that is, the quantities for each repeat order may vary in terms of color, size, and style details. Substantial preproduction stages are needed to move from the production of small scale sample designs for showing or merchandising purposes to large scale volume production capable of sustaining multiple repeat orders with varying mix over a season. Thus, for each unique style variant, garment specifications need to be defined, including sizing and pattern making and providing relevant instructions for cutting, assembly, sewing, finishing, and packing.

A key part of ensuring that volume garment production can be initiated for a new style or range of related styles is the sourcing of the required fabrics and accessories in the required volumes and with appropriate timings. Multiple garment styles may often be produced from a specific fabric type. Fabric supply is a substantial part of the overall supply process, with typically substantially longer lead times than garment production cycles. Having a ready source of fabric that is delivered with the anticipated volume of orders is therefore important to ensure quick response to volume orders. However, this can pose significant challenges for fashion garments.

Figure 2 illustrates conceptually a simplified generic process. In practice, there may be iterations and overlaps among the design, garment engineering, and fabric sourcing functions, for example; sampling may be done by a company in one country interpreting the design concept from another. Fabric selection may stimulate the design process, with fabric sourcing being initiated concurrently with design and garment engineering.

Garment production is typically a process of cutting, making up (sewing garment components together), pressing, and packing. For some basic garments, cutting may be done in separate production units before being sent to one or more production units for making up into finished garments. Making up of garments is usually the longest process, typically involving multiple skills and a significant garment production costs. However, as illustrated in Fig. 2, manufacturing lead times may be less significant than the combined lead times in upstream design, specification, and textile sourcing and the downstream logistics and distribution processes. Some of the technical aspects noted here vary for knitwear and hosiery garments.

Depending on where a garment is produced (which could involve multiple locations), logistics and distribution must be considered from production sites into retailing distribution networks, possibly through producer or logistics providers' warehouses. In volume retailing systems this may just mean fitting into an existing logistics and distribution system. These are typically managed by third party logistics providers to feed into the retailer's distribution centers serving the markets where garments are destined (Tokatli et al. 2008). For smaller and more specialized outlets, specific systems may have to be designed.

Two further issues that need to be considered are the coloring process and accessories. Garments may be produced from fabric that does not need coloring or from fabric that is subject to coloring after fabric production. A third possibility is that the finished garments may be colored once produced. In the second case, the coloring process may add to lead times or complicate fabric sourcing. Sometimes, the garment producer may store fabric in a "grey" undyed state and wait until orders are confirmed before sending fabric for dyeing. If whole garments are dyed, then this additional process must be factored into the garment production cycle.

Although the sourcing and supply of garment accessory items may seem a relatively trivial part of the overall process, they can be problematic. Often accessory items may be the distinguishing feature of a particular style variant or be required to match other aspects of the garment style in some way. Coordinated sourcing for highly mixed orders is therefore important. Special processes such as embroidery or adding sequins may also be problematic if they require specialist skills or involve outside service suppliers, complicating process routes and adding to lead time.

4.2 Three Key Processes

GQR must be considered with respect to the generic garment industry structure and processes described above and the requirements, opportunities, and challenges that arise. Here we identify three key processes:

1. The new garment design and development process
2. The initial volume order process
3. The replenishment or repeat order process

In traditional systems these processes occur sequentially and are affected by different constraints in the supply system. Here we consider these processes in the context of the global supply network and the factors affecting lead time and the ability to respond.

4.2.1 The New Garment Design and Development Process

Typically, design samples require only relatively small lengths of sample fabrics usually available from fabric suppliers based on standard fabrics that are always in demand and new or special fabrics produced by the fabric producers based on expected fashion trends in anticipation of garment designers' needs.

The new garment design process requires not only new garment designs to be produced quickly but it must also enable quick "ramp up" to volume production. The rapidity of new product introduction is a feature of current fast fashion retailers (Oxborrow 2000; Barnes and Lea-Greenwood 2006; Tokatli 2007). This requires capabilities to extract and utilize relevant market information, leverage design resources, modify existing designs, and understand what is practicable and realizable with available manufacturing resources (Ferdows et al. 2004; Tyler et al. 2006).

The value to designers of having local sampling facilities that can produce samples quickly is great (Tokatli 2007). Where sample garments are produced using global resources, they may use specific plants with which the design group has a special relationship (Ferdows et al. 2004; Tokatli 2007).Fast turnaround times are important at this stage and may require sample garments to be expedited using expensive transport options in small volumes (Ferdows et al. 2004; Doyle et al. 2006; Tokatli 2007).

The time taken for cost estimation for a new design may also have to be factored into the new garment development process. When pricing needs be done before a garment is offered to retail buyers or merchandisers, then decisions on where volume production is to be carried out, as well as detailed garment engineering and specification details need to be completed. Estimation done by a contracting garment manufacturer may add to new garment development time and may incur risks if approximations and assumptions are made with respect to supply and production costs.

An important trend in a number of industrial sectors has been the move towards concurrent engineering for new product design and development (Barclay and Dann 2000; Koufteros et al. 2001). Concurrent engineering is particularly important and challenging when design, development, and production are not co-located but dispersed internationally (Abdalla 1999). Concurrent engineering principles are well developed for engineered products in sectors such as aerospace and automotive and there is significant potential for the clothing sector to exploit concurrent product development concepts in a *GQR* context.

4.2.2 The Initial Volume Order

Decisions on the most appropriate plants in which to produce a new garment are typically based on technical, cost, contractual, and logistical factors relating to the supply of inbound fabric and accessories and outbound distribution (Tyler et al. 2006). Not all plants in a network will have the capability to produce all garment designs. Key issues are technical competence to manufacture, capacity to supply, and pre-existing contracts for agreed volumes (Doyle et al. 2006; Tyler et al. 2006). In buyer-driven supply networks, the brand owner, branded manufacturer, or major retailer may control fabric supply (Tokatli 2007; Tokatli et al. 2008). Garment producers in the network may be mandated to use specific fabric suppliers with whom the buyer or prime supply network controller has established contracts. This may guarantee adequate fabric supply and also, importantly from the controller's perspective, may help to assure quality.

Initial volume orders may enable significant learning, for example, in regard to quality and distribution. Lessons learned from a new supply route may well mean changes for subsequent orders – for instance, if the anticipated capacity to supply has not been realized or if logistical difficulties prove insurmountable. At the very least, there will be learning opportunities for repeat orders or new styles using the supply route.

4.2.3 The Repeat and Replenishment Order Process

A dependable network is needed for replenishment orders. The network needs to be capable of working at the required pace for the supply chain and, importantly, be capable of accommodating changes in volume and mix requirements (Hunter et al. 2002; Storey et al. 2005; Birtwistle et al. 2006). Quality and logistics issues need to have been eliminated to ensure that a supply route can respond to mix changes and costs with the required speed and responsiveness (Forza and Vinelli 2000). Fabric sourcing should be agreed and capable of supplying at the rate required (Hunter et al. 2002). An effective order placing and confirmation process must be in place (Hunter et al. 2002).

Supply networks cannot maintain high levels of unutilized capacity in antic-ipation of demand. The potential downside of a strongly demand-driven order fulfillment system is that volume sales opportunities that arise quickly may not be capable of being fulfilled. The market may demand some items in high volumes that could only have been satisfied by prior production based on forecasts (Fisher et al. 1994; Fisher 1997). Increases and changes in the level of product variety add to complexity in international supply chains (Er and MacCarthy 2006).

Both QR and GQR systems must have sufficient supply capacity (Forza and Vinelli 1997; Barnes and Lea-Greenwood 2006; Reichhart and Holweg 2007), accu-rate market intelligence (Forza and Vinelli 1996; Kritchanchi and MacCarthy 1999; Catalan and Kotzab 2003), and effective controls (Forza and Vinelli 1997; Hunter et al. 2002) to deal with both the volume and the mix issues. Supply networks need to be able to absorb the negative effects of volume and mix changes. A key issue in designing effective GQR systems is good decision making with respect to when to commit to volume and mix, discussed below.

5 Enablers for GQR

GQR needs to incorporate many of the elements of QR systems, but do so in the context of globally dispersed production and supply resources. A number of researchers have presented different aspects and requirements for QR initiatives (e.g., Hunter 1990; Hunter et al. 1992; Forza and Vinelli 1997, 2000; Lowson et al. 1999; Perry and Sohal 2001; Oxborrow 2000; Al-Zubaidi and Tyler 2004; CRPM report 2005; Birtwistle et al. 2006; Gunasekaran et al. 2008). Typically researchers highlight that QR needs operational systems in place that facilitate responding quickly and flexibly to changing demand signals. Here we synthesize and summarize the essence of QR.

- *Strive for fast and accurate information transmission*: The processes and speed of transmission of both product and order information need to be analyzed (Forza et al. 2000; Sheridan et al. 2006; Birtwistle et al. 2006; Reichhart and Holweg 2007). The formats for design and garment specifications need to facil-itate both rapid transmission of design requirements and the rapid production of new designs. An issue in the sector is that no standard universal product data formats exist for garments, unlike engineering design information. Speed and accuracy are also important in the transmission of order information, particularly for replenishment orders where time is of the essence.

- *Develop flexible production resources*: Traditional garment manufacturing uses batch production methods. Many opportunities exist to reconsider layouts and organization of factory processes, particularly cellular manufacturing where whole garments or parts of garments are produced or assembled in flow driven cellular processes (Pieter et al. 2007; van Donk and van der Vaart 2007). If such cells are rapidly reconfigurable, then advantages can be gained in quickly responding to the required mix changes. In addition, flexible human skills are valuable in responding to changing garment designs (CRPM Report 2005; Pieter et al. 2007; van Donk and van der Vaart 2007). This is critical, particularly in the time consuming making up processes in garment production. When flexible skills are combined with cellular team-based production, then rapid response to design and mix changes can be enacted without incurring significant set up costs.

- *Utilize technology and automation where appropriate:* In general, the garment manufacturing sector is less automated than many other industrial sectors, particularly the engineering sector. Human skills perform much of the value adding activities in garment production. However, every opportunity needs to be taken to adopt new technology in areas such as laying up and marking of fabric, cutting, sewing, pressing, and packing (Lowson et al. 1999; Forza et al. 2000; Hunter et al. 2002; Hayes and Jones 2006). Also technologies that assist in rapid material identification, material handling, and material flow (Rho and Yur 1998; Reichhart and Holweg 2007) and technologies that enable flexibility need to be adopted, particularly for quick changeovers and set up processes (Lowson et al. 1999; Hunter et al. 2002; Barnes and Lea-Greenwood 2006; Reichhart and Holweg 2007).

- *Develop fast logistics:* Rapid material flow needs to be encouraged and enabled in any QR system. The corollary to this is that stationary material and large inventory buffers should be avoided. The entire distribution channel from production to the retail floor needs to be considered. Implementing fast logistics for inbound fabric supply, for material flow within plants, and outbound into the distribution channels is important (Forza et al. 2000; Lummus et al. 2003; Christopher et al. 2004; Reichhart and Holweg 2007). The technologies noted above can assist in achieving this. The last "50 m" of the supply chain should not be ignored, hence the importance of "floor ready" garments that are appropriately tagged and packaged for immediate display once delivered.

- *Exploit all opportunities for lead time compression*: The combination of the above initiatives reduces many of the time delays affecting overall response times. All aspects of processes, systems, and procedures for gathering and transmitting demand information and for the design, production, and distribution of garments must be looked at for opportunities to compress lead times. One of the keys to compressing overall response times is to ensure fabric availability (Forza and Vinelli 2000). As noted earlier, this can be challenging for fashion or innovative garments. Comparative data on relative lead times is given by Oxborrow (2000, 2006). In addition, QR initiatives will try to identify specific opportunities for lead time compression in the systems and processes of any specific producer or supply chain prime partner and those aspects of the system that need close management and control.

- *QR must be a key part of an organizations strategy and have a supportive organizational culture*: An organization that seeks to pursue QR must see it as a fundamental part of its business strategy. Not all organizations should attempt or will be successful at QR. In pursuing a QR strategy, every effort needs to be made to develop a supportive organizational culture (Forza and Vinelli 1997; Hunter et al. 2002; Sheridan et al. 2006).

Strong QR basics are needed in GQR systems. However, much of the emphasis in QR initiatives has focused on internal production systems. Achieving GQR in globally dispersed clothing supply networks requires much more – a *total systems focus*.

The key processes highlighted in Sect. 4.2 above need to be considered with respect to the global structures outlined in Fig. 1 and the overall generic process outlined in Fig. 2. In the reminder of this section we consider GQR in buyer-driven supply networks with respect to (1) market intelligence and rapid new product introduction, (2) network structure and composition, (3) network planning and staged postponement, (4) network capability, performance, and health.

5.1 Market Intelligence and Rapid New Product Introduction

Given the increased complexity in a GQR system compared to a locally based supply system, more and better market intelligence is required. Earlier and greater sensitivity to changes are needed particularly in new product introduction and in specifying repeat orders.

The whole of the clothing sector is influenced by trade and fashion shows for yarns, fabrics, and garments. These strongly influence new styles and the fabrics and materials used (Forza and Vinelli 2000; Tyler et al. 2006). Whether for commodity products or for fast fashion, they provide important signals in understanding what future demand may look like. However, although such events strongly influence what is designed and produced, they cannot dictate consumer behavior. Receiving accurate consumer-based market intelligence is equally important. Effective systems need to be in place to gather and utilize the information emanating from downstream consumer behavior and preferences (Birtwistle et al. 2006). Opportunities for lead time compression may be possible in all parts of this process – information gathering, information interpretation, and in dissemination to designers.

Design capabilities, skills, and expertise are needed that can utilize market information and that can manage the sampling process. For rapid new product introduction, it is important to understand garment architecture and those details of garment styles that are important to the customer. Thus, the range of garment styles that can be produced from a specific fabric can be maximized. By offering only relevant variety that customers value in terms of ranges, styles, colors, and sizes, the potentially negative impacts of variety in sourcing, production, and distribution can be minimized.

5.2 Network Structure and Composition

A strong supply network with multiple capabilities that can respond appropriately to diverse and changing demands is essential in achieving GQR. Although some brand owners and retailers may be able to use global production resources on an ad-hoc contractual basis, more generally a well developed cohesive network is needed to guarantee continued response and replenishment in appropriate volumes and mixes and also to innovate where appropriate. Hence the nature of the supply chain partners, their relationships, and locations within the network are important (Doyle et al. 2006). Desirable network structure will depend on factors that include costs, quality, reliability of delivery, access to quality inputs, and transport and transaction costs (Doyle et al. 2006; Bruce and Daly 2006; Sen 2008).

Some supply networks may be based on traditional contractual relationships, while others may be fully integrated with long-term relationships based on trust. Purely contractual relationships may have benefits in terms of achieving volume and limiting the liabilities for the contracting producer. However, they are more limited in terms of responsiveness to mix changes, in season refreshing, and in changing pre-agreed contracts. A fully integrated network structure may positively affect the reputation of a brand, facilitating the close monitoring of the entire sourcing process. However, a fully integrated network may also be costly to maintain and may result in slow response in some circumstances when it is centrally controlled. A combination of contractual and integrated partnerships may provide the optimum level of network flexibility.

Although various forms of ownership, joint ventures, equity stake holdings, strategic alliances, and contractual relationships may exist in a network, the development of strong mutually beneficial partnerships is central to establishing an effective supply network. Partners who agree to adopt a GQR strategy in a supply network are more likely to be successful in adopting effective processes and practices over time. Network structures operating on a purely contractual basis are likely to take longer to set up, have longer lead times, and be less flexible and responsive to market changes. However, there are difficulties in maintaining long-term partnerships unless mutual benefits accrue (Birtwistle et al. 2006). Making partnerships work involves sharing the benefits of improved margins and guaranteed volumes rather than benefits accruing only to the prime partner or retailer.

Bruce et al. (2004) highlight the importance of partnerships and the careful selection of partners based on the specific competencies they offer and the contributions they make to the network. Building strong relationships is identified as important, not just at the company level but at the functional level as well. They note the importance of specific relationships and interfaces in the supply networks they analyze, for example, between designers and manufacturers and between sales and development functions.

Although GQR is premised on utilizing global supply networks to gain cost, capability, and volume advantages, some local production resources may be important for some retail and brand strategies to enhance flexibility and speed. Thus, a GQR strategy may combine both local and global production resources to cater for some aspects of the dynamics of the market quickly and flexibly (Bruce et al. 2004; Birtwistle et al. 2006; Tyler et al. 2006; Tokatli 2007; Tokatli et al. 2008). An important issue is to decide the right balance between local and global production resources to meet specific market requirements.

Network partnerships involve not just fabric and garment producers but potentially many other service providers. Effective logistics is central to a successful GQR strategy. This may be facilitated by using experienced Third Party Logistics (3PLs) providers (Fisher and Raman 1996; Fernie 1994; Forza and Vinelli 2000) with knowledge and expertise of global distribution. Such organizations can provide the "glue" to enable a GQR network to operate effectively and efficiently. Third Party Logistics providers can enhance the operation of supply networks by utilizing their expertise in deciding appropriate modes of transportation, in facilitating cross border trade, and in providing contract warehousing facilities with the latest automation in materials storage and handling. Logistics partners can organize and facilitate cross-docking initiatives to minimize stationary time and reduce the need for intermediate storage in supplying retail markets (Fernie 1994; Ferdows et al. 2004; Tokatli 2007). In addition, GQR networks may require other services for the gathering of market data, for product design, for merchandising, and for marketing.

Ethical issues are increasingly important in supply chain management in general and in the clothing sector in particular (Iwanow et al. 2005; Joergens 2006; Pretious and Love 2006). The globalization of the clothing industry has increased competition amongst suppliers and indeed between countries, and this has put pressure on the adoption and maintenance of strong ethical practices. However, globalization also opens up supply networks to greater scrutiny and public awareness. Non-ethical practices are more likely to be exposed than in the past. The adoption of ethical practices may have positive effects on brand image, perception, and loyalty both in customers and in suppliers, although how these issues affect consumer purchasing decisions is open to debate (Iwanow et al. 2005; Joergens 2006). Many retailers and brand owners have developed ethical frameworks, policies, and practices, including the two examples given in Sect. 6: Zara (www.inditex.com) and Primark (www.ethicalprimark.com). A full discussion of ethical issues and how they affect global network design and management is outside the scope of this chapter. However, we note that failure to have ethical policies or to apply them in practice exposes the major companies in the supply chain to significant risks with respect to both brand perception and legal issues. Ethical issues can be expected to play an increasingly significant role in influencing and affecting network design and composition in the future.

5.3   Network Planning and Staged Postponement

A supply network must be capable of producing and delivering efficiently at the anticipated demand and variety level. Although at the detailed mix level forecasting is likely to be inaccurate (Christopher et al. 2004; Tyler et al. 2006), in GQR systems some aspects of future requirements can and indeed must be predicted at the volume level, starting with a retailer's target sales volumes. Inaccurate volume estimation will result in either a network that cannot supply the required volumes because of capacity limitations or one with costly unutilized spare capacity.

Effective supply network planning and management is important, particularly for ongoing repeat ordering and replenishment where market requirements are changing dynamically. There may be a tension here between the retailer's perspective and the producer's perspective. The former tends to prefer to delay committing to precise orders until as late as possible on the basis that later information will result in precise requirements being known with greater accuracy and thus entailing less risk. However, the producer values long planning lead times to ensure that production resources can be marshaled efficiently and that stable plans can be put in place, avoiding frequent changeovers and giving reasonable lead times to suppliers. A type of *staged postponement* described here helps to balance these opposing needs.

The postponement principle delays commitment to final product attributes until close to the point of real demand (Van Hoek 2001). It avoids the risks and costs of carrying large inventories. Postponement can be applied in different ways and the terminology used differs. The most common type of postponement – form postponement – delays commitment to the final product form until a late point in the production process. This is often associated with "late point differentiation" strategies. However, this approach is not of great value in a GQR clothing context. As illustrated in Fig. 2, the relative time in production is outweighed by the time taken for preproduction, fabric sourcing, and distribution. In addition, a late point differentiation strategy is difficult to apply in the sequence of operations in garment production. All the key product attributes – fabric/style/color/size – are committed to in the cutting process. Once fabric is cut, precise style commitments are made. However, the cutting process is the first value adding operation in garment production.

Place postponement occurs when the final destination of finished garments is left undecided until clear demand signals are received. This has some value in a GQR system. Finished goods inventory may be pooled in central downstream warehouses and "called off" for different locations as local demand requires. Place postponement may also be important for fabric sourcing when fabrics can be used by various garment producers in the network and allocated dynamically to garment manufacturing plants depending on current demands. There are some applications in apparel products combining late point differentiation and place postponement – so called *customizing in the channel*– where centrally stored inventory is worked on within logistics facilities for such finishing operations such as tagging, labeling, printing, or specialized packing appropriate for particular markets, particularly for promotional items.

A type of postponement that is less commonly discussed is postponement in planning. The most valuable and important type of postponement in dynamically managing a GQR clothing network is *structured and staged planning postponement*, illustrated in Fig. 3.

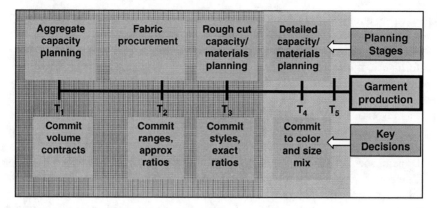

Fig. 3 Staged planning postponement and flexible open pipelines

Well designed *staged planning postponement* strategies operating over a rolling planning horizon have great potential to enable effective dynamic planning to meet changing market requirements. Essentially, aggregate volumes are committed to at an early stage of the planning process, but commitments to precise mix requirements are delayed as late as possible in the planning process, thus maintaining an open flexible planning pipeline, but allowing the network to prepare for volume production.

Figure 3 illustrates a generic process with planning stages from aggregate capacity planning to detailed capacity and materials planning. At each stage, commitments to order details become more precise – initially just volume contracts but eventually commitment to precise mix ratios in terms of color and size. The precise stages and timings (T_1 to T_5 in Fig. 3), as well as the associated planning activities, will depend on the nature of demand, the nature of the supply network, how responsive it is, and also on the retailer's strategy. The global dispersal of production units needs to be factored in – geographical distance may determine the latest point at which commitments can be made and how much flexibility there is in the planning pipeline. Market knowledge is also important. The details of a staged planning postponement strategy will differ depending on whether basic, seasonal, fashion, or fast fashion garments are being produced.

5.4 Network Capability, Performance, and Health

Planning for capacity is one thing. Capability – the range of garment styles that a network can produce – is another. Both the capability and performance of the supply network must be assessed. Although fashion trends can and do go through sudden, perhaps seismic changes from one season to the next, for many seasons range changes can be more gradual and planning at the mix level is more important. Ensuring an appropriate range of network capabilities, particularly when major changes are anticipated, is therefore important, that is, the "health" of the network must be maintained.

For retailers and brand owners with established networks, it is important to track performance, understand where critical interfaces occur (e.g., interfaces with the greatest influence on responsiveness and lead time), and where additional capabilities may be required. Managing across critical interfaces with supply network partners is important. The power of rapid information gathering needs to be leveraged with appropriate IT systems to highlight underperformance and to assess where additional or different capabilities may be desirable.

Dynamic networks that attempt to match more precisely real demand with supply will inevitably have some problems, but valuable learning can occur by addressing problems proactively and jointly. The powerful player in a supply network can benefit from managing the development of capability, capacity, and performance of the supply base. Supplier development programs (Handfield et al. 2000) can benefit the long-term health of a network by enabling appropriate and timely capacity expansion (perhaps through joint investment), by developing quality standards, and by having proactive and joint approaches to problem solving.

6 Global Supply Chain Solutions: Examples from Practice

Different retailers, brand owners, and branded manufacturers have evolved, developed, and deployed different strategies to achieve GQR with different levels of network integration. Here we discuss briefly two examples of different approaches with respect to the nature of the networks they use.

Inditex, the Spanish textile, clothing, and retailing company, and its Zara brand have been noted frequently in both the academic and practitioner literature for the radical changes they have brought to the way fashion clothing is sourced, produced, and sold (Barnes and Lea-Greenwood 2006; Hayes and Jones 2006). Their supply network has traditionally been in Northern Spain and Portugal but increasingly they have used an international supply network, sourcing from countries such as Turkey, Morocco, India, Pakistan, Bangladesh, Sri Lanka, and Indonesia (Tokatli 2007). However, their network remains strongly integrated – 60% of the production is carried out in-house in Europe and in neighboring countries; 40% of its fabric is sourced from Inditex companies; it has its own design resources and systems, has centralized and automated fabric cutting and dyeing, and has its own distribution centers (Tokatli 2007; Gallaugher 2008). They are therefore more vertically integrated than many of the major clothing retailers or brand owners operating globally.

Zara prioritizes responsiveness to its global retail network over production efficiency (Tokatli et al. 2008). They are willing to tolerate surplus capacity to enable responsiveness (Ferdows et al. 2004). Their operating philosophy emphasizes well-designed systems that are focused on compressing the time taken from receiving market information to delivering the right products to Zara's retail stores. Ferdows et al. (2004) describe the dominant "rhythm" that drives design, forecasting, planning, and replenishment across the entire network. In deploying these principles, Zara uses typical good practices, for example, state-of-the-art IT, warehousing, and distribution systems. Their distribution centers enable rapid dispatch of garments to stores all over the world, for example, within 24 h for the EU and within 48 h for North America and Asia (Tokatli 2007). However, they also adopt less common approaches. Co-location of designers, production, and distribution staff has a major positive effect on achieving rapid response (Ferdows et al. 2004).

By deploying "end-to-end" control of both physical supply and information transmission, Zara achieves rapid time to market for new products in small batches, resulting in reduced markdowns and less stock holding overall than competitors. Tokatli (2007) notes that its inventory-to-sales ratio is better than many of its competitors. Furthermore, Zara maintain different mixes of products across their retail outlets and offers large assortments of garments to their customers (Tokatli 2007; Ferdows et al. 2004). They are prepared to tolerate stock-outs, reasoning that it may encourage customers to make frequent visits to stores (Kumar and Linguri 2006).

Figure 4 illustrates Zara's overall approach that enables it to achieve time compression in supplying garments to retail stores that will best appeal to customers. It is based on strong market intelligence to understand what is selling and customer preferences for specific garments, styles, colors, and combinations. Retail stores operate on a tight schedule for replenishment orders that are fed into the forecasting, planning, and scheduling system to drive both the production and the distribution networks. This enables rapid dispatch of garments driven by real demand. Zara is prepared to hold significant stocks of fabric to enable the garment production system to be decoupled from the longer lead time fabric production system. This is helped by having a significant level of fabric supply originating within its parent company group.

Zara's new garment design cycle may be seen as a form of "time postponement." Market intelligence is used for designing and developing new garments quickly. Zara has invested significant resources into design and garment engineering to interpret market intelligence and to enable new garment variants to be developed, evaluated, costed, and planned for production rapidly. Thus, Zara can delay or postpone the final design until it has a clear view of likely demand for the new variant, knowing that its design and development system can respond quickly with garment designs that can be successfully engineered and brought into production.

Primark is a good example of the recent trend for "fast fashion." However, its systems have been less frequently described in the literature. It has become one of the most successful clothing retailers in the UK. It is second in the value clothing category (Financial Times 2009; Belfast Telegraph 2007) and has won the "UK Retailer of the year" award in the Global RLI Awards 2008 (www.primark.co.uk). Sayid (2008) notes that "Primark has the ability to take a catwalk idea and run with it at very affordable prices."

Primark's strategy is an interesting blend of fashion, volume, and low price. Primark claims that it focuses on simple "classic" designs at low prices but without compromising on quality. As with Zara, its strategy is built on high stock

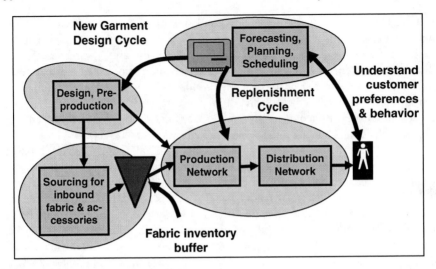

Fig. 4 Zara's demand-driven approach

turnover, striving to always offer something new in its stores and thus creating an ever changing retail experience (www.primark.co.uk).

Unlike Zara, however, Primark is a branded retailer that does not own production facilities but uses large scale and long-term contracting and sub-contracting on a global scale. Primark operates a highly flexible supply network, utilizing a strategic combination of UK, European, and off-shore suppliers to react quickly to the volatile fashion market (www.sdlgreenstone.com 2008). Primark has contractual relationships with over 400 suppliers in countries such as India and Bangladesh. It uses sub-contractors for processes such as embroidery, printing, and sequins work. O'Donoghue (2008) notes that a key part of Primark's business model is the sourcing of products from the cheapest possible supplier while offering the supplier high volume contracts.

Primark has developed highly responsive global supply chain management practices that enable it to stop or change production even in the middle of a season. It uses advanced inventory management and tracking systems that can monitor the movement of goods on an hourly basis in all the stores (Sunday Tribune 2005). It makes use of state-of-the-art third party logistics and warehousing facilities that enable flexibility, speed, productivity, and low costs. This has allowed Primark to increase volumes and capacity utilization within its warehouses without significant increases in staffing levels in their UK National Distribution Centre (www.sdlgreenstone.com 2008).

Primark has been highly innovative and successful in supplying fast fashion to the marketplace. It has done so using a GQR model based on large-scale global contracting, while ensuring that the supply network is actively managed to meet the dynamics of the fast changing fashion market.

7 Conclusions

The production, distribution, and retailing of clothing and apparel products represent a truly global and internationally dispersed industry. It is highly dynamic in many ways: where value adding activities take place; the speed with which new garment designs are introduced to the marketplace; and how different retailers, brand owners, and branded manufacturers have developed their supply network and how they manage them to meet market demands.

In this chapter the emergence of buyer-driven supply networks in the clothing and the apparel sectors has been noted. We have re-examined the concept of QR in the context of globally dispersed production, distribution, and retailing networks and have defined and described a new concept – GQR. We have examined GQR with respect to the new garment design and development process; the initial volume order process; and the replenishment order process. Enablers for GQR have been discussed in detail. In addition to the basic requirements for QR, a GQR strategy requires detailed consideration of (1) market intelligence and rapid new product introduction, (2) network structure and composition, (3) network planning and staged postponement, and (4) network capability, performance, and health. The concept of maintaining a degree of flexibility through well designed staged planning postponement over a rolling planning horizon is highlighted. Two contrasting examples with respect to the nature of their supply networks have been noted.

The theory and practice of GQR in the clothing sector offers much potential for further research both in the strategies and practices adopted by different prime entities and in different sub-sectors and categories of the clothing industry. There are also opportunities for the development of models to analyze and support GQR practice, in particular, simulation and optimization models. The adoption of GQR strategies in other sectors also has significant potential for further research.

References

Abdalla HS (1999) Concurrent engineering for global manufacturing. Int J Prod Econ 60–61: 251–260

Abernathy FH, Volpe A, Weil D (2006) The future of the apparel and textile industries: prospects and choices for public and private actors. Environ Plann A 38:2207–2232

Al-Zubaidi H, Tyler D (2004) A simulation model of quick response replenishment of seasonal clothing. Int J Retail Distrib Manag 32(6):320–327

Audet D (2007) Smooth as silk? A first look at the post MFA textiles and clothing landscape. J Int Econ Law 10(2):267–284

Barclay I, Dann Z (2000) Management and organisational factors in new product development (NPD) success. Concurrent Engineering 8(2):115–132

Barnes L, Lea-Greenwood G (2006) Fast fashioning the SC: shaping the research agenda. Intern J Fashion Market Manag 10(3):259–271

Belfast Telegraph (2007) Cheap chic? (By Chrissie Russell. www.belfasttelegraph.co.uk.) Accessed 7 Nov 2007

Birtwistle G, Fiorito SS, Moore CM (2006) Supplier perceptions of quick response systems. J Enterprise Inform Syst 19(3):334–345

Bruce M, Daly L (2006) Buyer behaviour for fast fashion. J Fashion Market Manag 10(3):329–344

Bruce M, Daly L, Towers N (2004) Lean or agile: A solution for supply chain management in the textiles and clothing industry?. Int J Oper Prod Manag 24(2):151–170

Catalan M, Kotzab H (2003) Assessing the responsiveness in the danish mobile phone supply chain. Int J Phys Distrib Logist Manag 33(8):668–685

CBARSL-Central Bank Annual Report Sri Lanka (2005–2007)

Christopher M, Lowson R, Peck H (2004) Creating agile supply chains in the fashion industry. Int J Retail Distrib Manag 32(8):367–76

Cooper MC, Lambert DM, Pagh JD (1997) Supply chain management more than a new name for logistics. Int J Logist Manag 8(1):1–14

CRPM report in Macedonia (2005) World trends in clothing manufacturing. Occasional Paper No 9, Center for Research and Policy Making, 31 Nov 2005. www.crpm.org.mk. Accessed 18 Oct 2008

Doyle SA, Christopher MM, Morgan L (2006) Supplier management in fast moving fashion retailing. J Fashion Market Manag 10(3):272–281

EMCC – European Monitoring Centre on Change (2008) Trends and drivers of change in the european textiles and clothing sector: Mapping report. European Foundation for the Improvement of Living and Working Conditions. www.eurofound.europa.eu/pubdocs/2008/15/en/1/ef0815en.pdf. Accessed 27 Oct 2008

Er M, MacCarthy BL (2006) Managing product variety in multinational corporation supply chains: A simulation study. J Manuf Technol Manag 17(8):1117–1138

Ferdows K, Lewis MA, Machuca JAD (2004) Rapid-Fire fulfillment. Harv Bus Rev 82(11):104–110

Fernie J (1994) Quick response: An international perspective. Int J Phys Distrib Logist Manag 22(6):38–46

Financial Times (2009) Primark sparkle brightens resilient associate British foods. (By Maggie Urry) 16 Jan 2009

Fisher M, Raman A (1996) Reducing the cost of demand uncertainty through accurate response to early sales. Oper Res 44(1):87–99

Fisher ML (1997) What is the right supply chain for your product? Harv Bus Rev 75(2):105–115

Fisher ML, Hammond JH, Obermeyer WR, Raman A (1994) Making supply meet demand in an uncertain world. Harv Bus Rev 83–93

Forza C, Vinelli A (1996) An analytical scheme for the change of the apparel design process towards quick response. Int J Clothing Sci Technol 8(4):28–43

Forza C, Vinelli A (1997) Quick response in the textile-apparel industry and the support of information technologies. Integrated Manuf Syst 8(3):125–136

Forza C, Vinelli A (2000) Time compression in production and distribution with the textile-apparel chain. Integrated Manuf Syst 11(2):138–146

Forza C, Romano P, Vinelli A (2000). Information technology for managing the textile apparel chain: current use, shortcomings and development directions. Int J Logist 3(3):227–243

Gallaugher JM (2008) Zara case: Fast fashion from savvy systems. www.gallaugher.com. Visited on 8 Feb 2009

Gereffi G (1999) International trade and industrial upgrading in the apparel commodity chain. J Int Econ 48(1):37–70

Gunasekaran A, Laib K, Cheng TCE (2008) Responsive supply chain: A competitive strategy in a networked economy. Int J Manag Sci 36:549–564

Handfield RB, Krause DR, Scannell TV, Monczka RM (2000) Avoid the pitfalls in supplier development. Sloan Manag Rev 37–49

Hayes SG, Jones N (2006) Fast fashion a financial snapshot. J Fashion Market Manag 10(3):282–300

Holweg M (2005) The three dimensions of responsiveness. Int J Oper Prod Manag 25(7):603–622

Hunter NA (1990) Quick reponse in apparel manufacturing. The Textile Institute, UK

Hunter NA, King RE, Nuttle HLM (1992) An apparel – Supply system for quick response retailing. J Textil Inst 83(3):462–471

Hunter A, King R, Lowson RH (2002) The textile/clothing pipeline and quick response management. The Textile Institute, UK

Iwanow H, McEachern MG, Jeffrey A (2005) The influence of ethical trading policies on consumer apparel purchase decisions: A focus on the Gap Inc. Int J Retail Distrib Manag 33(5):371–387

Joergens C (2006) Ethical fashion: myth or future trend?. J Fashion Market Manag 10(3):360–371

Koufteros X, Vonderembse M, Doll W (2001) Concurrent engineering and its consequences. J Oper Manag 19(1):97–115

Kritchanchi D, MacCarthy BL (1999) Responsiveness of the order fulfilment process. Int J Oper Prod Manag 19(8):821–833

Kumar N, Linguri S (2006) Fashion sense. Bus Strat Rev 17(2):80–84

Lambert MD, Cooper MC (2000) Issues in supply chain management. Ind Market Manag 29:65–83

Lowson B, King R, Hunter A (1999) Quick response: managing the supply chain to meet consumer demand. Wiley, NY

Lummus RR, Duclos LK, Vokurka RJ (2003) Supply chain flexibility: building a new model. Global J Flex Syst Manag 4(4):1–13

Martin MF (2007) US clothing and textile trade with china and the world: trends since the end of quotas. CRS Report for Congress, A Report Prepared for Members and Committees of Congress on July 10 2007. Order Code RL34106. www.fas.org/sgp/crs/row/RL34106.pdf. Accessed 18 Oct 2008

Nordas HK (2004) The global textile and clothing industry post the agreement on textiles and clothing. Discussion Paper No 5, World Trade Organization Geneva, Switzerland. www.trade. wtosh.com/english/res_e/booksp_e/discussion_papers5_e.pdf. Accessed 21 Oct 2008

O'Donoghue B (2008) Primark director. www.primark.co.uk

Oxborrow L (2000) Changing practices in the uk apparel supply chain: results of an industry survey. Research Project Paper for Harvard Business Center for Textile and Apparel Research. www.hctar.org/pdfs/GS04.pdf. Accessed 17 Oct 2008

Oxborrow L (2006) Customer responsiveness: curse or salvation? Issues facing the UK's apparel labour market. Accessed via Google 11 Nov 2008

Perry M, Sohal AS (2001) Effective quick response practices in a supply chain partnership an australian case study. Int J Oper Prod Manag 21(5–6):840–854

Pieter D, van Donk, Taco van der Vaart (2007) Responsiveness through buyer-focused cells: exploring a new supply strategy. Int J Oper Prod Manag 27(12):1362–1379

Pretious M, Love M (2006) Sourcing ethics and the global market: the case of the UK retail clothing sector. Int J Retail Distrib Manag 34(12):892–903

Reichhart A, Holweg M (2007) Creating the customer-responsive supply chain: a reconciliation of concepts. Int J Oper Prod Manag 27(11):1144–1172

Rho B-H, Yur Y-M (1998) A comparative study on the structural relationships of manufacturing practices, lead time and productivity in Japan and Korea. J Oper Manag 16(2–3):257–270

Sayid R (2008) Budget store primark to overtake marks & spencer. The Daily Mirror, Ruki Sayid, 23/04/2008. www.mirror.co.uk

Sen A (2008) The US fashion industry: a supply chain review. Int J Prod Econ 114(2):571–593

Sheridan M, Moore, Nobbs K (2006) Fast fashion requires fast marketing the role of category management in fast fashion positioning. J Fashion Market Manag 10(3):301–315

Storey J, Emberson C, Reade D (2005) The barriers to customer responsive supply chain management. Int J Oper Prod Manag 25(3):242–260

Sunday Tribune (2005) Primark takes a giant leap in the space race (By Aine Coffey, 17 July 2005, www.tribune.ie)

The US Department of Trade (www.osha.gov/pls/imis/). Accessed 4 April 2009

The US Department of Labour (www.bls.gov/news.relese/ecopro.t02.htm). Accessed 11 March 2009

Tokatli N (2007) Global sourcing: insights from the global clothing industry – The case Of Zara, A fast fashion retailer. J Econ Geogr; Advance Access Published in Oct 23, Oxford University Press, London

Tokatli N, Wrigley N, Kizilgun O (2008) Shifting global supply networks and fast fashion: made in turkey for marks & spencer. Global Network 8(3):261–280

Tyler D, Heeley J, Bhamra T (2006) Supply chain influences on new product development in fashion clothing. J Fashion Market Manag 10(3):316–328

UNCTAD Current Studies on FDI and Development (2005) TNCs and the removal of textiles and clothing quotas. United Nations, New York and Geneva. www.unctad.org/en/docs/iteiia20051_en.pdf. Accessed 2 Nov 2008

van Donk DP, van der Vaart T (2007) Responsiveness through Buyer-focused cells: exploring a new supply strategy. Int J Oper Prod Manag 27(12):1362–1379

Van Hoek RI (2001) The rediscovery of postponement a literature review and directions for research. J Oper Manag 19:161–184

Wadhwa S, Saxenay A, Chanz FTS (2008) Framework for flexibility in dynamic supply chain management. Int J Prod Res 46(6):1373–1404

www.sdlgreenstone.com/files/case-study-primark.pdf. Accessed 15 April 2009

Part II
Modelling and Analysis of QR Programmes

Procurement Flexibility under Price Uncertainty

Qi Feng and Suresh P. Sethi

Abstract This chapter examines the interaction between supply price uncertainty and demand uncertainty. We consider a manufacturer who sources a key component using different procurement options: a long-term order on a price-only contract, short-term orders on an adjustment contract, and short-term purchases directly from the market. At the beginning of the planning cycle, the manufacturer places a long-term order and reserves a certain amount of supply capacity for the purpose of adjusting the long-term order, if needed. Before the selling season, the manufacturer has multiple opportunities of supplementing the long-term order from the reserved capacity or from the market. We compare two types of capacity arrangements: dedicated capacity and overall capacity. Under a dedicated capacity arrangement, the manufacturer reserves a capacity for each adjustment order in the contract. Under an overall capacity arrangement, she keeps the flexibility of using the reserved capacity in any periods during the planning cycle. We discuss the optimal procurement strategies and the criteria for capacity allocations, as well as the policy behavior and service performance under different arrangements.

Keywords Base-stock policy · Capacity · Price risk-sharing · Procurement flexibility · Supply contract

1 Introduction

Rapid adoption of internet-based technologies has enabled firms to quickly acquire supply information, shorten procurement leadtimes, and reduce transaction costs. Many business-to-business platforms have played critical roles in commodity supply chains. A manufacturer can monitor market price changes and place orders through the internet. Although the spot markets of electricity, crude oil, and steel

---

Q. Feng (✉)
McCombs School of Business, The University of Texas at Austin, Austin, TX, USA
e-mail: annabelle.feng@mccombs.utexas.edu

T.C. Edwin Cheng and T.-M. Choi (eds.), *Innovative Quick Response Programs in Logistics and Supply Chain Management*, International Handbooks on Information Systems, DOI 10.1007/978-3-642-04313-0_4,
© Springer-Verlag Berlin Heidelberg 2010

have become major source of supply for these products, the commodity spot markets of most products are far from maturity because of the concerns about the credibility of the suppliers and the product quality. As a result, firms prefer to maintain contractual relationship with their key suppliers, while using spot market as a supplementary supply source.

Studies of flexibility contracts are motivated by industry practices in companies including HP (Martínez-de-Albéniz and Simchi-Levi 2005), Sun Microsystems (Tsay 1999), Blockbuster (Gerchak et al. 2006), etc. Recent trends in business (e.g., shrinking product life cycle, globalization, outsourcing) have increased uncertainties in sourcing decisions. Flexibility is especially desired to manage procurement risk, respond quickly to market changes, and maintain core competence in the business world. For example, replenishment leadtimes for key components of mobile phones range from 6–12 months. Procurement orders are typically placed when the product is still in the design phase. Mobile technology advances quickly and product life cycle of a particular model is very short. It is thus critical to introduce a new model in a timely fashion. Bulk demand is usually expected right after a new launch. If no flexibility is provided to revise early orders when the competitive conditions and customer requirements are better understood, the company may have to stick to the production quantity planned in the design stage and lose opportunities in market competition.

Flexibility in supply contract can be provided in many ways – quantity, time, and price. The goal of this study is to characterize the optimal procurement strategy of a manufacturer when various flexibilities are provided in procurement contracts. We consider a manufacturer who purchases a standard component and produces a finished product with a short-life cycle. Examples of such products are consumer electronics and fashion goods. In these industries, the firm often experience bulk demand during a single selling season. Because of long production and transportation leadtimes, the manufacturer has to place purchase orders and the suppliers have to set up their capacities long before the selling season. As the demand information unfolds over time, the manufacturer would like to have the opportunity to adjust her early order. Two major issues are considered in the contract: price-risk sharing and capacity agreements.

In many industries, production input sourcing involves substantial price fluctuation. For example, the spot prices for fiber, petrochemical, electronics, and textile are highly uncertain. If the price is expected to be high, then a subsequent adjustment via spot purchasing would be costly to the manufacturer. If the price is anticipated to be low, the suppliers may not be willing to produce enough for future supplemental orders. To hedge the price risk, both the manufacturer and the suppliers would like to have some price arrangement. We propose a price-risk sharing scheme by which the suppliers' risk is reduced by a prepaid capacity reservation price and the manufacturer's risk is reduced by a procurement price lower than the market price. We study the effect of different price parameters on the optimal procurement strategy.

Our analysis shows that the manufacturer's purchasing strategy may also be affected by the type of capacity arrangement. If there is a capacity constraint for each order, then the manufacturer should behave *greedily* (as the situation described in Martínez-de-Albéniz and Simchi-Levi 2005). At each replenishment epoch, she should always use the cheapest available source first because any left-over capacity is of no benefit in the future. If, however, only an overall supply capacity before the selling season is given and there is no restriction on individual replenishment opportunity, then the manufacturer has the *flexibility* to execute the contact at any time within the contractual time frame. This requires an appropriate trade-off between the cost and the information at each adjustment time. In a procurement system with multiple ordering options and random ordering prices, different capacity arrangements lead to different "preferences" to the ordering options. In general, a dedicated capacity arrangement leads to an optimal base-stock policy, since the preference of the options is according to the cost ranking, which can be determined in advance. However, the preference depends also on the updated market information when an overall capacity arrangement is adopted. In this case, a speculative behavior may turn out to be optimal and the optimal replenishment strategy may not be a base-stock policy.

We also show that the added flexibilities decrease the operating cost of the system. Interestingly, they do not change the overall service performance with adequate supply. If supply capacity is limited, however, introducing flexibilities in the system may result in a decreased overall service performance.

This chapter is organized as follows. A brief literature review is provided in Sect. 2. In Sect. 3, we describe the model assumptions and discuss the risk-sharing contract. In Sect. 4, we examine a simplified two-stage model. The general multi-stage problem is studied in Sect. 5. Finally, we conclude the study in Sect. 6.

2 Literature Review

Various supply contracts have been studied in the literature. Recent surveys can be found in Cachon (2002) and Lariviere (1999). We shall briefly review the studies on flexible contracts, with a particular emphasis on the discussion of optimal procurement strategy.

Several types of contracts provide the buyer flexibility in adjusting her early order at a deterministic price. For example, Sethi et al. (2004) formulate a multi-period model to study procurement strategy under a quantity-flexible contract with a spot market purchasing opportunity. The quantity flexible contract is very similar to a call option. The difference is that the reservation capacity in the quantity flexible contract is a fixed fraction of the early order rather than a separate decision variable. Li and Ryan (2004) propose an adjustment contract in which the buyer can adjust her early order, up or down, at a predetermined unit price. Our work generalizes that of Li and Ryan (2004) in the following aspects. We allow for a general adjustment price scheme and endogenous capacity decisions. Also, we consider a general demand updating process and allow spot market purchases.

In the supply chain literature, most studies on procurement contracts with price-sharing agreement focus on the option contract. The underlying theory and practice of option contract are discussed by Kleindorfer and Wu (2003). Several authors (e.g., Cachon and Lariviere 2001; Barnes-Schuster et al. 2002; Martínez-de-Albéniz and Simchi-Levi; 2005) have shown that quantity flexible contracts, buy-back contracts, and pay-to-delay contracts are special cases of a combination of a price-only contract and a call-option contract.

Barnes-Schuster et al. (2002) consider an option contract in a two-period setting. The spot market is not explicitly modeled and thus the price risk is not considered. Cheng et al. (2008) consider a single-period contract with a precommitted order and an option. They assume fixed salvage values for both buyer and seller instead of the spot price and derive a put-call parity relation under a normal demand assumption. Golovachkina (2003), Wu et al. (2001, 2002), and Deng and Yano (2002) study two-stage problems involving a call option contract combined with a spot market purchasing opportunity. Martínez-de-Albéniz and Simchi-Levi (2005) consider a manufacturer who purchases the suppliers' capacities using call option contracts at the beginning of the planning horizon. Contracts are executed after the spot price and the demand are observed, and unsatisfied demand is lost. We generalize the above studies by allowing for a general price scheme.

Another stream of research concerns contractual relationships between suppliers and buyers in a competitive market. Examples can be found in Lee and Whang (2002) and Sethi et al. (2005). These studies examine an endogenous price determined via the market mechanism. We refer the reader to the survey paper by Kleindorfer and Wu (2003) and references therein.

The literature has not paid much attention to *time flexibility* in procurement decisions. Milner and Kouvelis (2005) study two-stage inventory systems under different settings to compare quantity flexibility and time flexibility. Li and Kouvelis (1999) propose a supply contract in an environment of deterministic demand and uncertain prices modeled as a geometric Brownian motion. The contract specifies a risk-sharing scheme with a piecewise linear price that provides the buyer a time flexibility. Exact time of purchasing is not specified in the agreement. A special case of our model concerning an overall capacity agreement solves a version of this problem with stochastic demand.

We demonstrate that the time flexibility can be provided through an overall capacity agreement. Several papers have studied the impact of capacity agreements on procurement strategies in different contexts. Bassok and Anupindi (1997) study a supply contract with a total minimum commitment on orders over a finite planning horizon. They show that the optimal ordering policy is a base-stock policy. Bonser and Wu (2001) develop a heuristic to determine the optimal procurement schedule when a minimum commitment and a maximum allowable ordering quantity are imposed.

3 Model Development

A manufacturer needs to source from its supplier to meet an uncertain demand. The supplier provides two procurement options to the manufacturer: a price-only contract for an early (long-term) order and an adjustment contract for future purchases (via short-term orders). The long-term contract specifies a unit price w. The adjustment contract specifies a prepaid reservation price v for each unit of capacity reserved for future purchases and a procurement price agreement $g(s)$ when the market price is s at that time. At the beginning of the planning horizon ($t = 0$), the manufacturer decides on the early order quantity q and the reservation capacities for future adjustments. The demand information unfolds and the market price evolves over time. At each adjustment time t, $t = 1, \ldots, n$, a demand signal I_t is updated and the current market price S_t is observed. The manufacturer may supplement the early order by purchasing additional units q_t^c from the reserved supply capacities at the contract price $g(S_t)$. The exercised contract order q_t^c must not exceed the available reserved capacity for time t. In addition, the manufacturer may also purchase q_t^s from the spot market at the market price S_t. Orders are delivered right before the selling season ($t = n + 1$). Then, the demand D materializes and the manufacturer pays penalty for unsatisfied demand or salvages left-over inventory. The cost of x units of ending inventory/lost sales is given by

$$H(x) = \begin{cases} h^+x & \text{if } x \geqslant 0, \\ h^-x & \text{if } x < 0, \end{cases}$$

with $h^- > h^+$. A positive h^+ represents the disposal cost and a negative h^+ stands for the salvage value of the unsold inventory. The sequence of events is presented in Fig. 1

We assume that the demand signal process $\{I_1, \ldots, I_n, D\}$ and the market price process $\{s_1, \ldots, s_n\}$ are two independent Markov processes. Also, the expected demand at any given time is stochastically increasing in the observed signals. Let $\mathcal{F}_n$ be the underlying history or the filtration of the system time $n \geqslant 1$ generated by $\{(I_1, S_1), \ldots, (I_n, S_n)\}$.

3.1 Price Risk-sharing Agreement

The short-term contract $(v, g(\cdot))$ is designed to share the risk of commodity price uncertainty. The idea comes from the common practice of hedging financial risk through contingent claims. However, commodity markets have certain

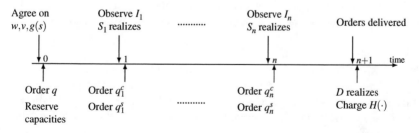

Fig. 1 The time line of events

characteristics different from the capital market. The commodity procurement decisions are based not only on the price, but also on the demand of a certain product.

According to the contract, the manufacturer pays the reservation price v for each unit of the contract capacity, which secures the supplier's risk of production. The execution price $g(s) \leq s$ reduces the manufacturer's risk of procurement. An example of $g(\cdot)$ is

$$g(s) = \begin{cases} (1 - \lambda)s + \lambda \bar{s} & \text{if } s > \bar{s}, \\ s & \text{if } s \leq \bar{s}, \end{cases} \tag{1}$$

for some $\lambda \in [0, 1]$. When $\lambda = 0$, the manufacturer will not reserve any positive capacity. The problem reduces to a mix of a long-term order and a spot market. When $\lambda = 1$, the adjustment contract is equivalent to a call option, with the exercise price of $\bar{s}$. In this case, v represents the cost of buying a call option. Note that the assumption $g(s) \leq s$ is reasonable because the manufacturer normally obtains a better price from her long-term supplier than from the market. Throughout our analysis, we assume a general price scheme $(v, g(\cdot))$ with $g(s) \leq s$ and $g(\cdot)$ nondecreasing.

3.2 Capacity Specification

In most studies of capacitated multistage model, it is assumed that there is a capacity limit at procurement opportunity. Such an assumption is reasonable when the adjustment points can be identified in advance. However, when future market changes are highly unpredictable, it is hard to determine in advance when the adjustment will take place. In such cases, the supplier may specify only a maximum total supply capacity before the selling season, and thus only an overall capacity constraint for future purchases is imposed.

We examine both types of capacity constraints. Under a dedicated capacity agreement, denote K_t to be the supply capacity and L_t to be the reservation capacity at time t. The capacity constraints are expressed as

C1: $q \leq K_0, q_t^c \leq L_t \leq K_t$ for $t = 1, \ldots, n$, with $K_t = \alpha_t K$ and $\sum_{t=0}^{n} \alpha_t = 1$.

Under a total capacity agreement, denote K to be the total supply capacity and L to be the reserved capacity for adjustments. The capacity constraints are written as

C2: $q + L \leq K$ and $\sum_{t=1}^{n} q_t^c \leq L$.

Under C1, the supply capacities are dedicated to different stages, and the manufacturer has to determine how much capacity is reserved for each later adjustment. Under C2, only a total reservation capacity is required. Later we show that the structure of the optimal procurement strategy is closely related to the type of the capacity specification.

4 A Single Adjustment Opportunity

We first study a simplified model with $n = 1$ in this section and examine the general problem in Sect. 5.

At the adjustment point ($t = 1$), the manufacturer's problem is to determine the contract order q^c and the market order q^s to obtain the minimum expected cost:

$$V_1(y, L; s, i) = \min_{0 \leqslant q^c \leqslant L, q^s \geqslant 0} \{g(s)q^c + sq^s + E[H(y + q^c + q^s - D)|i]\}, (2)$$

where y is the post-order inventory position at time 0, s is the spot price at $t = 1$, and i is demand signal at $t = 1$.

At the beginning of planning cycle ($t = 0$), the manufacturer decides the long-term order q and the reserved capacity L. The minimum expected cost is given by

$$V(x) = -wx + \min_{q \geqslant 0, L \geqslant 0} \{wq + vL + EV_1(x + q, L; S, I)\}, (3)$$

where x is the initial on-hand inventory. Note that $y = x + q$.

We denote F_D and F_I to be the distribution functions of D and I evaluated at time 0, respectively. Also denote $F(\cdot|i)$ as the updated demand distribution after observing $I = i$ at time 1.

4.1 The Optimal Policy

To derive the optimal replenishment policy, we begin with a discussion of the properties of the cost functions. The following theorem states that the cost functions are convex, which ensures that the optimal solution is essentially unique.

Theorem 1. $V_1(y, L; s, i)$ is jointly convex in (y, L) and $V(x)$ is convex in x.

Proof. We need to show that if $J_1(\cdot, \cdot)$ is convex, then $V_1(y, L; s, i) = \min_{0 \leqslant q^c \leqslant L, q^s \geqslant 0} J_1(y + q^c + q^s, L - q^c)$ is jointly convex in (y, L). Let $\beta \in [0, 1]$, $\bar{\beta} = 1 - \beta$, and the superscript $*$ denote the minimizer. Then

$$\beta V_1(y_a, L_a; s, i) + \bar{\beta} V_1(y_b, L_b; s, i)$$
$$= \beta J_1(y_a + q_a^{c*} + q_a^{s*}, L_a - q_a^{c*}) + \bar{\beta} J_1(y_b + q_b^{c*} + q_b^{s*}, L_b - q_b^{c*})$$
$$\geqslant J_1\Big((\beta y_a + \bar{\beta} y_b) + (\beta q_a^{c*} + \bar{\beta} q_b^{c*}) + (\beta q_a^{s*} + \bar{\beta} q_b^{s*}), (\beta L_a + \bar{\beta} L_b)$$
$$- (\beta q_a^{c*} + \bar{\beta} q_b^{c*})\Big)$$
$$\geqslant V_1(\beta y_a + \bar{\beta} y_b, \beta L_a + \bar{\beta} L_b; s, i).$$

The first equation follows from the definition of V_1, the second inequality follows from the convexity of J_1, and the third inequality follows from the minimality of V_1. It follows that $V_1(y, L; s, i)$ is convex in (y, L).

Similar arguments lead to the convexity of $V(x)$. ☐

4.1.1 The Optimal Adjustment Strategy at Time 1

At the adjustment point $(t = 1)$, we have two purchase options, that is, the contract purchase q^c and the market purchase q^s. Let $y^c = y + q^c$ and $y^s = y^c + q^s$ be the post-order inventory positions at time 1 relevant to the contract and market purchases, respectively. It can be shown that the cost function is separable in (y^c, y^s), and the optimal ordering policy follows a base-stock type policy. The next result has been proven by several authors (e.g., Sethi et al. 2004, Martínez-de-Albéniz and Simchi-Levi 2005).

Theorem 2. *Suppose that the observed demand signal is $I = i$ and the realized market price is $S = s$ at the adjustment point $(t = 1)$. There exist optimal base-stock levels $(\bar{y}^c, \bar{y}^s)$, independent of (y, L), such that $\bar{y}^c > \bar{y}^s$ and the optimal ordering policy follows a modified base-stock policy.*

$$\begin{cases} q^{c*}(y, L) = (\bar{y}^c - y)^+ \wedge L, \\ q^{s*}(y, L) = (\bar{y}^s - y - L)^+. \end{cases}$$

Theorem 2 indicates that a market purchase is used only when the contract capacity is exhausted. This is because the contract price is always lower than the market price. The optimal base-stock levels are given by the newsvendor formula, that is,

$$\bar{y}^c(s, i) = F_D^{-1}\left(\left.\frac{h^- - g(s)}{h^- + h^+}\right| i\right), \quad \bar{y}^s(s, i) = F_D^{-1}\left(\left.\frac{h^- - s}{h^- + h^+}\right| i\right).$$

The post-order inventory positions depend on the realizations of demand signal $I = i$ and the market price $S = s$. The optimal base-stock levels $\bar{y}^c$ and $\bar{y}^s$ are nondecreasing in i and nonincreasing in s. To characterize the policy in (s, i)-space, we let $A = y + L$ and define

$$I^c(s, \mu) = \{i \mid \bar{y}^c(s, i) = \mu\}, \quad I^s(s, \mu) = \{i \mid \bar{y}^s(s, i) = \mu\},$$

where μ may take the value y or value A. There are four possible cases at time 1 as demonstrated in Fig. 2. In region I, a high spot price and a low demand signal is observed. In this case, no adjustment order is placed. In region IV, a low spot price and a high demand signal is obtained. In this case, the contract capacity is fully executed and an additional quantity is ordered from the market. There are two intermediate cases: II and III. In region II, a part of contract capacity is used and no order is placed for market purchasing. In region III, all the contract capacity is executed and market procurement option is not used. An alternative view of Fig. 2

Fig. 2 Different ordering regions according to realization (i, s)

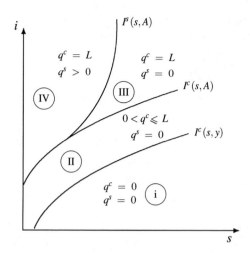

suggests that for each demand signal i, there are two thresholds of the market price, one for contract purchasing and one for market purchasing. An order is placed only when the market price is lower than the corresponding threshold.

4.1.2 The Optimal Capacity Allocation Strategy at Time 0

For simplicity of exposition, assume that all the distribution functions involved are differentiable. Denote $J(y, A) = wy + v(A - y) + EV_1(y, A - y; s, i)$ as the function inside "min" of (3). Then

$$\frac{\partial J(y, A)}{\partial y} = w - v + E_S \left[\int_0^{I^c(S,y)} \frac{\partial E[H(y - D)|I]}{\partial y} \, dF_I - \int_{I^c(S,y)}^{\infty} g(S) \, dF_I \right],$$

(4)

$$\frac{\partial J(y, A)}{\partial A} = v + E_S \left[\int_{I^c(S,A)}^{I^s(S,A)} \left(g(S) + \frac{\partial EH[(A - D)|I]}{\partial A} \right) dF_I \right.$$

$$\left. + \int_{I^s(S,A)}^{\infty} (g(S) - S) \, dF_I \right].$$

(5)

Note that (4) does not depend on A and (5) does not depend on y, which imply that $J(y, A)$ is separable in (y, A). Thus, we can write

$$J(y, A) = J^1(y) + J^2(A),$$

with $J^1(\cdot)$ and $J^2(\cdot)$ both convex. The first-order condition of $J^1(\cdot)$ and $J^2(\cdot)$ can be computed from (4) and (5). Denote $\tilde{y} = \arg\min_y J^1(y)$, $\tilde{a} = \arg\min_A J^2(A)$,

$\hat{b} = \arg\min_y\{J^1(y) + J^2(y)\}$, and $\check{b} = \arg\min_y\{J^1(y) + J^2(y + K_1)\}$. Then we have the following result.

Theorem 3. *There exist optimal base-stock levels* $(\bar{y}, \bar{a})$ *such that the optimal capacity allocation strategy at time* 0 *follows a modified base-stock policy.*

(i)   *If constraint* C1 *is imposed, then* $\bar{y} = \tilde{y} \wedge \hat{b} \vee \check{b}$, $\bar{a} = \tilde{a}$, *and*

$$\begin{cases} q^* = (\bar{y} - x)^+ \wedge K_0, \\ L^* = (\bar{a} - q^* - x)^+ \wedge K_1. \end{cases} \tag{6}$$

   Moreover, $\bar{y}$ *depends on* K_1 *and is independent of* (x, K_0), *and* $\bar{a}$ *is independent of* (x, K_0, K_1).

(ii) *If constraint* C2 *is imposed, then* $\bar{y} = \tilde{y} \wedge \hat{b}$, $\bar{a} = \tilde{a}$, *and*

$$\begin{cases} q^* = (\bar{y} - x)^+ \wedge K, \\ L^* = (\bar{a} - q^* - x)^+ \wedge (K - q^*). \end{cases} \tag{7}$$

   Moreover, $\bar{y}$ *and* a *are independent of* (x, K).

Proof. Denote (y^*, a^*) as the minimizer of $\{J^1(y) + J^2(A)|x \leqslant y \leqslant K_0, y \leqslant A \leqslant y + K_1\}$.
   (i) Under C1, we define

$$\begin{aligned} J(y) &= J^1(y) + \min_{y \leqslant A \leqslant y + K_1} J^2(A) \\ &= \begin{cases} J^1(y) + J^2(y) & \text{if } \tilde{a} \leqslant y, \\ J^1(y) + J^2(\tilde{a}) & \text{if } y < \tilde{a} < y + K_1, \\ J^1(y) + J^2(y + K_1) & \text{if } \tilde{a} \geqslant y + K_1. \end{cases} \end{aligned} \tag{8}$$

Clearly, $F(y)$ is convex in y and its unconstrained minimizer does not depend on K_0. It is easy to check that

$$\bar{y} = \arg\min_y F(y) = \begin{cases} \hat{b} & \text{if } \tilde{y} \geqslant \tilde{a}, \\ \tilde{y} & \text{if } \tilde{a} - K_1 < \tilde{y} < \tilde{a}, \\ \check{b} & \text{if } \tilde{y} \geqslant \tilde{a} - K_1. \end{cases} \tag{9}$$

Also, we shall check that

$$\min\{\tilde{y}, \tilde{a}\} \leqslant \hat{b} \leqslant \max\{\tilde{y}, \tilde{a}\}, \tag{10}$$

$$\min\{\tilde{y}, \tilde{a} - K_1\} \leqslant \check{b} \leqslant \max\{\tilde{y}, \tilde{a} - K_1\}. \tag{11}$$

The former is proven in Feng et al. (2005, 2006a, 2006b) and the latter follows in a similar way. Hence, we have $\bar{y} = \tilde{y} \wedge \hat{b} \vee \check{b}$ and $y^* = (x \vee \bar{y}) \wedge (x + K_0)$.

   To see that the optimal base-stock level for the reservation capacity L is $\tilde{a}$, we check three possible cases in (8). If $y^* \geqslant \tilde{a}$, then $a^* = y^* = (\tilde{a} \vee y^*) \wedge (y^* + K_1)$.

If $\tilde{a} - K_1 \leqslant y^* \leqslant \tilde{a}$, then $a^* = \tilde{a} = (\tilde{a} \vee y^*) \wedge (y^* + K_1)$. If $y^* \geqslant \tilde{a} - K_1$, then $a^* = y^* + K_1 = (\tilde{a} \vee y^*) \wedge (y^* + K_1)$. Hence, the result follows.

(ii) The argument is similar to (i) by removing the constraint $y \leqslant x + K_0$ and replacing $A \leqslant y + K_1$ to $A \leqslant K$. □

Theorem 3 suggests an optimal policy that can be implemented in the following manner. We first place a long-term order to bring the inventory level up to the base-stock level $\bar{y}$ or the capacity level K_0 under C1 (K under C2), depending on which one is smaller. Then, we treat L as a virtual order whose post-reservation position is $q^* + L$, reference position is q^*, and capacity is constrained by K_1 under C1 ($K - q^*$ under C2). The optimal reservation policy is to reserve up to the level $\bar{a}$ or to the capacity level.

4.2 Comparisons

In the previous section, we have characterized the optimal policies under the dedicated C1 and the overall C2 capacity constraints, respectively. At the adjustment point ($t = 1$), the optimal ordering policy under C1 and C2 are base-stock policies with the same policy parameters. At the beginning of the planning horizon ($t = 0$), the optimal capacity allocation policies under C1 and C2 have the same structure, but with different policy parameters. In Sect. 4.2.1, we compare the policy behavior at time 0 when different capacity agreement are applied. In Sect. 4.2.2, we discuss the overall service performance of the systems under the optimal policies.

4.2.1 Capacity Allocations

Figure 3 compares the base-stock levels at time 0 when C1 and C2 are imposed. We use subscripts C1 and C2 to distinguish the two cases. We have several observations.

Proposition 1.

(i) If $\tilde{y} \geqslant \tilde{a}$, then $\bar{y}_{C1}(\alpha_1) = \bar{y}_{C2} = \hat{b}$. If $\tilde{y} < \tilde{a}$, then

$$\bar{y}_{C1}(\alpha_1) = \begin{cases} \check{b}(\alpha_1) & 0 < \alpha_1 < (\tilde{a} - \tilde{y})/K, \\ \bar{y}_{C2} = \tilde{y} & \alpha_1 \geqslant (\tilde{a} - \tilde{y})/K, \end{cases}$$

with $-K \leqslant d\check{b}/d\alpha_1 \leqslant 0$ and $\tilde{y} \leqslant \check{b}(\cdot) \leqslant \tilde{a}$.

(ii) $q_{C1}^* + L_{C1}^* \leqslant q_{C2}^* + L_{C2}^*$.

Proof. (i) Note that $\tilde{a}$, $\tilde{y}$, $\hat{b}$ do not depend on $K_1 = \alpha_1 K$. From the proof of Theorem 3, we have $\tilde{y} \leqslant \hat{b} \leqslant \tilde{a}$ when $\tilde{y} \leqslant \tilde{a}$. Consider an α_1^u with $\hat{b}^u = \check{b}(\alpha_1^u)$. By definition,

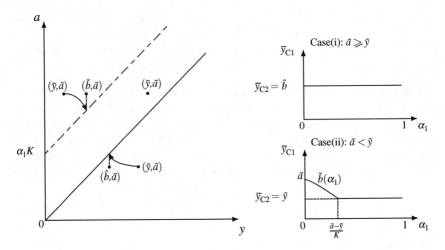

Fig. 3 The base-stock levels

$$J'(\check{b}^u) = J^{1'}(\check{b}^u) + J^{2'}(\check{b}^u + \alpha_1^u K) = 0. \tag{12}$$

Since $\check{b}^u \geqslant \tilde{y}$, we have $J^{1'}(\check{b}^u) \geqslant 0$ and $J^{2'}(\check{b}^u + \alpha_1^u K) \leqslant 0$. Hence, we deduce from (12) that $\check{b}^u$ is decreasing in α_1^u.

Consider the first-order derivative at $\check{b}^u - \delta K$ when α_1 increases to $\alpha_1 + \delta$. Then,

$$J'(\check{b}^u - \delta K) = J^{1'}(\check{b}^u - \delta K) + J^{2'}\left((\check{b}^u - \delta K) + (\alpha_1^u + \delta)K\right)$$
$$= J^{1'}(\check{b}^u - \delta K) + J^{2'}(\check{b}^u + \alpha_1^u K)$$
$$\leqslant J^{1'}(\check{b}^u) + J^{2'}(\check{b}^u + \alpha_1^u K) = 0.$$

By the convexity of F, we deduce that $\check{b}(\alpha_1^u + \delta) \geqslant \check{b}^u - \delta K$. Hence, we have

$$\check{b}'(\alpha_1) = \lim \frac{\check{b}(\alpha_1^u + \delta) - \check{b}(\alpha_1^u)}{\delta} \geqslant -K.$$

(ii) The result follows directly from comparing the solutions obtained in the proof of Theorem 3. □

Proposition 1 indicates that the overall capacity arrangement C2 induces higher total capacity reservation at time 0 than the dedicated capacity arrangement C1 does. When the second-stage supply capacity $K_1(= \alpha_1 K)$ is large enough (i.e., when an increase of the capacity does not increase the corresponding order), the optimal base-stock levels under C1 are the same as those under C2. When the second-stage capacity is limited, the optimal policy under C1 tends to increase the base-stock level of the long-term order $\bar{y}_{C1}$ to compensate for the reduced capacity of the adjustment contract. Moreover, the base-stock level $\bar{y}_{C1}$ increases at a rate lower than the decreasing rate of K_1.

In general, the overall capacity arrangement leads to better cost performance than the dedicated capacity arrangement. There is always a capacity specification (α_0, α_1) (See Fig. 4) under which the dedicated capacity system is equivalent to the overall capacity system.

Proposition 2. *For given x and K, the cost function $V_{C1}^{\alpha_1}(x)$ is convex in α_1, and it satisfies*

$$V_{C1}^{\alpha_1}(x) \begin{cases} \leqslant V_{C2}(x), & decreasing\ in\ \alpha_1, & if\ 0 \leqslant \alpha_1 < \underline{\alpha}_1, \\ = V_{C2}(x), & constant\ in\ \alpha_1, & if\ \bar{\alpha}_1 \leqslant \alpha_1 \leqslant \underline{\alpha}_1, \\ \leqslant V_{C2}(x), & increasing\ in\ \alpha_1, & if\ \underline{\alpha}_1 < \alpha_1 \leqslant 1, \end{cases} \qquad (13)$$

where $\bar{\alpha}_1 = 1 - (\tilde{y} \vee \hat{b} - x)^+/K$ and $\underline{\alpha}_1 = (\tilde{a} \wedge (x + K) - \tilde{y} \vee x)^+/K$.

Proof. The convexity of the cost function in α_1 follows in a similar way as in Theorem 1. We prove (13) for the case when $(\tilde{y}, \tilde{a}) \in N = \{(y, a) | x \leqslant y \leqslant a \leqslant K\}$ (Other cases can be similarly deduced). Clearly, the optimal solution to the problem under C2 is $(\tilde{y}, \tilde{a})$. As shown in Fig. 4, there are $(\bar{\alpha}_0, \bar{\alpha}_1)$ and $(\underline{\alpha}_0, \underline{\alpha}_1)$ such that $\bar{\alpha}_0 K = \tilde{y}$ and $\underline{\alpha}_1 K = \tilde{a} - \tilde{y}$.

Now consider the problem under C1, that is, $\min\{J^1(y) + J^2(a) | N\}$. Denote (y^*, a^*) as the minimizer. For any $\alpha_1 \geqslant \bar{\alpha}_1$, the minimizer satisfy $y^* = \alpha_0 K \leqslant \tilde{y}$ and $a^* = \tilde{a}$. By the convexity of the cost function, the optimal cost is increasing in α_1. For any $\alpha_1 \leqslant \alpha_1^b$, the minimizers satisfy $y^* = \check{b} - \alpha_1 K \geqslant \tilde{y}$ and $a^* = \check{a} \leqslant \tilde{a}$. By the convexity of the cost function, the optimal cost is decreasing in α_1. For any $\underline{\alpha}_1 \leqslant \alpha_1 \leqslant \bar{\alpha}_1$, the minimizers are $y^* = \tilde{y}$ and $a^* = \tilde{a}$. The cost function is the same as that under C2. □

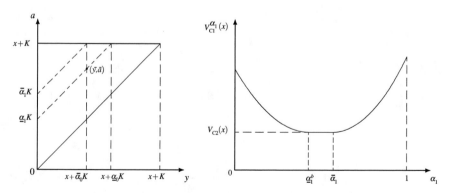

Fig. 4 Comparison of the optimal cost functions

4.2.2 Service Performance and Adjustment Opportunities

In this section, we examine service performance of the optimal policy under different capacity arrangements (for comparison purposes, we assume that the initial inventory x is small enough so that a long-term order q is always placed). The performance measure evaluated here is the overall service level, that is, the probability that the demand is satisfied.

To study the impact of introducing the adjustment contract, we also consider a system that is not flexible (NF), in which only the long-term order and the market purchases are available.

Proposition 3. *Let P_k denote the probability that demand is satisfied in system k, $k = \text{NF, C1, C2}$. Then,*

(i)

$$
\begin{cases}
P_{C2} = P_{NF} = \frac{h^- - w}{h^- + h^+} & \text{if } \hat{b} \vee \tilde{a} \leqslant K + x, \\
P_{C2} = P_{NF} < \frac{h^- - w}{h^- + h^+} & \text{if } \hat{b} \wedge \tilde{y} > K + x, \\
P_{C2} < P_{NF} \leqslant \frac{h^- - w}{h^- + h^+} & \text{if } \tilde{y} \leqslant K + x, \tilde{a} > K + x.
\end{cases}
$$

(ii)

$$
\begin{cases}
P_{C1} = P_{C2} = \frac{h^- - w}{h^- + h^+} & \text{if } \tilde{y} \leqslant K_0 + x, \tilde{a} \leqslant \tilde{y} + K_1, \\
P_{C1} < P_{C2} \leqslant \frac{h^- - w}{h^- + h^+} & \text{if } \tilde{y} > K_0 + x, \\
P_{C1} = \frac{h^- - w}{h^- + h^+} > P_{C2} & \text{if } \tilde{y} \leqslant K_0 + x, \tilde{a} > \tilde{y} + K_1.
\end{cases}
$$

Proof. (i) We prove the three cases separately.

Case 1: We first compute P_{C2} when $\tilde{y} < \tilde{a} < K$. In this case $\tilde{y} < \hat{b} < \tilde{a}$. Let $\Theta^k, k = \text{I, II, III, IV}$ be the corresponding events in Fig. 2. From (4) and (5), we have

$$
P\{Q \geqslant D, \Theta^I\}
$$
$$
= \frac{1}{h^+ + h^-} E_S \left[-w + v + \int_0^{I^c(S,\tilde{y})} h^- \, dF_I + \int_{I^c(S,\tilde{y})}^\infty g(S) \, dF_I \right], \quad (14)
$$
$$
P\{Q \geqslant D, \Theta^{III}\}
$$
$$
= \frac{1}{h^+ + h^-} E_S \left[-v + \int_{I^c(S,\tilde{a})}^{I^s(S,\tilde{a})} [h^- - g(S)] \, dF_I + \int_{I^s(S,\tilde{a})}^\infty [S - g(S)] \, dF_I \right]. \quad (15)
$$

Also note that

$$
P\{Q \geqslant D, \Theta^{II}\} = \frac{E_S \int_{I^c(S,\tilde{y})}^{I^c(S,\tilde{a})} [h^- - g(S)] \, dF_I}{h^+ + h^-}, \quad (16)
$$
$$
P_{C2}\{Q \geqslant D, \Theta^{IV}\} = \frac{E_S \int_{I^s(S,\tilde{a})}^\infty [h^- - S] \, dF_I}{h^+ + h^-}. \quad (17)
$$

Thus,

$$P = \sum_{j=I,II,III,IV} P\{Q \geqslant D, \Theta^j\} = \frac{h^- - w}{h^+ + h^-}. \tag{18}$$

Note that when $\tilde{y} \geqslant \tilde{a}$, (10) indicates $\tilde{y} \geqslant \hat{b} \geqslant \tilde{a}$ and the optimal solution becomes $(\hat{b}, \hat{b})$. In this case, the sum of (4) and (5) is zero at $A = y = \hat{b}$. Thus, $P\{Q \geqslant D, \Theta^I \cup \Theta^{II}\}$ is the sum of (14) and (15) with $(\tilde{y}, \tilde{a})$ replaced by $(\hat{b}, \hat{b})$. Also Θ^{II} is empty. As a result, the service level is still $(h^- - w)/(h^+ + h^-)$.

To derive P_{NF}, we first note that when the optimal base-stock level for the long-term order is $\hat{b}$, there are two possible events at time 1, namely $\Lambda_1 = \{Q = \hat{b}\}$ and $\Lambda_2 = \{Q > \hat{b}\}$. By the argument in the last paragraph, $P\{Q \geqslant D, \Lambda_1\}$ can be derived similarly as $P\{Q \geqslant D, \Theta^I \cup \Theta^{II}\}$ for $A = y$. Thus, we conclude the result.

Case 2: When $\hat{b} \wedge \tilde{y} > K + x$, no contract capacity is reserved under C2. Then the two systems are equivalent. Since $\hat{b} > K + x$ and J is convex, we have $\frac{dJ(y,y)}{dy}|_{y=K+x} < \frac{dJ(y,y)}{dy}|_{y=\hat{b}} = 0$, and we deduce that

$$P_{NF}\{Q \geqslant D, \Lambda_1\} < \frac{1}{h^+ + h^-} Es\left[-w + \int_0^{I^s(S,x+K)} h^- dF_I + \int_{I^s(S,x+K)}^{\infty} S dF_I\right].$$

Hence, $P_{C2} = P_{NF} \leqslant (h^- - w)/(h^+ + h^-)$.

Case 3: When $\tilde{y} \leqslant K + x, \tilde{a} > K + x$, the optimal solution under C2 is $(\tilde{y}, K + x)$. Using an argument similar to that in Case 2, we can show that $P_{C2} \leqslant (h^- - w)/(h^+ + h^-)$. If $\hat{b} \leqslant K + x$, we have $P_{C2} = (h^- - w)/(h^+ + h^-)$ from Case 1. When $\hat{b} > K + x$, we have $P_{C2} < (h^- - w)/(h^+ + h^-)$ from Case 2. The market order is placed when the event $\Theta^{IV} = \Lambda_2 = \{I > I^s(S, K + x)\}$ happens. Also under NF, $Q = K + x$ when Λ_2 does not happen; while under C2, $Q \leqslant K + x$ whenever Θ^{IV} does not happen. In this case, the long-term order under NF is always higher than that under C2. Hence, we conclude the result.

(ii) The proof is similar to that of (i). $\qquad\square$

The ratio $(h^- - w)/(h^+ + h^-)$ is the critical fractile of a single-stage newsboy model with a unit ordering cost w. In this case, no flexibility of adjusting the long-term order is allowed. When adjustments are allowed and the supply capacity is sufficiently large, the service level in each of the system equals $(h^- - w)/(h^+ + h^-)$. This implies that additional flexibilities (provided by an adjustment contract or spot market purchase) do not change the service performance.

When procurement flexibilities are provided under a limited supply capacity, the service performance may decrease. If the adjustment contract is introduced with the overall capacity arrangement C2, then the overall service performance is always lower than that without adjustment contract NF. If the adjustment contract is introduced with the dedicated capacity arrangement C1, then the overall service level remains at $(h^- - w)/(h^+ + h^-)$ as long as the first-stage capacity K_0 is sufficient.

If the first-stage capacity is not enough in the dedicated capacity system, then its overall service performance is always lower than that of the overall capacity system.

5 Multiple Adjustments

In this section, we study the situation where the manufacturer has multiple opportunities to adjust her early order prior to the selling season. The decisions are based on demand updating and price evolution. In Sect. 5.1, we characterize the structure of the optimal strategies. In Sect. 5.2, we examine the policy behavior under certain contract price schemes and market price processes. In Sect. 5.3, we study the service performance under the optimal policies.

5.1 Policy Structure

We discuss the dedicated and overall capacity arrangements in Sect. 5.1.1 and Sect. 5.1.2, respectively. In the first scenario, the manufacturer specifies a reservation capacity for each adjustment point, and the leftover capacity at a given stage cannot be carried over for future purchasing. In the second case, the manufacturer purchases a total reservation capacity for future adjustment purchase, and keeps the time-flexibility of exercising the reserved capacity.

5.1.1 Dedicated Capacity Agreement

Under C1, the dynamic programming equations are

$$V(x) = \min_{\substack{0 \leq q \leq K_0, \\ 0 \leq L_t \leq K_t, \\ t=1,\dots,n}} \left\{ wq + v \sum_t L_t + EV_1(q + x, L_1, \dots, L_n; S_1, I_1) \right\}, \quad (19)$$

$$V_t(y_t, L_t, \dots, L_n; s_t, i_t) = \min_{\substack{0 \leq q_t^c \leq L_t, \\ q_t^s \geq 0}} \left\{ g(s_t)q_t^c + s_t q_t^s \right. \tag{20}$$

$$\left. + EV_{t+1}(y_t + q_t^c + q_t^s, L_{t+1}, \dots, L_n; S_{t+1}, I_{t+1}) \right\}$$

for $t = 1, \dots, n-1$,

$$V_n(y_n, L_n; s_n, i_n) = \min_{\substack{0 \leq q_n^c \leq L_n, \\ q_n^s \geq 0}} \left\{ g(s_n)q_n^c + s_n q_n^s + EH(y_n + q_n^c + q_n^s - D) \right\}. \quad (21)$$

Theorem 4. *Suppose that the capacity constraint is of* C1 *type.*

(i) *The cost function* $V_t(y_t, L_t, \ldots, L_n; s_t, i_t)$ *is jointly convex in* $(y_t, L_t, \ldots, L_n)$
for $t = 1, \ldots, n$, *and* $V(x)$ *is convex in* x.

(ii) *There exist optimal base-stock levels* $(\bar{y}_t^c, \bar{y}_t^s)$, *independent of* $(y_t, L_1, \ldots, L_t)$,
such that $\bar{y}_t^c \leqslant \bar{y}_t^s$ *and the optimal replenishment quantities at time* t *are*

$$
\begin{cases}
q_t^{c*} = (\bar{y}_t^c - y_t)^+ \wedge L_t, \\
q_t^{s*} = (\bar{y}_t^s - y_t - L_t)^+, & t = 1, 2, \ldots, n.
\end{cases}
$$

(iii) *There exist an optimal base-stock level* $\bar{y}$, *independent of* (x, K_0), *such that
the optimal long-term order quantity at time* 0 *satisfies*

$$
q^* = (\bar{y} - x)^+ \wedge K_0.
$$

Proof. (i) follows from an induction on t and an argument similar to Theorem 1,
and the proof of (ii) is similar to that of Theorem 1 in Martínez-de-Albéniz and
Simchi-Levi (2005). To see (iii), we rewrite $V(x)$ as

$$
V(x) = -wx + \min_{x \leqslant y \leqslant x + K_0} \left\{ wy + \min_{\substack{0 \leqslant L_t \leqslant K_t \\ t=1,\ldots,n}} \left[v \sum_t L_t + E V_1(y, L_1, \ldots, L_n; S_1, I_1) \right] \right\}
$$

$$
= -wx + \min_{x \leqslant y \leqslant x + K_0} \left\{ wy + G(y) \right\},
$$

with $G(y)$ convex in y. Thus, $\bar{y}$ is the unconstrained minimizer to $wy + G(y)$, which
depends on $(K_1, \ldots, K_n)$ and is independent of (x, K_0).   □

The optimal replenishment policies at the adjustment points have the same
structure as that in the single-adjustment case. Because the reservation capacity is
specified for each adjustment point and the leftover capacity is of no use in the
future, the optimal replenishment strategy tends to use up the cheaper source first.
This result can be generalized to the case when price scheme is $g_t(S_t)$, that is, when
it is different for different t.

Convexity of the cost function $V_1(x)$ ensures an optimal solution at time 0. However, the dependence among $(L_1, \ldots, L_n)$ is quite complex and the optimal policy
for capacity reservation does not have a simple structure.

5.1.2 Overall Capacity Agreement

Next we consider the situation under C2 is imposed. The manufacturer reserves L
units of capacity at time 0, and her total ordering quantity from the adjustment contract is constrained by L. Let L_t be the available contract capacity at time t. Then,
L_t depends on the orders $\{q_1^c, \ldots, q_{t-1}^c\}$ and is random before t. The optimality
equations are

$$V(x) = \min_{\substack{q \geqslant 0,\, L \geqslant 0. \\ q+L \leqslant K}} \left\{ wq + vL + EV_1(q + x, L; S_1, I_1) \right\}, \quad (22)$$

$$V_t(y_t, L_t; s_t, i_t) = \min_{\substack{0 \leqslant q_t^c \leqslant L_t. \\ q_t^s \geqslant 0}} \left\{ g(s_t) q_t^c + s_t q_t^s \right. \quad (23)$$

$$\left. + EV_{t+1}(y_t + q_t^c + q_t^s, L_t - q_t^c; S_{t+1}, I_{t+1}) \right\}$$

for $t = 1, \ldots, n-1$,

$$V_n(y_n, L_n; s_n, i_n) = \min_{\substack{0 \leqslant q_n^c \leqslant L_n. \\ q_n^s \geqslant 0}} \left\{ g(s_n) q_n^c + s_n q_n^s \right.$$

$$\left. + EH(y_n + q_n^c + q_n^s - D) \right\}. \quad (24)$$

At any adjustment point, the manufacturer reviews the current inventory position y_t and the available contract capacity L_t and makes the decision on the ordering quantities q_t^c and q_t^s according to the observed demand information i_t and the current market price s_t. Then, the inventory position is updated to $y_{t+1} = y_t + q_t^c + q_t^s$ and the available contract capacity becomes $L_{t+1} = L_t - q_t^c$.

Theorem 5. *Suppose that the capacity constraint is of C2 type.*

(i) *The cost function $V_t(y_t, L_t; s_t, i_t)$ is jointly convex in (y_t, L_t) for $t = 1, \ldots, n$, and $V(x)$ is convex in x.*

(ii) *There exist optimal base-stock levels $(\bar{y}_n^c, \bar{y}_n^s)$, independent of (y_n, L_n), such that $\bar{y}_n^c \leqslant \bar{y}_n^s$ and the optimal replenishment quantities at time n are*

$$\begin{cases} q_n^{c*} = (\bar{y}_n^c - y_n)^+ \wedge L_n, \\ q_n^{s*} = (\bar{y}_n^s - y_n - L_n)^+. \end{cases}$$

There exist optimal base-stock levels $(\bar{\zeta}_{n-1}^s, \bar{\zeta}_{n-1}^c)$, with $\bar{\zeta}_{n-1}^c$ independent of (y_{n-1}, L_{n-1}) and $\bar{\zeta}_{n-1}^s$ independent of y_{n-1}, such that the optimal replenishment quantities at time $n-1$ are

$$\begin{cases} q_{n-1}^{s*} = (\bar{\zeta}_{n-1}^s - y_{n-1})^+, \\ q_{n-1}^{c*} = (\bar{\zeta}_{n-1}^c - y_{n-1} - q_{n-1}^{s*})^+ \wedge L_{n-1}. \end{cases} \quad (25)$$

Proof. (i) follows from a direct extension of Theorem 1 and induction. The details are omitted here.

We focus on proving (ii). The optimality of the base-stock policy at t_n can be deduced directly from Theorem 2. When $t = n-1$, let $v_n(y, A) = v_n(y, y + L) = V_n(y, L)$. Then, $Ev_n(y, A)$ is separable in (y, A). Define $\zeta_{n-1}^s = y_{n-1} + q_{n-1}^s$ and $\zeta_{n-1}^c = y_{n-1} + q_{n-1}^s + q_{n-1}^c$. Then,

$$V_{n-1}(y_{n-1}, L_{n-1}; s_t, i_t)$$

$$= \min_{\substack{y_{n-1} \leqslant \zeta_{n-1}^s \leqslant \zeta_{n-1}^c \\ \zeta_{n-1}^c \leqslant \zeta_{n-1}^s + L_{n-1}}} \left\{ -s_{n-1} y_{n-1} + [s_{n-1} - g(s_{n-1})] \zeta_{n-1}^s \right.$$

$$\left. + g(s_{n-1}) \zeta_{n-1}^c + E v_n(\zeta_{n-1}^c, L_{n-1} + \zeta_{n-1}^s; S_{t+1}, I_{t+1}) \right\}.$$

The right-hand side is separable in $(\zeta_{n-1}^c, \zeta_{n-1}^s)$. Define $(\bar{\zeta}_{n-1}^c, \bar{\zeta}_{n-1}^s)$ as the minimizer to the above over the region $\{\zeta_{n-1}^s \leqslant \zeta_{n-1}^c \leqslant \zeta_{n-1}^s + L_{n-1}\}$. Then, the optimal ordering quantities are defined in (25). Hence the result follows. □

At the last adjustment point, any leftover capacity $L_n - q^{c*}$ is wasted. Thus, we should use the cheap contract order, and order from the market only when there is not enough contract capacity. At the $(n-1)^{\text{st}}$ adjustment point, however, the ordering decision (q_{n-1}^c, q_{n-1}^s) depends on the realization of the market price S_{n-1} and the perception of the future market price S_n. It may be economic to leave some contract capacity to time n and order some units from the market at time $n - 1$. Note that the base-stock policy at time $n - 1$ is different from that at time n in their definitions of reference inventory positions.

The optimal replenishment strategy does not follow a base-stock policy at the early adjustment points ($t < n - 1$), because the cost function $E V_{n-1}(y_{n-1}, L_{n-1})$ is not separable in $(y_{n-1}, y_{n-1} + L_{n-1})$ in general. The optimal replenishment does not necessarily prefer the contract purchasing to the market purchasing at any adjustment point. It is possible that market order is placed when there is still a positive available capacity on contract. Thus, the possible ordering regions cannot be completely characterized by the iso-quants of y_t and $y_t + L_t$ as in Fig. 2 (See Table 1). As a result, the cost function V_t does not satisfy the desired separability condition that leads to the optimality of a base-stock policy.

The optimal adjustment policy described in Theorem 5 reveals a speculative nature. In reality, the operational decisions are often restricted to nonspeculative policies. That is, the preferred procurement source is always the supplier with a long-term agreement. Only when the contact capacity is not enough are the alternative sourcing options like spot market purchase used. Thus, under the nonspeculative policy, we enforce $q_t^s = 0$ whenever $q_t^c < L_t$. Then, (23) can be rewritten as

Table 1 Possible ordering regions ($A_t = y_t + L_t$)

Possible cases	Order quantities quantities	Ending state		
		Optimal C1	Optimal C2	Non-spec. C1
Case I	$q_t^c = 0, q_t^s = 0$	$(y_t, L_{t+1}, \ldots, L_n)$	(y_t, A_t)	(y_t, A_t)
Case II	$0 < q_t^c < L_t, q_t^s = 0$	$(y_t^c, L_{t+1}, \ldots, L_n)$	(y_t^c, A_t)	(y_t^c, A_t)
Case III	$q_t^c = L_t, q_t^s = 0$	$(y_t + L_t, L_{t+1}, \ldots, L_n)$	(A_t, A_t)	(A_t, A_t)
Case IV	$q_t^c = L_t, q_t^s = 0$	$(y_t^s, L_{t+1}, \ldots, L_n)$	(y_t^s, y_t^s)	(y_t^s, y_t^s)
Case V	$0 < q_t^c < L_t, q_t^s > 0$	—	$(y_t^s, A_t + y_t^s - y_t^c)$	—
Case VI	$q_t^c = L_t, q_t^s > 0$	—	$(y_t^s, A_t + y_t^s - y_t)$	—

$$V_t(y_t, L_t; s_t, i_t) = \min_{y_t \leqslant y \leqslant y_t + L_t} \left\{ J_t(y, y_t, L_t; s_t, i_t) \right\},$$

where

$$J_t(y, y_t, L_t; s_t, i_t) \tag{26}$$
$$= \begin{cases} g(s_t)L_t + s_t(y - y_t - L_t) + EV_{t+1}(y, 0; S_{t+1}, I_{t+1}), & y \geqslant y_t + L_t, \\ g(s_t)(y - y_t) + EV_{t+1}(y, L_t - (y - y_t); S_{t+1}, I_{t+1}), & y_t \leqslant y < y_t + L_t. \end{cases}$$

In this case, the problem reduces to a one-dimensional minimization problem. The possible ordering cases at each adjustment point (see Table 1) is similar to that in Fig. 2. However, the cost function $V_t(y_t, L_t; s_t, i_t)$ may not be convex. Thus, the optimal ordering policy is not a base-stock policy in general. Our next result implies that if the optimal procurement policy is a nonspeculative policy, then the optimal policy is once again a base-stock policy.

Proposition 4. *If $\{s_t - g(s_t)\}_{t \geqslant 1}$ is a martingale or a supermartingale, then a nonspeculative policy is optimal. Moreover, there are optimal base-stock levels $(\bar{y}_t^c, \bar{y}_t^s)$, independent of (y_t, L_t), such that $\bar{y}_t^c < \bar{y}_t^s$ and the optimal ordering policy at time t follows a base-stock policy, that is,*

$$\begin{cases} q_t^{c*} = (\bar{y}_t^c - y_t)^+ \wedge L_t, \\ q_t^{s*} = (\bar{y}_t^s - y_t - L_t)^+, \quad t = 1, \dots, n. \end{cases} \tag{27}$$

Also, there exist optimal base-stock levels $(\bar{y}, \bar{a})$, independent of (x, K), such that the optimal capacity allocation strategy at time 0 follows a modified base-stock policy defined in (7).

Proof. Suppose that the optimal ordering quantities at the tth adjustment point satisfy $q_t^{s*} > 0$ and $q_t^{c*} < L_t$. Let $L_{t+1} = L_t - q_t^{c*}$, $y_{t+1} = y_t + q_t^{s*} + q_t^{c*}$, and $y_{t+2} = y_{t+1} + q_{t+1}^{s*} + q_{t+1}^{c*}$. Note that $q_{t+1}^{s*}, q_{t+1}^{c*}$, and y_{t+2} are random variables at the tth adjustment point. By the optimality of (q_t^{s*}, q_t^{c*}), we have

$$V_t(y_t, L_t; s_t, i_t)$$
$$\leqslant [g(s_t)(q_t^{c*} + \varepsilon) + s_t(q_t^{s*} - \varepsilon) + EV_{t+1}(y_{t+1}, L_{t+1} - \varepsilon; S_{t+1}, I_{t+1})].$$

for a small enough ε. That is,

$$EV_{t+1}(y_{t+1}, L_{t+1} - \varepsilon; S_{t+1}, I_{t+1}) - EV_{t+1}(y_{t+1}, L_{t+1}; S_{t+1}, I_{t+1}))$$
$$\geqslant \varepsilon[s_t - g(s_t)]. \tag{28}$$

Let $q_{t+1}^{c'} = (q_{t+1}^{c*} - \varepsilon)^+$ and $q_{t+1}^{s'} = q_{t+1}^{s*} + (q_{t+1}^{c*} - q_{t+1}^{c'})$. Note that

$$EV_{t+1}(y_{t+1}, L_{t+1} - \varepsilon; S_{t+1}, I_{t+1})$$
$$< Eg(S_{t+1})q_{t+1}^{c'} + S_{t+1}q_{t+1}^{s'} + EV_{t+2}(y_{t+2}, L_{t+2}; S_{t+2}, I_{t+2}).$$

Thus,

$$EV_{t+1}(y_{t+1}, L_{t+1} - \varepsilon; S_{t+1}, I_{t+1}) - EV_{t+1}(y_{t+1}, L_{t+1}; S_{t+1}, I_{t+1})$$
$$\leqslant E(q_{t+1}^{c'} - q_{t+1}^{c*})g(S_{t+1}) + E(q_{t+1}^{s'} - q_{t+1}^{s*})S_{t+1}$$
$$= E(q_{t+1}^{s'} - q_{t+1}^{s*})[S_{t+1} - g(S_{t+1})] \leqslant \varepsilon E[S_{t+1} - g(S_{t+1})]. \qquad (29)$$

Then, (29) and (28) imply that $s_t - g(s_t) \leqslant E[S_{t+1} - g(S_{t+1})]$. This contradicts the fact that $\{S_t - g(S_t)\}_{t \geqslant 1}$ is a supermartingale. Hence, we conclude that $q_t^{s*} > 0$ only if $q_t^{c*} = L_t$.

Next we prove the optimality of the policy defined in (27). We show by induction that $Ev_t(y_t, A_t) = EV_t(y_t, A_t - y_t; S_t, I_t)$ is separable in y_t and A_t. Clearly, this is true for $t = n$. Assuming $Ev_{t+1}(y_{t+1}, A_{t+1}) = F^1(y_{t+1}) + F^2(A_{t+1})$. Now consider the optimal ordering decision at the tth adjustment point. By induction hypothesis, the first and the second function in (26) are both convex in y. Define $y_t^c = y_t + q_t^c$ and $y_t^s = y_t + q_t^c + q_t^s$. Let $\bar{y}_t^c = \arg\min_{y_t^c}\{g(s_t)y_t^c + F^1(y_t^c)\}$ and $\bar{y}_t^s = \arg\min_{y_t^s}\{s_t y_t^s + F^1(y_t^s) + F^2(y_t^s)\}$. Then, $\bar{y}_t^s$ and $\bar{y}_t^c$ are the unconstrained minimizer to the first and the second functions in (26). Note that the pair $(\bar{y}_t^c, \bar{y}_t^s)$ does not depend on (y_t, A_t). We show by contradiction that $\bar{y}_t^c > \bar{y}_t^s$. Suppose $\bar{y}_t^c < \bar{y}_t^s$. Let $J(y_t^c, y_t^s) = g(s_t)y_t^c + s_t(y_t^s - y_t^c) + Ev_{t+1}(y_t^s, A_t + (y_t^s - y_t^c))$ be the objective function at time t. Note that the unconstraint minimizer to J_t must satisfy either $y_t^c = y_t^s$ or $y_t^c = A_t$. We have two cases (see Fig. 5):

Case 1: $J_t(\bar{y}_t^c, \bar{y}_t^c; s_t, i_t) < J_t(A_t, \bar{y}_t^s; s_t, i_t)$. Define two sets of points: $(y_t^{c\delta}, y_t^{s\delta}) = (\bar{y}_t^c + \delta(A_t - \bar{y}_t^c), \bar{y}_t^c + (\bar{y}_t^s - \bar{y}_t^c)\delta)$ and $(y_t^{c\epsilon}, y_t^{s\epsilon}) = (\bar{y}_t^c + \epsilon(A_t - \bar{y}_t^c), \bar{y}_t^c + \epsilon(A_t - \bar{y}_t^c)$ for some $0 < \delta < 1$ and $0 < \epsilon < 1$. Then by convexity, $J_t(y_t^{c\delta}, y_t^{s\delta}; s_t, i_t) < J_t(\bar{y}_t^c, \bar{y}_t^c; s_t, i_t) < J_t(y_t^{c\epsilon}, y_t^{s\epsilon}; s_t, i_t)$. This indicates that

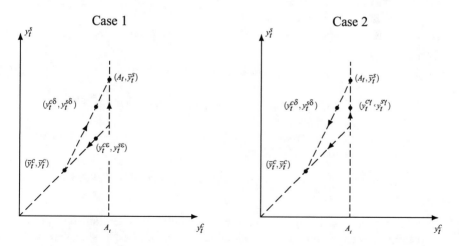

Fig. 5 Two possible cases in the proof of Proposition 4

$(y_t^{c\delta}, y_t^{s\delta})$ yields a lower cost than $(y_t^{c\epsilon}, y_t^{s\epsilon})$, which contradicts the fact that the optimal solution satisfies either $y_t^c = y_t^s$ or $y_t^c = A_t$.

Case 2: $J_t(\bar{y}_t^c, \bar{y}_t^c; s_t, i_t) < J_t(A_t, \bar{y}_t^s; s_t, i_t)$. Define $(y_t^{c\gamma}, y_t^{s\gamma}) = (\bar{y}_t^c, \bar{y}_t^c + \gamma(\bar{y}_t^s - \bar{y}_t^c))$ for $0 < \gamma < 1$. By convexity we have $J_t(y_t^{c\delta}, y_t^{s\delta}; s_t, i_t) < J_t(A_t, \bar{y}_t^s; s_t, i_t) < J_t(y_t^{c\gamma}, y_t^{s\gamma}; s_t, i_t)$. Again, this contradicts the fact that the optimal solution satisfies either $y_t^c = y_t^s$ or $y_t^c = A_t$.

Hence, we must have $\bar{y}_t^c < \bar{y}_t^s$. Then we can define critical signals $I_t^c(s_t, y_t) = \{I_t | \bar{y}_t^c = y_t\}$, $I_t^c(s_t, A_t) = \{I_t | \bar{y}_t^c = A_t\}$, and $I_t^s(s_t, A_t) = \{I_t | \bar{y}_t^s = A_t\}$. Similar to the analysis given in Fig. 2, we can establish the separability of the cost function $Ev_t(y_t, A_t)$, which in turn leads to the optimality of a base-stock policy defined in (27). Finally, we apply the result in Theorem 3 (ii) to establish the optimal policy at time 0. □

Proposition 4 suggests that when the price advantage of the contract diminishes over time, the optimal policy tries to exercise the contract capacity as early as possible. The resulting portfolio selection and procurement strategies have a base-stock structure.

It is easily deduced from the proof of Proposition 4 that the base-stock policy is optimal when market procurement is never used (e.g., when market price is too high). Thus, a single-option procurement system with uncertain procurement prices $g(\cdot)$ and a maximum allowable total order quantity L follows a base-stock policy. This result is closely related to Bassok and Anupindi (1997) in which a base-stock policy has been shown to be optimal for a stationary single-source ordering system with a deterministic ordering price and a minimum commitment total order quantity.

5.2 Discussions on Price Parameters

Proposition 5. *The optimal solution at time 0 has the following properties.*

(i) *If $w \geqslant ES$, then $q^* = 0$.*

(ii) *If $w + h^+ < v$, then $q^* = 0$ whenever $\sum_t L_t^* < \sum_t K_t$ under C1 or $q^* = 0$ under C2.*

(iii) *If $v \geqslant E[S_t - g(S_t)]$ for some t, then $L_t^* = 0$ under C1. If $v \geqslant \sum_{t=1}^n E[S_t - g(S_t)]$, then $L^* = 0$ under C2.*

(iv) *If $w \geqslant v + Eg(S_t)$ for some t, then $q^* = 0$ whenever $L_t < K_t$ for any t under C1 or $q^* = 0$ under C2.*

Proof. The proof involves a sample path argument similar to that of Proposition 4. The details are omitted here. □

Note that conditions in Proposition 5 are only sufficient to determine the preference of procurement options. These conditions become necessary when demand is deterministic or when the only underlying randomness is the market price process, as it is in the financial markets. Such an example can be found in Wu et al. (2002), where the commodity demand is modeled as a deterministic function of the market price and the supply contracts are call option contracts. They obtain a preference order of procurement options according to expected unit purchasing cost. However, different procurement options cannot be ordered in one dimension (expected cost) when the demand process is random. This is a key difference between contingent claims in the financial markets and procurement contracts in the commodity markets.

When the market price is stable or downward trending, the optimal replenishment policy calls for postponing adjustment procurement. If enough reservation capacity is available, then the supplementary orders are only placed at time n when the lowest purchasing prices are expected and the most accurate demand information is acquired.

Proposition 6. *If the market price process is a martingale or a supermartingale, then we have the following results.*

(i) *There is an optimal solution such that $q_t^s = 0$ almost surely for any $t < n$.*
(ii) *If, in addition, $g(\cdot)$ is concave, then there is an optimal solution that satisfies the following:*

    (a) *Under C1, $L_t > 0$ only when $L_p = K_p$ for each $p > t$, and the optimal (q, L_t) takes the form of (6).*
    (b) *Under C2, $q_t^c = 0$ almost surely for any $t < n$, and the problem reduces to a two-stage problem with the solution at time 0 given in (7).*

Proof. Proof of (i) is straightforward. We show that under C1, $L_t > 0$ only if $L_p = K_p$ for each $p > t$. Suppose $L_t > 0$ and $L_p < K_p$ for some $p > t$. Since $g(s)$ is nondecreasing concave in s, we have

$$g(S_t) \geqslant g(E S_t) \geqslant E g(S_t).$$

Then, $\{g(S_t)\}_{t \geqslant 1}$ is also a supermartingale. Thus, the result follows.

The proof for C2 is similar and is omitted. $\square$

Note that a concave price scheme is not a very restrictive assumption. In fact, most price risk-sharing schemes satisfy this assumption, for example, a call option or the price function as proposed in (1). In this case, the contract price increases slower than the market price, which ensures that the manufacturer's price risk is indeed hedged by the agreement.

It is intuitive to argue that an increasing price trend does not necessarily favor early adjustment because of possibly higher demand signals in the future. However, a submartingale price process does not necessarily induce early procurement even when demand signals give worthless information.

Proposition 7. *If $(v, g(\cdot))$ is a call option contract, then there is an optimal solution that satisfies the following.*

(i) *Under C1, $L_t > 0$ only when $L_p = K_p$ for each $p > t$.*
(ii) *Under C2, $q_t^c = 0$ almost surely for any $t < n$.*

Proof. Note that at time t, if $S_t < \bar{S}$, then there is an optimal solution in which $q_t^c = 0$. If $S_t > \bar{S}$, then we can always postpone market procurement to time n and get a price $g(S_n) \leqslant \bar{S}$. Thus, there is an optimal solution in which $q_t^c = 0$ for any $t < n$. The remainder of the proof is similar to that of Proposition 6. □

Under a call option contract, the manufacturer can always buy adjustment units at a price no higher than $\bar{S}$. Thus, it is optimal to hold contract capacity until the last stage and take advantage of possibly low realizations of market prices.

5.3 Overall Service Performance

Here we examine the overall service level under different capacity arrangements. Similar to the result in Sect. 4.2.2, when the initial inventory x is low enough, the critical ratio $(h^- - w)/(h^+ + h^-)$ defines the upper bound on the overall service level. In a dedicated capacity system, the overall service level under the optimal policy is at the upper bound as long as the capacity for the long-term order q is sufficient. In an overall capacity system, the overall service level under the optimal policy or the optimal nonspeculative policy is at the upper bound as long as the total capacity is sufficient.

Proposition 8. *Let Q be the total inventory available at time n to satisfy demand D. The probability of meeting the demand, evaluated at time 0, is given by*

$$P(Q > D) = \frac{h^- - w}{h^+ - h^-},$$

when

(i) *C1 is imposed and the optimal solution is applied in which $0 < q^* < K_1$; or*
(ii) *C2 is imposed and the optimal nonspeculative policy is applied in which $0 < q^* + L^* < K$; or*
(iii) *C2 is imposed and the optimal solution is applied in which $0 < q^* + L^* < K$.*

Proof. We provide a proof for (ii). Let Θ_t^j, $j = I, II, III, IV$, as the corresponding (see Table 1) ordering regions at the tth adjustment point. Define $\chi_{\{\theta\}}^t(f) \equiv \int_{\{\theta\}} f \, d\mu_{t-1}$ for $\theta \in \mathcal{F}_{t-1}$, where μ_{t-1} is the corresponding measure defined on $\mathcal{F}_{t-1}$. Then, $\chi_{\{\theta_1\}}^t(f) + \chi_{\{\theta_2\}}^t(f) = \chi_{\{\theta_1 \cup \theta_2\}}^t(f)$ for $\theta_1 \cap \theta_2 = \emptyset$. Also, define $\chi_{\{\theta_j, \theta_t\}}^j \equiv \chi_{\{\theta_j\}}^j[\chi_{\{\theta_t\}}^t(f)]$ for $j < t$ and $\chi_{\{\theta\}}(f) \equiv E_{\mathcal{F}_0} \chi_{\{\theta\}}^t(f)$.

Denote $v_t(y, A) = V_t(y, A - y)$ and $v_t(y) = y_t(y, y)$. When the event Θ_t^{II} happens at time t, then q_t^{c*} can be determined by solving for y_t^c in the following equation:

$$g(S_t) + \frac{\partial E_{\mathcal{F}_t} v_{t+1}(y_t^c, A)}{\partial y_t^c} = 0.$$

Then,

$$\rho_t = \chi^t_{\{\Theta^I_t\}}\left[g(S_t) + \frac{\partial E_{\mathcal{F}_t} v_{t+1}(y^c_t, A)}{\partial y^c_t}\right] = 0. \tag{30}$$

Similarly, when the event Θ^{IV}_t happens at time t, we have

$$\varpi_t = \chi^t_{\{\Theta^{IV}_t\}}\left[S_t + \frac{\partial E_{\mathcal{F}_t} v_{t+1}(y^s_t)}{\partial y^s_t}\right] = 0. \tag{31}$$

Now define

$$\Upsilon_t = \frac{\partial E_{\mathcal{F}_{t-1}} v_t(y, A)}{\partial y} \tag{32}$$

$$= \chi^t_{\{\Theta^I_t\}}[\Upsilon_{t+1}] - \chi^t_{\{\tilde{\Theta}^I_t\}}[g(S_t)] + \varrho_t$$

$$= \chi^t_{\{\Theta^I_t \cup \Theta^{II}_t\}}[\Upsilon_{t+1}] - \chi^t_{\{\Theta^{III}_t \cup \Theta^{IV}_t\}}[g(S_t)]$$

$$= \ldots\ldots$$

$$= \chi^t_{\{\Theta^I_t \cup \Theta^{II}_t,\ldots,\Theta^I_n \cup \Theta^{II}_n\}}[P\{Q \geqslant D\}(h^+ + h^1) - h^-] - \chi^t_{\{\Theta^{III}_t \cup \Theta^{IV}_t\}}[g(S_t)]$$

$$- \sum_{j=t+1}^{n} \chi^t_{\{\Theta^I_t \cup \Theta^{II}_t,\ldots,\Theta^I_{j-1} \cup \Theta^{II}_{j-1},\Theta^{III}_j \cup \Theta^{IV}_j\}}[g(S_j)].$$

Then, y^* is determined by

$$w - v + \Upsilon_1 = 0. \tag{33}$$

Also note that

$$\frac{\partial E_{\mathcal{F}_{t-1}} v_t(y_t, A_t)}{\partial A_t} \tag{34}$$

$$= \chi^t\{\Theta^I_t\}\left[\frac{\partial E_{\mathcal{F}_t} v_{t+1}(y_t, A_t)}{\partial A_t}\right] + \chi^t_{\{\Theta^{II}_t\}}\left[\frac{\partial E_{\mathcal{F}_t} v_{t+1}(y^c_t, A_t)}{\partial A_t}\right]$$

$$+ \chi^t_{\{\Theta^{III}_t\}}\left[\frac{dE_{\mathcal{F}_t} v_{t+1}(A_t)}{dA_t}\right] + \chi^t_{\{\Theta^{III}_t \cup \Theta^{IV}_t\}}[g(S_t)] - \chi^t_{\{\Theta^{IV}_t\}}[S_t]$$

$$= \sum_{j=t+1}^{n-1} \chi^t_{\{\Theta^I_t \cup \Theta^{II}_t,\ldots,\Theta^I_{j-1} \cup \Theta^{II}_{j-1},\Theta^{III}_j\}}\left[\frac{dE_{\mathcal{F}_j} v_{j+1}(A_t)}{dA_t}\right] + \chi^t_{\{\Theta^{III}_t\}}\left[\frac{dE_{\mathcal{F}_t} v_{t+1}(A_t)}{dA_t}\right]$$

$$+ \sum_{j=t+1}^{n} \chi^t_{\{\Theta^I_t \cup \Theta^{II}_t,\ldots,\Theta^I_{j-1} \cup \Theta^{II}_{j-1},\Theta^{III}_j \cup \Theta^{IV}_j\}}[g(S_j)] + \chi^t_{\{\Theta^{III}_t \cup \Theta^{IV}_t\}}[g(S_t)]$$

$$- \sum_{j=t+1}^{n} \chi^t_{\{\Theta^I_t \cup \Theta^{II}_t,\ldots,\Theta^I_{j-1} \cup \Theta^{II}_{j-1},\Theta^{IV}_j\}}[S_j] - \chi^t_{\{\Theta^{IV}_t\}}[S_t].$$

Define

$$\kappa_t = \chi^t_{\{\Theta^{I\!I}_t\}}\left[\frac{\mathrm{d}E_{\mathcal{F}_t}v_{t+1}(A)}{\mathrm{d}A}\right] + \chi^t_{\{\Theta^{I\!I}_t \cup \Theta^N_t\}}[g(S_t)] - \chi^t_{\{\Theta^N_t\}}[S_t]. \tag{35}$$

Then, the optimal A^* is determined by

$$v + \kappa_1 + \sum_{t=2}^{n}\chi_{\{\Theta^I_1 \cup \Theta^I_1, \dots, \Theta^I_{t-1} \cup \Theta^I_{t-1}\}}[\kappa_t] = 0. \tag{36}$$

Note that

$$\Gamma_t = \frac{\mathrm{d}E_{\mathcal{F}_{t-1}}v_t(A)}{\mathrm{d}A} \tag{37}$$
$$= \chi^t_{\{\tilde{\Theta}^N_t\}}[\Gamma_{t+1}] - \chi^t_{\{\Theta^N_t\}}[S_t] + \varpi_t$$
$$= E_{\mathcal{F}_{t-1}}[\Gamma_{t+1}]$$
$$= E_{\mathcal{F}_{t-1}}[P_{\mathcal{F}_n}\{Q \geqslant D\}(h^+ + h^-) - h^-].$$

Thus,

$$\kappa_t = \kappa_t + \rho_t + \varpi_t \tag{38}$$
$$= \chi^t_{\{\Theta^{I\!I}_t\}}[\Gamma_{t+1}] + \chi^t_{\{\Theta^{I\!I}_t \cup \Theta^N_t\}}[g(S_t)] - \chi^t_{\{\Theta^N_t\}}[S_t] + \chi^t_{\{\Theta^N_t\}}[\Gamma_{t+1} + S_t]$$
$$= \chi^t_{\{\Theta^{I\!I}_t \cup \Theta^N_t\}}[P_{\mathcal{F}_n}\{Q \geqslant D\}(h^+ + h^-) - h^-] + \chi^t_{\{\Theta^{I\!I}_t \cup \Theta^N_t\}}[g(S_t)].$$

From (33) and (36), we have

$$0 = w - v + \Upsilon_1 + v + \kappa_1 + \sum_{t=2}^{n}\chi_{\{\Theta^I_1 \cup \Theta^I_1, \dots, \Theta^I_{t-1} \cup \Theta^I_{t-1}\}}[\kappa_t]$$

$$= w + \chi_{\{\Theta^I_1 \cup \Theta^I_1, \dots, \Theta^I_n \cup \Theta^I_n\}}[P\{Q \geqslant D\}(h^+ + h^1) - h^-] - \chi_{\{\Theta^{I\!I}_1 \cup \Theta^N_1\}}g(S_1)$$

$$- \sum_{j=2}^{n}\chi_{\{\Theta^I_1 \cup \Theta^I_1, \dots, \Theta^I_{j-1} \cup \Theta^I_{j-1}, \Theta^I_j \cup \Theta^N_j\}}[g(S_j)]$$

$$+ \sum_{t=2}^{n}\chi_{\{\Theta^I_1 \cup \Theta^I_1, \dots, \Theta^I_{t-1} \cup \Theta^I_{t-1}, \Theta^{I\!I}_t \cup \Theta^N_t\}}[g(S_t)]$$

$$+ \sum_{t=2}^{n}\chi_{\{\Theta^I_1 \cup \Theta^I_1, \dots, \Theta^I_{t-1} \cup \Theta^I_{t-1}, \Theta^{I\!I}_t \cup \Theta^N_t\}}[P_{\mathcal{F}_n}\{Q \geqslant D\}(h^+ + h^-) - h^-]$$

$$+ \chi_{\{\Theta^{I\!I}_1 \cup \Theta^N_1\}}[P_{\mathcal{F}_n}\{Q \geqslant D\}(h^+ + h^-) - h^-]$$

$$= w + P_{\mathcal{F}_n}\{Q \geqslant D\}(h^+ + h^-) - h^-.$$

Hence the result follows.   □

6 Concluding Remarks

This chapter investigates a procurement system involving both long-term capacity allocation and short-term procurement decisions. We proposed a general price risk-sharing scheme to respond to uncertainties associated with the product demand and the procurement price. Our study indicates that when multiple procurement options with random prices are involved, a pre-determined preference order of the procurement options leads to an optimal base-stock policy. Under such a policy, the definition of the reference inventory positions reflects the preference order, that is, preferred source is ordered first. We also remark that the models and the results mentioned above can be easily extended to multi-period case as in Sethi et al. (2004) and Li and Ryan (2004).

Procurement flexibilities typically lead to reductions in the expected cost and the risk. It is interesting to note that the introduction of additional flexibilities does not improve the overall service level performance. Instead, the service level may even decrease if the supply capacity is limited. When enough supply capacity is provided, the overall service level depends only on the price of the long-term contact and not on the adjustment price scheme and/or the market price process.

References

Barnes-Schuster D, Bassok Y, Anupindi R (2002) Coordination and flexibility in supply contracts with options. Manuf Serv Oper Manag 43: 171–207

Bassok Y, Anupindi R (1997) Analysis of supply contracts with total minimum commitment. IIE Trans 29: 273–381

Bonser JS, Wu SD (2001) Procurement planning to maintain both short-term adaptiveness and long-term perspective. Manag Sci 47: 769–786

Cachon GP (2002) Supply coordination with contracts. In: Graves S, Kok T (eds.) Handbooks in Operations Research Management Science, North-Holland

Cachon GP, Lariviere MA (2001) Contracting to assure supply: how to share demand forecasts in a supply chain. Managment Sci 47: 629-646

Cater JR, Vickery SK (1998) Managing volatile exchange rats in international purchasing. J Purch Mater Manag 24:13–20

Cheng F, Ettl M, Lin GY, Schwarz M, Yao DD (2008) Designing flexible supply chain contracts via options. In: Kempf KG, Keskinocak P, Uzsoy R (eds.) Planning in the Extended Enterprise: A State of the Art Handbook, Springer, Berlin

Deng S, Yano C (2002) On the role of a second purchase opportunity in a two-echelon supply chain. Technical report, University of California, Berkeley, CA

Feng Q, Gallego G, Sethi SP, Yan H, Zhang H (2005) Periodic-review inventory model with three consecutive delivery modes and forecast updates. J Optim Theor Appl 124:137–155

Feng Q, Sethi SP, Yan H, Zhang H (2006a) Optimality and nonoptimality of the base-stock policy in inventory problems with multiple. J Ind Manag Optim 2:19–42

Feng Q, Sethi SP, Yan H, Zhang H (2006b) Are base-stock policies optimal in inventory problems with multiple delivery modes? Oper Res 54:801–807

Golovachkina N (2003) Supplier-Manufacturer Relationships Under Forced Compliance Contracts. Manuf Serv Oper Manag 5(1):67–69.

Gerchak Y, Cho R, Ray S (2006) Coordination and dynamic shelf-space management of video movie rentals. IIE Trans 38:525–536

Kleindorfer PR, Wu DJ (2003) Integrating long-and-short term contracting via Business-to-Business exchanges for capacity intensive industries. Manag Sci 49:1597–1615

Lariviere M (1999) Supply chain contracting and coordination with stochastic demand. In: Tayur S, Ganeshan R, Magazine M (eds.) Quantitative Models for Supply Chain Management, Kluwer Academic Publisher, Boston

Lee H, Whang S (2002) The impact of the secondary market on the supply chain. Manag Sci 45:719–731

Li CL, Kouvelis P (1999) Flexible and risk sharing supply contracts under price uncertainty. Manag Sci 45:1378–1398

Li R, Ryan JK (2004) Inventory flexibility through adjustment contracts. Working paper, Purdue University, West Lafayette, IN

Martínez-de-Albéniz V, Simchi-Levi D (2005) A portfolio approach to procurement contracts. Prod Oper Manag 14:90–114

Milner JM, Kouvelis P (2005) Order quantity and timing flexibility in supply chains: the role of demand characteristic. Manag Sci 51:970–985

Tsay A (1999) The quantity flexibility contract and supplier-customer incentives. Manag Sci 45:1339–1358

Tsay A, Nahmias S, Agrawal N (1999) Modeling supply chain contracts. In: Tayur S, Magazine M, Ganeshan R (eds.) A review, Quantitative models for supply chain management, Kluwer Academic, Boston

Sethi SP, Yan H, Zhang H (2004) Quantity flexible contracts in supply chains with information updates and service-level constraints. Decis Sci J 35:691–712

Sethi SP, Yan H, Zhang H (2005) Analysis of a Duopoly Supply Chain and its Application in Electricity Spot Markets. Ann Oper Res 135:239–259

Wu DJ, Kleindorfer PR, Zhang JE (2001) Integrating contracting and spot procurement with capacity options. Working Paper, LeBow College of Business, Drexel University, Philadelphia, PA

Wu DJ, Kleindorfer PR, Zhang JE (2002) Optimal bidding and contracting strategies for capital-intensive goods. Euro J Oper Res 137:657–676

The Value of Information in Quick Response Supply Chains: An Assortment Planning View

Hajnalka Vaagen and Stein W. Wallace

Abstract Many see timely accurate information availability as the key of successful customer-behaviour-reactive, wait-and-see planning in agile environments. Because of the extensive use of lean retailing, these quick response (QR) strategies require substantially reduced lead times across the supply chain, with the competitive advantage of enabling constant new product supply. However, successful market attempts are rapidly copied by the competition, leading to an accelerating spiral of variety-pricing games, with the inevitable result of often trivial product differentiation, reduced quality and pressure on prices. The environmental, psychological and operational effects of this spiral are severe. This work discusses the operational aspects from an assortment planning point of view, referring to the products to be included in the portfolio, as well as their inventory levels. The aim is to *shift focus* from timely information availability across the supply chain and wait-and-see planning, to the actual information needed to make substantial and potentially important changes, and to information available at the time when important decisions are to be taken. A proposed decision support framework - with corresponding tool set of estimation and optimization methods - helps evaluating this, by measuring the value and risk of different assortment strategies, and decisions taken at different information levels. The estimation and optimization models presented here are consistent in their use of subjective knowledge and in emphasizing the importance of attribute-based assortment planning in contemporary QR supply chains.

Keywords Attribute based planning · Assortment risk · Bi-modal distribution · Correlation · Quick response · Substitutable newsvendor

H. Vaagen (✉)
Molde University College, P.O.Box 2110, NO-6402 Molde, Norway
e-mail: hajnalka.vaagen@himolde.no

T.C. Edwin Cheng and T.-M. Choi (eds.), *Innovative Quick Response Programs in Logistics and Supply Chain Management*, International Handbooks on Information Systems, DOI 10.1007/978-3-642-04313-0_5,
© Springer-Verlag Berlin Heidelberg 2010

1 Introduction

In this chapter we analyse the value of information in assortment planning in highly volatile environments. Research on this is motivated by the observation that, despite the focus on information being crucial for successful planning in agile industries, various quick response (QR) programs adopted to create market mediated value chains often fail or have limited value. We point out that our aim is neither to suggest ways of increasing available early information or yet again illustrating the value of having the necessary information, nor to illustrate the value of information-sharing in QR supply chains. We provide a *decision support framework*, with corresponding tool set, that allows us to measure the value of available information and helps us evaluate supply chain changes to support the strategically defined performance and risk measures. Available information, in this chapter, is not limited to real-time customer orders. Subjective knowledge - on particular trend estimates, demand driver attributes and relationships among these attributes - is not only allowed but is also of great importance in the presented models.

Volatile areas such as fashion apparel, also called agile environments in the literature (Gunasekaram 1999; Yusuf et al. 1999 and 2004; van Hoek et al. 2001; Naylor et al. 1999; Mason-Jones et al. 2000), are characterized by high levels of product variety and uncertainty, with customer demand as the driving force of design, planning and logistics activities. Abernathy et al. (2004) view the adaptation to *lean retailing* (retail orders made on real-time sales information) and *product proliferation* (constant demand distributed across a higher level of variety) as the key determinants for a future global success. To respond to the challenges arising from agility, various QR strategies are adopted to create market-mediated value chains. Lowson et al. (1999) defines QR as follows:

> A state of responsiveness and flexibility in which an organisation seeks to provide a highly diverse range of products and services to a customer/consumer in the exact quantity, variety and quality, and at the right time, place, price as dictated by real-time customer/consumer demand. QR provides the ability to make demand-information driven decisions at the last possible moment in time ensuring that diversity of offering is maximised and lead-times, expenditure, cost and inventory minimized. QR places an emphasis upon flexibility and product velocity in order to meet the changing requirements of highly competitive, volatile and dynamic marketplace. QR encompasses an operations strategy, structure, culture and set of operational procedures aimed at integrating enterprises in a mutual network through rapid information transfer and profitable exchange

A well-known QR initiative, from product management perspective, is increased product variety by mass-customization, achieved by common platforms for different product families and customization on the 'top'. From a supply–demand management perspective, market-mediated inventory/production allocation planning models are adopted.

Although these programs theoretically allow for supply chain flexibility, there is limited focus on defining the level of information required for implementing these strategies, so as to enable quick response without substantial increase in supply chain costs. In other words, although timely and accurate information flows may enable fast and accurate response, it is possible that the information needed to make substantial and potentially important changes in the supply chain arrives at a point in time when the changes are not compatible with supply chain capabilities. It is still not uncommon in the industry to implement different technologies and particular procedures, without the strategic underpinnings, and hence end up in suboptimal performance (Lowson 2002). A common example is the implementation of sophisticated planning systems connected to timely information-update software, but without substantial changes in the supply chain structure. Also, there is limited investigation of the risks taken by the adopted QR strategies, given a particular information level.

Product assortment and uncertainty being the major driving factors when designing a particular supply chain strategy, we believe that it is of both theoretical and practical interest to better understand the interaction between these factors. As we see it, this chapter is a step towards a more holistic view on assortment planning, with a critical focus on the information level available at any given point in time when decisions are taken, and hence towards the convergence of academia and industry practice.

To illustrate the challenges of assortment planning in dynamically changing contemporary markets, we provide the following two real cases from textile apparel. Although other agile supply markets, such as mobile phones, electronic equipment, movies, games, point to characteristics similar to that of textiles, we believe that the apparel industry examples are better suited to show the pitfalls of replicating particularly successful QR strategies.

1. Zara, the Spanish high-fashion producer, has a successful QR strategy with a new product launch 'every second week', including few products in small quantities, enabled by close daily interaction among design, production, marketing and retail activities, and closeness to the core markets (McAfee et al. 2004). A distinguishing feature of companies like Zara is their use of flexible arrangements with a large number of small manufacturers specialized in a particular garment type or material. In addition to daily point-of-sale data and supply chain flexibility, strong focus on understanding the trend drivers in the different markets defines their success. A two-week collection designed for a specific market can be seen as a project with low value compared to the overall wealth of the company, hence with low risk due to its impact, even though the project-risk itself can be high. Under a QR strategy like this, it might be appropriate for a decision maker to be risk-neutral and maximize expected profit of each small decision instead of focusing on risk aversion. In light of stochastic utility theory, pure profit maximization can be seen as maximizing expected utility with a risk-neutral attitude. And a linear utility function creates easier problems to solve.

2. Now take a brand-name technical outdoor and sportswear supplier, still having two major collections per year, with implemented collaborative planning, forecasting and replenishment systems, enabling continuous forecast and production updating and the use of sophisticated planning tools. Product development takes from a few months to 2 years. Production is largely located in the far east, with major markets in Europe and North America. Although the firm has an up-to-date QR

information system, the highly specialized structure of the manufacturing plants, all of substantial size, distant from the core markets, and the fact that the raw materials are not readily available, hinder quick response in production and supply. Traditionally, sportswear products have strong focus on the performance attributes and require highly specialized production lines, which makes 'shopping' among small manufacturers (Zara's approach) difficult. On the other hand, the fashion element is becoming more and more important, increasing the volatility in demand. Retailers respond to this by applying a late-ordering strategy, and hence forwarding their risks to the suppliers. Because of this, the amount of information required for establishing reliable demand estimates arrives at a point in time when updating production schedules leads to unreasonably high supply chain disturbances, which, in order, leads to a reduction of the value of the innovative market-mediated planning systems. Each collection stands for a significant share of the total result; hence, it is clear that risk should indeed be taken into account. Also, replicating Zara's strategy would lead to loss of core technical competence, and focus changed toward fashion-trend based attributes rather than innovation and functionality. It could also lead to weakening of the brand name. We mention that several technical sportswear specialists "marry" high-fashion designers to combine artistic vision with technical know-how, as the French ski specialist Rossignol and the Italian haute couture designer Emilio Pucci. The result is a juxtaposition of two highly distinctive areas, contributing to the brand name exclusivity, rather than diluting it to the fast changing street-wear market. Despite this, and in an attempt to quickly respond to market demand variations caused by the new emerging trends and to maintain market shares, several technical sportswear producers enter the street-wear segment as well, and increase the number of yearly collections; this, while still having the traditional supply chains with long lead-times.

Although both industrials require quick response, the market characteristics faced by them trigger substantially different assortment planning approaches and, hence, different supply chain strategies. While high-fashion suppliers can, indeed, focus on the ephemeral trends, "designed to capture a particular mood of the moment" (Christopher et al. 2004), sporting goods suppliers have to face the challenges arising from the emerging conflicting goals, to maintain a highly specialized performance focus, while satisfying customers with a strong fashion orientation. High-fashion products trigger customer needs in the moment by being available for only a short time. Customers impulsively react to the influence from movie/pop stars, athletes, and others; as such, demand is highly volatile. Hence, the street-wear supplier environment is demanding QR with frequent supply of new designs. Sports equipment and apparel products, on the other hand, traditionally are designed to satisfy high-performance requirements, intended to have longer product-life-cycles, and are less impulse-purchase driven. Although these characteristics suggest a 'less uncertain' environment, the introduction of the fashion element makes it more volatile. While many 'pure' fashion producers have, more or less, successfully, adapted QR strategies with lead-times reduced by as much as 70%, many sports apparel suppliers still suffer from the lack of a clear strategy. Despite the fact that sporting goods suppliers acknowledge the operational challenge of offering constant new products, there is limited knowledge on how to successfully handle the problem. Generally, there is an increasing academic and practical focus on real-time customer orders and on replicating QR strategies from successful high-fashion practitioners.

As a result, we believe that before adapting a particular QR strategy, it is important to understand how the different product characteristics (such as, performance attributes and fashion trends) behave in particular markets and establish the distinct value segments requiring different strategies. In other words, an attribute-based view of the assortment problem might be necessary to understand what type of information is required to adapt sudden changes. Hence, we deliberately limit the scope of this paper. Although we discuss neither specific trend drivers nor product-market combinations, we survey the models that are able to integrate such knowledge and to measure the value of early information.

There is extensive literature on assortment planning, and we refer to the reviews provided by Mahajan and van Ryzin (1998) and Kök et al. (2008). The focus is particularly on the exogenous demand multi-item newsboy models (Khouja et al. 1996; Bassok et al. 1999; Rajaram and Tang 2001; Netessine and Rudi 2003, and others) and individual customer preference multinomial logit models (see among others Mahajan and van Ryzin 2001; Gaur and Honhon (2006). Most supply chain policies discussed in these reviews focus on improving efficiency with a risk neutral attitude, that is, expected performance in terms of costs and profits. However, when the variance of profit is high relative to the overall wealth, this might lead to suboptimal decisions by ignoring the supplier's risk aversion. Accordingly, we find it important to include portfolio-risk considerations in this chapter, illustrating the risks taken at different information levels. Although the literature on this issue is still very new, there are important inventory-risk models to be found (Lau 1980; Chen and Federgruen 2000; Van Mieghem 2003; Choi 2008; Choi et al., 2008a and 2008b; Vaagen and Wallace 2008, and others). Relevant work will be discussed where appropriate throughout this chapter. Unfortunately, most existing models require substantial simplifying assumptions on the demand drivers, leading to reduced complexity, and also decisions that do not reflect reality. The models developed by Vaagen and Wallace (2008) and Vaagen et al. (2008 and 2009) avoid simplifications on the central terms and, by allowing for an attribute-based view of the problem, integrate subjective knowledge about the demand drivers. As such, they are well suited to measure the value and risk associated with different levels of information. In Sect. 2 we provide a decision support framework that helps in defining adequate QR strategies by (1) connecting supply chain capabilities and available information, and (2) allowing us to evaluate the value of information under the existing supply chain properties and the risk associated with decisions taken in light of different information levels. Simply stated, we provide a tool set that helps defining the point in time when different actions need to be taken. Optimisation and estimation models suited to evaluate decisions are given in Sect. 3. We conclude in Sect. 4.

2 Decision Support Framework to Value Potential QR Strategies

The core material of this chapter is given in the following sections. We provide a decision support framework that allows us to evaluate potential QR strategies to support the strategically defined performance and risk measures. Although it is not the aim of this chapter to deeply discuss the strategic implications of QR on organisations, we find it appropriate to provide the reader with a brief presentation on the subject (based on Christopher et al. 2004). This understanding is important while designing quick response strategies and when using the decision support framework suggested by us in this section: (1) The alignment of organisational activities to demand – such as design, marketing, production, retailing, and financial activities. (2) Linkages between demand and supply – by understanding the demand drivers and their connections to supply. (3) Understanding of unique product–market combinations that require different supply chain strategies. In other words, different groups of customers within the total market value different product attributes. This is reflected for instance by the market specific product selection of brand-name technical sportswear suppliers. While high performance attributes are the buying criteria in Scandinavia, style and brand name strength has higher added value in Hong Kong. (4) Resource configuration must reflect and build on customer values and perceived benefits for operations. (5) The ability to compress time, so as to enable accurate response to real-time demand - the fundamental of QR philosophies, successfully achieved by high-fashion suppliers like Zara, with lead times reduced to between 2 and 4 weeks. (6) Primacy of information – crucial to enable fast and accurate response without unnecessary costs. (7) A series of win–win business alliances.

When designing a particular QR strategy, the present supply chain flexibility must be connected to the information flow. The following questions structure the logic of this task, and as such, form the 'backbone' of our decision support system.

1. *What is the existing supply chain strategy* and *what are the goals* – the strategically defined performance measures, such as minimal acceptable assortment profit and maximal acceptable profit risk (i.e. the downside variance of the expected profit)?
2. What is the *present upstream supply chain flexibility,* described by different supplier *lead-times* (as given by Christopher et al. (2004)? – *Time-to-market:*the time between recognizing a particular demand driver and, hence, a market opportunity, translating this into a product and bringing it to the market. *Time-to-serve:* the time it takes from receiving a concrete customer order and until the product reaches the retail customer. *Time-to-react:* the time it takes to adapt sudden changes. In an assortment planning setting this refers to the ability and speed to update assortment with respect to both the products to be included and their inventory levels.
3. What is the structure of the *present downstream information availability*? What type of information becomes available from customers and when does that happen? Here we consider real customer orders as well as pre-season aggregated estimates and recognition of specific trend and demand driver attributes.

4. To reach the goals with the present supply chain strategy, what information, how much and when is it needed?
5. Is the present information flow defined in (3) in line with the information needed to support the goals (4)?
6. If the answer in step (5) is 'yes', an appropriate supply chain strategy is already in function and the process stops here.
7. If the answer in step (5) is 'no', an iterative analysis is required, by (a) *revising the supply chain strategy* – for example, evaluating different QR programs or hedging; (b) *revise the goals* – accept lower expected minimal profit or higher risk; or (c) *revise both* until convergence between the strategy and the goals is achieved. This step refers to evaluating available options to handle demand uncertainty. The choice of a particular option is a trade-off between costs and benefits.

To illustrate how our decision support framework can be used, consider the sports apparel supplier from Sect. 1. The company's logistics planning calendar for summer season products- indicating the supplier's product development, assortment planning and production periods, the retail selling season, information flow from customers and upstream flexibility - is given in Fig. 1. The winter season follows the same structure with 6 months delay. Although the planning period here is divided into months, this can be converted into weeks or days (at Zara for instance) to express the grade of QR with reduced reaction lead times. The time from product development until the retail selling season starts takes up to two years. Regular retail orders and reorders do not overlap. As opposed to the regular orders, reorders are mostly a reaction to customer behaviour. Although at our particular supplier the reorder period starts before the main selling season, at this point there are much stronger indications about the major trend patterns. First, the retailers' portfolios consist of several brands; some of them are launching new products already before the main selling season. Second, catalogues are often available to illustrate for customers the new trends and new arrivals. These, together, help retailers improve their own predictions and make necessary changes. That said, a large share of the reorders is based on real-time customer demand. Retail orders are updated continuously and production plans accordingly. About half of the total production needs to be committed at the beginning of the production season (August on the calendar). At this point, available information is limited to trends and sales estimates; estimates that are often wrong. Technical products are traded from overseas manufacturers with lead times up to 4 months. To a limited extent, extra production capacity reserved and express delivery is used to enable flexibility. Small and flexible, close-to-market production plants are largely used for less complex brand name profiling products, like t-shirts.

Assume that despite the ability to update information continuously, the amount of information needed to establish reliable assortment plans arrives late in the planning season. Increasingly, retailers transfer their risks to suppliers by postponing a large share of their orders until close to the start of the selling season. Further, assume that the existing upstream flexibility does not support radical assortment changes at such a late point in time. The following options are then available. The supplier can revise the goals and lower the expected minimal profit bound, accept higher risk (a decision to be taken by the owners), or revise the strategy as follows: (a) Evaluate options to 'influence customers' so that they deliver their orders earlier.

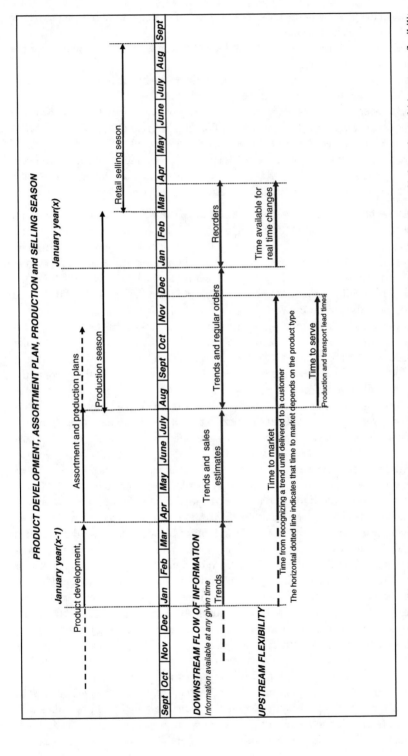

Fig. 1 Logistics planning calendar with (**a**) product development, production and selling seasons, (**b**) downstream flow of information and (**c**) upstream flexibility

Although this is a commonly appraised strategy, we point out that, due to highly uncertain demand patterns, lean retailing is increasingly dominating. Several brand name suppliers establish concept stores, hence 'buy' the retailers in an attempt to solve the lean retailing problem. (b) Offer a hedging portfolio, built by strategically chosen competing and substituting items; (c) Design a particular QR strategy with reduced reaction lead times. 'Onshore', close-to-market production increases production costs but allows for reduced lead times. The risk of expensive onshore production can be reduced by an increased 'number of seasons', each of them with lower variety and inventory levels, and the possibility to frequently update decisions as uncertainty reveals.

In this work, we particularly focus on assortment planning strategies and only briefly discuss the remainders. However, we provide the necessary tool to evaluate each of them as needed. We summarize the iterative decision support framework in Fig. 2. Note that this is not limited to the textile apparel industrial environment.

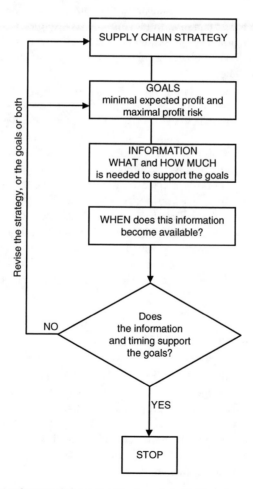

Fig. 2 Decision support framework for evaluating the value of information

3 Estimation and Optimisation Tools for Measuring the Value of Information

To evaluate the type and degree of quick response appropriate for a given practitioner, a set of integrated optimisation and estimation tools are needed. Particularly, it is important that these tools are compatible with each other and are connected by a common information base. In this section we provide the reader with a set of tools that, we believe, are consistent with regard to the information available at the moment of planning. Particularly, these optimisation and estimation models accept that information in QR supply chains is largely limited to knowledge on trends and demand driver attributes, rather than real-time customer orders. Concretely, the summarized tools provide decisions on items to include in the portfolio and their inventory levels, while allowing for an attribute-based view of the assortment problem. Although the core of this chapter is general in nature, the textile apparel examples used, and the industry situation, are well-suited to illustrate the need for attribute based planning models in QR environments. As such, the optimisation and estimation tools presented here are well-suited for most dynamically changing newsvendor-like products, like sports equipment, electronic equipment, music, video, and games.

Available information and uncertainty being crucial when estimating the model parameters, we start this in Sect. 3.1 by a qualitative discussion on the uncertainty and agility arising from the competitive situation in the apparel industry. The environmental and sustainability arguments included here intend to provide the reader with intuitive understanding of why some genuine quick response strategies might lead to unsustainable solutions for the industry. These arguments, in turn, are helpful to understand the focus of this chapter. In Sect. 3.2 we give the estimation methods suited for integrating subjective knowledge on demand driver attributes. Particularly, we focus on parameters that directly or indirectly define individual item demand distributions. Models suited to evaluate particular assortment planning options are given in Sect. 3.3, all of which analyse the same problem from different, but interrelated perspectives. The value of information is established in Sect. 3.4. Numerical examples are provided by a real case from the sports apparel industry.

3.1 Uncertainty and Information

In decision making and operations, the underlying assumption of demand being genuinely exogenous or endogenous, and its uncertainty external or internal, is a defining starting point. When differentiating between the external and internal natures of the uncertainty, we follow the terminology of Kahneman and Tversky (1982). External randomness cannot be controlled and the goal is to plan for it by creating flexibility. Internal randomness can be reduced or eliminated by better understanding and knowledge of the problem or by creating flexibility. This latter is a trade-off between costs and benefits. However, this trade-off cannot be properly translated into supply chain strategies without deep understanding of what drives uncertainty and why.

In dynamically changing, uncertain, industrial arenas it is commonly accepted that demand is exogenous and its uncertainty external. We believe this assumption is unrealistically strong, leading to a dynamic, accelerating spiral of variety-pricing games. In highly competitive markets, successful quick response implementations, such as risk dispersion by frequent new product supplies in lower quantities, are rapidly copied by the competition. This process, in turn, leads to substantially reduced lead times to enable constant 'new' product supply and increased variety to hedge against uncertainty around the products' market acceptance. The inevitable results of this dynamics are not only variety explosion, but also often trivial product differentiation, reduced quality and pressure on prices (Poiesz 2004). Despite the waste reduction in terms of 'time', there is a general agreement that the physical waste created has severe environmental consequences (Morley et al. 2006; Luz 2007). "There are nowhere near enough people in America to absorb the mountains of castoffs, even if they were given away." (Luz 2007). In the UK, the apparel offered to the market increased by over 60% just during the last 10 years (Morley et al. 2006). As prices and quality of new clothing continue to decline, so too will the demand for used clothing diminish affecting the long term viability of the textile recycling industry. First, low quality will not justify the energy and labor used to sort, wash and transport second hand clothes. Second, new clothing can be bought almost as inexpensively as used clothing; hence the attractiveness will be reduced. Canning (2006) points to similar supply market characteristics in the mobile phone industry and identifies the rate of new model introduction and low unit value as being the triggers of burning environmental problems, specifically emphasizing the waste's toxicity.

Furthermore, the immense variety offered, high technological sophistication and often banal differentiation among the products severely affect rational consumer choice (Dougherty and Hunter 2003), hence violates the assumption of demand exogeneity. Low risk implied by low prices and often trivial product differentiation does not motivate customers to carefully compare and judge. It rather motivates for more buys due to unfulfilled needs and budgets left for consumption. The enormous variety offered, communicated via a large number of distribution channels, lead to disturbing information overloads (Poiesz 2004). The amount of information that can be perceived by humans is limited and, for most consumers, dynamically changing markets are highly complex (Dougherty and Hunter 2003). The information absorption capability and motivation is further reduced by the limited amount of time available for decision making (short product life-cycles, short-time bargains). This interpretation implies that, to consumers, the disadvantages of the competitive environments might outweigh the advantages, and that purchases may not originate in product needs but may be a bi-product of psychological 'pressure' or social exchanges (Poiesz 2004).

The contemporary market characteristics clearly indicate the emergence of unsustainable solutions on operational, as well as environmental and psychological level.

From a supplier perspective, substantially increased variety for a rather stable aggregated demand and poor understanding or ignorance of the dependencies among the products offered might lead to internal randomness. Although QR suppliers acknowledge the operational and environmental challenges of offering constant new products, there is limited knowledge on how to successfully handle the problem. Furthermore, although existing planning support systems acknowledge market complexity and uncertainty, they still perform poorly in providing reliable decision support to industrials. Particularly, models suited to solve complex uncertainty-related problems with dependencies among the individual products, and models suited to measure the risk of decisions regarding variety, are not yet common in production planning and control. Existing analytical assortment and production planning models frequently assume external randomness and demand distributions are established by various methods, using historical data and dynamic purchasing processes, and production plans are made accordingly. Mahajan and van Ryzin (2001) point out that when applying inventory models in practice it is quite common to use simple distributional assumptions such as the normal, Poisson, negative binomial and multinomial distributions (Fisher and Raman 1996; Eppen and Iyer 1997; Nikhil and Anand 2001; Zhao et al. 2002; Donohue, 2000; Chen et al. 2006). Dependency patterns are allowed between the individual item demands however, often with strong assumptions and simplifications (Netessine and Rudi 2003; Rajaram and Tang 2001; Mahajan and van Ryzin 2001). In addition, strategic model parameters defining the demand patterns, such as substitution measures, are also simplified to make the models solvable (Rajaram and Tang 2001). In summary, the complexity of the uncertainty is somehow reduced, and available information possibly 'distorted', when used in the analytical planning models. Model solutions, hence, might not reflect reality. Despite these analytical approaches, the fact that demand for trend-driven products cannot or is difficult to forecast is now gradually accepted both by academics and practitioners. This recognition gave rise to the various QR strategies, with change from forecast driven to information-based supply chains. We find it appropriate to mention here that the forecasting methods commonly applied by both academics and practitioners largely use end-product level information. Although an attribute-based view of the assortment problem, and hence an attribute-based forecasting, is emphasized by Kök et al. (2008) to be important in the future, there is limited amount of work in this direction. Consumer choice models allow for this, however, with severe limitations with regard to dependencies among the attributes and end products. This, in turn, makes them less useful in agile environments. The following innovative initiatives show the importance of an attribute-based approach: the integration of textile technology and information-communication technology (ICT) to develop new materials with membranes and catalytic reactors for integrated communication systems, and 'green' material properties, achieved by organic–inorganic hybrids developed by nanotechnologies. When new products made of such materials are launched on the consumer market, it might be appropriate to analyse the market demand for *'green' properties, shape memory, integrated ICT* and *ephemeral seasonal trend* separately, before aggregating these into end-product demand.

Despite the 'chaotic' behaviour of individual product demands, there are some major patterns found to be common in product portfolios. In the textile apparel, several case studies indicate that nearly half of the variety offered becomes obsolete, and that the structure of an assortment can be described by some Pareto rule, with few items standing for a large share of the portfolio profit and large number of items ending up with marginal sales (Vaagen and Wallace 2008; Raman et al. 2001). Ex-ante the assortment planning, however, there is no way to say which items become popular; hence for many of them the world takes two possible states: *State 1* when they become popular and *State 2* when unpopular (Vaagen and Wallace 2008). On an aggregated level demand is not very uncertain as it refers to demand across whatever will become popular. On this lower level, demand uncertainty can be described by some doubly differentiable unimodal distribution. On a higher level, however, decision makers need to cope with the complexity in individual level uncertainty, frequently characterized by the existence of the two states of the world, and hence, bi-modal distributions. Although bi-modally distributed demand might seem to be specific for fashion and sports apparel, this is not the case. Sports equipment, electronic devices, videos and games follow the same market behaviour pattern, to a lower extent though. As such, we do not find it obscure to use textile apparel examples for illustration of difficult contemporary operational challenges.

3.1.1   Case analysis to illustrate the above discussed complex uncertainty patterns

Take the brand name sportswear supplier introduced earlier, with the 2005 summer season portfolio of about 900 new designs, continuing life-cycle and specially engineered products (about 20% of the total portfolio) excluded. To evaluate the predictability of the individual item demands we have performed an ex-post analysis based on observed total demand and monthly accumulated retail orders. About 50% and 80% of the total production is expected to be committed at the beginning of and 2 months into the production season, respectively. Figure 3 illustrates the observed demand measured at the end of the season relative to cumulative 2 months orders (denoted $cumX2\_New$). Our aim is not to predict demand, but to ex-post evaluate its predictability. Observe that at this point in time there is still substantial uncertainty to cope with. The 98% confidence interval allows for as much as ± 120 units of demand variation for each individual item (see the standard deviation S of 61 units on the figure). The situation is similar for the preceding five seasons as well (both summer and winter); seasons for which we actually ex-post evaluated the demand predictability.

Further, observe how the plot diagram clearly indicates the existence of the two states of the world, by two major patterns. However, the states of the world cannot be separated until well into the production season. With a portfolio of about 1,000 new designs and with the given supply chain capabilities, postponing decisions until the point in time when the popularity of items is revealed can be very risky. To enable decisions that are *reactive to real orders*, substantially reduced

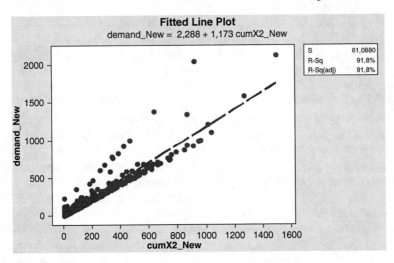

Fig. 3 Fitted line plot for observed end-season demand relative to cumulative two-months orders for about 900 new designs in the summer season of 2005

production and transportation lead times are needed. Reserving protective capacity seems not to properly solve the problem when the uncertainty around the popularity affects a large share of the portfolio. The technology now enables information flow from the point of actual demand directly to the focal supplier. Information provides the driving force to design quick response by reduced lead times, so as to reduce the risk presented above. However, lead time pressed down to a minimum, with the consequence of reduced quality and price, is not necessarily appropriate for high quality performance-wear suppliers. Hence, we suggest shifting focus to planning under available information, rather than applying particular wait-and-see strategies. In this sense, we emphasize the importance of understanding available information at the time when important assortment decisions are taken (might be vague trends or real-time orders), and how this information can be used to enable flexible strategies, without actually losing core competence attributes, like high performance and quality. Customized engineering is not to be confused by mass-customization of ephemeral trend attributes, often achieved by minimal changes in the product design.

3.2 Demand

Earlier we discussed that (1) real-time customer orders available at the time of assortment planning do not indicate which items become popular (hence are of limited value), and (2) creating flexibility by constant new product supplies has severe operational (and environmental and psychological) consequences for particular suppliers. For these reasons, we focus on the information available before real-time customer orders arrive, that is information on demand driver attributes and aggregated estimates and how this can be interpreted and integrated in the planning models. Note that we do not discuss particular product attributes, but we show how they drive the dependencies among the individual items in a portfolio and, hence, the demand. As such, in addition to real-time customer orders, we allow for subjective knowledge (e.g. ephemeral seasonal trends, image, particular technical features of the materials used). Qualitative understanding is repeatedly emphasized to be the key success factor at innovative dynamically changing agile suppliers (Kök et al. 2008; Christopher et al. 2004). The well-known 'Obermeyer case' from the sports apparel industry (Fisher et al. 1994) is the first work using subjective knowledge when establishing demand distributions. The method uses an expert team to give an initial forecast figure for each individual item. Based on this data, demand distributions (with mean and standard deviation) are constructed on distinct item level. The method is used to separate between uncertain and less uncertain products. The knowledge, then, is used to separate between first and second production runs, postponing the production of the very uncertain items (Fisher and Raman 1996). The idea is adopted by several agile industrials and the method further developed and included in sophisticated planning systems - like *A3 Forecast Solutions,* http://www. a3forecastsolutions.com/, applied by a wide range of fashion and sports apparel producers (among others, Levis, Helly Hansen, Tommy Hilfiger Europe). In our setting, the blind forecasting method can be used to separate the items that are very uncertain and subject to both states of the world (popular or unpopular).

3.2.1 Demand Driver Parameters

In this section we focus on the operational parameters directly/indirectly affecting the individual item demands, and further, how available trends and knowledge on demand driver attributes can be expressed by them. The discussion is based on Vaagen and Wallace (2008) and Vaagen et al. (2009).

Selling price is generally an important demand driver. However, in this work we do not consider price/cost parameters to be strategic; we assume homogeneity across a reference group, consisting of items directly competing with each other (such as high performance winter jackets for men from a particular brand name supplier, distinguished by style and colour combinations). Previous research indicates that the lean retail strategy is increasingly dominating, and influencing customers is more and more difficult (Campo et al. 2003). At 'our' sports apparel supplier, early-season discount strategies did not have the desired effect. For a customer, the negative consequences of purchasing the 'wrong' products are much higher than the winnings by early season discounts. That said, dynamic pricing strategies are indeed to be considered in an extended market-level analysis, involving distinct product–market combinations.

Parameters directly defining the demand distributions are the *mean demand*, its *variance* and *correlation values* expressing the dependencies among the individual item demands. In addition, *substitution measures* drive the *effective demand*, consisting of the direct demand of a particular item and substitution demand from other items (Kök and Fisher 2007; Rajaram and Tang 2001). Customers are often willing to substitute when their first preference is not available. Vaagen et al. (2009) recognize that trends drive the dependencies between the individual items, dependencies that can be 'translated' to correlation and substitution measure values. To do that, a decision independent approach is required. Traditional estimation methods are based on real-time sales transaction and inventory data and poorly suited to integrate subjective knowledge. Also, inventory and sales transaction data naturally indicate the necessity of dynamic data tracking. But even so, existing analytical assortment planning models are, as far we can understand it, still static. Accordingly, inconsistency between the dynamic data needed for establishing substitution shares and the static nature of the optimisation models might arise. For reviews on this subject we refer to Mahajan and van Ryzin (1998) and Kök et al. (2008).

In the following we summarize important *rules driving the inter-item dependencies*. First, the existence of the two states of the world for some items, paired with 'competition' for popularity, drives the strong negative correlations between certain individual item demands. Correlations are denoted $c_{ij} \in [-1, +1]$.

Second, additional trend patterns, like the popularity of a specific style across different colours, or the preference of a specific brand, drive the positive correlations.

Finally, the grade of similarity between the items with regard to the demand driver attributes is expressed by the decision independent substitution measure a priori *substitutability* $\alpha_{ij} \in [0, 1]$, indicating the portion of customers willing to replace item j with item i. The n items offered are potential substitutes for each other, with heterogeneous substitutability values. This measure differs from the *factual substitution*; a decision dependent outcome of a particular optimisation process, constrained by unsatisfied demand and the variants available at the moment of purchase.

The common information base (on product attribute level, rather than end-product level) naturally connects correlation and substitutability values. Below we use an apparel example to illustrate this, as well as important connections between the substitution possibilities and inter-item dependencies expressed by the correlations. Note that the connections among different types of dependencies are not textile industry specific. The style-colour combinations used and corresponding substitutability and correlation values are summarized in Table 1.

Take four high-performance winter jackets for women, distinguished by two styles (1 and 2) and three colours (skyblue, golden and white). Assume that, while the technical attributes define aggregated level demand, choices on individual item

Table 1 Style and colour combinations and corresponding substitutability and correlation values

α_{ij}/c_{ij}	1-Skyblue	1- Golden	2-Golden	2-White
1-Skyblue	1/+1	0.2/-0.6	0/-0.6	0.5/+0.2
1-Golden	0.2/-0.6	1/+1	0.7/+0.6	0.5/+0.2
2-Golden	0/-0.6	0.7/+0.6	1/+1	0.3/0
2-White	0.3/+0.2	0.3/+0.2	0/0	1/+1

level are driven by the highly uncertain trend attribute colour. Further, assume that golden and skyblue are seasonal high-fashion colours, competing on popularity. That is, we know that one of them will become popular, not the other.

(1) *Positively correlated first and substitute preferences:* Consider styles 1 and 2, in golden colour. Assume 'colour' has about 70% impact on customer choice, given the requested technical attributes. Hence the two items can be replaced by each other with substitutability probability about 0.7. Further, if golden becomes the popular colour (while skyblue unpopular), the demand goes up for both items, and vice versa, implying strongly positively correlated individual demands (such as +0.6). Despite the high grade of similarity between the two items, they might face stockout or overproduction simultaneously, implying 'diminishing' value of strong substitutability. The above understanding indicates that *a particular hedging strategy of including substitutes, with substitutability based on the 'similar and strong trend driver attributes'* (colour here), is poor.

(2) *Negatively correlated first and substitute preferences:* Consider now style 1 in the competing colours golden and skyblue, with strongly negatively correlated individual item demands (−0.6). Because of the competition between the two colours the items are not substitutes. Assume now that golden turns out to be popular. Further, assume that style is a particular trend driver, 'weaker' than colour. Accordingly, if golden faces stockout we can expect some substitution sale of skyblue, due to style similarity. However, the substitutability rate cannot be high (0.2 in the table). A large share of the unsatisfied demand for golden is more likely to be purchased from competitors. We indicate that, when demand is driven by trends, high negative correlation paired with high substitutability, is an unlikely case. This pattern can be observed, though, when offering bundles vs. individual standard/household articles.

(3) *Negatively correlated second choice possibilities:* Take style 1 in golden and skyblue, with negatively correlated individual demands (−0.6); each facing two possible states of the world, popular or unpopular at opposite times. Assume now that whenever one of them is popular, it is also a fair substitute for the first preference white (e.g. with substitutability probability 0.3). Now, if there is unsatisfied demand for white, according to our substitutability matrix, golden and skyblue are equally likely to substitute white, in each scenario. This is intuitively unrealistic, as one of them turns out to be unpopular with insignificant demand. There might be some substitution to an unpopular item (as described in (2)); however, assuming high probability is incorrect. Vaagen et al. (2009) solve this problem by allowing for state of the world dependent substitutability matrices, with changes applied only to the substitution choices manifesting this specific behaviour, everything else equal.

Finally, a substitutability matrix is not required to be symmetric. It is likely that there is high substitutability from a high-fashion colour to a more stable one (from skyblue to white e.g.). However, customers looking for a more subdued look are less likely to substitute to a high fashion colour.

3.2.2 Demand Distributions

In this section we provide the reader with a method appropriate to build demand distributions for short life-cycle highly uncertain products. All the optimization models presented in the next section need discrete approximations of the direct demand distributions. These approximations are often referred to as scenarios.

An important observation is that the overall demand distribution is very complex, due to the existence of distinct states of the world. On the other hand, the distributions conditional on the states of the world (i.e. distributions once we know the state) are much simpler and therefore easier to discretize. To define the state conditioned distributions we use aggregated demand data across whatever will become popular items. Hence, instead of trying to approximate the overall distribution, we generate scenarios for each state of the world independently, using some appropriate scenario-generation tool. In our case, we have assumed that the direct demand in each of the states is log-normally distributed, and used a method by Kaut and Lium (2007). This is a special version of the moment-matching algorithm from Høyland et al. (2003), which allows for generating scenarios from distributions specified by their marginal distributions and a correlation matrix. The assumption of log-normal marginal distribution is based on empirical evidence for several seasons and product groups at 'our' high performance sportswear supplier.

The overall distribution is then built by connecting all the scenarios. Probabilities are assigned to the states; probabilities that sum up to one. This way, the uncertainty around the particular items' popularity is easily captured. Under limited information, the two states occur with equal probabilities. Figure 4 illustrates the constructed demand distributions for two competing items, namely golden and skyblue from our example.

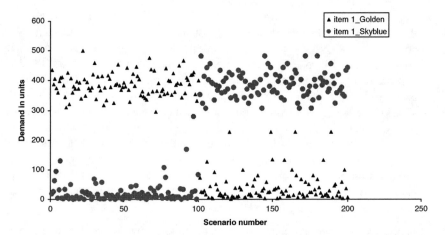

Fig. 4 Constructed demand distributions for two competing items, namely golden and skyblue – distributions that capture the two states of the world, with log-normally distributed demands in each state

3.3 Optimisation Models to Evaluate the Value of Information in Terms of Expected Assortment Profit and its Risk

In a decision making process, the outcomes of these optimisation models are compared to the predefined goals by particular industrials (the strategic performance measures to be achieved, expected profit and its risk). This is reflected by steps (5) and (6) in the decision support framework from Sect. 2.

3.3.1 The Vaagen–Wallace Assortment-Risk Model

The Vaagen and Wallace (2008) model is developed to study product variety decisions in light of uncertainty, with a particular focus on expected profit and risk. The optimal assortment structure, with items to include and corresponding inventory levels, is found. Assortment risk – constrained by minimal acceptable expected profit and maximal variety – is minimized by combining the mean-variance Markowitz model from finance and the multi-item newsvendor model from operations. Maximum variety is the maximum number of style-colour combinations in a reference group, which can be handled by existing supply chain capabilities. Semi-variance is used as risk measure, based on the observation that measuring portfolio volatility by variance implies minimizing both positive and negative deviations, hence limiting the possibility of high profits. Subjective knowledge on demand drivers is included by the correlations and possible states of the world defining the distributions. The available information, in order, is reflected by the correlations and the probabilities assigned to the particular states of the world.

The Model
Sets:

S – variety scenarios;
I – set of items in the reference group portfolio
Variables
x_i = production of item i
y_i^s = sale for item i scenario s
π_s = profit on scenario s
$E\pi$ = expected profit over all scenarios
$\Delta\pi_s^-$ = negative deviation from expected profit for scenario s
Parameters
d_i^s = demand of item i scenario s
p^s = probability scenario s
v_i = selling price of item i
c_i = purchasing cost of item i
g_i = salvage value of item i
B_i = stock-out costs, penalty beyond the lost profit for not satisfying the demand
μ = lower bound on the portfolio mean profit

$$\text{Minimize SemiVar}(\pi)_{PG} = \sum_{\text{Scen } S} p^S \left(\Delta \pi_S^-\right)^2 \tag{1}$$

Subject to:

$$\pi^s = \sum_{\text{SKU } i} \left\{ -c_i x_i + \left[v_i y_i^s + g_i \left(x_i - y_i^s\right) - B_i \left(d_i^s - y_i^s\right) \right] \right\} \quad \forall s \in S(2) \tag{2}$$

$$E\pi = \sum_{\text{Scen} S} p^S \pi^S \tag{3}$$

$$E\pi \geq \mu \tag{4}$$

$$\Delta \pi_s^- \geq E\pi - \pi_s \quad \forall s \in S \tag{5}$$

$$y_i^s \leq d_i^s \quad \forall i \in I, s \in S \tag{6}$$

$$y_1^s \leq x_i \quad \forall i \in I, s \in S \tag{7}$$

$$x_i \geq 0 \quad \forall i \in I \tag{8}$$

$$y_i^s \geq 0 \quad \forall i \in I, s \in S \tag{9}$$

$$\Delta \pi_s^- \geq 0 \quad \forall s \in S \tag{10}$$

Profit risk is minimized by using (1). Equation (2) defines the newsvendor profit for the reference group, containing i SKUs for each scenario. Equation (3) calculates expected profit, while in (4) this expected profit is constrained by a given bound. Equation (5) measures the negative deviation from expected portfolio profit. Equation (6) constrains the sales for each scenario and SKU, while (7–10) define the non-negativity of the variables.

3.3.2   The Vaagen–Wallace–Kaut Substitution Model

The Vaagen–Wallace model above shows the positive value of hedging portfolios. We recognize that this value can be further increased by designing the competing items so as to be each other's partial substitutes, and by that, allowing for lower production levels, lower costs and, hence, increased profitability. See Sect. 3.2.1 for an example on how to strategically design the substitutability of competing items. Accordingly, in this section we discuss a model that integrates substitutability. We treat substitution as a hedging strategy; a motivation arising from the recognition that postponing assortment decisions is of limited value. Substitution, as a strategy to increase market share, is not considered here.

When discussing substitution, we need to distinguish between consumer-directed and producer-directed substitution (see Mahajan and van Ryzin 2001 for a discussion). In consumer directed substitution models, the consumer is always free to buy any of the available items in stock (or buy nothing), while in producer-directed models, the producer is free to offer individual consumers any item he sees fit, and the consumer's only choices are to reject or accept. In particular, in a producer-directed context, a consumer may be offered his second choice even if the first choice is on stock, since the producer may want to reserve this item for another customer.

Since our focus is on information availability and demand volatility arising from the dynamics and uncertainty in customer choice processes, we need to model the consumer directed substitution problem. That is, we cannot assume that we are able to directly affect consumer choices other than by our inventory policy.

The consumer directed substitution choice process is hard to formulate; hence, it is also hard to define what constitutes optimal policies. Mahajan and van Ryzin (2001) capture the dynamic nature of the problem and provide nearly optimal solutions by applying a sample path algorithm and basing customer decisions on utility maximization. However, because of the limitations provided by the multinomial logit models' IIA property (Independence of Irrelevant Alternatives), these models cannot properly handle complex dependency patterns. This limitation makes those models inappropriate for our use, as we find it important to understand and include complex dependencies into the estimation/optimisation models for assortment planning. Vaagen et al. (2009) discuss several approximations to the problem; all of them able to handle complex dependencies. A simulation-based optimisation approach that captures some of the dynamics of the problem is proposed. However, it is only an approximation, as it assumes independence among the substitute choice possibilities. Also, it is only suited for problems of moderate size. A *stochastic programming formulation* is also proposed, only partially solving the true consumer-directed substitution problem. The partial solution assumes that demand is generated in two stages: the primary demand is realized in the 'first stage', substitution demand (with a nearly optimal substitution plan) in the 'second stage'. That said, this solution closely describes the situation of QR suppliers, who can (to some extent) control which retail customers to serve when the first preference is out of stock. In reality, this decision is based mainly on the customers' strategic importance. Hence, as such, this formulation is suited for the purpose of this volume treating QR supply chains with the supplier as a potential focal part. The stochastic programming formulation, alike the Vaagen–Wallace risk model above, is computationally efficient; an important point, given our strong emphasis on the ability to handle complex dependencies in large problems.

This model does not directly measure the assortment risk; however, it is similar in spirit to the risk model presented above, in that it introduces similar qualitative and quantitative concepts, and also directly uses insights from the risk model. Substitution variables are added to the basic multi-item newsvendor model, formulating the manufacturer directed substitution problem (Vaagen et al. 2008). A simple heuristic implying discounted substitution sales, then, enforces as much as possible primary demand in a 'first stage'. Finally, the true expected profit corresponding to the found solution is recalculated by an undiscounted objective function.

Although this model builds on a producer-directed substitution model, the interpretations of solutions provided by the two models are not to be confused. We mention this based on the observation that several analytical models claiming to treat the consumer-directed substitution problem actually solve the producer directed one (Rajaram and Tang 2001; Bassok et al. 1999).

The Vaagen–Wallace–Kaut substitution model is a step forward in attribute-based operational assortment planning and in providing consistency throughout the parameter estimation and optimisation process. Substitutability shares α_{ij} (defined in Sect. 3.2.1) entering the optimization model and the actual optimization are consistent in reflecting the same available information.

In addition to the notations used in Sect. 3.3.1, the following substitution related parameters and variables are needed.

Variables

z_{ij}^s = substitution sale of item i, satisfying excess demand of item j in scenario s
zt_i^s = substitution sale of item i, satisfying excess demand from all j's in scenario s
w_i^s = salvage quantity for item i in scenario s

Parameters

$\alpha_{ij} \in [0,1]$ – the grade of substitutability from item j to item I,indicating the portion of customers willing to replace item j with item i.
$q \in [0,1]$ – discounted-substitution-factor; the measure $q * v_i$ defines the discounted value of the substitution sale.

The true objective function (1) maximizes expected profit from ordinary sales, substitution sales and salvage, over all items and all scenarios.

$$\text{Max } E\Pi = \sum_{\text{Scen } S} p^S \sum_{\text{SKU}i} \left(-c_i x_i + v_i y_i^S + v_i zt_i^S + g_i w_i^S \right). \qquad (11)$$

Together with the rest of the model, (11) represents manufacturer directed substitution. To enforce direct sales before substitution, equation (11*) is used, with discounted substitution sales. The true value is then found by putting the optimal solution using (11*) into (11).

$$\text{Max } E\Pi = \sum_{\text{Scen } S} p^S \sum_{\text{SKU}i} \left(-c_i x_i + v_i y_i^S + q v_i zt_i^S + g_i w_i^S \right). \qquad (11^*)$$

The objective is constrained by the followings:

$$y_i^s + \sum_{j \neq i} z_{ji}^s \leq d_i^s \quad \forall i \in I, s \in S, \qquad (12)$$

$$z_{ij}^s \leq \alpha_{ij} \left(d_j^s - y_j^s \right) \quad \forall i, j \in I, i \neq j, s \in S, \qquad (13)$$

$$zt_i^s = \sum_{j \neq i} z_{ij}^s \quad \forall i \in I, s \in S, \qquad (14)$$

$$w_i^s = x_i - \left(y_i^s + zt_i^s \right) \quad \forall i \in I, s \in S, \qquad (15)$$

$$x_i \geq 0 \quad \forall i \in I, \qquad (16)$$

$$y_i^s \geq 0 \quad \forall i \in I, s \in S, \tag{17}$$

$$z_{ij}^s \geq 0 \quad \forall i, j \in I, i \neq j, s \in S, \tag{18}$$

$$zt_i^s \geq 0 \quad \forall i \in I, s \in S, \tag{19}$$

$$w_i^s \geq 0 \quad \forall i \in I, s \in S \tag{20}$$

Equation (5) states that item i sales – coming from primary demand for i plus sales of all j that substitute unmet demand for i – cannot exceed total demand for item i. Note that this constraint can be re-organized as

$$\sum_{j \neq i} z_{ji}^s \leq d_i^s - y_i^s \quad \forall i \in I, \forall s \in S, \tag{12a}$$

stating that substitution sales from item i cannot exceed available unsatisfied demand for i. Equation (13) define the upper bound for substitution sale of item i for item j, that is excess demand for item j with given substitutability probability α_{ij}. In (14) we calculate substitution sale of item i from all j's. Equation (15) gives the salvage quantity, the quantity of item i left after satisfying primary demand and substitution demand from all j. Equations (16–20) define the non-negativity of the variables.

3.4 Measuring the Value of Information

In this section we show how the value of information is measured in two distinct ways. Note that we neither discuss directly the information available before real-time orders arrive, nor particular demand driver attributes; these are built into the presented models by the correlation and substitution values and the existence of the particular states of the world. What we do is to illustrate what happens when these are ignored or mis-specified. First we assume that information is defined by the knowledge of which items will become popular (the existence of the two states of the world). We analyze the changes in expected portfolio profit and its risk while increasing the belief in one of the states. Second, we measure the performance errors when available information is 'distorted' by simplifying assumptions.

At the beginning of the assortment planning season there is limited information about the individual items' popularity, hence the two possible states of the world occur with equal probabilities: $Prob(State1) = Prob(State2) = 0.5$. Recall that the demand scenarios are constructed so as to reflect the different states of the world.

As demand is revealed (resulting in inventory changes and factual substitution), information about the states increases. The decision-independent substitution measure a priori *substitutability*, and on the other hand, is not affected by knowledge about the states of the world, as it defines the similarity among the products.

3.4.1 Numerical Results

The models have been implemented in AMPL with CPLEX as the underlying solver (see http://www.ilog.com/ for details on both systems), for an assortment case of 15 items, at the introduced sportswear supplier. The models are small and well structured, with negligible computation times.

The following results are obtained. Given the strong focus on lean retailing and the long lead times, the value of information is limited from an assortment planning point of view. Although the technology enables timely information flow, and hence enables fast response, the information required to make substantial and important assortment changes needs to be very accurate. This accuracy is reached at a point in time when the changes are not compatible with the supply chain capabilities. Reduced (but still rather large) production levels are indicated for some items when the probability for one of the states of the world exceeds 70%. However, there is no clear change in the assortment structure until we are 90% sure which state will occur, and the supply chain flexibility does not allow us to wait for such accurate information. Following our decision support framework, we must therefore look for alternative strategies.

Possible Solutions to the Problem

A. *Redesign the supply chain to enable QR by substantially reduced lead times:*

In this paper we do not aim to discuss particular QR strategies enabled by reduced lead times. However, the tool provided by us helps evaluating whether a new strategy is needed. The choice between a hedging strategy or a particular QR strategy is a trade-off between costs, benefits and risk.

B. *Hedging portfolios – strategic pairing of competitor and substitute items so to enable optimal hedging.*

The value of a hedging portfolio, indicated by Vaagen–Wallace, can be increased by designing the assortment items so as to be each other's strategic substitutes. Substitutability largely compensates for the negative effects of mis-specifying distributional parameters like mean and variance. However, to really benefit from substitution as an assortment planning strategy, an attribute based approach is required. Particularly the following are needed: (1) Understanding the existence of distinct states of the world, hence, the drivers of *negative correlations* between the individual demands (Note though that negative correlations do not imply two states of the world.); (2) Understanding the *similarity of the products (substitutability)* in a purchasing setting; (3) Understanding the *connections between correlations and substitutability*; (4) The use of an interdisciplinary team (designers, product developers, trend and operational analysts) to establish the correlation and substitutability values and to avoid information distortion by simplifications.

Below we give two examples on the effects of information distortion: first *we illustrate the error of substantially simplifying substitution measures*, second we measure *the error of being wrong in terms of distributions*. In this work we emphasize the value of qualitative information and that integrating such knowledge into the models as truthfully as possible is crucial. As discussed before, simplifying distributional and dependency assumptions are common in the literature - like the use of normal approximation and average correlation and substitution fraction value. This is caused by most existing analytical models' limited ability to handle the real complexity. Vaagen and Wallace (2008) discuss the effects of mis-specifying distributions in the fashion apparel supplier's environment. The authors conclude that, by simplifications, fashion and sports apparel actors introduce internal uncertainty into their planning processes, and hence increase the risks in their future payoffs. Vaagen et al. (2008) further investigate the effect of information distortion by a producer-directed substitution model.

Motivated by the numerical example in Rajaram and Tang (2001), where the authors assume an average substitution fraction value, parametrically varying from 0 to 1, we measure the effects of replacing the assumed 'true' matrix by a matrix where all elements equal the average value of the true matrix. Consider the true case being the one with bi-modally distributed individual item demands for about half of the portfolio and dependencies expressed by given correlation and substitutability matrices. Table 2 summarizes over the distributional assumptions used in the tests. The different distribution–correlation combinations are numbered 1 to 4; with Case 1 describing the true assortment problem. All four cases are solved with the full substitutability matrix (denoted mix), as well as a matrix where all elements equal 0.15 – the average of the entries in mix. The lognormal distribution has the same mean and variance as the bimodal distribution.

The expected profit (as measured within the model) is found to be higher for all cases using the average substitutability value 0.15 rather than the true matrix, see Fig. 5. Under the bimodal distributional assumption (Case 1), the expected profit using average substitutability of 0.15 and the true matrix (mix) are 1,874,581 and 1,777,850, respectively. If the decision corresponding to substitutability of 0.15 is used, but we assume that the true matrix actually describes the world, the producer will see neither what he thinks he will see (1,874,581), nor what he would have seen had he used the true substitutability matrix when planning (1,777,850), but rather the more moderate 1,720,068. This is caused by lower production levels in the average case (see Fig. 6.), implying lack of flexibility when facing the actual demand and substitution willingness. The actual profit observed will be about 6% below what the producer expected to see. Further, if we assumed the slightly higher 'average' substitution 0.2 (see dotted line in Figs. 5 and 6), the actual profit observed

Table 2 Distributional assumptions under which the value of information is measured

Case no.	Distribution Correlation values – c
1	Bimodal True matrix
2	Lognormal 0 – assumed zero correlation
3	Lognormal 0.5 – homogeneous value
4	Lognormal True matrix

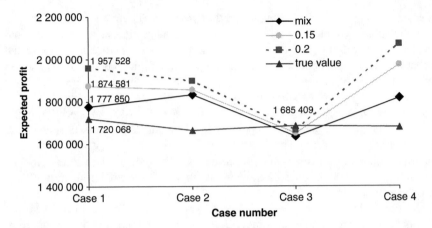

Fig. 5 Expected profit for the different cases for the 'true' mix matrix and its average 0.15, as well as the slightly higher fixed value 0.2, plus the true profit when the average substitutability 0.15 is assumed, but the reality is 'mix' and Case 1

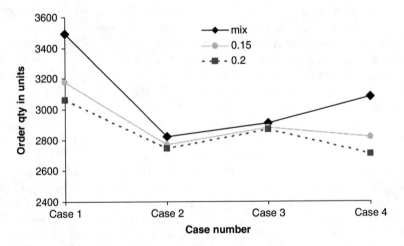

Fig. 6 Order quantity for the different cases for the 'true' mix matrix and its average 0.15, as well as the slightly higher fixed value 0.2

would be 25% below the expected one (the true profit 1,563,704 vs. the expected profit 1,957,528). This observation is important, in that it illustrates the sensitivity in substitution values; hence further strengthens our observation of potentially high negative effects of simplifications.

Observe further that if the decision corresponding to Case 3 and substitutability of 0.15 is used, but we assume that Case 1 and the true matrix actually describe the world, the error is approximately the same as when measured with the assumption of average substitution 0.15 under the true bimodal distribution Case 1 (about 5%; 1,685,409 vs. the optimal 1,777,850). Why do we not get higher error when

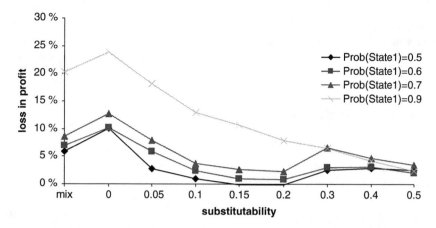

Fig. 7 Percentage loss in expected profit under the incorrect lognormal distributional assumption of Case 2 vs. the true bimodal Case 1; evaluated at different information levels for the true as well as different fixed substitution values

we have both the distributional and substitutional assumptions incorrect? It can be explained by the high average correlation value of 0.5 assumed in Case 3, indicating demands for all 15 items 'strongly' going in the same direction. This means that the items might face stockout or overproduction simultaneously. Substitution cannot really be leveraged on; hence, the effects of using the 'wrong' substitution values are diminished. It should be noted that high homogeneous correlations across a group of items is not very likely to occur. However, we chose to include the test motivated by Rajaram and Tang (2001).

Figure 7 summarizes the effects of being wrong in terms of distributions. We study Case 2, where we incorrectly assume log-normality, rather than the 'true' bi-modal marginal distributions of Case 1. The figure shows how much we lose in percent by this assumption for different substitution levels. We start with the case of maximal uncertainty, that is with $prob(State1) = 0.5$. Production decisions obtained from Case 2 (X_i^{Case2}) are evaluated using the distributions for Case 1. The result, in order, is compared with the optimal solution for Case 1 for corresponding substitution values to find the profit loss. Observe that the error is highest when there is no substitution between the individual items indicating that substitution partially compensates for being wrong in terms of distributional assumptions.

In a second step, the loss in expected profit is evaluated at different information levels (prob(State1)> 0.5). Production decisions are re-optimized for both the 'incorrect' Case 2 and the correct Case 1. Recall that throughout the bi-modal and the log-normal distributions have the same mean and variance. Figure 7 shows that, even with very accurate information, distributional assumptions are important. Note the high error under almost full information. The explanation is the following. Information needs to be very accurate (over 90% probability for one of the states, Vaagen and Wallace 2008) to make potentially important and substantial changes in the portfolio structure, that is, to drop hedging and substantially reduce production levels.

Drop in production levels, in order, contributes to a large increase in expected profit under the correct bi-modal assumption, and as a consequence, substantial increase in error under the incorrect log-normal assumption compared to the bi-modal one.

4 Concluding Remark

In contemporary, competitive, fast-changing markets demand is commonly assumed to be exogenous and its uncertainty external. As such, timely, accurate information availability is seen to be the key of successful QR initiations. Estimation and planning models reflect the same belief, and are largely based on end-product level customer information. Because of the agility caused by extensive use of lean retailing and product proliferation, these strategies require substantially reduced lead times across the supply chain, with the competitive advantage of enabling constant new product supply. However, successful market attempts are rapidly copied by the competition, leading to an accelerating spiral of variety-pricing-lead-time reduction games, with the inevitable result of often trivial product differentiation, reduced quality and pressure on prices. The environmental, psychological and operational effects of this spiral are severe. Although suppliers in agile markets acknowledge the operational and environmental challenges of constant new product supplies, there is limited knowledge on how to successfully handle the problem. Particularly, there is limited knowledge on the extent of internal randomness introduced by not properly understanding the effects of substantially increased variety and the dependencies among the choice possibilities. Existing planning support systems acknowledge market complexity and uncertainty; however, they still perform poorly in providing reliable decisions support to industrials. Particularly, models suited to solve complex uncertainty related problems with dependencies among the individual items, and models suited to measure the risk of decisions regarding variety, are not yet common in production planning and control.

This chapter contributes to quick response decision making by providing a comprehensive decision support framework, with corresponding set of newly developed estimation and optimisation tools. The focus is particularly on assortment planning, with decisions on which items to include in the portfolio and their inventory levels; this being the major decision in dynamic and uncertain industrial environments. The suggested decision support makes it possible to evaluate the value and risk of different assortment decisions taken at different information levels. As such, it is valuable in defining the trade-off between the grade of flexibility needed by practitioners and flexibility actually allowed by 'own' supply chain capabilities. In other words, it provides comprehensive operational control when evaluating appropriate QR strategies.

The value of this work, as we see it, lies in the focus shift from timely, end-product level information availability across the supply chain and wait-and-see assortment planning, to the actual information needed to make substantial and potentially important changes, and to what information is available when important decisions are to be taken. We emphasize that, at the point in time when important assortment decisions are taken, information is often limited to knowledge on demand driver attributes (may be qualitative or quantitative) and aggregated estimates. Given this, and given the repeated emphasis on subjective knowledge being the key success factor at innovative quick response suppliers, we focus on planning models that are actually able to handle such information. An attribute-based view of the assortment problem not only allows the use of qualitative information, but also for handling the strong dependencies among the individual items in the assortment (these, driven by the particular product attributes). As such, this approach attempts to control the operational internal randomness. Internal randomness is often introduced by both academia and practice by not correctly understanding how the different instruments in the portfolio affect each other. To conclude, the estimation and optimisation models included here are compatible with each other, and present a comprehensive tool-set for operational attribute-based assortment planning.

We do not mean to 'devalue' speed and planning for timely accurate information, neither to argue against specific quick response strategies. What we argue against is the accelerating dynamics of variety-pricing games, leading to the belief among practitioners that competitiveness can only be achieved by reaction to real-time customer orders and lead times pressed to a minimum, with the inevitable consequence of reduced differentiation, reduced quality and pressure on prices.

Acknowledgements

We thank Michal Kaut for helping us with all aspects of scenario generation in this paper. Both authors are partially supported by The Research Council of Norway under grant 171007/V30.

References

Abernathy FH, Dunlop JT, Hammond JH, Weil D (2004) Globalisation in the Apparel and Textile Industries: What is New and what is Not? In: Kenney M and Florida R (Eds). Locating Global Advantage: Industry Dynamics in the International Economy. Stanford Business Books, Stanford, CA, pp 23–51

Bassok Y, Anupindi R, Akella R (1999) Single-period multi-product inventory models with substitution. Oper Res 47(4):32–642

Canning L (2006) Rethinking market connections: Mobile phone recovery, reuse and recycling in the UK. J Bus Ind Market 21(5):320–329

Campo K, Gijsbrechts E, Nisol P (2003) The impact of retailer stock-outs on whether, how much, and what to buy. Int J Res Market 20(3):273–286

Chen F, Federgruen A (2000) Mean-variance analysis of basic inventory models. Working paper, Columbia University

Chen H, Chen J, Chen Y (2006) A coordination mechanism for a supply chain with demand information updating. Int J Prod Econ 103(1):347–361

Choi TM (2008) Mean-Variance Analysis for the Newsvendor Problem. IEEE Trans Syst Man Cybern Syst Hum 38:1169–1180

Choi TM, Li D, Yan H, Chiu CH (2008a) Channel coordination in supply chains with agents having mean-variance objectives, Omega: The Int J Manag Sci 36:565–576

Choi TM, Li D, Yan H (2008b) Mean-variance analysis of a single supplier and retailer supply chain under a returns policy. Eur J Oper Res 184(1):356–376

Christopher M, Lowson R, Pack H (2004) Creating Agile Supply Chains in the Fashion Industry. Int J Retail Distrib Manag 32(8):367–376

Donohue KL (2000) Efficient Supply Contracts for Fashion Goods with Forecast Updating and Two production Modes. Manag Sci 46(11):1397–1411

Dougherty MRP, Hunter JE (2003) Hypothesis Generation, Probability Judgment, and Individual Differences in Working Memory Capacity, Acta Psychol 113(2):263–282

Eppen GD, Iyer AV (1997) Backup Agreements in fashion buying – The value of Upstream Flexibility. Manag Sci 43(11):1469–1484

Fisher M, Hammond JH, Obermeyer WR, Raman A (1994) Making Supply Meet Demand in an Uncertain World. Harv Bus Rev 5/6:83–94

Fisher M, Raman A (1996) Reducing the Cost of Demand Uncertainty through Accurate Response to Early Sales. Oper Res 44(1):87–99

Gaur V, Honhon D (2006) Assortment Planning and Inventory Decisions under a Locational Choice Model. Manag Sci 52(10):1528–1543

Gunasekaram A (1999) Agile manufacturing: A framework for research and development. Int J Prod Econ 62(1/2):87–105

Høyland K, Kaut M, Wallace SW (2003) A heuristic for moment-matching scenario generation. Comput Optim Appl 24(2–3):169–185

Kahneman D, Tversky A (1982) Subjective probability: A Judgement of Representativeness. In: Kahneman D, Slovic P, Tversky A (Eds) Judgement under Uncertainty: Heuristics and Biases. Cambridge University Press, Cambridge, pp 32–47

Kaut M, Lium AG (2007) Scenario generation: Property matching with distribution functions. Working paper, available from http://work.michalkaut.net/

Khouja M, Mehrez A, Rabinowitz G (1996) A two-item newsboy problem with substitutability. Int J Prod Econ 44(2):267–275

Kök AG, Fisher ML (2007) Demand Estimation and Assortment Optimization under Substitution: Methodology and Application. Oper Res 55(6):1001–1021

Kök AG, Fisher M, Vaidyanathan R (2008) Assortment Planning: Review of Literature and Industry Practice. In: Agrawal N, Smith SA (Eds) Retail Supply chain managment. Kluwer Publishers, Boston

Lau HS (1980) The newsboy problem under alternative optimization objectives. J Oper Res Soc 31(6):525–535

Lowson RH (2002) Strategic Operations Management: The new competitive advantage. Routledge, London

Lowson RH, King R, Hunter NA (1999) Quick Response: Managing the supply chain to meet consumer demand. John Wiley & Sons, Chichester

Luz C (2007) Waste Couture: Environmental Impact of the Clothing Industry. Environ Health Perspec 115(9):A448–454

Mahajan S, van Ryzin G (1998) Retail Inventories and Consumer Choice, Chapter 17. In: Tayur S, Ganeshan R, Magazine M (Eds) Quantitative Methods in Supply Chain Management, Amsterdam, Kluwer Publishers, USA

Mahajan S, van Ryzin G (2001) Stocking retail assortments under dynamic consumer substitution. Oper Res 49(3):334–351

Mason-Jones R, Naylor B, Towill DR (2000) Engineering the leagile supply chain. Int J Agile Manag Syst 2(1):54–61

McAfee A, Dessain V, Sjöman A (2004) Zara: IT for Fast fashion. Harvard Case Collection, HBC Publishing, 9-604-081

Morley N, Slater S, Russell S, Tipper M, Ward GD (2006) Recycling of Low Grade Clothing Waste. Oakdene Hollins Ltd, Salvation Army Trading Company Ltd, Nonwovens Innovation & Research-Institute-Ltd., http://www.oakdenehollins.co.uk/pdf/Recycle-Low-Grade-Clothing.pdf. Accessed 10 Desember 2008

Naylor JB, Naim MM, Berry D (1999) Leagility: integrating the lean and agile manufacturing paradigm in the supply chain. Int J Prod Econ 62:107–118

Netessine S, Rudi N (2003) Centralized and Competitive Inventory Models with Demand Substitution. Oper Res 51(2):329–341

Nikhil J, Anand P (2001) A Generalized Model of Operations Reversal for Fashion Goods. Manag Sci 47(4):595–600

Poiesz ThBC(2004) The Free market Illusion Psychological Limitations of Consumer Choice. Tijdschr Econ Manag 49(2):309–338

Rajaram K, Tang CS (2001) The impact of product substitution on retail merchandising. Eur J Oper Res 135(2):82–601

Raman A, Fisher ML, McClelland A (2001) Supply Chain Management at World Co. Ltd. Harvard Case Collection, HBC Publishing, USA, p 21

Vaagen H, Halskau Ø (2005) Strategic planning under conditions with agile supply. Proceedings of the 17th Annual Conference for Nordic Researchers in Logistics. ISBN 87–988392–1–7. NOFOMA 2005, pp 347–363

Vaagen H, Wallace SW (2008) Product variety arising from hedging in the fashion supply chains. Int J Prod Econ 114(2):431–455

Vaagen H, Wallace SW, Kaut M (2008) The value of numerical models in quick response assortment planning. Working paper/Molde University College, no. 2008:16. Molde, Norway, Molde University College

Vaagen H, Wallace SW, Kaut M (2009) Modelling consumer-directed substitution. Forthcoming in International Journal of Production Economics, Special Issue on Robust Optimisation in Supply Chain Management

Van Hoek RI, Harrison A, Christopher M (2001) Measuring agile capabilities in the supply chain. Int J Opera Prod 21(1/2):126–147

Van Mieghem JA (2003) Capacity management, investment, and hedging: Review and recent developments. Manuf Serv Oper Manag 5(4):269–301

Yusuf YY, Gunasekaram A, Adeleye EO, Sivayoganathan K (2004). Agile supply chain capabilities: Determinants of competitive objectives. Eur J Oper Res 159(2):379–392

Yusuf YY, Sarhadi M, Gunasekaram A (1999) Agile manufacturing: The drivers, concepts and attributes. Int J Prod Econ 62(1–2):33–43

Zhao X, Xie J, Wei JC (2002) The Impact of Forecast Errors on Early Order Commitment in a Supply Chain. Decis Sci 33(2):251–280

Improving Revenue Management: A Real Option Approach

Wai-Ki Ching, Xun Li, Tak Kuen Siu, and Zhenyu Wu

Abstract In this article, we apply a real option approach for improving revenue management regarding fluctuating commodity prices and time-varying strike prices in the field of operational research. We also take into account the cyclical nature of commodity prices, which is an important "stylized" fact in the empirical behavior of commodity prices. Two typical examples are provided to illustrate how real options can be used for enhancing profits and managing risk, which are important in revenue management. Valuation of these real options via a semi-analytical algorithm is also discussed.

Keywords Air transportation · Energy · Real options · Revenue management · Risk management · Stochastic processes

1 Introduction

Many firms from various industrial sectors face a common important problem of increasing or maximizing their revenues by selling a fixed stock of products or certain amount of services due to the limitation of the production or service capacity in a fixed time period. This is commonly known as the problem of revenue management. In many cases, those products or services will have a very low value or even zero value if they are not used by the end of the selling period. Typical examples of industries offering such products or services include airlines, hotels, rental cars and fashion goods. See the surveys by Belobaba (1987), Weatherford and Bodily (1992), and Geraghty and Johnson (1997) for detail.

Some previous researches on revenue management mainly focus on the analysis of firms' pricing policy and selling strategy under the assumption that they

T.K. Siu (✉)
Department of Mathematics and Statistics, Curtin University of Technology, Perth, W.A. 6845, Australia
e-mail: T.Siu@curtin.edu.au

T.C. Edwin Cheng and T.-M. Choi (eds.), *Innovative Quick Response Programs in Logistics and Supply Chain Management*, International Handbooks on Information Systems, DOI 10.1007/978-3-642-04313-0_6,
© Springer-Verlag Berlin Heidelberg 2010

are the driving force in price-setting acting as monopolists in these industries (see, e.g., Gallego and Van Ryzin (1994) and Feng and Gallego (2005), and others). Although a model with price certainty works well under such an assumption, the price of the underlying capacity or commodity is usually driven by market forces in practice (see, e.g., Deng et al. (2006) for discussions). This makes the model with price certainty not satisfactory. When the price of the underlying capacity or commodity is fluctuating due to changes in economic factors, revenue management not only plays an important role for enhancing or maximizing profit, but also plays a significant role for risk management. This extends the domain of revenue management from enhancing or maximizing profit to both managing risk and enhancing or maximizing profit.

Traditionally, the main focus of the literature on revenue management concerns profit enhancement or profit maximization for industries, such as the airline industry and the car rental industry, with fluctuating commodity prices (see, e.g., Anderson et al. 2004). There is a limited amount of literature concerning the issue of risk management in revenue management when the price of the underlying commodity or capacity fluctuates randomly over time.

In this paper, we shall address the two important aspects, namely, profit enhancement and risk management, in revenue management. In particular, we shall apply a special type of options written on the underlying commodities to achieve the goals of profit enhancement and risk issues in revenue management. To further illustrate applications of the theoretical results, we also consider two typical industrial examples in revenue management to illustrate how the two goals can be achieved through the use of the options.

First, an example from the airline industry is provided for studying profit enhancement. The price of the airticket fluctuates randomly over time due to market forces, economic conditions and travel seasons. In reality, many travelers buy airline ticket from travel agents, which play an important role as an intermediation between airline companies and travelers. Here, we introduce a callable ticket or a discount ticket sold by a travel agent to a traveler, which gives the travel agent the right to buy back or call back the ticket at the last minute at which the agent can still sell the ticket. Since the travel agent has the right to buy back the ticket, the travel agent have to sell the callable ticket at a lower price compared with the original ticket. Travelers who do not have definite or exact travel plans may consider buying callable tickets. We shall consider the valuation of these discounted tickets. Besides determining the price of a discount ticket, it is an important practical problem about the determination of the optimal time at which the agents should buy back the ticket to maximize their payoffs or profits. We shall determine the optimal time by solving an optimal stopping problem.

The second example based on strategic petroleum reserve in the energy industry is to examine the risk management issue in revenue management. Li et al. (2008) state that, due to the special nature of energy commodities, longing call options while selling the energy commodities to the strategic petroleum reserve builders may help the producers to hedge risk. To provide more flexibility, Li et al. (2008) present a theoretical model to consider both the European-style and American-style energy options with time-varying strike prices so as to enhance the profits or achieve better risk management results. Different from the regime-switching methodology adopted by Li et al. (2008), we apply real option-based revenue management models and price the options using a semi-analytical algorithm in this study. This approach provides practitioners with a much more convenient way to value the real options compared with some numerical methods, such as the finite-difference method. To illustrate the estimation accuracy of our approach, we present numerical examples and compare the approximated results with those obtained from the finite-difference method. Results show that our semi-analytical approach does not deteriorate the accuracy of option pricing.

Recently, techniques for real option valuation have been applied to investigate the decision making in this field in the presence of uncertainty (Anderson et al. 2004). In the traditional financial economics literature, effects of random fluctuation in spot prices and limited capacity are often ignored in studies on option contracts and real options (Allaz and Vila 1993) for analytical simplicity. In particular, revenue management on callable products has received considerable interest, and some previous studies (for example, Gallego et al. 2004; Feng and Gallego 2005) have made significant contributions to this literature.

As one of the pioneer studies in this literature, Wu and Kleindorfer (2005) incorporate option-based contracts in supply management into a game-theoretic model and focus on electricity markets. As discussed by Gallego et al. (2004), in addition, the nature of callable products provides us with a different angle to examine revenue management. However, the issues of using callable products to enhance profit profiles and to improve the practice of risk management have not been extensively explored yet. More interestingly, one realizes that one of the most important features of the underlying commodities in revenue management is their price fluctuations over time (Anderson et al. 2004; Gallego et al. 2004; Feng and Gallego 2005). Thus, real options need to have time-varying strike prices so as to enhance profits and/or to hedge risk.

Multiple contributions are made to the literature by this paper. First, we provide a new real option approach to deal with both of the issues of profit enhancement and risk management, which are important in the revenue management. Second, we highlight the special feature of fluctuating commodity prices in revenue management and adopt an effective semi-analytical algorithm for pricing real options with time-varying strike prices. Third, it sheds lights on the risk management issues in energy financing and risk hedging using real options. Last, it provides testable implications for the airline industry and for energy finance and economics regarding the demand–supply equilibrium in building strategic petroleum reserve. This is mainly because changes in demand or supply influenced by many factors in the economy may affect the profit-enhancement and risk-management strategies significantly. The first example is highly relevant to the theme of quick response in this handbook. Indeed, the proposed call option that is purchased by the traveling agent can help traveling agents handle urgent purchase of air tickets from their customers and make higher profit.

The rest of this paper is structured as follows. Section 2 describes a general problem setting for the real option with a time-varying strike price. An example from the airline industry for profit enhancement is presented in Sect. 3, followed by Sect. 4 which provides an example of SPR from the energy industry for examining the risk-management issues. Concluding remarks and further implications are included in Sect. 5.

2   A General Problem Setting for Real Options with Time-varying Strike Prices

To construct a real option with a time-varying strike price, we denote K_t as the strike price depending on time t. For analytical simplicity, we define $K_t = K e^{rt}$, where K is predetermined in the options contract and r is a constant risk-free rate.

We suppose there is an underlying commodity S with spot price S_t at time t. The spot price of S fluctuates randomly over time according to a stochastic process, which will be specified in the next two sections for different commodities. A call option written on S with time-varying strike K_t and maturity T has a discounted payoff $e^{-rT}(S_T - K_T)^+$. Note that the option is a European option if it is not allowed to be exercised before the maturity T; otherwise, it is an American option, and there could be an optimal early exercise time $\tau^* \in (0, T]$. The early exercise feature of the American option with time-varying strike poses additional difficulty in its pricing issue.

Wu et al. (2002) present a model for pricing capacity options on non-storeable goods, and Xia and Zhou (2005), a pioneer study in option valuation, provide a closed-form formula for pricing perpetual American options with time-varying strike prices. Although Xia and Zhou (2005) pave the road for further research on this topic, exploring the use of options with both time-varying strike prices and finite maturities in revenue management and valuing these options have not been explored in the literature. It is of practical relevance to explore the use of these options to improve revenue management when the underlying commodity prices are fluctuating and/or capacity is limited.

In the next two sections, we explore the use of these options in the airline industry and the energy sector and consider the valuation of these options. We shall adopt a semi-analytical algorithm for pricing these options on commodities, with fluctuating prices in the airline industry and in the energy industry, respectively.

3   Profit Enhancement: An Example from the Airline Industry

In the airline industry, capacity is limited and therefore revenue management, including both the determination of prices over time and booking process, plays a key role in airline companies' profits. Previous studies (for example, Gallego et al.

2004) treat airline tickets as callable products for revenue management and discuss some alternatives such as bumping, flexible products and last-minute discounts.

In this section, we present a real option-based revenue management model with a call option purchased by travel agents, and the main objective is to enhance the agents' profits by purchasing call options from their customers while selling them air tickets. The call option premium appears in the form of a discount off the regular airfare. Customers who are flexible regarding all aspects of their trips and have the possibility of changing their travel plans are willing to accept the deal. In this case, travel agents can call back these tickets when some other customers need to travel with necessity or purchase air tickets shortly before departure at much higher prices. This can enhance the profits of the agents.

To illustrate the real option approach in this model, we assume that a customer purchases an air ticket at a discounted price cS_0 at time t_0, where $0 < c < 1$. S_0 is the regular airfare. At the same time, the deal is that, with the call option, the travel agent can buy back the ticket at the price K_t at any time $t \in (0, T]$, where T is the last minute at which the agent can sell the ticket and T represents the maturity of the embedded call option.

As defined in Sect. 2, the time-varying strike price $K_t = S_0 e^{rt}$ and S_t is the spot price of the air ticket at time t. Suppose C_0 is the price of a call option written on the ticket S, with strike K_t and maturity at time T. For analytical simplicity, we follow Li et al. (2008) and determine the discount coefficient c using

$$(1 - c)S_0 = C_0.$$

Furthermore, since airfare has the property of seasonality, we introduce an additional factor to the model to describe it following Elliott et al. (2003) and Li et al. (2008). Thus, the spot price of the air ticket under a real-world probability $\mathcal{P}$ follows

$$S_t = S_0 g_t e^{X_t},$$

where g_t is the seasonality factor defined as

$$g_t = e^{\delta \int_0^t \sin(2\pi s + \xi) ds}$$

and

$$dX_t = (\mu - q)dt + \sigma dW_t.$$

Here μ is the long-run mean return, q is a dividend-like term, σ is volatility, and W_t is a standard Brownian motion. In general, one can consider that parameters r, μ, q, σ, and S_t are deterministic functions of time t following prior research (for example, Duffie and Richardson 1991), and therefore, for analytical simplicity, we assume they are constant. A more general case can be extended easily by following the same method presented in the following.

By Itô's lemma, we have

$$dS_t = \left(\delta \sin(2\pi t + \xi) + \mu - q + \tfrac{1}{2}\sigma^2\right)S_t\, dt + \sigma S_t\, dW_t$$
$$= (b_t - q)S_t\, dt + \sigma S_t\, dW_t,$$
(1)

where $b_t = \delta \sin(2\pi t + \xi) + \mu + \tfrac{1}{2}\sigma^2$.

For pricing options, we need to work in a risk-neutral world. First, we suppose that there is a constant market price of risk λ. Let $\mathcal{F}_t$ denote the information set generated by the values of the Brownian motion W up to and including time t. Define a risk-neutral measure $\mathcal{Q}$ equivalent to $\mathcal{P}$ on $\mathcal{F}_T$ by the following Radon–Nikodym derivative:

$$\left.\frac{d\mathcal{Q}}{d\mathcal{P}}\right|_{\mathcal{F}_T} := \exp(-\lambda W_T - \frac{1}{2}\lambda^2 T)\,.$$
(2)

From Girsanov's theorem,

$$W_t^{\dagger} := \lambda t + W_t$$
(3)

is a standard Brownian motion with respect to $\{\mathcal{F}_t\}$ under $\mathcal{Q}$.

Let $\mu^{\dagger} := \mu - \lambda\sigma$. Write $b_t^{\dagger} := \delta \sin(2\pi t + \xi) + \mu^{\dagger} + \tfrac{1}{2}\sigma^2$. Then the risk-neutral dynamic of S under $\mathcal{Q}$ is

$$dS_t = (b_t^{\dagger} - q)S_t\, dt + \sigma S_t\, dW_t^{\dagger}\,.$$
(4)

3.1 Discounted Airfare with a European Option

We first present the fair value of the discounted airfare when a European call option is purchased by a travel agent. The European call option gives the agent the right, but not the obligation, to buy or call back the ticket. However, the agent cannot exercise the option before its maturity T. We can determine the value of the European option, given that

$$(1 - c)S_0 = e^{-rT} E\big[(S_T - K_T)^+\big|S_0\big],$$

where E is the expectation with respect to the risk-neutral probability $\mathcal{Q}$ defined above.

Note that the discount c offers to customers by the agent can be determined completely once we have determined the premium of the European option with payoff $(S_T - K_T)^+$ at the maturity T. Hence, we first consider the following problem according to risk-neutral spot price (4):

$$C(t, S) = e^{-r(T-t)} E\big[(S_T - K_T)^+\big|S_t = S\big].$$
(5)

In the above European option, K_T is used only at the maturity and regarded as fixed. Then the above (5) satisfies the partial differential equation (PDE)

$$\begin{cases} \frac{\partial C}{\partial t} + \frac{1}{2}\sigma^2 S^2 \frac{\partial^2 C}{\partial S^2} + (b_t^\dagger - q)S \frac{\partial C}{\partial S} - rC = 0, \\ C(T, S) = (S - K_T)^+. \end{cases} \tag{6}$$

As shown in Wilmott et al. (1996), solving (6) yields

$$\begin{cases} C(t, S) = S_0 \, e^{\int_t^T (b_s^\dagger - q - r)\,ds} N(d_1(t, S)) - K \, e^{rt} N(d_2(t, S)), \\ d_1(t, S) = \frac{\ln(S) - \ln(Ke^{rT}) + \int_t^T (b_s^\dagger - q + \frac{1}{2}\sigma^2)\,ds}{\sigma\sqrt{T - t}}, \\ d_2(t, S) = d_1(t, S) - \sigma\sqrt{T - t}. \end{cases} \tag{7}$$

Hence, the discount factor c is expressed by

$$c = 1 - e^{\int_0^T (b_s^\dagger - q - r)ds} N(d_{10}) - KN(d_{20})/S_0, \tag{8}$$

where

$$\begin{cases} d_{10} = \frac{\ln(S_0) - \ln(Ke^{rT}) + \int_0^T (b_s^\dagger - q + \frac{1}{2}\sigma^2)\,ds}{\sigma\sqrt{T}}, \\ d_{20} = d_{10} - \sigma\sqrt{T}. \end{cases}$$

3.2 Discounted Airfare with an American Option

However, the travel agent can have more flexibility if he relaxes the restrictions in the above European option by longing an American option instead. In this case, both the optimal exercise time τ^* and the value of c, where

$$(1 - c)S_0 = E[e^{-r\tau^*}(S_{\tau^*} - K_{\tau^*})^+],$$

need to be determined.

We now consider the following optimal stopping problem, which is different from pricing a standard American call option since the strike price is time-varying. At time t, the American call option price is

$$C^A(t, S) = \max_{\tau \in T_{t,T}} E\left[e^{-r(\tau - t)}(S_\tau - K_\tau)^+ \,\middle|\, S_t = S\right]. \tag{9}$$

This is the risk-neutral valuation of American option, where the value of an option is given by the expected payoff of the option when it is exercised at random time

τ discounted by the risk-free interest rate under the risk-neutral pricing probability Q. Since the holder of an American option has the privilege to exercise the option at any time from the current time t to the maturity T, the price of the American option should take into account this additional privilege and is given by the maximum of the expected payoff received by the option's holder under the risk-neutral measure where the option is exercised optimally. Consequently, to solve the American option valuation problem, one has to determine both the value of the option and its optimal exercise strategy. Note that the optimal exercise strategy is determined under the risk-neutral probability and the assumption that the holder acts rationally. In practice, the exercise strategy of the option's holder may deviate from the optimal one.[1]

Once $C^A(t, S)$ is determined, we can determine the value of the discount factor c. Note that the optimal exercise time τ^* is the same for $C^A(t, S)$ and c.

The above (9) satisfies the following free-boundary PDE problem or variational inequality:

$$
\begin{cases}
\frac{\partial C}{\partial t} + \frac{1}{2}\sigma^2 S^2 \frac{\partial^2 C}{\partial S^2} + (b_t^\dagger - q)S \frac{\partial C}{\partial S} - rC \leq 0, \\
C(t, S) - (S_t - K_t)^+ \geq 0, \\
\left(\frac{\partial C}{\partial t} + \frac{1}{2}\sigma^2 S^2 \frac{\partial^2 C}{\partial S^2} + (b_t^\dagger - q)S \frac{\partial C}{\partial S} - rC\right)\left(C(t, S) - (S_t - K_t)^+\right) = 0, \\
C(T, S) = (S - K_T)^+,
\end{cases} \tag{10}
$$

or

$$
\begin{cases}
\min\left\{-\frac{\partial C}{\partial t} + \frac{1}{2}\sigma^2 S^2 \frac{\partial^2 C}{\partial S^2} - (b_t^\dagger - q)S \frac{\partial C}{\partial S} + rC, C(t, S) - (S_t - K_t)^+\right\} = 0, \\
C(T, S) = (S - K_T)^+.
\end{cases} \tag{11}
$$

The above variational inequality (10) is an alternative characterization of the optimal stopping problem. It can be easily understood by looking at the third equality. If it is optimal to exercise the option at time t, the value of the option must be identically to its intrinsic value $(S_t - K_t)^+$, (i.e., the payoff of the American option when it is exercised), so $C(t, S_t) = (S_t - K_t)^+$, and

$$
\frac{\partial C}{\partial t} + \frac{1}{2}\sigma^2 S^2 \frac{\partial^2 C}{\partial S^2} + (b_t^\dagger - q)S \frac{\partial C}{\partial S} - rC < 0.
$$

---

[1] For technically inclined readers, the "max" should, in general, be replaced by "ess-sup," where "ess-sup" means the essential supremum and is defined as the smallest essential upper bound. That is, for any real-valued function f defined on a measure space (X, Σ, μ), ess-sup$_{x \in X} f(x) :=$ inf$\{l \in \Re | \mu(x \in X | f(x) > l) = 0\}$. The notion of "ess-sup" is relevant in probability theory, or in general, measure theory, where one usually considers statements that are not valid everywhere, but only valid almost everywhere. Intuitively, since both sides of the above (9) are random variables, we only require the optimal result holds true almost surely with respect to the probability measure $\mathcal{P}$ instead of for all sample points $\omega \in \Omega$.

If the option has not yet been exercised at time t, $C(t, S_t) > (S_t - K_t)^+$ and

$$\frac{\partial C}{\partial t} + \frac{1}{2}\sigma^2 S^2 \frac{\partial^2 C}{\partial S^2} + (b_t^\dagger - q)S \frac{\partial C}{\partial S} - rC = 0.$$

This is similar to the standard Black–Scholes–Merton PDE for a European-style option. The condition $C(t, S_t) \geq (S_t - K_t)^+$ states that the value of the American option must always be greater than or equal to its intrinsic value $(S_t - K_t)^+$. If this were not true, arbitrage opportunities exist. For example, if $C(t, S_t) < (S_t - K_t)^+$, one may lock in a positive amount of profit without taking any risk by selling the option and exercising it immediately. Since the option is valued based on the no-arbitrage principle, we must rule out the possibility that the value of the option falls below its intrinsic value. The last condition $C(T, S_T)$ is just the terminal pay-off of the option at its maturity. The variational inequality (11) is just a short, or convenient, form of (10).

Note that a closed-form solution to the variational inequality (11) rarely exists. Here we give an analytically approximate solution to the value of the American option. The main result of this analytically approximate solution is summarized in Theorem 1. Note that the approximation method and the corresponding assumptions are presented in the proof of Theorem 1.

Theorem 1. *The value of the American option can be approximated by*

$$C^A(t, S) = \begin{cases} C(t, S) + A_t \left(\frac{S}{S^*}\right)^{\gamma_t}, & \text{if } S < S^*, \\ S - Ke^{rt}, & \text{if } S \geq S^*, \end{cases} \tag{12}$$

where

$$A_t = \frac{S^*}{\gamma_t}[1 - e^{b_t^\dagger - q - r}N(d_1(t, S^*))] \quad \text{and} \quad \gamma_t = \frac{1}{2}\left(-(\beta_t - 1) + \sqrt{(\beta_t - 1)^2 + \frac{4\alpha}{h}}\right).$$

Proof. Since both American and European options satisfy the same PDE in the continuation region where the option has not been exercised yet, so does the early exercise premium

$$\epsilon(t, S) := C^A(t, S) - C(t, S).$$

Thus, $\epsilon(t, S)$ satisfies

$$\frac{\partial \epsilon}{\partial t} + \frac{1}{2}\sigma^2 S^2 \frac{\partial^2 \epsilon}{\partial S^2} + (b_t^\dagger - q)S \frac{\partial \epsilon}{\partial S} - r\epsilon = 0. \tag{13}$$

Following the plan in Li et al. (2008), we approximate the solution for the above PDE by assuming that $\epsilon(t, S)$ is approximately given by the separated form

$$\epsilon(t, S) \approx H(S, h)h(t).$$

We further assume that

$$h(t) = 1 - e^{-r(T-t)}, \tag{14}$$

and therefore,

$$\frac{\partial h}{\partial t} = r(h - 1). \tag{15}$$

Then

$$h \frac{\partial H}{\partial h} \frac{\partial h}{\partial t} + H \frac{\partial h}{\partial t} + (b_t^\dagger - q) S h \frac{\partial H}{\partial S} + \frac{1}{2}\sigma^2 S^2 h \frac{\partial^2 H}{\partial S^2} - rHh = 0.$$

With appropriate substitutions and variable changes, this gives

$$S^2 \frac{\partial^2 H}{\partial S^2} + \beta_t S \frac{\partial H}{\partial S} - \frac{\alpha}{h} H = (1 - h)\alpha \frac{\partial H}{\partial h}, \tag{16}$$

where

$$\alpha = \frac{2r}{\sigma^2} \quad \text{and} \quad \beta_t = \frac{2(b_t^\dagger - q)}{\sigma^2}.$$

Equation (16) can be approximated by

$$S^2 \frac{\partial^2 H}{\partial S^2} + \beta_t S \frac{\partial H}{\partial S} - \frac{\alpha}{h} H = 0, \tag{17}$$

since the right-hand side of (16) is generally fairly small and can be ignored. When $T - t$ is large, $1 - h$ is close to zero; when $T - t$ is small, on the other hand, $\frac{\partial H}{\partial h}$ is close to zero. Solving (17) and applying boundary conditions lead to the analytically approximate result.

Note that in Theorem 3.1 the variable S^* is the critical stock price above which the option should be exercised. It can be estimated by solving the equation

$$S^* - K e^{rt} = C(t, S^*) + A_t$$

iteratively.

In short, travel agents can be better off if they long options while selling air tickets. The prices of the call options appear in the form of discounts off the regular airfare. However, it is worth noting that this example is not exactly the same as that in the revenue management in prior research, since we focus on an intermediate party in the airline industry.

3.3 Numerical Examples

In this subsection, we use numerical examples for the European and American call options embedded in the discounted airfare to further illustrate profit maximization in revenue management of the airline industry described in Sects. 4.1 and 4.2. Assuming that

$$r = 0.05, \ q = 0.08, \ \mu^{\dagger} = 0.065, \ \xi = 1, \ \delta = 0.01, \ \sigma = 0.3$$

we price the embedded options and the discounted airfare for various values of initial spot price S_0 and maturity T. We suppose that T takes values 0.25, 0.5 0.75 year and 1 year, respectively, and S_0 ranges from 100 to 140 with an increment of 10. The figures we have assumed are consistent with the corresponding figures in the industries. For example, the spot price of the ticket can be from £100 to £140, which are compatible with the prices of tickets for UK internal flights or tickets from UK to other EU regions. The maturity T from 0.25 year and 1 year is also compatible with the real time duration for a ticket, which is available for sale.

We shall compare the option prices obtained from the semi-analytical algorithm with those from the finite difference scheme. Since there is no closed-form solution to the pricing problem we considered above, one might use some numerical method, such as the finite-difference scheme to solve the pricing PDEs. The finite-difference scheme has the advantage of giving a good approximate pricing result when an appropriate or a fine grid for discretizing the space and the time domains of the pricing PDEs is used. However, the computational time and effort required to implement the finite-difference scheme can be substantial. The semi-analytical algorithm we proposed can provide a convenient way to determine the option prices. We shall demonstrate the accuracy of the semi-analytical algorithm by comparing it with a finite-difference scheme with a fine grid, which can deliver accurate approximation results.

Table 1 presents the European and the American call option prices obtained from the BAW quadratic approximation (Barone-Adesi and Whaley 1987) when the initial price of underlying commodity and the maturity take different values, respectively. Comparing the option prices obtained from the above semi-analytical algorithm with those from the finite difference scheme, we find that the relative errors are negligible. Corresponding values of the discounted airfares are also presented in Table 1, and we find that the approximation algorithm provides accurate estimation and is easy to implement.

4 Risk Management: An Example from the Energy Industry

In the energy industry, revenue management is also one of the critical issues. Li et al. (2008) apply a real-option approach in a regime-switching model to address the risk-management and risk-hedging issues in strategic petroleum reserve. Unfortunately, their approach is not easy to implement in practice, and therefore, we present a numerical example on the basis of these issues using problem setting similar to the one presented in Li et al. (2008) by taking mean-reversion and time-varying strike prices into consideration.

Table 1 European and American option prices in the airline industry

S_0	European (fin. diff.)	(7)	Discounted airfare	American (fin. diff.)	(12)	Discounted airfare
			$T = 0.25$ year			
100	3.5359	3.5357	96.4643	3.6015	3.6125	96.3875
110	3.8892	3.8892	106.1108	3.9614	3.9738	106.0262
120	4.2422	4.2428	115.7572	4.3211	4.3350	115.6650
130	4.5965	4.5963	125.4037	4.6819	4.6963	125.3037
140	4.9503	4.9499	135.0501	5.0422	5.0576	134.9424
			$T = 0.5$ year			
100	4.6123	4.6113	95.3887	4.8304	4.8441	95.1559
110	5.0742	5.0724	104.9276	5.3140	5.3285	104.6715
120	5.5350	5.5336	114.4664	5.7968	5.8129	114.1871
130	5.9968	5.9947	124.0053	6.2802	6.2973	123.7027
140	6.4577	6.4558	133.5442	6.7631	6.7817	133.2183
			$T = 0.75$ year			
100	5.2358	5.2351	94.7649	5.6326	5.6848	94.3152
110	5.7594	5.7586	104.2414	6.1959	6.2532	103.7468
120	6.2828	6.2821	113.7179	6.7591	6.8217	113.1783
130	6.8063	6.8056	123.1944	7.3223	7.3902	122.6098
140	7.3302	7.3291	132.6709	7.8858	7.9587	132.0413
			$T = 1$ year			
100	5.7857	5.7870	94.2130	6.2690	6.4255	93.5745
110	6.3643	6.3656	103.6344	6.8960	7.0680	102.9320
120	6.9430	6.9443	113.0557	7.5229	7.7106	112.2894
130	7.5216	7.5230	122.4770	8.1499	8.3531	121.6469
140	8.1002	8.1017	131.8983	8.7768	8.9957	131.0043

Following the problem setting in Li et al. (2008), the strike price of the options is time-varying such as $K_t = K e^{rt}$, $t \in (0, T]$, where K is usually taken to be S_0, and $K_T = K e^{rT}$ for European options. Given that the spot price of an underlying energy commodity is S_0 at time t_0, for analytical simplicity, we define the energy commodity price producers sell at is $S_0 - C_0$ at time t_0, where C_0 is the call option premium. Li et al. (2008) also define the spot price of the underlying energy commodity as $S_t = S_0 g_t e^{X_t}$ under a real-world probability $\mathcal{P}$, where $g_t = e^{\delta \int_0^t \sin(2\pi s+\xi) ds}$ and

$$ dX_t = \kappa(\gamma - X_t)dt + \sigma \, dW_t. $$

κ is the strength of mean-reversion, which determines the speed of adjustment pulling the randomly moving value of the mean-reverting asset toward a central location γ, and γ is also referred to the long-run mean return.

By Itô's lemma, one can follow Li et al. (2008) approach and get

$$
\begin{aligned}
dS_t &= \left(\delta \sin(2\pi t + \xi) + \kappa\gamma + \tfrac{1}{2}\sigma^2 - \kappa \ln S_t\right) S_t dt + \sigma S_t \, dW_t \\
&= (\bar{b}_t - \kappa \ln S_t) S_t dt + \sigma S_t \, dW_t,
\end{aligned}
\tag{18}
$$

where $\bar{b}_t = \delta \sin(2\pi t + \xi) + \kappa\gamma + \tfrac{1}{2}\sigma^2$.

From (18), we see that the drift coefficient, or the expected rate of return from the commodity, can incorporate the seasonality effect, which is one of the major empirical effects of commodity prices.

Again, we need to adopt the risk-neutral valuation to price the option. This can be done by finding the dynamics of the commodity S under the risk-neutral probability. To find the dynamics under the risk-neutral probability, we need to employ a standard result for changing probability measures for Brownian motion, namely, Girsanov's theorem. The Girsanov theorem lies at the heart of the modern theory of option pricing, in particular risk-neutral valuation, and is an important tool in financial mathematics. In the context of option valuation, the Girsanov theorem tells how the price dynamics of the underlying risky asset change when we convert from the real-world probability to a risk-neutral probability. In general, the Girsanov theorem tells how the probability laws of stochastic processes change when changing the probability measures. In the current context with Brownian information, the Girsanov theorem gives us the following result for the price dynamics of the commodity S under the risk-neutral probability Q. For the detail about the Girsanov theorem, interested readers may refer to Shreve (2004).

Let $\kappa^\dagger := \kappa + \bar{\lambda}\sigma$. Then, under a risk-neutral measure Q, the dynamic of S is

$$
dS_t = (\bar{b}_t - \kappa^\dagger \ln S_t) S_t dt + \sigma S_t \, d\bar{W}_t^\dagger,
\tag{19}
$$

where

$$
\bar{W}_t^\dagger := W_t + \int_0^t \bar{\lambda} \ln S_u \, du
\tag{20}
$$

according to the Girsanov theorem.

At time t, thus, the American call option price is

$$
C^A(t, S) = \max_{\tau \in T_{t,T}} E\left[e^{-r(\tau-t)} (S_\tau - K_\tau)^+ \,\middle|\, S_t = S \right].
\tag{21}
$$

The above optimal stopping problem (21) for valuing an American option is the same as the one (9), except that they have different state processes, or price dynamics.

Again, there is an alternative characterization to the solution of the optimal stopping problem based on a variational inequality. Indeed, the American call price $C^A(t, S)$ satisfies the following free-boundary PDE problem, or variational inequality:

$$
\begin{cases}
\frac{\partial C}{\partial t} + \frac{1}{2}\sigma^2 S^2 \frac{\partial^2 C}{\partial S^2} + (\bar{b}_t - \kappa^\dagger \ln S)S \frac{\partial C}{\partial S} - rC \leq 0, \\
C(t, S) - (S_t - K_t)^+ \geq 0, \\
\left(\frac{\partial C}{\partial t} + \frac{1}{2}\sigma^2 S^2 \frac{\partial^2 C}{\partial S^2} + (\bar{b}_t - \kappa^\dagger \ln S)S \frac{\partial C}{\partial S} - rC\right)\left(C(t, S) - (S_t - K_t)^+\right) = 0, \\
C(T, S) = (S - K_T)^+
\end{cases}
\tag{22}
$$

The interpretation of the above variational inequality (22) is the same as that of the variational inequality (10). So we do not repeat it here.

4.1 Numerical Examples

To further illustrate the implementation of the algorithm introduced in Sect. 4.1, we consider the following numerical experiments using some specimen values for the model parameters such as $r = 5\%$; $\kappa = 0.15$, $\gamma = 0.5$, $\xi = 1$, $\delta = 0.01$, $\bar{\lambda} = 0.06$, and $\sigma = 0.3$. For different values of the initial price of the energy commodity S_0 and the time to maturity T, we price European and American call options purchased by energy commodity, and calculate their corresponding real energy commodity prices defined by $S_0 - C_0$. We suppose that S_0 ranges from 30 to 70 with an increment of 10, while T can be 0.25, 0.5, 0.75, and 1 years. Table 2 presents the numerical results for the European and American call option prices approximated by the finite-difference scheme and their corresponding real commodity prices.

Note that we have assumed zero dividend payment in the numerical examples, and therefore, according to the standard finance theory, the American call option prices should have been the same as the corresponding European counterparts due to the absence of dividend payment. However, this is not the truth here since the strike prices of the American call options are time-varying. This makes their behaviors totally different from those predicted from the standard option pricing theory. We can see that the gaps between the American call option prices and the European ones are quite substantial, and they increase in the length of maturity. In other words, an early exercise premium for the American call option is present due to the presence of the time-varying-strike-price (TVSP) effect, and this illustrates that the TVSP effect on option premium is significant.

One noticeable feature of the embedded European and American call options is that the strike price depends on both the initial price of the energy commodity S_0 and the time to maturity T. This makes the behaviors of call option prices as functions of the initial underlying price S_0 different from those of the standard call option prices with constant strike prices. This difference becomes more pronounced when we consider a European call option with longer time to maturity, and it is mainly due to the feature of seasonality.

Table 2 European and American option prices in the energy industry

S_0	European (C_0) (dinite difference)	Real commodity price ($S_0 - C_0$)	American (C_0) (finite difference)	Real commodity price ($S_0 - C_0$)
		$T = 0.25$ year		
30	0.4903	29.5097	0.8444	29.1556
40	0.5622	39.4378	1.0583	38.9417
50	0.6233	49.3767	1.2626	48.7374
60	0.6767	59.3233	1.4597	58.5403
70	0.7243	69.2757	1.6511	68.3489
		$T = 0.5$ year		
30	0.3279	29.6721	0.9274	29.0726
40	0.3416	39.6584	1.1468	38.8532
50	0.3502	49.6498	1.3553	48.6447
60	0.3558	59.6442	1.5557	58.4443
70	0.3595	69.6405	1.7500	68.2500
		$T = 0.75$ year		
30	0.2051	29.7949	0.9560	29.0440
40	0.1954	39.8046	1.1745	38.8255
50	0.1863	49.8137	1.3822	48.6178
60	0.1779	59.8221	1.5820	58.4180
70	0.1702	69.8298	1.7756	68.2244
		$T = 1$ year		
30	0.1299	29.8701	0.9687	29.0313
40	0.1138	39.8862	1.1859	38.8141
50	0.1012	49.8988	1.3925	48.6075
60	0.0911	59.9089	1.5914	58.4086
70	0.0827	69.9173	1.7844	68.2156

As shown in Table 2, the European call option prices decrease in the initial price of the underlying energy commodity when $T = 0.75$ year and when the maturity is 1 year. Please note that this does not violate the features of European call option prices defined in the Black–Scholes formula since the underlying security in the Black–Scholes model follows a log-normal process. The phenomena shown in our numerical experiments reflect the special feature, seasonality, of energy commodities. We also find that the influence of seasonality does not appear when call options are of the American style, and this is mainly because of the self-adjustment made by the option holders when they can choose an optimal early exercise time.

In short, we find that the seasonality have significant effects on European call option prices but insignificant effects on the American ones. This is mainly caused by the early-stopping characteristics of American options; in other words, American option holders can adjust again the seasonality effects by deciding when to exercise the options. On the contrary, the TVSP effect is significant when call options are of the American style, but insignificant when they are of the European style. Similar to the discussion earlier, this is also due to the optimal-stopping features of American options, while European option holders can do nothing against the TVSP effects.

5 Concluding Remarks and Further Implications

While revenue management has attracted serious attention of academic researchers in various disciplines and practitioners in different sectors, profit maximization has been the major focus of previous studies. Although more and more people have realized the importance of the risk-management issues, in particular the risk-hedging issues, in this field, they have not been extensively studied in the literature. This study introduces a real-option approach to deal with both profit enhancement and risk hedging issues in revenue management.

On the basis of the studies on callable products in revenue management (for example, Gallego et al. 2004; Feng and Gallego 2005), we used two typical examples in two industries, the airline industry and the energy industry, to illustrate the proposed approach. Because of the special features of airline tickets and energy commodities, in addition, we incorporate the seasonality and TVSP effects into the models, and propose a semi-analytical algorithm for pricing the real options. It develops the approach presented in Xia and Zhou (2005), which gives a closed-form expression for pricing perpetual American options with time-varying strike prices. Numerical examples are also presented to illustrate the estimation accuracy of the proposed approach by comparing with results obtained from the finite difference scheme.

In the airline industry, travel agents can buy call options from their customers while selling air tickets so as to be able to call back these tickets if they can sell them at much higher prices. To enhance their own profits, in other words, travel agents long call options to purchase the tickets back from their customers if some other customers travel with necessity and would like to pay higher prices. Customers who are flexible regarding their trips and those who can change their travel plans are willing to accept the deal. The option premium appears in the form of a discount offered to the customers when they purchase air tickets. In the energy industry, we follow the problem setting proposed by Li et al. (2008) to further address risk-hedging in strategy petroleum reserve using call options. While Li et al. (2008) adopt a regime-switching model to address this issue theoretically, we show how to implement the idea numerically so that it can be used in practice.

Using the models constructed on the basis of real options and incorporating seasonality, mean-reversion and time-varying strike prices into the models, we examine both aspects of revenue management, profit enhancement and risk management. Besides that we show the effectiveness and the estimation accuracy of the proposed approach, we also find that seasonality has significant effects only on European call prices, but the TVSP effects are significant only on the American ones, in the energy industry. In future studies, it is of interest to investigate these effects in other aspects of operations research and finance, especially in those related to the demand–supply equilibrium. For instance, it is important to consider the effects of term structure in addressing credit risk using the approach presented in this article.

Acknowledgements Research supported in part by HKU CRCG Grants and Strategic Research Theme Fund on Computational Physics and Numerical Methods. The second author acknowledges financial support from PolyU grants A-SA28 and G-YH20. The third author acknowledges the Discovery Grant from the Australian Research Council (ARC), (Project No.: DP1096243). The fourth author acknowledges the financial support of the University of Saskatchewan Research Grant #407294.

References

Allaz B, Vila JL (1993) Cournot competition, forward markets and efficiency. J Econ Theor 59:1–16

Anderson CK, Davison M, Rasmussen H (2004) Revenue management: a real options approach. Nav Res Logist 51:686–703

Barone-Adesi G, Whaley R (1987) Efficient analytic approximation of American option values. J Finance 42:1–20

Belobaba P (1987) Airline yield management: an overview of seat inventory control. Transport Sci 21:63–73

Deng SJ, Feng Y, Li X (2006) A real options analysis for optimal dynamic pricing of perishable products tradable in spot markets. The Chinese University of Hong Kong, Hong Kong (Preprint)

Duffie D, Richardson HR (1991) Mean-variance hedging in continuous time. Ann Appl Probab 1:1–15

Elliott RJ, Sick GA, Stein M (2003) Modeling electricity price risk. Working paper, University of Calgary and University of Oregon

Feng Y, Gallego G (2005) Optimal booking control with a callable booking class. Working paper, Chinese University of Hong Kong and Columbia University in the City of New York

Gallego G, Kou SG, Phillips R (2004) Revenue management of callable products. Working paper, Columbia University

Gallego G, Van Ryzin G (1994) Optimal dynamic pricing of inventories with stochastic demand over finite horizons. Manag Sci 40:999–1020

Geraghty MK, Johnson E (1997) Revenue management saves national car rental. Interfaces 27:107–127

Li X, Siu TK, Wu Z (2008) Risk hedging for strategic petroleum reserve. Math Model Appl Comput

Shreve S (2004) Stochastic calculus for finance. Springer, New York

Weatherford L, Bodily S (1992) A taxonomy and research overview of perishable-asset revenue management: yield management, overbooking, and pricing. Oper Res 40:831–844

Wilmott P, Howison S, Dewynne J (1996) The mathematics of financial derivatives. Cambridge University Press, USA

Wu DJ, Kleindorfer PR (2005) Competitive options, supply contracting, and electronic markets. Manag Sci 51:452–466

Wu DJ, Kleindorfer PR, Sun Y, Zhang JE (2002) The price of a real option on capacity. Working paper, Drexel University, University of Pennsylvania, and Hong Kong University of Science and Technology

Xia J, Zhou X (2007) "Stock loans" (pdf), Mathematical Finance, 17:307–317

Supply Chain Scheduling under Quick Response

Xiang Li and Yongjian Li

Abstract Quick Response has become one of the most important requirements in a well-designed and operated supply chain system. This chapter focuses on the scheduling problem within supply chain environment regarding Quick Response to customer orders as the ultimate objective. We introduce some recent and important research developments, including the customer order scheduling problems on either parallel machines or dedicated machines, the scheduling problems with outsourcing consideration, and the conflict and coordination of scheduling decisions among different supply chain members. For each problem, the scheduling model is presented and the main results are elucidated. Finally, the further research directions are also pointed out.

Keywords Customer order scheduling · Outsourcing · Quick response · Supply chain coordination

1 Introduction

In the middle 1990s, Quick Response (QR) became popular as a new concept aimed at rapidly satisfying the needs of end consumers. It was first described as an "initiative intended to cut manufacturing and distribution lead times through a variety of means" (Fisher and Raman 1996) within the apparel industry, soon adopted among a variety of industry fields, and further strengthened with the development of supply chain management. On the other hand, scheduling is a relatively old topic regarding the decisions on how to commit resources (so-called machines) among a set of possible tasks (so-called jobs). It is the supply chain management conception and practice that opens up new research fields and poses new problems in the scheduling area. The main objective of the scheduling in a supply chain is to

X. Li (✉)

Research Center of Logistics, College of Economic and Social Development, Nankai University, Tianjin 300071, P.R. China

e-mail: xiangli@mail.nankai.edu.cn

T.C. Edwin Cheng and T.-M. Choi (eds.), *Innovative Quick Response Programs in Logistics and Supply Chain Management*, International Handbooks on Information Systems, DOI 10.1007/978-3-642-04313-0_7,

produce and deliver finished products to end consumers in the most cost-effective and timely manner (Kreipl and Pinedo 2004), which corresponds to the essence of QR.

This chapter focuses on the supply chain scheduling under QR, hoping to establish a theoretical foundation and introduce some recent research developments in the area. More specifically, there are three streams of research drawing our attention: the scheduling of customer order, the scheduling regarding third-party logistics (3PL) and outsourcing, and the supply chain scheduling problem. First of all, when a large demand or customized demand occurs, each customer order usually contains a set of several prespecified products. This forces the firm to consider the scheduling problem of customer order where each order consists of multiple jobs, under the objective of minimizing the average completion time or lateness with respect to the customer order instead of the related jobs. In other words, different from the traditional objective with respect to the job completion time, these so-called *customer order scheduling* problems are to minimize the (weighted) average order completion time, hence the traditional result and method might not be applicable to these new problems. Both cases of scheduling customer orders have been studied when each job can be processed on any one of the machines and when each job has to be processed on a dedicated machine. Some related works include Blocher and Chhajed (1996); Ahmadi et al. (2005); Yang (2005); Yang and Posner (2005), etc.

Outsourcing is a natural phenomenon with the development of the supply chain and 3PL. It is adopted not only as a strategic tool to reduce the operational cost, but also as a tactical means to hedge against the capacity shortage for a large demand. When the demand is beyond the production capacity, the firm has the option to outsource part of or the entire orders to available subcontractors so that all orders can be completed as early as possible. This is also consistent with the high service level and QR requirement. However, in this case some factors such as costs for the outsourced jobs and the transportation back to the firm have to be taken into consideration.

The study of scheduling under the outsourcing environment has been explored for a few years. For example, Chung et al. (2005) studies a job shop scheduling model where temporal relaxation of the machine capacity constraint is possible through outsourcing. The objective is to effectively decrease the tardiness measure by rescheduling or outsourcing the operations on the bottleneck machines. Lee et al. (2002) presents an advance planning and scheduling model considering the selection of the best machine for operation, the operations to be outsourced and the sequence of operations, to minimize the makespan of the due date of each order. Chen and Li (2008) also studies a scheduling problem with outsourcing options, but it assumes that the subcontractor has unlimited capacity and thus no schedule is needed for the outsourced jobs. Other related literatures include Ruiz-Torres et al. (2006); Vairaktarakis and Cai (2007); Lee and Sung (2008a,b), etc. In this chapter, we first consider a scheduling problem where all jobs are to be processed by the machines of 3PL but only discontinuous time periods are available. Then we introduce the model studied in Qi (2008), which integrates the major issues of the scheduling with outsourcing option: the selection between in-house production and outsourcing, the machine scheduling for both in-house production and outsourcing, and the transportation for outsourced jobs.

Furthermore, the above models assume that the system is operated by a single controller and the objective is to optimize the centralized system. In fact, the planning and scheduling may be processed by different members in the supply chain in pursuit of the local optimization. The supply chain members therefore need to coordinate and collaborate in their schedulings on the job sequencing, production planning and transportation batching, to improve the channel performance. In this aspect, we introduce the work on supply chain scheduling by Hall and Potts (2003), which evaluates the benefit of coordinated decision making in a supply chain where a supplier makes deliveries to several manufacturers, who in turn supply several customers. Under the objective to minimize the total scheduling and batch delivery costs, the algorithms for both supplier and manufacturer are developed and the cost reduction through supply chain coordination is shown to be from 20% to 100%. The follow-up research on supply chain scheduling in assembly system is also presented in this chapter and the significance of benefits gained from coordinating scheduling decisions is once again validated. The majority of other recent papers related to conflict and coordination in supply chain scheduling include Hall and Potts (2005); Agnetis et al. (2006); Chen and Pundoor (2006); Chauhan et al. (2007); Sawik (2009), etc.

Finally, we point out that all problems discussed in this chapter are classified into the category of static scheduling. In real world environment scheduling is an ongoing process frequently revised in response to disruptions, such as machine failures, material shortages, urgent order arrival or order cancelation, etc. New scheduling might be required due to these disruptions, in that the initial solution could not be efficient or even feasible any more. The research on this field, usually referred to as "rescheduling" or "dynamic scheduling," has begun since early 1990s. Examples include Wu (1993); Ovacik and Uzsoy (1994); Abumaizar and Svestka (1997); Li et al. (2000); Alagoz and Azizoglu (2003); Caricato and Grieco (2008), etc. These problems are also highly relevant to the core spirit of QR; however, we do not include them here. One reason is due to the limited space of this chapter and another one is that there has already been an excellent recent review: Ouelhadj and Petrovic (2009) presents an overview of the state-of-the-art research on dynamic scheduling, illustrating in detail the current state and recent progress on not only the problems but also the dynamic scheduling techniques as well. We therefore refer the interested reader to Ouelhadj and Petrovic (2009) regarding this research stream.

2 Scheduling of Customer Orders for Quick Response

While the traditional scheduling literature cares about the job completion time, models based on the characteristics of customer orders are more realistic in the current QR environment. Each order consists of a known number of inside jobs to be processed on a set of machines. For the customer, the finish date of the entire order instead of the individual job is surely more relevant to satisfy their QR requirement. Shapiro et al. (1992) presents a good example in which a company completes 99% of all order components (referred to as "jobs" in our paper) on time, but only 50% of all customer orders can be shipped punctually. Therefore, though it seems to be satisfactory from the traditional view of job completion performance, the response standard of this system is far from acceptable to serve the customer. In the following, we classify the scheduling problems of customer orders into two classes: scheduling on parallel machines and scheduling on dedicated machines.

2.1 Scheduling of Customer Orders on Parallel Machines

Consider a problem of scheduling n customer orders on m parallel machines. Each order is composed of a set of jobs whose sizes are known beforehand. The machines are called "parallel" because each job can be processed on any of m machines with identical processing time. All machines are available from the very beginning and the objective is to minimize the average order completion time.

It is easy to see when there is only one order, the problem becomes equal to minimizing the makespan on parallel machines $P//C_{\max}$, which is one of the basic NP-complete problems. Therefore, the scheduling of customer orders on parallel machines is NP-hard. Another special case is that each order consists of only one job. Then the problem is equivalent to a flow-time minimization problem on parallel machines and can be solved by sequentially assigning the jobs to each machine in a shortest processing time (SPT) order.

Given by Blocher and Chhajed (1996) are two classes of heuristics, named two-component sequential heuristics and two-component dynamic heuristics. The intuitive of sequential heuristics is simple: first it determines the sequence of orders based on SPT idea, then sequentially assigns the jobs of each order to the machines based on longest processing time (LPT) idea.

For example, we define the average order processing time T_i/m as the sum of processing time T_i of jobs belonging to order i divided by the number of machines m. Then a simplest two-component heuristic is to select the unscheduled job with the longest processing time in the uncompleted order with the shortest average order processing time, whenever a machine becomes available. The detailed algorithm is as follows.

0. Reindex the batches so that $T_i/m \leq T_{i+1}/m$ for $i = 1, 2, \ldots, n$. For $i = 1, 2, \ldots, m$, reindex the jobs so that $p_j \geq p_{j+1}$ if $j, j+1 \in O_i$. Set $i = j = 1$ and $F_k = 0$ for $k = 1, 2, \ldots, m$.

1. Select the first available machine $u = argmin_{k=1,2,\ldots,m}\{F_k\}$. Assign job j in order i to machine u. Set $F_u = F_u + p_j$ and $j = j + 1$.

2. Repeat Step 1 until all jobs in order i are scheduled.

3. Set $C_i = \max_{k=1,2,\ldots,m}\{F_k\}$. If $i < n$, then set $i = i + 1$ and go to step 1. Otherwise, output $\sum_{i=1}^{b} C_i/m$ and stop.

In this algorithm we use SPT on the average processing time when sequencing the order, so we call it shortest-order average processing time (SOAPT). And because we simply apply LPT when scheduling the jobs within one specified order, we call this entire heuristic SOAPT-LPT. The underlying intuition of this heuristic is that, since the performance depends on the order completion time, we can view each order as a job, and thus SPT is preferred when sequencing the order since SPT is optimal in the special case when each order consists of only one job. When scheduling the jobs within one order, LPT is preferred as it provides a good heuristic solution of $P//C_{max}$: there is only one order consisting of several jobs.

However, SOAPT-LPT is not the only sequential heuristic. If we assume that each order is processed on m machines and LPT is applied to assign the jobs within the order, then we calculate the makespan of each order, which is used as the measure of the order's length. If we apply SPT based on this measure, the shortest-order longest-processing-time rule (SOLPT) is obtained.

As for assigning the jobs, we can also use the idea of bin packing instead of LPT. We first set a goal completion time (bin size) of each order as the completion time of the order when using LPT to assign the jobs. Then we assign the job with the longest processing time in that order to the machine with the least assigned works, which can finish the job within the goal time. If assigning the job to the machine with the least amount of works still exceeds the goal, then assign it to this machine, reset the goal to its completion time, and continue assigning the remaining jobs using the new goal. This rule is called BIN. Thus, four heuristics can be obtained by combining two rules of sequencing orders and two rules of sequencing jobs to the machines, within the class of two-component sequential heuristics.

Two-component dynamic heuristics also use the basic rules for assigning jobs (the second component), LPT and BIN. However, the order sequence (the first component) is determined dynamically. After making a trial to assign the jobs of all remaining orders by either LPT or BIN, we select the order with the smallest completion time as the next one to be processed. This approach is called greedy algorithm and thus two heuristics are obtained as Greedy-LPT and Greedy-BIN. Readers can find the detailed algorithms in Blocher and Chhajed (1996).

The problem can be formulated as a mixed-integer programming and the lower bound can be obtained by relaxing a certain of constraints to be linear (Blocher and Chhajed 1996). Some other tighter lower bounds can also be developed. The above heuristics are shown to be effective for a wide variety of problems since the lower bound and heuristic solutions appear quite close through a rather extensive numerical experiments and no heuristic dominates another. The most important affecting factors are shown to be the number of jobs/orders/machines dependent on different situations.

2.2 Scheduling of Customer Orders on Dedicated Machines

The background of the problem is similar to the former one: each customer order can be shipped only if all its jobs are completed. The difference is that now the jobs are distinct from each other and have to be processed on different dedicated machines. We suppose there are m dedicated machines available at the very beginning and n customer orders. Each order is composed of up to m jobs to be processed. The objective is to minimize the weighted average completion times of n orders $\sum_{i=1}^{n} w_i C_i$, where C_i is the completion time of order i and w_i is the corresponding weight. This problem is called scheduling of customer orders on dedicated machines, which is first studied in Ahmadi et al. (2005).

This is also an NP-hard problem; however, the proof is not as straightforward as the scheduling problem on parallel machines. On the other hand, similar with the one on parallel machines, there exists an optimal schedule satisfying the following "aligned" property: if a job of order h precedes a job of order k, then $C_h < C_k$. Thus the optimal schedule can be fully characterized by a single permutation Ψ. Other used notations are listed below:

i index of orders, $i = 1, 2, \ldots, n$,

j index of machines, $j = 1, 2, \ldots, m$,

$J(i)$ set of machines required by order i,

$p_{i,j}$ processing time of order i on machine j,

$C_{i,j}$ completion time of order i on machine j,

Φ set of all Ψ

Before discussing on the heuristic, we introduce the aligning procedure, which turns any semiactive schedule without preemptions into an aligned schedule.

Aligning Procedure (AP):

0. Let $U = \{1, 2, \ldots, n\}$.

1. Select the order $C_k = \mathrm{argmax}_{u \in U}\{C_u\}$ and delete k from U.

2. For all $j \in J(k)$, let $V_j = \{i \in U, s.t. \text{ job } J_k \text{ precedes job } J_i \text{ on machine } j\}$ and exchange job k with set V_j such that $C_{k,j} \to C_{k,j} + \sum_{i \in V_j} p_{i,j}$ and $C_{i,j} \to C_{i,j} - p_{k,j}, \forall i \in V_j$. Then go to Step 1 till $U = \emptyset$.

A special case is $m=1$ and the problem becomes a single machine total weighted completion time problem, which can be easily solved by sorting the processing times of jobs. Applying this intuition to each machine, we first sequence the orders in a nondecreasing order of $p_{i,j}/w_i$ on each machine j. From all these schedules an aligned schedule can be generated by AP. This algorithm is called weighted shortest processing times heuristic (WSPT).

Simpler heuristics without using AP are also proposed. One is greedy heuristics, which greedily schedules the order with the smallest weighted completion time as the next one. Another is referred to as bottleneck heuristic, which just schedules the orders in a nondecreasing "bottleneck" machine processing time, that is, in a nondecreasing order of $\{max_j\{p_{i,j}\}\}/w_i$.

More complicated heuristics are also presented in Ahmadi et al. (2005). The first one is based on the similarity between the problem and the single-machine total weighted tardiness problem. The basic idea is that, in the optimal schedule, the schedule on any machine minimizes the total weighted tardiness supposing that the due date of each order is the maximum of its completion time on the remaining machines. Another heuristic is based on adding some dual constraints to a mathematical formulation as an assignment problem, which results from the alignment property. Both heuristics require quite sophisticated computational technique to implement.

As a summary of this section, we point out that the introduced models can be applied to many practical problems. For instance, if a printing company receives orders from various customers consisting of several printing jobs per order, the primary concern of the company is usually to make all the jobs of one customer to be completed as soon as possible, thus the customer order completion time becomes the main focus. If the printing machines in the company are identical and each job can be processed on anyone among the machines, it can be reduced to a customer order scheduling problem on parallel machines. However, if each order consists of different types of jobs, for example, three jobs: printing, bookbinding and copying, and each job has to be processed on the dedicated machines, that is, a printing machine cannot copy papers, then the model of scheduling on dedicated machines should be adopted.

3   Scheduling the Outsourcing for Quick Response

Outsourcing refers to the case of subcontracting an entire section of production or service, which allows the firm to concentrate on its own core competency, reduce the operational cost, and lower the financial risk. In the current globalization trend and supply chain environment, it has become prevalent as a competitive weapon to hedge against capacity shortage when facing a large demand. Therefore, taking a good advantage of outsourcing helps the firm to improve its QR to the customer demand.

The traditional scheduling research carries the assumption that one always possesses all machines needed to process his jobs, which is no longer applicable for the widespread outsourcing practice. Therefore, it poses new challenge to consider the hire of additional machines from 3PL and the job sequence on them. The main objective of this section is to introduce some recent models to solve this problem. The first subsection considers a scheduling problem where all jobs are to be processed by machines of 3PL, and the jobs have to be transported back from the 3PL after completion. The second subsection extends the model by including the selection decision of a job between in-house production and outsourcing.

3.1   Scheduling on Single Outsourcing Machine

We first consider that a manufacturer receives n jobs at time 0 and outsources the jobs to a 3PL for processing due to his own limited capacity. However, only discontinuous time intervals at 3PL can be used for the job processing, which are referred to as manufacturing windows. The problem differs from the conventional scheduling problem with machine availability constraints in that, the outsourcing costs are considered in our model, including the booking cost of manufacturing windows and the overtime cost. The following notations are used:

i	index of jobs, $i = 1, 2, \ldots, n$
p_i	processing time of job i on the outsourcing machine
d_i	due date of job i
$W_k = [a_k, b_k]$	the kth manufacturing window
h_k	outsourcing cost of booking the kth manufacturing window
O_k	maximum overtime allowed in the kth manufacturing window
α	unit processing overtime cost

Here the setup time between jobs is neglected, and a job can be preempted in a manufacturing window and resumed during another. Moreover, the transportation issue is not considered after the jobs are finished at the 3PL location, with assumption that all completed jobs have a fixed delivery time from the 3PL to the manufacturer. The problem faced by the manufacturer is to determine a permutation of jobs in a subset of manufacturing windows among all S windows offered by the 3PL, with the objective to minimize the weighted sum of outsourcing costs and the number of tardy jobs.

The decision variables to be determined are overtime $x_k, k = 1, \ldots, S$. The overtime cost of extending the kth manufacturing window is denoted by $\Delta_k = x_k/\alpha$. Moreover, $y_i^k, k = 1, \ldots, S, i = 1, \ldots, n$ are 0–1 indicators to show whether job i is completed during W_k or not, representing the selected manufacturing windows. Denote k_i as the smallest integer k such that $a_k \geq d_i$. Cai et al. (2005) formulates the problem as a mixed-integer programming:

$$
\begin{aligned}
\min \ & \{\textstyle\sum_{k=1}^{S} h_k \max_{1 \leq i \leq n} y_i^k + \sum_{k=1}^{S} x_k + \beta \sum_{i=1}^{n} \sum_{k=k_i}^{S} y_i^k\} \\
s.t. \ (a) \ & \textstyle\sum_{k=1}^{r} \sum_{i=1}^{n} p_i y_i^k \leq \sum_{k=1}^{r} (b_k + \alpha x_k - a_k), \quad r = 1, \ldots, S, \\
(b) \ & \textstyle\sum_{k=1}^{S} y_i^k = 1, \quad i = 1, \ldots, n, \\
(c) \ & x_k \leq M \textstyle\sum_{i=1}^{n} y_i^k, \quad k = 1, \ldots, S, \\
(d) \ & \alpha x_k \leq O_k, \quad k = 1, \ldots, S, \\
(e) \ & y_i^k \in \{0, 1\}, x_k \geq 0, \quad i = 1, \ldots, n, k = 1, \ldots, S.
\end{aligned}
\tag{1}
$$

The objective in (1) is to minimize the total cost, including the booking cost of manufacturing windows, the overtime cost of extending the window and the tardiness penalty for late jobs. Here β can be regarded as a weight of the late job numbers to the outsourcing cost in the optimization objective.

This is an NP-hard problem too. However, efficient algorithms can be developed for some special cases, such as constant-length manufacturing windows and constant overtime upper bound, that is, $b_k - a_k = R$ and $O_k = O$ for all k. For example, the polynomial time algorithm can be derived when the set T of tardy jobs is known in advance. In this case, the scheduling of on-time jobs is more complicated than the scheduling of tardy jobs, in that the latter can simply be assigned at unused windows that incurs the smallest unit cost. Therefore, the subschedule of on-time jobs can be considered first to minimize the sum of booking and overtime costs. Cai et al. (2005) introduces an algorithm based on a max-flow min-cost network. Then the optimal schedule for the tardy jobs can also be obtained. Another practical special case is when the cost of late jobs is relatively trivial related to the outsourcing cost. In this case, a fast algorithm based on the earliest-due-date (EDD) sequence can also be developed to solve the hierarchical problem to minimize the number of jobs subject to the minimum total booking and overtime costs. We refer the reader to Cai et al. (2005) for the detailed algorithms in this aspect.

3.2   Scheduling on In-house and Outsourcing Machines

Consider that a manufacturer owns a single machine and n jobs to be processed at time 0. The jobs can be also outsourced to a 3PL with a single outsourcing machine. Each job j has an integer processing time p_j on the in-house machine, and an integer due date d_j. An outsourcing cost is βp_j, which is proportional to the processing time, is incurred if the job j is outsourced, and the processing time is αp_j on the outsourcing machine. We also assume that the outsourced jobs have to be transported back to the firm in batches. Each batch incurs a fixed transportation cost K and a transportation delay τ for the jobs.

The scheduling plan includes the following decisions: the jobs to be outsourced, the processing sequences for the jobs on the in-house and outsourced machines of 3PL, and the transportation batches for the outsourced jobs from the 3PL to the firm location. Note that this is a centralized optimization case in which, for example, the manufacturer can prescribe to 3PL the sequencing and batching requirements for the outsourced jobs by a specific contract. The objective is to minimize the sum of the outsourcing/transportation costs and the external cost, which are related to the customer service performance and measured by the following alternative targets: the total completion time $\sum C_j$, the makespan $C_{max} = \max C_j$, the maximum lateness $L_{max} = \max\{C_j - d_j\}$, and the number of late jobs $\sum U_j$, where U_j is an indicator to show whether job j is late or not. The problem is defined in Qi (2008), according to convention of the scheduling literature, as $1 + 1||f$, where f is an objective relevant to one of the above four performance measures.

As the time complexity is concerned, the problem $1+1||\sum C_j$ can be regarded as two parallel-machine problems with a batch delivery decision on only one machine and is solvable in polynomial time. The remaining three problems under different objectives are NP-hard. However, it can be shown that, for any problem $1 + 1||f$ of above four cases, there exists an optimal schedule, in which the processing sequence on either the in-house machine or outsourced machine of 3PL is the same as that in the corresponding conventional single-machine problem. The above property is the key to solve the model.

Consider, for example, the problem of minimizing the total completion time. According to the above key property, we only need to consider the schedule in which jobs are sequenced in an SPT order on both the in-house and outsourcing machines.

Without loss of generalization, we assume that n jobs are indexed by an SPT order, $p_1 \leq p_2 \leq \cdots \leq p_n$. A cost function $F(j, m, h, h')$ is also defined as the minimum cost for such a subschedule that satisfies (1) jobs $j, j + 1, \ldots, n$ are scheduled on the in-house machines and outsourced machines of 3PL; (2) m jobs are scheduled on the outsourced machines; (3) the earliest job on the outsourced machines belongs to, say a batch B, in which h jobs are to be scheduled; and (4) h' jobs have already been scheduled in the batch B. Then, based on the SPT property, Qi (2008) proposes a dynamic programming algorithm as follows:

$$F(j, m, h, h') = \min\{F(j + 1, m - 1, h, h') + m p_j,$$
$$F(j + 1, m - 1, h, h') + (n - j + 1 - m + h - h')\alpha p_j \quad (2)$$
$$+\tau + \beta p_j\}$$

for $h' > 1$, and

$$F(j, m, h, 1) = \min\{F(j + 1, m - 1, h, 1) + m p_j,$$
$$K + (n - j - m + h)\alpha p_j + \tau + \beta p_j \quad (3)$$
$$+ \min_{h'' \leq n - j - m} F(j + 1, m - 1, h'', h')\},$$

with boundary conditions

$$F(j, n, 0, 0) = \begin{cases} \sum_{k=j}^{n} n(n - k + 1)p_k & m = n - j + 1 \\ +\infty & m \neq n - j + 1 \end{cases} \quad (4)$$

and, for $h \neq 0$,

$$F(n, 0, h, h') = \begin{cases} K + h p_n + K, & \text{when } h' = 1 \\ +\infty, & \text{when } h' > 1. \end{cases} \quad (5)$$

The first term in the right-hand of (2) or (3) is the cost of putting job j on the in-house machine, and the second is that of scheduling it on the outsourcing machine. The difference lies in that when $h' = 1$ and job j is outsourced, the job has to be put in a new batch, and a fixed transportation cost K is incurred. Above all, the objective is to utilize the above dynamic recursion to minimize $F(1, m, h, h)$ over all $m = 0, 1, \ldots, n$ and $h = 0, 1, \ldots, n - m$. The optimal schedule can be obtained in $O(n^4)$ time.

The problem of minimizing the total completion time is studied in Qi (2008). For minimizing the makespan, the problem is equivalent to allocating all jobs into two sets: in-house machine set and outsourcing machine set, and in each set the job sequence is arbitrary since the makespan will be the same for different sequences. A dynamic programming algorithm with the time complexity of $O(nP)$ can be derived, where $P = \sum_{j=1}^{n} P_j$ is the total processing time of all jobs. For the problems of minimizing the maximum lateness and the number of late jobs, it is considered among the schedules where the jobs and on-time jobs are scheduled in an EDD order on both the in-house and outsourcing machines, respectively, and dynamic programming algorithms can be derived similarly to that in the makespan problem. The time complexities are $O(n^2 P^2)$ and $O(n P^3)$, respectively. This implies that the latter three problems are NP-hard as we have mentioned beforehand.

4 Supply Chain Scheduling for Quick Response

Optimal supply chain performance requires precise execution and perfect management on the processes, assets, flows of material, and information to respond to the customer's demand. Unfortunately, the supply chain member usually cares more about their own objective, resulting in poor system performance and lower customer service level. Therefore, a critical issue has been concerned on the coordination among different decision makers so that the entire supply chain efficiency is raised and each member is better off at the meantime.

As it has been extensively studied on the supply chain coordination, most literature concerns about the inventory control decision, less about the supply chain scheduling. The idea of coordination within the supply chain scheduling is relatively new. Because of the emphasis on the customer satisfaction, the necessity of collaboration on the scheduling decision among different supply chain members has become prominent to achieve the goal of QR. It has been shown of great importance to study the related scheduling problems, where the time value holds a dominant status. Consider the simplest supply chain consisting of a supplier and a manufacturer, for example. The service to customer would be improved if the manufacturer receives parts from the supplier as early as possible since this enlarges the manufacturer's scheduling options. However, the scheduling at the supplier's side has to take consideration of various factors, such as its own resource constraints and gained profits, etc. Thus some particular parts could not be processed by the sequence as the manufacturer expects. The objective of this section is to study this conflict and relevant issues and to validate the potential benefit that a cooperative scheduling decision could bring about, which has been revealed in some recent researches.

4.1 Batch and Delivery Scheduling in Supply Chain

We start from a supply chain where a supplier processes jobs and delivers to several manufacturers, who in turn satisfy the demand of several customers. The focus is on the scheduling, batching, and delivery decisions of both the supplier and the manufacturers, and the objective of each member is to minimize his own costs, respectively, including the batch delivery cost plus the scheduling cost based on the batch delivery time. Thus the batch release dates of the manufacturers are defined by the supplier's decision, which results in some conflicts of interests. For example, the manufacturer may prefer to receive frequent deliveries of small batches but the supplier may be reluctant to do so considering the possible high fixed-cost of each batch. Therefore, it would be an important problem to evaluate the cost of this conflict and the benefit from an effective coordination on the related scheduling and batching decisions.

More specifically, the supplier S has jobs $N^S = \{1, \ldots, n^S\}$ to be processed on a single machine. Each job is produced for one of G manufacturers: $M_1, \ldots, M_G$, and the jobs for manufacturer M_g are denoted as $(1, g), \ldots, (n_g, g)$, where $g \in \{1, \ldots, G\}$. Similarly, each manufacturer, say M_1, for example, uses jobs from the supplier to produce jobs $N^M = \{1, \ldots, n^M\}$ on a single machine, for customers $\zeta_1, \ldots, \zeta_H$. The jobs for customer ζ_h are denoted as $(1, h), \ldots, (n_h, h)$, where $h \in \{1, \ldots, H\}$. These jobs are scheduled and delivered in batches to the customers. The due dates of jobs submitted by the supplier are prescribed by the manufacturer based on a specific schedule for processing its jobs, and the due dates of the customer jobs are specified ideally, which are one type of performance measures of the manufacturer.

To specify the objective of this problem, the notations related to the supplier's performance measure are introduced as follows.

C_j^S the completion time at which job j is delivered to manufacturer

F_j^S the flow time of job j for the supplier, which is equal to C_j^S

d_j^S the due date of job j for the supplier

L_j^S the lateness of job j for the supplier, the value of which is equal to $C_j^S - d_j^S$

U_j^S the indicator of whether or not job j is delivered to the manufacturer by its due date

y_g^S the number of deliveries (or batches) to manufacturer M_g

D_g^S the delivery cost of each batch to manufacturer M_g

Similarly, for the manufacturer's problem, C_j^M, L_j^M, U_j^M, y_g^M, D_g^M can be defined too. Let r_j^M be the release date of job j characterizing the earliest date this job can be processed by the manufacturer, and $F_j^M = C_j^M - r_j^M$. The measure of the centralized system is defined analogously through changing superscripts of all notations into C. In the decentralized scenario, the supplier and manufacturer make their own scheduling planning and seek to minimize the sum of their internal cost and external cost, respectively. In the centralized scenario, the decisions are made cooperatively by the two partners to minimize the total cost of the entire supply chain. The external cost is relevant to the service performance and measured by one of the following factors:

$\sum w_j F_j^X$ the total weighted flow time of the jobs,

$\max_{i \in N} \{C_j^X - d_j^X\}$ the maximum lateness of jobs,

$\sum w_j U_j^X$ the total weighted number of late jobs,

where $X = S, M, C$ are for the supplier, manufacturer, and centralized system, respectively. The internal cost is measured by the delivery cost $\sum D_g^X y_g^X$

for $X = S, M$, and $\sum D_g^S y_g^S + \sum D_g^M y_g^M$ for $X = C$. Moreover, when the objective is to minimize the number of late jobs, it is assumed that any late jobs would never be produced and delivered.

For the supplier's problem under the objective of minimizing the sum of flow times and the delivery cost, which is denoted as problem $1 || \sum C_j^S + \sum D_g^S y_g^S$, the optimal schedule is to sequence jobs of each manufacturer by a shortest-processing-time (SPT) order. Let $f(q) = f(q_1, \ldots, q_G)$ denote the minimum total cost for processing and delivering jobs $(1, g), \ldots, (q_g, g)$ for $g = 1, \ldots, G$. Then, a dynamic programming algorithm can be derived accordingly:

$$f(q) = \min_{(q_g', g) \in J} \{(q_g - q_g')T + D_g^S + f(q')\},$$

where

$$J = \{(q_g', g)\} | 1 \le g \le G, q_g > 0, 0 \le q_g' < q_g\}; \quad T = \sum_{g=1}^{G} \sum_{j=1}^{q_g} p_{ig}^S;$$

and

$$q' = (q_1, \ldots, q_{g-1}, q_g', q_{g+1}, \ldots, q_G),$$

with the boundary condition $f(0, \ldots, 0) = 0$.

While the above algorithm is optimal when minimizing the cost related to the total flow time, the weighted version of the problem belongs to the kind of unary NP-complete. For the problem of maximum lateness and number of late jobs, similar dynamic programs can be formulated by the idea of sequencing jobs according to the earliest due date (EDD) rule. Note that when minimizing the number of late jobs, we suppose that the late jobs are never produced and delivered, thus the schedule focuses on only on-time jobs and the late ones are ignored. The detailed algorithm can be found in Hall and Potts (2003).

For the manufacturer, neither the SPT ordering nor the EDD ordering stated above can be directly used for the job scheduling for the customers, because the release dates of jobs for the manufacturer are the delivery dates from the supplier, and thus might be different from each other. In this case, the schedule is designed based on the so-called "batch consistency" rule, which implies that if job i is received by the manufacturer before job j, then job i cannot be scheduled to deliver later than job j for the manufacturer. This assumption will simplify the problem largely, in that it allows some scheduling decisions to be made without waiting for the next incoming batch. For example, in the problem of minimizing the sum of flow times (and the delivery costs), a dynamic programming algorithm can be derived for the manufacturer by the following SPT-batch consistency rule: the jobs for the same customer and with the same release date are scheduled in the SPT order, which is motivated by the optimal scheduling rule when minimizing the total flow time within a batch. Similarly, EDD-batch consistency can be defined and applied into the problems of minimizing the maximum lateness and number of late jobs. Again, the consistency rule is used only for the on-time jobs in the latter problem.

In the centralized scenario, the supplier and manufacturer cooperate to solve a combined problem to minimize the total cost of the entire supply chain. The following three problems should be considered in a coordinating way: how to schedule the job processing at the supplier and manufacturers, how to schedule the job deliveries from the supplier to the manufacturers, and how to schedule the job deliveries from each manufacturer to customers. The problems can also be solved based on the SPT and EDD idea. For example, in the total flow time problem, a dynamic programming algorithm can be derived for the manufacturer by the following "total SPT within group" rule: the jobs for the manufacturers are sequenced in the SPT order according to the processing time of the supplier, and the jobs for each customer are sequenced in the SPT order according to the processing times of the two parties. Similarly, the "total EDD within group" rule can be defined and applied to the problems of maximum lateness and number of late jobs. Again, the rule is used only for the on-time jobs in the latter problem.

By comparison of the decentralized and centralized scheduling cases, we can find that substantial benefit is obtained from the cooperation between the supplier and manufacturers. The examples provided by Hall and Potts (2003) show that 20%, 25%, or up to arbitrarily close to 100% cost reduction can be achieved by the cooperation, under the objective of minimizing the flow time, the maximum lateness, or the number of late jobs, respectively. Different mechanisms should be provided to inspire the cooperation, such as offering incentives to encourage the supplier to deliver the entire jobs in a same order, or offering incentives to encourage the supplier to deliver part of the order earlier, depending on the specific case.

4.2 Assembly Supply Chain System

If a manufacturer requires jobs that are customized and supplied by multiple suppliers, an assembly system is to be adopted. Each supplier provides parts to the manufacturer, who has to wait until all parts of a job have been delivered and then start the final stage of the process. More specifically, we suppose that the manufacturer M receives from its customers n jobs, each of which consists of several parts to be processed at suppliers $S_1, \ldots, S_s$. The parts of one job can be processed concurrently by different suppliers. Each job j has a due date d_j, and let $p_{i,j}$ be the total processing time of parts of job j processed by supplier S_i. The delivery time from each supplier to the manufacturer and the processing time of each job at the manufacturer are both regarded as negligible.

Similarly with the previous subsection, the following notations are used to measure the performance of this supply chain.

C_{ij} the completion time at which the parts of job j are delivered from supplier S_i to the manufacturer

C_j the completion time of job j at the manufacturer, the value of which is equal to $\max_{1 \leq i \leq s} C_{ij}^S$

L_j^S the lateness of job j, the value of which is equal to $C_j^S - d_j^S$

Each schedule in the system consists of $n + 1$ subschedules faced by S suppliers $S_1, \ldots, S_S$ and one manufacturer M. In the decentralized scenario, each supplier S_i minimizes its work-in-process cost, which is measured by the total completion time of all jobs at the particular supplier, $\sum_{j=1}^{n} C_{ij}$. On the other hand, the QR environment requires the manufacturer to provide a higher customer service level. Therefore, the objective of the manufacturer is to minimize the total completion time of jobs, $\sum_{j=1}^{n} C_j$, which measures the average customer service, or to minimize the maximum lateness of jobs, $L_{\max} = \max\{L_j | 1 \leq j \leq n\}$, which measures the customer service in the worst case. In the centralized scenario, all the suppliers and the manufacturer jointly minimize the total system cost, measured by the total weighted cost of the suppliers and the manufacturer. The weight parameter α is used to convert the performance of the suppliers and manufacturer into common cost units. Thus, if we denote F_i as the objective of supplier i and G as one of the individual manufacturer, then the centralized system seeks to minimize the objective measured by $\alpha \sum_{i=1}^{n} F_i + (1 - \alpha)G$.

What the manufacturer cares about is the delivery date of the last part of each job, because the final stage of the job processing in the manufacturer requires all parts of that particular job simultaneously. Therefore, the performance of the manufacturer is dependent on the delivery time the supplier delivers the last part of the job, and thus the schedule planning of all suppliers. However, the suppliers focuses on minimizing their own costs, which are not, in general, in accordance with the manufacturer's best interest. Let ν and γ be (near) optimal schedules under a specific objective, respectively, and denote the relative error as the cost increment for the manufacturer when utilizing the optimal schedule for the suppliers $\frac{\sum_{j=1}^{n} C_j(\nu) - \sum_{j=1}^{n} C_j(\gamma)}{\sum_{j=1}^{n} C_j(\gamma)}$ or $\frac{L_{\max}(\nu) - L_{\max}(\gamma)}{L_{\max}(\gamma)}$. Note here $C_j(x)$ and $L_{\max}(x)$ denote the completion time of job j at the manufacturer and the maximum job lateness under schedule x, respectively. Extensive numerical studies show that in most cases the related error is above 10%, and for the maximum lateness case the error becomes arbitrarily large when n goes to infinity.

The incentive mechanism to solve these significant conflicts depends on specific scenarios for the relative bargaining power of the suppliers and manufacturer. For example, in the case of "suppliers dominate, manufacturer negotiates," the suppliers have a dominant bargaining power over the manufacturer and determine their optimal schedule ν. The manufacturer may prefer another schedule σ for its own interest and has to provide some incentive to induce the suppliers to choose σ rather than ν. Denote π as the optimal schedule for the centralized problem. In this case, it can be easily seen that the optimal strategy of the manufacturer is to offer an incentive $u_i = \alpha[F_i(\pi) - F_i(\nu)]$ to each supplier S_i; therefore, schedule π can be automatically implemented. Other scenarios, such as "manufacturer dominates, suppliers negotiate," "manufacturer dominates, supplier adjust," and "suppliers and manufacturer cooperate" can also be investigated and we refer the reader to Chen and Hall (2007) for the detailed discussion.

5 Conclusion

Nowadays, enterprises are facing crucial challenges from competitors and serving more demanding consumers in the global market. To remain competitive, establishing an efficient QR system becomes a common and important practice for enterprises in terms of cost reduction and customer satisfaction improvement. The topic of this chapter is related to supply chain scheduling under QR, with a discussion on the following three classes of problems.

The first problem refers to the scheduling of customer orders, motivated by the fact that today's customers usually place orders consisting of several different components or in need of several job operations. The customers are more focusing on the performance with respect to the entire order rather than some specific job within the order. We study the problems of scheduling jobs on either parallel machines or dedicated machines and present efficient heuristics to minimize the (weighted) average order completion time in each case. The second problem involves in the scheduling with outsouring option. We first study the case in which the jobs have been selected on single outsourced machine, which has discontinuous available time shifts. Then we study a logistics scheduling model for the coordination of in-house production and outsourcing, with the consideration of batch transportation issue and related costs.

All above models belong to the class of centralized optimization. However, a dominant partner in the supply chain may dictate terms to other supply chain members, thereby squeezing out the system profit while decreasing the overall performance of the entire supply chain. It is the objective of Sect. 4 to investigate this conflict and also the coordination issue on the supply chain scheduling. We consider first the case where a supplier makes deliveries to several manufacturers, who may in turn supply several customers, and then the case where multiple suppliers provide parts to a manufacturer. The models for both centralized and decentralized scenarios are introduced and analyzed. It has been pointed out that conflicting scheduling decisions of the supply chain members will generate significant cost and the cooperation mechanism is in need to solve this conflict.

We believe there is still great potential in the field of supply chain scheduling under QR. Possible further directions include the problem with more complicated supply chain structure, for example, the problem with multiple subcontractors, or one subcontractor concentrating on a two-stage supply chain, etc. Another promising research opportunity might be the negotiation problem between the manufacturer and subcontractor, within the framework of bargaining theory or other cooperative game theory.

Acknowledgements This work is partly supported by National Nature Science Foundation of China (No. 70501014, 70971069), 985 Project of National Center on Business Management and Institutional Innovation of China in Nankai University, and 2009 Humanities and Social Science Youth Foundation of Nankai University NKQ09027.

References

Abumaizar RJ, Svestka JA (1997) Rescheduling job shops under random disruptions. Int J Prod Res 35(7):2065–2082

Agnetis A, Hall NG, Pacciarelli D (2006) Supply chain scheduling: sequence and coordination, Discrete Appl math 154:2044–2063

Ahmadi RH, Bagchi U, Roemer T (2005) Coordinated scheduling of customer orders for quick response. Nav Res Logist 52:493–512

Alagoz O, Azizoglu M (2003) Rescheduling of identical parallel machines under machine eligibility constraints. Eur J Oper Res 149:523–532

Blocher JD, Chhajed D (1996) The customer order lead time problem on parallel machines. Nav Res Logist 43(5):629–654

Cai XQ, Lee CY, Vairaktarakis GL (2005) Optimization of processing and delivery decisions involving third-party machines. Nonlinear Anal 63:2269–2278

Caricato P, Grieco A (2008) An online approach to dynamic rescheduling for production planning applications. Int J Prod Res 46(16):4597–4617

Chauhan SS, Gordon V, Proth JM (2007) Scheduling in supply chain environment. Eur J Oper Res 183(3):961–970

Chen ZL, Hall NG (2007) Supply chain scheduling: Conflict and cooperation in assembly systems. Oper Res 55(6):1072–1089

Chen ZL, Li CL (2008) Scheduling with subcontracting options. IIE Trans 40:1171–1184

Chen ZL, Pundoor G (2006) Order assignment and scheduling in a supply chain. Oper Res 54: 555–572

Chung D, Lee K, Shin K et al (2005) A new approach to job shop scheduling problems with due date constraints considering operation subcontracts. Int J Prod Econ 98(2):238–250

Fisher M, Raman A (1996) Reducing the cost of demand uncertainty through accurate response to early sales. Oper Res 44(1):87–99

Hall NG, Potts CN (2003) Supply chain scheduling: Batching and delivery. Oper Res 51(4): 566–584

Hall NG, Potts CN (2005) The coordination of scheduling and batch deliveries. Ann Oper Res 135:41–64

Kreipl S, Pinedo M (2004) Planning and scheduling in supply chains: An overview of issues in practice. Prod Oper Manag 13(1):77–92

Lee IS, Sung CS (2008a) Minimizing due date related measures for a single machine scheduling problem with outsourcing allowed. Eur J Oper Res 186:931–952

Lee IS, Sung CS (2008b) Single machine scheduling with outsourcing allowed. Int J Prod Econ 101:623–634

Lee YH, Jeong CS, Moon C (2002) Advanced planning and scheduling with outsourcing in manufacturing supply chain. Comput Ind Eng 43:351–374

Li H, Li Z, Li LX, Hu B (2000) A production rescheduling expert simulation system. Eur J Oper Res 124(2):283–293

Ouelhadj D, Petrovic S (2009) A survey of dynamic scheduling in manufacturing systems. J Scheduling 12(4):417–431

Ovacik IM, Uzsoy R (1994) Rolling horizon algorithms for a single-machine dynamic scheduling problem with sequencedependent set-up times. Int J Prod Res 32(6):1243–1263

Qi XT (2008) Coordinated logistics scheduling for in-house production and outsourcing. IEEE Trans Autom Sci Eng 5(1):188–192

Ruiz-Torres AJ, Ho JC, Lopez FJ (2006) Generating pareto schedules with outsource and internal parallel resources. Int J Prod Econ 103:810–825

Sawik T (2009) Coordinated supply chain scheduling. Int J Prod Econ doi:10.1016/j.ijpe.2008.08.059

Shapiro BP, Rangan VK, Sviokla JJ (1992) Staple yourself to an order. Harvard Business Rev
    70(4):113–121

Vairaktarakis G, Cai XQ (2007) Cooperative strategies for manufacturing planning with negotiable
    third-party capacity. Working Paper. http://weatherhead.case.edu/academics/departments/
    operations/research/
    technicalReports/Technical%20Memorandum%20Number%20820.pdf

Wu SD, Storer RH, Chang PC (1993) One machine rescheduling heuristics with efficiency and
    stability as criteria. Comput Oper Res 20(1):1–14

Yang J (2005) The complexity of customer order scheduling problems on parallel machines.
    Comput Oper Res 32(7):1921–1939

Yang J, Posner ME (2005) Scheduling parallel machines for the customer order problem.
    J Scheduling 8:49–74

Dynamic Pricing of Seasonal Product without Replenishment: A Discrete Time Analysis

Zhongjun Tian

Abstract We study dynamic pricing of seasonal product in the revenue management context. A retailer places an order a long time before the beginning of a
short selling season, knowing that dynamic pricing will be applied. There is no
opportunity of inventory replenishment. Customer arrival follows a Poisson process.
The realized demand intensity is price sensitive. We analyze this intensity control
problem in a discrete time framework. The approach is applicable to all but one
(the multiplicative) common demand models. Our numerical study shows that this
approach is accurate. We also compare the performances of dynamic pricing and
static pricing. We find that the value of dynamic pricing is significant as long as
inventory is not abundant. We provide useful managerial insights for retailers and
managers on when to adopt dynamic pricing policy and when to switch between the
two pricing policies.

Keywords Dynamic pricing · revenue management · inventory control

1 Introduction

Dynamic pricing in the revenue management context is characterized by (1) perishable products; (2) no inventory replenishment; and (3) stochastic and price sensitive
demand. It has been widely applied in traditional revenue management dominated
industries such as airlines, hotels, cruise lines, and rental cars. Recent years have
seen a spread of dynamic pricing to other industries. For example, more and more
retail stores have adopted dynamic pricing as a reaction to the lengthened lead time
due to outsourcing and the fast changing customer tastes.

In a typical single retail product dynamic pricing settings, a retailer places an
order a long time before the beginning of the selling season, knowing that dynamic

Z. Tian
School of International Business Administration, Shanghai University of Finance and Economics
777 Guoding Road, Shanghai, 200433 China
e-mail: tian.zhongjun@mail.shufe.edu.cn

T.C. Edwin Cheng and T.-M. Choi (eds.), *Innovative Quick Response Programs*   159
in Logistics and Supply Chain Management, International Handbooks on Information
Systems, DOI 10.1007/978-3-642-04313-0_8,
© Springer-Verlag Berlin Heidelberg 2010

pricing will be applied. There is no opportunity of inventory replenishment. Customer arrival is a continuous stochastic process, while demand realization is price sensitive. At the end of the selling season, all leftovers are salvaged, and any unsatisfied demand is lost with no penalty cost. Upon the arrival of the order, the retailer's problem is to find a pricing policy that maximizes the total expected revenue generated over the selling season. This is a continuous time stochastic optimal control problem.

For this optimal control problem, Kincaid and Darling (1963) present the optimality condition (the HJB equation) when prices are posted in their seminal work. They also study the case where prices are not posted and in the multiple products case. Gallego and van Ryzin (1994) (GvR94 for short hereafter) re-derive the HJB equation and prove structural properties of optimal policies for homogenous Poisson demand process. GvR94 point out that obtaining a unique solution to the HJB equation is quite difficult for arbitrary regular demand functions, although they do find an exact solution for the exponential demand model. If no solution to the HJB equation can be found, one way to solve such an optimal control problem is discretizing the time horizon and converting the continuous optimal control problem to a discrete time dynamic programming problem.

In this chapter, we present a discrete time dynamic programming approach, which works effectively for large number of time period and is applicable to all but one (the multiplicative) common demand models. In each period, price is adjusted according to the latest information on the inventory level and the remaining time periods. In modeling, we consider a Poisson demand process and approximate it by a Binomial process to implement dynamic pricing in discrete time framework.

There are a considerable body of literature on dynamic pricing. Three up-to-date papers provide thorough review of the literature from different perspectives. McGill and van Ryzin (1999) focus on the research in revenue management in transportation, covering pricing as well as many other issues, such as forecasting, overbooking, and seat inventory control. Bitran and Caldentey (2003) dedicate to the pricing models for revenue management, mainly in the retail environment. Elmaghraby and Keskinocak (2003) take inventory into consideration in a dynamic pricing context. To save space, only closely related papers will be reviewed here. Readers are referred to the above review papers for complete bibliography.

Following Kincaid and Darling (1963) and GvR94, a bunch of papers study single product dynamic pricing with Poisson demand process. Zhao and Zheng (2000) extend the problem to nonhomogeneous demand and derive new structural properties of optimal policies. Bitran and Mondschein (1997) study periodic pricing of seasonal products in retailing. They consider a situation where prices are allowed to change only at specific instants in time, along with monotonically decreasing price paths. Bitran et al (1998) extend the model in Bitran and Mondschein (1997) to a retail chain. Netessine (2006) studies the case where there is a limit on the number of times that price can be adjusted, but the timing of price change is also a decision variable. Some other papers add restrictions on the number of the admissible prices but not on the number of possible price changes and the timing of such changes, for example, Chatwin (2000), Feng and Xiao (2000a), and Feng and Xiao (2000b). Gallego and van Ryzin (1997) extend the basic model in GvR94 to network revenue management. They derive the HJB equation for the multiple product case and study two heuristics based on the solution of the deterministic version of the problem. Other works on multiple product dynamic pricing include Talluri and van Ryzin (2004) and Maglaras and Meissner (2006).

Two recent papers approach the single product dynamic pricing problem with non-Poisson demand process. Monahan et al (2004) study the dynamic pricing problem from a newsvendor's perspective. They assume isoelastic demand function but the random demand process is general. They find a strong parallelism between the dynamic pricing problem and dynamic inventory models. They develop structural properties and present an efficient algorithm for computing the optimal prices. Xu and Hopp (2006) assume that customer arrival follows a geometric Brownian motion and homogeneous customers have an isoelastic demand function. They find a closed-form optimal pricing policy under which the inventory clearance price is optimal.

The rest of this chapter is organized as follows. In the next section, we introduce the control model of dynamic pricing in the continuous time framework. In Sect. 3, we present the discrete time approach and apply it to some common demand models. We also provide a theoretical pricing guideline for retailers and managers. In Sect. 4, through extensive numerical study, we investigate the accuracy of the discrete time approach and the value of dynamic pricing compared to static pricing. Some extensions are discussed in Sect. 5, followed by our conclusions in Sect. 6. All proofs are placed in the Appendix.

2 Control Model

2.1 Timing and Assumptions

In our model, time is indexed backward following the convention in the revenue management literature, that is, the beginning and end of the selling season is represented by $t = T$ and $t = 0$, respectively. Besides, the ordering time is denoted by $T_+, T_+ > T$. We use the subscript t to denote time and $[t, s]$ with $t \geq s$ to represent the time horizon from t to s. At T_+, the retailer places an order specifying the initial inventory $x_T \in \mathbb{N}^+$. We assume that the delivery lead-time is too long and the selling season is too short to allow replenishment during the selling season. The retailer receives the shipment of the order by the beginning of the selling season $t = T$ when customers start to arrive. Customer arrival is a homogeneous Poisson process with time-invariant intensity $\lambda_0 \in (0, \infty)$ (the nonhomogeneous Poisson process is discussed in the extension section). If the product is priced at r, an arrived customer buys a unit of the product with probability $P(r)$. We assume that customers are non-strategic, and so $P(r)$ depends only on the current price $r_t \in \mathbb{R}^+$. We also assume that there always exists a no-purchase choice for the customer, and thus $P(r)$ is nonincreasing in r. We call $P(r)$ the *purchase probability* and $P_0(r) = 1 - P(r)$ the *no-purchase probability*. Therefore, the expected demand rate is a Poisson process with intensity $\lambda_0 P(r)$. We assume that the selling season is closed whenever the product is sold out at any time $t > 0$; otherwise, the selling season ends at time $t = 0$ with all unsold units salvaged.

At any time t during the selling season, the retailer monitors the inventory level x and sets the price r_t to control the demand rate $\lambda_0 P(r_t)$. We use $\mathbf{r} = \{r_t, 0 \leq t \leq T\}$ to denote the sequence of price and call it the *pricing policy* or *price scheme*. As λ_0 is beyond the control of the retailer, controlling demand rate is equivalent to controlling the purchase probability $P(r_t)$. Hence, without loss of optimality, we work on $P(r)$ hereafter. We assume that $P(r)$ is a *regular* function satisfying the following assumptions proposed in GvR94.

1. There is a one-to-one correspondence between prices and purchase probabilities so that $P(r)$ has an inverse, denoted by $r(P)$.
2. The *revenue rate*

$$\zeta(P) = \lambda_0 P r(P) \tag{1}$$

satisfies $\lim_{P \to 0} \zeta(P) = 0$, is continuous, bounded and concave, and has a bounded least maximizer defined by $P^* = \min\{P : \zeta(P) = \max_{P \geq 0} \zeta(P)\}$.

Assumption (1) allows us to use the purchase probability $P(r)$ instead of the price r to control the dynamic system, while assumption (2) ensures that the optimal control can be obtained by solving the Hamilton–Jacobi–Bellman equation. The limitation in assumption (2) also implies the existence of a null price $r_{+\infty}$ for which $\lim_{r \to r_{+\infty}} P(r) = 0$ and $\lim_{r \to r_{+\infty}} r P(r) = 0$. The null price acts to turn off the demand process and is applied only when the product is sold out.

2.2 Control Problem

Let N_t denote the counting process of the number of sales up to time t. N_t is a stochastic point process with Markovian intensity controlled by a nonanticipating pricing policy $\mathbf{r}$ through the purchase probability function $P(\mathbf{r})$. If a customer arrives and chooses to buy a unit of the product at time t, then $dN_t = 1$, otherwise, $dN_t = 0$.

For a given selling season with length T and initial inventory level x_T, the expected revenue of a price scheme $\mathbf{r}$ is

$$J_T^{\mathbf{r}}(x_T) = E_{\mathbf{r}}\left[\int_0^T r_t \, dN_t\right]. \tag{2}$$

The retailer's problem is to find a pricing policy $\mathbf{r}^*$ that maximizes the total expected revenue generated over the selling season, denoted by $\pi_T(x_T)$. Equivalently,

$$\pi_T(x_T) = \sup_{r \in \mathbb{R}^+ \times [T,0)} J_T^r(x_T). \tag{3}$$

An optimal solution to (3) can be found in principle through the HJB sufficient condition:

$$\frac{\partial}{\partial t} \pi_t(x) = \sup_{P \in [0,1]} \lambda_0 P[r(P) - \Delta \pi_t(x)], \tag{4}$$

where $\Delta \pi_t(x) = \pi_t(x) - \pi_t(x-1)$ and π_t satisfies boundary conditions

$$\pi_t(0) = 0 \ \forall t, \tag{5}$$
$$\pi_0(x) = 0 \ \forall x. \tag{6}$$

Note in (6) that the salvage value is normalized to zero without loss of generality.

With the optimal expected revenue given by (3), we determine the optimal initial inventory level. Since we consider a short selling season, the holding cost is assumed negligible and the revenue flow is not discounted. Also, following the convention in the revenue management literature, all unsatisfied demand is lost with no penalty cost. We assume constant procurement cost, but it is readily to extend the model to any convex cost function. Denote the unit procurement cost by c and define the expected profit at time T as

$$V_T(x_T) = \pi_T(x_T) - c x_T. \tag{7}$$

The initial inventory decision made at time T_+ is then formulated as

$$x_T^* = \underset{x_T \in \mathbb{N}^+}{\operatorname{argmax}} V_T(x_T). \tag{8}$$

3 Optimal Pricing Solutions

In dynamic pricing, one has to take into account the future value of the marginal unit inventory when setting the current price. This value is represented by $\Delta \pi_t(x)$ in (4). $\Delta \pi_t(x)$ also can be understood as the marginal opportunity cost, as it is the expected loss of selling this particular unit rather than holding it to the remaining selling season. We define the *adjusted revenue rate* as

$$\xi_t(x) = \lambda_0 P[r(P) - \Delta \pi_t(x)]. \tag{9}$$

If an optimal solution to (4) exists, then $\sup \xi_t(x) = \max \xi_t(x)$. Thus, to solve (4), it suffices to find a maximizer of $\xi_t(x)$. The value of $\Delta \pi_t(x)$ depends on both x and t but not on P, as P is the retailer's action. So $\Delta \pi_t(x)$ is a constant when we maximize $\xi_t(x)$ by changing P. As $\zeta(P) = \lambda_0 P r(P)$ is concave, $\xi_t(x)$ is concave in P, too. Thus, the first order condition gives

$$r(P) + P r'(P) = \Delta \pi_t(x). \tag{10}$$

Let $P_t^*(x)$ denote the optimal purchase probability and define

$$m_t(x) = -P_t^*(x) r'(P_t^*(x)). \tag{11}$$

Then, the optimal price is

$$r_t^*(x) = \Delta \pi_t(x) + m_t(x). \tag{12}$$

The implication of (12) is clear. As $\Delta \pi_t(x)$ is the opportunity cost of selling a marginal unit of inventory, the product must be priced higher than $\Delta \pi_t(x)$, with the difference representing profit. Thus, $m_t(x)$ in (12) is the net revenue margin of one sale at price $r_t^*(x)$. Note that $m_t(x)$ is always non-negative, as $r'(P) \leq 0$ by the assumption of nonincreasing property of $P(r)$.

Substituting (12) into (4) gives

$$\frac{\partial}{\partial t} \pi_t(x) = \lambda_0 P_t^*(x) m_t(x). \tag{13}$$

From (10) and (11), $P_t^*(x)$ depends only on $\Delta \pi_t(x)$, while $m_t(x)$ is a function of $P_t^*(x)$. Thus, (13) is a difference-differential equation (DDE) of $\pi_t(x)$. By (12), the pricing problem reduces to solving a DDE. In general, there is no exact closed-form solution to this DDE. Probably the only exception is the case of exponential demand. As discussed in both Kincaid and Darling (1963) and GvR94, for exponential demand function defined by $D(r) = \lambda_0 e^{-br}$, $b > 0$, the optimal solution to (13) is

$$\pi_t(x) = \frac{1}{b} \ln \left(\sum_{i=0}^{x} (\lambda_e^* t)^i \frac{1}{i!} \right), \tag{14}$$

where $\lambda_e^* = \lambda_0/e$ is the myopic demand rate.

In the case of $b = 1$, (14) is identical to (9) of GvR94. We should note that here we do not normalize b to 1 as GvR94 does. From our numerical results we find that a general b makes it easier to compare the performance of dynamic pricing policy for different demand functions.

3.1 Discrete Time Approach

We use a discrete time approach to apply dynamic pricing to more general demand models. First we discretize the time and rescale the time horizon so that the intensity of the customer arrival process, which is now the expected arrival per unit time period, is much less than one. With such small λ_0, the probability of one arrival in each period is approximately λ_0, and the probability of no arrival is approximately $1 - \lambda_0$, while the probability of more than one arrival is negligible. Then we approximate the Poisson demand process by a Binomial process. The event of a sale in one period is a successful trial in a Bernoulli trial. The probability of such an event is $\lambda_0 P(r)$, which implies that a customer arrives and makes a purchase. On the other hand, the probability of no sale is $1 - \lambda_0 P(r)$, which results from either no arrival, with probability $1 - \lambda_0$, or no purchase upon arrival, with probability $\lambda_0[1 - P(r)]$. The discrete time adjusted revenue rate is

$$\xi_t^d(x) = \lambda_0 P[r(P) - \Delta \pi_{t-1}(x)]. \tag{15}$$

As $\Delta \pi_{t-1}(x)$ is independent of P, $\xi_t^d(x)$ is concave in P. Thus, both the Principle of Optimality and the HJB sufficient condition apply to the discrete time version optimization problem. Specifically, the control problem is to find a pricing policy $\mathbf{r}^*$ that maximizes the total expected revenue generated over the selling season, denoted by

$$\pi_T(x_T) = \sup_{r \in \mathbb{R}^+ \times T} J_T^r(x_T),$$

where $J_T^r(x_T)$ is the expected revenue of a price scheme $\mathbf{r}$ for a giving selling season with periods T and initial inventory level x_T, denoted by

$$J_T^r(x_T) = E_{\mathbf{r}} \left[\sum_{t=1}^{T} r_t \, dN_t \right].$$

The new HJB sufficient condition is

$$\nabla \pi_t(x) = \sup_{P \in [0,1]} \lambda_0 P[r(P) - \Delta \pi_{t-1}(x)],$$

where $\nabla \pi_t(x) = \pi_t(x) - \pi_{t-1}(x)$ and $\pi_t(x)$ satisfies the boundary conditions (5)–(6).

3.2 Optimal Discrete Time Solutions

Replacing $\Delta \pi_t(x)$'s in (10)–(13) by $\Delta \pi_{t-1}(x)$, we have the following discrete time optimal solutions.

Proposition 1. *Suppose the purchase probability function $P(r)$ is regular. For any time $t \in \{T, \ldots, 1\}$ with inventory $x \in \mathbb{N}^+$,*

(1) The optimal purchase probability $P_t^*(x)$ is the unique solution of

$$r(P) + P r'(P) = \Delta \pi_{t-1}(x)$$

(2) The optimal price is

$$r_t^*(x) = \Delta \pi_{t-1}(x) + m_t(x)$$

(3) The maximum expected revenue is

$$\pi_t(x) = \pi_{t-1}(x) + \lambda_0 P_t^*(x) m_t(x) \tag{16}$$

We apply Proposition 1 to various demand functions. We consider all common demand functions except the constant-elasticity demand in the form of $D(r) = \lambda_0 a r^{-b}, a, b > 0$, as it does not satisfy our second assumption. The purchase probability $P(r)$ corresponding to the demand functions to be discussed is defined in Table 1. The last column of Table 1 gives the derivative of $P(r)$ in r, which will be used in the next section.

3.2.1 Linear Demand

To ensure $P \in [0, 1]$, we define the linear demand function as $D(r) = \lambda_0 P(r) = \lambda_0(1 - br), b > 0$, for $r \in [0, r_{+\infty}]$, where $r_{+\infty} = 1/b$ is the null price to shut down the demand process.

Corollary 1. *Suppose the purchase probability is linear in price, that is, $P(r) = 1 - br, b > 0$. For any time $t \in \{T, \ldots, 1\}$ with inventory $x \in \mathbb{N}^+$,*

(1) The optimal revenue margin is $m_t(x) = \frac{1}{2b} - \frac{1}{2} \Delta \pi_{t-1}(x)$
(2) The optimal purchase probability is $P_t^*(x) = \frac{1}{2} - \frac{b}{2} \Delta \pi_{t-1}(x)$
(3) The optimal price is $r_t^*(x) = \frac{1}{2b} + \frac{1}{2} \Delta \pi_{t-1}(x)$
(4) The maximum expected revenue is $\pi_t(x) = \pi_{t-1}(x) + \frac{b \lambda_0}{4} \left[\frac{1}{b} - \Delta \pi_{t-1}(x) \right]^2$

Table 1 Purchase probability

Demand	$P(r)$	$P_0(r)$	$P'(r)$
Linear	$1 - br$	br	$-b$
Exponential	e^{-br}	$1 - e^{-br}$	$-bP(r)$
MNL	$\frac{e^{a-r}}{1+e^{a-r}}$	$\frac{1}{1+e^{a-r}}$	$-P(r)P_0(r)$
MCI	$\frac{ar^{-b}}{1+ar^{-b}}$	$\frac{1}{1+ar^{-b}}$	$-\frac{b}{r} P(r) P_0(r)$

3.2.2 Exponential (Log-Linear) Demand

The exponential demand is defined as $D(r) = \lambda_0 P(r) = \lambda_0 e^{-br}$, $b > 0$, for $r \in \mathbb{R}^+$. The null price is $r_{+\infty} = \infty$.

Corollary 2. *Suppose the purchase probability is exponential in price, that is,* $P(r) = e^{-br}$, $b > 0$. *For any time* $t \in \{T, \dots, 1\}$ *with inventory* $x \in \mathbb{N}^+$,

(1) The optimal revenue margin is $m_t(x) = \frac{1}{b}$
(2) The optimal purchase probability is $P_t^*(x) = e^{-b\Delta\pi_{t-1}(x)-1}$
(3) The optimal price is $r_t^*(x) = \Delta\pi_{t-1}(x) + \frac{1}{b}$
(4) The maximum expected revenue is $\pi_t(x) = \pi_{t-1}(x) + \frac{\lambda_0}{b} e^{-b\Delta\pi_{t-1}(x)-1}$.

3.2.3 MNL Demand

The MNL demand function is based on the Multinomial Logit model, one of the two well-known market share attraction (MSA) models in determining the market shares of competitive products. In the basic "us/(us+them)" form of the MSA models, us and them represent the attractiveness of a particular retailer and all its competitors, respectively, and the ratio is the retailer's market share. In the MNL model, the attractiveness of each alternative is denoted by $e^{(a_i-r_i)/\mu}$, where a_i and r_i are the quality index and price, respectively, and $u_i = a_i - r_i$ is the mean utility. μ is the common scale parameter of the i.i.d. Gumbel random variables, which reflect the stochasticity of consumer utility. Since we do not explicitly model the competition between the retailer and its competitors, all the alternatives from the competitors are modeled as an outside choice with attractiveness $e^{u_0/\mu}$, while u_0 is the mean utility of the outside choice. Without loss of generality, we can assume $u_0 = 0$ and $\mu = 1$. Also, we drop the subscript of a_i and r_i. Then the purchase probability is defined by

$$P(r) = \frac{e^{a-r}}{1 + e^{a-r}}, \tag{17}$$

where $r \in \mathbb{R}^+$. The null price is $r_{+\infty} = \infty$.

Corollary 3. *Suppose the purchase probability is given by the MNL model, that is,* $P(r) = e^{a-r}/(1 + e^{a-r})$, *where a is a finite constant. For any time* $t \in \{T, \dots, 1\}$ *with inventory* $x \in \mathbb{N}^+$,

(1) The optimal revenue margin $m_t(x)$ *is the unique solution of*

$$(m - 1)e^m = e^{a-\Delta\pi_{t-1}(x)} \tag{18}$$

(2) The optimal purchase probability is $P_t^*(x) = 1 - \frac{1}{m_t(x)}$
(3) The optimal price is $r_t^*(x) = \Delta\pi_{t-1}(x) + m_t(x)$
(4) The maximum expected revenue is $\pi_t(x) = \pi_{t-1}(x) + \lambda_0[m_t(x) - 1]$

3.2.4 MCI Demand

Now we consider the other one of the two well-known MSA models, the multiplicative competitive interaction (MCI) model. In the MCI model, the attractiveness of each individual product is denoted by $u_i = a_i^{\alpha_i} r_i^{-b_i}$, where a_i and r_i are the quality index and price of product i, respectively, and α_i and b_i are positive parameters that reflect customer sensitivity to the quality and price, respectively. We model all the products of the competitors as an outside choice with attractiveness u_0. We also drop the subscript of a_i, r_i, α_i, and b_i. Without loss of generality, we assume $u_0 = 1$ and $\alpha = 1$. Then the purchase probability is defined by

$$P(r) = \frac{ar^{-b}}{1 + ar^{-b}}, a > 0, b > 1, \tag{19}$$

where $r \in \mathbb{R}^+$. The null price is $r_{+\infty} = \infty$.

Corollary 4. *Suppose the purchase probability is given by the MCI model, that is, $P(r) = ar^{-b}/(1 + ar^{-b})$, $a > 0$, $b > 1$. For any time $t \in \{T, \dots, 1\}$ with inventory $x \in \mathbb{N}^+$,*

(1)   The optimal revenue margin $m_t(x)$ is the unique solution of

$$(b - 1)m - \Delta\pi_{t-1}(x) = a[m + \Delta\pi_{t-1}(x)]^{1-b} \tag{20}$$

(2)   The optimal purchase probability is

$$P_t^*(x) = 1 - \frac{1}{b} - \frac{\Delta\pi_{t-1}(x)}{bm_t(x)} \tag{21}$$

(3)   The optimal price is $r_t^*(x) = \Delta\pi_{t-1}(x) + m_t(x)$

(4)   The maximum expected revenue is $\pi_t(x) = \pi_{t-1}(x) + \frac{\lambda_0}{b}[(b-1)m_t(x) - \Delta\pi_{t-1}(x)]$

It is clear from Corollaries 1–3 that, in the linear and MNL demand models, the optimal revenue margin $m_t(x)$ is decreasing in $\Delta\pi_{t-1}(x)$, while in the exponential demand model, $m_t(x)$ is a constant. Thus, $m_t(x)$ is nonincreasing in $\Delta\pi_{t-1}(x)$ in all these models. But it is not always the case in the MCI model. Taking the derivative of m in $\Delta\pi_{t-1}(x)$ on both sides of (20) gives

$$m' = \frac{(2 - b)m + \Delta\pi_{t-1}(x)}{(b - 1)m}.$$

For $b = 2$, $m' = \Delta\pi_{t-1}(x)/m > 0$. Thus, $m_t(x)$ is strictly increasing in $\Delta\pi_{t-1}(x)$ (in fact, (20) becomes $m = [a + (\Delta\pi_{t-1}(x))^2]^{1/2}$ for $b = 2$). For $b > 2$, the denominator is positive but $(2 - b)m < 0$, so m' might be positive or negative, which implies that $m_t(x)$ does not necessarily change in $\Delta\pi_{t-1}(x)$ monotonically.

3.3 Pricing Guideline

From Corollaries 1–4, at any time t during the selling season, all $r_t^*(x)$, $P_t^*(x)$, and $\pi_t(x)$ depend only on $\Delta\pi_{t-1}(x)$, directly or indirectly through $m_t(x)$. This property not only enables us to implement the dynamic pricing policy through backward dynamic programming, but also implies some pricing guideline to the retailers.

It is useful to introduce here the notion of inventory scarcity in the context of discrete time dynamic pricing. We say that inventory is scarce if the inventory level is lower than the maximum possible demand in the remaining selling season. For a Poisson arrival process, the maximum possible demand is infinite for any length of remaining season. Thus, in our original continuous time model, inventory is always scarce, unless it is infinite. In contrast, for the approximate binomial process, the demand in each period is either one or zero, and consequently, the maximum possible demand in any remaining season is no more than the number of the remaining periods. Therefore, in the discrete time model, at any time t during the selling season, if the inventory level x is lower than the number of the remaining periods t, inventory is scarce; otherwise, there is no inventory scarcity. Equivalently, $\Delta\pi_{t-1}(x) > 0$ if $x < t$ and $\Delta\pi_{t-1}(x) = 0$ if $x \geq t$. Moreover, as the demand in each period is at most one, once $x_t \geq t$ holds for some t, $x_s \geq s$ holds for any time $s < t$. In such a case, there is no inventory scarcity at any time in the remaining season in any sample path. This observation implies the following property.

Corollary 5. *Suppose the purchase probability function $P(r)$ is regular. For any $t \in \{T,\ldots,1\}$ and $x \in \mathbb{N}^+$,*
(1) If $x < t$, $r_t^*(x)$ is strictly decreasing in x and strictly increasing in t
(2) If $x \geq t$, $r_t^*(x)$ is equal to the myopic price and the price is fixed for the remaining selling season

Corollary 5(1) is the discrete time version of the price part of Theorem 1 of GvR94. Corollary 5(2) highlights the role of inventory scarcity in dynamic pricing. That is, if the number of the remaining periods reaches the inventory level, fixed pricing is optimal. Although the optimal inventory decision usually leads to some initial inventory scarcity for nonzero procurement cost, as the arrivals follow Poisson process, there exists a positive probability of no sale for a long time and subsequently the inventory level and the remaining time periods match. In this case, the retailer should simply fix the price at the myopic price from that time point on. *Therefore, Corollary 5(2) gives an important guideline on when to switch from a dynamic pricing policy to a static pricing policy without loss of optimality.*

4 Numerical Study

Our numerical study focuses on two aspects: (1) the performance of the discrete time approach in terms of *accuracy* relative to the original continuous time dynamic pricing; (2) the value of dynamic pricing, that is, the revenue/profit gain compared to static pricing.

Through this section, the Poisson arrival rate is $\lambda_0 = 0.1$ for all $t \in [T, 0]$. Such homogeneous Poisson arrival process enable us to compare the performance of dynamic pricing to static pricing. The parameters of the demand functions are given in Table 2. It can be verified that, with these parameters, the myopic prices for the six demand functions are all equal to 5, which ensure that the comparison of the performance of dynamic pricing for different demand functions is fair. Recall that for the MCI demand, the revenue margin $m_t(x)$ behaves differently for $b = 2$ and $b > 2$. So we consider three cases, $b = 2, 3, 4$, and denote them by MCI-b2, MCI-b3, and MCI-b4, respectively.

Before moving on to the investigation of the accuracy, we take a brief look at the behavior of the optimal price and the optimal revenue margin. Consider a remaining selling season with 500 periods. Figure 1 shows the optimal price $r_t^*(x)$ and its two components $m_t(x)$ and $\Delta\pi_{t-1}(x)$ for $x = 1, \ldots, 50$. Not surprisingly, both $r_t^*(x)$ and $\Delta\pi_{t-1}(x)$ strictly decrease in x in all the six demand models, but the behavior of $m_t(x)$ is not always consistent. In particular, $m_t(x)$ does not change in $\Delta\pi_{t-1}(x)$ monotonically for MCI-b3 and MCI-b4, which verifies the discussion at the end of

Table 2 Demand parameters (b in linear and exponential and a in the others)

	Linear	Exponential	MNL	MCI-b2	MCI-b3	MCI-b4
	0.1	0.2	6.39	25	250	1875

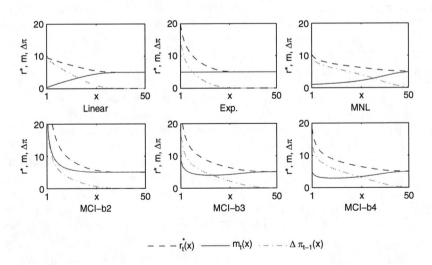

Fig. 1 Optimal price and its components, $t = 500$

the last session. The same behaviors can be observed if we fix the inventory x and change the remaining time t.

In the rest of this section, we consider a time period $t = 500$ in two scenarios: (1) dynamic pricing for given inventory; and (2) joint dynamic pricing and inventory setting. While the second scenario corresponds to a typical joint inventory and pricing decision made at time T^+ (with $t = T$), the first scenario involves the pricing decision only and may occur at any time before and during the selling season. In the second scenario, the procurement cost plays a role in the initial inventory decision and should be taken into account.

4.1 Accuracy

The existence of the closed-form solution (14) enables us to evaluate the accuracy of the discrete time approach for exponential demand. We consider the two scenarios with and without inventory decision.

In the first scenario, we let x range from 1 to 50 to see the accuracy in situations with different inventory scarcity. As the expected arrivals in the remaining season is $\lambda_0 t = 50$, a small x means severe inventory scarcity and a large x close to 50 implies mild inventory scarcity. In Fig. 2, the left and middle column show the results given by the continuous (cont.) and discrete (disc.) time models, respectively, while the right column shows the accuracy, where ε's are defined by

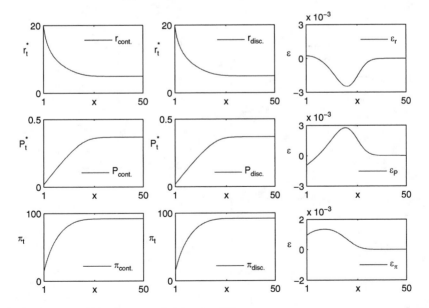

Fig. 2 Accuracy without inventory decision, $t = 500$

$$\varepsilon_\kappa = \frac{\kappa_{\text{disc.}} - \kappa_{\text{cont.}}}{\kappa_{\text{cont.}}}, \ \kappa = r, P, \pi. \tag{22}$$

From Fig. 2, the price given by the discrete time approach is very close to the price of the original continuous time model. The deviation is within 0.3% for all $x = 1, \dots, 50$. For x close to 50, the deviation vanishes as the inventory scarcity decreases, and both the discrete price and the continuous price converge to the myopic price. The deviation of the purchase probability is also within 0.3%, while the deviation of the expected revenue is within 0.2%. The reason for the higher accuracy of the expected revenue is that the expected revenue is determined by the price and the purchase probability, but they deviate in reverse directions.

In the second scenario, we look at the performance of the discrete time approach in the presence of inventory setting. We let the procurement cost c increase from 0.5 to 5. Figure 3 shows that the discrete time approach provides exactly the same optimal initial inventory level as the original continuous model does. From Fig. 3, we can see that the initial inventory level decreases in c, which is intuitive, as higher c means less profitable and results in lower initial inventory level. We note that the deviation of the expected profit, which is defined by (22) with $\kappa = V$, is larger than that of the expected revenue for the same x. The reason is that, for same x, $\pi_{\text{disc.}} - \pi_{\text{cont.}} = V_{\text{disc.}} - V_{\text{cont.}}$ but $V_{\text{cont.}} < \pi_{\text{cont.}}$, and thus, $\varepsilon_V > \varepsilon_\pi$.

Another observation worthy of being mentioned is that the discrete time approach tends to overrate the expected revenue/profit, as $\varepsilon_V > 0$ and $\varepsilon_\pi > 0$ for all c. This is the result of the binomial process approximation, as it underestimate the variance of

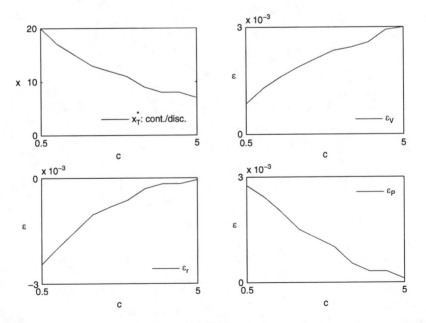

Fig. 3 Accuracy with inventory decision, $T = 500$

the customer arrivals. For a Poisson process, the expectation of the demand in each period is $\lambda_0 P(r)$, which is also the variance. Meanwhile, for a binomial process, the expectation is also $\lambda_0 P(r)$, but the variance is $\lambda_0 P(r) P_0(r)$, which is smaller than $\lambda_0 P(r)$, as $P_0(r) < 1$.

4.2 Value of Dynamic Pricing

The value of dynamic pricing is reflected by the revenue/profit gain compared to the static (i.e., nondynamic) pricing policy. We investigate the revenue gain in the first scenario, where inventory is given, and the profit gain in the second scenario, where inventory is a decision variable.

4.2.1 When Inventory is Given

From Fig. 1 we can see that the optimal price is sensitive to the inventory level for small x, but when x is close to 50, the optimal price converges to the myopic price. The convergence occurs much earlier in the linear, exponential, and MCI-b2 models than in the others. Suppose that from some time point on, the retailer fixes the price in the rest of the selling season. He will suffer a revenue loss due to the adoption of the fixed price, as he is no longer able to adjust the price according to the actual demand realization. In contrast, suppose the retailer switches from static pricing to dynamic pricing at any time during the selling season, he will enjoy a revenue gain. Intuitively, the revenue gain depends on the inventory scarcity and the demand model. Figure 4 shows the relative revenue gain of dynamic pricing (DP) compared to static pricing (SP), that is, $[\pi_{DP}(x) - \pi_{SP}(x)]/\pi_{SP}(x) \times 100\%$.

From Fig. 4, there exists a threshold of inventory level in each demand model. When inventory is higher than the threshold, the value of dynamic pricing vanishes.

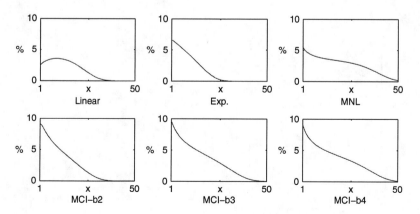

Fig. 4 Value of dynamic pricing for given inventory, $t = 500$

In the MNL, MCI-b3, and MCI-b4 models, the threshold is very close to 50, but in
the linear, exponential, and MCI-b2 models, it is much lower than 50. In any case,
the threshold is around or lower than the expected arrivals in the remaining selling
season ($\lambda_0 t = 50$), and is much lower than the number of the periods in the remaining season (t = 500). *Therefore, this observation provides a much more practical
pricing guideline than the analytical result presented in Sect. 3.3, which requires the
inventory being higher than or equal to t to fix the price without loss of optimality.*
We note that the revenue gain is strictly decreasing in inventory level in all
demand models except for small x in the linear demand. This exception is caused by
the noninfinite null price of the linear demand. If inventory level is low, the advantage of dynamic pricing is significant, as the retailer can increase the price to control
the demand rate so that the expected revenue is maximized, which is infeasible for
static pricing. In all other demand models, the lower the inventory, the higher the
advantage, and hence, the higher the revenue gain. Moreover, there is no limitation
of the revenue gain, as the null price, which acts to shutdown the demand, is infinite.
Nevertheless, in the linear demand model, the null price is $1/b$, which means that if
the price is higher than $1/b$, the demand is lost. Therefore, when x decreases in a
low range, the price increase is limited by the null price, and thus, the advantage of
dynamic pricing decreases.

4.2.2 When Inventory is a Decision Variable

Now we incorporate the initial inventory decision to investigate the value of dynamic
pricing. For this purpose, we compare the maximum expected profit of the optimal
dynamic pricing with that of the static pricing at the corresponding optimal inventory levels. Such comparison is of great interest to firms seeking justifications of or
implementing dynamic pricing practice at the ordering time.
Figure 5 shows the relative profit gain of dynamic pricing compared to static
pricing, that is, $[V^*_{DP}(x^*_{DP}) - V^*_{SP}(x^*_{SP})]/ V^*_{SP}(x^*_{SP}) \times 100\%$, for c from 0.5 to 5. We

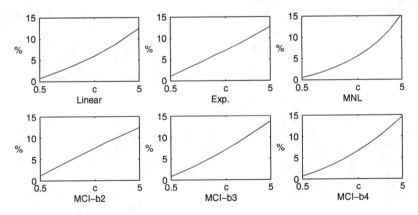

Fig. 5 Value of dynamic pricing with inventory decision, $T = 500$

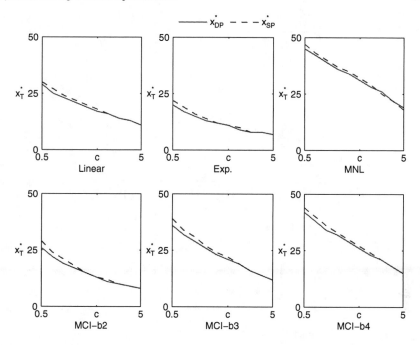

Fig. 6 Optimal initial inventory in c, $T = 500$

note that V_{DP}^* and V_{SP}^* are achieved at x_{DP}^* and x_{SP}^*, respectively. These two x^*'s may be the same or different for given c, as shown in Fig. 6.

From Fig. 5, we see that the value of dynamic pricing is significant so long as c is not too low, and the value of dynamic pricing is more sensitive to the procurement cost than the demand types and parameters. On the one hand, in all demand models, the profit gain is above 5% for $c = 2.5$, which is 50% of the myopic price, and is about 10% for $c = 4$, which is 80% of the myopic price. On the other hand, as c increases, the trajectories of the profit gain in different demand models are much closer than the trajectories of the revenue gains in Fig. 4. Therefore, after the inventory decision is incorporated, dynamic pricing becomes an attractive tool, regardless of the demand models.

One observation from Fig. 6 is noticeable. We note that the optimal initial inventory level given by dynamic pricing is almost always lower than that given by static pricing. More interestingly, this difference shrinks as c increases. Now suppose the initial inventory level is determined by static pricing, but the retailer decides to switch to dynamic pricing at the beginning of the selling season. The maximum expected profit after switching to dynamic pricing is $V_{DP}^*(x_{SP}^*)$. We call the dynamic pricing starting with inventory x_{DP}^* the *original*, and the one starting with inventory x_{SP}^* the *hybrid*. Figure 7 shows that the relative revenue gain from hybrid dynamic pricing is very close to that from original dynamic pricing. On the one hand, if c is high, the initial inventory given by static pricing is near optimal for dynamic pricing.

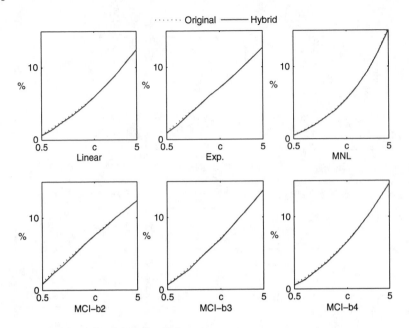

Fig. 7 Value of dynamic pricing, $T = 500$

On the other hand, if c is low, the initial inventory given by static pricing is higher than the optimal level corresponding to dynamic pricing; but since c is low, the profit loss due to overstocking is small. Therefore, in both cases, the maximum expected profit of hybrid dynamic pricing is very close to that of the original dynamic pricing. The managerial insight we can derive from this observation is that, *even if the retailer determines the initial inventory and places order using static pricing, he still can enjoy the benefit of dynamic pricing by changing pricing policy at the beginning of the selling season.*

5 Extensions

The discrete time approach can be applied in a straightforward manner to two extensions of the model. First, it can apply to an environment where the demand parameters evolve over time. For example, the quality index in the MNL model decays as time passes. One way of modeling such change is to allow b (resp., a) to increase (resp., decrease) over time in a deterministic fashion. All previous results hold by changing b (resp., a) to b_t (resp., a_t). Second, it can apply to an environment where the customer arrival rate is nonhomogenous in time. For example, traffic to stores might be higher on weekend than on week days; traffic to websites may vary from day time to night time. All previous results hold by replacing λ_0 by λ_t, where λ_t is a function of t.

Another natural extension is from the single product case to the multiproduct case. Suppose that a customer has more than one choice (excluding the no-purchase choice) from the retailer. For example, the retailer may sell two or more differentiated products. Then we have to consider the substitution effect, which cannot be well modeled by the linear and exponential demand models. In contrast, the MNL and the MCI models are two well-known market share attraction models in determining the market shares of competitive products. Dong et al (2009) study the joint problem of dynamic pricing and inventory control of substitute products. They adopt the MNL model to capture the customer choice behavior, that is, the demand substitution effect. They show that there exists a revenue margin $m_t(x)$, which acts as the common lower bound of the optimal prices. For any product i in stock at time t, the optimal price $r_t^{i*}(x)$ is composed of $m_t(x)$ and its own marginal future value, denoted by $\Delta^i \pi_t(x) = \pi_t(x) - \pi_t(x - e^i)$. There is only one equation of m to solve for given time and inventory level, but the number of possible inventory levels at consequent time periods increase sharply as the size of the assortment increases. Because of such curse of dimensionality, the backward dynamic programming does not work as well as in the single product case.

The application to the MCI model is limited to the special case of $\alpha_i \equiv \alpha$ and $b_i \equiv b$ for all products. In such a symmetric case, the revenue margin must be equal for all products, and thus, the problem can be solved in a similar way as in the MNL model. In all other cases, the situation is much worse. For example, if $b_i \equiv b$ for all products but $\alpha_i \neq \alpha_j$ for some products i and j, the difference between $r_t^{i*}(x)$ and $\Delta^i \pi_t(x)$ varies from product to product. In other words, each product has its own revenue margin and there does not exist a common revenue margin. Because of the demand substitution effect, these revenue margins must be obtained by solving multiple equations of the prices jointly, which could be very complicated.

6 Conclusions

We have presented a discrete time approach for the classic dynamic pricing problem in the revenue management context, where the product is perishable and there is no opportunity of inventory replenishment. The approach is applicable to all but one common demand models. Through extensive numerical study, we have shown that the discrete time approach is accurate in applying dynamic pricing to general regular demand models. We also have shown that, when inventory is scarce, dynamic pricing dominates static pricing by bringing significant revenue/profit gain. Our numerical study provides some useful managerial insights. On the one hand, unless the procurement cost is very low, dynamic pricing is always preferred in the joint decision of pricing and inventory setting. Even if the amount of the order is determined by static pricing, the retailer can use dynamic pricing from the beginning of the selling season and still enjoy significant benefit of such hybrid dynamic pricing. On the other hand, at any time during the selling season, if inventory is close to the expected arrivals in the remaining selling season, the retailer can switch back to static pricing to save the additional management cost of dynamic pricing.

Appendix: Proof of Theoretical Results

Proof of Proposition 1. Omitted.

Proof of Corollary 1. We show the regularity of the purchase probability function first. As $P'(r) = -b < 0$, $P(r)$ is strictly decreasing in r and there exists a one-to-one correspondence between r and P. The inverse of $P(r)$ is $r(P) = (1 - P)/b$. Also, it is easily seen that the revenue function $\zeta(P) = \lambda_0 P(1 - P)/b$ is continuous and satisfies $\lim_{P \to 0} \zeta(P) = 0$. As $\zeta' = \lambda_0(1 - 2P)/b$ and $\zeta'' = -2\lambda_0/b < 0$, ζ is concave and there is a unique maximizer $P_l^* = 1/2$ given by the FOC. As $\zeta(P) \geq 0$ for $P \in [0, 1]$ and $\zeta(P_l^*) = \lambda_0/(4b)$ is finite, ζ is bounded. So, all the assumptions of a regular demand function are satisfied.

As $r'(P) = -1/b$, $P_t^*(x)$ is given by $(1 - P)/b - P/b = \Delta\pi_{t-1}(x)$. By definition, $m_t(x) = -P_t^*(x)r'(P_t^*(x)) = 1/(2b) - \Delta\pi_{t-1}(x)/2$. Then $r_t^*(x) = \Delta\pi_{t-1}^*(x) + m_t(x) = 1/(2b) + \Delta\pi_{t-1}(x)/2$ and $\pi_t(x)$ follows from (16). $\qquad\square$

Proof of Corollary 2. As $P'(r) = -be^{-br} < 0$, $P(r)$ is strictly decreasing in r and there exists a one-to-one correspondence between r and P. The inverse of $P(r)$ is $r(P) = -(\ln P)/b$. The revenue function is $\zeta(P) = -\lambda_0 P(\ln P)/b$, which is continuous. By l'Hospital's rule, $\lim_{P \to 0} P \ln P = 0$, so $\lim_{P \to 0} \zeta(P) = 0$. As $\zeta' = -\lambda_0(1 + \ln P)/b$ and $\zeta'' = -\lambda_0/(bP) < 0$, ζ is concave and there is a unique maximizer $P_e^* = 1/e$ given by the FOC. As $\zeta(P) \geq 0$ for $P \in [0, 1]$ and $\zeta(P_e^*) = \lambda_0/(be)$ is finite, ζ is bounded. So, all the assumptions of a regular demand function are satisfied.

As $r'(P) = -1/(bP)$, $P_t^*(x)$ is given by $-(\ln P)/b - 1/b = \Delta\pi_{t-1}(x)$. By definition, $m_t(x) = -P_t^*(x)r'(P_t^*(x)) = 1/b$. Then $r_t^*(x)$ follows and so does $\pi_t(x)$. $\qquad\square$

Proof of Corollary 3. As $P'(r) = -e^{a-r}/(1 + e^{a-r})^2 < 0$, $P(r)$ is strictly decreasing in r and there exists a one-to-one correspondence between P and r. The inverse of $P(r)$ is $r(P) = a + \ln(1/P - 1)$. The revenue function is $\zeta(P) = \lambda_0 P[a + \ln(1/P - 1)]$, which is continuous. By l'Hospital's rule we have $\lim_{P \to 0} P \ln(1/P - 1) = 0$, so $\lim_{P \to 0} \zeta(P) = 0$. As $\zeta' = \lambda_0[a + \ln(1/P - 1) - 1/(1 - P)]$ and $\zeta'' = -\lambda_0/[P(1 - P)^2] < 0$, ζ is concave and there is a unique maximizer implicitly given by the FOC. Specifically, P^* satisfies $a + \ln(1/P^* - 1) = 1/(1 - P^*)$. Then $\zeta(P^*) = \lambda_0 P^*/(1 - P^*)$. As $P^* \in [0, P(0)]$ and $P(0) = e^a/(1 + e^a) < 1$, $\zeta(P^*) < \infty$, that is, ζ is bounded. Thus, all the assumptions of a regular demand function are satisfied.

As $r'(P) = -/[P(1 - P)]$ and $m_t(x) = -P_t^*(x)r'(P_t^*(x))$, we have $m_t(x) = 1/[1 - P_t^*(x)]$, which gives $P_t^*(x) = 1 - 1/m_t(x)$. Substituting $P_t^*(x)$ into $r(P_t^*(x)) = \Delta\pi_{t-1}(x) + m_t(x_t)$ gives $m_t(x) + \ln[m_t(x) - 1] = a - \Delta\pi_{t-1}(x)$, which is equivalent to (18). The uniqueness of the solution to (18) comes from the fact that the LHS is monotone increasing in m, while the existence is straightforward since the RHS is a finite positive number and the LHS is zero for $m = 1$ and infinite for $m = \infty$. □

Proof of Corollary 4. As $P'(r) = -(b/a)r^{b-1}/(r^b/a + 1)^2 < 0$, λ is strictly decreasing in r and there exists a one-to-one correspondence between r and P. The inverse of $P(r)$ is $r(P) = [a(1/P - 1)]^{1/b}$. The revenue function is $\zeta(P) = \lambda_0 P[a(1/P - 1)]^{1/b}$. It is easily seen that $\zeta(P)$ is continuous and satisfies $\lim_{P \to 0} \zeta(P) = 0$. As $\zeta' = \lambda_0[1 - 1/(b(1 - P))]r(P)$ and $\zeta'' = -(b - 1)\lambda_0 t r(P)/[b^2 P(1 - P)^2] < 0$, ζ is concave and there is a unique maximizer $P^* = 1 - 1/b$ given by the FOC. As $\zeta(P) \geq 0$ for $\lambda \in [0, 1]$ and $\zeta(P^*) = \lambda_0(1 - 1/b)[a/(b - 1)]^{1/b}$ is finite, ζ is bounded. So, all the assumptions of a regular demand function are satisfied.

As $r'(P) = -r(P)/[bP(1 - P)]$ and $r(P_t^*(x)) = r_t^*(x) = \Delta\pi_{t-1}(x) + m_t(x)$, we have $m_t(x) = -P_t^*(x)r'(P_t^*(x)) = [m_t(x) + \Delta\pi_{t-1}(x)]/[b(1 - P_t^*(x))]$, which gives (21). We need to show that $m_t(x)$ is uniquely given by (20). As $r(P) = [a(1/P - 1)]^{1/b}$, substituting (21) into $[a(1/P_t^*(x) - 1)]^{1/b} = m_t(x) + \Delta\pi_{t-1}(x)$ gives (20). The existence and uniqueness of the solution to (20) comes from the fact that the LHS (resp., RHS) is monotone increasing (resp., decreasing) in m, while for $m = 0$ the LHS (resp., RHS) is negative (resp., positive). □

Proof of Corollary 5. Omitted.

References

Bitran G, Caldentey R (2003) An overview of pricing models for revenue management. Manuf Serv Oper Manag 5:203–209

Bitran G, Caldentey R, Mondschein S (1998) Coordinating clearance markdown sales of seasonal products in the retail chains. Oper Res 46:609–624

Bitran G, Mondschein S (1997) Periodic pricing of seasonal products in retailing. Manag Sci 43:64–79

Chatwin R (2000) Optimal dynamic pricing of perishable products with stochastic demand and a finite set of prices. Eur J Oper Res 125:149–174

Dong L, Kouvelis P, Tian Z (2009) Dynamic pricing and inventory control of substitute products. Manuf Serv Oper Manag 11:317–339

Elmaghraby W, Keskinocak P (2003) Dynamic pricing in the presence of inventory considerations: research overview, current practices and future directions. Manag Sci 49:1287–1309

Feng Y, Xiao B (2000a) A continuous-time yield management model with multiple prices and reversible price changes. Manag Sci 48:644–657

Feng Y, Xiao B (2000b) Optimal policies of yield management with multiple predetermined prices. Manag Sci 48:332–343

Gallego G, van Ryzin G (1994) Optimal dynamic pricing of inventories with stochastic demand over finite horizons. Manag Sci 40:999–1020

Gallego G, van Ryzin G (1997) A multiproduct dynamic pricing problem and its application to network yield management. Oper Res 45:24–41

Kincaid W, Darling D (1963) An inventory pricing problem. Math Anal Appl 7:183–208

Maglaras C, Meissner J (2006) Dynamic pricing strategies for multi-product revenue management problem. Manuf Serv Oper Manag 8:136–148

McGill J, van Ryzin G (1999) Revenue management: research overview and prospects. Transport Sci 33:233–256

Monahan G, Petruzzi N, Zhao W (2004) The dynamic pricing problem from a newsvendor's perspective. Manuf Serv Oper Manag 6:73–91

Netessine S (2006) Dynamic pricing of inventory/capacity with infrenquent price changes. Eur J Oper Res 174:553–580

Talluri K, van Ryzin G (2004) Revenue management under a general discrete choice model of consumer behavior. Manag Sci 50:15–33

Xu X, Hopp W (2006) A monopolistic and oligopolistic stochastic flow revenue management model. Oper Res 54:1098–1109

Zhao W, Zheng Y (2000) Optimal dynamic pricing for perishable assets with nonhomogeneous demand. Manag Sci 46:375–388

Supplier Selection in Make-to-Order Manufacturing

Jinfeng Yue, Yu Xia, Thuhang Tran, and Bintong Chen

Abstract When make-to-order (MTO) manufacturers receive unpredictable custom orders, they face a common challenge: quick supplier selection of custom parts and components. This challenge becomes even more serious when the order's customization level is high, the MTO's committed delivery time is short, the desired service level is high, and the missing delivery time penalty is severe. This chapter considers an MTO manufacturer who produces a product consisting of several custom parts that cannot be pre-inventoried. To respond to the custom order quickly, the MTO manufacturer can follow the procedures in this chapter to allocate orders to each supplier for each custom part and calculate the associated replenishment cost as well as the probability of meeting the delivery date, using the suppliers' jobs on hand, availability, process speed, and defective rate. For a given delivery time and service level, a replenishment cost frontier can be generated to provide a range of options to meet customer requirements. This innovative method can be further extended to the case when the delivery time is not fixed and the manufacturer needs to reduce its delivery time to win a customer bid.

Keywords Delivery time · Frontier portfolio · Make-to-order · Supplier selection

1 Introduction

Quick response to custom orders is a critical attribute for make-to-order manufacturer (MTO) operations. When receiving an unscheduled custom order with a short delivery deadline, an MTO manufacturer must quickly decide how much to order from each qualified supplier for each un-inventoried custom part. It is a key step

J. Yue (✉)
Department of Management and Marketing, Jennings Jones College of Business, MTSU Box 75
Middle Tennessee State University, Murfreesboro, TN 37132, USA
e-mail: jyue@mtsu.edu

T.C. Edwin Cheng and T.-M. Choi (eds.), *Innovative Quick Response Programs in Logistics and Supply Chain Management*, International Handbooks on Information Systems, DOI 10.1007/978-3-642-04313-0_9,
© Springer-Verlag Berlin Heidelberg 2010

for the MTO manufacturer to assure meeting the desired service level to maintain customer satisfaction. When the MTO manufacturer is in a bidding process for a customer contract, a short committed delivery time and a competitive offering price are key factors to winning contracts. If the manufacturer commits to an earlier date that is too short for production, it may win the contract at the risk of missing the delivery schedule, harming its reputation, and incurring late penalties. On the other hand, the manufacturer risks losing the contract altogether with a later committed delivery time. Similarly, a high price is a barrier to winning the contract while a low price may erode the MTO's profit. The decision of how much to order from each supplier for any custom part significantly influences the MTO manufacturer's lead time and cost, which affects the committed delivery time and price for contract bidding. Therefore, quick response in supplier selection also affects whether the MTO manufacturer wins the customer contract or not in a bidding process. How to respond quickly to the supplier selection issue is a challenge in practice.

Traditionally, Deming's 14 points would suggest that the manufacturer moves toward a single supplier for any one part based on the supplier's quality, loyalty, and reliability. This idea is valid for mass production systems with consistent demand. However, for custom orders with a limited timeframe, the sole part supplier may not have sufficient capacity to provide all the quantities required by the due date, and so it must use other suppliers to subcontract the part order. As a result, the MTO manufacturer may lose control over the subcontractor supplier selection, which affects quality and increases delivery time uncertainty. As an alternative, the MTO manufacturer can make its own selection by determining the multiple suppliers who are qualified for certification, and so any one custom part can have several certified suppliers available. When the MTO manufacturer receives a custom order, using information about supplier's quality, available capacity, costs, processing time, etc., it can determine the component portfolio for each supplier (i.e., which supplier produces what component and in what quantity) to achieve the desired service level or to shorten the delivery time. The innovative use of multiple suppliers for a single custom part does not contradict Deming's quality ideals from the suppliers' point of view. By selecting the suppliers and determining its portfolios, the MTO manufacturer may have better control, better product quality, more on-time delivery, and higher customer satisfaction for the custom order. This exemplifies the concept of vertical integration, where the manufacturer expands into the area of supplier selection.

This chapter aims to provide an analytical tool for MTO manufacturers to quickly select their suppliers while considering the on-time delivery and replenishment cost simultaneously through a systematic study of the trade-offs between these two factors. This innovative tool provides a pool of supplier selection options; among which, no option is better than another in terms of both cost and service level. The MTO manufacturer can choose a favored option based on its preference.

2 Literature Review

In a customer–manufacturer–supplier supply chain, an MTO manufacturer can gain competitive advantage in fulfilling the customer's contract (or bid on a contract) by how it manages its supplier selection and production processes. Because an MTO manufacturer cannot begin without an order, it must be able to control its lead time from the start of the supplier selection process until the order is delivered (Cakravastia et al. 2002). Consequently, the extant research on controlling delivery time for MTO manufacturers has focused in three general areas along the supply chain.

The first research stream examines how the manufacturer can improve its delivery time through its production facilities using job sequencing and queuing. Recommendations include sequencing policies, such as first-come-first-served (FCFS) or earliest due date (EDD), to take into account customer preferences for due date and price trade-offs (Duenyas 1995; Keskinocak et al. (2001) and to account for the manufacturer's capacity constraints (Duenyas and Hopp 1995). Various factors can be taken into consideration to improve the MTO manufacturer's due date quotes, including information about work-in-progress (WIP), demand, lost sales, batch size, quality, and capacity (Hopp and Roof Sturgis 2000; Zipkin 2000). Dellaert (1991) developed a queuing model based on estimated arrival times, setup times, and service times to generate acceptable delivery times while minimizing storage and penalty costs. While some research have examined policies to minimize average lead times (Wein 1991; Spearman and Zhang 1999), Bookbinder and Noor (1985) included service-level constraints with exponentially modeled processing times to determine delivery time.

The second research area shifts the focus to the customer and examines the impact of the manufacturer's capacity, pricing, and lead-time policies on the customer's bid acceptance. In managing delivery time, the manufacturer can choose one of the two strategies: maintain a consistent and short lead-time by varying price and capacity or have variable lead times through stable pricing and capacity (Webster 2002). The first strategy would enable the manufacturer to earn higher but variable premiums, while the second option yields lower but consistent profits. To hedge against possible contract cancellations with fixed capacity, the MTO manufacturer may optimize price and lead time while considering contingent orders from other customers (Easton and Moodie 1999; Watanapa and Techanitisawad 2005). So and Song (1998) examined the interaction among capacity, delivery time, and price under different market conditions. Through their mathematical framework, they conclude that the ability to increase capacity at low costs gives the manufacturer more delivery time and pricing flexibility, though pricing flexibility is largely determined by the customer's delivery time elasticity. This flexibility gives the manufacturer more bargaining power in the bidding process with its customer (Lawrence 1994; El-Hafsi and Roland 1999; Moodie 1999). Research on lead-time quoting recognizes the need for coordination between the customer and the manufacturer's internal operations to determine attractive delivery dates for bidding. Researchers have used a Nash game theory model (Erkoc and Wu 2000), multistage decision-making model (Weng 1999), and information sharing between departments to develop marketing quotation policies (Chatterjee et al. 2002).

The third research stream moves backward along the supply chain to examine the impact suppliers have on delivery time. For a sole supplier, the manufacturer can improve delivery time through negotiations, but in the more typical case of multiple suppliers, both negotiation and selection are important. The supplier negotiation literature has focused on developing models to account for joint costs between the manufacturer and the supplier (Miller and Kelle 1998), using integrated data-envelopment analysis as a negotiation tool to assist the manufacturer in identifying efficient supplier points (Weber and Desai 1996), determining price and delivery times in multiple rounds of negotiation (Cakravastia and Nakamura 2002), and negotiating in noncooperative environments (Weber et al. 1998). As the number of available suppliers increases, bargaining power shifts to the manufacturer, and supplier selection becomes the main sourcing issue in terms of which suppliers and what order quantity. A review by De Boer et al. (2001) reveals that supplier selection models examined by previous researchers include rating/linear weighting, total cost approaches, mathematical programming, statistical models, and artificial intelligence-based models. Previous studies have focused primarily on either minimizing costs or minimizing lead time while using the other along with quality, discounts, or capacity as constraints (Jayaraman et al. 1999; Aissaoui et al. 2007).

This chapter introduces the concepts and methods in a research paper by the authors (Yue et al. 2009) that can address irregular custom orders. It provides an innovative and practical tool for an MTO manufacturer, whose custom product has a delivery time set by the customer (or is bid by the MTO manufacturer), but whose ability to fulfill the order by the delivery time is determined by the custom part suppliers. As the custom parts are the bottleneck, the manufacturer cannot improve its performance only through internal methods such as better job scheduling or sequencing to meet the delivery time. This method enables the MTO manufacturer to respond quickly to the customer's order by deciding how to select custom part suppliers and allocate quantities among selected suppliers under this restrictive case.

The proposed method is innovative in several ways. First, the model connects all three major players in the supply chain by incorporating the customer's desired delivery time (or a reasonable bid date), the MTO manufacturer's internal processing time, and the suppliers' costs, defect rate, capacity, and processing time. The inclusion of all three members in the supply chain model provides a more integrated, realistic, and complete picture. Second, the method extends other supplier selection methods by considering dual objectives: increasing service level (on time probability) and decreasing cost to meet a customer-defined delivery time. By using two factors in the selection model, the manufacturer can have multiple options, which form a selection "frontier" for a given delivery time. This method allows the MTO manufacturer to have flexibility in choosing its own preferred custom part suppliers by trading between cost and service level without additional investment in manufacturing capacity or other resources. Third, the method can help an MTO manufacturer determine the delivery time and cost for bidding a customer's contract in a competitive environment. Using this model, the MTO manufacturer can determine its shortest delivery time while still satisfying the desired service level. When the delivery time is reduced through "crashing," the MTO manufacturer can obtain a preferred option for contract bidding from the possible frontier choices with associated costs and service level.

3 Model Description

In this study, we consider the case where an MTO manufacturer needs several types of custom parts, and each type of custom part requires multiple units from a few certified suppliers. Once the manufacturer receives all the custom parts, it then assembles the parts to make the final MTO products. The customer may demand that the final products are finished before a certain delivery time, or the MTO manufacturer may establish an attainable delivery time for bidding. To meet the delivery time requirement, the MTO manufacturer has to determine the portfolio, that is, the order quantity for each supplier. The portfolio should be based on suppliers' availability, process speed, process quality, and cost as well as the customer's delivery time and manufacturer's service level. Since standard parts can be efficiently managed by material requirement planning methods and are usually not the bottleneck in finishing a custom order, this chapter focuses on the critical custom parts.

Assuming one particular order contains m custom parts; for each custom part $i (i = 1, 2, \ldots, m)$, N_i units are needed, and k_i certified suppliers (denoted as $S_{ij}, j = 1, 2, \ldots, k_i$) are available. The MTO manufacturer assembly time is assumed to be fixed. We are interested only in the custom part required time T, the time left for the suppliers to provide the custom parts to the manufacturer for final assembly, which equals the customer's order delivery time less the manufacturer's assembly time. Initially, we examine T as a given value, and later, we investigate how to "crash" or shorten T (Stevenson 2007). We also assume that the MTO manufacturer has a desired service level P, the required on time probability to complete the order by the customer's delivery time, or the probability of the manufacturer receiving all parts by time T. In the manufacturer's portfolio, the order quantity for supplier S_{ij} is n_{ij} units $(i = 1, 2, \ldots, m; j = 1, 2, \ldots, k_i)$, which is decided by the MTO manufacturer. To satisfy the assembly requirements, custom part i should meet the relationship

$$\sum_{j=1}^{k_i} n_{ij} = N_i.$$

Figure 1 describes the structure of this customer–manufacturer–supplier supply chain.

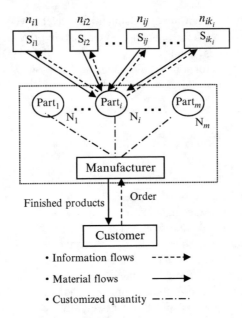

Fig. 1 Flows for multi-parts make-to-order manufacturer

3.1 Individual Supplier Performance

In this subsection, we focus on any individual supplier's performance. An individual certified supplier may not work exclusively for the manufacturer under consideration, but instead, it may have numerous jobs from various sources. Without losing generality, we assume that the supplier must finish some on hand jobs before processing the manufacturer's order. In practice, each supplier may have a different processing time for one unit of the custom part and a different quality level measured by the defect rate. The supplier under consideration may also process parts that are different from the particular custom part for the MTO manufacturer. According to the aggregate planning concept, the part quantity for the existing jobs can be converted to the MTO manufacturer's particular custom part quantity. In addition, since the supplier's quality should be consistent regardless of the various orders, the defect rate is assumed to remain the same when the existing jobs are converted to the manufacturer's particular custom part. When the manufacturer has a good relationship with its suppliers, the information about the suppliers' existing jobs can be shared between the two. Otherwise, the MTO manufacturer will have to estimate it from the suppliers' bidding or offering time (e.g., see Sahin and Robinson 2005). The need for this information highlights the importance of maintaining a good relationship with suppliers, as suggested by Deming.

Following the previous notation, supplier S_{ij} spends t_{ij} time to process one unit of custom part i, whether it is good or defective. The defect rate of supplier S_{ij} to process custom part i is $(1 - R_{ij})$, where R_{ij} is an index to show the quality differences among part suppliers. Before supplier S_{ij} starts work on the manufacturer's order, the existing on hand jobs aggregate to O_{ij} units of custom part i. If supplier S_{ij} cannot finish the on hand jobs by time T, it cannot be selected by the manufacturer for the new order; thus, one validation condition for supplier S_{ij} for the new order is

$$O_{ij} \times t_{ij} < T. \tag{1}$$

Within T, supplier S_{ij} can produce at most $\lfloor T/t_{ij} \rfloor$ units of aggregated custom part i (where $\lfloor x \rfloor$ represents the highest integer no larger than x), including both good and defective units. Therefore, the order quantity of custom part i for supplier S_{ij}, n_{ij}, has the upper bound $\overline{n_{ij}}$ defined as

$$n_{ij} \leq \overline{n_{ij}} = \lfloor T/t_{ij} \rfloor - O_{ij}. \tag{2}$$

The MTO manufacturer can assign the upper bound quantity to supplier S_{ij} only when the defect rate is zero.

Supplier S_{ij} needs to produce O_{ij} good aggregated part i before processing the manufacturer's order with assigned n_{ij} units of custom part i. To be able to produce $(n_{ij} + O_{ij})$ good units of (aggregated) part i to fulfill the order, the number of total units (both good and defective) produced ranges from any number no less than $(n_{ij} + O_{ij})$ up to infinity. Furthermore, to finish the assigned job by time T, the total number of units (both good and defective) should be no more than $(\overline{n_{ij}} + O_{ij})$. Theoretically, the probability for the total number of units produced follows a negative binomial (Pascal) distribution, which has appeared in the extant literature in operations management (e.g., Nandakumar et al. 1993; Yue and Wang 2004). The on time probability for supplier S_{ij} for assigned n_{ij} units by time T is determined by

$$P_{ij}(n_{ij}) = \begin{cases} 0, & n_{ij} > \overline{n_{ij}}; \\ \sum_{k=n_{ij}+O_{ij}}^{\overline{n_{ij}}+O_{ij}} \binom{k-1}{n_{ij}+O_{ij}-1} \\ (R_{ij})^{(n_{ij}+O_{ij})}(1-R_{ij})^{(k-n_{ij}-O_{ij})}, & 0 < n_{ij} \leq \overline{n_{ij}}; \\ 1, & n_{ij} = 0. \end{cases} \tag{3}$$

As mentioned in Deming's 14 points, the replenishment cost from a supplier is not only the tagged price, but it also includes the costs to build and maintain the relationship to assure quality. We use F_{ij} to describe the fixed cost (e.g., the relationship maintenance and quality assurance cost) and V_{ij} to describe the unit variable cost of replenishing from supplier S_{ij}. Therefore, the total cost to replenish n_{ij} units of part i from supplier S_{ij} is

$$C_{ij}(n_{ij}) = F_{ij} \times b_{ij} + V_{ij} \times n_{ij}, \quad \text{where} \quad b_{ij} = \begin{cases} 0 & n_{ij} = 0; \\ 1 & n_{ij} > 0. \end{cases} \tag{4}$$

In the above equation, b_{ij} is a binary variable to indicate if supplier S_{ij} is selected by the MTO manufacturer. Equations (3) and (4) provide the on time probability for the given delivery time and the associated total cost for any certified supplier, respectively.

3.2 Multiple Suppliers Performance for a Particular Part

For a particular custom part, the MTO manufacturer may select multiple suppliers to fulfill the customer's order by the delivery time. This subsection determines the probability function and the associated cost function for finishing a particular custom part by a given time if multiple suppliers are involved.

In practice, the longest finishing time of the selected suppliers determines the finishing time for a custom part. An order for a particular custom part is fulfilled by part required time T only when all selected suppliers have finished their assigned quantities on time. Therefore, for a given set of quantity assignment $n_{ij}(j = 1, 2, \ldots, k_i)$, the on time probability for custom part i for a given part required time T is the multiplication of all k_i certified suppliers' on time probabilities:

$$P_i(n_{ij}, j = 1, 2, \ldots, k_i) = \prod_{j=1}^{k_i} P_{ij}(n_{ij}). \tag{5}$$

The associated cost function for replenishing part i is obtained by the sum of the cost functions of all k_i certified suppliers

$$C_i(n_{ij}, j = 1, 2, \ldots, k_i) = \sum_{j=1}^{k_i} C_{ij}(n_{ij}). \tag{6}$$

How to decide the set $n_{ij}(j = 1, 2, \ldots, k_i)$, called the *part portfolio*, for custom part i, to maximize the probability in (5) with the smallest possible cost in (6) is discussed in Sect. 4.

3.3 All Parts for a Custom Order

Before final assembly, the MTO manufacturer should receive all custom parts so that the starting time for assembly is given by the longest finishing time of all custom parts. To fulfill the customer order, the MTO manufacturer must have all custom parts ready and begin assembly before time T. Therefore, the probability of no delays for an order is the on time probability for all parts by a given part required time T, which equals the multiplication of the on time probabilities for each individual custom part by time T

$$P(i = 1, 2, \ldots, m; n_{ij}, j = 1, 2, \ldots, k_i) = \prod_{i=1}^{m} P_i(n_{ij}, j = 1, 2, \ldots, k_i). \quad (7)$$

The associated total part replenishment cost is the addition of the replenishment costs of all custom parts

$$C(i = 1, 2, \ldots m; n_{ij}, j = 1, 2, \ldots k_i) = \sum_{i=1}^{m} C_i(n_{ij}, j = 1, 2, \ldots, k_i). \quad (8)$$

Once the MTO manufacturer determines the portfolio for each custom part, the on time probability for the order is obtained by (7). If this probability is greater than the desired service level P, the portfolio, denoted as $n_{ij}(i = 1, 2, \ldots, m; j = 1, 2, \ldots, k_i)$, called the *order portfolio*, is valid for the given order. In addition, knowledge about the total replenishment cost can help the manufacturer success-fully bid on the customer contract. Thus, both decreasing the part replenishment cost and increasing the on time probability for the order are major considerations when the manufacturer chooses the order portfolio. In Sect. 4, we demonstrate how these two factors can be combined to select the portfolios when a delivery time is given. Then, we show how a manufacturer can reduce the committed delivery time for bidding purposes with this approach.

4 Frontier Portfolio Solutions

In Sect. 3.2, we defined a part portfolio as a part quantity assignment for all valid suppliers for a particular custom part and an order portfolio as a valid combination of part portfolios for all custom parts to finish the order. We also calculated the on time probabilities and the part replenishment costs for both the part and order portfolios. Both factors are used to evaluate both part and order portfolios. In com-paring two portfolios A and B, if A has lower cost and equal or higher probability than B, or A has equal or lower cost and higher probability than B, then A is supe-rior to B and B is inferior to A. However, a superior relationship may not always exist between two portfolios. Since a single optimal portfolio with both the highest probability and lowest cost may not exist, we obtain several portfolios that form a frontier. Both a part frontier portfolio and an order frontier portfolio have the follow-ing properties: any frontier portfolio is not superior to any other frontier portfolio, but any non-frontier portfolio is inferior to at least one frontier portfolio. See Fig. 3 for an example with the on time probability for the order represented on the Y-axis, cost on the X-axis, and the points denote portfolios, with linked points identifying the frontier portfolios. The part and order frontier portfolios have the following rela-tionships: (1) any part frontier portfolio is a candidate for the order frontier portfolio but may not necessarily be chosen for the order portfolio, and (2) any order frontier portfolio must contain only part frontier portfolios. Therefore, the search for the final order frontier begins with the search for the part frontiers for all critical custom parts.

4.1 Part Portfolio Frontier Search

This subsection describes the part portfolio frontier search process for a particular custom part i ($i = 1, 2, \ldots, m$) with N_i units and k_i certified suppliers. Only l_i number of suppliers ($l_i \leq k_i$) can satisfy (1) and are valid for the new job. To determine the frontier, all combinations of suppliers are examined. First, we look at the case of one supplier to finish the entire units for the custom part i. To be placed into the initial frontier pool, a single supplier must have sufficient capacity to finish the job with the desired service level and is not inferior to any other supplier. The reason for satisfying the desired service level is that if the part on time probability is less than the desired service level, the final order cannot meet the desired service level.

Next, all possible combinations of multiple suppliers are tested to see if any can improve the frontier. To ensure that the final order service level is met, only the portfolio that maximizes the on time probability while satisfying the desired service level is considered. It is compared with all existing frontier pool portfolios. If it is not inferior to any frontier pool portfolios, it is placed into the frontier pool. If any existing frontier pool portfolio is inferior to this portfolio, the existing pool portfolio is removed from the frontier pool.

Without losing generality, the valid suppliers S_{ij} ($j = 1, 2, \ldots, l_i$) are re-ranked in increasing order of their unit variable cost V_{ij} ($V_{i1} \leq V_{i2} \leq \cdots \leq V_{il_i}$) to keep costs low. The search process follows the steps in *Search Procedure I*.

Search Procedure I

Step 1. We start with an empty frontier pool, $\Omega = (\emptyset)$

Step 2. Consider the portfolio with only one supplier, let $j = 0$;

2.1 Let $j = j + 1$, check condition (2) for supplier S_{ij}. If the upper bound meets the condition $\overline{n}_{ij} \geq N_i$, supplier S_{ij} may be able to complete the job by itself, go to 2.2. Otherwise, supplier S_{ij} does not have enough capacity to finish the job alone and is not considered for the pool. Check if $j = l_i$; if yes, go to Step 3, otherwise go to 2.1.

2.2 Calculate the on time probability $P_{ij}(N_i)$ from (3) for the supplier S_{ij}. If $P_{ij}(N_i) \geq P$, calculate the replenishing cost $C_{ij}(N_i)$ from (4) for the supplier S_{ij}, go to 2.3. Otherwise, supplier S_{ij} cannot satisfy the desired service level, and is not considered for the pool. Check if $j = l_i$; if yes, go to Step 3, otherwise go to 2.1.

2.3 Compare the portfolio ($n_{ij} = N_i$) with all pool portfolios. If this portfolio is inferior to any pool portfolio, it should not be in the pool. Otherwise, put portfolio ($n_{ij} = N_i$) into pool Ω. If any existing pool portfolio is inferior to the portfolio ($n_{ij} = N_i$), remove the inferior pool portfolio from the pool Ω. Check if $j = l_i$; if yes, go to Step 3, otherwise go to 2.1.

Step 3. Consider the portfolio with multiple valid suppliers. Let $j = 1$.

3.1 Let $j = j+1$. Consider the portfolios with j number suppliers
3.2 Determine all possible combinations of j number suppliers among the valid l_i suppliers
3.3 Check if a combination can be put into the pool
3.3.1 For a combination of suppliers, find the highest probability portfolio by *Search Procedure II*
3.3.2 If the probability is higher than the desired service level P, calculate the associated cost by (6). Otherwise, go to Step 3.3.4
3.3.3 Compare the portfolio with all portfolios in the pool Ω. If this portfolio is inferior to any pool portfolio, it should not be in the pool. Otherwise, place it into the pool Ω. If any existing pool portfolio is inferior to the portfolio, remove the inferior pool portfolio from the pool Ω
3.3.4 Confirm all combinations of j number suppliers have been checked. If no, for another combination, go to 3.3.1
3.4 Check if $j = l_i$, if no, go to 3.1. Otherwise, the part frontier is obtained. Stop the procedure

Search Procedure II finds the highest probability portfolio for any combination of j number of suppliers. To keep costs low, the maximum possible quantity is first assigned to the supplier with the lowest variable cost, and only one unit is assigned to each remaining supplier. The portfolio is adjusted by moving one unit from one supplier to another to incrementally maximize the on time probability. Once the probability can no longer be improved by moving one unit, the highest probability portfolio for this combination is found.

Search Procedure II

Step 1. Without losing generality, order the j suppliers by increasing unit variable cost. Denote the suppliers as $S_1, S_2, \ldots, S_j$.

Step 2. Initially assign $q_1 = N_i-(j-1)$ quantity to supplier S_1, and $q_2 = q_3 = \cdots = q_j = 1$ unit to the remaining $(j-1)$ suppliers.

Step 3. Calculate the probability $P_i(q_1, q_2, \ldots, q_j)$ by (5) and let $\tilde{P} = P_i(q_1, q_2, \ldots \ldots, q_j)$.

Step 4. Find the maximum probability portfolio by moving only one unit from one supplier to another supplier,

4.1 Let $r = 1$
4.2 Check if $q_r = 1$, if yes, go to step 4.4
4.3 Calculate the probabilities of moving one unit from supplier r to one of the remaining suppliers using (5). Compare the highest probability with $\tilde{P}$; if it is more than $\tilde{P}$, then it replaces $\tilde{P}$
4.4 $r = r + 1$. Check if $r = j + 1$, if not, go to 4.2

Step 5. If there is a replacement in step 4, update the portfolio with the new $\tilde{P}$. Go to Step 4 until no further improvement is possible. The remaining portfolio provides the highest probability for the given combination of suppliers. Calculate the related cost $C_i(q_1, q_2, \ldots, q_j)$ per (6). The search is finished.

In most cases, the maximum number of iterations in *Search Procedure II* for custom part i with a combination of j available suppliers is estimated as $(N_i-j)(j-1)$.

Search Procedure II finds the part portfolios with the highest probabilities for each combination of suppliers. Although this procedure may not provide all possible portfolios with lower probabilities and lower costs, there are several reasons for this simplification. First, the delivery time is often a primary concern for manufacturers and the main decision criteria. Second, without this simplification, the number of calculations can be prohibitive. Third, the simplification ensures that a feasible portfolio can be found as long as it exists.

The maximum possible number of iterations to find the part frontier portfolios for custom part i in *Search Procedures I* and *II* combined is

$$ l_i + \sum_{j=2}^{l_i} \frac{l_i!}{(l_i - j)! j!} (N_i - j)(j - 1). \tag{9} $$

The number of iterations increases approximately linearly with the part units (N_i), but exponentially with an increase in the number of valid suppliers (l_i). This procedure is not efficient for cases with a large number of suppliers. For example, when l_i is 3 and N_i is 50, the estimated maximum possible number of iterations is 1,755, but when l_i doubles to 6, the maximum possible number of iterations increases to 741,906. However, in practice, the number of iterations is much less than the maximum cap shown in formula (9). In addition, the number of suppliers is limited due to the administrative cost, the prequalification process, and capacity constraints of suppliers. Deming's philosophy on supply chain integration and cooperation also suggests a small number of suppliers. Therefore, very large calculations can be avoided when suppliers are few in number.

4.2 Order Portfolio Frontier Search

Once the part portfolio frontiers are determined for all custom parts, the MTO manufacturer can find the order portfolio frontier from the part portfolio frontiers. One frontier part portfolio for each part is chosen and combined to form an order portfolio frontier candidate. Again, the order frontier candidate must be checked to ensure that it can meet the desired service level. To make the order frontier, eligible candidates are compared against one another to remove any inferior order portfolios.

For any possible order portfolio frontier candidate, (7) is used to calculate the order on time probability. If the probability is lower than the desired service level, then the search moves to the next order portfolio frontier candidate until one is found for the desired service level. If no candidate can meet the desired service level, then the manufacturer cannot fulfill the order by the delivery time with the given service level. Once the search finds a candidate that can meet the desired service level, it is placed in the order frontier pool and the associated cost is calculated as per (8).

As soon as the pool has at least one candidate, each remaining candidate is compared to any order pool portfolio. If it is not inferior to any pool portfolio, then it is added into the pool. If any pool portfolio is inferior to this one, then the pool portfolio should be removed. Once all candidates are checked, the portfolios remaining in the pool form the frontier, which provides the options available to the manufacturer. To obtain the order frontier, the number of iterations is the multiplication of the number of part frontier portfolios for all custom part. Since the number of custom parts is limited for the MTO manufacturer, the number of order frontier iterations is not large.

5   Committed Delivery Time Reduction ("Crashing")

Previously, Sect. 4 provided procedures to obtain both the part and order frontier portfolios under the assumption of a customer given delivery time. In practice, the MTO manufacturer may need to determine and quote a contract due date for bidding. Of course, the shorter delivery time has a higher chance of winning the bid. To reduce the delivery time, the manufacturer can engage in "crashing," which is traditionally achieved by investing additional labor, money, and other resources in critical activities. However, the MTO manufacturer may not have control over how much resources suppliers use. Even if the manufacturer can do so, this process may place tremendous pressure and strain on the suppliers.

Using the suppliers' operating parameters and coordinating with them, the MTO manufacturer can use this procedure to obtain a different order frontier for each crashed delivery time. Without putting additional pressure on the suppliers, the manufacturer always knows its options, which suppliers to choose and what quantity to assign to each supplier. This process helps to improve customer service between the MTO manufacturer and its suppliers.

Because delivery time is the sum of the part required time T and the manufacturer's fixed assembly time, crashing the delivery time is equivalent to crashing the part required time T. The crashing process starts with an arbitrary part required time T_0 with which the manufacturer is confident. The part required time is decreased by one unit of time (e.g., 1 day, 1 week, or any meaningful time measure for a particular contract) each time. The procedure in Sect. 4 is used to find the new order frontier for each crashed part required time. As long as there are still portfolios in the frontier, the part required time can be crashed further, and the process is repeated. When one more time unit reduction generates no portfolio in the frontier, the last successfully attempted part required time T is the shortest possible part required time for the desired service level. This shortest part required time plus the manufacturer's assembly time provides the shortest delivery time that the manufacturer can submit for bid.

Table 1 Parts and certified supplier characteristics

Part # # units	Suppliers	Aggregated jobs on hand (O_{ij}: unit)	Unit production time (t_{ij}: day/unit)	Quality (R_{ij})	Fixed cost (F_{ij}: \$)	Variable cost (V_{ij}: \$/unit)
Part 1	S_{11}	0	0.20	0.85	410	30
40 units	S_{12}	20	0.10	0.90	360	45
	S_{13}	10	0.15	0.85	300	46
	S_{14}	20	0.20	1.00	380	50
	S_{15}	50	0.25	0.90	350	52
Part 2	S_{21}	0	0.60	0.95	800	100
20 units	S_{22}	10	0.50	0.90	760	112
	S_{23}	8	0.45	0.85	740	120
Part 3	S_{31}	10	0.20	0.85	80	40
60 units	S_{32}	0	0.25	0.90	70	45
	S_{33}	20	0.35	0.99	60	45
Part 4	S_{41}	0	0.35	0.90	880	30
40 units	S_{42}	10	0.40	0.90	850	35
	S_{43}	10	0.45	0.95	820	40
	S_{44}	5	0.50	0.90	800	42
	S_{45}	18	0.50	0.99	750	45

6 Numerical Example

In this example, the MTO manufacturer has a custom part required time of 12 days ($T = 12$) for four custom parts and a desired service level of 90% ($P = 90.0\%$). Table 1 shows the certified suppliers and their associated information for all four custom parts.

6.1 Part Portfolio Frontier Search for Given Delivery Time

To find the part frontier portfolio for Part 1, all five certified suppliers for Part 1 are checked first for availability per condition (1) to ensure each has excess time to take the manufacturer's order. Because supplier S_{15} has too many jobs on hand, it is not available ($O_{15} \times t_{15} = 50 \times 0.25 = 12.5 > 12$). *Search Procedure I* generates the part frontier portfolios for Part 1 for the remaining suppliers S_{11}, S_{12}, S_{13}, and S_{14}.

The procedure starts by checking to see if an individual supplier can finish the entire job as per (2). For instance, supplier S_{11} can produce 60 units ($\overline{n_{11}} = \lfloor 12/0.2 \rfloor - 0 = 60 > 40$), which is equal to or greater than the required 40 units. If S_{11} is assigned the whole job, its on time probability is 100.0% per (3) with a cost of \$1,610 per (4), making portfolio ($n_{11} = 40, P_1 = 1.000, C_1 = \$1,610$) the initial frontier candidate. A check of remaining suppliers and all possible combinations of multiple suppliers per *Search Procedure I* shows that they are all inferior to portfolio ($n_{11} = 40$, $P_1 = 1.000$, $C_1 = \$1,610$), which remains the only Part 1 frontier portfolio.

For Part 2, all suppliers are available for the customer's order, but no single supplier is capable of providing the needed 20 units with probability higher than 90%. If both suppliers S_{21} and S_{22} are chosen to do the job, the portfolio with the maximized probability can be determined by *Search Procedure II* as ($n_{21} = 15$, $n_{22} = 5$; $P_2 = 1.000$, $C_2 = \$3,620$). Since other possible portfolios are inferior to it, portfolio ($n_{21} = 15$, $n_{22} = 5$; $P_2 = 1.000$, $C_2 = \$3,620$) is the only Part 2 frontier portfolio. Similarly, the Part 3 frontier has a single frontier portfolio ($n_{31} = 31$, $n_{32} = 29$; $P_3 = 1.000$, $C_3 = \$2,695$).

All five suppliers for Part 4 are available for the job, but none of them can finish the job individually. An examination of two-supplier combinations yield an initial frontier portfolio ($n_{41} = 27$, $n_{42} = 13$; $P_4 = 0.975$, $C_4 = \$2,995$). A check of other two-supplier combinations shows that the only portfolio comparable to the initial frontier portfolio is portfolio ($n_{41} = 27$, $n_{44} = 13$; $P_4 = 0.976$, $C_4 = \$3,036$), which is added to the frontier. From the remaining three-, four-, and five-supplier combinations, one more comparable frontier portfolio can be inserted into the frontier, giving Part 4 these three final frontier portfolios: ($n_{41} = 27$, $n_{42} = 13$; $P_4 = 0.975$, $C_4 = \$2,995$), ($n_{41} = 27$, $n_{44} = 13$; $P_4 = 0.976$, $C_4 = \$3,036$), and ($n_{41} = 24$, $n_{42} = 10$, $n_{44} = 6$; $P_4 = 1.000$, $C_4 = \$3,852$).

6.2 Order Portfolio Frontier Search for Given Delivery Time

The possible number of order frontier portfolios equals the multiplication of the number of part frontier portfolios for each part. In this example, there are three ($1 \times 1 \times 1 \times 3 = 3$) combinations from the four parts, which are all order frontier portfolios, shown in Fig. 2. The MTO manufacturer, depending on its preference for reliability and cost, can choose any listed frontier portfolio for the order.

6.3 Delivery Time Reduction

Previously, the delivery time is assumed given by the customer. In actual bidding, the MTO manufacturer may need to shorten the delivery time to be more competitive while maintaining a desired service level. To do so, the manufacturer may try to crash T in incremental units (days in this example) from an arbitrary part required time of 12 days to find the associated order frontier until no frontier is available.

First, we reduce T to 11 days, which gives 36 combinations that qualify as frontier candidates with an on time probability higher than 90%, but only ten portfolios belong to the order frontier. Figure 3 depicts the order frontier portfolio candidates with the ten order frontier portfolios linked.

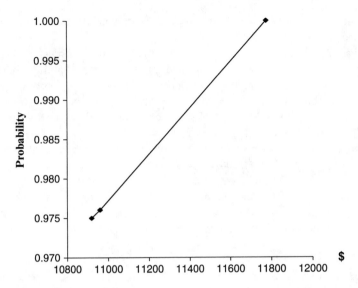

Fig. 2 Order frontier portfolios for $T = 12$

When $T = 10$ days, six portfolios are on the order frontier (see Fig. 4). A reduction to $T = 9$ days yields two possible order portfolios, shown in Fig. 5, but neither can achieve the 90% desired service level and do not qualify as order frontier candidates. Therefore, the most time-competitive bid the MTO manufacturer can make is 10 days with any of the six order frontier portfolios. If the manufacturer is willing to reduce the desired service level and crash one more day to win the contract, 9 days part required time with 89.6% service level is manageable and may also be considered an option.

7 Numerical Example Discussion

The numerical example highlights several interesting points. When the delivery time is sufficiently long, a single supplier for each custom part is the best likely choice for most parts, giving the MTO manufacturer very few frontier portfolio options. Deming's quality point of using a single supplier for each part is ideal when the delivery time is very long. When the delivery time is crashed or shortened, a single supplier may not have sufficient capacity to finish the entire job by itself. Consequently, several supplier combinations are comparably capable of fulfilling each part requirement, increasing the number of frontier portfolios. When the delivery time is shortened further, the number of supplier combinations that can finish the job for each part declines, and the number of frontier portfolios decreases. This explains why the number of order portfolios first increases then eventually decreases when the delivery time is shortened (see Figs. 2–5).

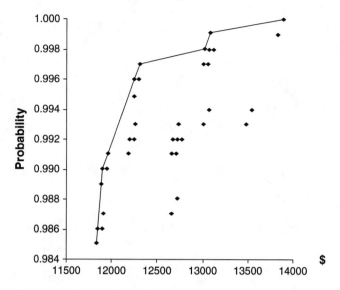

Fig. 3 Order frontier portfolios for $T = 11$

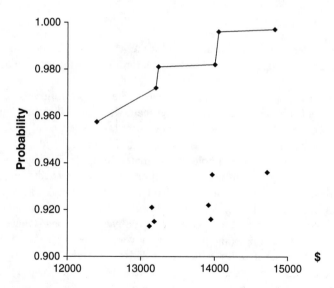

Fig. 4 Order frontier portfolios for $T = 10$

The order frontier portfolio is highly dependent on the part frontier portfolio. A part frontier portfolio with a higher probability is more likely to be a candidate for the order frontier, and a part portfolio with a lower probability is unlikely to qualify. Conversely, a candidate may not be on the frontier if its cost is too high.

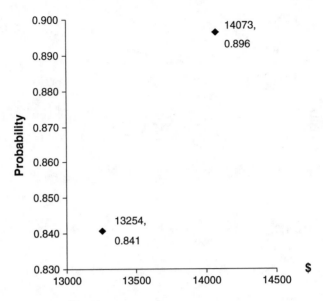

Fig. 5 Order portfolios for $T = 9$

In sum, the order frontier portfolio provides the MTO manufacturer with a range of supplier choices depending on the manufacturer's need for high reliability and low cost.

When the part required time T is shortened, some part portfolios no longer qualify because their probabilities have dropped below the desired service level while others that were not candidates before now qualify for the part frontier. As a result, the order frontier portfolio may have different valid suppliers and quantity allocations as T is crashed. In this example, the number of order frontier options changed from 3 to 10, 6, and 0 when the part required time was crashed from 12 to 11, 10, and 9 days, respectively. A shorter delivery time corresponds with a more inferior order frontier (i.e., a higher cost and/or lower probability), shown in Fig. 6. This phenomenon makes sense because reducing the delivery time means more resources are needed. For this example, the procedure shows that the MTO manufacturer can maintain its service level while reducing the delivery time by 2 days. By choosing an option from the order frontier for a particular delivery time, the MTO manufacturer not only knows how to assign jobs to each part supplier for a desired service level, but also knows the precise part order costs. Two key issues in the bidding process, namely delivery time and price, can be accurately determined by vertically integrating the MTO manufacturer and part suppliers.

There are some limitations and concerns associated with this procedure. First, this process performs better when the number of custom parts and the number of qualified suppliers for each part are few. When the number of suppliers increases, the maximum possible number of iterations increases exponentially, which makes

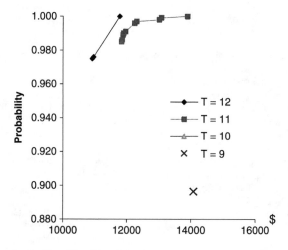

Fig. 6 Order frontier for $T = 12$ to $T = 9$

this procedure less efficient. Second, this procedure requires good communication and information sharing between the MTO manufacturer and custom parts suppliers. If there is no information sharing, the manufacturer will need to estimate the suppliers' parameters, which will lead to less certainty in meeting the customer's delivery time. Third, this model is not efficient in the case of repeated interactions (i.e., negotiations) between the suppliers and MTO manufacturer. A change in any of the initial assumptions will require a recalculation to find new solutions.

8 Conclusions

The method presented in this chapter offers a quick response to a real world problem commonly found in today's global manufacturing environment. Internalizing key suppliers allows the manufacturer to retain its manufacturing capabilities and avoid some potential problems of outsourcing. When the MTO manufacturer receives a custom order, it can first request timely information from the available suppliers, then follow the proposed method to generate possible supplier allocation options that take into account both the replenishment cost and the on time probability to choose a preferred supplier option. When it bids on a contract, the MTO manufacturer can quickly determine the shortest committed delivery time for a desired service level and find the supplier allocation options for all possible delivery times. The given options allow the MTO manufacturer to generate a practical and competitive bidding plan. This innovative method can substantially reduce the decision making time and allow the MTO manufacturer to quickly respond to an unpredictable business environment.

References

Aissaoui N, Haouari M, Hassini E (2007) Supplier selection and order lot sizing modeling: a review. Comput Oper Res 34(12):3516–3540

Bookbinder JH, Noor AI (1985) Setting job-shop due dates with service-level constraints. J Oper Res Soc 36(11):1017–1026

Cakravastia A, Nakamura N (2002) Model for negotiating the price and due date for a single order with multiple suppliers in a make-to-order environment. Int J Prod Res 40(14):3425–3440

Cakravastia A, Toha IS, Nakamura N (2002) A two-stage model for the design of supply chain networks. Int J Prod Econ 80(3):231–248

Chatterjee S, Slotnick SA, Sobel MJ (2002) Delivery guarantees and the interdependence of marketing and operations. Prod Oper Manag 11(3):393–410

De Boer L, Labro E, Morlacchi P (2001) A review of methods supporting supplier selection. Eur J Purch Supply Manag 7(2):75–89

Dellaert NP (1991) Due date setting and production control. Int J Prod Econ 23(1–3):59–67

Duenyas I (1995) Single facility due date setting with multiple customer classes. Manag Sci 41(4):608–619

Duenyas I, Hopp WJ (1995) Quoting customer lead times. Manag Sci 41(1):43–57

Easton FF, Moodie DR (1999) Pricing and lead time decisions for make-to-order firms with contingent orders. Eur J Oper Res 116(2):305–318

El-Hafsi M, Roland E (1999) Negotiating price/delivery date in a stochastic manufacturing environment. IIE Trans 31(3):255–270

Erkoc M, Wu SD (2000) Competitive due-date coordination between marketing and manufacturing. Manufacturing and Service Operations Management Conference Proceedings, Ann Arbor, MI, June 29–30

Hopp WJ, Roof Sturgis ML (2000) Quoting manufacturing due dates subject to a service level constraint. IIE Trans 32(9):771–784

Jayaraman V, Srivastava R, Benton WC (1999) Supplier selection and order quantity allocation: A comprehensive model. J Supply Chain Manag 35(2):50–58

Keskinocak P, Ravi R, Tayur S (2001) Scheduling and reliable lead-time quotation for orders with availability intervals and lead-time sensitive revenues. Manag Sci 47(2):264–279

Lawrence SR (1994) Negotiating due dates between customers and producers. Int J Prod Econ 37(1):127–138

Miller PA, Kelle P (1998) Quantitative support for buyer-supplier negotiation in just-in-time purchasing. Int J Purch Mater Manag 34(2):25–30

Moodie DR (1999) Demand management: The evaluation of price and due date negotiation strategy using simulation. Prod Oper Manag 8(2):151–162

Nandakumar P, Datar SM, Akella R (1993) Models for measuring and accounting for cost of conformance quality. Manag Sci 39(1):1–16

Sahin F, Robinson EP (2005) Information sharing and coordination in make-to-order supply chain. J Oper Manag 23(6):579–598

So KC, Song JS (1998) Price, delivery time guarantees, and capacity selection. Eur J Oper Res 111(1):28–49

Spearman ML, Zhang RQ (1999) Optimal lead time policies. Manag Sci 45(2):290–295

Stevenson WJ (2007) Operations management, 5th edn. McGraw-Hill/Irwin, Boston

Watanapa B, Techanitisawad A (2005) Simultaneous price and due date settings for multiple customer classes. Eur J Oper Res 166(2):351–368

Weber CA, Desai A (1996) Determination of path to vendor market efficiency using parallel coordinates representation: A negotiation tool for buyers. Eur J Oper Res 90(1):142–155

Weber CA, Current JR, Desai A (1998) Non-cooperative negotiation strategies for vendor selection. Eur J Oper Res 108(1):208–223

Webster S (2002) Dynamic pricing and lead-time policies for make-to-order systems. Decision Sci 33(4):579–599

Wein LM (1991) Due date setting and priority sequencing in a multiclass M/G/1 queue. Manag Sci 37(7):834–850

Weng ZK (1999) Strategies for integrating lead time and customer-order decisions. IIE Trans 31(2):161–171

Yue JF, Wang MC (2004) Robust commit time decisions and bounds for measuring demand-side quality costs. Int J Syst Sci 35(11):649–660

Yue J, Xia Y, Tran T, Chen B (2009) Using frontier portfolios to improve make-to-order operations. Prod Oper Manag 18(2):226–239

Zipkin PH (2000) Foundations of inventory management. McGraw-Hill, Boston

Part III
Enabling Technologies for QR Programmes

Enhancing Responsiveness for Mass Customization Strategies through the Use of Rapid Manufacturing Technologies

Hartanto Wong and Daniel Eyers

Abstract Today, when more and more industries move towards creating markets of one, the satisfaction of increasingly individualized consumer demand is a challenge faced by many manufacturing organizations. Consequentially, this situation has led to a rapid growth in the attention given to mass customization for the fulfillment of individual consumer requirements. This chapter explores the opportunities afforded by a group of new manufacturing technologies known collectively as Rapid Manufacturing as an innovative enabler for mass customization. In particular, we consider the opportunities offered by these technologies to enhance the responsiveness of mass customization strategies. Using a stylized model and case examples, we show the potentials of the technologies as well as some challenges that still need to be overcome to achieve the ideal situation of individualized production.

Keywords Integrated production-marketing problem · Mass customization · Rapid Manufacturing technologies

1 Introduction

In proposing mass customization, Davis (1987) envisaged a situation whereby the demand for customized products could be satisfied through individualized manufacturing, while still maintaining the economies of scale prevalent in mass production. By exploiting manufacturing and communications technologies, combined with changes in the organization's approach to the provision of goods, Pine (1993) proclaimed that mass customization could not only compete but also triumph over mass production by fulfilling the exact requirements of the customer without a corresponding increase in costs.

The central motivation for businesses to adopt a mass customization strategy has often been attributed to increasing business competitiveness, and thereby gaining

H. Wong (✉)
Innovative Manufacturing Research Centre, Cardiff University, Wales, UK
e-mail: wongh@cardiff.ac.uk

T.C. Edwin Cheng and T.-M. Choi (eds.), *Innovative Quick Response Programs in Logistics and Supply Chain Management*, International Handbooks on Information Systems, DOI 10.1007/978-3-642-04313-0_10,
© Springer-Verlag Berlin Heidelberg 2010

an advantage over rival companies. By providing customers with products that meet their requirement, mass customization has been heralded as being "the New Frontier in Business Competition" (Pine 1993). Porter (1998) identifies two core strategies for the achievement of a competitive advantage – price and differentiation. Competing on price is often an undesirable consequence of the commoditization of products, resultant from an absence of differentiation opportunities (e.g., as in generic pharmaceuticals). Consequentially, negative effects such as margin erosion are typical of competition based on price. Differentiation can be vertical (typically differentiating on product quality) or horizontal (differentiating on product attributes). For mass production it may be difficult to increase the horizontal differentiation without incurring greater costs of manufacture. However, for companies pursuing a mass customization strategy this is the primary focus, and therefore competitiveness is theoretically increased.

Empirical evidence suggests that the customization is not "free" and needs to be traded-off against lead time, cost, and other factors (Squire et al. 2006). In particular, the notion of responsiveness in the context of mass customization has been exemplified by McCutcheon et al. 1994) in their work considering "the customization-responsiveness squeeze," discussing how companies could offer customized products while still ensuring quick delivery times. Following Chopra and Meindl (2007), who introduced the concept of *cost-responsiveness efficient frontier* in explaining the trade-off between supply chain efficiency and supply chain responsiveness, we argue that conceptually there exists a *customization-responsiveness efficient frontier* as shown in Fig. 1. The figure indicates the highest possible responsiveness to achieve a given level of customization based on the existing technologies. One of the main challenges pertinent in mass customization is how to shift the efficient frontier closer towards the ideal state where firms are able to provide customized products at a comparable speed of equivalent standardized offerings.

It is evident that the current state of mass customization is achievable through the adoption of flexible manufacturing systems, introduction of modularization and postponement, combined with e-commerce. Such continuous developments

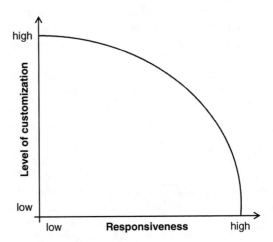

Fig. 1 The customization vs. responsiveness efficient frontier (Adapted from Chopra and Meindl 2007)

of innovative technologies and techniques have been shown to facilitate a more responsiveness means of introducing customization. In line with the spirit of enhancing the responsiveness of mass customization strategies, this chapter introduces a group of new manufacturing technologies known collectively as "Rapid Manufacturing" (RM) as an emerging enabler for mass customization. The advent of RM technologies, which is considered by some authors to be "an industrial revolution for the digital age" (Hopkinson et al. 2006), may offer a significant leap forward to reach the ideal state of mass customization.

RM is a collective term for a range of additive layer manufacturing technologies, whereby layers of material are joined together to form parts, enabling virtually any product shape to be created from a range of engineering materials (including metals, resins, composites, and thermoplastics). RM has already achieved extensive usage in medical applications, where customized products are necessary to best suit the individual's physiology, and is emergent in many other sectors of low volume and custom manufacture. There are several characteristics of RM that make it attractive in a mass customization scenario, particularly in the achievement of responsive manufacturing. The most relevant attribute is the capability to achieve highly sophisticated geometries in manufacture, but without the need for manufacturing aids such as moulds and tooling, which are usually requisite in many conventional manufacturing technologies. For conventional standardized production, development of tooling and moulds is performed prior to the product launch to promote responsiveness. Where customized manufacture results in changes to the geometry, this cannot be prepared in advance and consequentially manufacturing lead-times are likely to be extended. Through RM, the elimination of these requirements not only simplifies the overall tasks of the product designer and eliminates cost, but also makes an important contribution to addressing the responsiveness of the manufacturer.

This chapter aims to examine the potentials of RM, particularly in enhancing the responsiveness of mass customization strategies (i.e., being able to shift the efficient frontier much closer to the ideal state). Consequently, our analysis will be focusing on the economic rather than technical aspects of the technologies. We present a stylized model used to generalize the economic implications of the technologies. More specifically, we compare two manufacturing configurations. The first configuration is mass producer (MP) working in a make-to-stock mode to provide a limited number of standard products, which do not meet customer preferences exactly but are available immediately (or with a relatively short lead time). The second configuration is mass customizer (MC) working in a make-to-order mode to provide custom products, which meet customer preferences exactly but are available only after a certain lead time. The model we develop captures the integration of production-inventory as well as marketing related factors. We consider the fact that customer demand is influenced by product variety and lead time apart from the product's price. Increasing the variety for standard products or shortening the lead time for custom products can enhance the sales and margin. The model can be exploited to explain the potential of RM to enhance the responsiveness of mass customization.

The rest of the chapter is organized as follows. In the next section we provide a survey of the relevant literature. In Sect. 3 we present our stylized model, and Sect. 4

presents and discusses numerical examples. In Sect. 5 we close the chapter with a concluding discussion and some suggestions for future research.

2 Literature Background

In this section we discuss the relevant literature, with emphasis on two streams of research considered most relevant to this work. The first stream of research is on different enablers of mass customization that particularly contribute to the enhancement of quick response strategy. The second stream of research focuses on examining the business implications of RM as mass customization enabler. Examples of RM-enabled mass customized products are also presented.

2.1 Responsiveness in Mass Customization

Mass customization was first introduced as being when "the same large number of customers can be reached as in mass markets of the industrial economy, and simultaneously be treated individually as in the customized markets of pre-industrial economies" (Davis 1987). Adopting mass customization combines the best of the craft era, where products were individualized but costly, with the best of the mass production era, where everybody could get the standardized, affordable products (Fralix 2001). Though for many industries customization was largely discarded in favor of standardization during the twentieth Century as seemingly inefficient (Lampel and Mintzberg 1996), the implementation of the mass customization concept has been identified as a consequence of changing consumer requirements, with individualism of demand becoming increasingly apparent and homogenous markets ceasing to exist (Hart 1995).

This apparent market demand for customized products should promote MC, where in ideal situations it should be able to achieve individualized manufacturing without incurring tradeoffs when compared to conventional approaches. Three core attributes of MC are outlined by Tseng and Jiao (1998): quick response, customization, and the achievement of economies of scale. Responsiveness is discussed throughout the MC literature; however, we note that the intended meaning of authors with regards to the term responsiveness may differ. There is much scholarly discussion as to what constitutes responsiveness, with the terms of *agility* and *flexibility* often being used interchangeably with *responsiveness* in operations management literature, despite being distinctly different in their meaning (Bernardes and Hanna 2009). Several reviews of the concept have been conducted (Bernardes and Hanna 2009; Holweg 2005; Kritchanchai and MacCarthy 1999; Reichhart and Holweg 2007), each identifying different interpretations in the literature for responsiveness. Consequentially in this chapter, we are mindful to consider the intention of authors who discuss responsiveness in the context of MC.

As stated earlier, the notion of responsiveness in the context of mass customization has been exemplified by McCutcheon et al. (1994). In their study, the notion of "responsiveness" equates to the total manufacturing and delivery lead-time for the custom product, and is an interpretation echoed throughout MC literature. However, while the authors emphasize the potential costs and risks resultant from needing to address the difficulties of responsiveness, a later survey of MC companies (Åhlström and Westbrook 1999) ranked increased order response times with other customization negatives, finding (to their surprise), companies reporting this of lesser importance than other attributes such as material and manufacturing costs. These findings are from the perspective of the company towards responsiveness and do not consider the perceptions of the end customer. In a more recent consumer study, Endo and Kincade (2008) highlight the importance of how quickly a company is able to supply custom products as a determinant of choosing customized over standardized offerings, which is further supported by the findings of Piller and Müller (2004) that customers may expect a financial discount to compensate from extended delivery times. Hence, it is evident that MC companies should focus their attention not only on achieving mass production level costs, but also on the achievement of responsiveness to satisfy customer demands.

To achieve both production economics and responsive manufacturing, one widely implemented method of mass customization enablement is modularity, originally envisaged by Pine to promote economies of both "scale and scope" (Pine 1993). For mass customization to minimize costs while maximizing individualization, modularity is often applied (Feitzinger and Lee 1997; Pine 1993). An exact definition of modularity is uncertain in the literature; however, a consensus exists that modularity entails the combination of a series of modular components in the creation of a modular product (Gershenson et al. 2003). In mass customized manufacture, this equates to the manufacture of a variety of standardized components, which are then integrated as part of the overall customized product. Through this approach, not only should costs be maintained at mass production levels, but also issues of responsiveness addressed. McCutcheon et al. (1994) discussed how an organization adopting modularity of its components could make some effort to address the "customization-responsiveness squeeze," resulting in greater substitution to satisfy customer orders. It was observed that, although this is beneficial to the organization's responsiveness, unless all core components can be modularized, it will not be possible to completely address the squeeze through modularity. Furthermore, in order to accommodate the large variety of demand but still satisfy customer delivery time expectations, the evidence is that the firms increase inventories of potential components. Customized mainframe manufacturer Amdahl is widely cited as attempting to provide customized built computer in a week by stocking every potential component, but at the cost to the business of holding millions of dollars in excess inventory (Pine et al. 1993; Radder and Louw 1999).

Another concept recognized as mass customization enabler is *postponement* or *delayed product differentiation*. The concept is appealing particularly in dealing with uncertainty due to proliferation in product varieties and uncertain demands from customers. This is achieved by properly designing the product structure and the manufacturing and supply chain processes so that one can delay or postpone the final customization of the product to the maximum extent possible, pending more accurate product demand information. One of the classic examples of successful postponement application is Hewlett–Packard (HP) for their DeskJet printers (Lee et al. 1993; Feitzinger and Lee 1997). The company opted to customize the printers at its local distribution centers rather than at its factories. For example, instead of customizing the DeskJet at its factory in Singapore before shipping them to Europe, HP has its European distribution center near Stuttgart, Germany, perform this job. HP restructured its printer production process by manufacturing a generic DeskJet printer and later localizing the generic product by integrating in the localized modules (power supplies, packaging, and manuals) at its local distribution centers. This way, HP was able to maintain the same service levels with an 18% reduction in inventory, saving millions of dollars. Another celebrated example is Benetton who used postponement to cope with volatile fashion trends and long production lead-times (Signorelli and Hesket 1984; Dapiran 1992). By using un-dyed yarn to knit about half of its clothing and delaying the dying process to a later stage, Benetton has a better idea of the popular colors for the season. Other examples include IBM (Swaminathan and Tayur 1998), Whirlpool (Waller et al. 2000), and Xilinx (Brown et al. 2000). We refer the reader to Van Hoek (2001); Swaminathan and Lee (2003); Yang et al. 2004) for a comprehensive review of research on postponement.

2.2 Rapid Manufacturing as an enabler for mass customization

Through the application of RM technologies, it is possible to manufacture parts of highly sophisticated and complicated geometries, but without the need for costly tooling. It is this absence of tooling that promotes the feasible production of parts in quantities as needed, rather than in large batches that Hopkinson et al. (2006) claim may make "volume of one" manufacturing economically viable. However, despite the recognized potential for RM to enable the mass customization concept, there has been limited research conducted in this field, and almost no consideration of the implications for manufacturing responsiveness.

RM has evolved from the technology origins of rapid prototyping (RP), where the research literature is predominantly based on the engineering capabilities of emergent technologies, used to create one-off products for the prototyping industries. However, some of these technologies appeared promising for actual production environments, and the term rapid manufacturing has started to become a familiar vocabulary. One of the defining texts during this transition was that of Pham and Dimov (2001), who provided an extensive review of the process technologies and the applications, particularly from an engineering viewpoint. Although RP and RM both utilize the same principal technologies, the distinction between the two is usually classified on the final application of the created part, with RM featuring only parts that will be used in end-use finished goods.

While a large body of literature exists for RP (and, to a lesser extent, RM), the limited research into enablement of mass customization using these has predominantly employed case studies to showcase both opportunities and constraints of the technologies. In a medical context, Hieu et al. (2005) identified medical applications to include biomodels, surgical aids, implants, training models, and scaffolds for tissue engineering, using reverse engineering (RE) scanners and computer tomography (CT) scans as a basis for generating 3D models needed to create RP/RM components. Further work related to customization for individual human geometries can also be found in the work of Tuck et al. (2008), who explored the opportunities to reduce pilot fatigue using RM to produce custom seating and Barrass et al. (2008) who considered customization in tennis racket grips.

Within the field of mass customization, the involvement of customers is an important concept, with early involvement in the production cycle leading to higher degrees of customization in the finished product (Duray et al. 2000). Hague et al. (2003) discussed how customers could be involved in the design stages of the production cycle for customized products, suggesting limitations in their abilities for this task and proposed options to overcome this issue. Hague noted the use of the internet for codesign of customized products, a theme also explored by Bateman and Cheng (2006) through several case scenarios. Their work outlined both the techniques for eliciting customization preferences for products via the internet and also the realization of these through RM processes.

One case example of RM for mass customization is that of customized hearing aid shells. In traditional manufacture, shells would be manually created by a skilled technician as described by Cortex et al. (2004). Having achieved a cast from the supplied mould, nine further steps involving recasting, trimming, and drilling are necessary to create the final product. This manual process takes an experienced technician approximately three hours to achieve and suffers from high variability in product quality. The technician's continual cutting and trimming of the shell down to size is highly error prone, and often it is necessary to reattach erroneously removed material using adhesives. In severe cases, the shell must be discarded, significantly affecting the responsiveness of the manufacturer. Resultantly, manufacturing lead-times were often quoted at approximately 1 week, and typically about 35% of the dispatched products are returned to the manufacturer for adjustment (a "first-fit" rate of 65%).

Using RM technologies, manufacturing responsiveness and quality can be improved. Moulds are 3D scanned and this data file is used by the RM equipment for manufacture. Although each hearing aid will be of different shape, in actual manufacturing environments the simultaneous production of multiple customized products is commonplace (as shown in Fig. 2). Through this technique, setup and fixed costs can be amortized across a larger production run, improving the commercial viability of the process. Therefore, while demand from an individual customer in MC manufacturing requirement will typically be low (i.e. one-off), as the actual processes of manufacturing do not need to differentiate between products, many items can be produced in a single build, resulting in the achievement of "mass" volume in mass customization.

In terms of responsiveness, the application of RM technologies together with efficient operations management results in an improved situation. Under normal circumstances, devices can be designed, manufactured, configured, tested, and

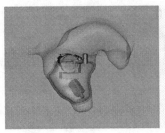 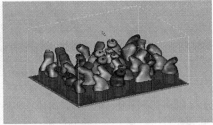

Fig. 2 *Left*: 3D Model of configured ITE device; *Right*: multiple batched devices for manufacture (Courtesy of Materialise)

dispatched within a single working day, with first-fit rates in excess of 95%. Resultantly, the use of RM technologies for the commercial manufacture of hearing aid devices is commonplace, displacing the conventional craft approach to customized manufacture.

A second case example is that of customized lamps, which are often formed from modular components, allowing the selection of base and shades in terms of shape and color from a predetermined catalogue of options. While this encompasses the efficiencies of mass production in the production of shades and bases, the limitations of this assemble-to-order approach can be observed in the restricted number of permutations possible in the final product. However, since the component parts are mass produced, these costs should remain unchanged. For more extensive customization of lamps, the convention is to engage the services of a designer. While this approach will enable a higher level of product customization, this tends towards the craft approach and often results in higher unit costs and significantly extended response times, moving away from the ideal state of MC. A hybrid strategy is also evident from some companies, whereby modularity of components is maintained, but with each component hand-crafted. Resultantly, product options are constrained in a similar manner to mass production, but individually crafted by hand on a make-to-order basis with a manufacturing lead-time of 4–6 weeks.

Through RM, highly sophisticated lamp designs can be made without affecting the delivery lead time of the product (Fig. 3 shows a range of MGX designer lamps). Customers may affect attributes such as size, color, and embedded text, or for some designs perform customizations by supplying parameters for mathematical expressions but control the placement of product features.

MGX lamps combine component modularity with RM technologies to facilitate product customization. For these products, both the base and the shade can be customized, with bases selected from a modular range of possibilities and shades individually manufactured. Despite the extent of customizations which can be made to the shade, achieving these with RM does not significantly affect the manufacturing costs. For MGX lamps, the customizations require relatively trivial intervention by the manufacturer, requiring only parameter changes in the CAD model prior to submission for building. This compares favorably to the expenses that would be incurred in injection molding, whereby a mold would require design and fabrication

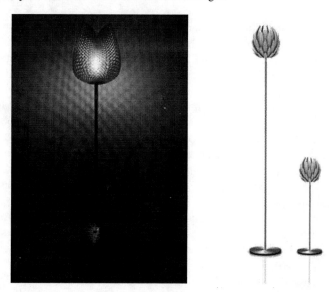

Fig. 3 *Left*: Tulip.MGX by Peter Jansen; *Right*: Lily.MGX by Janne Kytannen (both images are courtesy of Materialise)

to enable manufacture, or in craft manufacture, where the time of the designer/maker will also increase the product costs. In RM, greater costs will be incurred only if more material is used, or the geometry increases the overall size of the build. Where customization does not affect these attributes, there will be no increase in costs compared to standardized items, achieving one of the main prescribed principles of mass customization.

The absence of molds not only eliminates a cost of production, but also results in improved responsiveness. Compared to standardized manufacturing, the principal delays resultant from customization in RM are the reconfiguration of the electronic model of the product to accommodate customization; however, these do not extend the normal 2–3 week manufacturing lead-time. Resultantly, customers will receive either custom or standardized RM lamps within the same timescale.

We would like to close this section by emphasizing the importance of this chapter in enhancing the awareness of academics as well as practitioners, particularly those working in the area of mass customization, of the emerging RM technologies that seem to offer opportunities in advancing the current state of mass customization.

3 Model

We now present a stylized model used to generalize the economic implication of the technologies. Our model is similar to those considering the coordination of marketing and operations decisions in the context of mass customization as studied by some authors, including, for example, Jiang et al. (2006); Alptekinoglu and Corbett (2008); Mandelson and Parlaktürk (2008). In comparison to Jiang et al. (2006), our model is different mainly in the following aspects. First, we specifically consider a pure customization based on a make-to-order configuration while they do not. Second, their model ignores the effect of congestion at the production facility, while we explicitly model the queuing effect as a result of considering a capacitated production facility. The other two studies, Alptekinoglu and Corbett (2008); Mandelson and Parlaktürk (2008), model competition between two multiproduct firms, where one firm is a mass customizer while the other is a mass producer. Our analysis is different from theirs as we do not model competition, and furthermore, they focus on firms' product and pricing decisions without considering lead time as a factor affecting customer purchase decisions.

We consider a market with customers who have heterogeneous preferences for product attributes. Similar to De Groote (1994), we model the product space $\Theta = [0, 1]$ using the spatial location model of Hotelling (1929) and its extensions by Lancaster (1990). To make the model more tractable and focus on product line decisions associated with a horizontal differentiation, customer ideal tastes are assumed to be uniformly distributed on Θ. This assumption is commonly used in the Hotelling-style models. Each product is characterized by $x \in \Theta$, a single point on the unit product line segment. This can represent, for example, the size or color attribute of the product. As stated earlier, we intend to compare two types of manufacturing configurations: MP that produces standard products and MC that produces individually customized products. The two configurations will be assessed on the basis of their respective expected profit. Our notation and parametric assumptions are summarized in Table 1.

3.1 Customer Choice

Our model captures the situation in which customer demand is sensitive to price, product characteristics, and also delivery lead time. Specifically, the utility of a type-θ customer derives from buying a product with characteristic x, price p, and lead time T is equal to

$$U(\theta, x, p, T) = r - p - v|\theta - x| - wT, \tag{1}$$

where the reservation price $r > 0$ is the customer's willingness to pay for her ideal product (all customers are assumed to have a common reservation price). We assume that r is large enough so that the net utility is always greater than zero and so all customers will buy a product. Products are offered with price p, assumed to be identical for all products. The uniform pricing scheme is reasonable when the products are horizontally differentiated (in which qualities of products are at the same level). The customer's disutility of misfit relative to her ideal preference is expressed as $v|\theta - x|$, where $v > 0$ is the linear transportation cost, which also represents the intensity of customer preference, and $|\theta - x|$ is the distance from her ideal product

Table 1 List of Notation

Demand parameters	
λ_0	Total potential demand rate
π_i	First choice probability of product i
λ_i	Demand rate for product i
r	Customers' reservation price
Production input parameters	
μ	Production rate for the MP configuration
μ'	Production rate for the MC configuration
Cost parameters	
h	Unit inventory holding cost for MP
c	Unit production cost for the MP configuration
c'	Unit production cost for the MC configuration
F	Product proliferation cost for the MP configuration
v	Linear transportation cost (customers' preference intensity)
w	Linear waiting cost (customers' sensitivity to delay)
Decision variables	
S_i	Base stock level for MP's finished goods
$\mathbf{S}$	Vector of base stock levels
n	Number of product lines
x_i	Product i's characteristic
$\mathbf{x}$	Vector of product characteristics
p	Product price
T	Average delivery lead time (determined by inventory policy)
Performance measures	
I_i	Expected on-hand inventory level
Z	Expected total profit

attribute. Further, the disutility of waiting is represented by wT, where $w > 0$ is the customer's sensitivity to delay and T is the expected delay.

We assume that demands arrive according to a Poisson process with rate, or demand intensity λ_0, and they differ only in their ideal products $\theta \in \Theta$. Upon arrival, the customer observes the product offerings and selects the product that maximizes her utility, provided that it is nonnegative, otherwise she does not make a choice. Product i is said to be the first choice of a given customer if it gives a non-negative utility to that customer and its utility is the maximum among all products offered by the manufacturer. Denote π_i as the *first choice probability* of product i, and the demand rate for product i can be defined as $\lambda_i = \pi_i \lambda_0, i = 1, 2, \ldots, n$. Consistent with the assumption of non-negative net utility, we also assume that complete market coverage is optimal. This assumption is common in the marketing and economics literature (Alptekinoglu and Corbett 2008).

3.2 The MP Configuration

In this configuration the manufacturer offers n standard products, indexed by $i = 1, 2, \ldots, n$. This configuration is modeled as a single stage production-inventory system. We assume that the processing times are i.i.d. random variables and exponentially distributed with rate $1/\mu$. These assumptions make the problem tractable, without a significant loss in accuracy, especially as our emphasis is deriving qualitative patterns and managerial insights. For stability, we require that the utilization rate $\lambda_0/\mu = \rho < 1$. Demand is satisfied from stock unless the corresponding inventory is empty. All shortages are backlogged. We assume that a base-stock policy is used for the inventory control. Let S_i denote the base stock level for finished product i. Furthermore, changeover times between products are assumed to be negligible.

Let c denote the unit production cost incurred for this configuration. Also, we assume that the cost is the same for all standard products. For each unit in stock, the manufacturer also incurs inventory holding cost h per unit time. Further, there is a product proliferation cost F, incurred every time the manufacturer offers a new product variant. This cost could include redesign, tooling, and setup costs. We assume that the cost of variety is linear in the number of products offered, which is in line with common observation in the operations literature (Dobson and Waterson 1996; Benjaafar et al. 2004). The manufacturer makes simultaneous decisions regarding how many products to offer and their characteristics, base stock level of finished products, and price, maximizing the expected profit. Note that the decision on the base stock level will also influence the average lead time experienced by customers.

3.2.1 Evaluation model

Following Buzacott and Shanthikumar (1993), for a given base stock level S_i, the expected inventory for finished product i is given by

$$I_i(S_i) = S_i - \left(\frac{\lambda_i}{\mu - \lambda_0}\right)\left(1 - \hat{\rho}_i^{S_i}\right), \tag{2}$$

where $\hat{\rho}_i = \lambda_i / (\mu - \lambda_{-i})$ and $\lambda_{-i} = \sum_{j \neq i} \lambda_j$.

The expected lead time for a given S_i is given by

$$T = \frac{\hat{\rho}_i^{S_i}}{\mu - \lambda_0}. \tag{3}$$

3.2.2 Optimization

Define $x = [x_1 \, x_2 \ldots x_n]$ as a vector of product characteristics and $S = [S_1 \, S_2 \ldots S_n]$ as a vector of base stock levels. We formalize the manufacturer's optimization problem as follows.

$$\text{Max } Z(n, x, S, p) = \sum_{i=1}^{n} (p - c) \cdot \lambda_i(n, x_i, S_i, p) - h \cdot I_i(S_i) - Fn. \tag{4}$$

Following de Groote (1994), an optimal design of the product line can be determined as follows. For a given n, the optimal product line has a simple structure: the market should be partitioned in segments of equal lengths, the characteristics of the products should correspond to the taste of the customers located in the middle of the segments, and the manufacturer should set prices as to make the customers located at the extreme of the segments indifferent between buying and not buying. To put it more formally, given that n, T, v, and w are fixed, we obtain full market coverage with the maximum revenue by setting

$$x_i^* = \frac{2i-1}{2n}, \quad i = 1, 2, \dots, n \text{ and} \tag{5}$$

$$p^* = r - wT - \frac{v}{2n}. \tag{6}$$

Following (5), the optimal product line has a structure in which the market should be partitioned in segments of equal lengths. This means for a given n, $\pi_1 = \pi_2 = \cdots = \pi_n$ and so $\lambda_1 = \lambda_2 = \cdots = \lambda_n$, and as a consequence, we have identical optimal base stock levels for all products, that is, $S_1^* = S_2^* = \cdots = S_n^*$.

The problem in (4) can now be solved in two stages. In the first stage, we fix n and find the optimal $\mathbf{S}$. And in the second stage we optimize n. From (3) it can be shown that the promised lead time T is decreasing with S_i before reaching a zero level. It can also be proven that $I_i(S_i)$ is increasing and is a convex function of S_i. The optimal n can be determined by gradually increasing n starting from $n = 1$. For each value of n we optimize $\mathbf{x}$, p, and $\mathbf{S}$. The search can be terminated when the condition $(r-c)\lambda_0 \leq Fn$ is met. The first term $(r-c)\lambda_0$ is a constant and represents the maximum profit, which can be gained by setting the price equal to the reservation price. The second term Fn represents the product proliferation cost, which is linearly increasing with n. This condition ensures that no better improvement is possible by increasing n.

3.3 The MC Configuration

In this configuration the manufacturer offers individualized customized products, which means no decision to be made on the number of products. As for MP, this configuration is also modeled as a single stage production-inventory system, with the only difference being that this configuration does not hold any finished goods inventory. Hence, we have a special case of the MP configuration with zero base stock levels. The processing times are i.i.d. random variables and exponentially distributed with rate $1/\mu'(\leq 1/\mu)$. This reflects our attempt to capture the potential of RM technologies in reducing the total manufacturing lead time. Let c' denote the unit production cost incurred for this configuration. To reflect a premium cost associated with the adoption of new technology, we assume that the direct cost of manufacturing is nondecreasing when switching from MP to MC (i.e., $c' \geq c$). The new cost c' already includes the amortized value of such premium cost. To reflect the highly flexible feature of RM technologies, we assume that there is no proliferation cost incurred for this configuration. However, this is not for free as the development of such a flexible technology will certainly incur a high investment and production cost, which in our model has been reflected by a higher unit cost c'.

3.3.1 Evaluation

For this special case, the expected inventory level is zero and the average lead time is given by

$$T = \frac{1}{\mu - \lambda_0}. \tag{7}$$

3.3.2 Optimization

For this configuration, price is the only relevant decision variable. The profit maximization problem can be formulated as

$$\text{Max } Z[p] = (p - c')\lambda_0. \tag{8}$$

Solving the above problem is very straightforward as we just need to find the maximum price value that does not give a negative utility for customers. From (6) and (7), the optimal price can be determined as follows:

$$p^*_{\text{MC}} = r - wT = r - w\frac{1}{\mu - \lambda_0}. \tag{9}$$

4 Numerical Examples

In this section we present several numerical examples to enhance the understanding of how different factors may affect the preference of one configuration to the other. In particular, we intend to generalize how the advent of advanced manufacturing technologies such as RM enhances the responsiveness of mass customization strategies as indicated by increased profitability of the MC configuration relatively compared to the MP configuration.

4.1 Base example

In this example we present a situation in which all the parameters are identical for both the MP and MC configurations. Both configurations are different only with respect to finished goods inventory. Consider the following system parameters:

- Aggregate demand rate $\lambda_0 = 5$/time unit
- Reservation price $r = 500$

- Production rate $\mu = \mu' = 6/$time unit
- Product proliferation cost $F = 10$ (only for MP)
- Unit production cost $c = c' = 100/$unit

As the expected profits for both configurations are influenced by the customer's sensitivity to delay and preference intensity, a range of w and v values were experimented. It is also notable to mention that as the sensitivity of the profit function to each of the two parameters can be different, some preliminary experiments were conducted to find a sensible range of values from which we are able to derive insights. The following values are used: $w = [2, 4, 6, 8, 10, 12,$ and $14]$ and $v = [20, 40, 60, 80,$ and $100]$.

For the MP configuration, the main results from this example are summarized in Table 2. In the table we show the expected profit as well as the optimal number of product variety for each combination of v and w.

It is indicated in the table that the average profit first decreases as a function of the waiting cost, but there is a threshold value of waiting cost after which the profit becomes constant. This occurs because by increasing the waiting cost, the MP configuration will react by holding a higher inventory level. From a certain w value, however, the inventory level is high enough to cause a zero lead time, thereby making the profit function constant. The table also shows how the customers' preference intensity influence the number of product variety, that is, increasing v values tends to increase n^*.

For the MC configuration, the results are presented in Table 3. As MC is able to offer individual customized products, the profit is affected only by the customers' sensitivity to delay, that is, there is no effect of the customers' preference intensity.

It is obvious that the expected profit is linearly decreasing as a function of w. Given all other parameters are fixed, the profit for MC depends only on the optimum

Table 2 Optimal profit and number of products for different v and w(MP)

	$w = 2$	$w = 4$	$w = 6$	$w = 8$	$w = 10$	$w = 12$	$w = 14$
$v = 20$	1,916	1,883	1,863	1,861	1,859	1,859	1,859
	$n^* = 2$	$n^* = 2$	$n^* = 2$	$n^* = 2$	$n^* = 2$	$n^* = 2$	$n^* = 2$
$v = 40$	1,898	1,863	1,838	1,836	1,834	1,834	1,834
	$n^* = 3$	$n^* = 3$	$n^* = 2$	$n^* = 2$	$n^* = 2$	$n^* = 2$	$n^* = 2$
$v = 60$	1,883	1,847	1,821	1,818	1,816	1,815	1,814
	$n^* = 4$	$n^* = 4$	$n^* = 3$	$n^* = 3$	$n^* = 3$	$n^* = 3$	$n^* = 3$
$v = 80$	1,871	1,834	1,806	1,802	1,800	1,798	1,797
	$n^* = 4$	$n^* = 4$	$n^* = 3$	$n^* = 3$	$n^* = 3$	$n^* = 3$	$n^* = 3$
$v = 100$	1,861	1,823	1,794	1,786	1,784	1,782	1,782
	$n^* = 5$	$n^* = 5$	$n^* = 4$	$n^* = 4$	$n^* = 4$	$n^* = 4$	$n^* = 4$

Table 3 Optimal profit for different w (MC)

$w = 2$	$w = 4$	$w = 6$	$w = 8$	$w = 10$	$w = 12$	$w = 14$
1,990	1,980	1,970	1,960	1,950	1,940	1,930

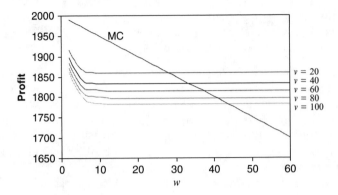

Fig. 4 Maximum waiting cost w^0 for different values of v

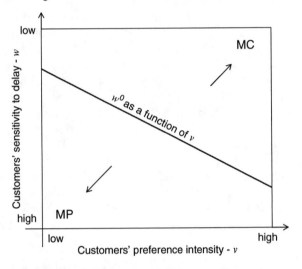

Fig. 5 Maximum waiting cost w^0 separating MC and MP areas

price, which is a linear function of w. For the selected range of w, the MC config-uration seems to be superior compared to the MP configuration, giving indication that the selected parameters do not really represent situations in which customers are concerned about the lead time. As expected, increasing w further may lead to observations where MC is less profitable than MP. In relation to this, we suggest to use w^0, defined as the value of w at which the profits for both MP and MC are equal. A small w^0 can be seen as an indicator of nonsupportive environment for mass customization strategies, and vice versa. Determining w^0 is straightforward as we know that MP's profit is a constant and the MC's profit is a linear function of w. We summarized the results in Fig. 4.

Conceptually, the preference of offering individual customized products to stan-dardized products as influenced by customer's sensitivity to delay and preference intensity, that is, the lead time vs. product variety trade-off can be represented in a diagram depicted in Fig. 5. In this diagram we show that offering customized products is preferable when customers are willing to wait longer for a product that matches very well with their ideal preference. In contrast, offering standard products is more likely to be more profitable when lead time is more an issue compared to product variety. The maximum waiting cost function, w^0, as defined above serves as the separation line of the two extreme markets.

4.2 The effect of increased production rate

We now extend the base example by capturing the fact that the total manufacturing lead time is reduced due to the exploitation of new technologies. We use the following values for the production rate for the MC configuration: $\mu' =[6, 7, 8, 9,$ and $10]$, while the production rate for MP is kept at $\mu = 6$. All the other parameter values are not changed. Figure 6 is presented to show the benefit of increasing production rate for MC as indicated by larger w^0 values.

By using the concept introduced in Fig. 5, we can explain that technologies such as RM that are able to enhance responsiveness by reducing the total manufacturing lead time (without sacrificing quality) will increase the maximum waiting cost w^0 for a fixed v value, that is, shift the w^0 function down, thereby expanding the total market potential for customized product offerings (see Fig. 7).

4.3 The effect of increased production rate and production cost

We now present the final example to represent the most realistic situation for RM in which the increased production rate needs to be balanced against the higher unit production cost. Five values are chosen for the MC's unit production cost: $c' =[100, 105, 110, 115,$ and $120]$. Similar to the previous analysis, we determine

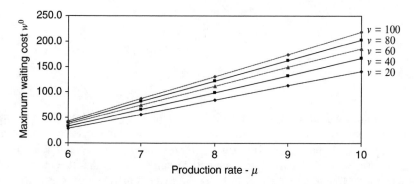

Fig. 6 Maximum waiting cost w^0 affected by production rate

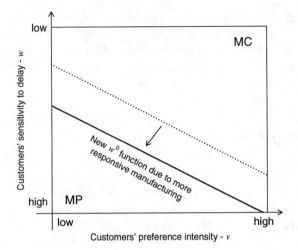

Fig. 7 Expansion of MC's market potential

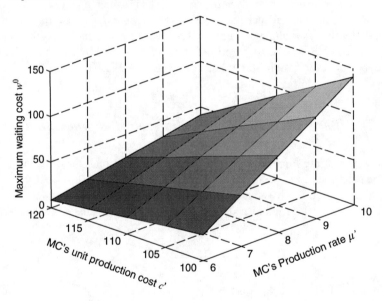

Fig. 8 Maximum waiting cost w^0 as a function of c' and μ'

the maximum waiting cost w^0 for each combination of production rate and unit production cost. The results (only for $v = 20$) are depicted in Fig. 8.

In Fig. 8, the lighter area of the surface represents the situations that are more favorable for mass customization strategies. Despite the fact that it remains challenging for RM-enabled mass customization to reach this light area, especially due to the cost issue, the successful application of RM in the hearing aids industry gives indication that this area is not unachievable. Significant year-on-year growth in the

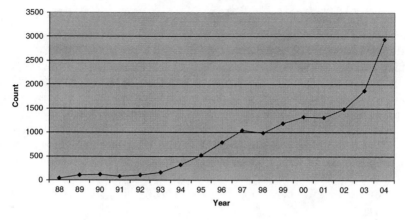

Fig. 9 Additive systems worldwide sales 1988–2004 (Wohlers 2007)

RM industry (as shown in Fig. 9), together with the launches of new machines and products, suggests a wide scale confidence in the opportunities for the RM technologies. Furthermore, as the industry develops, competition between vendors is likely to reduce both maintenance and material costs (Hopkinson et al. 2006).

5 Conclusion

This chapter explores the opportunities afforded by the emerging RM technologies as a promising enabler for enhancing the responsiveness in the provision of mass customized products. The topic is of great relevance, because today, where more and more industries move towards creating markets of one, the use of innovative technologies and methods that are capable of enhancing responsiveness can be seen as a competitive advantage.

Through our case examples, we present two applications of mass customization, and consider the implications for responsiveness and cost using both conventional and RM approaches. Though the products are from very different markets, we find some commonalities consistent with the prescribed methods of mass customization envisaged by Pine (1993). The elimination of molds in production increases the geometric customizations possible without incurring additional manufacturing costs, supported by the use of modularity for some components of the products. By adopting these approaches, responsiveness between customized and standardized has been improved in both examples when compared to conventional manufacturing involving higher degrees of customization.

The stylized model developed in this chapter helps us gain more insights into the potentials as well as the limitations of the RM technologies. The model captures the interaction of production-inventory and marketing factors that are prevalent in the context of mass customization, and in particular, is helpful to explain how the

RM technologies may affect the existing trade-off between responsiveness vs. customization. Through numerical examples we show how some advantages offered by RM technologies such as reduced lead times and improved flexibility are beneficial for mass customization strategies. More specifically, as market segments can be represented by the customer's preference intensity and sensitivity to lead time, we show how those advantages may result in an expansion of the total market potential for mass customized products. Further, the examples also demonstrate how the high cost attribute associated to RM technologies may inhibit successful applications RM-enabled mass customization. This is in accordance with some emergent applications discussed earlier, where highly customized products serve only a niche market that can afford a high premium. However, it is encouraging to see a very active research in this new area that may eventually rule out the cost as a major constraint.

Many opportunities for future research arise from this work. Empirical research to assess different parameters in real settings is a challenge. In particular, research to estimate customer preference intensity and sensitivity to lead time would be very valuable. This research will reveal which sectors are favorable (or indeed unfavorable) for the implementation of RM-enabled mass customization strategies. We believe such information is very useful to further assess the viability of the technologies in the long term. Another opportunity is to extend the model by incorporating the fact that products manufactured by the two configurations may co-exist in the market. Such a study will complement the existing models analyzing competition between mass producers and mass customizers. Another possible extension is to extend the market demand model by, for example, allowing customers to have uncommon reservation price for their ideal products as well as by allowing customer preferences to follow any distribution rather than the more usual and restricted uniform distribution. Such extensions would certainly make the model more realistic and may lead to some interesting managerial insights.

References

Åhlström P, Westbrook R (1999) Implications of mass customization for operations management: An exploratory survey. Int J Oper Prod Manag 19(3):262–273
Alptekinoglu A, Corbett C (2008) Mass customization vs. mass production: Variety and price competition. Manuf Serv Oper Manag 10:204–217
Barrass DF, Roberts J, Jones R, Hague R, Dickens P (2008) The use of structured relationship modelling techniques as a tool to elicit customizable product features. Proc IME C J Mech Eng Sci 222(2):247–255
Bateman RJ, Cheng K (2006) Extending the product portfolio with 'devolved manufacturing': methodology and case studies. Int J Prod Res 44(16):3325–3343
Benjaafar S, Kim JS, Vishwanadham N (2004) On the effect of product variety in production-inventory systems. Ann Oper Res 126:71–101
Bernardes ES, Hanna MD (2009) A theoretical review of flexibility, agility and responsiveness in the operations management literature. Int J Oper Prod Manag 29(1):30–53

Brown AO, Lee HL, Petrakian R (2000) Xilinx improve its semiconductor supply chain using product and process postponement. Interfaces 30:65–80

Buzacott J, Shanthikumar JG (1993) Stochastic Models of Manufacturing Systems. Prentice-Hall, Upper Saddle River

Chopra S, Meindl P (2007) Supply Chain Management: Strategy, Planning and Operation. Pearson Prentice Hall, Upper Saddle River

Cortex R, Dinulescu N, Skafte K, Olson B, Keenan D, Kuk F (2004) Changing with the Times: Applying Digital Technology to Hearing Aid Shell Manufacturing. Hear Rev 11:30–38

Dapiran P (1992) Benetton – Global logistics in action. Int J Phys Distrib Logist Manag 22:7–11

Davis SM (1987) Future Perfect. Addison-Wesley, Boston, MA

De Groote X (1994) Flexibility and marketing/manufacturing coordination. Int J Prod Econcs 36:153–167

Dobson P, Waterson M (1996) Product range and inter-firm competition. J Econ Manag Strat 35:317–341

Duray R Ward PT, Milligan GW, Berry WL (2000) Approaches to mass customization: configurations and empirical validation. J Oper Manag 18(5):605–625

Endo S, Kincade DH (2008) Mass customization for long-term relationship development: Why consumers purchase mass customized products again. Qual Market Res 11(3):275–294

Feitzinger E, Lee HL (1997) Mass customization at Hewlett Packard: the power of postponement. Harv Bus Rev 75:116–121

Fralix (2001) From mass production to mass customization. J Textil Apparel Tech Manag 1(2):1–7

Gershenson JK, Prasad GJ, Zhang Y (2003) Product modularity: definitions and benefits. J Eng Des 14(3):295–313

Hague RJM, Campbell I, Dickens P (2003) Implications on design of rapid manufacturing. Proc IME C J Mech Eng Sci 217:25–30

Hart C (1995) Mass customization: conceptual underpinnings, opportunities and limits. Int J Serv Ind Manag 6(1):36–45

Hieu LC, Zlatov N, Vander-Sloten J, Bohez E, Khanh L, Binh PH, Oris P, Toshev Y (2005) Medical rapid prototyping applications and methods. Assemb Autom 25(4):284–292

Holweg M (2005) The three dimensions of responsiveness. Int J Oper Prod Manag 25(6):603–622

Hopkinson N, Hague RJM, Dickens PM (2006) Rapid Manufacturing: An Industrial Revolution for the Digital Age, Wiley, Chichester

Hotelling H (1929) Stability in competition. Econ J 39:41–57

Jiang K, Lee HL, Seifert RW (2006) Satisfying customer preferences via mass customization and mass production. IIE Trans 38:25–38

Kritchanchai D, MacCarthy B (1999) Responsiveness of the order fulfillment process. Int J Oper Prod Manag 19(7):812–833

Lampel J, Mintzberg H (1996) Customizing Customization. Sloan Manag Rev Fall 21–30

Lancaster K (1990) The economics of product variety: A survey. Market Sci 9:189–206

Lee HL, Billington C, Carter B (1993) Hewlett Packard gains control of inventory and service through design for localisation. Interfaces 23:1–11

Mandelson H, Parlaktürk AK (2008) Product-Line Competition: Customization vs. Proliferation. Manag Sci 54(12):2039–2053

McCutcheon DM, Raturi AS, Meredith JR (1994) The Customization-Responsiveness Squeeze. Sloan Manag Rev 35(2):89–99

Pham DT, Dimov S (2001) Rapid Manufacturing: The Technologies and Applications of Rapid Prototyping and Rapid Tooling, Springer, London

Piller FT, Müller M (2004) A new marketing approach to mass customization. J Comput Integrated Manuf 17(6):583–593

Pine BJ (1993) Mass Customization: The New Frontier in Business Competition, Harvard Business School Press, Boston, MA

Pine BJ, Victor B, Boynton AC (1993) Making mass customization work. Harv Bus Rev 108–119

Porter ME (1998) Competitive advantage: creating and sustaining superior performance, Free Press, NY

Radder L, Louw L (1999) Mass customization and mass production. The TQM Magazine 11(1):35–40

Reichhart A, Holweg M (2007) Creating the customer-responsve supply chain: a reconciliation of concepts. Int J Oper Prod Manag 27(11):1144–1172

Signorelli S, Hesket JL (1984) Benetton A, Harvard Business School Case, 9–685–014

Squire B, Brown S, Readman J, Bessant J (2006) The impact of mass customization on manufacturing trade-offs. Prod Oper Manag 15:10–21

Swaminathan JM, Tayur S (1998) Managing broader product lines through form postponement using vanilla boxes. Manag Sci 44:S161-S172

Swaminathan JM, Lee H (2003) Design for postponement, In: Graves S, de Kok (Eds) Handbooks in Operations Research and Management Science: Supply Chain Management: Design, Coordination and Operation. Elsevier Publishers, pp 199–228

Tseng MM, Jiao J (1998) Concurrent design for mass customization. Bus Process Manag J 4(1): 10–24

Tuck CJ, Hague RJM, Ruffo M, Ransley M, Adams P (2008) Rapid manufacturing facilitated customization. Int J Comput Integrated Manuf 21(3):245–258

Van Hoek RI (2001) The rediscovery of postponement: a literature review and directions for research. J Oper Manag 19:161–184

Waller MA, Dabholkar PA, Gentry JJ (2000) Postponement, product customization, and market-oriented supply chain management. J Bus Logist 21:133–159

Wohlers TT (2007) Wohlers report 2007: State of the Industry Annual Worldwide Progress Report. Wohlers Associates Inc

Yang B, Burns ND, Backhouse CJ (2004) Postponement: a review and an integrated framework. Int J Oper Prod Manag 24:468–487

Innovative Process in E-Commerce Fashion Supply Chains

Margaret Bruce and Lucy Daly

Abstract Fashion is price sensitive and runs on tight margins. Consumers expect high quality fashion at competitive prices, and in a recession falling prices and demand are particularly acute. This presents challenges for the supply chain. The sector is driven by cost and the need to manage the supply chain more effectively to reduce excess stock and risk in product forecasting. Increasing competition from low labour cost countries puts pressure on manufacturers to push down prices and, at the same time, to offer exceptional levels of service. Manufacturers may not wish to compete on the basis of price, and thus must find some other means of differentiation to remain competitive. E-commerce allows companies to improve communications within the supply chain and enhance service offering, thus providing opportunities for competitive differentiation. However, companies may not have the skills to develop e-commerce operations immediately, nor be able to realise revenue stream from investment in this technology and so may be unable to assess fully the risk of investment. Through the presentation of primary research, this chapter addresses the adoption process and the use of e-commerce in the textiles and clothing supply chain.

Keywords E-commerce · supply chain management · adoption of technologies · textiles and apparel supply chains

1 Key Drivers Affecting Change

The textiles and apparel industry in the UK is facing tremendous competition and is currently undergoing substantial change, particularly in a recessionary environment. Underlying clothing sales for Christmas 2008 were an estimated 6–9% lower

M. Bruce (✉)
Professor of Design Management and Marketing, Marketing, International
Business and Strategy Division, Manchester Business School, Booth Street West, Manchester
M15 6PB, UK
e-mail: margaret.bruce@mbs.ac.uk

T.C. Edwin Cheng and T.-M. Choi (eds.), *Innovative Quick Response Programs in Logistics and Supply Chain Management*, International Handbooks on Information Systems, DOI 10.1007/978-3-642-04313-0_11,
© Springer-Verlag Berlin Heidelberg 2010

than that for 2007 (The Observer 28.12.08). Consumers are reluctant to spend on discretionary items, and when they do, they expect fashion, quality and low cost items. The reduction in sales and the expectation of customers to pay less for a comparable quality resulted in one-day flash sales in the run-up to Christmas 2008, with discounts of up to 20% (The Observer 04.01.09). However, these figures did little to quell the effects of the economic environment, with reported third quarter sales down at least 5.5% on previous years (The Observer 04.01.09).

The Western textiles and apparel manufacturing industry can no longer compete on price alone, and thus is facing tough competition from low labour cost countries (Jones 2002). On 1 January 2005, the Agreement on Textiles and Clothing (ATC) was terminated. Consequently, world trade of textile and apparel products is no longer governed by quotas, but is instead governed by the rules and disciplines within the multilateral trading system (WTO.org, 01.06.2009). The impact of this is an increase of imports from countries with low labour costs. At the same time, the speed of replenishment is important in some areas to satisfy customer demand, thus making "countries with proximity more competitive for those goods where replenishment is important and these economic factors will intensify" (Abernathy et al. 2004). Therefore, there are two drivers underpinning sourcing decisions: cost and location. This is true for the US and the UK, where the general trend of a steady decline of indigenous production of textiles and apparel is ongoing (Abernathy et al. 2004)

The apparel manufacturing industry in the UK is also highly fragmented (Da Silva et al. 2000). There are a small number of large companies, and it is these companies that tend to be the main UK suppliers to the major retailers in the country, such as Marks and Spencer PLC, and the other high street stores. However, the majority of companies are small (Stengg 2001).

Notably, small firms often have limited manpower, time, expertise within the organisation and financial resources (Burns 1996; Bridge et al. 1998). This has an impact on the firm's ability to invest in new technologies such as e-commerce. Often the skills are not available in-house, increasing the cost implications and perceived risk. Typically, learning new skills is carried out 'on-the-job'. This has implications for adopting innovation in the management of the supply chain, as in-house skills and expertise may not be readily available and may need to be outsourced.

Apparel manufacturing is labour intensive, and the UK and the US has a high wage rate compared to many less developed countries. Many brands and retailers in both countries have increased overseas sourcing, thus resulting in a reduction of domestic production (Textiles and Apparel Strategy Group 2000). This raises the issue of how indigenous companies, and in particular the small and medium enterprises (SMEs), obtain competitive differentiation, as they are unable to compete on price. The industry has a number of characteristics, namely short product lifecycles, high volatility of demand, low predictability and high incidences of impulse purchase (Christopher and Peck 1998). These factors result in difficulties in forecasting demand, and the need for a constantly changing product portfolio places further pressures on the textiles and apparel supply chain.

Table 1 Market size and forecast of online retail sales of clothing and footwear, 2003–2008 (Source: Mintel 2008b)

	Online retail sales of clothing and footwear		Change year-on-year	At 2003 prices[a]	
	£m	Index	%	£m	Index
2003	1,089	100	20.1	1,089	100
2004	1,519	140	39.5	1,563	144
2005	1,691	155	11.3	1,780	163
2006	2,037	187	20.4	2,174	200
2007	2,377	218	16.7	2,556	235
2008 (est)	3,002	276	26.3	3,259	299

[a]Calculated using Mintel's clothing deflator

The UK and US high street clothing retail sectors have also seen increasing levels of competition, not only from overseas with new entrants, such as Zara and Mango with their efficient supply chains, rapid stock turnover and increasing numbers of seasons – the 'fast fashion', but also from the growth of supermarket fashion from traditional food retailers, such as Asda Wal-Mart and Tesco. Such companies have developed highly successful clothing ranges: Asda Wal-Mart with George, Tesco with Florence and Fred and Sainsburys with Tu. This has further increased competition and also redefined how consumers shop for fashion, with time-starved customers able to purchase cheap fashionable clothing as part of their weekly food shop, rather than visiting the high street specifically for clothes. Again, this is changing the dynamics of the sector as a whole, as there is an increasing emphasis on quick replenishment and rapid turnover of stock. Zara is a specialist fashion chain and an important example of a fast fashion retailer, with rapid stock turnaround and vertical integration. Indeed, Zara is credited with being a leader in fast fashion (The Economist 2005; Strategic Direction 2005; Foroohar and Stabe 2005). However, contributing to Zara's success is its focus on a limited range, basic shapes and small sizes, so that it deals with a rather narrow product range.

Simultaneously, online fashion retailing has continued to grow steadily, as indicated in Table 1. It is predicted that online retailing could account for between 10 and 15% of clothing sales in the coming years (Mintel 2008a). In real terms, the market trebled in size between 2003 and 2008 (Mintel 2008b). Table 2 indicates that this growth will continue in future years.

It is expected that the online fashion market will be worth £6.8 billion by 2013 (Mintel 2008b).

2 The Textiles and Apparel Supply Chain

Fashion and textiles is a volatile industry, and getting the right product in the right place at the right time can be difficult to achieve (Fernie 1999). Response times in the textiles and clothing supply chain can be lengthy, resulting in the distributor

Table 2 Market size and forecast of online retail sales of clothing and footwear, 2003–2013 (Source: Mintel 2008b)

	Current Prices	Year-on-year		At 2008 prices		Year-on-year
	£m	%	Index	£m	Index	%
2003	1,089		36	1,002	33	
2004	1,519	39.5	51	1,439	48	43.5
2005	1,691	11.3	56	1,639	55	13.9
2006	2,037	20.5	68	2,000	67	22.0
2007	2,377	16.7	79	2,353	78	17.6
2008 (est)	3,002	26.3	100	3,002	100	27.6
2009 (proj)	3,695	23.1	123	3,732	124	24.3
2010 (proj)	4,507	22.0	150	4,642	155	24.4
2011 (proj)	5,309	17.8	177	5,524	184	19.0
2012 (proj)	6,154	15.9	205	6,480	216	17.3
2013 (proj)	6,844	11.2	228	7,207	240	11.2

ordering up to 8 months in advance of when the goods are required in store (Forza and Vinelli 1997). Longer supply chains require more 'pushing' of merchandise and result in less accurate forecasts. This can lead to excess inventory, increased discounting and consumer dissatisfaction (Mattila et al. 2002). It is estimated that 33% of merchandise is sold at mark-down prices, and that only one in three customers are able to find the right product in stock (Fisher et al. 2000, cited in Mattila et al. 2002).

Fast fashion has the objective of getting clothing into store within the shortest time possible. This has resulted in an increasing number of 'seasons', and shipping times from suppliers must be taken into consideration (Mintel 2008a). Distance is key-goods from China can have a shipping time of 22 days, compared to five days from Turkey (The Financial Times, August 30, 2005). Retailers are switching production for replenishment to countries that are close to the market and have good infrastructure to move goods. And so, Eastern Europe, Turkey and India are benefiting in response to competition from fast fashion specialists, such as Zara, who are able to push the latest trends quickly by sourcing closer to home (The Financial Times, August 30, 2005). Some high street retailers are sourcing and buying on a weekly basis to introduce new fashionable items and to replenish stock.

Changes to fashion sale patterns in the UK and the US as a result of increased competition and changes in consumer purchasing behaviour have meant that retailers are now buying in smaller quantities. Sourcing has become more systematic with a greater emphasis placed on supplier involvement (Jackson and Shaw 2001). Because of competitive forces and reducing fashion cycles, retailers have been forced to develop strategies, enabling them to control the supply chain more closely, thus allowing them to source quality products at competitive prices (Bruce and Moger 1999).

The UK and the US industries need to concentrate on quick response methods to counteract the threat of the increasing number of imports and levels of overseas sourcing (Bhamra et al. 1998; Abernathy et al. 2004). This includes ensuring accurate response to overcome industry characteristics, such as short product lifecycles, high volatility, low predictability and high impulse purchase (Chandra and Kumar 2000). These include flexible delivery through domestic sourcing, reduced levels of stock and increased net margins. In addition, there is an increased opportunity for improved innovation, quality and style. There is a growth in 'local' manufacturers in lower cost European countries such as Romania and Slovakia. By sourcing from lower cost countries in Europe, rather than countries further afield such as Asia, companies are able to realise shorter lead times, while still benefiting from lower costs. This, then, raises the issue of how the UK and the US indigenous companies can enhance their offering in order to obtain a competitive differentiation.

Information and Communication Technology (ICT) plays an important role in such activities by facilitating efficient ordering and tracking of goods within the supply chain, particularly when the supply chain is operating on a global basis. Many retailers are now using ICT to gain improved control over product development and supply chain processes (Jackson and Shaw 2001).

2.1 E-Commerce in the Textiles Supply Chain

Research has shown that through e-commerce, businesses are able to use the Internet to reduce costs associated with purchasing, to manage supplier relationships, to streamline logistics and inventory, to plan production and to reach customers in a more effective manner (Margherio et al. 1999) and to develop strategic advantage and successful implementation of business re-engineering (Strempek and Alexander 2000).

Hines (2001) argues that the 'e-revolution' is transforming how interaction occurs in business-to-business markets. This change has occurred not only because of technological advances, but also because of factors such as globalisation, organisational restructuring, information and communication technologies, increased focus on differentiation over cost-cutting and rise in consumerism. However, in contrast, Van Hoek (2001) argues that, in reality, e-business is still largely focussed on sales and marketing, rather than becoming an integral business model for transactions and operations management. Building on from this, Murphy and Bruce (2001) suggest that many companies entering into e-commerce activity do so purely so as not to be left behind by competitors and with little regard to strategy and return on investment. They fail to consider their target customer, and whether their web offering is targeting this group, attracting a new customer and, perhaps most importantly, what value the site offers to either group. This raises the question of to what extent are companies in the textiles and clothing supply chain taking advantage of e-commerce technologies.

E-commerce, and its predecessor EDI, has had a considerable impact on the transference of product requirement information through the supply chain. The textiles and apparel supply chain is becoming increasingly global, as retailers transfer sourcing to low labour cost overseas suppliers in a bid to meet consumers' value for money requirements and increase profit margins. E-commerce technologies have the potential to considerably ease problems of communicating worldwide across time zones and enable immediate transfer of information between companies.

Characteristics of the textiles and apparel industry include short product lifecycles, demand volatility, difficulties in forecasting and impulse purchasing (Christopher and Peck 1998), and so make the issue of information distortion in the sector a particular problem. E-commerce may have an impact on the accuracy and speed of information flow. It allows companies to share information within the supply chain and provides customers with the ability to input order data and check the status of this.

Given the large proportion of SMEs in the sector, it is important to also consider SME use of e-commerce. Chapman et al. (2000) suggest that internet applications provide an opportunity for small firms to improve competitiveness. SMEs tend to use the Internet as a communication medium, and websites often provide information about the company and its products and services in order to increase awareness rather than to conduct business (Elsammani and Scown 2000). E-commerce holds benefits for smaller suppliers as well, as it allows them to collaborate with other small manufacturers, or even to work together with a large manufacturer, who can help with aspects such as warehousing (Loughlin 1999).

2.2 Adoption of E-Commerce Technologies

Thus, research indicates some of the salient benefits of using e-commerce in the textiles and apparel sector. So, what is the process of adopting this technology by companies in the sector and what are the challenges? Pires and Aisbett (2003) suggest that investment decisions about e-commerce must be considered in conjunction with internal, competitor and market analysis, and that e-commerce adoption may also require the adoption of new business strategies. Power (2002) also notes that websites tend to be used to establish a presence and providing information on the company, products and general PR, rather than as a transactional tool.

From the e-commerce adoption literature, the adoption process is presented as a stage process and different stages are presented by different researchers. Pires and Aisbett (2003) suggest that these move from basic use of communication technology through to the realm of business transactions. Work by Ellis-Chadwick et al. (2002) focusses on stages of e-commerce amongst retailers and suggests that the following stages apply:

- *Communication platform*: providing generally available information (financial, store location, mission statement and terms of customer service).
- *Electronic shop*: the retailer offers their offline shop online.

Critical success factor	Phase
Commitment	Start-up
Content	Start-up
Price sensitivity	Start-up
Convenience	Start-up
Control	Growth/start-up
Interaction	Growth/start-up
Brand image	Growth/start-up
Community	Growth
Partnership	Maturity
Process improvement	Maturity
Integration	Maturity

Fig. 1 Critical success factors by phase of development (adapted from Jeffcoate et al. 2002)

- *Trading community*: the development of portals that are inward looking (linking together the various companies under a single holding group) or outward looking (linking together companies outside the holding group).

Also, Jeffcoate et al. (2002) identify key stages in the adoption process. They suggest that three phases in the development of an e-commerce business can be found, namely start-up, growth and high volume business/maturity. And that they tend to move from an informational website to a transactional (i.e. cost effective selling) during these phases. They also identify a number of critical success factors for e-commerce, and argue that these become applicable during the different phases (Fig. 1). This approach raises the question of whether these issues apply in this sequence to the textiles and apparel sector, or whether certain phases such as brand image and partnership will apply earlier. For example, SMEs are restricted by a lack of in-house skills and may have to outsource or develop partnerships in order to move into e-commerce.

Again, it is important also to consider SME adoption of e-commerce, given the large proportion of SMEs in the UK textiles and apparel sector. Walczuch et al. 2000) identify uses of e-commerce by SMEs and also the frequency by which they are used (Fig. 2). Again this suggests activities that a firm starts with and indicates a progression to other activities. It also indicates that uses of e-commerce are far broader than merely launching a promotional website.

SME adoption of the Internet can be restricted by a number of factors, especially a lack of understanding of the opportunities available to small business, a lack of understanding on how to implement these techniques, a lack of skills amongst the workforce to use them, price of technology and a lack of willingness to dedicate the time and resources to resolve this paucity of understanding and skills (Chapman et al. 2000). One aspect of the adoption process is that it allows knowledge and insight to be gained to maximise the return from this investment at a later stage in

	Percentage of companies
E-mail address	97
To provide rational information	90
To promote company and/or products	86
To order	31
Customer service	21
To search for suppliers	10
To pay	7
Built-in security	7
To offer job vacancies	3
Information for personnel (intranet)	0
Extranet	*0*

Fig. 2 Website applications (Source: Walczuch et al. 2000)

the process. However, recent research by Ashworth et al. (2006) shows that smaller retailers can make revenue at the outset from their investment in e-commerce, if planned and managed effectively. They are critical of the stage models that tend to pass mechanically from information to transactional sites and which indicate that revenue gains can only be made at the later stages of adoption. From Ashworth et al.'s research, they found that successful e-tailers operated a transactional site at the outset. 'Web-weaving' is an approach they have identified as typical of successful e-tailers. These have evolved through a successive activity of venturing, learning and developing the business and have found a 'strategic fit' with their offerings and the market and continually evolved their businesses to meet new opportunities, adding value, for example through new services like fitting guides online, personal shopper, etc. In this way, they have benefited from cost savings and spreading expenditure to 'fast track' profits, and have generated revenue from the outset.

3 Adoption and Use of E-Commerce in the Fashion Supply Chain

To gain insight into the adoption process and utilisation of e-commerce in fashion supply chain, research was conducted with the US and the UK textiles and apparel companies at all stages in the supply chain. The sample selection included both large international corporations and SMEs to provide a greater breadth across the sector. Research was conducted through face-to-face, open-ended and semi-structured interviews with key personnel involved in the e-commerce operations of the company, and a set of constructs of themes were developed and some comparisons made,

Attribute	UK	US
Benefits	• Cost reduction • Expansion of customer base	• Ease of access • Cost reduction • Expansion of customer base
Challenges	• Lack of skills in-house requiring outsourcing • Changes to the customer base • Lack of information available • Lack of funds • Challenging existing work practices and attitudes	• Lack of information available to show successes and failures • High levels of risk • Channel conflict • Challenging existing work practices and attitudes
Development	• Important to take a gradual well managed approach	• Important to take a gradual well managed approach
Supply chain	• Not concerned with channel conflict generally • Facilitates overseas communication within the chain • Not strategic in approach to e-commerce	• Channel conflict a major concern • Facilitates overseas communication within the chain • Strategic in approach to e-commerce
Supply chain relationships	• No partnering for e-commerce ventures • Companies felt e-commerce benefited relationship • Customers felt e-commerce did not affect the relationship • Important not to lose personal contact with customers	• Partnerships to develop e-commerce ventures considered important • Important to consider impact of e-commerce on existing relationships – e-commerce may not benefit the relationship

Fig. 3 Comparison between the UK and the US companies

as shown in Fig. 3. The results from this research were then used to develop a process of e-commerce adoption for the sector.

The US research was conducted with eight companies, and companies involved in the US study showed varied experience of e-commerce. Some companies were technology providers with considerable knowledge of the possibilities of e-commerce, and others were large organisations at various stages of e-commerce integration. UK research was carried out with five small companies in the textile and clothing industry. Companies involved in the UK study were all at different stages of e-commerce use, with one company very new to e-commerce and one company with considerable experience. Themes from the US and the UK studies are compared as shown in Fig. 3.

3.1 Costs and Benefits

US companies involved in the study noted that e-commerce provided organisational benefits, including ease of access to technology, cost reduction and expansion of the customer base. Companies were operating within a global supply chain with many sourcing product from low labour cost countries, and e-commerce was deemed to be simpler than its predecessor EDI to implement in companies operating in less developed countries, due to its lower cost. UK companies in the study also noted cost reduction as a benefit, as it facilitated cost savings in promotional activities. However, ease of access and use was not a benefit recognised by the majority of the UK companies, as due to the size they did not have the skills in-house to develop and manage e-commerce operations, and thus had to outsource the activity. Further benefits noted by the UK companies included the ability to expand the customer base, although this then had implications of meeting demand and delivery, particularly with overseas requests.

A major concern of the US companies was the lack information available for a company moving into e-commerce. A common view was that information of past successes, failures and experiences of other organisations would be a useful aid for a company developing an e-commerce operation. This was echoed to some extent by the UK companies, although the information they required was with regards to where to source skills when outsourcing, as many were not in the position to carry out the activity in-house.

> We'd outsource it, we don't have the skills. We wouldn't employ someone at this stage because we're more comfortable with outsourcing because they're contracted to do a specific task so, meta-tagging, things like that, they will be updated to the search engine and all the rest of it would be done on either a monthly or weekly basis, by someone who's contracted to do it.

(Small UK soft furnishings manufacturer)

Both the UK and the US companies, particularly those operating within manufacturing and retailing sectors, noted that it was important to take a gradual approach to e-commerce and to develop operations as skills and confidence increased within the organisation. For example, many companies regarded that an organisation should not develop a fully transactional site before the company was in a position to be able to respond to the number of orders that may arise, and ensure that they had addressed issues such as delivery and fulfilment.

> You used to hear a lot about first mover advantage. I think it is less pertinent, I believe it is less important to be absolutely first, it is more important to do it correctly. We're taking a little bit more time I would say to do it correctly.

(Large US based international clothing brand)

UK companies noted that global reach was a major consideration with the introduction of e-commerce, and as a result of their internet presence had seen a considerable increase in interest from potential overseas customers. This was not the case with the US companies in the study. However, the US companies were all large, established organisations currently operating on a global level, while the UK companies were all SMEs, which often only have a localised customer base.

3.2 Challenges

The issue of customer base was a critical one for the US companies involved in the study. Manufacturers strongly believed that an e-commerce operation did not mean that they would then be able to sell directly to the end consumer, as this would result in channel conflict occurring between themselves and their current customer base of retailers. This was less of an issue to the UK companies involved in the study, and one company made deliberate moves to sell to its original customer base of retailers and also to a new target market consisting of the end retailer. This was justified by the fact that the company would be able to achieve greater profit margins when selling directly to the end consumer. It is possible that the reduced concern regarding channel conflict amongst SMEs was due to less advanced marketing skills, and their location in the supply chain, as small manufacturers. The large US organisations all had strong brand equities to protect, and did not want these damaging by any online activity. The UK SMEs in the study did not show concern regarding their existing brand and saw e-commerce as a move to target more customers.

Both the US and the UK companies stated that e-commerce functions such as e-mail, intranets and extranets were particularly beneficial when communicating with customers and suppliers overseas. However, the US companies were much more advanced in their use of e-commerce systems than the UK companies. The US companies were using systems that allowed them to electronically transfer design work and order information through extranets with the supply chain.

"You're going to see suppliers becoming part of your design team."

(US not for profit research and education consortium)

In comparison, many UK companies were using methods such as e-mail to communicate. This was as a result of the fact that they were much less advanced in their e-commerce activities and had not developed to the stage where they were implementing complex systems. The UK companies were at earlier stages of the e-commerce adoption and process and also had fewer resources to invest in e-commerce technologies.

The US companies all noted that business-to-business e-commerce was an area where they expected to see the greatest benefits for the organisation, and were actively considering ways in which they would be able to capitalise on this.

There's our public website which is there to build brand presence and to drive business to our existing channels and that seems to be a pretty common trend over here... we focussed on business to business. We really have two major initiatives going. One is around customer relationships management which was the driving force for our extranet application. What we wanted to do is give our customers the same information that our internal customer service reps have...

(US based sportswear brand)

However, the UK companies were much less strategic in their approach and were developing websites to target customers, but had not evaluated ways in which they could utilise e-commerce operations for the greatest benefit for the organisation. Only one UK company had actively developed systems which would enhance its service offering within the supply chain by providing customers with access to account information, thus benefiting from reduced administrative work.

Majority of the UK companies involved in the study had not developed fully transactional websites. However, the view was taken amongst these companies that, even if they were to sell online, it was important to still keep some form of direct contact with customers, and not to become so completely e-commerce enabled that it is not possible for the customer to contact the organisation to speak with someone directly. US companies did not demonstrate this view.

We have e-mail, online ordering, dedicated account ordering, we have a facility where our customers can log onto a secure portal on our server and buy, account information, print copy, invoices, statements, that sort of thing. They are the facilities that we offer currently.

(Small UK based workwear manufacturer)

4 Discussion

There is a wealth of e-commerce literature discussing the benefits to companies of the use of various e-commerce technologies. However, a key outcome of this study is that in reality companies are not leveraging fully the technology, suggesting that much of e-commerce literature takes a blue-sky approach to e-commerce technology, rather than documenting how e-commerce is being used in an industry. The purpose of this study is to document how e-commerce as a technology is actually being taken up and utilised in the textiles and clothing supply chain. This study has identified that, despite the widely cited benefits of e-commerce, there is a considerable and notable degree of cautiousness in the uptake of e-commerce technologies, amongst companies of all sizes, as opposed to much of the e-commerce literature, which does not take into account actual e-commerce uptake from a practical point of view.

This study has indicated that the uses and benefits of e-commerce, such as order tracking and streamlining of logistics, that are widely cited in the literature are not an immediate reality for companies developing an e-commerce activity. A key issue for all the companies involved in the study was the need to ensure that any e-commerce development was carried out at a rate that the company could sustain. It is essential

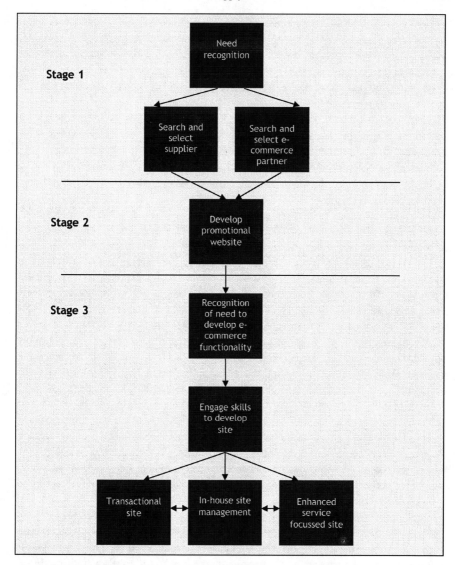

Fig. 4 Stage approach to e-commerce adoption in the textiles and apparel sector

that companies developing e-commerce functions do so at a rate that is appropriate to the skills within the organisation. This is echoed by Ashworth et al. (2006).

From the research reported here, it was apparent that a stage process could be identified for the adoption of e-commerce in the fashion supply chain. And that this did correspond to the stages presented by Jeffcote et al. (2002). Figure 4 presents the stage approach of e-commerce adoption that has been developed as an outcome of this study.

Figure 4 illustrates the process that companies follow when developing e-commerce functions. The speed at which companies move through the process will depend on the capabilities within the organisation, and so a company with skills in-house at the beginning of the process will move through stages at a faster rate than a company with no experience of e-commerce. All companies will begin the process by recognising a need to develop an e-commerce function of some sort. This is likely to occur as a result of competitor analysis or a desire to offer customers potential customers with improved ways of accessing company information. However, after need recognition, companies will take one of the two routes – either source a supplier, as in the case of many UK based SMEs, or identify an e-commerce partner, as in the cases of some of the large US corporations. Both routes provide e-commerce expertise for the company.

The company then enters stage two of the process model, which is development of a promotional website. It is highly likely that a company will develop an informational website when initially moving in to e-commerce.

Companies then move on to stage 3, which is the recognition of the need to develop e-commerce, facilities from a promotional site to an interactive site. Again, the length of time elapsed between stage 2 and stage 3 will depend on company skills and confidence levels. And this is reinforced by Ashworth et al.'s (2006) notion of 'web-weaving'. After need recognition, the company will source the skills to develop e-commerce functions. This level of the model refers to a company outsourcing the development of the stage of e-commerce if they do not have the in-house skills. However, companies with the in-house capability will by-pass this level and move directly to the final level of the model, which echoes the findings of Ashworth et al. This includes developing the in-house capability, which can occur either by training existing staff or recruiting new staff to manage e-commerce operations. This occurs as the need to manage the site in-house increases as a result of increased demand, either training or recruiting. Ashworth et al. (2006) note that accumulated learning occurs that feeds back into the development of the e-commerce activity and so may result in the rapid development of new functions and offerings and expansion into new niche markets.

The final level of stage 3 is to develop the advanced e-commerce capability, and again companies may find that they develop a transactional site allowing companies to purchase goods, or a site offering enhanced services such as tracking of goods and management of inventory. Companies may also decide to offer both facilities, either with or without a time-lapse. This is the stage where companies may use their e-commerce facilities to share information regarding scheduling and planning throughout the chain, and utilise e-commerce technologies to assist in achieving flexible manufacturing for fast fashion.

However, it should be recognised that it is not necessary that companies progress through all stages. In some cases it may be more consistent with company strategy to stop at stage 2 of the model, rather than to always plan to end at stage 3. Not all companies will have the resources in terms of capital and competencies to move to stage 3, and attempting to do so may damage company reputation. Others may plan from the outset to develop a transactional site, and as Ashworth et al have shown, this can enable 'fast track' revenue gain on the investment.

5 Conclusion

With globalisation of the supply chain, companies face complications of communicating across time zones. E-commerce technologies facilitate this, as it enables information to be transferred electronically. However, much of the e-commerce literature presents a blue-sky approach to e-commerce that is not immediately achievable for many companies developing e-commerce operations. This study has identified that, despite the widely cited benefits of e-commerce, there is a notable degree of cautiousness in the uptake of e-commerce technologies, amongst companies of all sizes. More detailed cases of e-commerce take up and utilisation would help to disseminate know-how and give exemplars of success and so could encourage further adoption and utilisation of e-commerce in the sector.

References

Abernathy FH, Volpe A, Weil D (2004) The apparel and textile industries after 2005. Prospects and choices. Unpublished paper, Harvard University

Ashworth CJ, Schmidt RA, Pioch EA, Hallsworth A (2005) An approach to sustainable "fashion" e-tail: a five-stage evolutionary strategy of "clicks-and-mortar" and "pure play" enterprises. J Retailing Consum Serv 13(4):289–299

Ashworth CJ, Schmidt RA, Pioch EA (2006) "Web-weaving": an approach to sustainable e-retail and online advantage in lingerie fashion marketing. Int J Retail Distrib Manag 34(6):297–511

Bhamra T, Heeley J, Tyler D (1998) A cross-sectional approach to new product development. Des J 1(3):2–15

Bridge S, O'Neill K, Cromie S (1998) Understanding enterprise, entrepreneurship and small business. Macmillan Press Ltd., UK

Bruce M, Moger S (1999) Dangerous liaisons: an application of supply chain modelling for studying innovation within the UK clothing industry. Tech Anal Strat Manag 11(1):113–125

Burns P (1996) Small business and entrepreneurship. In: Burns, Paul, Dewhurst, Jim (eds) 2nd edn. Macmillan Press Ltd., UK

Chandra C, Kumar S (2000) An application of a system analysis methodology to manage logistics in a textile supply chain. Int J Supply Chain Manag 5(5):234–244

Chapman P, James-Moore M, Szczygiel M, Thompson D (2000) Building internet capabilities in SMEs. Logist Inform Manag 13(6):353–360

Christopher M, Peck H (1998) Fashion logistics. In: Fernie J, Sparks L (eds) Logistics and retail management, insights into current practice and trends from leading experts. Kogan Page Ltd., London, UK, pp 88–109

Da Silva R, Davies G, Naude P (2000) Marketing to UK retailers: understanding the nature of UK retail; buying of textiles and clothing. J Fashion Market Manag 4(2):162–172

Ellis-Chadwick F, Doherty N, Hart C (2002) Signs of change? A longitudinal study of internet adoption in the UK retail sector. J Retailing Consum Serv 9(2):71–80

Elsammani Z, Scown P (2000) How SMEs perceive and develop their web presence. Int J New Prod Dev Innovat Manag March/April

Fernie J (1999) Relationships in the supply chain. In: Fernie J, Sparks L (eds) Logistics and retail management, insights into current practice and trends from leading experts. Kogan Page Ltd., London, UK, pp 23–46

Foroohar R, Stabe M (2005) Fabulous fashion: low-cost companies like Zara and Topshop are emerging as defining and dominant players, not just followers. Newsweek International Oct 17, p 30

Forza C, Vinelli A (1997) Quick response in the textile-apparel industry. Integrated Manuf Syst 8(3):125–136

Hines T (2001) From analogue to digital supply chains: implications for fashion marketing. In: Tony H, Margaret B (eds) Fashion marketing, contemporary issues. Butterworth and Heinemann, Oxford, pp 34–36

Jackson T, Shaw D (2001) Mastering fashion buying and merchandising management. Palgrave, Hampshire, UK

Jeffcoate J, Chappell C, Feindt S (2002) Best practice in SME adoption of e-commerce. Benchmark Int J 9(2):122–132

Jones R (2002) The apparel industry. Blackwell Science Ltd, Aylesbury

Loughlin P (1999) Viewpoint: e-commerce strengthens suppliers' position. Int J Retail Distrib Manag 27(2):69–72

Margherio D, Henry S, Cooke S, Montes S, Hughes S (1999) The emerging digital economy. Secretariat on electronic commerce. Washington, www.ecommerce.gov/viewhtml.htm. Accessed 15 Apr 1998

Mattila H, King R, Ojala N (2002) Retail performance measures for seasonal fashion. J Fashion Market Manag 6(4):340–351

Mintel (2008a) Clothing retailing in the UK. September 2008

Mintel (2008b) Fashion online UK. August 2008

Murphy R, Bruce M (2001) B2C Online strategies for fashion retailers. In: Tony H, Margaret B (eds) Fashion marketing, contemporary issues. Butterworth and Heinemann, Oxford

Pires G, Aisbett J (2003) The relationship between technology adoption and strategy in business-to-business markets: the case of e-commerce. Ind Market Manag 32(4):291–300

Power D (2002) Application of established and emerging B2B e-commerce technologies: Australian empirical evidence. Integrated Manuf Syst 13(8):573–585

Strategic Direction (2005) How Zara fashions its supply chain. 21(10):28–31

Strempek B, Alexander L (2000) The adoption of electronic commerce in the United States hosiery industry. Int J New Prod Dev Innovat Manag March/April

Textiles and Apparel Strategy Group (2000) A national strategy for the UK textile and clothing industry. June 2000

The Economist (2005) The future of fast fashion: Inditex. June 18, 375(8431), p 57

The Financial Times (2005) Retailers move production from China in response to demands of "fast fashion" August 30th p 1

The Observer 28.12.08 If you thought the Christmas price cuts were good.... www.guardian.co.uk/business/2008/dec/28/high-street-new-year-sales/print

The Observer 04.01.09 M&S reveals scars of high street slump, www.guardian.co.uk/business/2009/jan/04/marks-and-spencer-sales-figures/print

The Times (2009) 100, ASOS strategic growth in the fashion retail industry. www.thetimes100.co.uk

Van Hoek R (2001) E-supply chains – virtually non-existing. Supply Chain Manag Int J 6(1):21–28

Walczuch R, Van Braven G, Lundgren H (2000) Internet adoption barriers for small firms in the Netherlands. Eur Manag J 18(5):561–572

Stengg W (2001) The textile and clothing industry in the EU: a survey. Enterprise Papers, No 2, June 2001

The Next Generation Demand Network in Quick Response Systems: Intelligent Products, Packet Switching and Dynamic Information

Jeff Barker and Gavin Finnie

Abstract This chapter discusses several innovations in information and communication technology and develops their potential to radically alter our view of the supply chain in quick response applications. Using the packet-switching framework as an analogy, it explores the way in which intelligent products may operate to dynamically adjust to market volatility. The changes will require new thinking in areas such as supply chain optimization and the handling of services in the supply chain or demand network. The main contribution here is to extend the research framework for dynamic information management for quick response networks.

Keywords Delivery time · Demand network · Information generation 3 · Intelligent product · Lead time · Packet switching · Quick response system · RFID · Supply chain · Packet switching

1 Introduction

The concept of a quick response (QR) system cannot be easily separated from those of efficient consumer/customer response systems (ECR), agile systems or other variations on the theme. The Council of Supply Chain Management Professionals' (CSCMP) definition of QR is: "A strategy widely adopted by general merchandise and soft lines retailers and manufacturers to reduce retail out-of-stocks, forced markdowns and operating expenses. These goals are accomplished through shipping accuracy and reduced response time. QR is a partnership strategy in which suppliers and retailers work together to respond more rapidly to the consumer by sharing point-of-sale scan data, enabling both to forecast replenishment needs"

J. Barker (✉)
School of Information Technology, Bond University, Gold Coast, QLD 4229, Australia
e-mail: jbaker@bond.edu.au

T.C. Edwin Cheng and T.-M. Choi (eds.), *Innovative Quick Response Programs in Logistics and Supply Chain Management*, International Handbooks on Information Systems, DOI 10.1007/978-3-642-04313-0_12,
© Springer-Verlag Berlin Heidelberg 2010

(Supply Chain Management Terms and Glossary 2009). Although originating in the apparel industry, the QR concept appears to have broader implications than just this field. Efficient Consumer Response, although focused more on the grocery sector, is characterised as "a process that tightly integrates demand management, production scheduling and inventory deployment to allow the company to better utilize information, production resources and inventory" (Weeks and Crawford 1994).

Christopher and Towill (2002) describe agility as a supply chain philosophy with six dimensions: marketing, production, design, organization, management and people. They define agility as "a business-wide capability that embraces organisational structures, information systems, logistics process and in particular, mindsets". The common theme across QR, agile and ECR is the effective rapid sharing of information using information and communication technology to deal efficiently with market volatility.

Rapid changes in technology allow industry to continuously adapt its view of "traditional" ways of doing things. Given the major financial return of effective supply/demand chain management for QR to market changes, this is an obvious target for the use of new technologies. However, this is an area in which these technologies have radically changed the way in which we view the management of the flow of materials and information from the raw material supplier to the final customer. Although the traditional term is "supply chain", the move to provide more customer focus refers to these as demand-driven supply chains, demand-driven value chains, demand chains or demand networks (Almirall et al. 2003). The principle here is that customer demand should be fuelling the need for supply fulfilment. As discussed later most demand "chains" are not linear relationships, and this chapter will generally use the term demand network rather than supply chain.

RFID (radio frequency identification) and intelligent products, supply/demand networks, multi-agent systems and information generation three (IG3) type technologies provide an opportunity to review the concepts supporting the traditional view of the demand chain. Most present day systems, including the current barcode systems, are still operating within the realms of information generation two (IG2). (The IG2 and IG3 terms are further developed below). Most current assessment of the implications of RFID in demand networks seem to deal primarily with low cost passive tags. The economics of basic RFID vs. barcodes does not in many cases appear to justify the investment (e.g. Tellkamp 2006). Any effective use of RFID must add value to the process, and one way to do this is to improve not only the visibility of information (the current approach and available via using bar codes) but also the processing and the location of that processing, that is by adding some enhanced capability to the RFID component.

The dynamics of information has undergone a significant transition. "Information now is global rather than local and dynamic rather than static" (Barker and Finnie 2004). Current barcode systems are only able to provide "semi-dynamic" information to enterprise systems, as information can only be obtained at limited, designated segments in the demand chain. There is an information deficiency at many stations in the demand chain due to the lack of visibility and ability to capture real-time information. This creates bottlenecks and places various limitations on the efficiency and effectiveness of managing these demand networks, obviously putting constraints on the ability for rapid response.

An interesting intermediate technology to extend the capability of barcodes is the emergence of the 2D or the matrix barcode. With a 2D structure these barcodes can store significantly more information (up to 2 KB at present) and can include redundancy and error-correction capability. One interesting application that opens up the dynamic capability of these codes is the embedding of URL information in the code, which can be detected from a mobile phone camera and used to link a WAP phone directly to the information source. However, the information source (the data matrix) is still static information with any active processing being performed elsewhere.

RFID technology and silent commerce offer the possibility of providing enterprise systems with truly dynamic information throughout the demand chain/network. The silent commerce concept was introduced by Accenture to describe the use of wireless, tagging and sensor technologies to make objects intelligent and interactive. Combining this with the internet enables new ways of gathering data and delivering services without human interaction. Real-time information can be captured throughout the entire global demand chain irrespective of its scale and complexity. However, current RFID applications tend to remain focused on an IG2 perspective of information and the view that RFID tags provide little more than replacement for barcodes. The emphasis has been placed on lowering the costs of passive tags with limited storage capability – in fact little more than is available on a bar code. The marriage of the "smart chip" (i.e. incorporating processing capability) and RFID technology occurring in parallel in applications such as the Octopus card has not rated much consideration in the demand chain.

This chapter will explore some of the potential provided by linking "intelligence" (or smart technology) to RFID capability in the demand network. Although the idea has attracted some interest, it has not been developed to any significant extent in supply chains, despite the potential for significant financial return in certain applications. The concept has, however, attracted some attention in manufacturing (see, e.g. Meyer et al. 2009). The technology enables us to consider the concept of the intelligent product, that is a product that carries with it some processing capacity and memory. The relationship between lead times and demand times in any supply/demand network defines the constraints under which the network operates and the way in which technologies like RFID can contribute to improving the efficiency and effectiveness of the network. The packet switching paradigm will be discussed as a construct for reviewing the way demand networks operate. The foundation of a QR system is rapid and effective information visibility and the packet switching view provides the vision of dynamic information and the capacity to speed up delivery and order fulfillment, even to the point of dynamic re-routing of products as needed.

2   The Role of Lead Times and Delivery Times in Demand Networks

The need to supply any product or service is defined by the demand for that product. A considerable amount of the research in supply chains/demand networks relates to establishing the estimated or forecast demand. In fact, a fundamental premise of movements like QR is that known demand can be rapidly communicated to the supply partners. However, the constraints on manufacturing any product are based on the lead times for the components of that product. It is in fact somewhat surprising that so little attention is paid in research to lead times and delivery times and the effects these times will have on the companies in a demand network. This section develops some of the backgrounds of these key issues, which will be addressed later in the chapter.

For the following, assume that the supply chain is a simple linear supply chain with every company having only one supplier and one customer as shown in Fig. 1.

Let l be the manufacturing lead time of a product and d be the acceptable delivery time of the same product. It is important to note that delivery time is the customer expectation of what the delivery should be, not the physical constraints on moving the product from one location to another. The latter is incorporated as a component of the lead time. It could possibly better be defined as "expected" delivery time.

The lead time l is the manufacturing lead time within one company in the demand network. It does *not* include the suppliers' lead times (for any necessary raw materials). The delivery time d is effectively driven by the demand and is set by the market, not the supply chain. The relationship

$$l : d \tag{1}$$

is crucially important and very often overlooked.

The following usually determine the necessity or otherwise of forecasting within a company:

$$l \leq d, \text{ forecasting is not required} \tag{2}$$

$$l > d, \text{ forecasting is required} \tag{3}$$

As an example, if it takes only 1 week to make the product ($l = 1$) and the delivery time is 2 weeks ($d = 2$), then no forecasting is required. Consequently, the product can be "engineered-to-order" (ETO) or "made-to-order" (MTO). If, however, it takes 6 weeks to make a product (i.e. $l = 6$) but the market will only accept a delivery time of 3 weeks ($d = 3$), then forecasting is required. Typically, such products are "made-to-stock" (MTS) or "assembled-to-order" (ATO).

Shingo (1981) used the terms production lead time (P) for l and delivery lead time (D) for d. Based on the $P{:}D$ ratio, Wikner and Rudberg (2005) proposed which manufacturing strategy should be used.

The lead time l can be made smaller by the following:

- Reducing set-up times, move times, run times and/or clean-down times
- Expanding capacity via the following:
  - Purchasing extra machines
  - Improving manufacturing efficiency
  - Purchasing newer machines

- Simplifying product design
- Using different materials, etc.

Now consider all the companies in this simple supply chain. For the purposes of the following analysis, it is assumed that the manufacturing (demand) network is linear, that is each company in the chain has one supplier and one customer, except of course, for the company at the tail of the chain and the company at the head of the chain.

Assume

n companies in simple supply chain, where $n \geq 2$

- The initial upstream company is number 1
- Final downstream company is number n
- The companies in between (if any) are numbered sequentially from 2 to $n - 1$, for $n > 2$

Note that within this supply chain, companies may be using ETO, MTO, ATO and MTS. Regardless of which manufacturing strategy or strategies companies in the chain use, each company will have a resultant lead time, which includes any decoupling point locations in the chain (see Sharman 1984; Hoekstra and Romme 1992; Olhager 2003; Rudberg and Wikner 2004).

Then the lead time and delivery time of company i is $l(i)$ and $d(i)$, respectively. Therefore, the *total* lead time for the whole manufacturing chain is the sum of each company's lead time:

$$L = l(1) + l(2) + \cdots + l(n) = \sum l(i) \text{ for } i = 1 \text{ to } n, \qquad (4)$$

and the *total* delivery time is

$$D = d(1) + d(2) + \cdots + d(n) = \sum d(i) \text{ for } i = 1 \text{ to } n. \qquad (5)$$

Therefore, the lead time to delivery time comparison ($l : d$ above) becomes, for the manufacturing chain,

$$L : D. \qquad (6)$$

However, we hypothesise that the final customer is only prepared to wait $d(n)$ time units. Hence, the comparison $L:D$ is replaced with

$$L : d(n), \qquad (7)$$

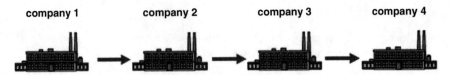

company 1   company 2   company 3   company 4

Fig. 1 Simple supply chain

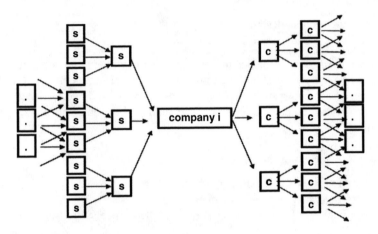

Fig. 2 Suppliers have suppliers and customers have customers

which is somewhat different from (6). L is, of course, the total lead time of say company 4, which is its own manufacturing lead time, $l(4)$, plus the suppliers lead times, $l(1) + l(2) + l(3)$. QR is addressing the constraints placed on the demand network due to (7).

It is important also to realise that neither l nor d is fixed. Unless all demand is specifically MTO, it must be assumed that demand will change. This will be discussed in further detail below. The $l{:}d$ ratio contributes towards the categorisation of Lean Supply or Agile Supply as given in Christopher (2000).

However, the supply chain is not as simple as that given in Fig. 1. An entity in the chain (a factory or distributor) may have many suppliers and many customers as depicted in Fig. 2. Each supplier and customer may, in turn, also have many potential suppliers and customers creating a network rather than a chain. Note that for x suppliers, the lead time to company i is now the maximum lead time from the x suppliers.

Figure 2 shows the network as seen by company i, which has three suppliers and three customers. Each of its suppliers has suppliers and each of its customers has customers.

What are not shown in Fig. 2 are the other customers of company i's suppliers and the other suppliers of company i's customers. Figure 3 includes these. Silisque et al (2003) noted that supply chains will develop into networks that adapt to consumer demand in almost real time, hence the term "demand networks".

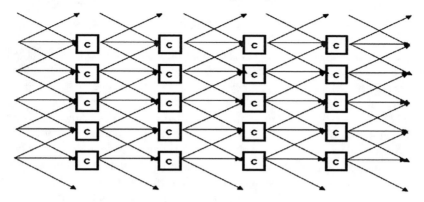

Fig. 3 Demand network

3 RFID in Demand Networks

In demand networks, an RFID device is a radio frequency identification tag that is attached to a physical item. Detailed coverage of the history and applications of RFIDs is given in Schuster et al. (2007).

The tag data needs to be converted to information and be made available to various information systems, for example Transaction Management Systems (TMS), Warehouse Management Systems (WMS), Advanced Planning and Scheduling (APS) systems, etc. Since the system is global, certain standards and processes need to be introduced. These standards, developed at MIT, include the following:

- EPC (electronic product code), a simple serial numbering data system to identify the item
- PML, a physical markup language based on XML to describe the item, which effectively converts the EPC data to useful information
- ONS (object naming service), a mapping technique to link the EPC and PML
- Savant, data handling software

More detail on the standards can be found at the auto-id laboratories website (www.autoidlabs.org). The reader captures the EPC data from the RFID tag and relevant environmental and location information. It interacts with the Savant, which uses the ONS to retrieve information on the item. The accumulated information is then written to corporate databases using PML. By strategically placing readers in the supply chain, an item can be identified and traced locally. Because of the weak strength of the signal, this cannot be done globally. Further, the current cost of RFIDs has limited their use to items based on appropriate size or value. Items that do not satisfy these criteria are identified and located with a packaging unit such as a carton, a palette, etc. Applications of RFID in supply/demand networks include identity, track and trace, theft prevention, expiration dates for food and pharmaceuticals, counterfeit prevention and security (Asif and Mandiwala 2005). Bardaki et al. (2007) describe eight RFID-enabled supply chain collaboration services such as dynamic pricing and smart recall.

A common framework to assess the value of information technology (IT) is based on the view that IT creates business value via automational, informational and transformational effects. (Mooney et al. 1996). They define these as follows: "automational effects refer to the efficiency perspective of value deriving from the role of IT as a capital asset being substituted for labor. Within this dimension, value derives primarily from impacts such as productivity improvements, labor savings and cost reductions. Informational effects emerge primarily from IT's capacity to collect, store, process and disseminate information. Following these effects, value accrues from improved decision quality, employee empowerment, decreased use of resources, enhanced organizational effectiveness and better quality. Third, transformational effects refer to the value deriving from IT's ability to facilitate and support process innovation and transformation. The business value associated with these effects will be manifested as reduced cycle times, improved responsiveness, downsizing and service and product enhancement as a result of re-engineered processes and redesigned organizational structures".

The PhD research by Tellkamp (2006) focused on the impact of low cost passive tags and showed that in many cases the use of RFID purely as an identification device offered little if any economic benefit over the use of bar codes. In particular, the informational gains did not appear to justify the expenditure in readers and tags as the basic POS (point of sale) data was already available. However, our view in this chapter is that the major gains that are likely to appear in the longer term from RFID technology will be primarily transformational. Although the provision of better quality information can and probably will improve supply chain efficiency, the use of the technology to alter the way in which products and information flow is likely to be the most significant gain in effectiveness. The capability of the technology to provide more than just identification and, in particular, the possibility of some local processing or enhanced information capability allows us to look at ways in which the product itself can contribute to the operation of the chain.

4 The Next Generation Demand Network and Quick Response Systems

In moving towards the effective utilization of new technologies in QR demand networks, we can identify a number of key "change agents" that are driving the need to view demand networks differently. These include the following:

- A new dynamic view of information that we have termed "information generation three or IG3"
- Global track and trace
- Intelligent products and local intelligence capability
- Multi-agent systems

4.1   Information Generation Three: IG3

With the advent of the world-wide-web, the world has moved into an information age that is changing not only the way we do business and commerce but also our lifestyles. To help define this emerging environment, the following simple terminology and concepts are used. An information generation (IG) can be defined by the availability and general distribution of non-verbal information. Using this definition, there have been three "information generations" to date: IG1, IG2 and IG3.

IG1 is the information generation that started with rock drawings and paintings, and progressed through hieroglyphics to written language on scrolls and hand-written manuscripts. IG2 started with the invention of the printing press, which was the first "machine" to become involved in the storing and distribution of information. The availability and accuracy of information grew by orders of magnitude, resulting in the biggest increase in productivity to that time. IG3 started with the introduction of the world-wide-web ("the web") and owes its existence mainly to innovations in information and communication technology (ICT). It again resulted in orders of magnitude increase in the accuracy and availability of information and associated knowledge.

In IG3, as soon as information is updated, it is virtually, instantly and globally available through passive and active methods. Such information can be termed "dynamic" to differentiate it from the static information used in IG2. Physical devices such as GPS (global positioning systems), satellite navigation, smart cards, RFIDs and cell phones gather dynamic information as and when required. Using smart phones and personal calendars, it is now possible to know where people are and where they plan to be. Various techniques and facilities such as intelligent agents, data-mining, knowledge engineering and many others use dynamic information to add to knowledge and intelligence.

The business ecosystem (Moore 1993) is dynamic, volatile and complex in IG3. As stated by Watson (2007), with globalization, environments for organisations, both business and world governments, are becoming more complex. The reason for this increased environmental complexity include "the four V's", specifically:

- Increased Volume (from local to global context in terms of transactions)
- Increased Velocity (faster transactions between people)
- Increased Volatility (organisations change and reorganize faster)
- Increased concerns regarding Veracity (the truth is harder to distinguish)

In IG3,

- The amount of information is orders of magnitude greater than in IG2
- "Dynamic" information is replacing "static" information
- Information access is much faster
- The information has become truly global
- Information is more accessible
- In addition to information, processes can be exchanged

- Different search parameters can be utilized
- Visual communication is used more extensively
- Intelligence and knowledge retention are replacing data and information retention

This dynamic information and intelligence on things and people was not available in IG2 and was therefore not used in systems and methodologies designed and implemented in IG2. IG3 should be the foundation of modern QR systems, although much of the view of information currently employed in QR networks is from the IG2 era. Note that IG3 is not a system; it is the information environment we are progressively moving into.

4.2 Global Track and Trace

It is helpful to envisage a spectrum of devices to identify, locate and provide input on individual items. At one end of the spectrum used to provide dynamic information are GPS devices (the macro end), and at the other end of the spectrum are small RFID devices (the micro end). Other devices such as e-tags, sat-nav, smart cards, mobile phones, etc. are positioned along the spectrum. All these devices supply dynamic information. Bar codes can also be included in the spectrum, although they have limited locational dynamic information. It is possible to strategically place RFID readers and so the global location of individual items with attached RFIDs is known.

As an example, assume that the cost of RFIDs is such that it is feasible to put them onto individual widgets. Each widget can then be traced locally at a warehouse, a manufacturing plant or a retail outlet as is done now to. It can then be packaged into a carton that will have a separate RFID. Current thought is that individual item RFIDs and packaging unit RFIDs may have different frequencies (Schuster et al. 2007). As the item is loaded onto the carton, the relevant data structures will be updated so that each individual widget knows which carton contains it and each carton knows what widgets it contains.

The process is repeated when cartons are packaged onto palettes. If an RFID reader is placed around a truck loading space, relevant data structures can then be updated so that the truck knows what palettes its carrying and the palettes know which truck they are in. By reading the relevant data structures, the location of each widget (RFID), carton (RFID), palette (RFID) and truck (GPS) is known. This process can then continue when the palette is loaded off the truck and into a container (GPS), which has an RFID reader around its opening, for shipping the item to any global location. As is done now, the locations of the container and the truck are provided via GPS. Therefore, by strategically placing RFID readers, updating information system data structures, and using existing GPS devices and RFIDs, it is possible to locate an individual widget anywhere on the globe that has GPS coverage.

4.3   Intelligent Products

With each generation of RFID, there is increasing capability and potential to include local processing capacity. Current RFID technology provides a range of solutions. Simple EPC codes such as EPC-64 and EPC-96 provide 64 and 96 bit data structures to identify static product information. At the other extreme there is the US DOD RF-Tag data Format that has a standard non-volatile memory of 128–256 bytes and extended memory of 128 K bytes of battery-backed RAM. The military 412 tag has 4,096 bytes of EEPROM, with additional space for a number of commodity records. Tags may be further divided into active and passive tags, that is those that respond to a signal but have no local power source and those with battery power.

Much of the debate and commercial evaluation of RFID technology has been on cutting costs of passive RFID tags to make it competitive with bar code technology. In many cases the cost of the products being moved or the cost of a container load of product would make it worthwhile to consider more powerful devices. The DOD has taken this view with its increased storage capacity RF-Tags. With the continuing fall in smart card costs, the provision of intelligent RFID devices is financially viable for certain classes of product or product package.

The boundary between RFID tags, "Smart RFID" devices and "Smart Sensors" is becoming increasingly blurred, as is the place where specific computation occurs. The original RFID concept used RFID middleware and the object name service (ONS) to identify and process particular EPC codes. This middleware provides messaging, routing and connectivity to backend ERP systems and databases. This middleware processing capability tended to be centralized. More recently, the idea of edge processing has been proposed to deal with the high volumes of data generated by RFID devices. Hanebeck (2006) claims that "intelligence and data processing capabilities should not be located in large-scale remote systems but rather need to be readily available at the edge of the network where the individual items, cartons and pallets live". This "edgeware" deals with filtering, cleaning and eliminating redundant data before transmission to interfacing systems. The processing capability has moved to "smart RFID sensors", which can handle local activity.

Smart sensors (Culler and Mulder 2004) are a key component of the move towards pervasive and ubiquitous computing. Smart sensors incorporate both RFID capability and local processing capability and can form perceptive networks to monitor complex environments such as a factory.

Although the technology exists and there is a move to perform more local processing at key points in the demand chain, there does not appear to have been any significant move to provide intelligent or smart RFID sensors in demand chain applications. The question arises as to what benefit there can be in proving some autonomy for each product or pallet in the network. Schuster and Brock (2004) introduce the concept of "smart products" that "sense and respond with the physical world". They consider that "smart objects within the consumer demand chain might dynamically change price based on sensing demand at retail stores".

Karkkainen et al. (2003) also describe "intelligent products" as a potentially valuable tool in international projects where a large number of individualized deliveries need to be managed through a sizable demand network. Since the products and product delivery in such projects tend to be customized, the ability of products to actively participate in the demand network can significantly improve overall project productivity. In their HUT system, deliveries can communicate their identity and handling instructions directly to the information system. This information can be changed as conditions change. In the HUT system, each product is managed by a software agent who is external to the product. Wong et al. (2002), based on research at the Auto-ID centre at the University of Cambridge, also investigate the role of intelligent products in the demand chain. They define an intelligent product as having part or all of the following characteristics:

- Possesses a unique identity
- Is capable of communicating effectively with its environment
- Can retain or store data about itself
- Deploys a language to display its features, production requirements, etc.
- Is capable of participating in or making decisions relevant to its destiny

Such products can negotiate resources via their software agents, adapt objectives based on updates from the environment, advise on adjusted picking schedules, etc. Intelligent products may be considered at the case or pallet level to make the option cost-effective.

Although the intelligent product was proposed at this stage, there appears to have been little follow-up in more recent work in supply chain management. However, the idea has been further developed in manufacturing with the work on product-driven control systems. The Holonic Manufacturing Systems approach is predicated on the view that autonomous production units (holons) can work together to make products in a dynamically reconfigurable environment (e.g. Leitao and Restivo 2006). Product-driven control systems are "dealing with products whose information content is permanently bound to their material content and which are able to influence decisions made about them" (Pannequin et al. 2009). Allied with the holonic manufacturing systems approach based on intelligent agents, product-driven control offers the potential for increased flexibility and rapid adjustment to dynamic information to meet business demands (Haouzi et al. 2009; Gouyon and David 2008; Morel et al. 2003).

In this chapter, we extend this intra-organizational shop floor view to extra organizational supply networks. We consider the implication of intelligent products allied with a packet-switching view of the demand network. In particular, we consider the implications of embedding the intelligent agent capability in the RFID tag itself, rather than relying on an external agent to manage the product.

4.4 Multi-agent Systems (MAS) in Demand Networks

There is a considerable body of research on the use of multi-agent systems on demand chain management, and this section provides only some examples of the area. Autonomous software agents have been considered for multiple applications such as managing scheduling, procurement, negotiation, etc. There is in fact a competition (The Trading Agents Competition) that enables competitors to compare different agent strategies in a simulated supply chain environment (Arunchalam and Sadeh 2005). The MAS approach provides a useful programming paradigm for the provision of local intelligence by autonomous entities.

To provide a framework to consider MAS in supply chains, Ahn and Lee (2004) suggest that studies in agent-based supply chain management can be put into three categories: using the technology to improve the operational efficiency of supply chains, using dynamic information to improve network adaptability and using efficiency and effective agent-based architectures for supply chain management. As examples in the first area, an agent-based framework that simulates the supply chain with agents at each station was defined by Fox et al. (2000). Andrews et al. (2007) analysed the features that distinguished winning agents from losers in the TAC competition. Cao and Leggio (2008) showed that a multi-agent approach could reduce the bull-whip effect as opposed to conventional supply chain management approaches.

The discussion in the current chapter falls into the second category concerning the use of dynamic information. The paper by Ahn and Lee (2004) proposes an agent-based network where agents form dynamic information networks to coordinate production and order planning. Luh et al. (2003) have investigated a price-based approach for activity coordination using mathematical optimisation and the contract net protocol. The use of auctions to form optimal dynamic demand networks has been investigated by Kim and Segev (2003). Hanebeck and Raisinghani (2007) discuss the use of RFID technology as a supply chain coordination mechanism.

In the third category a large number of approaches to different architectures have been suggested. As an example, Sadeh et al. (2003) have worked on an agent-based decision support environment for dynamic supply chain management. In the system, called MASCOT, each agent uses a blackboard architecture for coordination and control and an agenda to drive activity. Finnie et al. (2004) have proposed a two-tier architecture of buyer/seller agents with buyer and seller coordinator agents. Nissen (2001) describes a design for agent federation, where the agent activities are defined using a Petri-net-based approach. Monteiro et al. (2007) describe an architecture based on "virtual enterprise nodes" to distribute decision making in a multi-site system where each VEN is implemented using two types of agent.

For the intelligent product as envisaged in this chapter, the intelligent agent approach provides a flexible programming methodology that suggests a distributed solution to controlling the demand network. It does not matter whether the agent is embedded at the individual product level or higher in the process, for example in the edgeware or at the smart sensor level, provided that the communications language and infrastructure are well defined.

5 Circuit-Switching, Packet-Switching and QR Systems

In the context of the IG3 concept and the role of RFID devices in dynamic information, this chapter considers how we could apply some packet-switching concepts to "dynamic demand networks". This section defines and contrasts the concepts of circuit-switching and packet-switching, considers the impact of demand in QR systems and the effect of lead times before looking at how a packet-switching view can change the way in which we consider demand networks.

5.1 Circuit-Switching vs. Packet-Switching

The term packet-switching is a telecommunications term, but it is used in this work to describe the model for demand networks. Both circuit-switching and packet-switching are used for high-capacity network communications. In circuit-switching networks, the connection is made between the sender and the receiver before the start of the communication and the "line" remains dedicated to that connection until closed by the sender or receiver. In packet-switching, the message is divided into packets that can each take a different path through the network from the source to the destination, where the packets are then recompiled into the original message. Packet-switching and circuit-switching networks are used to exchange information. However, in this discussion, we are using the switching networks as models to exchange inventory in demand network management rather than information. The enterprises exchanging inventory in the demand network are equivalent to nodes in a switching network exchanging information.

The current view of the demand network can be seen to be equivalent to circuit-switching, where connections are made between the customer and a limited number of suppliers. In both the out-dated MRPII and JIT theories, customers are recommended to have only one supplier and to develop a very close relationship to that supplier. We are proposing that the circuit-switching model was appropriate for SCM in IG2 as mainly only static information was available, but given the dynamic information facilities in IG3, the packet-switching model, with multiple suppliers rather than one source, for demand networks can and should be used in IG3.

5.2 The Impact of Demand in QR Systems

QR requires a high level of transparency and rapid availability of demand information. As products are sold, the information about that sale is recorded and made available to suppliers to plan production. Current approaches use scanners and barcodes, and the use of RFID purely as a product information source will not add much (other than some possible information on product detail, e.g. colour, etc.). With the addition of features such as temperature sensing, the use of RFID in fast moving consumer goods (FCMG) chains for products like perishable goods begins to make more economic sense. However, a key weakness in much of the assessment of agile and quick response systems is that demand, once known, is static. The demand for a product is itself a dynamic information, with the actual volume and location of demand possibly changing between the point of estimate and time of delivery. The longer the time interval, the higher is the probability that some change will occur. Viewing demand as static information reduces the flexibility offered by new technologies. As discussed later, the ability to view the demand network as a packet-switching environment allows us to consider multiple sourcing and dynamic re-direction of products as needed. The details of the sale are fed as far back in the demand network as needed. Various points in the network may form decision points, which will decide how to source (or multi-source) product (in the information flow) or how to reroute product (in the product flow) as needed.

As discussed earlier, the relationship between lead times and delivery times defines the constraints on meeting demand within a specified period. The total lead-time is the sum of each company's lead time, and minimising the response time could depend on how effectively the lead-times can be reduced (where $l(i) > d(i)$). On the other hand, if $d(i) > l(i)$, where $d(i)$ is the expected quick response time, there is no need to work on reducing this delivery time. In either case, the ability to partition and review the demand network components is enhanced by the intelligent packet-switched product view developed below.

5.3   Packet-Switching in the Demand Network

Christoper and Towill (2002) consider developing "market-specific" supply chains and the concept of matching the pipeline to the product. They use the example of the Spanish fashion retailer Zara to show that quick response and agility is achieved by compressing the total pipeline. In Zara, raw materials are sourced from low-cost off-shore suppliers. Approximately 40% of garments with low volatility are imported as finished goods. The rest are produced by QR in Spain, using their own factories for economies of scale operations (e.g. dying, cutting, etc.) and a network of small contractors for labour-intensive finishing stages.

Instead of dealing with demand for a product as a single value, Zara is categorizing such demand into two; a longer-term less volatile demand which can be serviced by cheaper overseas suppliers and a shorter-term volatile demand which can be serviced by local, more expensive suppliers.

The d for a product given in (1) has been broken up into components (in the Zara example, into two components):

$$d = d_{st} + d_{lt}, \tag{8}$$

where st is for short term and lt is for longer term

Thus, Zara split its sourcing to matched suppliers with suitable lead times to d_{st} and d_{lt}, and so the original $l : d$ (1) was satisfied by

$$l_{lt} : d_{lt} \text{ and } l_{st} : d_{st}. \tag{9}$$

Splitting sourcing provides a possible source of competitive advantage for a range of companies. Ordering of components or material in advance of demand and assembling or manufacturing the final product locally to enable responsiveness satisfied the d_{st} requirements. In effect, Zara is compressing the total pipeline by effective balancing of lead and delivery times.

The packet switching view of materials in the demand network enables us to view material as composed of local packets with addressing and content information attached and dynamically accessible. Niederman et al. (2007) hold the view that trading communities will "move from a world of point-to-point relationships to massive collaboration".

Traditional packet-switching has data packets arising from a single source and being reassembled at a single destination. Our packet-switching view allied with the intelligent product concept allows us to consider multiple sourcing of materials and the ability to dynamically complete shipments as requirements change. The corollary with packets lies in viewing each chunk or packet of supply as an addressable unit that can be redirected as needed and reassembled at the destinations(s) as required. Instead of the traditional view of inventory tied to a specific supplier or warehouse, we can rather consider virtual inventory, that is it exists somewhere in the pipeline. This may be in transit or resident in a supplier warehouse. Its location, volume, etc. can be determined dynamically. This is equivalent to Intel's view of "Inventory in Motion", where inventory is in the pipeline and products can be shipped before orders are received (Leach 2004). The demand network is self-adjusting, in that inventory will be re-routed as demand appears. For certain materials, there are a range of potential suppliers and the type and quality of material is relatively consistent across suppliers. Dynamic information also suggests the ability to deal dynamically with excess inventory in the demand network. As a customer requires an order to be completed, it is feasible to consider the following scenario:

The customer seeks order fulfillment. The order can be split into the most efficient delivery patterns and directed to relevant locations. Priorities can be established based on criteria such as delivery history, other CRM type factors, etc. Each location can be queried for its potential to deal with the order. Once an order is completely assembled, the component orders can be confirmed and initiated.

Dealing with products that require an agile response (e.g. local manufacture or assembly from components) could fit the packet-switching concept. The ability to dynamically adapt the ordering process allows for rapid response to changing conditions, for example if a shipment is delayed it can be replaced as needed by another order. Multiple sources of material can be considered and the most effective combination selected. The flexibility inherent in this approach allows both assemble-to-order and make-to-order to be dealt with. The inventory in the pipeline

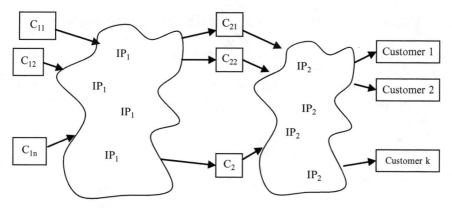

Fig. 4 Demand network with intelligent products IP_j and companies C_{ij}

can if necessary be redirected elsewhere. Although human management of this type of situation is feasible but not practical in terms of the complexity, a multi-agent environment could deal with this complexity and optimize delivery rates. For situations where the lead time exceeds the delivery time, the packet-switching view enables the supplier to identify any re-routing or alternative sourcing, which may reduce lead-time for product development. If the constraint is delivery time based, redirection and the inventory in motion view could be used to reduce the delivery time. This concept is illustrated in Fig. 4, which uses the cloud analogy to represent the flexibility of dynamic response to changing orders. Any one of the company type C_1 can provide intelligent products of type IP_1, which are required by companies of type C_2. Companies C_2 produce products of type IP_2, which in this example are then supplied to customers.

It is possible to envision an environment in which products can act as agents with local processing capability and some autonomy. In keeping with the intelligent product concept discussed earlier, such a product would be capable of reporting its status and evaluating whether action needs to be taken. The processing model would be partially decentralized (based on a multi-agent system and smart sensors view) with some central control, for example to coordinate actions between products. As an example, one could consider perishable goods or materials that may be subject to change during transit. If there is any delay, a smart product could evaluate its status and report to the nearest sensor that action needs to be taken. This action may involve negotiating with another product elsewhere in the demand network for redirection, for example to a more convenient location. Any product with a use-by date, for example a shipment of fruit, may encounter some delivery delay or unusual conditions such as excessive heat. This shipment could be dynamically redirected to a more suitable destination. Another example is where a number of buyers may have need for a generic type of product such as PVC piping. Depending on current availability in the warehouse "cloud", intelligent products could negotiate to reach an optimal delivery schedule based on time, distance and dynamic demand.

Intelligent products provide an embodiment of the packet-switching view of the demand chain. Each product with local processing capability can act as a packet, with the capability of being redirected as needed and with the capacity to develop its own knowledge on its environment. Another scenario that could be considered would be to assist backroom visibility. A cluster of similar products could negotiate to decide which is the most sensible to go next, that is to be moved to the retail shelves.

6   Conclusion

The packet switching view of intelligent products is a new paradigm that suggests a wide range of opportunities for quick response environments. One can envision products that can be dynamically redirected as needs change or constraints develop. Complete product packages can be assembled for a number of product components that can be optimized for such factors as delivery time, cost, etc. Each product or product grouping (at case or pallet level) could have sufficient decision making logic to decide whether to participate in a delivery, negotiate with other products of the same category for sequencing, etc. The traditional view of the supply chain is that products (transactions) are buffered until required and much of the supply chain optimization relates to issues of static buffer management. With intelligent products buffering may in effect act as redirection of products to the next destination. Further, such buffering will include any decoupling point analysis if and where required. The demand-driven supply network must be seen as a dynamic structure and not as a static structure as per current Supply Chain Management theory. As in packet-switching communication networks, "packets" of inventory will be routed in real-time as demand dictates and as constrained by the effect of lead time.

With a new view of the demand network and products, there is a need to redefine business processes to deal with this dynamic environment. Processes must be capable of quick response and adaptation as needed. The current processes were designed in IG2 for the IG2 supply chain. The service-oriented approach suggests one way of dealing with the issue.

Western economies are moving steadily towards a service-based rather than a manufacturing-based economy. The Economist Intelligence Unit (EIU 2006), in its Foresight 2020 report, notes "In the US employment in services industries is expected to increase from an already high rate of some 85% to well over 90% of total employment in the non-farm sector." One area of research that is of interest to this chapter is how to deal with services in a dynamic demand network. Virtually all research to date in this area has focused on static supply chains with materials movement and inventory management.

Services have particular features of interest to demand networks, that is they are perishable, cannot be buffered or stored and have tight constraints on their use. Traditional supply chain thinking tends to take a capacity limit view of products when trying to optimise utilisation of production capability. However, it can be shown that by taking a constraint-based view, it is possible to achieve a better overall use of productive capacity. The demand-driven packet-switching network need not be restricted to physical inventory. It is also applicable to the services industry and to any business process that is part of a demand network. By bringing the overall measurement units down to $/time, it no longer matters whether one is dealing with static products, dynamic intelligent products or services.

This chapter has attempted to define the role of several new concepts of interest in the rapidly changing supply chain field. The authors believe that changes in technology and ways of thinking provide the opportunity to develop a new theory of demand networks, which can deal with dynamic information, intelligent products, services as well as physical products and locally intelligent agents. The packet switching view of products and services in the supply network provides a simple conceptual framework for visualizing the way this could operate. Further research in this area will involve investigation of possible industry partners and suitable industries to develop the concept further as well as the development of a simulation environment to investigate the economic effect of intelligent products and dynamic information.

References

Ahn HJ, Lee H (2004) An agent-based dynamic information network for supply chain management. BT Tech J 22(2):18–27

Almirall E, Brito I, Silisque A, Cortés U (2003) From supply chains to demand networks: the electrical bazaar-agents in retailing. http://www.minds-on-fire.com/zupc/publ/AiRCaepia2003.pdf

Andrews J, Benisch M, Sardinha A, Sadeh, N (2007) What differentiates a winning agent: an information gain based analysis of TAC-SCM. AAAI-07 Workshop on trading agent design and analysis (TADA'07), Vancouver, Canada

Arunachalam R, Sadeh N (2005) The supply chain trading agent competition. Electronic Commerce Research and Applications, 4(1)

Asif Z, Mandiwalla M (2005) Integrating the supply chain with RFID: a technical and business analysis. Comm Assoc Inform Syst 15:393–427

Bardaki C, Pramatar K, Doudakis GI (2007) RFID-enabled supply chain collaboration services in a networked retail business environment. 20th Bled econference emergence: merging and emerging technologies, processes and institutions. Slovenia

Barker JR, Finnie G (2004) A model for global material management using dynamic information, Americas conference on information systems, New York, USA

Cao Q, Leggio KB (2008) Alleviating the bullwhip effect in supply chain management using the multi-agent approach: an empirical study. Int J Comput Appl Tech 31(3–4):225–237

Christopher M (2000) The agile supply chain: competing in volatile markets. Ind Market Manag 29(1)

Christopher M, Towill D (2002) Developing market specific supply chain strategies. Int J Logist Manag 13(1)

Culler DE, Mulder H (2004) Smart sensors to network the world. Sci Am 290(6):85–93

Economist Intelligence Unit (2006) Foresight 2020: economic, industry and corporate trends. Available from http://www.eiu.com/site_info.asp?info_name=eiu_Cisco_Foresight_2020&rf=0

Finnie G, Barker JR, Sun Z (2004) A multi-agent model for cooperation and negotiation in supply networks. Americas conference on information systems, New York, USA

Fox MS, Barbuceanu M, Teigen R (2000) Agent-oriented supply-chain management. Int J Flex Manuf Syst 12:165–188

Gouyon D, David M (2008) Implementing the concept of product-driven control using wireless sensor networks: some experiments and issues. Proceedings 17th IFAC World Congress, Korea

Hanebeck C (2006) Managing data from RFID & sensor-based networks: implications and considerations for data management challenges. Available at http://www.globeranger.com/pdfs/futureoftheedge/GlobeRangerRFIDData.pdf

Hanebeck HL, Raisinghani MS (2007) Delivering on the promise of auto-ID through intelligent agent technologies. Int J Innovat Learn 4(4):411–424

Haouzi HE, Petin JF, Thomas A (2009) Design and validation of a product-driven control systems based on a six sigma methodology and discrete event simulation. Prod Plann Contr 20:142–156

Hoekstra S, Romme J (1992) Integrated logistics structures: developing customer oriented goods flow. McGraw-Hill, London

Karkkainen M, Holmstrom J, Framling K, Artto K 2003, Intelligent products: a step towards a more effective project delivery chain. Comput Ind 50(2):141–151

Kim JB, Segev A (2003) Multi-component contingent auction (MCCA): a procurement mechanism for dynamic formation of supply networks. Proc ACM conf electron commerce 78–86

Leitao P, Restivo F (2006) ADACOR: A holonic architecture for agile and adaptive manufacturing control. Comput Ind 5:121–130

Luh PB, Ni M, Chen H, Thakur LS (2003) Price-based approach for activity coordination in a supply network. IEEE Trans Robot Autom 19(2):335–346

Leach PT (2004) Inventory in motion. J Commerce 29

Meyer GG, Framling K, Holmstrom J (2009) Intelligent products: a survey computers in industry 60(3):137–148

Mooney JG, Gurbaxani V, Kraemer KL (1996) A process oriented framework for assessing the business value of information technology. ACM SIGMIS Database Adv 27(2):68–81

Monteiro T, Roy D, Anciaux D (2007) Multi-site coordination using a multi-agent system. Comput Ind 58(4):367–377

Morel G, Panetto H, Zaremba M, Mayer F (2003) Manufacturing enterprise control and management system engineering: rationales and open issues. Annu Rev Contr 27–32

Moore JF (1993) Predators and prey: a new ecology of competition. Harv Bus Rev 71(3):75–86

Niederman F, Mathieu RG, Morley R, Kwon IW (2007) Examining RFID applications in supply chain management. Comm ACM 50(7):92–101

Nissen ME (2001) Agent-based supply chain integration. Inform Tech Manag 2(3):289–312

Olhager J (2003) Strategic positioning of the order penetration point. Int J Prod Econ 85:319–329

Pannequin R, Morel G, Thomas A (2009) The performance of product-driven manufacturing control: an emulation-based benchmarking study. Comput Ind. 60

Rudberg M, Wikner J (2004) Mass customization in terms of the customer order decoupling point. Prod Plann Contr 15(4):445–458

Sadeh-Koniecpol ND, Hildum J, Kjenstad H (2003) MASCOT: an agent-based architecture for dynamic supply chain creation and coordination in the internet economy. Prod Plann Contr 12(3)

Schuster E, Brock DL (2004) Creating an intelligent infrastructure for ERP: the role of auto-ID technology. This is a working paper for APICS

Schuster EW, Allen SJ, Brock DL (2007). Global RFID: the value of the EPCglobal network for supply chain management. Springer-Verlag, New York

Sharman G (1984) The rediscovery of logistics. Harv Bus Rev 62:71–80

Shingo S (1981) Study of Toyota production system from industrial engineering viewpoint. Japan Management Association, Tokyo

Silisque A, Brito I, Almirall E, Cortés U (2003) From supply chains to demand networks. Agents in retailing. The Electrical Bazaar Artificial Intelligence Research Report. LSI-03-41-R

Supply Chain Management Terms and Glossary (2009) Council of supply chain management professionals. http://cscmp.org/digital/glossary/glossary.asp

Tellkamp C (2006) The impact of auto-ID technology on process performance: RFID in the FMCG supply chain. Doctoral thesis, Universität St. Gallen

Watson RT (ed) (2007) Information systems. University of Georgia, http://globaltext.terry.uga.edu/books

Weeks D, Crawford FA (1994) Efficient consumer response: a mandate for food manufacturers? Food Process 55(2):34

Wikner J, Rudberg M (2005) Integrating production and engineering perspectives on the customer order decoupling point. Int J Oper Prod Manag 25(7):623–641

Wong CY, McFarlane D, Ahmad Zaharudin A, Agarwal A (2002) The intelligent product driven supply chain. IEEE Int Conf Syst Man Cybern

RFID's Applications in Quick Response Systems

Xiaowei Zhu, Samar K. Mukhopadhyay, and Xiaohang Yue

Abstract Quick response systems need all supply chain players to respond quickly to market changes and cut ordering lead time and cost on inventory control, increase the accuracy of inventory information, help avoid stock-outs, and boost the number of inventory turns. Radio frequency identification (RFID) is an emerging technology that is increasingly being used in quick response systems and supply chain management. RFID technology plays an important role in supporting logistics and supply chain processes because of its ability to identify, trace, and track information throughout the supply chain. In this chapter, we provide an overview of the current state of RFID applications in quick response systems and its impact on business operations. We give suggestions for future research areas at the end.

Keywords Quick response · RFID · Supply chain management

1 Introduction

RFID stands for radio-frequency identification. RFID technology has been used in everything from controlling buildings access to animal tracking. Until recent years, people realize that RFID holds great potential for logistic, supply chain management, and quick response systems. RFID can be used to identify and track the location of shipping containers and items (like apparel, book, drug, and others) in warehouses and whole shipping route. RFID also can be used to make the inventory control system more efficiently. With more and more companies using RFID, new challenges and opportunities arise for the application of quick response systems and supply chain management. RFID will be the fastest-growing segment of the smart label market through 2007, with an estimated annual growth of 180% from around ten million RFID labels sold in 2002 (Collins 2003). Collins (2003) states that

X. Zhu (✉)
College of Business and Public Affairs, West Chester University of Pennsylvania
West Chester, PA 19383, USA,
e-mail: xzhu@wcupa.edu

T.C. Edwin Cheng and T.-M. Choi (eds.), *Innovative Quick Response Programs in Logistics and Supply Chain Management*, International Handbooks on Information Systems, DOI 10.1007/978-3-642-04313-0_13,

further spurring demand of RFID-enabled labels through 2012 will be falling prices, technological advances, and the establishment of uniform RFID communications standards. Spiegel (2006) identified the United States as the largest adopter of RFID technology by a wide margin, followed by the United Kingdom, Japan, Germany, China, France, Australia, the Netherlands, Korea, and Canada, in that order.

Academic research in RFID has proliferated significantly over the last few years, and several journals, like *Production and Operations Management, International Journal of Production Economics*, and other journals, provided special issues on the topic. Ngai et al. (2008) gave a comprehensive review and classification of 85 academic journal papers that were published on the subject between 1995 and 2005. Chao et al. (2007) gave a history review of RFID research from 1991 to 2005 and explored RFID technological trends and forecasts. This chapter is not only serving as a literature review, but also cooperating with several real world RFID application examples.

In this chapter, we explore RFID usage in quick response systems and supply chain management. We focus on the management issues and applications of RFID instead of technical issue. We will briefly introduce RFID technology in Sect. 2. General RFID management issues will be reviewed in Sect. 3. We will comprehensively discuss RFID functions across different industries in Sect. 4 and further discuss RFID applications in several different fields in Sect. 5. We finish this chapter in conclusion in Sect. 6.

The purpose of this chapter is to review the extant literature on RFID and discuss the current RFID applications in real world. It is hoped that the finding of this study will highlight the importance of RFID technology and its application in quick response systems and supply chain management and provide insight into current RFID research for both academics and practitioners.

2 RFID Technology

RFID systems collect real-time data and communicate it via radio waves. RFID technology is composed of RFID tag and an RFID reader linked to a computer system. Most RFID tags consist of two parts, a small chip and an antenna. The chip is used to store and process information and the antenna is used to receive and transmit the information. The chip stores information about a product or shipment. Each RFID tag provides a unique identifier for that object. RFID tag must be read by RFID reader to retrieve the information, just as a bar code must be scanned to get the information. The information stored in an RFID tag is detected and recorded when a tag passes by an RFID reader that tracked the tag's movement in real time and passed its digital identity to a computer system.

RFID tag can be tagged into a product, animal, or person to track information. There are generally two types of RFID tags: active RFID tags, which contain a battery, and passive RFID tags, which have no battery. For the passive RFID tag, the antenna has the ability to collect power from the incoming signal and to transmit the signal back to the reader. Unlike passive RFID tags, the active RFID tags have their own internal power source, which is used to power the chip and to broadcast the response signal back to the RFID reader. The active tags may include larger memories than the passive tags and can be read/write from longer distance from the passive tags. The current price of the passive RFID tag is $0.04–0.10, and active tags are more expensive due to the price of the battery. The passive RFID tags are used in book product tracking, building access control, airline baggage tracking, and others. The companies like Wal-Mart, GAP, Old Navy, JC Penney, and P&G use passive RFID tags on supply chain management. Also, North American drivers use EZ-Pass highway toll lanes, even though they do not know that they are using the RFID (passive tag) technology. The United States Department of Defense has successfully used active tags to reduce search and loss in logistics and to improve supply chain visibility.

There are several issues that impede seamless integration of RFID tags in a supply chain, including technical problem, customer privacy, and RFID standards. Piramuthu (2008) studies RFID tags reading collision, which occurs when multiple tags transmit data to the same receiver slot. There are also some other technical problems. However, this chapter focuses on RFID applications, and we skip the details of technical issue. Besides the technical concerns, one of the big impediments to RFID implement is the customer privacy. Juels et al. (2003); Weis et al. (2004); Garfinkel et al. (2005); Ohkubo et al. (2005); Sackmann et al. (2006); Solanas et al. (2007); Chen et al. (2008), and others study the consumer privacy issue related to RFID. However, customer privacy is managed under national legislation and guidelines of good practice. Gillette and the MIT Auto-ID Center said they are taking precautions to protect consumer privacy. For instance, the Auto-ID Center's technical specifications call for retailers to be able to disable the tags after purchase at checkout counters. Wal-Mart could decide to disable the microchips in Gillette products before they leave the store. The security issues also have been extensively researched in literature. Kang and Gandhi (2003); Knospe and Pohl (2004); Phillips et al. (2005); Chien and Chen (2007); Piramuthu (2007); Jabbar et al. (2008), and others study the security and standard issue related to RFID.

The other stream of research is related to new technology development in RFID. Mazurek (2009) studies the active RFID system with spread-spectrum transmission. Yang et al. (2007) proposes to use inkjet-printing technology to make RFID tag and RF structures on a paper substrate. As discussed earlier, there are numerous technical, privacy, security, and standard issues. All these likely will be resolved with time, experience, and money. Thus, it is unclear just how RFID will be effectively used when RFID applications will become feasible (Zipkin 2006). We will devote the rest of this chapter to discuss RFID from management aspects and its business applications.

3   RFID on Management

In the section, we briefly discuss several general concerns and management issue related to RFID application. Initial RFID adoption efforts have occurred at the case/pallet level and are focused on improving backroom inventory-management

Table 1 The overview of RFID related management issues

Management issue	Contribution	Author
RFID deployment and return expectations	Proposes a theoretical framework for RFID adoption and benefits, and tests the framework using data on the US firms	Whitaker et al. (2007)
Allocating RFID cost among supply chain partners	Show how the cost of item-level RFID should be allocated among supply chain partners such that supply chain profit is optimized	Gaukler et al. (2007)
Business value from RFID technology	Examines three dimensions of the value proposition of RFID and identify areas for further investigation	Dutta et al. (2007)
Mandated RFID adoption and institutional responses	Explores the responses of four decentralized business units to institutional pressure to adopt RFID through a case study	Barratt and Choi (2007)
RFID's benefits and risks	Discuss the risks that accompany RFID adoption	Cannon et al. (2008)

practices. Now people started to pay more attention on item level RFID usage to explore more benefit from RFID technology. With RFID development, people raise several management issues, like RFID investment return expectations, RFID business value, RFID adoption process and people's attitude, RFID benefit and risk to the organizations. Table 1 gives an overview of RFID related management issues.

4 RFID Functionality

RFID technology demonstrates great potential on reducing shrinkage, preventing stockouts and excess stocks, improving data accuracy, and increasing information visibility of supply chain. The following section will discuss these functions.

4.1 RFID Used to Reduce Inventory Shrinkage

Shrinkage is a term that refers to loss of product through damage, misplacement, or theft from manufacture to retail and during the retailing process itself. When items are continuously monitored, inventory shrinkages can be avoided using RFID technology. de Kok et al. (2008) study that both manufacturers and retailers use RFID tag to control shrinkage. By comparing the situation with RFID and the one without RFID in terms of costs, an exact analytical expression is derived for the break-even prices of an RFID tag. It turns out that these break-even prices are highly related with the value of the items that are lost, the shrinkage fraction, and the remaining shrinkage after implementing RFID.

4.2   RFID Used to Improve Inventory Record Accuracy

Most retailers suffer from substantial discrepancies between warehouse quantities recorded in the system and stocks truly available to customers. RFID technology has often been suggested as a remedy to this problem. Heese (2007) considers the inventory record inaccuracy in a supply chain model, where a Stackelberg manufacturer sets the wholesale price and a retailer determines how much to stock for sale to customers. Rekik et al. (2008) considers the situation of a retail store subject to inventory inaccuracies stemming from operating errors.

4.3   RFID Enhances Information Visibility

RFID technology allows people to create end-to-end supply chain information visibility by enabling supplier, manufacturers, logistics providers, and retailers to track and trace item information through the whole supply chain at any time and at any locations. Information visibility is very critical to quick response systems to respond quickly to market changes and cut ordering lead times. Delen et al. (2007) show how information collected by RFID can be valuable to both the retail store operator and the supplier through a case study. Authors further discuss how these RFID measures can assist in improving logistical performance at a micro-supply chain level of operations between a distribution center and a retail store. Karaer and Lee (2007) quantify the visibility savings of RFID in the reverse channel as a candidate enabler technology. Ngai et al. (2007) presents a case study of the research and development of an RFID-based traceability system, which is to support the tracking and tracing of aeroplane repairable items in an aircraft engineering company in Hong Kong.

5   RFID Applications

We discuss the RFID usage according to its application in different fields or industries in this section. For each of the field, we explain the RFID application usage for that field, followed by real world examples. We also introduce the academic research in each field.

5.1 RFID in Retailing-CPG

Inventory management is an important aspect of supply chain management. RFID holds great potential to improve the inventory management for today's supply chains and quick response systems. Quick response systems require an effective inventory management, which depends upon consolidating, integrating, and analyzing data collected from many supply chain players such as supplier, manufacturer, distributor, wholesaler, shipper, and retailer. The traditional stocking shelves and managing inventory are labor intensive, time consuming, and error-prone. If products come with RFID tags, retailers could track them the moment they are delivered to the store. The information can then be used to minimize back room inventory over time and keep shelves full. Store security and analysis of sales data can also be improved. RFID Journal (2003) reported that Wal-Mart required its top 100 US suppliers to attach RFID tag on all pallets and cases of all products by the end of 2005. Songini (2007) reported that Procter & Gamble, one of Wal-Mart's top providers of consumer goods, had found success by following the RFID requirements of the retailer Wal-Mart. Weier (2008) brought the recent news that Wal-Mart got tough on RFID and Sam's Club suppliers were required to use RFID tags or face $2 fee by 30 January 2008. He also reported that Sam's Club's mandate to require its entire supplier to have cases and pallets RFID tagged for all distribution centers by October 2009 and for item-level RFID by 2010.

5.1.1 RFID Used in Smart Shelf

The smart shelf is designed to detect RFID tags affixed directly to individual products, informing retailer of the precise location of items on a shelf. In a replenishment-based system, whenever the total inventory at a warehouse or distribution center drops below a certain level, the RFID-enabled system could automatically place an order, either by informing a store retailer to retrieve more products from a storage room or by notifying the manufacturer that another shipment is needed. RFID-tagged products will allow retailer to track the location and count of inventories in real time. Manufacturers are interested in smart shelves as a tool to help increase sales by ensuring that store shelves are always stocked with their products. This will better monitor demand for certain products and place orders to prevent an out-of-stock situation. The high levels of inventory monitoring obtained using RFID can particularly benefit CPG (Consumer Packaged Goods) or called FMCG (Fast Moving Consumer Goods). Manufacturer or shipper can also attach the RFID tags to shipping containers and pallets in an effort to more efficiently locate and route merchandise in its journey from factory to store shelf. Wal-Mart tested the Gillette product using RFID to build smart shelf initially in a store located in Brockton, Mass, in 2003 (Gilbert 2003).

Bottani and Rizzi (2008) use quantitative method to assess the impact of RFID technology and electronic product code (EPC) system on the main processes of the CPG supply chain. A questionnaire survey was performed to collect both quantitative and qualitative data related to logistics processes of a three-echelon supply chain, composed of manufacturers, distributors, and retailers of CPG. Bottani and Rizzi (2008) conclude their research to state that RFID adoption with pallet-level tagging provides positive revenues for all supply-chain players. Conversely, adopting a case-level tagging, substantial costs arise for manufacturers, involving negative economical results. Outcomes of this study provide an economical justification to the RFID and EPC implementation in the CPG supply chain.

By further reducing the RFID tag price, we can believe that the RFID usage will become more and more popular in CPG field in the near future.

5.2   RFID in Retailing-Apparel

Several US apparel companies used RFID with the point of sale (POS) to improve supply chain performance. Customers in the US can find RFID tags in the cloth from GAP, Old Navy, Ann Taylor, Calvin Klein, American Apparel, and others. Of course, RFID can also be used in smart shelf, reducing inventory shrinkage and inventory control as described in the previous section. Besides these features, RFID show more applications in the apparel industry.

5.2.1   RFID Used with POS

On the retailing side, RFID technology at the POS can be used to monitor demand trends or to build a probabilistic pattern of demand. This application could be useful for apparel industry or products exhibiting high levels of dynamism in trends. The company uses RFID to record goods received, to deduct goods sold by recording them at POS, and to count inventory in the back room and retail floor. RFID tags are removed at the POS when products are sold.

American Apparel is a US Los Angeles-based leading basics brand for young adults and people of all ages, with both wholesale and retail divisions globally. Gaudin (2008) report that Zander Livingston, a research-and-development strategist at American Apparel, said that, to ensure product availability, American Apparel takes complete in-store inventories twice per week, then restocks and reorders as necessary. The inventory process typically occupies four employees for 8 h. At the RFID-enabled Columbia University-area store, it takes two employees just 2 h to take inventory. Livingston said as many as 10% of items that should be on the sales floor could be missing at any given time. Sales increase by 15–25% when all items are available on the floor. The RFID system has made 99% of sales-floor inventory available to customers, he said.

5.2.2   RFID Used in Fitting Room

Piquepaille (2007) introduced that RFID tags help customer to choose clothes. He wrote: "A German department store, the Galeria Kaufhof in Essen, part of the Metro retailing group, is using RFID technology in a new way.... Men buying clothes in this store will get automatic suggestions. For example, when you go to a dressing room to try a suit, a 'smart mirror' will tell you what kind of shirt or tie you need to buy with it...... An RFID reader on a 'smart mirror' in the change room determines which clothing has been brought into the room from the RFID tag attached to the apparel, then displays complementary clothing choices or accessories. The system is used in combination with 'smart shelves,' which can read what merchandise is currently in stock, so that customers can be shown choices in sizes that are available and in various styles and colors."

From the above discussion, we see the great potential of RFID application in various retailing market, including CPG and apparel industry. IDTechEx (2005) makes a summer on payback factors for item level RFID identified in various rollouts, , and studies. It shows that The GAP, US apparel company, increases over 2% sales by using RFID to reduce less stockouts; and J Crew, US apparel company, experiences a five to eight times faster in inventory counting. Szmerekovsky and Zhang (2008) study the effect on manufacturers and retailers of attaching RFID tags at the item level in a vendor managed inventory (VMI) system. They study and compare the inventory control with RFID system and non-RFID system. Authors derive the optimal inventory policies in a centralized system and decentralized system and show how the sharing of the tag price can be used to coordinate the supply chain and how it can be exploited in manufacturer and retailer dominated systems.

5.3 RFID in Food and Restaurant

A perishable product has limited useful life and if it is not handled properly while transporting, it may get spoiled and its useful life reduces. If this information is not updated, then it may be possible that an outdated item gets delivered to a customer. In such a case, there may be an additional cost of replacement of item and also loss of goodwill of customer. The US Food and Drug administration has assessed that: "Up to 20% of foods are discarded due to spoilage in the supply chain." Such spoilage could be reduced simultaneously with automating inventory management, by using RFID technology for product identification, while it moves through the supply chain. RFID system can track the items in real time without product movement, scanning, or human involvement. Using active RFID tags, it can be possible to update information on it dynamically.

RFID can be used to address the problem of food traceability and integrate agricultural firms into the food chain and slash product recall costs. Mennecke and Townsend (2005) reports on a project to examine the feasibility of extensive RFID tagging to determine product provenance in the meat production industry. The investigators examined existing technologies and meat production processes as well as emerging technologies in RFID tagging to assess the potential of RFID technologies for provenance assurance. Ngai et al. (2008) describes the design and development of RFID system in a conveyor-belt sushi restaurant to enhance operational efficiency. This study demonstrates the significance and benefits of using RFID technology specifically in the food industry.

5.4 RFID in Health Care

Health care provider are using RFID to improve patient monitoring and safety, increase asset utilization with real-time tracking, reduce medical errors by tracking medical devices, and enhance supply-chain efficiencies. Tzeng et al. (2008) proposes a framework for evaluating the business value of RFID technology. Emphasis is on delivering business value through refining business processes and expanding the business model. This research illustrates these concepts drawing on the experience of five early adopters from the Taiwan healthcare industry and formulates the framework as a set of propositions based on relevant literature. IDTechEX (2006) states that the market for RFID tags and systems in healthcare will rise rapidly from $90 million in 2006 to $2.1 billion in 2016. Primarily, this will be because of item level tagging of drugs and Real Time Locating Systems (RTLS) for staff, patients, and assets to improve efficiency, safety, and availability and to reduce losses. IDTechEX (2006) summarizes the main purposes of RFID application in healthcare that RFID has currently been used in healthcare in error prevention of product, patient tagging for error prevention, locating staff, and locating assets/speedy, accurate stocktaking, theft prevention, and cost control. The future RFID applications in healthcare include more functions, like locating visitor, behavioral studies to optimize operation, and tracking and tracing of most medicines, consumable, and assets.

Amini et al. (2007) presents a simulation study conducted at a regional hospital for which data related to trauma patient movement was collected with an RFID-based system. Authors find that not only does this data serve as the basis for successful simulation modeling, but that RFID technology may address several data-related challenges previously identified in the simulation literature.

5.5 RFID in Logistic

Fosso Wamba et al. (2008) studied how RFID technology and EPC network impacts on mobile B2B eCommerce. Based on empirical data gathered from interrelated firms of a supply chain, several scenarios integrating the RFID–EPC network have been tested in a pilot project and evaluated. Through a business process approach, authors have several findings: the RFID–EPC network can improve the "shipping," "receiving," and "put-away" processes; these technologies can cancel, automate, or automatically trigger some business processes; they foster a higher level of information sharing/synchronization between supply chain members; and they require to be integrated in a wider strategy.

Thiesse and Fleisch (2008) is concerned with the practical use of RTLSs in complex manufacturing processes. Starting from the case example of an RFID-based RTLS implementation in a semiconductor fab, authors investigate the value of RTLS information on the locations of physical objects in a production system to the problem of efficient job scheduling. Through building a simulation model, Thiesse and Fleisch (2008) indicate that the use of RTLS technology provides the opportunity for new levels of process visibility and control in comparison to conventional material-tracking systems. The benefits that can be drawn from the technology include not only an overall acceleration of the existing process but also an additional efficiency gain through novel dispatching rules that take into account real-time information on the logistic processes on the shop floor.

Lee et al. (2008) states that cost-conscious businesses traditionally have focused on using RFID systems to enhance the efficiency in the supply management/logistics process. These firms go through an implementation process that focuses on the supplier-facing, back-office operations. Through three case studies in the service sector, authors develop a complimentary customer-facing model, which focuses the diffusion of RFID as originating from those activities associated with the delivery of the actual service offering. Lee et al. (2008) found that by focusing a firm's RFID strategy on customer-facing activities, a firm can use the technology to change its basis of competition from an efficiency-oriented strategy to one where RFID has more strategic implications such as providing the foundation for new products or services or providing the infrastructure to enhance customers' value perceptions to strengthen customer loyalty.

5.6 Other RFID Applications

Other RFID applications include its usage in military. Doerr et al. (2006) report an analysis of the costs and benefits of fielding RFID/MicroElectroMechanical System (RFID/MEMS) technology for the management of ordnance inventory. Lehto et al. (2009) study the passive UHF RFID application in paper industry. Kim and Sohn (2009) propose a cost of ownership model to study the RFID logistics system of ubiquitous city (u-city). Wang et al. (2008) focus on the analysis of simulated impact of the RFID system on the inventory replenishment of the long life cycle product, thin film transistor liquid crystal display (TFT-LCD) supply chain in Taiwan.

Texas Instruments (2001) reports that RFID speed flower auction flow as below: "In the vast halls of the Bloemenveiling Holland flower auction, 6,000 growers generate 32,000 transactions, with orders being shipped to 2,000 buyers locally and abroad each day – all before 11:00 am. To correctly pack and ship this blossoming cargo, TI-RFid tags identify 100,000 trolleys as part of sophisticated automated logistics and tracking system. As trolleys move along miles of electric track and orders are picked, Ti-RFID tags are read by antennas in the floor communicating timely data to logistics software. Personnel can pinpoint the exact location of an order, its contents, and how quickly it will arrive at the dock door for shipping."

6 Conclusion

RFID is a promising technique that enables tracking of essential information about objects as they pass through supply chains. RFID technology also shows significant value for inventory systems by providing an accurate knowledge of the current inventory at lower labor cost and simplified business processes. Information tracked by RFID can be utilized to improve the whole supply chain efficiency and offer huge competitive advantage for the firms involved. Although there are numerous technical, privacy, and security issues, all these likely will be resolved with time, experience, and money.

Lee and Özer (2007) state that extant industry reports and white papers are now filled with estimates and proclamations of the benefits and quantified values of RFID, not based on detailed, model-based analysis. The authors argue that there is a huge credibility gap of the value of RFID, and that a void exists in showing how the proclaimed values are arrived at and how those values can be realized. They show that this credibility gap must be filled with solid model analysis, and therefore, presents a great opportunity for the Production and Operations Management (POM) research community. The paper further reviews some of the ongoing research efforts that attempt to close the credibility gap, and suggests additional directions for further strengthening the POM's contribution to help industry realize the full potentials of RFID.

The future research in RFID in quick response systems includes further reducing RFID system cost, make worldwide standard for RFID system, design better business process of RFID system, explore new RFID application on item level, and use RFID to increase the whole supply chain efficiency, like reducing bullwhip effect and reduce logistic cost. We have enough reason to believe that RFID technology have a bright future. We will see more RFID applications in various industries as the price of the technology decreases and technical, privacy, and security issues are resolved. We hope that this chapter will be a good resource for anyone who is interested in RFID research, including both academic researcher and industry practitioner, and will help to stimulate further interest in this area.

References

Amini M, Otondo RF, Janz BD, Pitts MG (2007) Simulation modeling and analysis: A collateral application and exposition of RFID technology. Prod Oper Manag 16(5):586–598

Barratt M, Choi T (2007) Mandated RFID and institutional responses: Cases of decentralized business units. Prod Oper Manag 16(5):569–585

Bottani E, Rizzi A, (2008) Economical assessment of the impact of RFID technology and EPC system on the fast-moving consumer goods supply chain. Int J Prod Econ 112(2):548–569

Cannon AR, Reyes PM, Frazier GV, Prater EL, (2008) RFID in the contemporary supply chain: Multiple perspectives on its benefits and risks. Int J Oper Prod Manag 28(5):433–454

Chen JV, Pfleuger Jr. P (2008) RFID in retail: A framework for examining consumers' ethical perceptions. Int J Mobile Comm 6(1):53–66

Chao CC, Yang JM, Jen WY (2007) Determining technology trends and forecasts of RFID by a historical review and bibliometric analysis from 1991 to 2005. Technovation 27:268–279

Chien HY, Chen CH (2007) Mutual authentication protocol for RFID conforming to EPC Class 1 Generation 2 standards. Comput Stand Interfac 29(2):254–259

Collins J (2003) Smart lables set to soar, RFID Journal. http:www.rfidjournal.com/article/articleprint/712/-1/1. Acessed Dec 23 2003

Delen D, Hardgrave BC, Sharda R (2007) RFID for better supply-chain management through enhanced information visibility. Prod Oper Manag 16(5):613–624

Doerr KH, Gates WR, Mutty JE (2006) A hybrid approach to the valuation of RFID/MEMS technology applied to ordnance inventory. Int J Prod Econ 103(2):726–741

Dutta A, Lee HL, Whang S (2007) RFID and operations management: Technology, value, and incentives. Prod Oper Manag 16(5):646–655

de Kok AG, van Donselaar KH, van Woensel T (2008) A break-even analysis of RFID technology for inventory sensitive to shrinkage. Int J Prod Econ 112(2):521–531

Garfinkel SL, Juels A, Pappu R (2005) RFID privacy: An overview of problems and proposed solutions. IEEE Security & Privacy Magazine 3(3):34–43

Gaudin S (2008) American Apparel uses RFID to take better stock of its stores Retailer credits tagging of every item with bumping sales in pilot store by 15% to 25%. http://www.computerworld.com/action/article.do?command=viewArticleBasic& taxonomyName=Mobile+Applications+and+RFID&articleId=9078338&taxonomyId=77& pageNumber=1

Gilbert A (2003) Major retailers to test 'smart shelves'. CNET News. http://64.233.169.132/search?q=cache:wEyOTJ4wCFIJ:news.cnet.com/Major-retailers-to-test-smart-shelves/2100-1017_3-979710.html± Wal-Mart± tested± the± Gillette± product± using± RFID± to± build± smart± shelf± initially± in± a± store± located± in± Brockton,± Mass,&hl = en&ct = clnk&cd = 1&gl = us. Accessed Jan 8 2003

Gaukler GM, Seifert RW, Hausman WH (2007) Item-level RFID in the retail supply chain. Prod Oper Manag 16(1):65–76

Heese HS (2007) Inventory record inaccuracy, double marginalization, and RFID adoption. Prod Oper Manag 16(5):542–553

IDtechEx (2005) Cost reduction in retailing & products using RFID. http://www.idtechex.com/research/articles/cost_reduction_in_retailing_and_products_using_rfid_00000205.asp . Accessed Apr 16 2008

IDtechEx (2006) Rapid adoption of RFID in healthcare. http://www.idtechex.com/research/articles/rapid_adoption_of_rfid_in_healthcare_00000470.asp. Accessed May 08 2006

Jabbar H, Jeong T, Hwang J, Park G (2008) Viewer identification and authentication in IPTV using RFID technique. IEEE Trans Consum Electron 54(1):105–109

Juels A, Rivest RL, Szydlo M (2003) The blocker tag: Selective blocking of RFID tags for consumer privacy. Proc ACM Conf Comput Comm Secur 103–111

Kang G, Gandhi OP (2003) Comparison of various safety guidelines for electronic article surveillance devices with pulsed magnetic fields. IEEE Trans Biomed Eng 50(1):107–113

Karaer Ö , Lee HL (2007) Managing the reverse channel with RFID-enabled negative demand information. Prod Oper Manag 16(5):625–645

Kim HS, Sohn SY (2009) Cost of ownership model for the RFID logistics system applicable to u-city. Eur J Oper Res 194(2):406–417

Knospe H, Pohl H (2004) RFID security. Inform Secur Tech Rep 9(4):39–50

Lee H, Özer Ö (2007) Unlocking the value of RFID. Prod Oper Manag 16(1):40–64

Lee LS, Fiedler KD, Smith JS (2008) Radio frequency identification (RFID) implementation in the service sector: A customer-facing diffusion model. Int J Prod Econ 112(2):587–600

Piramuthu S (2007) Protocols for RFID tag/reader authentication. Decis Support Syst 43(3): 897–914

Lehto A, Nummela J, Ukkonen L, Sydanheimo L, Kivikoski M (2009) Passive UHF RFID in Paper Industry: Challenges, Benefits and the Application Environment. IEEE Trans Autom Sci Eng 6(1):66–79

Mazurek G (2009) Active RFID System With Spread-Spectrum Transmission. IEEE Trans Autom Sci Eng 6(1):5–32

Mennecke B, Townsend A (2005) Radio Frequency Identification Tagging as a Mechanism of Creating a Viable Producer's Brand in the Cattle Industry. MATRIC Research Paper 05-MRP 8. http://www.card.iastate.edu/publications/DBS/PDFFiles/05mrp8.pdf

Ngai EWT, Cheng TCE, Lai KH, Chai PYF, Choi YS, Sin RKY (2007) Development of an RFID-based traceability system: Experiences and lessons learned from an aircraft engineering company. Prod Oper Manag 16(5):554–568

Ngai EWT, Moon KKL, Riggins FJ, Yi CY (2008) RFID research: An academic literature review (1995–2005) and future research directions. Int J Prod Econ 112(2):510–520

Ngai EWT, Suk FFC, Lo SYY (2008) Development of an RFID-based sushi management system: The case of a conveyor-belt sushi restaurant. Int J Prod Econ 112(2):630–645

Ohkubo M, Suzuki K, Kinoshita S (2005) RFID privacy issues and technical challenges. Commun ACM 48(9):66–71

Phillips T, Karygiannis T, Kuhn R (2005) Security standards for the RFID market. IEEE Secur Privacy Mag 3(6):85–89

Piquepaille R (2007) Personalization in Retail: How RFID tags are helping a German retailer to provide customization of the retail experience. http://mass-customization.blogs.com/mass_customization_open_i/2007/11/personalization.html

Piramuthu S (2008) Adaptive Framework for Collisions in RFID Tag Identification. J Inform Knowl Manag 7(1):9–14

RFID Journal (2003) Wal-Mart Details RFID Requirement. http://74.125.47.132/search?q=cache: c4JZ9HcCSGcJ:www.rfidjournal.com/article/view/642/1/1± walmart± rfid± 100± supplier&hl = en&ct = clnk&cd = 2&gl = us

Sackmann S, Stru¨ker J, Accorsi R (2006) Personalization in privacy-aware highly dynamic systems. Commun ACM 49(9):2–38

Songini ML (2007) Procter & Gamble: Wal-Mart RFID Effort Effective. Computer World. http:// www.computerworld.com/action/article.do?command=viewArticleBasic&articleId=284160

Spiegel R (2006) U.S. and U.K. top countries for RFID implementation. Supply Chain Management Review. http://www.scmr.com/article/CA6395552.html

Thiesse F, Fleisch E (2008) On the value of location information to lot scheduling in complex manufacturing processes. Int J Prod Econ 112(2):532–547

Rekik Y, Sahin E, Dallery Y (2008) Analysis of the impact of the RFID technology on reducing product misplacement errors at retail stores. Int J Prod Econ 112(1):264–278

Solanas A, Domingo-Ferrer J, Martinez-Balleste A, Daza V (2007) A distributed architecture for scalable private RFID tag identification. Comput Network 51(9):2268–2279

Szmerekovsky JG, Zhang J (2008) Coordination and adoption of item-level RFID with vendor managed inventory. Int J Prod Econ 114(1):388–398

Texas Instruments (2001). Holland Flower Auction Uses RFID Tags for Logistics Improvements. Texas Instrument eRFID news 2. http://www.ti.com/rfid/docs/news/eNews/eNEWS2.pdf

Tzeng SF, Chen WH, Pai FY (2008) Evaluating the business value of RFID: Evidence from five case studies. Int J Prod Econ 112(2):601–613

Fosso Wamba S, Lefebvre LA, Bendavid Y, Lefebvre É (2008) Exploring the impact of RFID technology and the EPC network on mobile B2B eCommerce: A case study in the retail industry. Int J Prod Econ 112(2):614–629

Wang SJ, Liu SF, Wang WL (2008) The simulated impact of RFID-enabled supply chain on pull-based inventory replenishment in TFT-LCD industry. Int J Prod Econ 112(2):570–586

Weier MH (2008) Wal-Mart Gets Tough On RFID, Sam's Club suppliers required to use tags or face $2 fee. InformationWeek January 21, 2008 issue. http://www.informationweek.com/news/mobility/RFID/showArticle.jhtml?articleID=205900561

Weis SA, Sarma SE, Rivest RL, Engels DW (2004) Security and privacy aspects of low-cost radio frequency identification systems. Lecture Notes in Computer Science, Springer Berlin/Heidelberg, 2802, pp 201–212

Whitaker J, Mithas S, Krishnan MS (2007) A field study of RFID deployment and return expectations. Prod Oper Manag 16(5):599–612

Yang L, Rida A, Vyas R, Tentzeris MM (2007) RFID tag and RF structures on a paper substrate using inkjet-printing technology. IEEE Trans Microw Theor Tech 55(12):2894–2901

Zipkin P (2006) The best things in life were free: On the technology of transactions. Manuf Serv Oper Manag 8 (4):321–329

Enterprise Resource Planning Systems for the Textiles and Clothing Industry

Patrick C.L. Hui, Kidith Tse, Tsan-Ming Choi, and Na Liu

Abstract The textiles and clothing (TC) industry is well-known to be highly intensive in labor, raw material, product, capital, and inventory. Nowadays, companies in the TC supply chains have employed a wide array of technologies for enhancing the efficiency and effectiveness of different business processes. In particular, the enterprise resource planning (ERP) system has been rather widely implemented, and it has proven to be critical to the success of many TC companies. This paper aims to investigate the applications of ERP systems and explore the respective enabling technologies in the TC supply chains via studying various real company cases and reviewing some real ERP solutions. In addition, the main barriers of implementing the ERP systems in the TC industry are identified. Various critical success factors for the implementation of ERP systems are discussed. We conclude by exploring some future development directions.

Keywords Enterprise resource planning · Management information systems · Supply chain management · Textiles and clothing

1 Introduction

The unprecedented growth of information and communication technologies has affected all facets of computing applications across companies in the textiles and clothing (TC) industry. At the same time, the business environment is becoming increasingly complex, with functional units requiring more and more inter-functional data flows within TC supply chains for timely and efficient procurement of product parts, management of inventory, accounting, human resources, and distribution of goods and services. To deal with these challenges, an enterprise

P.C.L. Hui (✉)
Institute of Textiles and Clothing, Faculty of Applied Science and Textiles
The Hong Kong Polytechnic University, Hunghom, Kowloon, Hong Kong
e-mail: tchuip@inet.polyu.edu.hk

T.C. Edwin Cheng and T.-M. Choi (eds.), *Innovative Quick Response Programs in Logistics and Supply Chain Management*, International Handbooks on Information Systems, DOI 10.1007/978-3-642-04313-0_14,
© Springer-Verlag Berlin Heidelberg 2010

resource planning (ERP) system is one of the proposed solutions, and it has been implemented widely, especially in the larger scale TC companies.

Over the past decades, most of the TC companies have used information technology (IT) in some areas such as payroll, purchase, store, accounting, and human resources. With the advance of technology and the need of enhancing operational efficiency, applications of IT have been extended to other fields such as data management system for monitoring production online data, and automatic computer-aided design and manufacturing systems. However, such kind of IT adoption, though traditional and classical, is inadequate for coping with the challenges in the global economic environment around the TC industry. A substantial degree of system integration among different functional units is hence necessary for not only allowing effective communication among various business units but also enhancing the efficiency in the TC supply chains by implementing various measures such as just-in-time inventory and delivery, quick response, collaborative planning and forecasting, and even vendor-managed inventory schemes.

An ERP system can be defined as an information system for identifying and planning the enterprise-wide resources needed to take, make, ship, and account for customer order (Hodge 2002). It is a method of effective planning of all resources in an organization. It covers the techniques and concepts employed for the integrated management of businesses as a whole, with a goal to improve the efficiency of the whole enterprise (Ganesan et al. 2001). Obviously, it comprises of a commercial software package that promises the seamless integration of all the information flowing through the enterprise – financial, accounting, human resources, supply chain, and customer information (Davenport 1998). ERP systems are designed to model and automate many of the basic processes of an enterprise from finance to the sales floor (Ganesan et al. 2001), even though the degree of integration may vary from one scenario to another one. An ERP system is also a "configurable information systems package" that integrates information and information-based processes within and across functional areas in an organization (Kumar and Van Hillsgersberg 2000). It helps to accomplish business goals by integrating the information system and helping the organization to work and move forward as a single entity (Ganesan et al. 2001). With these features of an ERP system, it is crystal clear that it has very good potential to be applied in the TC industry. However, ERP system projects are also notorious for its high failure rate, and even big name companies (such as Nike), which have spent a huge amount of investment, would fail. As a result, it is important for us to identify the main barriers and challenges in implementing and using ERP system in the TC industry. Measures, especially those which employ technological innovations, could hence be proposed.

The organization of this chapter is as follows. The literature review is conducted in the next section. After that, we study some real world cases of companies that have implemented ERP systems. We then proceed to explore the barriers and challenges in ERP system implementation and applications. Various critical success factors for ERP system development and measures which can be applied to increase the chance of success with ERP system project are proposed. Future developments are discussed in the last section.

2 Literature Review

Supply chains in the TC industry are highly dynamic, and different stages have different requirements with respect to information. In the literature, it is well-known that information sharing scheme can effectively fight challenges such as the Bullwhip Effect in the supply chain. To enhance information sharing and other crucial operations, many TC companies have employed the company-wide centralized ERP system as a solution (Callaway 1999). The main purpose of implementing an ERP system is to achieve integration and coordination both within the company and across the industry. This will in turn lead to cost reduction and hence profitability improvement (Koch et al. 1999). With successful implementation, the ERP system's influence is immense. However, there is no guarantee for success. In Stefanou (1999), it is argued that an effective application of ERP systems is closely related to a corresponding business process re-engineering (BPR) scheme. In particular, TC companies that have implemented the ERP systems should have re-focused and shifted from a functional to a cross-functional and inter-organizational operation mode. In many cases, the requirements of information used in companies become more advanced, and a "flexible, integrated, and modular" (see Stefanou (1999) for more) system is needed to support activities across the supply chain from upstream to downstream. It is known that companies that are motivated to implement ERP systems aim at achieving improvements in different aspects of the company (Callaway 1999). For instance, improvements can be along the supply chain via more coordinated applications within one company (Callaway 1999) and/or among channel members, with a seamless flow and sharing of information (Glenn 2008). These areas are all relevant to and are crucial for companies in the TC industry.

   In the literature, the importance of ERP system for TC supply chain management has been explored. In Au and Ho (2002), it is argued that ERP systems can support the TC industry by allowing the implementation of e-commerce models, which helps transform the channel into an "integrated, web-enabled supply chain." In addition, unlike many other industries' pattern of commodity flow, a "buyer-driven commodity chain" is extensively observed in the TC industry. Such a commodity chain incurs higher costs, and a better management of supply chain is desirable. Gereffi (1999) has observed that the ERP systems, with their ability to consolidate information across companies, are popularly adopted in the "full-package sourcing network" of the TC industry. Fast fashion (Sheridan et al. 2006) is another important topic associated with the use of ERP systems in the TC industry. Essentially, fast fashion leads to a more dynamic market with more frequently changing merchandising and purchasing decisions, and hence ERP systems can play a crucial role (Bruce and Daly 2006). ERP systems also provide companies with flexibility and help solve many operational problems such as achieving more coordinated decisions on material resource planning (MRP) and capacity scheduling (Doshi 2006).

   For the anticipated benefits of ERP systems for the TC industry, Callaway (1999) has proposed the following comprehensive dimensions: (1) inventory level, (2) personnel, (3) procurement costs, (4) transportation and logistics costs, (5) information technology costs, (6) systems maintenance, (7) productivity, (8) order management,

(9) financial cycles, (10) cash management, (11) profits earning, and (12) on-time delivery performance. Other benefits brought by ERP systems in the TC industry are visibility of company's information (such as inventory), increased responsiveness to markets, tightened system coordination, flexibility, and so on. Out of the mentioned advantages of ERP systems, Callaway (1999) has further identified two groups, namely strategic benefits and economic benefits. Nevertheless, implementation of ERP systems can incur hidden costs, and the disadvantages of using ERP systems in the TC supply chains include high costs, long system development cycle, challenges in data conversions, the requirements of substantial organizational changes, user resistance, etc. We will discuss more in the following sections.

3   ERP Systems in Textiles and Clothing

To learn more about the industrial practices of the implementation and application of ERP systems in the TC industry, we have conducted some interviews as well as reviewed some cases in the literature, and the findings are reported as follows.

3.1   Specific Cases[1]

Case 1: Company A: A Multiproduct Cooperation

As a multiproduct group, Company A designs and sells products such as apparels, leather products, watches, footwears, etc. In 2006, with a goal of optimizing the company's supply chain performance (sourcing capabilities, lead time reduction) and supporting the company's growth in retail business, Company A conducted a large-scale business processing re-engineering and invested substantially in an ERP solution. The company appointed a new information systems director for this project, who aimed to implement an ERP system that can be used and shared by all product categories. A high degree of integration with suppliers was also desirable. However, upon the implementation and changes, the attempt was deemed as a failure because the supply chain costs were over 50% higher than before, with only a very marginal single-digit increase of revenue recorded. Other problems such as a lack of data transparency and poor migration of data were reported. Finally, the major reasons that accounted for the failure of Company A's ERP system implementation project included the following: a lack of coordination for the project (the project leader and other related parties did not work closely together and most staff members did not get involved at all), top management lacked vision and offered limited support (the top management even failed to tell the staff members the importance of the project), over-ambitious in having all product lines integrated together, failure

---

[1] In the cases, Companies A, B, X, Y, Z are all fictitious names for real companies. These cases are either based on our discussions/interviews with various industrialists or from the literature.

to provide the right incentives to involve people in multiple disciplines to work together, failure to define roles of participants and goals to achieve.

Case 2: Company B: A Textiles Company

Company B is one of the market leaders in the industry, which supplies knitted fabrics. In the respective industry, the manufacturing process includes the following four standard steps: knitting, dyeing, printing, and finishing. Over 90% of the manufacturing of Company B is done in-house, and the company is a long-term supplier of many leading brands such as DKNY, GAP, etc. The market environment in which the company resides has created huge challenges to it in terms of inventory management. On one hand, the production yield rate of fabrics is uncertain, which means the production output is uncertain. This leads to many operational problems, which include delivery scheduling. On the other hand, customers of the company are constantly asking for a shorter lead time while their demand is highly volatile. Moreover, the price fluctuation of raw materials as well as the needs to manage a large variety of products (fabrics) are all challenges faced by Company B. In light of all these, Company B has implemented a versatile ERP solution, which was provided by a leading software company that provides specialized ERP solution to textiles companies. With an annual capacity of producing over 180 million pounds of fabrics and with a huge supplier base for yarns, this ERP system of Company B helps enhance partnership with suppliers and customers, and also provides decision support ability, which assists Company B in improving its operations. Some measures such as collaborative forecasting and even fabrics commitment are supported by the ERP system. With the ERP system, Company B has expanded its presence in big markets such as China and enlarged its production base to more countries.

Case 3: A Sewing Threads Manufacturer: Textile Plc

As a multinational textile group, Textile Plc. (TP) was studied by Holland and Light (1999) on its strategic context and implementation of its global ERP project in one of its international textile firms, Threads. Prior to ERP implementation, the workflow study reflected a fragmented use of over 40 legacy systems which led to the existence of compliance problems. Upon adoption of the global ERP system, TP could focus on its strategic vision and well-approach its target markets as customer services were standardized. The ERP system operated in parallel with the original systems in TP. For the resulted benefits, apart from being able to focus on strategic visions, the ERP system allowed TP to reduce overhead costs and gain better control by top management. However, to fully adopt the system, TP had spent 6 years for the entire re-engineering process, of which a total of three years were contributed to tracing and analyzing the ERP project scopes. Although the benefits brought by the ERP system in TP were tremendous, it costed the company substantially in staff training with numerous workshops, as well as the costs of configuration. (Please refer to Holland and Light (1999) for more details of this case)

Case 4: Company Z

Company Z is an international mass market fashion retail brand with its outlets located in countries all around the world. From a discussion with a senior manager of the company, it is known that the company has well-adopted ERP system mainly in its inventory management, and its applications include distribution management, production planning, size/color/SKU management, vendor management, replenishment control, and supply chain system. With the ERP module in inventory management, the company has successfully shortened its delivery lead time across its various target markets and has consequently reduced the logistics costs. The company is also capable of adopting quick response strategies in its manufacturing sector and the replenishment automation. In addition, vendor management is improved through sharing of information on the vendor platform. Management reports, financial data, and activity documentations can now be transmitted via the centralized database system, and are thus approved and shared among various departments in real time. Costs and human errors are therefore lowered.

Case 5: Adidas–Salomon (Adidas)

Adidas–Salomon (adidas) implemented the SAP ERP solutions, Apparel and Footwear (SAP AG 2004), in the mid-1990s, and prevented the company from losing in the market. With the implementation of the ERP system, adidas aimed at improving the customer service as well as its efficiency across countries. Adidas chose this ERP system as it supported the company's retailing strategy and the consolidation with other systems used in the company (SAP AG 2004). With the help of the respective ERP module, adidas was successful in boosting its sales up by 26% in 2001. Customer satisfaction and loyalty can be ensured by the system, and productivity also increased as a result, allowing the company to effectively allocate its resources and reduce costs (SAP AG 2004). The system also helped adidas in data mining its customers' order history, consumption patterns, and product needs, and enabling personalization of service such as personalized invitation of particular showrooms to retailers (SAP AG, 2004). This helps to achieve process and system standardization of adidas operations over the world (SAP AG 2003). In terms of product management, adidas used the ERP system to accommodate size, color, and style of its apparel products, and flexibly managed its product hierarchies and characteristics, as well as its inventory and shipment schedules (SAP AG 2003).

Case 6: A Textile and Garment Enterprise: Company Y

Company Y has her own textile and garment business and participates in the global trade. To facilitate tracking of customer information, the company adopts a module of an ERP system in the finance and accounting department with a secured online system that allows accessing to such information at anytime, from anywhere. This module is also used for cost control and cash flow management. The ERP accounting and finance module adopted by this company has assisted finance managers on accessing information and making decisions easily. However, the company installed the ERP system in only one department. The finance team is required to consolidate the data from different systems to generate reports using the ERP module. As different departments in the company use different systems, all of which do not integrate with one another or with a single, unified database, overall performance of the company has not been improved substantially, not to mention efficiency of the entire supply chain. The ERP in use has not yet been executed in the supply chain division. It is noticed that the company requires an integrated system in order to enhance efficiency and gain flexibility in business processes. Therefore, it needs a full implementation of the ERP instead of partial adoption of a few modules.

Case 7: A Textile Manufacturer: Company X

One of the interviewed textile manufacturers has indicated that the impact of international trade has led to the shortening of product life cycle in the textile and fashion industry, which makes production as well as delivery lead time a major concern in the industry. The issues of quality inconsistency, raw material price fluctuation, and ever-changing market demand are also challenges faced by this company. Company X realized that better internal and external communication and collaboration with employees, vendors, logistics partners, retailers, and customers are essential in the TC industry. Thus, it adopted the SAP ERP system and a productivity effective maintenance system to achieve effective system control and internal cooperation. The ERP system installed aimed at solving the problems of (a) miscommunication between workers and managers, (b) inaccurate demand forecast, and (c) delays in production and delivery. The ERP system also allows the company to synchronize with its global customers. The procurement cycle of the company has been enhanced greatly by the implementation of the SAP ERP system. On the other hand, however, apart from the customers whose requirements are better fulfilled with the customer service modules of the implemented ERP system of the company, there is no evidence showing that overall supply chain performance has been improved.

3.2   Common Features and Modules

In general, ERP systems used in textile and clothing industries are modular in structure and they can be tailored to the needs of companies, both large and small. The number and features of the modules vary. For example, Datatex's ERP system for TIM (Textile Integrated Manufacturing) is complete textile software to help control and manage textile and apparel business and manufacturing. It covers sales, production planning and scheduling, production and quality management, dyehouse management, and costing and accounting. The Parellax MAE Garment and Textile Industry ERP Solution is a solution for the entire industry supply chain from manufacturing (including product development, management in sales, purchase, inventory, import and export trading, shipping, human resources, financial, production planning and control.), distribution and retail (including POS, management in client relationship, logistics, inventory, distribution, sales, promotion management, and style documentation management) to trading and merchandising (including garment trading, product development, management in style documentation, sales, cost, sample production, sample invoice, and client portal).

In Table 1, we have summarized some real ERP systems in the TC industry. As we can see from them, the following modules and functional areas are commonly available in most ERP systems used in the TC industries:

Table 1 Modules, features, and functions of some real ERP systems in the TC industry[2]

Name	Description (Modules)
AMT Software orioninc.com	AMT is an ERP solution for apparels, footwear, and accessories importers and manufacturers. AMT is an application envisioned and developed by Orion Systems. It makes use of Microsoft's technologies like Microsoft.NET, SQL database server, and Microsoft SQL Report Writer. The major functionalities include the following: eliminate redundancies, enhance customer support, maintain vendor compliances, reduce charge backs, improve warehouse efficiencies, enhance on-demand management visibility and an overhead cost reduction.
ApparelMagic apparelmagic.com	ApparelMagic is a web-enabled ERP solution. ApparelMagic can be linked to the company's web store, which allows the company to manage e-commerce, purchasing, and replenishment at the same time. Using ApparelMagic's can enhance real-time inventory control. ApparelMagic also supports integration with logistics service providers such as UPS and FedEx.
Aria Systems ariany.com	Aria Systems' "Aria 4XP ERP Product Suite" is a kind of ERP solution which offers three modules: supply chain management (SCM), product lifecycle management (PLM), and electronic data interchange (EDI), and it is specifically designed for the apparel, accessories, footwear, and textiles industries. Aria Systems services include comprehensive training solutions, as well as business and process management consulting. The warehousing software developed by Aria Systems supports radio frequency identification (RFID) technology and can work with the Aria Apparel System.
A2000 Software by GCS a2000software.com	The A2000 ERP package provides integrated modules for production, forecasting and inventory, warehousing, order processing, sales, shipping, accounting, EDI, reporting, etc. and web-enabled consumer-based sales system.
Cantel Apparel Systems cantel-cams.com	Cantel Apparel Systems offer web-based ERP solution for apparel companies. The specific applications include the following: sales order processing, accounting, warehouse control, customer relationship management (CRM), forecasting, merchandising, production control, materials requirements planning, EDI, etc.
DataS Ltd. datas.ro	DataS Ltd. provides real time business and production process modeling software solutions for the management of middle sized apparel manufacturers. The main functions include the following: order management, production planning, processing bill of materials, monitoring work-in-process inventory, material assembly, inventory control, quality control, etc.
e-jing Technologies e-jing.net	The e-jing SCM module of the ERP systems developed by e-jing can be applied in both the woven garment and the sweater industries. For woven garment, the key functions include demand forecasting, fabric allocating, material quality controlling, order processing, inventory control, and cost analysis. For sweater, the core functions include sample management, yarn management, accessory management, procurement management, knitting control, sub-contracting management, quality control, and accounting. In addition, e-jing K-FS (APS) is an advanced module for companies to manage their production scheduling of computerized knitting machines. e-jing WMS is for enterprises to manage their warehouses. The solution can support both the barcode and RFID technologies.

Fashion Master fashionmastersoftware.com	Fashion Master provides an ERP solution for small and mid-sized companies in the wholesale garment industry. It runs on the Microsoft Windows. It has the following modules: customer database, supplier database, order processing, inventory management, complete reporting.
iGarment igarment.net	iGarment offers on-demand internet-based business applications for apparel enterprises. There are several modules: netGarment – a complete management system solution for streamlining business operations; iWork – a garment production management system, which provides visibility throughout the entire production process, facilitates workflow, and payroll management; iBrand – a brand distribution management system for logistics, distribution, and retail operations.
Just OnePlace Pty Ltd just1place.com	The company offers a web-based software solution for managing product data, product development process, and supplier relationships. Major features include creating critical path templates (including alerting function), enhancing visibility from design to delivery, and automating integration.
Lawson Software lawson.com/fashion	Lawson for Fashion is an ERP solution for apparel, footwear, home textiles, and accessory companies. The major functions include finance, manufacturing, distribution, maintenance, CRM, etc.
Pebblestone pebblestone.us	Pebblestone Fashion is a Microsoft Enterprise Resource Planning add-on solution for the apparel, footwear, and outdoor industries. The main functions include CRM, warehousing, and e-commerce.
Zymmetry Group www.zymmetry.com	The Zymmetry Group has developed ERP systems for sourcing and manufacturing in the textiles and apparel industry. The ERP systems can support vertical retailers, global brands, wholesalers, exporters, trading companies, buying offices, and manufacturers. Zymmetry Group's ERP systems include a combination of enterprise software applications, which support various technologies such as RFID.

[2]Sources: http://www.e-jing.net, http://www.orioninc.com/,
http://www.apparelmagic.com/, http://www.ariany.com/, http://www.a2000software.com/,
http://www.cantel-cams.com/, http://www.datas.ro/, http://www.fashionmastersoftware.com/,
http://www.igarment.net/, http://www.just1place.com/, http://www.lawson.com/fashion,
http://www.pebblestone.us/,
http://www.apparelsearch.com/software_erp_enterprise_resource_planning.htm,
www.zymmetry.com

1. *Finance*. In the finance area, an ERP system helps with calculating standard costs for all items, calculating profit margins, indicating the production mix, calculating production costs, estimating operational risk, and indicating variations from standard costs.
2. *Sales and Distribution*. In the sales and distribution area, an ERP system helps the company handle orders, assortments and samples, conduct order forecasting, manage a multi-dimensional size matrix, confirm multiple deliveries to multiple destinations, calculate commissions and discounts, make sure the availability of products and materials, enhance inventory visibility, answer online production order status inquiry, and provide a cross-reference utility for user styles and templates for sales documents like picking lists, packing list, bills of lading, invoices, etc.
3. *Production Planning and Scheduling*. In the production planning and scheduling area, an ERP system helps with the calculation of materials and capacity requirements for the completion of the specified processes, checking for stock availability and manufacturing capacity, allocating and scheduling resources to the critical production steps, launching production orders, and identifying divergence of orders being processed. It also provides a feasible production plan based on the sales forecast and analyzes the impacts of the respective production plan on revenues, inventory, and cash flows. It also gives a recommendation on replenishment orders and identifies the shortages and the "at-risk orders" to enhance customer communication. Online updates are one of the desirable features that can improve the efficiency of production planning.
4. *Manufacturing and Quality Management*. In the area of manufacturing and quality management, an ERP system allows planning, launching, and tracking of production activities across the whole production cycle. It helps textile manufacturers reach the production goals, including correct and thorough control of each production process to maximize volume and profits for each individual department, track production to find and prevent defective lots or defects in production, reduce production lead-times, improve quality by better managing both material usage and process parameter settings, reduce waste by properly defining the production standards and monitoring production processes, maintain close management of external operations involving shipping of items to be processed to the converter, delivery dates and processing prices, perfect communication between sales and production so that delays and problems can be identified before they affect customer service.
5. *Inventory Management*. In the area of inventory management, an ERP system can enhance inventory visibility. It also helps buyers and inventory managers reduce the amount of unsold and obsolete stocks and supplies through careful controls. Other key functions such as optimization of physical warehouse and location selection, and improvement of customer service in terms of quality and response-time can also be achieved. Inventory management function of an ERP system usually focuses on managing inventory levels, requisitions, and allocations of the related products or materials. Some interesting supply chain management

practices such as vendor-managed inventory programme can also be supported by the inventory management module of an ERP system.

6. *Global Enterprise Management.* In the area of global enterprise management, an ERP system could provide the supports of human resources, logistics, product data management, and business intelligence. It gives businesses a vehicle to manage information globally and uses it to increase their competitive advantage. An ERP system organizes data in a way that helps individual departments operate more efficiently, and it creates streamlined processes that help companies cut costs and move products along the supply chain more quickly.

7. *CRM.* In the area of CRM, an ERP system allows TC companies to conduct advanced planning and scheduling to attain efficient customer response.

4 Enabling Technologies

In virtually all ERP systems employed in the TC industry, centralized relational databases and secured networks are used as the core technologies to integrate different modules. Under secured networks such as virtual private network (VPN), intranet, and extranet, there are several technology related methods for supporting data integration.

1. A modular, table-driven design allows the ERP implementation in different processes to fit the company's requirements, with flexibility and easy adaption to environmental changes. For example, for the trading companies, their business activities mainly focus on the sales, finance, inventory, and distribution. They could use such four modules for ERP implementation. For the production companies, their business activities focus mainly on production, quality control, and costing, and these three modules of ERP system can be implemented to offer direct helps. Such modular design is widely observed and the majority of the ERP solution providers as listed in Table 1 are adopting this modular approach.

2. For information sharing, the protocols that are employed include electronic data interchange (EDI) and electronic business extended markup language (ebXML). Traditional ERP systems used in the TC industry, such as the ERP solutions developed by Aria Systems and Cantel Apparel, adopt EDI for data exchange among different companies. Recently, ebXML has been proposed to replace EDI for data exchange. Essentially, ebXML is a set of specifications that enable a modular electronic business framework. The key strength of ebXML is that it can support a global electronic marketplace where enterprises of any size and in any geographical location can meet and conduct business with each other through the exchange of XML-based messages.

3. An item code structure can be used along the supply chain from yarn spinning to garment production. It is an important element to implement data integration in the TC industry. However, different ERP solutions developed by different vendors may use different item code structure for implementation. This creates

challenges and hence it is desirable to have a compatible and standardized coding system developed by some international organization for solving this problem.

5 Main Barriers

After a full discussion with ten industrialists (including two yarn manufacturers, four fabric manufacturers, and four garment manufacturers) and reviewing various reported cases, it appears to us that the TC industry always strives hard for new product development and efficiency improvement in production and sales with the use of ERP systems. However, various barriers are reported to be especially significant:

1. Production workers at garment factories usually have a habit of keeping their job ticket. This not only increases the factories' overtime expenses due to compliance requirement of extra compensation but also prohibits the factories from accurately estimating its workers' productivity through the ERP system, because the manual operations have not been fully integrated into the system.
2. There is no real-time monitoring in many ERP systems. For example, when there is bottleneck in certain production steps in the line, the ERP system fails to issue a warning within a short period of time. This finally causes production jam.
3. There is usually no specialized function of the existing TC ERP system, which enables more specialized and in-depth analysis. In reality, a lot of manufacturers have used other technologies such as simulation techniques and statistical tools for analyzing their production performance. This will significantly increase their running costs.
4. Most existing TC ERP systems (except a few such as DataS' ERP solution) support only batch processing but not the real-time one. This heavily reduces the significance of a truly powerful well integrated real-time ERP system.
5. For some apparel manufacturers, one of the most crucial functional elements of their ERP systems is MRP. However, it is found that a lot of manufacturers, for example, those located in China and Hong Kong, still rely heavily on Ms Excel for exporting ERP data to plan for yarn, fabric, accessories, etc. Efficiency is hence low and it is also a big barrier for companies to realize the true benefits of ERP systems.

6 Critical Success Factors for Implementing ERP Systems

To successfully implement and use the ERP systems, several critical success factors are essential. Some of them are listed as follows:

1. Thorough analyses of business processes as well as top management support are most important for a successful implementation of ERP system. In addition, supports from department heads and process owners including warehouse managers,

accounting heads, buying and purchasing department managers, and so on should not be ignored as they understand the particular business process of the corresponding departments better. The case on Company A that we discussed in Sect. 3 provides a good example for the failure of an ERP implementation project because of a lack of top management support.

2. The needs to possess a clear business vision and understand the scope of installation complexity. One of the common causes of failure for ERP implementation is the lack of company vision and poor understanding of the company. In fact, failure during the diagnostic phase is also a common source of the ERP implementation failure. The scope of the complexity of the business processes should be understood and clarified thoroughly, and this especially applies to the TC companies that undertake "multiyear supply chain implementations." These companies are strongly suggested to reassess their plans of ERP implementation and their own business processes to better facilitate the installation (Farmer and Luening 2001). Reassessment of the ERP plans includes rethinking whether the expected outcomes match the company's vision. This point is also illustrated by the case on Company A.

3. Effective change management scheme including sufficient staff training is necessary. The lack of proper training throughout the process of an ERP system's implementation is often referred to as one of the common factors for failures (Bhatti 2005). According to Bill Wohl from SAP, who was involved in the ERP implementation project with Nike, "what we know about a software implementation project is that it's just not about turning on the software" and he referred to ERP implementation as a project "really wrenching changes in a company's business process". In other words, not only are business daily operations altered, employees are also affected (Farmer and Luening 2001). Trainings help incorporating the technology advances and ensure that human factors are not ignored. Therefore, managing changes to better enhance employees' acceptance is essentially important because employees have a natural tendency to resist changes. It should also be noted that training should not be limited to IT people, but key users as well as process owners should also be trained. The purpose of performing trainings is to allow the users to be more "comfortable with the system" as well as "increase the expertise and knowledge level of the people" (Bhatti 2005). Company Z is a very good example, which has done an excellent job in offering training to employees of all levels for the implementation of their self-developed ERP system.

4. Sufficient IT infrastructure, hardware, and network are essential for the implementation of an ERP system which involves complex systems and information transitions (Bhatti 2005). According to Chris Kohlsdorf, a consulting manager involved in the Hugo Boss' ERP implementation project, "strategically planning the technical infrastructure at an early stage" contributed to the success of the ERP installation and adoption at Hugo Boss (SAP AG 2007). In addition, it is critical to consult key-users of the system for a smooth ERP implementation process. The adidas ERP project team included end users of the adopted ERP

system, and this allowed adidas to implement an ERP system that focuses on the empowering users, and in return drives the project to a success (SAP AG 2008).

5. ERP systems can help a company in the TC industry to achieve a higher degree of collaboration with her vendors or customers. To achieve this goal, proper communication among the supply chain partners must be established, and this would also gradually develop a high level of trust. (Clark 2004).

6. Be patient and understand that it is impossible to set an ambitious goal of "accomplishing everything within a short period of time." The success of Textile Plc. and the failure of Company A all explain the importance of this point.

7. Pilot tests are critical in ERP system's implementation for many TC companies because their operations very likely will involve a global supply chain that sources and assembles in different countries as well as marketing in multiple places. A pilot run of the ERP system ensures that the software, hardware, and datasets as well as the business processes can combine and work together (Farmer and Luening 2001). The lesson learnt from many cases is that a pilot running is necessary for a proper system implementation process. It does not necessarily mean that the TC company fully conducts a big "pilot run/test" after all phases and modules of the ERP system have been implemented. Instead, like what adidas-Salomon did, it could be wiser to take "incremental steps" in its ERP system development cycle and gradually tested the running of some modules before the full rollout in the company's offices globally. For adidas-Salomon, the pilot test lasted for 18 months to ensure that problems are solved before the full adoption (SAP AG 2008). It is also argued that global bigger enterprises like Nike and adidas would face a higher chance of failure in terms of ERP systems implementation, because "when these systems fail, they fail big" (Farmer and Luening 2001). It is thus proposed that the pilot running and testing are especially important to them.

7 Conclusion and Future Developments

In this chapter, we have studied the applications of ERP systems and explored the respective enabling technologies in the TC supply chains via studying various real company cases and the specifications of real ERP systems for the TC industry. In addition, the main barriers and the critical success factors of implementing the ERP systems in the TC industry have been identified.

In our opinion, one important future development of ERP systems for the TC industry is to integrate the traditional ERP system with an intelligent decision support system (DSS). This idea has been proposed by ERP solution providers such as e-jing Technologies who developed their sense-and-respond module. The major benefits of such integration include the ability to improve the quality and visibility of information, increase intelligence density (the degree of intelligence provided by a decision support tool) (Dhar and Stein 1997) of an enterprise, and achieve multi-enterprise collaboration. An enterprise can integrate an ERP system with a DSS in one of the several ways. First, extend the functionality of current DSS so that they can easily access the data stored in an ERP system. Second, integrate existing DSS that currently sits on top of an enterprise's information system. Third, integrate existing DSS that currently sits on top of an ERP system across multiple enterprises. Finally, build a single, flexible, and comprehensive DSS that sits on top of an ERP system (Shafiei and Sundaram 2004). Through such integration, ERP system can provide the integrated data stored in the centralized common database and the DSS makes the transformation of data, which allows the TC companies to gain a higher-level view of the data, thus providing them with the ability to discover trends, patterns, and relationships in the data. Furthermore, DSS supports them through a period of learning and decision makers gain insights and understanding, thereby setting the platform for making accurate, timely, and knowledgeable decisions. In addition to DSS, several other areas of further development of ERP systems for the TC industry are listed as follows,

1. Selection of an appropriate data warehousing methodologies and artificial intelligence techniques for modeling decision processes in the industry: Investigations shall be made in the comparison of various data warehousing methodologies and artificial intelligence techniques (such as neural networks, genetic algorithms, and fuzzy logics) regarding the various enterprises' planning in the TC industry.
2. Construction of an enterprise's application integration (EAI): It is important to take into account that ERP and DSS integration may be achieved via an emerging class of integration technologies called EAI. EAI efficiently and effectively integrates functionalities from a variety of information systems, resulting in flexible and maintainable information technology infrastructures. The ability of EAI makes it a viable choice for integrating ERP and DSS systems both within an enterprise and in a multi-enterprise level.
3. RFID technology has been frequently applied in various industries. Earliest applications focused on very specific areas, for example, in livestock tracking (Beigel 2003). RFID is also used extensively to allow tracking and identification of products in a retail supply chain. Many retailers like GAP, Marks & Spencer, and Wal-Mart have implemented item-level RFID to monitor stock in retail stores. In addition, the RFID system could also be used in anti-counterfeiting applications (Hui et al. 2006). By employing RFID technology in ERP systems, the TC companies can benefit from enjoying smaller administrative costs and faster processes and feedback. In addition, RFID technology and ERP systems can work together for better management in areas of materials control, monitoring the production WIP progress, order tracing, storage, logistics, recording sales data, and related security to improve the efficiency of the entire business process. In Table 1, we can observe that a few ERP solution providers such as Aria Systems, e-jing Technologies, and Zymmetry have already incorporated RFID into their solutions. From our discussions with the TC industrialists, we expect to see more and more ERP systems for the TC companies being supported by the RFID technology.
4. Including manufacturing execution system (MES): MES can support ERP systems to collect order processing related data. This would be a big help to

overcome the challenges brought by the barriers such as a lack of real-time monitoring module in the ERP system.

Acknowledgements This piece of research is partially supported by the research funding provided by the Hong Kong Polytechnic University under grant numbers of J-BB6U and G-YH12. Thanks are given to Mr. Mark Lee of e-jing Technologies Ltd. for his kind comments and inputs.

References

Au KF, Ho CK (2002) Electronic commerce and supply chain management: value-adding service for clothing manufacturers. J Integrated Manuf Syst 13:247–254

Beigel M (2003) Taming the beast: the history of RFID. Invited Presentation. Smart Labels, USA, Cambridge, MA

Bhatti TR (2005) Critical success factors for the implementation of enterprise resource planning (ERP): epmirical validation. The 2nd international conference on innovation in information technology (IIT'05)

Bruce M, Daly L (2006) Buyer behavior for fast fashion. J Fashion Market Manag 10:329–344

Callaway E (1999) Enterprise resource planning: integrating applications and business processes across the enterprise, 1st edn. Computer Technology Research Corporation

Clark T (2004) Power users: nike leads a prominent pack of technology champions. Consum Goods Tech 15

Davenport H (1998) Putting the enterprise into the enterprise system. Harvard Business Review, Vol. 76, Issue 4, July–August, pp 121–131

Dhar V, Stein R (1997) Intelligent decision support methods: the science of knowledge work. Prentice Hall, Upper Saddle River, NJ, USA

Doshi G (2006) Information technology and textile industry. http://www.fiber2fashion.com

Farmer MA, Luening E (2001) i2-Nike fallout a cautionary tale. Staff Writers, CNET News 9 Mar, 4:00 AM PST.

Ganesan P, Hariharan S, Praddeep E, Prakash A (2001) ERP in apparel industry. http://www.fibre2fashion.com

Gereffi G (1999) International trade and industrial upgrading in the apparel commodity chain. J Int Econ 48:37–70

Glenn G (2008) Enterprise resource planning 100 success secrets: 100 most asked questions – the missing ERP software, systems, solutions, applications and implementations guide. Lightning Source UK Ltd. UK

Hodge GL (2002) Enterprise resource planning in textiles. J Textile Apparel Tech Manag (online publication)

Holland CP, Light B (1999) A critical success factors model for ERP implementation. IEEE Software 16(3):30–36

Holland CP, Light B (1999) Global enterprise resource planning implementation. Proceedings of the thirty-second annual Hawaii international conference on system sciences, 5–8 Jan 1999, p 7016

Hui CLP, Wong KMK, Chan CKA (2006) Cryptography and authentication on RFID passive tags for apparel products. Comput Ind 57:342–349

Koch C, Slater D, Baatz E (1999) The ABCs of ERP. London: CIO. http://www.scsolutions.com.au

Kumar K, Van Hillsgersberg J (2000) ERP experiences and evolution. Commun ACM 43:23–26

SAP AG (2003) SAP customer success story in apparel and footwear: Adidas-Salomon. SAP, 50 043 151 (03/09)

SAP AG (2004) SAP customer success story in apparel and footwear: Adidas-Salomon. SAP, 50 043 151 (04/06)

SAP AG (2007) SAP customer success story: consumer products – apparel and footwear: Hugo Boss. SAP, 50 084 085 (07/05)

SAP AG (2008) mySAP CRM customer success stories: a comprehensive reference guide. SAP, 50 079 396 (06/05), pp 312–315, 562

Shafiei F, Sundaram D (2004) Multi-enterprise collaborative enterprise resource planning and decision support systems. Proc Hawaii Int Conf Syst Sci

Sheridan M, Moore C, Nobbs K (2006) Fast fashion requires fast marketing. J Fashion Market Manag 10:301–315

Stefanou CJ (1999) Supply chain management (scm) and organizational key factors for successful implementation of enterprise resource planning (ERP) systems. Association for Information Systems, AMCIS 1999 proceedings

Simulation-based Optimization of Inventory Model with Products Substitution

Di Huang, Qiu Hong Zhao, and Cheng Cheng Fan

Abstract The substitution between products is a common phenomenon in supply chains when customers find their favorite product unavailable. Products substitution can improve the availability of products and further enhance the quick response ability of supply chains, especially when the products are perishable. In this chapter, a single-period newsboy framework is utilized in a multi-product environment, wherein one product may be taken as a direct substitute for the others. We present an inventory model allowing for free and full substitution among multiple products and provide the necessary and sufficient optimality conditions for the existence of the optimal solution (optimal quantity of each product ordered). With the demonstration that the objective function is both concave and submodular, a Monte Carlo simulation algorithm for finding the optimal solution is proposed, and computational experiments are conducted to analyze the impact of products substitution on expected profit and total inventory level.

Keywords Full product substitution · Monte Carlo simulation · Newsboy model

1 Introduction

Quick response (QR) aims at shortening manufacturing and distribution lead times by means of information technology such as electronic data interchange (EDI) and point of sale scanner, by utilizing faster modes of transportation, and also by organizing the manufacturing operations around cellular manufacturing concepts (Fisher and Raman 1996). QR is developed from the fashion apparel industry to reduce inventory costs, particularly the cost of excess inventory and inventory stockouts. These costs are high in apparel supply channels with short product life. The impact of QR is reported to be especially substantial in the supply chains with products of short shelf-life, high seasonality, and high complexity (Lowson et al. 1999, Fisher

Q.H. Zhao (✉)
School of Economics and Management, Beihang University,
37 Xueyuan Road, Haidian District, Beijing 100191, China
e-mail: qhzhao@buaa.edu.cn

T.C. Edwin Cheng and T.-M. Choi (eds.), *Innovative Quick Response Programs in Logistics and Supply Chain Management*, International Handbooks on Information Systems, DOI 10.1007/978-3-642-04313-0_15,
© Springer-Verlag Berlin Heidelberg 2010

et al. 1994, 2001). As a result, QR has become popular and has been used successfully by a number of major retailers in fashion retail supply chains in the US (Fisher
and Raman 1996).

Most researchers focus on how to use the QR approach to improve demand forecast accuracy and shorten lead times. But quite a few notice the fact that considering
the effects of products substitution in inventory decision-making can also achieve
the goal of QR: to reduce the level of excess inventory and inventory stockouts in
supply chains while improving the customer service level. From a practical point of
view, exploiting products substitution in supply chain management provides a new
method to support the implementation of QR strategy.

Products substitution becomes a more and more important consideration for the
retail inventory management problem since the retailers sell more similar products.
Product substitution problems have been the focus of many studies, most of which
have been motivated by real-world applications. In apparel, for example, style goods
in different colors, styles, or brands may act as substitutes. The benefits of products substitution have long been recognized. Substitution among products motivates
retailers to share the inventory of similar products in a substitutable manner, which
may offer opportunities for economies of scale in managing the cycle stocks of all
the products. Another significant benefit of product substitution is the possibility of
inventory pooling to hedge against demand uncertainties and to help reduce safety
stocks.

In this chapter, we study single-period multi-product newsboy inventory problems in which any product with a surplus (i.e., whose demand is below its order
quantity) can be used to substitute for other out-of-stock products. The effective
demand for each product consists of two parts: the original demand for that product
and the essential demand derived from other products' unmet demand. This effect of
products substitution on demand is considered when the optimal ordering quantity
for each product is determined.

2 The Literature

QR is both a management paradigm and a methodology that allows supply chain
systems to react quickly to changes while improving their performance (Lowson
et al. 1999). In general, uncertainty in customer demand forecast is higher when the
forecasting is conducted a long time before the selling season starts. As the selling season approaches, more information about the potential customer demand is
acquired and demand forecasts become more reliable. A common practice utilizing
information update in a QR system is to split the traditional single purchase order
into two lots (see, e.g., Iyer and Bergen 1997; Choi 2006; Choi and Chow 2008;
Serel 2009). Iyer and Bergen (1997) studied the QR strategy for a single manufacturer single retailer two-echelon supply chain. They divide the planning horizon
into two separate stages; information observed in the first stage is used to update
the distribution parameters by the Bayesian approach. Actions like wholesale price
commitment and service-level commitment that can make QR beneficial to both

the retailer and the manufacturer are proposed. Choi (2006) studied a supply chain similar to Iyer and Bergen's (1997) but with another information updating model. Measures that can help to create win–win situations for the supply chain, such as buy-back policies, have been proposed and discussed. Choi and Chow (2008) extend the results of Iyer and Bergen (1997) to the case where the impacts of a QR system on both the mean and the variance of the profit distribution are taken into account.

Product substitution was first studied by McGillivray and Silver (1978) in the economic order quantity (EOQ) context. The related literature can be classified as one-way substitution and two-way substitution.

The one-way substitution, which is generally driven by the retailers, usually assumes that the products are classified into different grades and that products with higher grades can be used to substitute for products with lower grades (see, e.g., Bitran and Dasu 1992; Bassok et al. 1999; Hsu and Bassok 1999; Hsu et al. 2005; Bayindir et al. 2007; Dutta and Chakraborty 2009). Bitran and Dasu (1992) modeled production problems where yields are stochastic, demands are substitutable, and several items are jointly produced. This problem is formulated as a profit maximizing convex program, and two approximation procedures are proposed. Bassok et al. (1999) studied a single period multi-product inventory problem with one-way substitution and proportional costs and revenues. It is shown that the function of the expected cost in their model is concave and submodular. A greedy allocation algorithm is given and several properties of the optimal policy are derived. Hsu and Bassok (1999) presented a single-period, multi-product, downward substitution model, where one raw material acts as the production input and N different products are the outputs. Their problem is modeled as a two-stage stochastic program, which can be decomposed into a parameterized network flow problem. Hsu et al. (2005) discussed a finite horizon, multi-product, dynamic lot size problem with one-way product substitution. They analyzed two scenarios in their models: with and without a conversion cost in product substitution. Dynamic programming algorithms and heuristics are developed to solve the problems. Computational experiments are conducted to test the effectiveness of the heuristic and the efficiency of the optimal algorithm. Bayindir et al. (2007) investigated the benefits of remanufacturing option under one-way substitution policy in which the manufactured and remanufactured products are segmented to different markets and the product capacity is finite. Dutta and Chakraborty (2009) studied a two-item newsboy problem with substitution in fuzzy environment, which has not been received much attention yet.

The two-way substitution, which can be driven by both the retailers and the customers, allows that each product can be used to substitute for all other products freely. A research stream has considered the partial substitution among products in which only a fraction of customers will buy a substitute when their favorite product is out of stock. In partial substitution, a product can substitute for another product with a certain substitution probability (substitution rate). A large amount of research has been devoted to the single-period inventory problem with partial substitution, such as Parlar and Goyal (1984); Parlar (1988); Khouja et al. (1996); Nesstine and Rudi (2003); Rajaram and Tang (2001); Nagarajan and Rajagopalan (2008). Parlar and Goyal (1984) discussed a two-item newsboy problem in which substitution rate lies between 0 and 1. They showed that the function of total expected profits is concave for a wide range of problems. Parlar (1988) discussed the competitive version of the two-item newsboy problem with partial substitution. Using a game-theoretic approach, Parlar (1988) proved the existence of a unique Nash equilibrium and obtained the analytical solution to the problem. Khouja et al. (1996) formulated a centralized two-item newsboy problem with substitutability. Upper and lower bounds on the optimal order quantities of the two items are developed and a Monte Carlo simulation is used to identify the optimal solution. Netessine and Rudi (2003) considered the problem of determining order quantities under partial substitution for two scenarios: without and with retail competition. They developed first-order conditions that can be used to estimate order quantities under these scenarios if the distribution of effective demand under substitution is available. Rajaram and Tang (2001) provided an approximation for the effective demand under partial substitution and developed a service rate heuristic to solve the noncompetitive version of a multi-item newsboy problem. Nagarajan and Rajagopalan (2008) derived the optimal inventory policy for a single decision maker in a model with two substitutable products whose demands are negatively correlated and that are partial substitutes in stockout situations in both single-period and multi-period scenarios.

Our paper follows another research stream in which all the customers will buy a substitute when their favorite product is out of stock. In contrast with partial substitution, under full substitution all the customers (not only part of the customers) who would initially purchase a product are willing to accept another product when the former is out of stock. By considering the two-item newsboy problem with full and free substitution, Pasternack and Drezner (1991) proved that the expected profit function is concave and derived the analytical solutions for the optimal inventory levels. They have shown numerically that the associated optimal order quantities can be larger or smaller compared to the case with no substitution.

This paper aims to provide a general model and algorithm for single-period multi-product inventory problem with full and free products substitution. While it is closely related to the works of Pasternack and Drezner (1991); Hsu and Bassok (1999) as well as Bassok et al. (1999), our work differs from these earlier achievements in several respects. First, we develop an objective function that allows for free and full substitution among multiple products, rather than being limited to only downward substitution as in Hsu and Bassok (1999); Bassok et al. (1999). Second, by relating the objective function with that appeared in Van Slyke and Wets (1966) and the transportation problem in Topkis (1998), we manage to demonstrate that the objective function is both concave and submodular. These two important properties show innovativeness of our study and enrich inventory management theory, guaranteeing the valid application of Monte Carlo simulation method in our model.

The rest of the paper is arranged as follows. In Sect. 3, we present the single-period multi-product inventory model with full and free substitution. The objective function is demonstrated to be concave and submodular. In Sect. 4, we propose the Monte Carlo simulation method to solve the problem. In Sect. 5, we perform a computational study to analyze the impact of products substitution on expected profit and total inventory level. In Sect. 6, we conclude this paper.

3 The Model

We employ a newsboy inventory framework (Nahmias 2004) and generalize the multi-product substitution model given in Bassok et al. (1999). The newsboy holds a set of products that have the same selling season during which products can be sold at a full price. At the end of the selling season, products not sold during the regular season must be liquidated at a discounted price or otherwise disposed of. The sequence of decision-making in our model is as follows: first, the newsboy determines how many to order for each product at the beginning of a selling season. It is assumed that these products become available before demands are realized. Next, demands are observed. A substitution decision is made and existing inventory of different products is used to satisfy each product's effective demand. Any unsatisfied demand is lost. Then, purchasing costs, inventory holding costs, shortage penalty costs, and substitution costs are incurred. Finally, all left-over inventory is salvaged at a discounted price.

3.1 Notations and Assumptions

Throughout, we will adopt the following notation, in particular, let i, j be the product indices, $i, j \in (1, 2, \ldots, N)$, and

p_i: sale price of product i per unit
c_i: purchasing cost of product i per unit
h_i: holding cost of product i per unit per period
s_i: salvage value of product i per unit
π_i: shortage penalty cost of product i per unit
b_{ij}: substitution cost per unit when product i substitutes for product $j, i \neq j$
r_{ij}: sale price of product i per unit when it is used to substitute for product j, in which $r_{ij} = p_i$, for $i = j$, and $r_{ij} = p_i - b_{ij}$, for $i \neq j$
D_i: demand for product i with mean μ_i and standard deviation σ_i
d_i: demand realization for product i
Q_i: order quantity of product i
Q_i^*: optimal order quantity of product i
A_{ij}: quantity of product i allocated to satisfy demand for product j
E_i: excess inventory of product i after all demands are satisfied
S_i: shortage of product i

In our model, it is assumed that total substitution costs are linear (i.e., proportional to the amount of substitution from i to j). The per unit substitution cost is (1) the cost of transshipping products among outlets before substitution; or (2) the lost goodwill or reduced revenue when i is substituted for j. This is consistent with assumptions made in the literature on substitution models. Unlike Hsu and Bassok (1999), we assumed that the revenue earned from substitution depends on the unit sale price of product j used to satisfy the 'spill over' demand from product i and the corresponding unit substitution cost b_{ij}.

To avoid anomalies in product allocation such as one product is ordered not for sale but only for substitution, Assumptions 1–4, for all $i, j \in (1, 2, \ldots, N), i \neq j$, should hold:

> *Assumption 1.* $p_i > c_i > s_i - h_i$, for $i = 1, 2, \ldots, N$
> *Assumption 2.* $p_i - b_{ij} > s_i - h_i$, for $i, j = 1, 2, \ldots, N$
> *Assumption 3.* $p_i - (s_i - h_i) > p_j - b_{ji} - (s_j - h_j)$, for $i, j = 1, 2, \ldots, N$
> *Assumption 4.* $b_{ij} + \pi_i > \pi_j$, for $i, j = 1, 2, \ldots, N$

Assumptions 1–4 are the necessary and sufficient optimality conditions for the existence of the optimal solution. Assumption 1 is the common assumption in newsboy-type problems. Assumption 2 states that the substitution revenue of one product per unit must be larger than its salvage revenue. If Assumption 2 does not hold, the excess inventory of one product may be sold for its salvage value rather than substituting other products. Assumption 3 states that the sales price of one product per unit subtracting its salvage revenue must be larger than the substitution revenue of another product per unit subtracting its salvage revenue. If Assumption 3 does not hold, one product will be substituted by another product even though it has no shortage. Assumption 4 states that the shortage cost of one product per unit plus its substitution cost must be larger than the shortage cost of another product. If Assumption 4 does not hold, one product will be used as a substitute for another product even though it has unmet demand. It should be noted that in the two substitutable products case considered in Pasternack and Drezner (1991), Assumption 2, 3, and 4 guarantee the existence of a global optimum in the profit function.

3.2 The Profit Function

Let $Q = (Q_1, \ldots, Q_N)$ be a vector of order quantities, and $G(Q, d)$ be the total profit derived from products substitution for a given inventory level Q and a set of realized demands $d = (d_1, d_2, \ldots, d_N)$. Then the maximum expected profit function of the newsboy in our model can be formulated as a two-stage stochastic program.

$$P(Q) = \text{Max} \left\{ -\sum_{i=1}^{N} c_i Q_i + E\left[G(Q, d)\right] \right\}, \tag{1}$$

where

$$G(Q, d) = \text{Max} \left(\sum_{i=1}^{N} \sum_{j=1}^{N} r_{ij} A_{ij} + \sum_{i=1}^{N} (s_i - h_i) E_i - \sum_{i=1}^{N} \pi_i S_i \right) \tag{2a}$$

subject to

$$\sum_{j=1}^{N} A_{ij} + E_i = Q_i, \quad \text{for } i = 1, 2, \ldots, N, \tag{2b}$$

$$\sum_{i=1}^{N} A_{ij} + S_j = d_j, \quad \text{for } j = 1, 2, \ldots, N, \tag{2c}$$

$$A_{ij} \geq 0, \quad \text{for } i = 1, 2, \ldots, N, \ j = 1, 2, \ldots, N, \tag{2d}$$

$$Q_i \geq 0, \quad \text{for } i = 1, 2, \ldots, N, \tag{2e}$$

$$E_i \geq 0, \quad \text{for } i = 1, 2, \ldots, N, \tag{2f}$$

$$S_i \geq 0, \quad \text{for } i = 1, 2, \ldots, N. \tag{2g}$$

In (1) the first term is the total purchasing cost, the second term is the expected profit based on the substitution decision. Equation (1) expresses the total net profit for an ordering decision and a substitution decision. The first term in (2a) is the revenue for satisfying demands because A_{ij} represents the amount of demand for product j that is satisfied by product i and r_{ij} is the unit revenue, the second term is the effective salvage value (the salvage value minus the holding cost) obtained from excess inventory, and the last term is the shortage cost. Equations (2b) and (2c) are the inventory balance equations for each of the products. In (2b), the inventory of a product i can be allocated to satisfy demand for all the products or may be salvaged as excess inventory E_i. In (2c), the demand for a product j may be satisfied by inventory allocated to it; any shortfall is represented by the shortage S_j. We call $G(Q,d)$ *the transportation problem* since it is concerned with a given set of supply Q to satisfy a given set of demands d.

Proposition 1. *The sub-problem $E[G(Q,d)]$ is concave and submodular.*

Proof. For a group of realized demand d, it is observed that $G(Q,d)$ is a standard transportation problem. Based on Theorem 3.4.1 of Topkis (1998) as well as Lemma 1 and Lemma 2 in Karaesmen and van Ryzin (2004), $G(Q,d)$ is both concave and submodular with respect to Q. Then $E[G(Q,d)]$ is also concave and submodular because the expectation operation preserves concavity.

Proposition 2. *The profit function $P(Q)$ is concave and submodular.*

Proof. The decision process in our model is similar to that in Van Slyke and Wets (1966). The newsboy first determines the order quantity $Q_i(i = 1, \ldots, N)$ of each product, next the random demand $D_i(i = 1, \ldots, N)$ is realized as $d_i(i = 1, \ldots, N)$, then the newsboy decides the allocation quantities $A_{ij}(i = 1, \ldots, N, j = 1, \ldots, N)$ among products. When $Q_i(i = 1, \ldots, N)$ is fixed and $D_i(i = 1, \ldots, N)$ is realized, the problem to find the optimal allocation quantities among products is a deterministic problem. Hence, from Proposition 7 of Van Slyke and Wets (1966), $P(Q)$ is concave in Q. It is observed that in (1) the first term is a *valuation* in Q and the second term is submodular in Q (based on Proposition 1), then $P(Q)$ is also submodular in Q.

Propositions 1 and 2 establish the concavity and submodularity of the profit function $P(Q)$, which enable us to provide a modified Monte Carlo simulation method
(described in Sect. 4) for finding the optimal solution to the model. Concavity of
$E[G(Q,d)]$ and $P(Q)$ guarantee the existence of global optimal solutions. Submodularity of $P(Q)$ implies that the additional profit for additional product i will
not increase if there is more of product j. This is certainly a reasonable condition
for products substitution when the constraint qualification condition holds.

4 The Algorithm

In this section, the solution method is presented for solving the problem of maximizing profit in the single-period, multi-product inventory system with products
substitution. To the best of our knowledge, there is no known accurate and efficient method that could directly solve the problem (1). Although Pasternack and
Drezner (1991) provided a pair of equations that can be used for finding the optimal
solutions to the two-product case, these equations are available only for a specific
distribution (*uniform distribution*) and one must solve two quadratic equations. Distinguished with them, we employ a linear programming approach to solve the model
by formulating the problem (1) as a stochastic linear program.

When the demands are fixed at $d_1, d_2, \ldots, d_N$, $G(Q,d)$ is a linear program for
the transportation problem and $P(Q)$ is a deterministic problem which is formulated
in (3).

$$\text{Max} \left(-\sum_{i=1}^{N} c_i Q_i + \sum_{i=1}^{N}\sum_{j=1}^{N} r_{ij} A_{ij} + \sum_{i=1}^{N} (s_i - h_i) E_i - \sum_{i=1}^{N} \pi_i S_i \right) \quad (3)$$

subject to

$$\sum_{j=1}^{N} A_{ij} + E_i = Q_i, \quad \text{for } i = 1, 2, \ldots, N,$$

$$\sum_{i=1}^{N} A_{ij} + S_j = d_j, \quad \text{for } j = 1, 2, \ldots, N,$$

$$A_{ij} \geq 0, \quad \text{for } i = 1, 2, \ldots, N, \ j = 1, 2, \ldots, N,$$
$$Q_i \geq 0, \quad \text{for } i = 1, 2, \ldots, N,$$
$$E_i \geq 0, \quad \text{for } i = 1, 2, \ldots, N,$$
$$S_i \geq 0, \quad \text{for } i = 1, 2, \ldots, N.$$

The deterministic problem (3) can be solved by using min-cost network flow algorithms or a standard linear programming solver such as *LINGO*. We also provide a

greedy allocation algorithm for the deterministic problem (3), which can be stated as:

The greedy allocation algorithm

Step 1. {Satisfy the demand for each product using its own inventory}

For $i = 1$ to N
$A_{ii} = \min\{d_i, Q_i\}, E_i = \max\{Q_i - A_{ii}, 0\}, S_i = \max\{d_i - A_{ii}, 0\}$

Step 2. {Determine substitution quantities among products}

For $j = 1$ to N
While $(S_j > 0)$
find $i^* = \max(r_{ij} + \pi_j)$ for $i = 1$ to N while $(E_i > 0)$
if $(E_{i^*} < S_j)$ $\{A_{i^*j} = E_{i^*}, E_{i^*} = 0, S_j = S_j - E_{i^*}\}$
if $(E_{i^*} > S_j)$ $\{A_{i^*j} = S_j, E_{i^*} = E_{i^*} - S_j, S_j = 0\}$

To model random demand, we can formulate a stochastic linear program wherein the demand distributions are represented by a collection of random scenarios. The technique of generating random scenarios is equivalent to Monte Carlo sampling and is often used in stochastic linear programming. The objective of the stochastic linear program is then to maximize the *expected* profit over the scenarios. We will let M denote the number of scenarios and superscript each of the following parameters and variables by the scenario index m: d_i^m, A_{ij}^m, E_i^m, and S_i^m. Each scenario may be given a probability weight a_m such that $a_m > 0$ and $\sum_{m=1}^{M} a_m = 1$. We now have the following formulation for the problem that models the demand distributions using the M scenarios.

$$\text{Max} \sum_{m=1}^{M} a_m \left(-\sum_{i=1}^{N} c_i Q_i + \sum_{i=1}^{N}\sum_{j=1}^{N} r_{ij} A_{ij}^m + \sum_{i=1}^{N} (s_i - h_i) E_i^m - \sum_{i=1}^{N} \pi_i S_i^m \right)$$
(4)

subject to

$$\sum_{j=1}^{N} A_{ij}^m + E_i^m = Q_i, \quad \text{for } m = 1, 2, \ldots, M, \ i = 1, 2, \ldots, N,$$

$$\sum_{i=1}^{N} A_{ij}^m + S_j^m = d_j^m, \quad \text{for } m = 1, 2, \ldots, M, \ j = 1, 2, \ldots, N,$$

$$\sum_{m=1}^{M} a_m = 1,$$

$A_{ij}{}^m \geq 0, \quad \text{for } m = 1, 2, \ldots, M, \ i = 1, 2, \ldots, N, \ j = 1, 2, \ldots, N,$
$Q_i \geq 0, \quad \text{for } i = 1, 2, \ldots, N,$
$E_i^m \geq 0, \quad \text{for } m = 1, 2, \ldots, M, \ i = 1, 2, \ldots, N,$
$S_i^m \geq 0, \quad \text{for } m = 1, 2, \ldots, M, \ i = 1, 2, \ldots, N.$

Using (4), we can obtain an optimal ordering quantity by solving the linear program. As an example, consider a problem with three products ($N = 3$) and the following parameters for the model:

In this example, demands are normally distributed with the given mean μ_i and standard deviation σ_i. The cost and demand parameters of the three products are listed in Table 1, while the substitution cost is listed in Table 2. We set the coefficient of variation, denoted by cv, < 0.3, then the left tail of the distribution can be truncated below 0, which slightly increases the mean above μ_i and slightly decreases the standard deviation. Following the approach that we developed, we generate M scenarios each with equal weight ($a_m = 1/M$) that reflect the demand distributions.

As has been studied in the theory of Monte Carlo sampling, the sample size M is determined as follows: given the marginal error E and the confidence level $1 - \alpha$, the sample size M is determined by $M = Z_{\alpha/2}^2 \sigma^2 / E^2$, where σ is the standard deviation of demand and $Z_{\alpha/2}$ is the critical value for the corresponding level of confidence. Define the relative sampling error as $\xi = E/\sigma$, then the sample size M is obtained by $M = Z_{\alpha/2}^2 / \xi^2$. Table 3 shows the sample sizes under different confidence levels and relative errors. It can be seen that as the confidence level and simulation accuracy increases, the sample size M grows dramatically.

Another factor that should be considered in choosing the sample size M is the computational ability of the mathematical tools employed to solve the problem (4), which consists of a large number of decision variables (directly proportional to the number of demand scenarios and the number of products considered). Hence, the upper bound of M depends on the maximum number of decision variables that can be processed by the mathematical tools and the number of products.

To generate samples representing demands with random distribution, random number generators are employed. However, it is reported that the default random number generator in software such as *Matlab* has a strong dependence in the generated sequence of numbers (Savicky 2006). It is not possible to eliminate the dependencies in the pseudorandom number generators due to systematic errors. Hence, we have to take measures such as increasing the sampling size to diminish the influence of bad samples on the simulation results. As the number of scenarios M is increased, there is a trade-off between the increased computation time to

Table 1 Cost and demand parameters in the three-product example

Product i	p_i	c_i	h_i	s_i	π_i	μ_i	σ_i
1	8.0	4.5	0.7	1.6	2.3	100	20
2	7.7	3.4	0.5	1.3	2.0	120	25
3	7.5	3.5	0.3	1.1	1.9	130	20

Table 2 Substitution cost in the three-product example

b_{ij}	1	2	3
1	0	0.5	0.7
2	1.1	0	0.6
3	0.7	0.2	0

Table 3 The sample sizes under different confidence levels and relative errors

Relative error	Confidence level			
	90%	95%	98%	99%
10%	271	385	542	664
5%	1,083	1,537	2,165	2,654
3%	3,007	4,269	6,013	7,372
2%	6,766	9,604	13,530	16,587
1%	27,061	38,416	54,117	66,348

Table 4 Simulation results for different sample sizes

Sample size	Order quantity	Expected profit	Calculation time (s)
271	(77,147,141)	1266.32	< 1
385	(77,148,145)	1268.62	< 1
542	(77,148,145)	1270.55	< 1
664	(75,147,146)	1269.58	< 1
1,083	(77,148,144)	1267.26	< 1
1,537	(78,147,144)	1271.24	1
2,165	(77,146,145)	1267.63	1
2,654	(77,147,144)	1265.46	1
3,007	(78,148,145)	1271.1	2
4,269	(78,148,144)	1270.65	2
6,013	(77,147,144)	1267.95	4
6,766	(77,147,144)	1267.08	4
7,372	(77,148,144)	1262.14	6
9,604	(77,148,144)	1269.93	7
13,530	(77,147,144)	1265.08	12
16,587	(77,147,144)	1266.89	15
27,061	(77,147,144)	1267.58	37
38,416	(77,147,144)	1267.19	75
50,000	(77,147,144)	1266.78	91

solve the model and the improved accuracy as a result of a better approximation of the model.

In this example, we use the default random generator in *Matlab* (version 7.1) to generate samples and use software *Lingo* (version 8.0) to solve the problem (4). We set the maximum sampling size M as 50,000 (i.e., the linear program contains at most 150,000 decision variables). The simulation results under different sample sizes are summarized in Table 4, including the optimal order quantity, the expected profit, and the calculation time (*using the Barrier solver in Lingo*). The calculation time consists of the solution time only (not including input/output time) and is in CPU seconds running on a computer with a CPU speed of 2.33 GHz and a RAM size of 1.96 GB. Table 4 also shows the robustness of the optimal solution to the problem (4) with respect to the number of demand scenarios M. The optimal solution converges to (77,147,144) when $M > 13,530$. This is because as the sampling size increases, the linear program (4) approximates the basic model (1) more accurately and always secures its optimum at the same point (the optimal solution). This conclusion demonstrates the efficiency of our Monte Carlo simulation method.

In this example, the demands are independent and follow a normal distribution. In fact, our simulation-based approach can also deal with correlated demands. However, in multivariate Monte Carlo simulation, multivariate random variates can be generated only for a few joint distributions such as multivariate normal, multivariate lognormal, and multivariate gamma. Chang et al. (1994) proposed a practical multivariate Monte Carlo simulation that preserves the marginal distributions of random variables and their correlation structure without requiring the complete joint distribution. This enables our simulation method to model any demand structure according to any distribution, whether correlated or not. Procedures of Monte Carlo simulation algorithm are briefly explained as follows:

Step 1. Generate M groups of pseudo-random numbers subject to the products' demand distribution (under a reasonable confidence level and a reasonable relative sampling error).

Step 2. Set a weight a_m for each group of realized demand.

Step 3. Find the optimal solution for the linear program (4).

Step 4. Increase the sample size M, and repeat the above procedures until the optimal solution converges to a stationary point or the sample size reaches the maximized M.

As mentioned earlier, the Monte Carlo simulation method has several advantages: the formulation is easy to verify and commercial linear program solvers are readily available. However, the solution of the linear program is computationally intensive, especially if the number of products N and the number of scenarios M are large.

5 Computational Study

In this section, a computational study is conducted to gain some insights on the effect of inventory pooling in the multi-product inventory systems with products substitution. Inventory pooling is that if the demands from all sources are pooled by a centralized system, then not only will expected profits increase, but also inventory levels and costs will decrease (Eppen 1979). We also notice the recent work of Yang and Schrage (2009), in which conditions that cause the increase of total inventory level in inventory pooling (*inventory anomaly*) for the full substitution structure are discussed.

We limit this study to the two-product problem to (1) evaluate the gains in expected profit due to products substitution, and (2) assess the impact of inventory pooling for different sets of parameters on total inventory level due to products substitution.

To estimate the proportion of the gain in expected profit due to products substitution, denote that $P(Q^0)$ corresponds to the expected profit associated with the optimal order quantity $Q^0 = (Q_1^0, Q_2^0, \ldots, Q_N^0)$ when the products are not substitutable, while $P(Q^*)$ corresponds to the expected profit associated with the optimal order quantity $Q^* = (Q_1^*, Q_2^*, \ldots, Q_N^*)$ when the products are not substitutable. Then the percentage gain from products substitution is

$$\text{Percentage gain} = \frac{P(Q^*) - P(Q^0)}{P(Q^*)} \times 100\%. \tag{5}$$

And the percentage decrease in total inventory level is

$$\text{Percentage decrease} = \frac{\sum_{i=1}^{N} Q_i^0 - \sum_{i=1}^{N} Q_i^*}{\sum_{i=1}^{N} Q_i^0} \times 100\%. \tag{6}$$

We conduct three set of computational experiments with normally distributed demand. In the first set, we analyze the impact of the *coefficient of variation* of demand on the total inventory level. The standard deviation of demand for each product σ_i is chosen so that the coefficient of variation, μ_i / σ_i, takes on values of 0.1, 0.15, 0.2, 0.25, and 0.3. The rest of the parameters are fixed at $p_1 = 125$, $p_2 = 50$, $c_1 = 70$, $c_2 = 30$, $s_1 = 50$, $s_2 = 25$, $h_1 = 20$, $h_2 = 5$, $\pi_1 = 25$, $\pi_2 = 10$, $b_{12} = 80$, $b_{21} = 20$, $\mu_1 = 900$, and $\mu_2 = 600$. In the second set, we analyze the impact of the *critical ratio* on the total inventory level. The purchasing costs, c_i, are chosen so that the critical ratio, $(p_i + \pi_i - c_i)/(p_i + \pi_i - s_i + h_i)$, is varied from 0.2 to 0.9 in steps of 0.1. The rest of the parameters are fixed at $p_1 = 150$, $p_2 = 100$, $s_1 = 80$, $s_2 = 60$, $h_1 = 72.5$, $h_2 = 55$, $\pi_1 = 15$, $\pi_2 = 10$, $\mu_1 = 1{,}000$, $\mu_2 = 800$, $\sigma_1 = 120$, $\sigma_2 = 100$, $b_{12} = 100$, and $b_{21} = 50$. In the third set, we analyze the impact of the *substitution cost* on the total inventory level. The substitution costs, b_{ij}, are varied from $0.2p_i$ to $0.6p_i$ in steps of $0.1p_i$. The rest of the parameters were fixed at $p_1 = 200$, $p_2 = 150$, $c_1 = 120$, $c_2 = 100$, $s_1 = 90$, $s_2 = 60$, $h_1 = 25$, $h_2 = 45$, $\pi_1 = 15$, $\pi_2 = 15$, $\mu_1 = 1{,}300$, $\mu_2 = 1{,}100$, $\sigma_1 = 200$, and $\sigma_2 = 90$. All the sets of parameters in computational experiments must satisfy *Assumptions* 1–4.

The demand scenarios were generated using the default random generator in *Matlab* (version 7.1). The number of demand scenarios generated for each product with the underlying normal distribution was 15,000 (at about a confidence level of 98% with a sampling relative error 1.9%). The average computational time required to solve the two-product problem is about 8 s.

Based on the results of the three set of computational experiments, we make the following observations:

1. *Coefficient of variation of demand*: The gains in profit increase with increasing coefficient of variation from 0.50% for cv $= 0.1$ to 1.88% for cv $= 0.3$. The amount of decrease in total inventory also increase with increasing coefficient of variation from 3.17% for cv $= 0.1$ to 9.21% for cv $= 0.3$. This observation is consistent with the fact that the benefits of inventory pooling are significant especially when the demand uncertainty is high.

2. *Critical ratio*: For the condition that the critical ratio is larger than 0.5, the gains in profit increase with increasing critical ratio from 0.0065% for a ratio of 0.6–0.037% for a ratio of 0.9, and the amount of decrease in total inventory increase with increasing critical ratio from 0.32% for a ratio of 0.6–1.68% for a ratio of 0.9. In this condition, the newsboy can improve the expected profit and the expected service level through products substitution without increasing the total inventory level.

However, for the condition that the critical ratio is no larger than 0.5, inventory anomaly occurs. The gains in profit decrease with increasing critical ratio from 0.44% for a ratio of 0.2–0.003% for a ratio of 0.5. The amount of decrease in total inventory increase with increasing critical ratio from -2.64% for a ratio of 0.2 to -0.11% for a ratio of 0.5 (the negative value of percentage decrease assesses the impact of inventory anomaly on total inventory level). On comparing with the case of no substitution, the newsboy is willing to hold a higher inventory level to catch the opportunity of exploiting products substitution when the expected service level (i.e., critical ratio) is very low.

3. *Substitution cost*: The gains in profit decrease with increasing substitution cost from 0.73% for $b_{ij} = 0.2 p_i$ to 0.005% for $b_{ij} = 0.6 p_i$. The amount of decrease in total inventory also decline with increasing substitution cost from 0.73% for $b_{ij} = 0.2 p_i$ to 0.29% for $b_{ij} = 0.6 p_i$. The reason is as the increase of substitution cost, the impacts of products substitution on increasing expected profit as well as reducing total inventory level will weaken.

In our computational study, we assume that the coefficient of variation, cv, <0.3, then the right skewness of demand distributions is trivial. This assumption avoids most of the inventory anomalies in the full substitution structure discussed in Yang and Schrage (2009). Another factor that may lead to the full substitution inventory anomaly is the *critical ratio* value, which is set larger than 0.5 in most literature of the news-type problems. Our observations show that when the *critical ratio* is <0.5, inventory anomaly occurs, which is quite different with the conclusion of Yang and Schrage (2009). Thus we conclude that the full substitution inventory pooling occurs in a problem with low demand uncertainty, high expected service level (i.e., high critical ratio), and high product substitutability (i.e., low substitution cost). This conclusion is important when the problem considers products substitution in a QR system.

6 Conclusion

Products substitution can enhance the availability of products, reduce the level of excess inventory and inventory stockouts, and improve the customer service level. From a practical point of view, considering products substitution in supply chain management provides a new method to support the implementation of QR strategy. In this paper, we introduce a single-period multi-product newsboy inventory model with free and full substitution. Our work differs from earlier achievements in several respects. First, we develop an objective function that allows for free and full substitution among multiple products, rather than being limited to only downward substitution as in Hsu and Bassok (1999); Bassok et al. (1999). Second, by relating the objective function with that appeared in Van Slyke and Wets (1966) and the transportation problem in Topkis (1998), we manage to demonstrate that the objective function is both concave and submodular. These two important properties show innovativeness of our study and enrich inventory management theory, guarantying the valid application of Monte Carlo simulation method in our model. Computational experiments are conducted to analyze the effects of considering products substitution in inventory decision-making. Computational results show that the full substitution inventory pooling occurs in a problem with low demand uncertainty, high expected service level, and high product substitutability. Further research should focus on multi-period, multi-product inventory problem, with the integration of method for precisely forecasting to the demand in QR system.

Acknowledgements The work of this paper was supported by National Natural Science Foundation of China under grant Nos. 70771001 and No.70821061. The work was also supported by New Century Excellent Talents in University of China under grant No. NCET-07–0049 and by China Scholarship Council (CSC) under grant No. 2005A03010.

References

Bassok Y, Anupindi R, Akella R (1999) Single-period multiproduct inventory models with substitution. Oper Res 47:632–642

Bayindir ZP, Erkip N, Güllü R (2007) Assessing the benefits of remanufacturing option under one-way substitution and capacity constraint. Comput Oper Res 34:487–514

Bitran GR, Dasu S (1992) Ordering policies in an environment of stochastic yields and substitutable demands. Oper Res 40:999–1017

Chang CH, Tung YK, Yang JC (1994) Monte Carlo simulation for correlated variables with marginal distributions. J Hydraul Eng 120:313–331

Choi TM (2006) Quick Response in fashion supply chains with dual information updating. J Ind Manag Optim 2:255–268

Choi TM, Chow PS (2008) Mean-variance analysis of quick response program. Int Prod Econ 114:456–475

Dutta P, Chakraborty D (2009) Incorporating one-way substitution policy into the newsboy problem with imprecise customer demand. Eur J Oper Res.12:011. doi:10.1016/j.ejor.2008

Eppen G (1979) Effects of centralization on expected costs in a multi-location newsvendor problem. Manag Sci 25:498–501

Fisher M, Raman A (1996) Reducing the cost of demand uncertainty through accurate response to early sales. Oper Res 44:87–99

Fisher M, Hammond JH, Obermeyer WR, Raman A (1994) Making supply meet demand in an uncertain world. Harv Bus Rev 83–93

Fisher M, Rajaram K, Raman A (2001) Optimizing inventory replenishment of retail fashion products. Manuf Serv Opera Manag 3:230–241

Hsu A, Bassok Y (1999) Random yield and random demand in a production system with downward substitution. Oper Res 47:277–290

Hsu VN, Li CL, Xiao WQ (2005) Dynamic lot size problems with one-way product substitution. IIE Trans 37:201–215

Iyer AV, Bergen ME (1997) Quick response in manufacturer– retailer channels. Manag Sci 43: 559–570

Karaesmen I, van Ryzin G (2004) Overbooking with substitutable inventory classes. Oper Res 52:83–104

Khouja M, Mehrez A, Rabinowitz G (1996) A two-item newsboy problem with substitutability. Int J Prod Econ 44:267–275

Lowson R, King R, Hunter A (1999) Quick Response: Managing the Supply Chain to Meet Consumer Demand. Wiley, Chichester

McGillivray AR, Silver EA (1978) Some concepts for inventory control under substitutable demands. Infor 16:47–63

Nagarajan S, Rajagopalan S (2008) Inventory Models for Substitutable Products: Optimal Policies and Heuristics. Manag Sci 54:1453–1466

Nahmias S (2004) Production and Operations Analysis. 5th edn. McGraw-Hill/Irwin

Netessine S, Rudi N (2003) Centralized and Competitive Inventory Models with Demand Substitution. Oper Res 51:329–335

Parlar M (1988) Game theoretic analysis of the substitutable item inventory problem with random demands. Nav Res Logist 35:397–409

Parlar M, Goyal SK (1984) Optimal ordering decisions for two substitutable products with stochastic demands. Opsearch 21:1–15

Pasternack BA, Drezner Z (1991) Optimal inventory policies for substitutable commodities with stochastic demand. Nav Res Logist 38:221–240

Rajaram K, Tang CS (2001) The impact of product substitution on retail merchandising. Eur J Oper Res 135:582–601

Savicky P (2006) A strong nonrandom pattern in Matlab default random number generator. http://www.cs.cas.cz/~savicky/papers/rand2006.pdf. Accessed 4 Nov 2008

Serel DA (2009) Optimal ordering and pricing in a quick response system. Int J Prod Econ.04.020. doi:10.1016/j.ijpe.2009

Topkis DM (1998) Supermodularity and Complementarity. Princeton University Press, NJ

Van Slyke R, Wets R (1966) Programming under uncertainty and stochastic optimal control. SIAM J Contr Optim 4:179–193

Yang H, Schrage L (2009) Conditions that cause risk pooling to increase inventory. Eur J Oper Res 192:837–851

Part IV
Applications and Case Studies

Fast Fashion: Quantifying the Benefits

Warren H. Hausman and John S. Thorbeck

Abstract For short-life-cycle or fashion industries, the concept of supply flexibility, also known as postponement or "fast fashion," has high potential for significant increases in both profits and market capitalization for brands and retailers. First, we present a model to analyze the benefits of supply flexibility (in particular, reduced stockouts and markdowns) on operational financial metrics: revenue, cost, and profit. Assuming conservative improvements of 5% of revenue in both reduced markdowns and reduced stockouts from implementing supply flexibility, the resulting estimates of profit percent increases range from 22 to 28%. Next, the price/earnings ratio for 53 firms in fast-fashion or short-product-life-cycle busi-nesses is used to estimate the corresponding increase in market capitalization. The results are percentage increases in market cap ranging from 30 to 37%; these increase even further to 35–43% if one anticipates a 15% reduction in inventory levels due to improved supply flexibility.

Keywords Financial performance · Markdowns · Market capitalization · Price-earnings ratio · Stockouts

1 Introduction

Demand for short-life-cycle products or fashion goods is extremely hard to forecast. Thus it is typical that at the end of a selling season, retailers and brand owners both suffer from markdowns (price reductions to move merchandise unsold at full price) and stockouts (sellouts of popular styles or lost sales). Estimates of the costs of markdowns and stockouts range widely, some as high as 30% of retail sales. Bain & Company estimates that companies employing "fast fashion" tend to have significantly lower markdowns (both in items and in magnitude of markdown) than other classes of retailers. Table 1 below presents their analysis (Bain & Company 2005).

W.H. Hausman (✉)
Management Science & Engineering Department, Stanford University, Stanford, CA 94305, USA
e-mail: hausman@stanford.edu

T.C. Edwin Cheng and T.-M. Choi (eds.), *Innovative Quick Response Programs in Logistics and Supply Chain Management*, International Handbooks on Information Systems, DOI 10.1007/978-3-642-04313-0_16,
© Springer-Verlag Berlin Heidelberg 2010

Table 1 Typical markdowns across retailer categories

Fast FASHION (ZARA)	Traditional European apparel retailer	Traditional US apparel retailer	US department store
15% of items	30–40% of items	50–60% of items	60–70% of items
15% markdown	30% markdown	40% markdown	40% markdown

AMR Research has stated that in trend-driven consumer products, product life-cycles are short, new product development lead times are long, demand uncertainty is high, markups are high, and the risk and impact of stockouts and markdowns are very high. Yet most supply chain execution software and optimization software is still focused on the characteristics of routine and stable products (AMR Research 2006).

Robert Zane, Chairman of the US Association of Importers of Textile & Apparel and former sourcing executive for Liz Claiborne, Inc., states: "Willingly or unwillingly, we happily trade time for comfort. The most expensive elements of a slow time to market do not even appear on the cost sheets: the costs of markdowns." (wwd.com 2006).

Since operating income averages around 10% of sales for this industry, improvements in the management of markdowns and stockouts have enormous profit leverage for supply chains involving fashion goods or short-life-cycle products.

This paper briefly describes the various supply flexibility solutions that have been proposed for management of markdowns and stockouts. It then presents a financial model to evaluate the profitability impact of improvements in markdowns and stockouts, and presents numerical results for several well-known retailers and brands using publicly available data. It also proposes a metric for markdowns and stockouts and a corresponding metric for financial performance, and calculates the so-called *Zara Gap*, the difference in performance between Zara, a well-known fast fashion retailer, and average category performance. Lastly, using price/earnings (P/E) ratio data from 53 fashion-goods companies, estimates of the increase in market capitalization associated with any given profit increase are provided.

2 Literature Review

Several researchers have modeled how to determine desired merchandise order quantities for fashion products at the beginning of the selling season. Murray and Silver (1966) present a Bayesian model for forecast revision and use dynamic programming for its solution. Fisher and Raman (1996) formulate a two-period model incorporating limited production capacity and forecast updating and describe how its use at Sport Obermeyer resulted in a profit increase of 60%. Related research is described in Fisher et al. (1994, 1997, 2000). Fisher and Rajaram (2000) offer a way to test fashion merchandise popularity prior to the main selling season, and report profit improvements of more than 100% using this approach.

Smith and Achabal (1998) present a model that includes both markdown pricing and inventory management and report on its use in three retail chains. Mantrala and Rao (2001) present a pair of nested dynamic programming models that perform both the optimal markdown pricing strategy and the optimal order quantity calculation and apply their model to an example taken from a company.

Raman (1999) presents a review of research on fashion products, classified as production and inventory planning models, pricing and related models, and approaches for parameter estimation (particularly demand forecasts and forecast error estimation). Subrahmanyan (2000) also reviews this research stream. Related papers include Eppen and Iyer (1997); Crowston et al. (1973); Hausman and Peterson (1972); Hausman and Sides (1973); and Mantrala and Rao (2001).

Gernaat (2006) identifies the sum of markdown costs, stockout costs, and inventory carrying costs (what he identifies as "opportunity cost") as the "biggest cost element in the fashion supply chain."

Our focus here is to assume that tools such as the models above exist to enhance supply flexibility; our objective is to estimate the change in profit from applying such tools via their impact on markdowns and stockouts. We also want to show how to estimate the corresponding increase in a firm's market capitalization due to enhanced supply flexibility.

3 Supply Flexibility Solutions

There is a well-known concept called *Postponement* in supply chain management. The goal of postponement is to delay, to the latest time possible, the transformation of a product into its final form as a specific SKU (Stock Keeping Unit) with style, color, and size determined. The idea is that delaying the point of product differentiation will enable the manager to tailor the assortment of SKUs as closely as possible to rapidly shifting demands in the fashion marketplace.

Application of postponement and related concepts, often called Supply Flexibility in fashion industries, involves the following elements:

- Assessing demand risk and forecast learning by SKU
- Prepositioning materials (not yet committed to individual SKUs)
- Precommitting manufacturing capacity
- Precommitting transportation capacity
- Postponing SKU quantity decisions as late as possible

An excellent description of postponement and its benefits in supply chain management is presented in Lee and Feitzinger (1997).

AMR Research feels such strategies have high payoff for fashion goods:

"Sourcing strategies that minimize inventory and demand risk by optimizing tradeoffs between lead times and landed costs give high risk, fashion-forward retail strategies more leverage on revenue and margins than does markdown optimization." (AMR Research 2002)

Postponement can cause major reductions in lead times for SKUs, reducing them from months to days in some instances. Such major reductions in lead times can lead to substantial improvements in supply chain performance via reductions in both markdowns and stockouts.

4 The Model

Below we present a simplified profit and loss financial model that is nevertheless able to illustrate how improvements in the management of markdowns and stockouts translate into profit improvements. Our starting point is the representation of *revenues that would have occurred if no markdowns were needed* (i.e., all sales at full price). While this quantity is of course never attained and hence never measured directly, it is a useful model construct.

Let:

$R^* =$ Hypothetical revenues of a typical brand company if no markdowns occurred (i.e., all sales at full price)

$R_{orig} =$ Original actual revenues, allowing for markdowns and stockouts experienced

$COGS =$ Cost of goods sold

$SG\&A =$ Selling, general, and administrative expenses

$\pi_{orig} =$ Original operating profit

$\alpha =$ % of units sold at a markdown price

$\beta =$ average % markdown

Assume that COGS and SG&A are proportional to actual reported revenue R_{orig} as follows:

$$COGS = c\, R_{orig}, \qquad (1)$$
$$SG\&A = s\, R_{orig}. \qquad (2)$$

Then actual revenue for the brand company experiencing markdowns (α, β) is

$$R_{orig} = (1 - \alpha)\, R^* + \alpha\, (1 - \beta)\, R^* = R^*\, (1 - \alpha\beta). \qquad (3)$$

Also, profit for the brand company with cost structure (c, s) and experiencing markdowns (α, β) is, using (1)–(3),

$$\pi_{orig} = R_{orig} - COGS - SG\&A = R_{orig}\, [1 - c - s]. \qquad (4)$$

Solving (3) for R^*, the relationship between R^* and R_{orig} is

$$R^* = R_{orig}/\, (1 - \alpha\beta). \qquad (5)$$

4.1 Markdowns Avoided by Supply Flexibility

Suppose the use of supply flexibility concepts can avoid markdowns equal to $X\%$ of hypothetical revenue. Then α in (3) is replaced by $(\alpha - X)$ by definition. Also, it is assumed that both COGS and SG&A values remain unchanged from their original values. The argument for these two assumptions is that acquiring more-popular SKUs instead of less-popular SKUs to decrease markdowns should not affect either COGS or SG&A (admittedly there will be a one-time implementation cost for implementing supply flexibility concepts). These are critical assumptions that give rise to a significant percentage increase in profitability from a relatively modest reduction in markdowns. The new values of revenue and profit, denoted by R_M and π_M, respectively, will be, from (3)–(4),

$$R_M = R^* [1 - (\alpha - X) \times \beta] = R_{\text{orig}} + X\beta R^*, \tag{6}$$
$$\pi_M = R_{\text{orig}} [1 - c - s] + X\beta R^*. \tag{7}$$

Using (3)–(7), the ratio of new to original revenue and profit can be calculated:

$$R_M / R_{\text{orig}} = 1 + [X\beta/(1 - \alpha\beta)], \tag{8}$$
$$\pi_M / \pi_{\text{orig}} = 1 + [X\beta/ (1 - \alpha\beta)] / [1 - c - s]. \tag{9}$$

Equations (8) and (9) can be used to estimate gross percentage increases in revenue and profit due to the specified increase in markdowns avoided. To provide concrete examples of possible improvements in markdowns and stockouts due to implementing supply flexibility, the results of five pilot opportunity assessments are presented in Table 2 below. Although there is considerable variation around the average values, note that the average markdown savings (as a percentage of current revenue) is 5.8% and the average stockouts avoided (as percentage of current revenue) is 7.3%. A conservative 5% value for each of these quantities will be assumed (as a percentage of hypothetical revenue or actual revenue, respectively) in our subsequent numerical illustrations.

Table 2 Estimated benefits of supply flexibility concepts: five pilot studies

Type of company	Selling season (weeks)	Estimated markdown savings (% of current revenue)	Estimated stockouts avoided (% of current revenue)
Apparel catalog	26	15.0%	10.8%
Apparel wholesaler	52	2.5%	2.0%
Apparel retailer	13–26	0.0%	7.2%
Apparel wholesaler	26	9.7%	10.0%
Footwear wholesaler	36–104	1.8%	6.5%
AVERAGES:		5.8%	7.3%

Table 3 below contains sample values for the model parameters c, s, α, and β based on public data, industry sources, and informed judgments. For the fashion goods industry, COGS averages close to 60% of revenue and SG&A averages about 28% of revenue (see Table 4 for supportive data). Based on Table 1, α (percentage of units sold at markdown) is conservatively set to 25%; β (average percentage markdown, conditional on a markdown) is also conservatively set to 25%.

Using (8) and (9), Fig. 1 below illustrates the behavior of the increase in revenue and profit as markdowns avoided (X) increases from 0% of hypothetical revenue to 10% of hypothetical revenue. For example, taking a conservative value of $X = 5\%$ of hypothetical revenue, revenue increases by only 1.13% over the base case, but profit increases by 11.1%.

This result occurs since all the increase in revenue becomes profit in this case (recall it was assumed that COGS and SG&A are unchanged while acquiring a more-popular mix of SKUs). Thus what appears to be a minor increase in revenue can have a significant effect on profitability.

Who actually bears the cost of markdowns, and should we care? Increasingly, retailers are requiring manufacturers to compensate them with "markdown money" for opportunity costs associated with sales at markdown prices instead of list prices; see Rozhon (2005). Retailers might thus appear less interested in reducing markdowns if they are fully compensated for these costs. However, manufacturers who pay markdown money would be highly interested in reducing markdowns! The payment of markdown money simply transfers the cost of markdowns from one party

Table 3 Model parameter values

Parameters	Values (%)
c	60
s	28
α	25
β	25

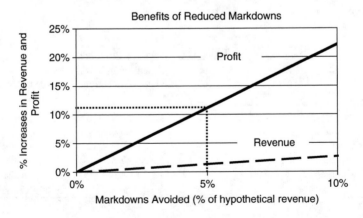

Fig. 1 Revenue and profit benefits from reduced markdowns

in the supply chain to the other and does nothing to reduce it; and in cases of private label product, even that transfer does not happen. Most importantly, many observers have noted that competition is now supply chain vs. supply chain, not company vs. company. Under this interpretation, it does not matter who bears the cost of markdowns, the retailer or the manufacturer – reductions in the cost of markdowns will be valuable to all participants.

Note that the considerable costs of implementing supply flexibility have not been included, including the requirement for change management due to changes in business processes. Thus the profit increases presented here are gross increases before costs of implementation.

4.2 Stockouts avoided by Supply Flexibility

Suppose the use of supply flexibility concepts avoids stockouts equal to $Y\%$ of reported revenue by providing an assortment of goods that more closely matches subsequent customer preferences. Then new revenue, denoted by R_S, increases $Y\%$ by definition:

$$R_S = (1 + Y) R_{\text{orig}}. \tag{10}$$

To gauge the impact of these no-longer-lost sales on profit, note that these sales would be at full price, not the usual blend of some full-price sales and some markdown sales that constitute a typical brand company's profit and loss statement. Furthermore, while COGS would certainly increase proportionally to cover the variable production and transportation costs associated with these increased sales, it may be reasonable to assume that SG&A expenses would not increase. In this case new profit, denoted by π_S, is calculated as follows:

$$
\begin{aligned}
\pi_S &= R_S - \text{new COGS} - \text{initial SG\&A} \\
&= (1 + Y) R_{\text{orig}} - (1 + Y) c R_{\text{orig}} - s R_{\text{orig}} = R_{\text{orig}} \left[(1 + Y)(1 - c) - s \right].
\end{aligned}
\tag{11}
$$

Also, the ratio of new to original revenue and profit is

$$R_S / R_{\text{orig}} = (1 + Y), \tag{12}$$

$$
\begin{aligned}
\pi_S / \pi_{\text{orig}} &= \left[(1 + Y)(1 - c) - s \right] / \left[1 - c - s \right] \\
&= 1 + \left[Y (1 - c) / (1 - c - s) \right].
\end{aligned}
\tag{13}
$$

Figure 2 illustrates the behavior of the increase in revenue and profit as stockouts avoided (Y) increases from 0% of revenue to 10% of revenue. For example, taking a conservative value of $Y = 5\%$ of revenue, revenue increases by 5% over the base case, but profit increases by 16.67%. This profit increase is due to both more full-price sales and also avoiding additional SG&A expenses in association with the sales that are no longer lost.

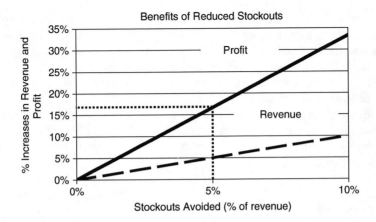

Fig. 2 Revenue and profit benefits from reduced stockouts

4.3 Combining Both Effects: Improved Markdowns and Stockouts

Now combine these two effects – suppose application of supply flexibility concepts can do two things at once: avoid markdowns equal to $X\%$ of hypothetical revenue and avoid stockouts equal to $Y\%$ of actual revenue. Then the new values for revenue $R_{M,S}$ and profit $\pi_{M,S}$ are

$$\begin{aligned} R_{M,S} &= (1+Y)\,R_{\text{orig}} + X\beta R^* \\ &= R^*\left[1 - (\alpha - X)\,\beta + Y\,(1 - \alpha\beta)\right], \end{aligned} \tag{14}$$

$$\begin{aligned} \pi_{M,S} &= R_{\text{orig}}\,(1 - c - s) + X\beta R^* + Y\,(1 - c)\,R_{\text{orig}} \\ &= R^*\left\{(1 - \alpha\beta)\left[(1 + Y)\,(1 - c) - s\right] + X\beta\right\}. \end{aligned} \tag{15}$$

As before, the ratios between new and baseline revenue and profit can be calculated as

$$R_{M,S}/R_{\text{orig}} = 1 + Y + [X\beta/(1 - \alpha\beta)], \tag{16}$$

$$\pi_{M,S}/\pi_{\text{orig}} = 1 + \{Y\,(1 - c) + [X\beta/(1 - \alpha\beta)]\}/(1 - c - s). \tag{17}$$

Figure 3 below illustrates the behavior of increased revenue as both markdowns and stockouts range over the same parameter values as before. Figure 4 below shows the corresponding behavior of increased profit. For midrange values of $X = 5\%$ and $Y = 5\%$, revenue increases by 6.3% due to both effects, and *profit increases by 27.8%*. (Note that (16) and (17) are linear in X and Y, so that changes in revenue and profit are proportional to changes in X and Y.)

Table 4 below presents an analysis of several large, well-known apparel companies involved with fashion goods. The input data (COGS, SG&A) is taken from each

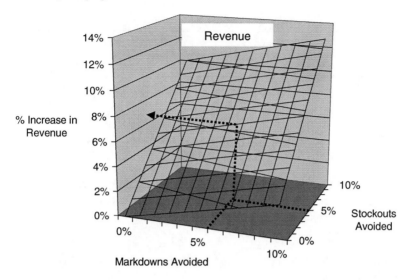

Fig. 3 Revenue benefits from reduced markdowns and stockouts

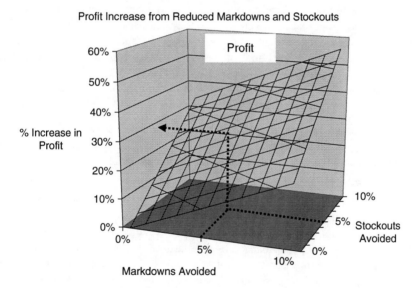

Fig. 4 Profit benefits from reduced markdowns and stockouts

company's most recent annual report. The output data are calculated by the model described above (16–17).

Note that while the revenue percent increase is 6.3% for all companies based on the stated assumptions, the profit percent increase ranges from 22.4 to 29.1% and averages 26.2% for these four companies. Thus supply flexibility has the potential to create truly dramatic percentage increases in profitability.

Table 4 Model applied to selected public companies

	COGS (% of revenue)	SG&A (% of revenue)	% Revenue increase	% Profit increase
Columbia Sportswear	56.4	27.9	6.3	22.4
Gap Inc.	63.4	25.7	6.3	29.1
Mattel	54.2	33.0	6.3	28.2
Nike	56.0	29.9	6.3	25.1
Averages:	57.5	29.1	6.3	26.2

In the next section these profit gains will be translated into increases in a firm's market capitalization, but first our metrics for markdown and stockout performance and financial performance are presented.

5 Metric for Markdowns and Stockouts and Financial Performance

Publicly available data do not allow direct observation of markdowns and stockouts; firms rarely break out markdown costs separately, and stockouts (lost sales) are by definition not incorporated in accounting results. Thus one needs to proceed indirectly and trace out the implications of improved markdown/stockout performance on operating income and inventory, two metrics that are available from public data.

Suppose markdowns and stockouts are both improved (i.e., are reduced) due to application of supply flexibility principles. Then logic would imply the following:

- Increased revenue (more full-price sales and also fewer lost sales)
- Increased operating income
- Decreased ending inventory (better inventory management)

Since markdown and stockout improvements increase operating income and decrease inventory, the ratio *Operating Income/Inventory* is proposed as a useful metric for markdown/stockout performance. Higher values of this metric are associated with improved markdown/stockout performance.

Regarding financial performance, the standard Wall Street metric for financial performance is the market capitalization of a company, abbreviated as market cap. However, to perform cross-company comparisons, this metric needs to be scaled. One way to scale it is to divide by a company's annual revenue:

$$\text{Scaled Market Cap} = \text{Market Cap}/\text{Annual Revenue}.$$

Again, higher values of this metric are associated with improved financial performance.

Table 5 Companies analyzed

Specialty Retail:	Department stores	Wholesale brands	Athletic brands
A&F	Dillard's	Brown Shoe	Adidas
American Eagle	Federated	Coach	K Swiss
Ann Taylor	J C Penney	Columbia Sportswear	Nike
Best Buy	Kohl's	Jones Apparel	Puma AG
Chico's	Marks & Spencer	Kellwood	Reebok
Circuit City	May Co.	Kenneth Cole	Saucony
Finish Line	Neiman Marcus	Liz Claiborne	Vans
Foot Locker	Nordstrom	Mattel	
Gap	Saks	Phillips-Van Heusen	
Genesco	Sears	Polo Ralph Lauren	
H&M		Russell Corp	
Inditex (Zara)		Stride-Rite	
Limited		Timberland	
Men's Wearhouse		Tommy Hilfiger	
Office Depot		VF Corp	
Payless ShoeSource		Wolverine	
Staples			
Talbots			
Toys "R" Us			

6 Data Analysis

Table 5 lists 53 companies dealing with fashion goods. Data was initially sought on 60 firms; only 53 had complete data available. Data was collected to compute both the markdown/stockout metric and the scaled market cap metric for each company. The scaled market cap data was calculated as of 30 June 2003 and the annual revenue, operating income, and inventory data were obtained from the fiscal year prior to and closest to 30 June 2003.

6.1 The "Zara Gap"

Zara (Inditex) is well known for operating in a "fast fashion" mode. It is instructive to compare Zara's performance vs. the averages for the four company categories in Table 5 (specialty retail, department stores, wholesale brands, and athletic brands). Table 6 presents these average metrics using our metrics for markdown/stockout performance and financial performance, and Fig. 5 plots the corresponding data.

Zara clearly outperforms all four category averages on both metrics. Some writers have observed that, for a significant percentage of its products, Zara has a supply chain that is mostly vertically integrated, while virtually all other apparel companies in our sample are not vertically integrated. However, we would argue that while

Table 6 Zara's performance on new metrics vs. category averages

Averages for	Metric for markdown & stockout performance: operating income/inventory	Metric for financial performance: market cap/revenue
Specialty retail	0.83	1.17
Department stores	0.33	0.59
Wholesale brands	0.88	1.17
Athletic brands	0.49	1.02
Zara (Inditex)	1.73	3.44

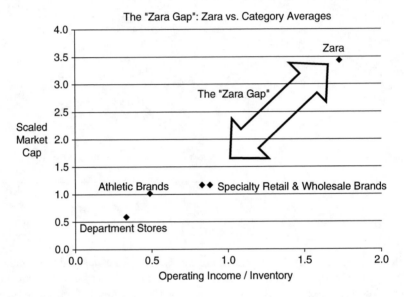

Fig. 5 Zara (Inditex) vs. four category averages

vertical integration may make it easier to implement Supply Flexibility, it is by no means essential.

As a quick diagnostic, any public company can plot their data values on Fig. 5 and compare their performance both with category averages and also with Zara (Inditex) and see whether they too are subject to the "Zara Gap."

6.2 Statistical Analysis

Figure 6 contains a scatter plot of our financial metric vs. our markdown/stockout metric for all 53 companies in Table 5. One can observe a reasonably strong and positive association simply from direct observation. This is as expected, since there is a close relationship between our two metrics and the familiar P/E ratio in financial analysis. Note that our ratio (scaled market cap/[income/inventory]) equals the

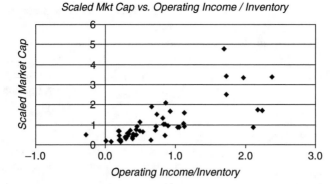

Fig. 6 Scaled market cap vs. (operating income/inventory) for 53 retail companies

P/E ratio (market cap/income) multiplied by (inventory/annual revenue). If the latter ratio has variability that is random and independent, then it simply introduces some "noise" into the P/E ratio.

A regression equation was estimated on this data (a zero intercept was used since the logic underlying the relationship is the P/E ratio, which has a zero intercept by definition) with the following results:

$$\text{Scaled Market Cap} = 1.293 \times (\text{Operating Income/Inventory}). \quad (18)$$

Just as a P/E ratio can be used to convert changes in earnings to corresponding changes in stock prices, the value of the slope coefficient ($+1.293$) in this regression can be used to estimate the change in *scaled market cap* associated with any particular change in the ratio (*operating income/inventory*).

Inventory levels are conservatively assumed to remain unchanged, although it is highly likely that supply flexibility would produce some reductions in inventory in addition to improved markdown and stockout performance; see the next section for an alternative assumption. Since

$$\text{scaled market cap} = (\text{market cap}) / (\text{annual revenue}), \quad (19)$$

any percentage revenue increase will also enter into the calculation for market cap:

$$\text{market cap} = \text{scaled market cap} \times \text{annual revenue}. \quad (20)$$

Using (20) and (18), one can show that the ratio of new market cap to original market cap is the following:

$$\frac{(\text{Operating Income/Inventory})_{\text{New}} \times R_{\text{New}}}{(\text{Operating Income/Inventory})_{\text{Orig}} \times R_{\text{orig}}}. \quad (21)$$

Equation (21) was used to calculate the estimated percentage increase in market cap for the four companies examined earlier in Table 6, using projected revenue and profit increases from Table 4 and actual market cap data as of December 2006; Table 7 contains the results. The percentage increases in market cap range from 30.1% to 37.2% and the corresponding dollar value increases range from $0.6 Billion to $8.1 Billion, averaging $4.3 Billion for this particular set of companies.

Table 7 Estimated increases in market cap for selected public companies

	% profit increase	Market cap ($ billions)	% Market cap increase	Absolute market cap increase ($ billions)
Columbia Sportswear	22.4	2.1	30.1	0.6
Gap Inc.	29.1	15.5	37.2	5.8
Mattel	28.2	8.5	36.3	3.1
Nike	25.1	24.7	32.9	8.1
Averages:	26.2	12.7	34.1	4.3

6.3 Effect of 15% Inventory Reduction

If one also anticipates a reduction in inventory of, say, 15% due to supply flexibility, then the ratio operating income/inventory would be 17.6% higher ($1/0.85 = 1.176$) and hence it would be associated with an increase in market cap of 35–43% instead of the 30–37% values in Table 7.

7 Conclusions

Our simplified financial model has shown that improved markdown and stockout performance obtained from supply flexibility solutions can provide a significant percentage increase in operating income for companies dealing with fashion goods. Further, using the familiar P/E ratio, a metric associated with improved markdown/stockout performance (namely, the ratio operating income/inventory) is linked to the financial metric "scaled market capitalization." This linkage is used to demonstrate dramatic percentage increases in market cap associated with improved management of markdowns, stockouts, and inventory. Thus companies that expend the effort to apply supply flexibility to their fashion-goods supply chains can expect to see not only significant improvements in operating income, but also significant increases in their market capitalization.

Acknowledgements Portions of this paper were presented at the INFORMS National Meeting in Denver, CO, in October 2004. We are indebted to the Infosys Offshore Research Center for their valuable aid in data analysis. We also thank Steve Smith and Narendra Agrawal of Santa Clara

University, Thomas Weber of Stanford University, and several anonymous reviewers for valuable suggestions on an earlier draft.

References

AMR Research (2002) "Price Optimization is Hot, But It's Just the Beginning", Greg Girard, AMR Report, August 2002

AMR Research (2006) "Episode II: The Future of Supply Chain Planning", Bruce Richardson, AMR Research Alert, March 2, 2006

Bain & Company (2005) Fast fashion retailers gaining speed in a slow market

Crowston WB, Hausman WH, Kampe WRII (1973). Multistage production for stochastic seasonal demand. Manag Sci 19(8):924–935

Eppen GD, Iyer AV (1997) Improved fashion buying with bayesian updates. Oper Res 45(6): 805–819

Fisher ML (1997) What is the right supply chain for your product? Harv Bus Rev 75(3):105–116

Fisher M, Rajaram K (2000) Accurate retail testing of fashion merchandise: methodology and application. Market Sci 19(3):266–278

Fisher ML, Raman A (1996) Reducing the cost of demand uncertainty through accurate response to early sales. Oper Res 44(1):87–99

Fisher M, Hammond JH, Obermeyer WR, Raman A (1994) Making supply meet demand in an uncertain world. Harv Bus Rev 72(5):83–93

Fisher M, Hammond JH, Obermeyer WR, Raman A (1997) Configuring a supply chain to reduce the cost of demand uncertainty. Prod Oper Manag 6(3):211–225

Fisher ML, Raman A, McClelland A (2000) Rocket science retailing is almost here–are you ready? Harv Bus Rev 78(7)

Gernaat MJ (2006) The impact of lead time on the fashion apparel supply chain. MSc Thesis, School of Management, Cranfield University

Hausman WH, Peterson R (1972) Multiproduct production scheduling for style goods with limited capacity, forecast revisions and terminal delivery. Manag Sci 18(7):370–383

Hausman WH, Sides R St.G (1973) Mail order demands for style goods; theory and data analysis. Manag Sci 20(2):191–202

Lee HL, Feitzinger E (1997) Mass customization at hp: the power of postponement. Harv Bus Rev 75(1):116–121

Mantrala MK, Rao S (2001) A decision-support system that helps retailers decide order quantities and markdowns for fashion goods. Interfaces 31(3):S146–S165

Murray GR Jr., Silver EA (1966) A bayesian analysis of the style goods inventory problem. Manag Sci 12(11):785–797

Raman A (1999) Managing inventory for fashion products. In: Tayur S, Ganeshan R, Magazine M (eds) Quantitative models for supply chain management. Kluwer Academic Publishers, Boston, MA

Rozhon T (2005) First the markdown, then the showdown. the new york times

Smith SA, Achabal DD (1998) Clearance pricing and inventory policies for retail chains. Manag Sci 44(3):285–300

wwd.com, Accessed Oct 25 2006

Subrahmanyan S (2000) Using quantitative models for setting retail prices. J Prod Brand Manag 9(5):304–315

Divide and Conquer: From MTO to ATO/MTO
A Case Study of an Electronics Manufacturer

Ying Wei, Frank Y. Chen, Mark Lee, Houmin Yan, Kenneth Kong, and Chi Ho Ng

Abstract In this chapter, we present a study of an electronics manufacturer that changed its manufacturing strategy from make-to-order to a combination of assemble-to-order and make-to-order. Faced with increasing pressures from its customers, this contract manufacturer had to implement a quick response program to reduce its manufacturing lead time and improve its on-time delivery rate. Based on an analysis of the product characteristics and demand pattern, we find that delayed differentiation in production becomes feasible. We divide the products into two categories and propose different manufacturing strategies, as well as different operating implementation programs. We highlight a missing link between the current Oracle ERP system and the proposed manufacturing programs, and further develop an efficient IT tool to support intelligent materials planning. The instant impact of the quick response program has been significant, with the on-time delivery rate being increased from under 50% to almost 90% within 6 months.

Keywords Assemble-to-order · Bullwhip effects · Delayed production · ERP · Inventory planning · Lead time · Make-to-order · Manufacturing strategy · MRP · On-time delivery · Quick response

1 Introduction

1.1 Background

Established in 1991, SUGA is an Asia-based electronics manufacturing services (EMS) provider, mainly engaged in the research and development, manufacturing, and sale of electronics products. Examples of products include consumer electronics products, physical training devices, networking devices, digital products, etc. Its

Y. Wei (✉)
Université catholique de Louvain, CORE, B-1348 Louvain-la-Neuve, Belgium
e-mail: ying.wei@uclouvain.be

T.C. Edwin Cheng and T.-M. Choi (eds.), *Innovative Quick Response Programs in Logistics and Supply Chain Management*, International Handbooks on Information Systems, DOI 10.1007/978-3-642-04313-0_17,
© Springer-Verlag Berlin Heidelberg 2010

core EMS business is mainly operated by four subsidiaries: Suga Electronics, Suga Networks, Pets & Supplies, and Precise. This case study focuses on a subsidiary of SUGA that manufactures electronic healthcare products for its US client, BTG.

The subsidiary is dedicated exclusively to BTG, while for BTG, this subsidiary is almost the sole supplier of its several product categories. Based in Chicago, Illinois, BTG is a privately held company and one of the industry leaders in physical training, health monitoring, and lifestyle products solutions. Physical training related business is highly specialized and enjoys a relatively high profit margin. Demand for these products is steadily increasing, especially in developed countries in North America, Europe, and Asia. Founded in 1991, BTG has grown rapidly in recent years, and has doubled its revenues of 2006 as compared to that of 2004. Aggressive and ambitious, BTG aims to become the most trusted brand in the healthcare industry. Accordingly, it has seen its market penetration rate increase from 2 to 20%, and has established its market leadership in key categories such as fitness monitoring, detector devices, and physical training. BTG has also introduced over 75 new products in the last 5 years. However, it still faces competition from both new entrants and existing competitors.

1.2 Challenges for SUGA

Catching up with the rapid growth of the healthcare industry and of BTG, SUGA has grown quickly in recent years. However, it also has to face rising expectations and pressures from its customer BTG.

To satisfy the giant retailers and maintain a high market penetration rate, BTG must hold a large amount of inventory in finished goods. In addition, long and unstable order fulfillment lead times have meant that the company must also maintain a high level of safety inventory, thus incurring significant costs. In response to this, BTG decided to push its inventory up the supply chain to mitigate its own cost and risk. This was achieved by delegating the purchase of key materials to the contract manufacturer.

To better control the whole supply chain and monitor supplier performance, BTG initiated the balanced score card system in 2006, and began to quarterly evaluate the performance of all its suppliers and contract manufacturers in terms of four categories: quality, delivery, cost, and new product development. According to BTG's latest supplier performance evaluation, SUGA performed poorly in the delivery category and was marked "at risk." SUGA was expected to take 70 days to fulfill an order, excluding 40 days lead time for ocean shipment. However, the actual order fulfillment cycles ranged from 90–180 days. This delay in manufacturing meant that the ocean shipment had to be changed from time to time to air shipment, in order to meet retailers' requirements. It resulted in significant increase in transportation cost in the past few years.

At the time of evaluation, SUGA produced all its products using make-to-order (MTO) manufacturing strategy. Although the company had introduced Oracle ERP before BTG's evaluation, its materials planning was still weak. In the worst case, purchase orders for certain raw materials were issued only after product orders had been received. Given that the longest component lead time was 16 weeks, manufacturing could, and indeed did, experience constant materials shortage.

In addition, SUGA had to handle internal resource competition of BTG. BTG was divided into strategic business units (SBUs) based on different product categories. Each SBU had an independent accounting system, its own market specialists, and dedicated engineers. This structure was to increase internal competition at BTG. Although two or more SBUs might share a sourcing planner, for SUGA, a good balance must be maintained among these SBUs in terms of resource allocation and priority setting.

SUGA was also facing increasing competition. BTG sought additional suppliers in China and worldwide to reduce sourcing risks. It also explored the possibility of starting its own materials distribution center in China to enhance sourcing security and key materials availability, and to reduce sourcing costs.

With increasing pressure from BTG, SUGA understood that it had to take action to respond to customer demands more quickly, speed up its supply chain, reduce the duration of the order fulfillment cycle, and improve its on-time delivery rate. The challenge was how to introduce and implement a quick response program.

The remainder of the paper is organized as follows. Section 2 describes the global supply chain for healthcare products. Section 3 analyzes the supply chain in terms of product characteristics and demand pattern. Section 4 proposes a solution strategy for SUGA and operational manufacturing programs. Section 5 discusses the implementation and its instant impact, and Section 6 concludes the whole paper.

2   The Electronics Supply Chain for Healthcare Products

For convenience, when no confusion could arise from the context, we use the present tense to describe the case, where "current" means at the time of case study. Without further explanation, the source for all the data and illustrations is from SUGA International Holding Ltd.

2.1   The Global Supply Chain

This is a typical global supply chain in which BTG designs and sells products to the US consumers, and SUGA is the contract manufacturer that sources materials and produces the required products. Figure 1 depicts the supply chain for a major training product.

BTG sells its products primarily through major retail chains, such as Macy's, J.C. Penney, Target, and Sam's. Sales to its top eight customers dominate BTG's US market share, constituting about 70% of the company's total sales volume. To maintain

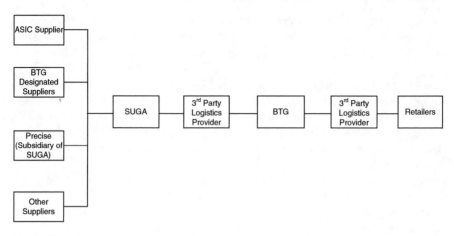

Fig. 1 Illustration of the global supply chain

a high market penetration rate, BTG must meet the high on-time fulfillment rates set by these leading retailers, which are normally 97–99%. Another sales channel is by catalogs, for example, Professional Devices. Products must be ready 5–6 weeks before the catalog is printed. This strict time constraint also causes BTG stocking a high level of finished goods at a significant cost. In 2005, the year-ending inventory cost was estimated to be more than US$15 million, and the inventory turnover rate was about four per year.

BTG stores all the finished goods in its distribution center at Nashville, from which they are delivered to retailers by third-party logistics service providers. BTG outsources its manufacturing processes in China and Mexico to reduce costs. SUGA is a major contract manufacturer responsible for more than 70% of its total products. BTG also has designated suppliers for certain raw materials or components. A typical example is application-specific integrated circuit (ASIC) cards and components supplied by Precise Plastic Injection Ltd ("Precise"), which is another subsidiary of SUGA. For other raw materials or components, SUGA selects and manages the suppliers itself.

2.2 BTG Ordering Process

Each month the planners in each of BTG's SBUs issue a purchase order (PO) to SUGA. The order quantity is decided based on the inventory level of finished goods at the distribution center and the sales data retrieved from *Atlas*, a software tool used by BTG's sales division. The planners also issue a planned order (PLO) to SUGA, which is based on the forecast sales determined by BTG sales managers. The forecast sales are based on historical sales data and expectations of future trends. In principle, BTG shares its forecasts with SUGA monthly, and the planners update their PLOs in 6-month rolling windows. However, in practice, the sharing of PLO information is neither consistent nor complete (e.g., that for some products was missing). The information updating is irregular, and there exists considerable variation between quantities of PLOs and corresponding POs. As a result, SUGA cannot make use of the PLO information efficiently and effectively. In addition, market demand spikes caused by promotion events, new channel (client) accounts (and existing clients' expansion), and emergency orders frequently catch SUGA by surprise.

A typical example of the timeline of the product ordering process is depicted in Fig. 2. Given that goods should be shipped to BTG's customers at the beginning of September 2005, BTG planners then need to issue the PO to SUGA 110 days in advance in May (70 days manufacturing lead time plus 40 days shipping time). The latest indicator of the order information should be revealed in the PLO issued at April, and the first indicator can be traced back to the PLO of December 2004 (6-month rolling window). (The PLOs are decided based on the sales forecast information, which was estimated even earlier.)

2.3 SUGA's Current Manufacturing Practice

Accordingly, a PO from BTG is the corresponding sales order (SO) to SUGA. Once SUGA sales department confirms the SO with BTG, it inputs SO into the Oracle system. The purchasing group in the Production and Manufacturing Control (PMC) department then generates a materials purchase plan by running the Oracle ERP System, and the production control group works out the production schedules manually. As soon as the production schedule plan has been issued, the Production department then sets up the production line and starts production.

The production process at SUGA can be divided into five stages, as shown in Fig. 3: surfaced mounting technology (SMT), bonding, printed circuit board assembly (PCBA), casing, and packaging. The work-in-progress (WIP) after the PCBA stage is transferred to the warehouse and sent to the next production stage (casing) for assembly. A typical production lead time is about 14 days if the materials are ready.

After production, the finished goods are transferred to and stored in the warehouse. Once they have passed the quality requirements, they are then shipped and delivered to BTG. In general, the agreed SUGA order fulfillment cycle length is about 70 days, counting from receiving the SO to delivering the finished goods. Ocean shipment takes around 40 days.

Noticing that a huge gap exists between the 70-day order fulfillment time and the 14-day production lead time, questions thus arise: what swallows the time? and how is the 14 days production time stretched fivefold and longer?

We first check the manufacturing strategy. SUGA employs a MTO strategy and starts manufacturing only once a confirmed SO has been received. By MTO, SUGA eliminates its finished goods inventory and stock obsolescence risk. However, MTO

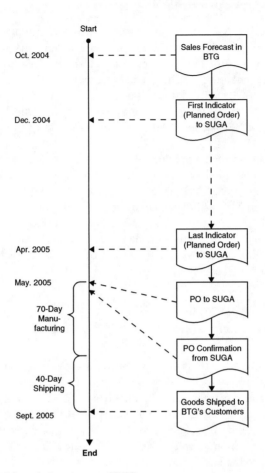

Fig. 2 Illustration of the ordering process of BTG

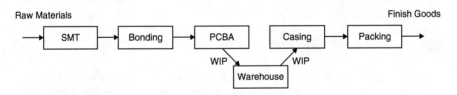

Fig. 3 Illustration of production process of SUGA

is vulnerable to market demand fluctuations and requires proactive demand management. As the contract manufacturer, SUGA uses the PLO of BTG as its demand forecast, but purchases materials based on the confirmed SO instead of the PLO. It is the materials purchasing delay that magnifies the 14-day production lead time to a great extent, and in the worst case the order fulfillment time length is prolonged to 131 days. SUGA uses the PLO information for advance purchasing only for certain designated suppliers, for example, ASIC components.

MTO is appropriate for short lead time manufacturing process and requires a high materials ready rate. However, at SUGA, there is a long lead time for materials purchasing, and production is often delayed due to a shortage of materials.

Two reasons explain why SUGA purchases materials based on the SO instead of the PLO. First, there is no formal agreement on purchasing long lead time materials according to the PLO. Second, the quantities of PLO are inconsistent with the corresponding SO; in addition, the PLO information is not updated regularly. Thus, SUGA is reluctant to purchase materials in advance or only at partial volume due to the cost and risk considerations.

Production is delayed mainly by material's shortage. Putting aside engineering problems such as the orders that require frequent engineering changes, the primary reason for materials shortage is poor inventory planning by SUGA, a problem which is prevalent among contract manufacturers in the Pearl River Delta of China because most of them are in transition from original equipment manufacturing (OEM) and processing with supplied materials to original design manufacturing (ODM). Another reason is the ineffective use of PLO. Finally, there is no systematic approach or supporting tools for the purchasing and handling of long lead-time materials, and the PMC department has to make decisions on advance purchasing based on manual calculations.

3 Analysis of the Supply Chain

3.1 Product Characteristics

We notice that although SUGA produces hundreds of SKUs, 95% share 10–15 common components. For example, the PP05 component is shared by Product A, Product B, and Product C. Products B and C belong to the Health Monitoring SBU, and Product A to Physical Training SBU. Figure 4 gives an illustration of the shared component, and Fig. 5 depicts the individual and aggregate demand information. If the demand for the shared components is high or medium and stable, they can then be produced in advance, and planned stock of such a component will be consumed by future demand. The order fulfillment lead time can thus considerably be reduced by saving the production time of the shared components. Such sharing of components results in a pooling effect, whereby the inventory is invested at the component level, rather than at the unique finished product level, thus creating a "delayed differentiation" in production.

It should be noted that ASIC, which is an important component and used in many BTG products and core units, however, requires a long lead time, that is, 16 weeks.

3.2 Consumer Demand Pattern

Investigating into market data, we are able to divide the products into "regular" and "irregular" demand types. We find that demand from existing giant retailers, such

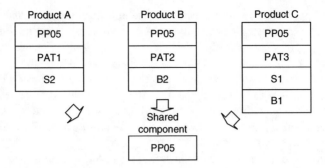

Fig. 4 Illustration of bill of materials for Products A, B, and C

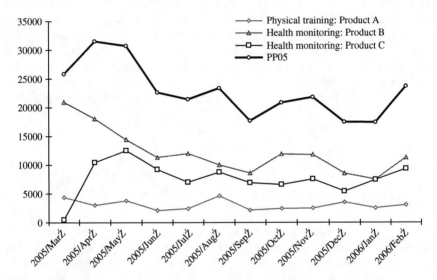

Fig. 5 Illustration of individual and aggregate demand for the shared component: PP05

as Macy's and Target, is relatively regular. In a "stable state," regular demand only deviates from the average monthly demand by up to 20%, and thus a high on-time fulfillment rate is achievable.

Irregular demand arises due to new channels, promotional activities, store expansions, etc. Typically, planners will not be informed of market activities 60 days ahead. It is thus difficult for them to forecast this portion of demand and on-time delivery for irregular demand becomes challenging.

3.3 Bullwhip effect

We observe a three-stage supply chain in this case. The retailers observe consumer demand, place orders with BTG, and receive products from the distribution center. BTG acts as a distributor and collects the orders from retailers and places orders

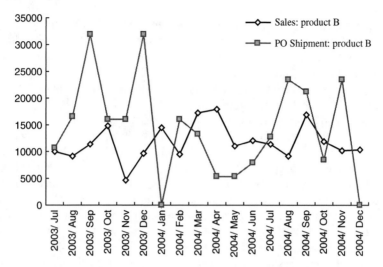

Fig. 6 Illustration of increase in demand variability in the supply chain – product B

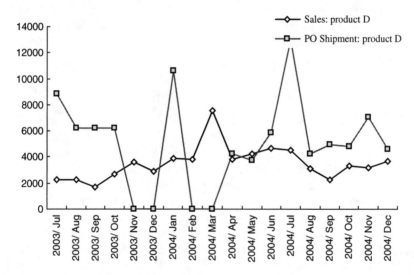

Fig. 7 Illustration of increase in demand variability in the supply chain – product D

to the contract manufacturer (SUGA). All finished goods are sent to the distribution center by the contract manufacturer, and from there are delivered to the various retailers. Thus, the sales information from the distribution center can be regarded as the retailers' order information, and the PO information is regarded as the distributor's order. Table 1 lists the sales information from the BTG distribution center and the corresponding PO issued to SUGA. Figures 6 and 7 provide a graphical representation of orders for two products placed separately by retailers (sales delivered from distribution center) and distributors (PO issued to SUGA) as a function of time. As can be observed, fluctuations in orders increase as they move up the supply chain from distributor to manufacturer, which is known as the "bullwhip effect." A large number of research papers and industrial reports investigate the reasons and impacts of bullwhip effect (see Lee et al. 1997).

Long lead time for manufacturing and transportation is one of the major reasons for the bullwhip effect. Long and uncertain lead times require a higher safety stock level, which leads to an increase in the demand variability.

Demand uncertainty is another reason for the bullwhip effect. In this case, the uncertainty of customer demand and the lead time for order fulfillment means that BTG has to stock a certain quantity of goods to satisfy the average demand during the lead time plus a multiple of the standard deviation of this demand. The latter quantity is referred to as the "safety stock." A standard approach to calculating the safety stock is given in Appendix 604. As the orders are estimated based on constantly updating market observations, the order quantities are changed frequently and the order variability thus increases.

The bullwhip effect is also magnified by information lag and a lack of information sharing. For example, promotional activities are foreseen by BTG, but are only perceived by the contract manufacturers as an inflated order signal. If SUGA uses the inflated order to forecast future demand, then the increase in orders will be interpreted as an increase in demand, which will leave the manufacturer with a surplus product and capacity.

4 Solution Strategy

Firms employ different manufacturing strategies to quickly respond to market demand change (Rajagopalan 2002). MTO systems are suitable for manufacturing with highly customized requirements and in situations where customers are willing to wait. However, in this case, the customer does not require mass customization and is not willing to wait. BTG also has to hold a large finished-goods inventory to maintain a 98% service level for its retail customers. Employing the MTO strategy, SUGA stores inventories of raw materials and starts the production process only after a confirmed SO has been received from BTG, and then issues purchasing orders (PO) to the next tier of suppliers. The subsequent materials delay increases the production lead times from 14 to 70 days. SUGA thus needs to find a more appropriate manufacturing strategy to reduce its order fulfillment lead times.

According to the production process in Fig. 3, WIPs are transferred to the warehouse after PCBA and issued to the next production stage (casing) for assembly. This, combined with the fact that some of the core components are shared, makes it possible to implement "delayed differentiation" in production. Delayed differentiation is widely used in industrial practices, which is to redesign the product or production process so that the point of differentiation (i.e., the stage after which the products assume their unique identities) is delayed as much as possible (Lee and Tang 1997).

Table 1 Sales in BTG distribution center and POs issued to SUGA (Data source: BTG Company)

		2003 Q3			2003 Q4			2004 Q1			2004 Q2			2004 Q3			2004 Q4		
—	—	07	08	09	10	11	12	01	02	03	04	05	06	07	08	09	10	11	12
Product B	Total sales in DC	10075	9190	11457	14750	4,628	9,683	14,490	9,527	17,319	17,891	10,950	12,125	11,438	9,064	16927	11904	10154	10261
—	PO to SUGA	10635	16484	31904	15952	15,952	31,904	0	15,952	13,293	5,317	5,317	7,976	12,762	23,396	21269	8508	23396	0
Product D	Total sales in DC	2230	2278	1721	2689	3605	2902	3924	3839	7,584	3,813	4,222	4,658	4,514	3,120	2,240	3,341	3,166	3,676
—	PO to SUGA	8869	6211	6211	6211	11	0	10635	0	0	4,254	3,722	5,849	13,028	4,254	4,963	4,793	7,093	4,615

We are now ready to propose different manufacturing strategies for different product types, and to use different matrix to measure the performance of different manufacturing process. We divide products into two types, taking into account both regular and irregular demand patterns:

Type I: products that have a high or medium and stable demand (A-level product), or products that have the same core unit as an A-level product

Type II: the other products

In what follows, we first discuss the approach of dividing these two product types and then provide with different manufacturing strategies, as well as details of operational procedures.

4.1 Strategic Manufacturing (the methodology of "divide")

The methodology of determining Type I products is as follows.

1. Define all core units.
2. Find products (SKUs) that share one or more core units and calculate the aggregate sales of these SKUs by month (at BTG distribution center).
3. Calculate the coefficient of variation (CV) of the aggregate sales associated with each core unit(s).
4. Products that have aggregate sales with a CV of less than or equal to 0.4 (suggested) are designated Type I products. All SKUs that share core units are Type I products.
5. If an SKU does not share a core unit but has aggregate sales with a CV of less than or equal to 0.4 and monthly sales larger than a certain amount, say 1,000 units, then it can also be considered a Type I product.

CV measures the relative variability of the demand and is calculated using the following formula.

$$CV = \text{Standard Deviation}/\text{Average}.$$

The smaller the CV, the more stable the demand pattern. To sum up, products with a stable demand, or that containing core units with a stable demand, are Type I products.

The manufacturing strategy differs for each product type to reduce the overall order fulfillment lead time as follows:

1. Assemble-to-order (ATO) strategy for Type I products. With ATO, inventories of core units are built up in advance and finished goods are produced from these core units upon the receipt of the customer PO. In SUGA's case, core units are built and stored in the warehouse as WIP and are then issued to the next casing or packing stage. It should be noted that the core units are produced once the stock levels fall below a certain level, according to the Make-to-Stock (MTS) strategy.

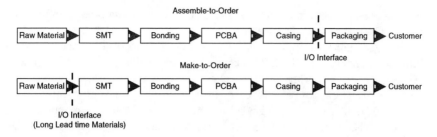

Fig. 8 Illustration of difference between ATO and MTO

2. MTO strategy for Type II products. With MTO, inventories of long lead-time materials are built up according to forecasts, and finished goods are produced from the raw materials upon the receipt of the customer PO.

The difference between ATO and MTO is illustrated in Fig. 8.

4.2 Operational Manufacturing (the art of "conquer")

4.2.1 ATO

With ATO, SUGA can reduce the order fulfillment lead time to less than 6 weeks, including 4 weeks for materials preparation and no more than 2 weeks for final production. As a result, BTG will be able to reduce its safety stock of these products by at least 5–6 weeks, thus making a one-and-a-half-month saving on its finished goods inventory.

For Type I products, the key issue in implementing ATO is to build the core units in advance. Core units may use long lead-time components, such as ASIC cards, which have a very long lead time of 16 weeks. Thus, the inventory planning for core units and raw materials for these long lead-time components is a key problem to be solved. In SUGA's case, we refer long lead-time materials to materials with lead times longer than 4 weeks.

The operating procedure for the ATO system is as follows:

1. The list of Type I products and core units is agreed upon by SUGA and BTG. If a core unit is made to stock, then all products derived from it will be assembled in order to streamline the operational planning.
2. BTG shares its demand information with SUGA, specifically the withdrawn quantity at its distribution center for all products derived from the same core unit.
3. For the stable demand part, SUGA negotiates with BTG for a minimal order quantity for each month, such as 2,000 units for July and 4,000 units for December, and seeks a pre-agreed demand variation percentage, for example, an increase of 20% of the PO quantity over the minimum order quantity. Core units are produced and replenished based on the minimum order commitment. Long

lead-time components are purchased based on the minimum order commitment, and PLOs are used as reference only.

4. For the uncertain irregular demand part, a safety stock of core units and long lead-time components is required. BTG keeps the cost of holding the safety stock with SUGA. This risk-sharing approach eliminates SUGA's materials shortage and prevents over-forecasting by BTG. At the same time, the inventory information is shared by both parties, and BTG has better control over the manufacturing process. BTG also benefits by investing in inventory at the raw materials level, rather than the finished goods level.

5. SUGA communicates with and obtains confirmation from BTG regarding the inventory status. BTG also shares information that implies a demand increase, such as upcoming promotional activities, so that SUGA understands the rational behind each SBU's order forecast and replenishment order quantity. Similarly, when a core unit or product is phased out due to product obsolesce; BTG gives SUGA a signal in advance, because otherwise BTG would need to pay for the remaining unconsumed stock of the obsolete core unit.

6. The "monthly wash" concept applies. For Type I products, POs received in the first month should be shipped in the second month. All unshipped POs will be cleared in the third month.

We notice that the risk-pooling effect of ATO can be best utilized when all SKUs that share the same core unit are considered together, because the ups and downs in demand of the different SKUs cancel out or at least partially compensate each other. Materials purchasing and production are smoother and more stable, and the level of safety stock is lower than that for individual products.

4.2.2 MTO

With MTO, the order fulfillment lead time can be reduced to 6 weeks, including 4 weeks for materials purchasing and 2 weeks for production. Again, inventory planning for raw materials, and especially those with long lead times, is the key to the success of the MTO system.

Each month, BTG provides SUGA with PLOs for the coming 6 months at the same time as it issues the POs. The PLOs are rolling monthly orders, the collection of which is called the "order book." The purchase of long lead-time components is issued based on the order book. An example of an order book is given in Table 2.

Taking the example of "PLO_3 (6)," the lower index "3" indicates the index month of March, and the number "6" in the brackets indicates the index of the PLO. Therefore, PLO_3 (6) represents the sixth PLO (or forecast) based on the demand for March.

As depicted in Fig. 9, for a PO issued at the beginning of July, the materials with the longest lead time (15–18 weeks) are purchased 3 months beforehand (in April) based on PLO_7 (4); the materials with the second longest lead time (11–14 weeks) are purchased 2 months beforehand (in May) based on PLO_7 (5); and the materials with the third longest lead time (7–10 weeks) are purchased 1 month beforehand

Table 2 An example of an order book for one product

–	Jan.	Feb.	Mar.	Apr.	May	June	July	Aug.	Sept.
Jan.	PO_1	$PLO_2(6)$	$PLO_3(5)$	$PLO_4(4)$	$PLO_5(3)$	$PLO_6(2)$	$PLO_7(1)$	–	–
Feb.	–	PO_2	$PLO_3(6)$	$PLO_4(5)$	$PLO_5(4)$	$PLO_6(3)$	$PLO_7(2)$	$PLO_8(1)$	–
Mar.	–	–	PO_3	$PLO_4(6)$	$PLO_5(5)$	$PLO_6(4)$	$PLO_7(3)$	$PLO_8(2)$	$PLO_9(1)$
Apr.	–	–	–	PO_4	$PLO_5(6)$	$PLO_6(5)$	$PLO_7(4)$	$PLO_8(3)$	$PLO_9(2)$
May	–	–	–	–	PO_5	$PLO_6(6)$	$PLO_7(5)$	$PLO_8(4)$	$PLO_9(3)$
June	–	–	–	–	–	PO_6	$PLO_7(6)$	$PLO_8(5)$	$PLO_9(4)$
July	–	–	–	–	–	–	PO_7	$PLO_8(6)$	$PLO_9(5)$
Aug.	–	–	–	–	–	–	–	PO_8	$PLO_9(6)$
Sept.	–	–	–	–	–	–	–	–	PO_9

(in June) based on PLO_7 (6). Note that all the PLO dates are adjusted by deducting 40 days of sea shipment time from the original PLO dates given by BTG.

The operating procedure for MTO is as follows.

1. Each month BTG provides SUGA with PLOs for the coming 4 months when it issues the PO. Again, the PLOs are updated on a 6-month rolling basis.
2. SUGA purchases in advance long lead-time materials, maintaining the agreed safety stock levels and sharing inventory information with BTG for forecasting.
3. SUGA is responsible for maintaining a list of long lead-time materials. If a material stops or starts having a long lead time, then SUGA must update and submit the list to BTG for confirmation. It is SUGA's responsibility if a delay in delivery is caused by having to purchase a long lead-time material that is not on the list. For its part, BTG signals when certain products are to be phased out.
4. Both BTG and SUGA generate a forecast discrepancy report for each rolling forecast period, which includes quantity differences between POs and PLOs.
5. Every 6 months or other agreed interval, SUGA submits a list of excess long lead-time material inventory with the corresponding costs caused by demand discrepancy. BTG acknowledges and pays for the excess inventory cost. This part of the inventory then becomes BTG's consigned inventory at SUGA. The consigned inventory is then taken into account by SUGA in the next round of purchasing and is consumed first.

4.2.3 Safety Stock for Long Lead-Time Materials and Forecast Error Measurement

The level of safety stock is determined by three factors: the materials purchasing lead time, the service level, and the variation between forecasted and real demand. Vertically, the longer the lead time, the higher the level of safety stock level. Horizontally, the higher the forecasted variation, the higher the level of safety stock.

The safety stock is calculated and adjusted dynamically based on the approach in Appendix 604. However, considering the lack of historical data in this case, we propose a simple and rough approach to initialize the implementation. The relationships

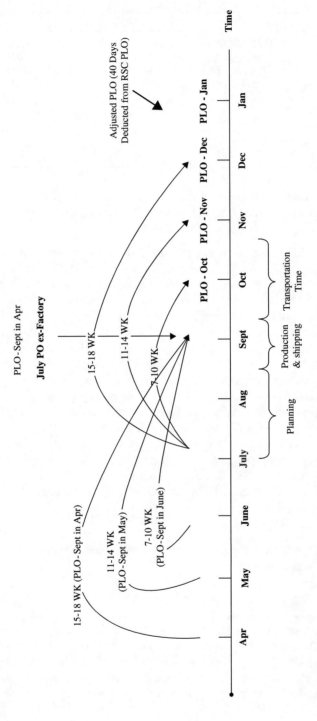

Fig. 9 Illustration of PO, PLO, and long lead-time materials purchasing

Table 3 Safety stock level of materials with different lead times vs. forecasted variation

Material Lead time	Forecast Variation Variation		
	10%	20%	30%
7–10 Weeks	10%	20%	30%
11–14 Weeks	21%	44%	69%
15–18 Weeks	33%	73%	120%

Table 4 SUGA's KPI system for suppliers

Category	KPI Title	Function	Review Period
Delivery	1. Order fulfillment lead time	To measure how long the supplier needs to fulfill an order	Monthly
	2. On-time delivery rate	To measure to the extent to which orders can be fulfilled on time	Monthly
	3. On-time fulfillment for samples	To measure the capability to manufacture newly developed products	Monthly
Quality	4. Average weighted defected rate	To measure the quality of incoming materials	Weekly
	5. Number of complaints from SUGA	To measure the number of complaints from the Production Department on the quality of raw materials	Weekly
Flexibility	6. Timely response to order changes	To measure the manufacturing flexibility of suppliers to cope with order changes in time	Monthly
	7. Successful pull-in-out orders	To measure the manufacturing flexibility of suppliers to cope with changes in order number	Monthly
Cost	8. Price changes rate	To measure suppliers' performance in terms of quotations and costs	Quarterly

between the safety stock level of materials with different long lead times and their forecasted variation level are shown in Table 3.

Within the agreed forecast variation rate and with the corresponding safety stock on hand, SUGA can achieve a 98% on-time and complete order delivery rate. The forecasted variation rate and safety stock level need to be decided and agreed upon by both SUGA and BTG.

4.2.4 Coordination Of Type I and II Products

Type I and II products may share certain long lead-time components, but the approaches to obtaining the components may be different. As elaborated in the previous sections, for Type I products, the requirement for long lead-time components is derived from the core units demand data, whereas for Type II products it is derived from the PLO and safety stock level data. Although these material requirements are consolidated when issuing a PO to a supplier, it is necessary to keep an internal record of the corresponding inventory to avoid confusion over inventory allocation. This requires the support of advanced IT system.

4.3 Reducing the Bullwhip Effect

To reduce the bullwhip effect, BTG must share sales information from its distribution center with SUGA. This sales information can be regarded as actual customer data. Based on the aggregate demand information and the PLOs issued by BTG, SUGA can make forecasts, then determine its target inventory level, and issue orders to its next-tier suppliers.

By employing the mixed manufacturing strategy of ATO and MTO, the order fulfillment lead time can be greatly reduced. The shorter the production lead time, the more accurate the forecast, and inventory can be better planned and material shortages are reduced. By collaborative planning and inventory control, SUGA can purchase raw materials in advance and prevent materials shortages, which would otherwise happen frequently.

BTG and SUGA must establish a close and integrated strategic partnership to improve their information sharing and inventory planning within the global supply chain. BTG has adopted the vendor managed inventory (VMI) system for some retailers, such as Wal-Mart. This system determines how much inventory to keep on hand and how much to ship to the retailer in every period. This helps BTG to connect directly to the end consumers and to replenish the inventory based on the demand information that comes direct from the market. By establishing a more collaborative approach to share information such as demand data and product obsolescence signals and by controlling inventory through the sharing of the risks associated with holding an inventory of long lead-time materials, the performance of the global supply chain can be greatly improved.

4.4 Performance Evaluation

In implementing a mixed ATO and MTO manufacturing strategy with information sharing and collaborative planning, a set of systematic measurements is necessary to monitor SUGA's progress toward attaining its strategic objective.

To improve SUGA's on-time delivery rate, a key performance indicator (KPI) system is proposed. The KPI system can be divided into three subsets: KPIs for suppliers and service providers, KPIs for internal departments, and KPIs for customers.

KPIs for suppliers measure supplier performance in terms of delivery, quality, flexibility, and cost. The definitions and functions of these are given in Table 4.

Table 5 Summary of the current and proposed manufacturing and inventory strategies

–	Current	Proposed
Manufacturing strategy	Partial MTO	Systematic MTO, ATO
Demand-supply planning	Independent	Collaborative
Information sharing	Manual-weak	Enhanced-integrated
Planning data analysis and tracking	Occasionally and manually	Periodical and electronically

Note: Partial MTO refers to MTO without a scientific inventory allocation policy.

KPIs for the internal departments of SUGA monitor the performance of the entire order fulfillment process in terms of order delivery, product quality, inventory planning, manufacturing and production process, innovation and creativity, and new product development.

KPIs for customers evaluate customer performance, including forecasting accuracy and information sharing.

We also develop an assessment matrix that defines the owners and target departments of each KPI, and clearly states the data sources and evaluation period. Each evaluation period is treated by the KPI implementation team as a project. First, they collect the KPI input data; second, they assess the data and calculate each KPI; third, they analyze the data and report the evaluation results; and fourth, they deliver the evaluation report and propose an improvement action plan.

5 Implementation and Impact

5.1 Current Status

We proposed an adaptive manufacturing strategy and the development of operating processes and a performance evaluation tool to help SUGA reduce its order fulfillment lead time, and increase its on-time delivery rate as well.

As an initial stage of implementation, SUGA is currently using MTO for most products and MTS for several core components. However, demand and inventory information sharing is better implemented than before, and collaborative inventory planning has also been initiated based on a long lead-time materials purchasing agreement with BTG. SUGA is using inventory planning tools, rather than manual planning, to support the mixed manufacturing strategy. In addition, 10 or 20% of the average month's demand is used as the safety stock level.

A comparison of the current and suggested manufacturing and inventory strategies is given in Table 5. Currently, SUGA employs MTO, or more precisely, partial MTO, for the lack of scientific inventory allocation policy. The planners in each SBU of BTG are independent, and the information sharing between BTG and SUGA is weak and manually operated. Inventory planning is manual, and data analysis and tracking is occasional and manual. With the proposed solution, the systematic ATO/MTO manufacturing strategy is to be employed. Demand planning is collaborative, and information sharing is enhanced or integrated with the supporting IT tools. Inventory planning is then executed periodically and electronically. In summary, the proposed strategy will improve the visibility, synchronization, interdependency, and accountability between SUGA and BTG.

Although the implementation is still at the initial stage, the improvements are significant. According to BTG's most recent performance evaluation, SUGA's on-time delivery rate has increased to 89% and its order fulfillment lead time has decreased to 67 days.

5.2 Technology Innovations

Since August 2005, SUGA has been using the Oracle ERP system replacing the previous BAAN system. The Oracle system provides multiple modules such as engineering, MRP, and inventory. The application of the Oracle system integrates the main internal supply chain operations. The MRP module meets most of the current planning requirements, but is still subject to the following functional shortcomings:

- Lack of direct pegging between SOs and POs. POs are pegged to Job Orders, which are created from SOs
- Inability to reserve materials for specific orders
- Inability to group POs by supplier. The PMC department therefore uses Excel to group POs manually
- A PO quantity change requires a total re-schedule. The previously calculated PO then becomes void, which confuses suppliers

Inventory planning is the most difficult part of the implementation. Because there are thousands of SKUs, it is impossible to plan manually: a decision support system is necessary. With a mixed manufacturing strategy inventory planning is more complicated as compared to the pure MTO strategy. Because of the limitations of the current MRP system, an advanced MRP tool to support decision making in a mixed manufacturing environment and materials control is necessary. This system should provide a platform for collaborative planning and advance inventory planning (inventory locking and sharing and adjustment of the input of the MRP to smooth production), and a seamless interface with the existing Oracle MRP system. In addition, it should provide a platform for performance evaluation, such as KPI data that are automatically acquired, calculated, and reported.

At the second stage of implementation, we develop an efficient IT tool – the Sense-and-Respond PMC Manager – that is tailored to SUGA's needs. PMC Manager is designed to help planners to intelligently utilize all available resources at the right time, at the right place, and in the right quantity for the right order. The logic of the system is presented in Fig. 10.

The advanced functions of PMC Manager are grouped into five modules.

Alternative Part Handler. This is one of the most important elements missing from standard MRP packages. Alternative parts are those that can substitute for a primary part when the primary part is not available in stock. With alternative part handler, the user can indicate the sequence in which the primary part and alternative parts in the inventory are consumed, and can determine which parts should be purchased after inventory consumption.

Multi-Location Planner. The multi-location planner is specially designed for enterprises with multiple and widely distributed factories. By balancing the supply demand condition among factories, a planner can help each factory to effectively calculate PLOs, re-schedule notices, and transfer orders for supplying other factories. For example, a company may have several factories, each of which has its own inventory, and a centralized distribution center that can provide materials for all the factories. The company planners will seek to use the

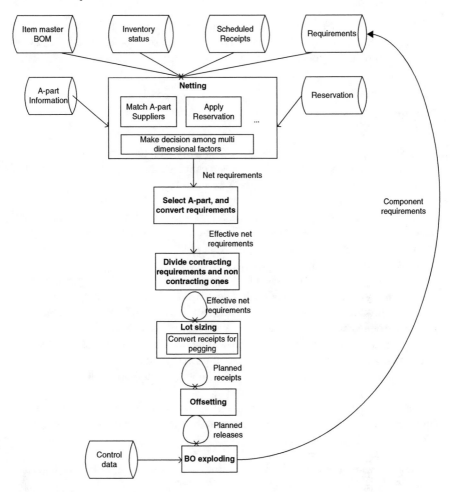

Fig. 10 Logic of the PMC Manager

materials in the local warehouse first. If the local supply is not sufficient, then the supply in the central distribution center will be considered.

Advanced Pegging and Reservation. As one of the core features of constrained and conditional MRP (C^2 MRP), pegging is vital for synchronizing supply-demand transactions and activities across the entire manufacturing supply chain. With pegging, supply can be exactly matched with demand, which ensures that changes can be effectively propagated to all related orders when there are supply or demand changes in any nodes in the supply chain.

Ad-hoc Lot Sizing for ATO. To enable an ATO manufacturing strategy, planners should be able to adjust and reschedule the production quantity of core units to ensure smooth production. The Ad-hoc Lot sizing module is designed to allow planners to intervene in the lot sizing process for a core unit order release schedule to achieve ATO flexibility.

Sub-Contracting Handling. This function allows users to define subcontracted parts (global, BOM specific, no materials provided by subcontractor) for assembly demand, and accordingly generate materials requirements.

6 Conclusion

Quick response was initiated in the apparel industry with the purpose to shorten lead time so as to adjust orders to market demand changes. Recently, quick response has been applied to other industries as well. In this chapter, we summarize a case of Hong Kong electronics manufacturer implementing quick response program.

Facing with increasing expectations and pressures of customer, SUGA, the manufacturer need to implement the program with the objective to speed up its supply chain, respond to customer demands more quickly, shorten manufacturing lead time, and improve its on-time delivery rate.

Based on the analysis of product characteristic and production process, delay in production becomes feasible. By further analysis of the market demand pattern, we can divide products into two different types. We propose ATO/MTO mixed manufacturing strategy and the operational procedures for different types of products. As a complementary, we propose a set of systematic measurements and selective key performance indicators to monitor the operating performance. We further develop an efficient IT tool, which is tailored to SUGA's needs, to support intelligent materials planning.

Even though it is at the initial stage of implementation, the improvements are still significant: the on-time delivery rate has increased to 89%, and its order fulfillment lead time has decreased to 67 days.

Acknowledgements This research was partly supported by the Li and Fung Institute for Supply Chain Management of the Chinese University of Hong Kong.

Appendix A

Abbreviation list

ASIC	Application-specific integrated circuit
ATO	Assemble-to-order
BOM	Bill of materials
C^2 MRP	Constrained and conditional MRP
CV	Coefficient of variation
KPI	Key performance indicator
MRP	Material requirements planning
MTO	Make-to-order

MTS   Make-to-stock
ODM   Original design manufacturing
OEM   Original equipment manufacturing
PCBA   Printed circuit board assembly
PLO   Planned order
PMC   Production and manufacturing control
PO   Purchase order
SBU   Strategic business unit
SKU   Stocking unit
SMT   Surfaced mounting technology
SO   Sales order
VMI   Vendor managed inventory
WIP   Work in progress

Appendix B

Safety stock calculation

Assumptions

> Forecast-demand errors are symmetric.
> Calculations are based on pooled PLOs and POs.

Formula

> The safety stock for each long lead-time material is

$$= \sqrt{\text{Lead} - \text{time}} \times \text{Service Level Factor} \times (1.25 \times \text{MAD}),$$

where
Lead-time = the purchasing lead time for a material,
Service Lever Factor = a multiplier to calculate a specific quantity to meet the specified service level. For a 98% service level (on time and complete delivery rate), the factor is 2.05
MAD = Mean Absolute Deviation: a measure of the variance between forecasted and real demand
MAD = Sum (|Sum (PLOt) – Sum (POt – 3)|) – N for the material with the longest lead time
    = Sum (|Sum (PLOt) – Sum (POt – 2)|) – N for the material with the second longest lead time
    = Sum (|Sum (PLOt) – Sum (POt – 1)|) – N for the material with the third longest lead time,
where t = period number and N = total number of periods.

References

Lee H, Padmanabhan V, Whang S (1997) Information distortion in a supply chain: the bullwhip effect. Manag Sci 43(4):546–558

Lee H, Tang CS (1997) Modelling the costs and benefits of delayed product differentiation. Manag Sci 43(1):40–53

Rajagopalan S (2002) Make to order or make to stock: model and application. Manag Sci 48(2):241–256

Vollmann TE, Berry WL, Whybark DC, Jacobs FR (2005) Manufacturing Planning and Control Systems for Supply Chain Management. 5th edn McGraw-Hill

Quick Response Practices in the Hong Kong Apparel Industry

Pui-Sze Chow, Tsan-Ming Choi, T.C.E. Cheng, and Shuk-Ching Liu

Abstract This chapter presents a study on innovative quick response (QR) practices in the apparel industry in Hong Kong. We conducted desk research, as well as in-depth face-to-face interviews, with six established apparel firms in Hong Kong. The purpose was to gain an understanding of the business environment in which the apparel industry operates, as well as the approaches the firms have taken to increase responsiveness to their customers' demands. Despite their different business nature and company background, we observed after a detailed examination of the various QR measures employed by these companies that a strong buyer–supplier relationship and frequent information sharing between channel members are crucial to the success of QR adoption.

Keywords Apparel industry · Hong Kong · Quick response

1 Introduction

Lead time management is crucial in modern supply chain management. Industries in all the sectors need to control order and transportation lead time, which in turn ensures that merchandise is delivered to the sales floor on time. This is especially prominent in industries such as fashion apparels, in which quick response (QR) practices, an approach to reduce lead time, emerged (Iyer and Bergen 1997).

Hong Kong is a logistics hub for apparel products in the Asia-Pacific region. As early as 1987, the Hong Kong Government hired consultants to identify the future direction of the region's textiles and clothing industry (KS Associates 1987). In that consultant report it was suggested that QR adoption was both a threat and an opportunity in the light of global competition. In the aftermath of the recent

P.-S. Chow (✉)
Business Division, Institute of Textiles and Clothing, Faculty of Applied Science and Textiles
The Hong Kong Polytechnic University, Hung Hom, Kowloon, Hong Kong
e-mail: linda.chow@polyu.edu.hk

T.C. Edwin Cheng and T.-M. Choi (eds.), *Innovative Quick Response Programs in Logistics and Supply Chain Management*, International Handbooks on Information Systems, DOI 10.1007/978-3-642-04313-0_18,
© Springer-Verlag Berlin Heidelberg 2010

global financial turmoil, Hong Kong's apparel industry is facing huge challenges, and competition has become very keen. To survive, apparel firms need to profoundly improve their operations and elevate their productivity; QR again holds the key to success of this campaign.

This chapter aims at exploring the adoption of QR strategy in some representative companies in Hong Kong's apparel industry. We first conducted desk research on two companies in the sector that are well-known in their QR practices. We then interviewed four companies that play different roles in the fashion supply chain to learn the current practices adopted by the clothing industry in Hong Kong. We also sought to understand these apparel firms' comments on QR practices from these interviews. We believe that these companies serve as illustrative examples for practitioners, whether within or outside the clothing industry, on the significance of QR and how it can be effectively adopted in different company situations.

The rest of this chapter is organized as follows. We provide a literature review in Sect.2. Afterwards, we review the QR practices in two established companies and summarize the findings of the interviews conducted with four apparel firms in Sect.3. Finally, we conclude and provide some managerial insights in Sect.4.

2 Literature Review

First established in the 1980s in American's apparel industry, QR has been a well-established and widely practised strategy. With a focus on responding to market changes quickly and cutting order lead time (Hammond 1990; Choi et al. 2006), QR concepts are now widely adopted in industries with products that have short life cycles and are subject to highly volatile demand. There are a wide variety of descriptions about the definition for QR (Lowson et al. 1999). From the perspective of the textiles and clothing sector, Hunter (1990) defined QR as integration of all the parts in the fashion supply chain (from fibre, textile and clothing manufacturing to retailing), with the use of innovative hard and soft technologies, into "a consumer responsive whole" that can provide the best product quality at every stage. A concise version of the definition is perhaps the one suggested by Fairbairn (1997): "QR is a technology-driven sourcing strategy that is based on a cooperation relationship between retailer and supplier that seeks to minimize slack resources (i.e. time and inventory) in the supply chain." It is generally agreed that firms increasingly adopt QR strategy as a means to enhance their competitiveness. Such competitiveness can be illustrated by the significant improvements in the participants' business performance reported in a government-funded QR programme for the Australian textiles, clothing and footwear industry (Perry et al. 1999). Results of a questionnaire survey on specialty retailers in the US also indicate that QR adoption could improve a firm's performance (Palmer and Markus 2000).

Nevertheless, implementation of QR programmes requires extra effort and cooperation from both retailers and suppliers. Larson and Lusch (1990) proposed that both parties should share mutual goals and treat their relationship as partnership to have QR successfully employed. In reality, such a cooperative spirit is not easy to accomplish as it requires complete trust between trading partners (Giunipero et al. 2001), while a stable relationship between channel members is related to achieving the goals of quality improvement in the supply chain as well (Lai et al. 2005). A good buyer–supplier relationship also has a positive effect on a company's financial performance (Carr and Pearson 1999). Several case studies, including those by Sullivan and Kang (1999); Perry and Sohal (2000); Giunipero et al. (2001); Fiorito et al. (1998); Fernie and Azuma (2004), used surveys to investigate the differing views of retailers and suppliers on QR. Mathematical models (e.g., Iyer and Bergen 1997; Al-Zubaidi and Tyler 2004; Choi and Chow 2008) and face-to-face interviews (e.g., Birtwistle et al. 2006) are alternative methods for studying the various issues related to QR practices. While a multitude of surveys have found that most companies agree that QR practices are useful, many firms still have prejudice and doubts about QR's actual value. Whiteoak (1999) raised some fundamental issues of practising QR in the grocer sector such as "Who should own the stock?" and "Who should pay?" These questions are imperative and meaningful, and require more careful consideration and up-front answers. Consequently, measures must be taken to help build trust between the parties engaged in QR practices, as mutual trust between trading partners provides the basis to resolve the above issues. One of such measures is the use of information technology. A recent exploration of the impact of electronic integration on logistical systems' performance was reported in Lai et al. (2008). Implementation of technology such as point-of-sale (POS) equipment, universal product code (UPC), and automatic checkout machines (ACM) to monitor different business processes and document mistakes (Larson and Lusch 1990; Birtwistle et al. 2006) is essential for efficient implementation of QR. These devices can strengthen communication between the retailer and the supplier to hold each party accountable for fulfilling their commitments through unbiased tracking (Giunipero et al. 2001). RFID technology is another emerging practice that can accelerate and smooth the logistics processes (e.g., container transport) in a supply chain. However, adequate equipment management and supply chain collaboration are key to gaining QR benefits (Lun et al. 2008). An obstacle to collaboration is that "suppliers may be reluctant to invest the capital required in new technologies to enable them to share information in real time, due to the dynamic and adversarial nature of the retail relationship." (Birtwistle et al. 2006). Therefore, strong incentives are needed to attract suppliers to faithfully join a QR partnership. This motivation can be in the form of equal and asymmetric information flow and many suppliers would request to take a bigger part in the decision-making process (Giunipero et al. 2001). Multi-directional information sharing includes wish lists and strategic planning to enhance product-related action plans, which improves ordering (and response) times (Perry et al. 1999). However, this is easier said than done since collaborative decisions require managers to share sensitive information that they may be hesitant to give (Perry and Sohal 2000). It can be argued that proper training is another important measure. Fiorito et al. (1998) surveyed various retail buyers and found most of them agree that QR would be beneficial, but QR training needs to be improved. If more training is conducted, most firms agreed with the notion that confidence in information sharing would be higher.

3 Current Practices in Hong Kong's Apparel Industry

Although the 15-day magic of Zara (Ghemawat and Nueno 2003) is a benchmark example of the successful deployment of QR strategy in fast fashion, many practitioners in the fashion industry are adopting various measures to quickly react to the highly volatile demand due to fierce competition in the industry and increasingly demanding customers. Hong Kong, as a regional apparel centre, has many apparel companies that are known to be effective QR adopters. In this section we present (1) a review of two companies renowned for their QR approaches, and (2) face-to-face interviews with four apparel companies to study their practices and attitudes towards QR.

The two desk-research examples presented in this section were the TAL Group and Moiselle International Holdings Limited. The former has been a textbook case example in supply chain management for years, whereas the latter is one of Hong Kong's local retailers having the reputation for flexibility in coping with customer demands in the industry. The four "in-depth interviewed" firms included (1) Magenta Wardrobe Fashion Associates Ltd., which is the strategic partner of the regional casual wear brand "eBase," (2) the regional buying office of an European brand in men's, women's, and children's wear, (3) a retailer of a local ladies' wear brand, and (4) a medium-sized apparel manufacturer. The interviews were conducted with the Managing Director, a Buying Coordinator, the Brand Manager, and a Senior Merchandiser of the four companies, respectively. Given their different business nature and roles in the fashion supply chain, we deem to have acquired a comprehensive understanding of the current state of QR practices in Hong Kong's apparel industry.

3.1 The TAL Group (TAL)[1]

Originating as a spinning mill for yarn production in Hong Kong in 1947, TAL has evolved into one of the largest garment manufacturers in the world that produces over 56 million pieces of clothing annually. With its main focus on the North American market, the Group's major customers include such branded apparel retailers as JC Penny, Brooks Brothers, Liz Claiborne, Polo Ralph Lauren, Land's End, and L.L. Beans. One of the Group's main corporate strategies is to transform itself

---

[1]Except for those with references provided, the sources of the information on the TAL Group were a seminar delivered by Professor Harry Lee, the Managing Director of the TAL Group, at The Hong Kong Polytechnic University in November 2007, as well as TAL's official website.

from a traditional manufacturer to a "Total Solution Innofacturer." Apart from the development of various edge-cutting performance product technologies, TAL also strives to provide innovative supply chain services. The Group had been investing in information and communications infrastructure long before the others realized such a need. Amongst the numerous innovative approaches implemented to help the company to quickly respond to customer demand, one of the earliest and most influential projects was its implementation of a powerful ERP system. By adopting the industry-specific Movex Fashion Solution (which was developed by Intentia International, a Sweden-based IT solutions provider), TAL is able to streamline its internal operations, as well as manage external relationships with trade partners (Farhoomand and Ho 2005). The integrated communication infrastructure also facilitates later IT enhancement and business process development.

Another ground-breaking QR-oriented achievement of TAL is its successful delivery of the vendor-managed inventory (VMI) programme to JC Penny. With direct access to the retailer's POS data, TAL can learn about the retailer's sales patterns and plan for its own production accordingly. As a result, inventory is reduced and replenishment cycles are shortened. In addition, the sophisticated pick-to-light racking system and cross docking also help streamline the warehousing and delivery processes and results in considerable savings in operational cost. It is worth noticing that strong trust and a shared goal between the retailer and the supplier are pre-requisites for successful collaboration on a VMI programme.

Taking a step forward, TAL is working with JC Penny to adopt Collaborative Planning Forecasting and Replenishment (CPFR). One of the weaknesses of the existing VMI programme is that forecasting is done by TAL based on sales data, but promotional events to be launched by JC Penny are not communicated. Such a lack of pro-active communication significantly affects the accuracy of demand forecasts. To cope with the problem, weekly video/teleconferences are arranged between the two parties to discuss the forthcoming production plan. At the moment, a new forecasting system is being installed between the two parties to facilitate the implementation of CPFR.

3.2 MOISELLE International Holdings Limited (Moiselle)

Established in 1997, Moiselle specializes in the design, development, manufacturing, distributing and retailing of prestigious high-end ladies' apparel. Publicly listed on the main board of the Stock Exchange of Hong Kong Limited since 2002, the company currently owns more than 120 retail shops and counters in Hong Kong and in various major cities in China and Taiwan. Apart from the in-house brand MOISELLE, the company also engages in exclusive distributorship of international brands like COCCINELLE, SEQUOIA and REISS (www.moiselle.com.hk).

Moiselle is renowned for its achievement in reducing order lead time to 14–30 days. Although the design theme would first come from most fashion brand owners for planning the forthcoming collection, the company deliberately puts the fabrication consideration prior to the design for many products. Specifically, Moiselle determines the fabrics to be used for the forthcoming season and arranges order placing at the very beginning of the development stage. Afterwards, it works on the designs and production with respect to the fabrics ordered. By smartly swapping the development procedure to a small extent, the order lead time is greatly reduced in the light of "faster" fabric availability. Besides, the small order quantities for individual styles (approximately 10–200 pieces per style) also contribute to shorter production time. Except for denim and sweater items that are outsourced to factories in southeast China, MOISELLE works with its vendors on a contract manufacturing basis. Besides, the company also has its own factories in the region for the production of its woven and basic styles. As a result, the company closely collaborates with its suppliers to monitor the production process and smoothly resolve issues that crop up.

3.3 Magenta Wardrobe Fashion Associates Ltd (Magenta)

Established in 1995, Magenta supplied women's and men's wear collections to various department stores in Hong Kong, such as Sogo, Jusco and Seiyu, on a wholesale basis under the brand names of "Magenta" and "Cyan." Recently, the company became an original design manufacturing (ODM) supplier to the Baleno Group, and in 2001, Magenta acted as a strategic partner of the group for developing the brand "ebase". Currently, there are over 50 ebase stores in various commercial locations in Hong Kong, China and Taiwan, providing over 2,000 fashionable styles on an annual basis.

According to Mr. Percy Yung, the Managing Director of Magenta, the order lead time for Magenta's merchandise has reduced to 60–90 days in recent years. Although the order lead times for fabrics and other raw materials are somewhat fixed and uncontrollable, Magenta has been striving hard to streamline its internal processes to further shorten the production lead time. At present, individual processes are isolated, which hinder information flow. In particular, when changes in schedules and production details take place during the course of production, it takes an enormous amount of time to make the necessary amendments. Meanwhile, the company is developing an information system to link up individual processes and expects that the new system will help reduce redundant work significantly. Being the "middleman" in the fashion supply chain, Magenta is well aware of the importance of information sharing amongst channel members. On the one hand, it needs to updated market information from retail outlets for design and production planning; on the other hand, it needs to keep its suppliers informed about any changes in production planning. In the light of this, Magenta is seriously considering the adoption of information technology to link up with the POS systems of its retailers, as well as to share information with its suppliers in a prompt and timely manner. Magenta believes that a good retailer–supplier relationship is the key to success in the highly competitive apparel industry nowadays. To facilitate the production process, the company currently shares style information with individual suppliers through a sophisticated information system. In the long run, Magenta plans to select "focus suppliers" that can provide ODM services and become strategic partners of the company.

3.4 DIS[2]: The Buying Office for a European Fashion Brand "M"

Founded in 1986, European brand M markets an extensive range of fashion apparel and accessories for women, men and children. Currently employing over 6,000 people worldwide, the brand has 9,000 selling points in more than 50 countries all over the world, including Europe, Canada, China, Singapore, Taiwan and Thailand. DIS is the buying office of Brand M in the Asia-Pacific region for ordering and sourcing coordination. Normally the order lead time for DIS is about 60–90 days. After the seasonal merchandise seminar, buyers from all over the world will determine their regional ordering quantities. To facilitate the production process, the company will inform their contract manufacturers for greige fabrics ordering 3–4 weeks before they submit the final order details. Buyers from all over the world then input their order details into the corporate purchase order (PO) system, which then consolidates the final orders and sends them to the manufacturers for order placing. Manufacturers of DIS are required to prepare the merchandise in sales-floor-ready conditions. In other words, all the hanging of labels, tags and bar-codes and packaging are to be done in the factories. DIS employs Paxar as its hang-tags and bar-code provider. Granted access to the company's database, Paxar prepares the tags and bar-code labels for DIS's merchandise according to order details. Individual manufacturers are then required to log into Paxar's system to arrange label/tags pick-up for the final packaging stage of their respective orders.

Over 60% of DIS's manufacturers are located in southeast China (e.g. Hong Kong and various cities in Guangdong Province). To facilitate shipment arrangements, the company appoints Maersk, a logistics service provider, as its designated forwarder in the region. When finished merchandise is ready for shipment, manufacturers in southeast China are required to input the shipment details into DIS's web-based shipping system for approval. Meanwhile, the electronic packing lists are sent to Maersk for reference. Upon approval, the manufacturers deliver their finished merchandise to Maersk's container freight station at the Kwai Chung Container Terminal in Hong Kong, where shipments are consolidated and arranged for delivery to Brand M's single distribution centre in Rotterdam, the Netherlands, before onward sending to respective retail outlets throughout the world. Thus with one-time data input from a single party (i.e. the supplier) into DIS' shipping system,

---

[2]From Sects. 3.4–3.6, the names of the companies are fictitious per request of the interviewees. For the sake of presentation, we call them DIS, RTL and MFR (with respect to their "distributing", "retail" and "manufacturing" business nature, respectively). Two fashion brand names that we mention, i.e., "M" and "X", are also fictitious names but all the cases are real.

shipment information is shared to all other parties involved in a real-time manner and the whole delivery process is streamlined.

3.5 RTL: A Hong Kong Branded Retailer in Ladies' Wear

Established in 2002, RTL is a retail subsidiary of its parent company as an extension from original equipment manufacturing (OEM) to original brand manufacturing (OBM). Although the main product category of the brand is targeted as ladies' wear, handbags, footwear and accessories constitute 30% of its merchandise. In terms of styling, 60% of its apparel products are fashionable items that change on a seasonal basis, while the remaining 40% are of basic designs that can be carried forward to the next season. Over 70% of the merchandise of RTL is produced by the two factories owned by the parent company, while the remaining portion is purchased from overseas importers. As of February 2008, there were three retail locations in Hong Kong and six in various major cities on the Chinese mainland, which generate an annual sales turnover of around HK$10,000,000 (equivalent to around 12,000 pieces of merchandise) for the company.

RTL undoubtedly recognizes the importance of short order lead time to retail operations. Contrary to common business practice, the order lead time for RTL is longer compared with that 5 years ago. Being a retail subsidiary of the parent company, RTL has a lower priority in using the production resources of its parent company's owned factories. Therefore, whenever the factories are fully occupied with OEM orders, production of RTL's merchandise is inevitably delayed. Besides, with high turnover rates in the factories, worker efficiency is not satisfactory due to the increased learning time. In addition, quality problems appear frequently so that extra time is required for remedies and remakes. As a result, most of the merchandises will be delivered to shops only after the selling season has started. Though the factories offer discounts in some cases, the delay inevitably causes stock-outs and in the long run jeopardizes RTL's market development.

In the light of its specific situation, RTL has adopted various policies to tackle its current challenges. First of all, it has introduced a year-round long-running collection that requires shorter production lead times. Since there is no strict seasonality for these regular items, factories can make use of their spare time and capacity to do the production whenever available. Also, the regular collection can serve as a substitute in case that there is a delay in seasonal collection launches. Nevertheless, fashionable items are essential to the future development of an apparel brand. To cope with the above challenges, RTL adopts the postponement approach by developing styles that can share common components amongst one another. By doing so, material procurement can be more focused and production quantities can be easily swapped amongst styles according to updated market information. Apart from this, RTL also keeps track of factories' material availability so that its designs are made of fabrics that the factories have sufficient stock. As a result, the lead time for fabric ordering can be reduced and, in turn, the production lead time can be shortened.

Moreover, the Design and the Buying Teams of RTL proactively keep contact with factories to monitor their production processes. From the frequent visits to factories, RTL discusses with the factories regarding their production progress. In case that any production obstacles are identified, it can react promptly and take remedial actions in all areas.

3.6 MFR: A Hong Kong "Small-Medium Enterprise" (SME) Manufacturer

Established in 1989, MFR is a Hong Kong-based SME apparel manufacturer that focuses its business on cut and sewn knitwear and basic woven shirts and trousers. In terms of seasonality, half of MFR's merchandise is fashionable items, while the other half is of basic styles. With the head office located in Hong Kong, MFR has three overseas factories, two in Vietnam and one in Cambodia. Over 90% of their customers are branded retailers and distributors in North America, examples of which include Meryns, JC Penny and Columbia. Over 5,000,000 pieces of merchandise are produced and sold by MFR every year, which accounts for an annual sales turnover of US$13,000,000. MFR is well aware of the industry-wise reduction in order lead time from 90–120 to 60–90/75 days over the past 5 years. It is well known that improvements in raw materials/product shipment schedules and advances in technology for fabric and clothing production have contributed significantly to order lead time reduction. Nevertheless, MFR also reflects on the problems that may take place and delay the original schedule. Fabric quality problem is one of such causes of delay, while customers' sudden requests for changes in product design, order quantity, and delivery schedule are other frequent reasons causing disturbance to the original production schedule.

MFR talked about a specific case whereby one of their long-term distributor customers (hereafter referred as Brand X) requested a shorter order lead time. Brand X requested to postpone its order placing time so that it can gather the order details from its wholesale/retail customers after their selling campaigns and make a more accurate ordering plan. Brand X used to provide some production forecasts for MFR's reference, but such forecasts tended to be not so accurate. On the other hand, MFR had to arrange packaging, wash labels, and stock allocation for different markets for Brand X with the allocation plans provided by Brand X. However, to cope with the sudden demand changes in various markets, Brand X frequently changed its allocation plans and delivery instructions. As a result, MFR had to redo the packaging to meet the updated requirements. Though MFR could charge back the extra cost for repackaging in some cases, redundant workload was wasted and errors would occur. In view of this, MFR did not object to Brand X's order placing postponement, provided that the order lead time does not fall below the threshold level of 75 days, which is the minimum production time MFR requires. If any client requires shortening the order lead time to less than 75 days, MFR demands the client to commit to the aggregated quantities of the styles using specialized fabrics at least 10 days before confirmation of order details, so that MFR can arrange fabric ordering in advance to "shorten" the overall order lead time.

3.7 Summary of the Review of Current QR Practices

From the desk research and the face-to-face interviews, we found that all the firms acknowledged the importance of short order lead time and they had adopted various QR measures in their quest for shortening order lead times. We summarize in Table 1 the various specific QR-related measures that the above-mentioned apparel companies in Hong Kong have put in place.

We found that most of the apparel companies under study had taken steps to shorten order lead times for raw materials, mostly fabrics. Some measures are rather innovative, for example Moiselle swaps the development stages to determine fabrics prior to design. Normally the order lead time for fabrics is around 3–4 weeks (for some companies, it can be as long as 6 months), which constitutes nearly half

Table 1 Summary of QR-related practices among companies discussed above

Scope	QR-oriented measure	Companies adopting the measure
Shortened lead time for raw materials	Designs made of fabrics on hand	RTL
	Fabric ordering in advance	Magenta, Moiselle, MFR, DIS
Easily adaptable designs	Design styles that can be easily swapped between (postponement approach)	RTL
Inventory practices	VMI programme	TAL
	CPFR	TAL
	Small order quantity	Moiselle
Information sharing–internal	ERP system	TAL
	Worldwide corporate PO system for order consolidation	DIS
Information sharing–external	Web-based quotation system	Magenta
	Granted access to styles database for individual suppliers	
	Worldwide corporate PO system for order consolidation	DIS
	Electronic packing lists prepared in web-based shipping information system	
	Order details linked up to label/bar-code provider	
Warehousing	Pick-to-light racking system	TAL
	Cross-docking	

of the production time and thus can be viewed as a bottleneck of the whole production process. To shorten the fabric ordering lead time, many apparel retailers book/commit fabrics in advance with their suppliers before order details are confirmed. In doing so, it requires strong mutual trust between both parties so that manufacturers are willing to act before order confirmation. On the other hand, frequent liaison between retailers and manufacturers is needed to resolve any issues coming up during the course of production. Hence, it is important for both parties to build up a positive relationship and trust for the sake of smooth supply chain collaboration. In this respect, effective and efficient information flow between channel members can improve communication and facilitate collaboration. It is seen from Table 1 that many apparel companies have made investments in employing innovative information technology to enhance information sharing.

4 Managerial Implications and Conclusions

In this chapter, we explored the current industrial practices associated with QR in Hong Kong's apparel industry. We interviewed four companies and performed desk research on two established companies in Hong Kong's clothing industry to gain an understanding of their business practices. We found that most practitioners fully recognize the importance of order lead time reduction. All the firms under study have adopted various measures pertinent to their own situations to strive for lead time reduction (and hence moving towards QR). In particular, we observed that some measures, which are relatively innovative to the fashion industry, such as VMI, CPFR, design procedure swap (to pre-determine fabric in advance) etc., had been adopted by these companies to facilitate the achievement of lead time reduction, which in turn becomes a critical success factor for QR strategy. In addition, various industrial practices, such as small order quantity, ERP and web-based quotation and shipping systems, were reported to be helpful in developing successful supply chains under QR in the apparel industry.

A close buyer–supplier relationship was shown to facilitate the adoption of QR practices. As substantiated by the experiences of RTL and MFR reported in their interviews, their close collaboration with their suppliers and retail-customers facilitate their prompt handling of unexpected events occurring during the course of production, thus minimizing possible delay to their original production schedules.

Information sharing between manufacturers and retailers are also deemed to be critical for successful QR adoption and conducive to enhancing company business performance. As illustrated by the supply chain of TAL and JC Penny, we strongly believe that fashion retailers that want to enhance their supply chain's efficiency should faithfully share information (such as sales data and market trend) with their upstream channel members. Furthermore, as suggested by Mr. Percy Yung, Managing Director of Magenta, in his interview, it is a general trend for fashion retailers and suppliers to form strategic partnerships to cope with the increasingly fierce competition nowadays. Thus from the whole supply chain's perspective, frequent exchange of timely information between channel members is essential and a pre-requisite for an efficient fashion supply chain.

Hence, we highly recommend that apparel companies make a greater effort to adopt appropriate information technologies that enable them to enhance the flexibility of their operations, achieve effective information flow (internally and externally) and facilitate ordering and production process follow-ups, which in turn will help them continuously shorten their order lead times. These actions not only help apparel firms to streamline their business processes, but also establish better buyer–supplier relationships. As discussed in the case report in Sect. 3.1, TAL is a company that is very successful in this aspect. Implementation of both the ERP systems and the VMI schemes has significantly contributed to the success of TAL's supply chain management. In the future, more innovative applications of technology, such as the RFID-based real-time decision support systems as well as intelligent data mining tools, can potentially further enhance the significance of QR practices in the apparel industry.

Acknowledgements We express our gratitude to Mr. Percy Yung of Magenta Wardrobe Fashion Associates Limited and the other three anonymous interviewees for their kind inputs. Thanks are also due to Na Liu and Carol Rego for rendering us various forms of assistance to carry out this research. Tsan-Ming Choi's research was partially supported by the RGC of Hong Kong under grant number PolyU5145/06E. Pui-Sze Chow's research was partially supported by the RGC of Hong Kong under grant number PolyU 5143/07E.

References

Al-Zubaidi H, Tyler D (2004) A simulation model of quick response replenishment of seasonal clothing. Int J Retail Distrib Manag 32(6):320–327

Birtwistle G, Fiorito SS, Moore CM (2006) Supplier perceptions of quick response systems. J Enterprise Inform Manag 19(3):334–345

Carr AS, Pearson JN (1999) Strategically managed buyer-supplier relationships and performance outcomes. J Oper Manag 17:497–519

Choi TM, Chow PS (2008) Mean-variance analysis of quick response program. Int J Prod Econ 114(2):456–475

Choi TM, Li D, Yan H (2006) Quick response policy with Bayesian information updates. Eur J Oper Res 170(3):788–808

Fairbairn LP (1997) Quick Response and global sourcing: Organizational and performance implications for U.S. retailers. PhD Thesis, Michigan State University, USA

Farhoomand A, Ho P (2005) TAL Apparel limited: stepping up the value chain. Asia case research centre case: 05/214C

Fernie J, Azuma N (2004) The changing nature of Japanese fashion: Can quick response improve supply chain efficiency? Eur J Market 38(7):790–808

Fiorito SS, Giunipero LC, Yan H (1998) Retail buyers' perceptions of quick response systems. Int J Retail Distrib Manag 26(6):237–246

Ghemawat P, Nueno JL (2003) Zara: fast fashion. Harvard business school cases: 9–703–497

Giunipero LC, Fiorito SS, Pearcy DH, Dandeo L (2001) The impact of vendor incentives on Quick Response. Int Rev Retail Distrib Consum Res 11(4):359–376

Hammond JH (1990) Quick Responses in the apparel industries. Harvard business school note: N9–690–038

Hunter NA (1990) Quick response in apparel manufacturing. The textile institute, Manchester, UK

Iyer AV, Bergen ME (1997) Quick response in manufacturer-retailer channels. Manag Sci 43(4):559–570

KS Associates (1987) Final report on techno-economic and marketing research study on the textiles and clothing industry for hong kong government industry department, Kurt Salmon Associates. Inc., GA

Lai KH, Cheng TCE, Yeung ACL (2005) Relationship stability and supplier commitment to quality. Int J Prod Econ 96(3):397–410

Lai KH, Wong CWY, Cheng TCE (2008) A coordination-theoretic investigation of the impact of electronic integration on logistics performance. Inform Manag 45(1):10–20

Larson PD, Lusch RF (1990) Quick response retail technology: integration and performance measurement. Int Rev Retail Distrib Consum Res 1(1):17–35

Lowson B, King R, Hunter A (1999) Quick response: Managing the supply chain to meet customer demand. Wiley, UK

Lun YHV, Wong WYC, Lai KH, Cheng TCE (2008) Institutional perspective on the adoption of technology for the security enhancement of container transport. Transport Rev 28(1):21–33

Palmer JW, Markus ML (2000) The performance impacts of quick response and strategic alignment in specialty retailing. Inform Syst Res 11(3):241–259

Perry M, Sohal AS (2000) Quick response practices and technologies in developing supply chains: A case study. Int J Phys Distrib Logist Manag 30(7/8): 627–639

Perry M, Sohal AS, Rumpf P (1999) Quick Response supply chain alliances in the Australian textiles, clothing and footwear industry. Int J Prod Econ 62(1–2):119–132

Sullivan P, Kang F (1999) Quick Response adoption in the apparel manufacturing industry: Competitive advantage of innovation. J Small Bus Manag 37(1):1–13

Whiteoak P (1999) The realities of quick response in the grocery sector - a supplier viewpoint. Int J Phys Distrib Logist Manag 29(7/8):508–519

Efficient Response Systems with RFID Technology: Cases in China

Hongwei Wang, Shuang Chen, Yong Xie, and Qing Ding

Abstract This paper studies four cases in China to illustrate the benefits of radio frequency identification (RFID) in efficient response systems. The first case discusses the warehouse management in the tobacco industry. We propose an RFID-based digital warehouse management system to tackle the low efficiency problem of barcode data collection. The new technology greatly improves the efficient response system in the following dimensions: visualization of inventory management, automatic guided forklift, and reduction of loading time. The second case introduces a communications system based on RFID technology in a primary school. The new system not only improves the management of school, but also enhances the security of the pupils and the supervision of parents. In our current studies, we separately discuss the implementation of our first case in the whole supply chain, and the implementation of RFID for the efficient response in an electronic toll collection system.

Keywords Efficient response · Radio frequency identification

1 Introduction

Nowadays, supply chain management (SCM) with short-life-cycle products is complicated by the short shelf-life of the products, a high number of product variants, a large volume of goods handled, and an unpredictable demand. All these challenges lead to more sophisticated supply chain operations, including production scheduling, capacity planning, and inventory management. These business processes are integrated from the original suppliers to the end customer in such a way so as to provide products and information that add value to both companies and customers. As

H. Wang (✉)
Institute of Systems Engineering, Huazhong University of Science and Technology
Wuhan 430074, PR. China
e-mail: hwwang@mail.hust.edu.cn

T.C. Edwin Cheng and T.-M. Choi (eds.), *Innovative Quick Response Programs*
in Logistics and Supply Chain Management, International Handbooks on Information
Systems, DOI 10.1007/978-3-642-04313-0_19,
© Springer-Verlag Berlin Heidelberg 2010

a result, the use of efficient logistics and innovative supply-chain management strategy, such as efficient response (ER), creates a chance for retailers of short-life-cycle products to tackle these challenges.

ER is a good fit as a SCM strategy that has been widely used in industry since the 1980s (Choi 2006). The two classical ER strategies for logistics management are known as efficient consumer response (ECR) and its variant for the general retail industry, which is known as quick response (QR). The ultimate goal of ER is a consumer-driven responsive system in which the supply chain members work together to maximize consumer satisfaction and minimize costs via improving efficiency of the logistics management (Carney 2003). Hoffman and Mehra (2000) defined the concept of ER as a "natural pull" strategy that uses scanned point-of-sale data to update inventory and trigger replenishment orders based on real-time demand through information technologies. ER allows manufacturers, suppliers, wholesalers, and retailers to work together and share information in near-real time, as well as to quickly respond to the customer's needs.

Although "real time" means something different to each person, the underlying idea is to respond efficiently and quickly to market changes and reduce the lead time for ordering (Hammond 1990). The factors that really make an ER program succeed are upper management's leadership and vision, strong partnerships with customers and suppliers, information technology (IT) that enables information sharing between partners, and a quick manufacturing response time (Blackburn 1991). ER is a series of technologies, such as scanning at checkout counters, which enables the tracking of goods through a supply chain and the sharing of information (Fernie 1994). The above definition indicates that one of the most important parts of an ER program is information sharing, which is traditionally carried out by information technologies such as electronic data interchange (EDI) and barcodes (Mackay and Rosier 1996; Massetti and Zmud 1996; McMichael et al. 1997; McMichael et al. 2000).

In the past decades, barcodes have long been an important technology for ER, which help the industry save production costs, reduce inventories, and prevent overstocking, by reducing manual data handling errors and providing visibility of SCM (Ko and Kincade 1997; Fiorito et al. 1998; Hill 2004). However, there are problems associated with barcode data collection. The disadvantages of using barcodes include a need for manual handling, short distance scanning only, and limited stored information. These disadvantages greatly lower the supply chain efficiency. Hence, there is a growing need for a new technology to sustain ER for tackling new challenges.

In the past decade, a new technology, radio frequency identification (RFID) has become popular in the industry, particularly in the logistics and SCM domain. RFID's advantages over barcodes include a larger memory space and the ability to have unique identification codes, identify multiple objects, scan objects from a long distance, store data dynamically, and be written over multiple times. These benefits have led RFID technology to be utilized in a wide variety of areas such as manufacturing, warehouse management, product tracking, retailing, physical security, and electronic toll collection (ETC) systems.

RFID has been presented as one possible key technology in building more efficient supply chains (Rizzotto and Wolfram 2002). In contrast to the barcode technology, RFID allows supply chain members to automate manual tasks, reduce human errors, and improve the traceability and availability of items, as well as to increase efficiency in the supply chain (Kärkkäinen 2003). Furthermore, items equipped with RFID (also called intelligent items) have the ability to communicate with their environment more efficiently and actively. Moreover, an RFID-based ER system, coupled with a wireless network, allows access to continuous real-time information on "smart items" any time, any where in the supply chain. Therefore, a visible SCM can be achieved. Thus, the unique potential of RFID may offer considerable improvements in ER systems (Bendavid et al. 2006).

In this paper, we describe the advantages of utilizing RFID in ER systems both in supply chains and social services by using a couple of case studies. Two of them have been successfully implemented in China, while the others are still being worked on. These cases should not be unfamiliar to those well acquainted with RFID applications. There are no complicated equations or propositions in this paper; its contribution lies in its rich description of the intuitive benefits brought about by the use of RFID in ER programs, on the basis of real examples. From these cases, we point out that RFID technology can be successfully used in wide areas for ER systems to improve supply chain performance efficiencies, information visibility, and social service efficient response.

2 Literature Review

The objective of SCM is to eliminate friction in the supply chain by enabling the synchronization and sharing of valuable information among trading partners (Kouvelis et al. 2006). The earliest literature about information and ER can trace back to the classic papers by Dvoretzky et al. (1952); Scarf (1959); and Murray and Silver (1966). They analyze the inventory decision policy with Bayersian information updates. After them, vast numbers of literature exploring QR for information collection and procession have come out, most of which focus on two categories in SCM: inventory management (Choi et al. 2004; Choi et al. 2006; Cheng and Wu 2005; Chen et al. 2006; Choi 2007; Choi and Chow 2008; and references therein) and industrial practice (Iyer and Bergen 1997; Ritu et al. 2004; Choi 2006; Choi and Chow 2008, and references therein). However, very few of them took into account the new, up-and-coming technology, RFID, which brings more benefits than the traditional information technology in SCM.

With the development of technology, more and more organizations have moved to RFID to improve the efficiency of material and information flow both within and between organizations. Alongside this industrial interest, academic research on RFID has also proliferated significantly in the last few years. In a related study, working towards elimination of the delay in information sharing, Yao and Carlson (1999) explored the impact of real-time data communication on inventory management in large distribution centers. The authors compared the traditional batch data reporting and RFID-based real time data collection in these centers. Their study results illustrate that the implementation of RFID greatly improved warehouse operations, such as receiving goods, processing orders, handling material, reserving stock, picking up orders, and shipping. Similarly, Lee et al. (2004) explored the impact of the information collected by RFID in a manufacturer-retailer supply chain. The authors compared the effect of inventory accuracy, inventory visibility, and shelf replenishment policy with and without RFID. Their simulation results demonstrated the potential benefits of RFID in terms of inventory reduction and an improvement in service levels.

Another research area on illustrating the impact of RFID technology on the reduction of inventory inaccuracies also attracts attention. Fleisch and Tellkamp (2005) studied the effects of inventory inaccuracies on a retail supply chain. By simulating a three echelon supply chain with one product, the authors proposed that automated identification technology has the greatest potential to achieve the desired inventory accuracies. Kok et al. (2008); Rekik et al. (2008); and Rekik et al. (2009) take into account the three main sources of inventory incorrectness: shrinkage, misplacement of products, and transactional errors. Their studies indicate that the inventory discrepancies can be detected in time and reduced efficiently. Using a theoretical analysis, Uçkun et al. (2008) consider a supply chain consisting of a retailer (distributor) and a supplier. They model a single-period newsvendor-type problem, and conclude that if the market is characterized by highly uncertain demand, making an investment in RFID technology to decrease inventory inaccuracy may be ill advised. Szmerekovsky and Zhang (2008) study the effects of attaching RFID tags at the item level to monitor performance of manufacturers and retailers in a vendor-managed inventory (VMI) system. By comparing the case of RFID enabled and non-RFID enabled VMI system, they conclude that RFID is more of a revenue-generating technology than a cost-saving one. A more comprehensive academic literature review from 1995 to 2005 on RFID technology can refer to Ngai et al. (2008a). The authors organize it into four main categories: technological issues, applications areas, policy and security issues, and other issues.

In contrast to the studies cited above, Chow et al. (2006) analyzed the effect of RFID in an ER system by using a real world case study instead of a simulation. They presented a design of an RFID-based resource management system (RFID–RMS) for use in a warehouse operations environment. The goal of the system was to formulate a resource usage package to enhance the effectiveness of resource operations by integrating RFID, case-based reasoning (CBR) technologies, and the programming model for forklift route optimization. The results of applying RFID–RMS to the GENCO Distribution System were very positive; the utilization of warehouse resources was maximized while work efficiency was greatly enhanced. The authors extend their works in Choy et al. (2008) and Poon et al. (2009).

Similarly, in order to explore the potential business case for RIFD in ER systems, Delen et al. (2007) conducted a case study using actual RFID data collected by a major retailer from the goods shipped by one of its major suppliers. The authors discuss how supply chain partners find information about themselves valuable to each other, and argue that RFID can help to eliminate the delay in information sharing by distributing information from different organizational levels (at the gates, at the shelves, points of sale, etc.) and of different types (backlogs, inventory levels, forecasts, etc.) in real time.

Research efforts to implement RFID for ER in SCM are also made by Ngai et al. (2007), who present a case study of the research and development of an RFID-based traceability system in an aircraft engineering company in Hong Kong. The study reveals that the successful implementation of RFID systems could effectively support the quick tracking and tracing of repairable items in an aircraft engineering company. Moon and Ngai (2008) show that RFID can be implemented in the fashion retailing, and bring the benefits on improving operational efficiency and effectiveness. In order to illustrate the impact of RFID in social services, Ngai et al. (2008b) design an RFID-based sushi management system in a conveyor-belt sushi restaurant. The authors point out that the implementation of RFID can achieve better inventory control, quick responsive replenishment, and food safety control, as well as improve the quality of service.

Since the successful implantation of RFID technology in Chinese national ID cards, China has become the world's biggest market for RFID. However, within our best knowledge, there are few technical articles or case studies to introduce RFID applications in China. Thus, different from the above articles, our paper focuses on the real successful RFID application cases in China, and illustrate that how RFID technology can be successfully used to improve the ER systems.

The rest of this paper is organized as follows. In Sects.3 and 4, we describe our findings from two different case studies on the use of RFID applications. Both sections are divided into three parts that detail the history and background of the particular application, the RFID-based solution, and the benefits of the solution. In Sect.5, we discuss two cases of our current works. We conclude with a summary of the main results and a discussion on the future uses of RFID in Sect.6.

3 Warehouse Management in Tobacco Industry

The tobacco industry is one of the biggest industries in China. Its profits tax accounts for 10% of the national financial revenue. To control tobacco production, the Chinese government requires that all tobacco products for sale should be affixed with a barcode, and that the combined barcode information should then be sent to a government database. In the past, these data were collected by manually scanning the barcode one by one when the products were shipped from the warehouse. It is clear that, with the large throughput of production, the cost of these warehouse operations formed a large part of total costs. Any time saved in handling would be an important competitive advantage. In such a case, most of the tobacco companies have adopted supply-chain management techniques, such as an ER system. However, limited with the lower efficiencies of bar codes scanning, ER did not play a significant role in this situation. In 2008, Wuhan Tobacco Corporation (WTC) of China has been greatly rewarded in that area by using RFID, which eliminated the need to hand-scan each product.

3.1 Company Background

WTC is the third biggest tobacco corporation in China. It has more than 100 warehouses with thousands of different products in different areas. As a short-life-cycle product, tobacco has its own particularities: strict fermentation time requirements, a large number of product variants with very similar appearances, real-time temperature control requirements, and small quantities of different varieties to suit certain customer demands. All these properties determine the complexity of warehouse operations in WTC.

However, due to the disadvantages of the barcodes, the products could not be identified automatically. With greater product variety and increasingly complex customer orders and underdeveloped management technology, products were often mixed up. As a result, operational efficiency has been greatly reduced, as well as inventory inaccuracy has been increased. Therefore, large-scale manpower is required to reorganize these products and prepare for orders. In the face of these problems, WTC's warehouse managers had decided to enhance their warehouse operations by using RFID technology. They specifically used it to achieve the following:

- Help operators pick the products more rapidly and accurately once the assignment decisions had been made
- Improve the operational efficiency of the warehouse as customer orders become more complex
- Improve inventory visibility in the supply chain, so as to better synchronize material and information flows and reduce inventory inaccuracy

3.2 Technology Solutions

In the past, automatic warehouses have played an important role in inventory management as they integrate multiple functions and possess advantages, such as a faster turnover speed, a lower rate of product dilapidation, and the ability to store more products in a smaller area. However, few enterprises can afford automatic warehouses, mainly because they require a large investment and a high level of technological and management capabilities. In addition, they have to be designed for the long term.

On the basis of the above considerations, WTC decided to implement an RFID-based digital warehouse management system (RFID–DWMS) to improve its warehouse operations and enhance its competitive advantage in the tobacco industry. Under the RFID–DWMS solution, pallet level tagging is adopted, as, in most cases, this is the most beneficial mode of RFID adoption in industry (Bottani and Rizzi

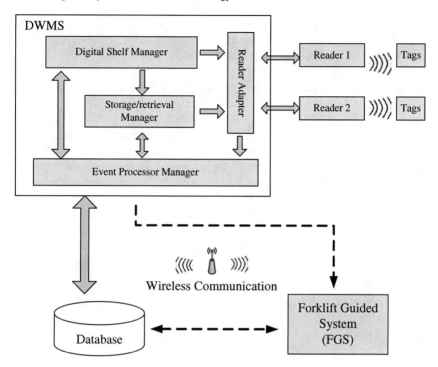

Fig. 1 System architecture of RFID–DWMS

2008).Thus, the RFID tags are placed on pallets, instead of individual products. The RFID tag is fixed in the center of pallet, and takes on the barcode's role, albeit with more automated and faster data collection. When products are transported into the warehouse, the corresponding barcode information will be collected. The RFID tag records the barcode information of all the products on the pallet, as well as other information as required. Two scanning readers, at the entrance and exit of the warehouse, automatically read the tags and collect the information from the pallets when they pass through.

RFID–DWMS integrates RFID and computer and wireless communication technology, and consists of three modules which play different roles. They are digital warehouse management system (DWMS), forklift guided system (FGS), and database, as illustrated in Fig. 1. The DWMS acts as an automatic warehouse manager, automatically collecting the barcode information by scanning the tags when the pallets are transported through the warehouse's doors. It is composed by four core components, digital shelf manager, reader adapter, storage/retrieval (S/R) manager and event processor manager (EPM). As the core component of DWMS, the digital shelf manager is designed to monitor the inventory events in the warehouse and provide a platform for operators to manage the inventory visually. In addition, it provides a digital shelf map to illustrate the real-time inventory status. From the map, the corporation knows where each product and pallet is located in its warehouses, when the products were produced, how long they have been stored, and the combined barcode information. The reader adapter performs as a bridge of relationship between DWMS and physical RFID readers, and collects the data from the pallets. All the collected data are transported to the EPM for advanced processing. As there must be much redundant data and error data collected by the reader, the EPM is designed to group and filter the raw data. In addition, the EPM also takes charge of communicating with the database and providing the corresponding real-time inventory information. The S/R manager is designed to improve S/R assignments. It performs on the basis of a set of basic S/R rules, which are predefined and stored in the database. By incorporating these S/R rules into the system, warehouse operations are no longer dependent on human memory. Instead, all of the operations are performed by RFID–DWMS. The required commands are automatically generated by DWMS and executed by forklifts. Each forklift has a touch-screen computer, called the FGS, which automatically guides the vehicle to transport the pallets, and communicates wirelessly with DWMS. For more details about this case study, we refer interested readers to Wang et al. (2008) (our previous working paper).

3.3 Benefits

By implementing RFID–DWMS, the operating performance in the distribution center warehouse has been improved in three ways. First, detailed inventory information is updated in real time and accurately shown on a map provided by DWMS. As the transported pallets are automatically detected by RFID readers, the inventory information is updated and easily shared in real time. As a result, mistakes resulting from fallible human memory are significantly reduced.

Second, with the help of the FGS, the warehouse operations are similar to those of an automatic warehouse. The managers do not need to notify the operators orally any more, as they can dispatch the relevant commands to the forklifts via the FGS. The drivers can then execute the orders by driving directly to the exact space according to the directions from the automated guided map on FGS, rather than having to search for the location by themselves. Thus, less manpower is wasted and the chances of mistakes in operation are reduced.

Third, loading time has been greatly reduced. As the delivered products are transported in the form of pallets when loading, there is no need for operators to scan the barcodes of individual products, and to manually verify that the right quantity of the right products has been picked. Now, once they drive their forklifts with pallets past the scanner, the barcode data is automatically collected by DWMS, which in turn verifies the validity of the products. If a pallet is picked incorrectly, DWMS will send a message to warn the driver to return it.

Table 1 compares warehousing performance with and without RFID–DWMS. The comparison illustrates that by implementing RFID–DWMS, the number of individuals needed for product loading has been reduced by half, while the average

Table 1 Comparison of warehousing performance without and with RFID–DWMS

Indexes	Without RFID–DWMS	With RFID–DWMS
Loading manpower	8 persons	4 persons
Average loading time	50 min	18 min
Loading ratio	800 boxes	480 boxes
Inventory accuracy	80%	99%

loading time is reduced from 50 to 18 min. In general case, the loading time is a significant part of the lead time. Hence, by implementing RFID, the lead time has been significantly reduced. As the products are transported in the form of pallets, the loading ratio is only 60% of the previous one. However, the drop in loading ratio can be counteracted by raising loading and unloading efficiency, as well as truck turnover, or by adjusting the size of the pallets or the trucks (Lu et al. 2007). Furthermore, using RFID–DWMS increases inventory accuracy from 80 to 99%. The 1% inaccuracy is mostly generated by misreading by RFID scanners. The proposed system shows an overall 98% read rate on the pallet RFID. It is believed that, as RFID readers and tags improve, inventory inaccuracy can be avoided.

4 Home–School Communications System in Primary School

In this section, a home–school communications system (HSCS) is introduced to illustrate that, not only in SCM, but also in social services RFID technology will be of great benefit for ER.

HSCS is an information exchange platform for timely communication between home and school. Research clearly illustrates that effective, responsive, well-planned home–school communication can lead to a positive influence on the children's learning. Bowman (1989) suggested that effective home–school communication can facilitate teachers' responsibility to interpret and relay the school's agenda to the parents. Bhattacharya (2000) identified a strong link between parents and teachers as a factor protecting children from dropping out of school. Henderson and Mapp (2002) analyzed 80 studies of parental involvement in schools, and pointed out that the effective communication can bring benefits for both home and school.

The traditional method for communication is to schedule and invite parents to school for face-to-face conversations, usually one or two times a semester. However, some families have busy lives and it is difficult for parents to be involved in school. Hence, more and more schools have to find new ways to establish relationships with parents without inviting them to school, such as telephone, message, newsletters etc. Dyson (2001) investigated 40 families in Canada and found that the most popular method among parents was still the in-person communication. A combination of in-person contact, written messages, and telephone conversations was the second-most popular option, followed by an augmentation of the mixture with newsletters or formal interviews. With the development of information technology and the popularization of internet, computers, and mobile phones, large HSCSs based on computer and mobile platform have been proposed (Chen 2006; Ma and Wu 2006; Gan et al. 2006; Wang et al. 2007; Jiao and Zhao 2007). As the function of these systems was limited to the simple mutual communication, another important function, a timely and effectively notice of the children's arrival/departure time for parents has been ignored. It will be more cared for by parents than any other information, especially by the pupils' parents.

Pupils are a special group. They have a limited ability to protect themselves, making it easier for them to, for example, be hurt in traffic accidents or be kidnapped. They also lack the capacity to restrain themselves; for example, they may play truant or not return home directly after class. However, most of the pupils travel to school by themselves. This may either be because their parents are too busy to accompany them, or because the parents would like to enhance their children's independence. Therefore, the guardianship, safety, and school attendance of school pupils cannot be guaranteed. In such cases, a timely and ER to emergencies is exceedingly important to school and parents.

On the other hand, a school also has, in general, the responsibility to guarantee the safety and attendance of pupils when they are in the school. It is also the biggest dispute between schools and parents. When something happens to children, parents usually assume that schools should bear the main responsibility. At the same time, the schools argue that the children are playing truant and are thus out of their guardianship. Therefore, a timely means of monitoring children is a significant issue that needs to be addressed.

4.1 Background of the Pilot Primary School

The pilot primary school in Wuhan has more than 2,000 pupils. As Wuhan is the biggest city in the center of China, most of the pupils live far away from the school. The traditional way, face-to-face conversation, is not suitable for the communication between home and school. Very few parents were present in the scheduled meeting in the past years. Also, it is difficult for teachers to visit home by home. That is why the school seeks new technology to build a bridge between home and school. The feedback of a set of questionnaires illustrated that the exact arrival/departure time of the pupils is the most concerned information by the parents. Thus, the school takes into account the adoption of RFID-based HSCS to achieve the following functions:

- Providing a platform for school to publish the various types of school information (e.g. homework) and the living and learning state of the pupils to their parents
- Detecting the exact time of the pupils' arrival/departure and reporting it to their parents in real time
- Providing a platform for parents to feed back their suggestions to school

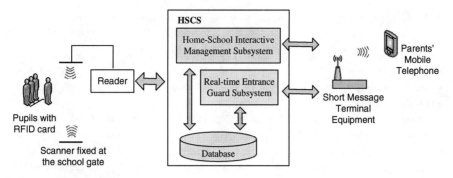

Fig. 2 System architecture of HSCS

4.2 Solutions

In this section, we proposed a HSCS that used RFID. HSCS is not only a home–school interactive management system, but also an entrance guard system that monitors pupils' access to the school. As shown in Fig. 2, HSCS consists of two subsystems, home–school interactive management subsystem (HSIMS) and entrance guard subsystem (EGS). And two terminal equipments are also contained in this system, RFID equipment for monitoring and collecting data and short message terminal equipment for sending and receiving corresponding information.

With the implementation of mobile communication network, HSIMS realizes the communication between school and home at any moment and any where. The relevant information, such as pupil's learning attitudes, behavior in school, school activities, and homework, will be inputted in the computer and sent to the parents' mobile phones as short messages. In addition, the parents can feed back their suggestions or their children's behavior at home to school via mobile phones.

An RFID tag is embedded in each student's identity card. As the tag ID is unique and cannot be over-written, the student's identity card can be detected and identified as the pupils' ID. All pupils are required to pass through the school gate with their student's cards, so that their information is collected in a timely manner, including the students' ID, names, entrance time, leaving time, and school attendance situation. The information is then sent via short message service (SMS) to their parents' mobile telephones in real-time.

The messages parents receive will provide them with real-time notification of their children's attendance, and understand whether or not the length of time taken by their children to reach school is regular. If parents do not receive a message in regular time, they can reasonably assume that either an accident has happened to their children or that they are playing truant. In such cases, an ER policy will be used to react to these emergencies.

4.3 Discussions

The real-time collection and notification of students' school attendance has greatly enhanced the safety and security of the pupils. Besides helping schools improve their management and supervision, it has also clarified the division of responsibilities for a child's guardianship between school and parents.

However, some issues still exist that should be taken seriously. First, since this system is based on the SMS platform, it requires the parents to have a mobile telephone. With economic development, this will be not a problem in the future. Second, while the multi-object identification property of RFID technology makes it possible to allow crowds of pupils to pass through the gate at the same time, it may be difficult to confirm that the reader has collected the right amount of the right information from the right pupil. This is especially when a single individual has multiple cards or no card at all. Schools should take additional measures to enhance the safety and security in school and prevent such things from happening. Finally, if a misreading occurs, it is difficult to find out which child's card was misread. Hopefully, the continued development of RFID technology will help overcome these challenges.

5 Extensions of RFID Application for Efficient Response in Other Ways

As more and more RFID applications have been successfully used in China, it is no doubt that RFID technology is of great benefit to the ER system in different areas. Therefore, we do not stop our steps at the above case studies. In this section, we give a brief discussion of extending RFID application for ER in the following two ways, on which we are have been focusing our efforts recently: extension of the RFID–DWMS application to the whole tobacco supply chain, and an RFID-based ETC System.

5.1 RFID–DWMS in the Whole Tobacco Supply Chain

As discussion in Sect. 3, the WTC's warehouse managers have greatly benefited from implementing RFID–DWMS and thus improving their warehouse operations. However, this system was only implemented in WTC's distribution center warehouses for an experiment. The upstream partners (e.g. production suppliers) and downstream partners (e.g. wholesalers and retailers) still operate in traditional ways by using barcode technology. Therefore, to save the cost, the tagged pallets should be returned back for reuse, when they are transported to the downstream partners. Although, RFID–DWMS improved the warehouse operations in the distribution center warehouses, an additional operation, separating pallets, must then be

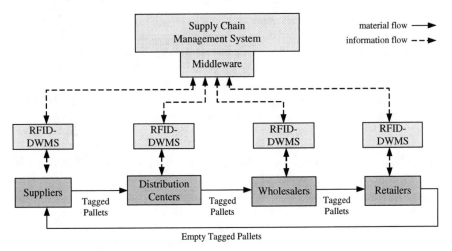

Fig. 3 System architecture of extended RFID–DWMS

incorporated. From the perspective of the total supply chain, this will greatly reduce, or even counteract the benefits of RFID.

The best solution to this problem is to develop a unified specification in the whole tobacco supply chain to make sure that products flow throughout the whole supply chain in the same forms between different partners. Hence, the RFID tagged pallet may become the norm, rather than the exception, in all distribution centers and even in the other supply chain sections. Furthermore, RFID–DWMS implemented in different areas can be in turn networked using middleware to a dedicated management system, which can be remote accessed by every member in the supply chain, as shown in Fig. 3. Only in this way, can the supply chain obtain the greatest benefits.

From the system architecture, it is clear that the products entering and exiting the warehouse's door can be easily detected. The information will then be collected and shared in the same management system. In such a case, real-time inventory information could be shared with all members of a supply chain. This would help synchronize information and material flow, as well as support the use of VMI in a supply chain. As a result, the ER policies of members of a supply chain will be more effective, and the bullwhip effect can be reduced.

5.2 RFID Applications in Electronic Toll Collection System

Another promising area for development of RFID application is the ETC. With the rapid development of the Chinese economy, more and more highways are being built as the number of vehicles increases. The traditional toll stations which necessitate stopping traffic have becomes the bottle-necks of the highways and result in bad congestions in southern China. To avoid these events happening again, the Chinese government has decided to invest in a new technology called ETC.

ETC is a system that makes use of automatic vehicle identification (AVI) technology based on RFID, to realize the wireless communication between vehicles and toll stations, and register automatic payment. An ETC system should consist of three sub-systems: automatic vehicle identification system (AVIS), short distance communication system (SDCS), and video enforcement system (VES).

AVIS, the most important function in ETC, is the process of determining the identity of the vehicles that have passed. Some early AVISs used barcodes technology to identify the vehicles, which were read optically at the tollbooth. However, the poor performance of barcode readers greatly decreases the efficiency of identification. In contrast, RFID tags will completely eliminate this problem. SDCS would determine the required payment of vehicles, and automatically deduct it from the amount stored in customer accounts. When the balance is running low, SDCS will send a warning message. The last sub-system, VES, is designed to photograph the vehicles that have passed without ETC cards.

By implementing ETC, vehicles will be allowed to pass through toll systems quickly without congesting nearby traffic. Even more, with the information sharing on networks, the information of when the vehicles passed by the station and where the vehicles have been passing by can be clearly collected for tracking them. However, we are still researching how to guarantee the accuracy of identification and adding the possible corresponding remedial measures.

6 Conclusion

The above case studies illustrate the benefits of utilizing RFID technology in ER programs. We aim to provide intuitive benefits for those who are interested in combining RFID technology with ER research. From these cases, it is clear that RFID technology has greatly improved ER programs in both SCM and social service areas.

As all the systems are pilot systems used by pioneering organizations, there are still some problems being uncovered with the implementation of RFID technology. First, cost is one of the major factors that influences whether RFID will be rapidly extended to different areas. The question that whether the attainable benefits can be off-set by the high capital investment required has been widely argued (Burnell 1999). Indeed, the current price of RFID facility is still too high to be afforded by most of the companies, especially in China, where most RFID facilities are imported from foreign markets. Therefore, the RFID systems must be designed as a closed-loop system, in which, the tags can be reused circularly. In such a case, the applications of RFID will be more acceptable for the implementers.

Second, the misreading made by RFID readers is a serious problem that reduces its credibility. Hence, the biggest problem for blocking the implementation of RFID technology in ER system must be how to make the managers believe the potential benefits of the new information technology and obtain the top management and executive support. It is clear that the top management support is the first step towards success in the implementation of the new technology. In order to get the management and user commitment and understanding on RFID, we suggest that a prototype system should be developed to test its feasibility and advantages before starting a real trial. With the help of prototype system, it gives the managers an intuitive understanding on RFID technology. Therefore, a prototype system is significantly necessary before a real trial. As technology develops, the above issues should not persist in the future. For more RFID applications, we refer interested readers to the free e-book edited by Polniak (2007), which contains the RFID implementation experiences of 25 different organizations from around the globe in different application areas.

In terms of future study in this domain, a challenging but useful extension might come from looking into possibilities of using RFID technology in anti-counterfeiting systems. With the benefits of large information storage space and the ability to be written over multiple times, we believe that there exists immense potential benefits from RFID combined with coding technology in this area.

References

Bendavid Y, Wamba SF, Lefebvre A (2006) Proof of concept of an RFID-enabled supply chain in a B2B e-commerce environment. Proceedings of the 8th international conference on electronic commerce 13–16 August, pp 564–568

Bhattacharya G (2000) The school adjustment of South Asian immigrant children in the United States. Adolescence 35(137):77–86

Blackburn JD (1991) The quick response movement in the apparel industry: a case study in time-compressing supply chains. In: Blackburn JD (Ed) Time-Based Competition. Richard D. Irwin, Homewood, IL, pp 246–269

Bottani E, Rizzi A (2008) Economical assessment of the impact of RFID technology and EPC system on the fast-moving consumer goods supply chain. Int J Prod Econ 112(2):548–569

Bowman BT (1989) Educating language-minority children. Phi Delta Kappan 71(2):118–120

Burnell J (1999) Users will overcome many obstacles and implement RFID, study predicts. Automat News 15(5):26

Carney V (2003) B2B eCommerce trading processes and the enabling technologies used in the retail industry – risks, benefits and future developments. http://veritycarneyalgebra.spaces.live.com/blog/cns!77D0B3E1ED13FACD!306.entry. Accessed 02 Feb 2003

Chen GH (2006) Short-message communication between family and school. Comput Syst Appl 6:72–75

Chen H, Chen J, Chen Y (2006) A coordination mechanism for a supply chain with demand information updating. Int J Prod Econ 103(1):347–361

Cheng TCE, Wu YN (2005) The impact of information sharing in a two-level supply chain with multiple suppliers. J Oper Res Soc 56(10):1159–1165

Choi TM (2006) Quick response in fashion supply chains with dual information updating. J Ind Manag Optim 2(3):255–268

Choi TM (2007) Pre-season stocking and pricing decision for fashion retailers with multiple information updating. Int J Prod Econ 106(1):146–170

Choi TM, Chow PS (2008) Mean-variance analysis of quick response program. Int J Prod Econ 114(2):456–475

Choi TM, Li D, Yan H (2004) Optimal single ordering policy with multiple delivery modes and Bayesian information updates. Comput Oper Res 31(12):1965–1984

Choi TM, Li D, Yan H (2006) Quick response policy with Bayesian information updates. Eur J Oper Res 170(3):788–808

Chow HKH, Choy KL, Lee WB, Lau KC (2006) Design of a RFID case-based resource management system for warehouse operations. Expet syst Appl 30(4):561–576

Choy KL, Chow KH, Moon KL, Zeng X, Lau HCW, Chan FTS, Ho GTS (2008) A RFID-case-based sample management system for fashion product development. Eng Appl Artif Intell. doi:10.1016/j.engappai.2008.10.011

Delen D, Bill CH, Sharda R (2007) RFID for better supply-chain management through enhanced information visibility. Prod Oper Manag 16(5):613–624

Dvoretzky A, Kiefer J, Wolfowitz J (1952) The inventory problem: II. Case of unknown distributions of demand. Econometrica 20:450–466

Dyson LL (2001) Home-school communication and expectations of recent chinese immigrants. Can J Educ 26:455–476

Fernie J (1994) Quick response: an international perspective. Int J Phys Distrib Logist Manag 22(6):38–46

Fiorito SS, Giunipero LC, Yan H (1998) Retail buyers' perceptions of quick response systems. Int J Retail Distrib Manag 26(6):237–246

Fleisch E, Tellkamp C (2005). Inventory inaccuracy and supply chain performance: A simulation study of a retail supply chain. Int J Prod Econ 95(3):373–385

Gan J, Peng, XG, Zhu B (2006) The research and realization of instant messaging system on family and campus network on network platform. Net Commun 9:85–87

Hammond JH (1990) Quick response in the apparel industries. Harvard Business School, (N9–690–038), Cambridge, MA

Henderson A, Mapp K (2002) A new wave of evidence: The impact of school, family, and community connections on student achievement. Annual synthesis, Austin: southwest educational development laboratory. eric document reproduction service, No. ED474521

Hill S (2004) Apparel logistics: new technology, trends, and industry developments: Management briefing: RFID. Just-Style 22–23

Hoffman JM, Mehra S (2000). Efficient consumer response as a supply chain strategy for grocery businesses. Int J Serv Ind Manag 11(4):365–373

Iyer AV, Bergen ME (1997) Quick response in manufacturer–retailer channels. Manag Sci 43(4):559–570

Jiao WF, Zhao JL (2007) Study on communication between home and school system based on mobile education platform. Inform Tech Appl Educat; IEEE Int Symposium 23–25 November, 478–482

Kärkkäinen M (2003) Increasing efficiency in the supply chain for short shelf life goods using RFID tagging. Int J Retail Distrib Manag 31(10):529–536

Ko E, Kincade DH (1997) The impact of quick response technologies on retail store attributes. Int J Retail Distrib Manag 25(2):90–98

Kok AGDe, Donselaar KHV, Woensel TV (2008) A break-even analysis of RFID technology for inventory sensitive to shrinkage. Int J Prod Econ 112(2):521–531

Kouvelis P, Chambers C, Wang H (2006) Supply chain management research and Production and Operations Management: review, trends, and opportunities. Prod Oper Manag 15(3):449–469

Lee YM, Cheng F, Leung YT (2004) Exploring the impact of RFID on supply chain dynamics. Simulation Conference, Proceedings of the 2004 Winter 2:1145–1152

Lu SP, Wu YH, Fu YT (2007) Research and design on pallet-throughout system based on RFID. Automat Logist IEEE International Conference on 18–21 August. 2592–2595

Ma S, Wu JS (2006) Development and testing of home-school communication software based on VSTS2005. Sci Tech Eng 6(17):35–48

Mackay DR, Rosier M (1996) Measuring organizational benefits of EDI diffusion: a case of the Australian automotive industry. Int J Phys Distrib Logist Manag 24(10):60–78

Massetti B, Zmud RW (1996) Measuring the extent of EDI usage in complex organizations: strategies and illustrative examples. MIS Quarterly 20(3):331–345

McMichael H, Mackay DR, Altmann GL (1997) Quick response in the Australian textile clothing and footwear industry. European Conference on Information Systems, University of Cork, Ireland, pp 295–312

McMichael H, Mackay D, Altmann G (2000) Quick response in the Australian TCF industy: a case study of supplier response. Int J Phys Distrib Logist Manag 30(7–8):611–626

Moon KL, Ngai EWT (2008) The adoption of RFID in fashion retailing: a business value-added framework. Ind Manag Data Syst 108(7):596–612

Murray GR, Silver EA (1966) A Bayesian analysis of the style goods inventory problem. Manag Sci 12(11):785–797

Ngai EWT, Cheng TCE, Lai K, Chai PYF, Choi YS, Sin RKY, (2007) Development of an RFID-based traceability system: experiences and lessons learned from an aircraft engineering company. Prod Oper Manag 16(5):554–568

Ngai EWT, Moon KKL, Riggins FJ, Yi CY (2008a) RFID research: An academic literature review (1995–2005) and future research directions. Int J Prod Econ 112(2):510–520

Ngai EWT, Suk FFC, Lo SYY (2008b) Development of an RFID-based sushi management system: The case of a conveyor-belt sushi restaurant. Int J Prod Econ 112(2):630–645

Polniak S (2007) The RFID case study book: RFID application stories from around the globe. Abhisam. http://www.rfidebook.com

Poon TC, Choy KL, Chow HKH, Lau HCW, Chan FTS, Ho KC (2009) A RFID case-based logistics resource management system for managing order-picking operations in warehouses. Expet Syst Appl 36(4):8277–8301

Rekik Y, Sahin E, Dallery Y (2008) Analysis of the impact of the RFID technology on reducing product misplacement errors at retail stores. Int J Prod Econ 112(2):264–278

Rekik Y, Sahin E, Dallery Y (2009) Inventory inaccuracy in retail stores due to theft: An analysis of the benefits of RFID. Int J Prod Econ 118(1):189–198

Ritu L, Xie T, Subramaniamb R (2004) Efficient consumer response in Japan Industry concerns, current status, benefits, and barriers to implementation. J Bus Res 57(3):306–311

Rizzotto P, Wolfram G (2002) Intelligent tagging - getting supply chain smart. The 2002 official ECR Europe conference, montjuïc 2 conference centre ECR Europe, Barcelona, Spain

Scarf H (1959) Bayes solutions of the statistical inventory problem. Ann Math Stat 30(2):490–508

Szmerekovsky JG, Zhang J (2008) Coordination and adoption of item-level RFID with vendor managed inventory. Int J Prod Econ 114(1):388–398

Uçkun C, Karaesmen F, Selçuk S (2008) Investment in improved inventory accuracy in a decentralized supply chain. Int J Prod Econ 113(2):546–566

Wang HQ, Cui XC, Cao ZH (2007) A framework of web-based mobile learning platform for teachers' professional development. Int Conf Comput Sci Educ 1226–1229

Wang HW, Chen S, Xie Y (2008) An rfid-based digital warehouse management system in tobacco industry: a case study. Working paper, Huazhong University of Science and Technology, Wuhan, PR China

Yao AC, Carlson JG (1999) The impact of real-time data communication on inventory management. Int J Prod Econ 59(1–3):213–219

The Emergence of the Fast Fashion Business Model and Imposed Quick Response Challenges for Chinese Fabric Manufacturers

Jennie Hope Peterson, Jimmy Chang, Yiu-Hing Wong, and Carl A. Lawrence

Abstract This chapter explores and develops fast fashion in the current retailing industry and its impacts on how the Chinese textile manufacturing industry has adjusted to remain competitive. Fast fashion evolved at the turn of the twenty-first century into a business approach characterized by fresh fashions, shorter life cycles, and faster production, placing significant pressure for rapid delivery, quality products, and low prices for each segment of the supply chain in a highly competitive environment. Manufacturers must utilize dynamic capabilities to maximize their competitive advantages in their production strategies, business models, and activities toward achieving retailers' fast fashion requirements. The main aims of this reported study were to examine the "need" for fast fashion in the current retailing industry and to look at its impacts on the Chinese textile manufacturing industry. The focus was therefore on textile suppliers' production strategies, and the suppliers' intentions and activities toward achieving their customers' fast fashion requirements. A study with Chinese fabric suppliers analyzes the dynamic capabilities and production methods applied in response to the fast fashion industry. Steps were taken to develop a framework for future research into the crucial production planning and manufacturing of fabrics for the fast fashion retail market. Attempt is made to identify the organizational changes following a shift in the industry environment, in the context of how a textile factory adapts to a change in its manufacturing as a result of the onset of fast fashion.

Keywords China · Dynamic capabilities · Fabric suppliers · Fast fashion · Production · Quick response · Retailers

J.H. Peterson (✉)
Institute of Textiles and Clothing, The Hong Kong Polytechnic University, Hunghom, Kowloon, Hong Kong
e-mail: jhopepeterson@yahoo.com

T.C. Edwin Cheng and T.-M. Choi (eds.), *Innovative Quick Response Programs in Logistics and Supply Chain Management*, International Handbooks on Information Systems, DOI 10.1007/978-3-642-04313-0_20,
© Springer-Verlag Berlin Heidelberg 2010

1 Introduction

The global clothing sector provides the world's second largest economic activity at a value of more than $1 trillion USD, encompassing a broad range of pursuits from textile and garment production to high profile celebrity and designer press coverage in the fashion media (Ruddock 2007; Jackson and Shaw 2006). The most recent business approach in the textile and clothing industry called "fast fashion" emerged at the turn of the twenty-first century, utilizing proven quick response (QR) manufacturing methods to secure current market trends and effectively reflect those fashions in constantly changing merchandise assortments to meet market demand. QR systems aim to reduce development and production lead times with more efficient manufacturing and enhanced information technology, thus reducing the transaction costs with improved time efficiencies, inventory reductions, and increased return on investments (Bruce et al. 2004; Bruce and Daly 2006; Hammond and Kelly 1990; Sen and Zhang 2009). In addition to prevailing QR methods, fast fashion companies compete further to differentiate their clothing through trend relevance and style, price, and quality (Bruce and Daly 2006; Fernie and Sparks 1999). Although the idea of fast fashion is relatively new, textile and clothing (T + C) companies world-wide are adopting this business strategy to further enhance their sales by embracing the latest fashions and consequently limiting over-stock items and discounted clothing. Competitive retailers optimizing this business approach move forward with hard line buying and sourcing standards through revised and precise production and logistic strategies, which require their suppliers to successfully manufacture products and services in-line with this new tactic (Bruce and Daly 2006; Sheridan et al. 2006). This chapter will explore the development of dynamic capabilities of the woven cotton piece-good supply chain in China and Hong Kong in response to the emergence of the relatively new "fast fashion" retail business strategy and the consequent manufacturing adjustments along the supply chain which improved production output and reduced production costs for the Chinese factories. In addition, the following text will overview a qualitative research study conducted by means of in-depth interviews with eight large Chinese textile factories to gain accurate data on the changes that are currently implemented to coincide with fast fashion's model. The data may be beneficial to buyers and suppliers in understanding difficulties faced by both producers and retailers in the fast fashion industry and may provide the possible changes China should make to further secure a competitive advantage in the global textile industry. Lastly, a model will be presented, which is useful to textile industry professionals for a better understanding of time management and costs associated with alternative production methods. Current research in fast fashion generally does not extend toward the manufacturing arm in China and to the reaction of the product suppliers; therefore, this work offers unique insight into the ways in which the T + C factories prioritise, manage, and innovate to remain competitive.

1.1 Fast Fashion

Fashion is about change and expression delicately intertwined with timelines and seasons which establish value. It is motivated by new styles and innovative designs, and also carries a sense of distinctiveness and imagination, which is risky and can offer fewer profits to large manufacturers if mainstream consumers do not embrace the look (Jackson and Shaw 2006). Luxury brands and couture houses demonstrate creativity and artistic styling through their fashion designs as art and market group association and symbolism with their goods, and so consumers' desires for new clothing and expressions have become both physical and emotional as societal changes reflect in fashion to communicate and convey consumer identity (Jackson and Shaw 2006; Tungate 2005). Modern technology and the mass media are key tools for consumer exposure to more styles and retail brands. These platforms provide instant and convenient access to today's ever-changing fashion realm through press coverage of designer fashion shows and celebrity trends from around the world (Jackson and Shaw 2006; Tungate 2005). High-street labels observe the newly broadcasted luxury designs, immediately begin manufacturing a similar version to be ready within just 6 weeks, and market the look in a way that is affordable and represents status to those without the means to buy true luxury goods (Jackson and Shaw 2006). The luxury lifestyle attached to new trends and celebrity adoration misleads consumers into believing they can assume new emotional identities by getting rid of previous fashions and buying new ones (Tungate 2005). As a result, the mass-produced items become somewhat disposable and quickly irrelevant, as new styles appear the next season in luxury brands, on celebrities, and in fashion shows (Menkes 2002). The idea of combining luxury and fashion is novel because luxury was once thought to be nearly unobtainable and reserved for the truly elite in society, while the term fashion today is ubiquitous and low prices make "fashion" in clothes and small accessories affordable to many, even in slow economic times (Bruce and Daly 2006; Jackson and Shaw 2006). It is a new concept and thus, fast fashion retailing is born.

Fashion retail brands are now divided into three categories: luxury, high street, and supermarket/discounter. As supermarkets such as Target and Wal-Mart enter the fashion realm and attract one-stop price conscious shoppers, competition on the high street has increased (Gannaway 1999). For most clothing companies, this competition within the past 5 years has led to price reductions and reflects the new democratization of fashion in which the majority of the population in developed nations can afford to buy high-street items, thus increasing consumer shopping power and the demand for fashionable clothing (Bruce and Daly 2006; Jackson and Shaw 2006; Ruddock 2007). With this in mind, clothing in the fast fashion sector of the market exists primarily in the middle and upper middle segments (see Fig. 1) which have lower prices, higher volumes, and a consumer who seeks a consistent variety in changing styles and colors (Eberle et al. 2004).

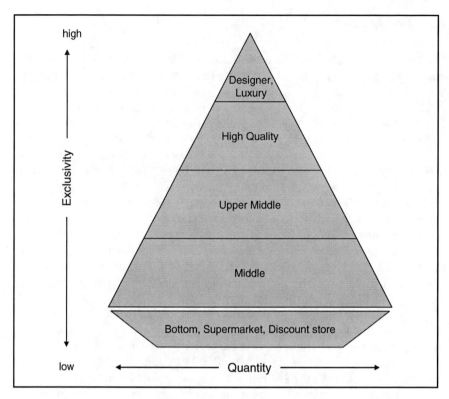

Fig. 1 Clothing quality levels (Eberle et al. 2004)

1.1.1 Zara's Business Model

Perhaps the most applauded business in the fashion industry for exemplifying QR and fast fashion with rapid stock delivery is the internationally sold Spanish clothing retailer Zara, with more than 400 stores in 25 countries (Economist 2005; Folpe 2000). With the latest trends distributed in an unprecedented 15 day lead-time, Zara far out-paces traditional retailing practice and has created a global phenomenon with low prices and high fashion looks straight off the catwalk (Ferdows et al. 2004; Folpe 2000). One key to Zara's success is the ability to maintain a focused product range which presents a collection of 79% commodity items with just 20% of the business falling into the fast fashion category (Mintel Group 2002). The company is 60% vertically integrated and therefore out-sources just 40% of its production to suppliers who accept fluctuations in order quantities, thus preventing costly overproduction, consequent merchandise discounts, and inventory risks which are characteristic of the retailing industry. As a result, stores receive rapid replenishment of on-trend merchandise in small batches, often using less expensive fabric, streamlined buying methods, and source from reputable suppliers to keep prices and transaction costs down (Ferdows et al. 2004; Folpe 2000). With so much stock turn-around in the merchandise, consumers in Central London visited Zara stores six times more often per year compared with the average store (BBC 2007; Ferdows et al. 2004).

1.2   Retail Buying Cycle: Traditional vs. Fast Fashion

The traditional fashion buying cycle is 9–12 months with a reliance on data from historical sales to forecast future business, and involves a production commitment of 6 months before the in-store date (Birtwistle et al. 2003). An example for such a buying and development plan (see Fig. 2) details the lengthy and highly specific calendar used by a large well-known American retail giant for their fabric development – from design and concept through bulk production.

The projected time for each fabric to evolve from idea to workable cloth is at least 9 months and significant buying time is invested in two separate rounds of fabric sample production before committing to a bulk order. Risks to this approach include inaccuracy from out-of-date information and difficulties targeting market changes (Bruce and Daly 2006). In today's media-based market, trends often evolve and evaporate within that time span and as a result approximately 33% of off-trend merchandise in traditionally operated retailer stores is marked down because consumers have changed their fashion preferences within the 9–12 month buying cycle (Bruce and Daly 2006). Shoppers want to see the freshest styles in stores and are no longer flexing their spending power in traditional retail stores which operate on the basis of calendars similar to that shown in Fig. 2.

In contrast, fast fashion retailers maintain a leading edge in the highly competitive clothing industry by implementing classic QR strategies, prompt and direct development with suppliers, and keen marketing sensibilities to mass-produce on-trend, inexpensive collections in record time with global distribution (BBC 2007; Bruce and Daly 2006; Ruddock 2007). The quick replenishment of products through frequent, smaller, repeat orders to suppliers is more expensive than traditional retail practices because retailers pay a premium to expedite transportation of garments for on-time delivery to the store and manufacturers charge higher prices for smaller order sizes (Birtwistle et al. 2003; Hammond and Kelly 1990; Mintel Group 2002). The faster a store displays new collections, the more it will sell (Eberle et al. 2004); therefore, fast fashion companies work on 6–15 week buying cycles and increase the number of delivered "seasons" for constant change in store merchandise. As a result, 12 seasons of styles (see Table 1) are produced rather than the traditional four. For example, the below back-to-school (BTS) season in August specifically targets children and college-aged students who do not wear uniforms and often shop for new school clothes at the end of the summer. Although more expensive, fast fashion companies reduce the marked-down stock and lost sales by focusing on consumer demand and building a progressive supply chain rather than sales forecasting (Birtwistle et al. 2003; Bruce and Daly 2006; Hammond and Kelly 1990; Kline and Wagner 1994; Mintel Group 2002). It was predicted that T + C companies which

		Annual Calendar of a Typical Fashion Label							
EVENTS	**LOGIC**	***SUM '08***	***FALL '08***	***HOL '08***	***RESORT '08***	***SP '09***	***SUM '09***	***FALL '09***	***HOL '09***
Begin Fabric Development	45 days prior to fabric selection	4/24	7/2-7/3	8/10-9/14	9/24	1/7	3/28-4/11	6/16	8/6-9/30
Design Concept Presentation	45 days prior to design handoff	5/11	8/1	10/2	12/13	2/11	5/1	7/28	9/15
Color handover with color names	7 days after concept turnover	5/11	8/1	9/17	11/6	2/18	5/5	8/1	9/30
Fabric / Yarn selection with preliminary colors assigned	45 days prior to design handoff	5/18	8/1	10/5	11/7	1/22-3/7	5/8-5/9	8/4	10/6
Handoff print artwork / Yarn dyes	6 weeks before samples	6/20	8/22	10/26	11/30	1/27-3/7	5/20-5/28	9/5	10/24 -11/14
Fabric Codes assigned	3 days after fabric selection	5/23	8/1	9/21-10/5	12/20	1/25-3/10	5/11	8/7	10/8
Order Development Yardage	40 days prior to proto yardage at factory	5/22	7/23-8/1	9/21-10/5	12/21	3/18	5/12-5/30	8/8-8/11	10/1-10/13
Development Yardage x - mill	40 days after order proto yardage	7/3	8/30	10/26	1/25	4/18 x-mill	6/6-7/2	8/27-9/8	10/27-11/12
Fabric quality / Lab dip / development approval due	7 days prior to order sample date	7/25	9/26	12/7	3/14	5/2	7/23	10/17	12/12
Order Fabric samples in each bulk color	45 days prior to all sample due in fty	8/1	10/3	12/14	3/21	5/9	7/30	10/24	12/15 -1/9
Samples in each color due at garment factory	7 days prior to sample fit approval deadline	9/14	11/19	2/1	5/2x-mill	6/27x-mill	9/22	12/5	2/23
Book Bulk Fabric	3 days before merch meeting	12/3-12/4	1/25-1/29	4/14	7/7-7/8	8/21-8/22	11/21	1/23	4/15
Bulk Fabric Ex-factory, Arrives Garment Factory	60 days after booking bulk order	2/4	3/29	6/14	9/9	10/22	1/20	3/23	6/15
Total time for only fabric development	***Allow 8-10 months for fabric development***	***7.5 mo.***	***7 mo***	***8 mo***	***10 mo.***	***8 mo***	***7 mo***	***8 mo***	***8 mo***
		4/24 -12/4	***7/2 -1/29***	***8/10-4/14***	***9/24-7/9***	***1/7-8/22***	***3/28-9/20***	***6/16-1/23***	***8/6-4/15***
Total time for fabric from development to bulk completion	***Allow 10-12 months for fabric production***	***9.5 mo.***	***9 mo.***	***10 mo.***	***12 mo.***	***10 mo.***	***9 mo***	***10 mo.***	***10 mo.***
		4/24 - 2/4	***7/2 - 3/29***	***8/10- 6/14***	***9/24-9/9***	***1/7-10/22***	***3/28-11/20***	***6/16-3/23***	***8/6-6/15***

Fig. 2 Calendar of traditional retailer (Borrowed from anonymous retailer)

Table 1 US and UK apparel seasons (Modified from Jackson and Shaw 2006)

Fashion seasons/sub-seasons	Months
Early spring (Resort)	Jan–Feb
Spring (Valentine's Day, etc)	Feb–March
Early summer	April–May
Summer	May–June
High summer	June
Summer Sale	June–July
Transitional fall	July–August
Back-to-school (BTS) (non-uniform)	August
Fall	Sept–Oct
Party wear	November
Christmas (Holiday)	December
Winter Sale	Dec–Jan

did not adapt to the new fast fashion business model would lose customer interest and likely be out of business by 2010 (Folpe 2000). In order to incorporate this new industry model, it is necessary for companies to not only modify design and marketing methods, but also to change businesses operation entirely, including information technology upgrades and sourcing strategies (Sheridan et al. 2006).

Textile suppliers are of particular interest as a link in the clothing supply chain because fabric sourcing is often the first step in a retailer's collection planning. Textiles are the essential building blocks to fashion trends and developing a clothing product as they convey fashion trends and influence the mood of a clothing collection (Bruce et al. 2004; Yu 2008). The ability for textile suppliers to refine their capabilities and adjust their fabric production methods to increase speed and/or reduce costs and thus improve efficiency and attractiveness to fast fashion retailers is paramount for survival in the modern clothing industry. Prior to evaluating individual supplier firms, however, a retailer must carefully determine the global location for establishing supply chain networks which are compatible with their business strategies and product development ideologies.

1.3 China's Competitive Advantages for Fast Fashion

In January 2004, the United States International Trade Commission (USITC 2001) stated, "China is expected to become the 'supplier of choice' for most US importers (the large apparel companies and retailers) because of its ability to make almost any type of textile and apparel product and any quality level at a competitive price..." (Helander and Möller 2007). Since the lifting of trade quotas, retailers have more options for determining where to set up their supply chain. In research literature on the topic of China's manufacturing in the face of trade liberalization, six key factors (A–F) established in an analytical framework by USITC (2004) were regarded as influential to the arrangement of retailer production and sourcing. We will refer to these six key factors to highlight China's competitiveness in the textile industry.

China's capabilities in all six categories help secure its competitive advantage in the global textile and clothing manufacturing industry.

1.3.1 Business Climate and Infrastructure

With regard to retailers' supplier selection, the primary considerations are the conditions of a country, including government policies, economic infrastructure, community harmony, limited barriers to market, and a clear respect for human ethics. Of critical importance and a huge determining factor for buyers who are setting up sourcing strategies and introducing suppliers into their buying matrix is also whether a country is able to support the retail buying process with solid infrastructure for telephone and computer communication, trade documentation and logistics, availability of shipping, transport, and other logistic support, and research and testing facilities for development and quality assurance purposes (Birnbaum 1993; Tait 2002; World Bank Report 2005) The 1977 Open Door Policy introduced market reforms in China which reduced government interference in the economy and paved the way for a new era of production in the textile and clothing industry which was in the forefront of the movement because of the ability to employ a large number of laborers from a country population of 690 million (Chi and Kilduff 2006; XINHUA 2005). Currently, textile and clothing production in the eastern areas of China offers ease of logistic handling and trading as a result of the efficient ports in Shanghai and Hong Kong with a huge investment to further improve transport systems and infrastructure for Western China where many raw materials and new factories are located for a smooth vein of delivery (Towers and Peng 2006). Furthermore, foreign retail corporations are attracted to the stability of modern China's government and swelling economy with 8–9% GDP growth per year (Jackson and Shaw 2006). Because of planned development, China's supply chain and textile industry have grown consistently and in a balanced way (Chan and Au 2007).

1.3.2 Proximity to Major Markets

Fast fashion requires rapid replenishment schemes with capable key suppliers; therefore, factory and supplier locations are critical in ensuring the fastest lead-times for the products to arrive to the store locations (Abernathy 2000; Appelbaum 2005). In determining supply chain members, retailers must weigh the importance of logistics and proximity between the fabric manufacturer and the clothing distribution center with regard to transportation prices and the cost of risks connected to buying fabrics in new locations and from new suppliers (Appelbaum 2003). Because of the far distance from the US and Europe, Chinese factories must aggressively compete with East European countries to earn key programs with retailers looking for opportunities to have products in-store quickly. China may be able to shorten its lead-times by quickening its manufacturing processes with efficient QR systems brought about with dynamic capabilities and at the same time, offering competitive prices. Although Romania, the Czech Republic, and Hungary are all within a few days travel to Europe (Tait 2005), they may not be able to compete against China's increasingly low communication and transportation costs (Someya et al. 2002; Towers and Peng 2006). China's success is further enhanced by the cluster approach which associates the economic success of firms within an area to the bond they have among their own nearby competitors in the region vs. their isolated rivals (Schiele 2006). Thus, manufacturers located in regional groups create an unspoken union which attracts buyers to easily source, develop, and communicate with a clustered manufacturing area which provides skilled labor, shorter lead-times due to a close-knit supply chain, access variety, knowledge, innovation, lower costs due to price competition, and other sourcing advantages which are unavailable with more isolated suppliers (Homburg and Kiedaisch 1999). However, innovation processes with the greatest success are established within close geographical proximity to buyers, so China-based companies should travel often to their western customers for development discussions (Garg et al. 2004).

1.3.3 Market Accessibility

China's entry into the WTO in 2001 and the reduction of quotas in 2004 helped to provide China with a better opportunity to access international markets, specifically Western Europe and North America. China's success and large surge of exports to these high-volume markets of developed countries was possible only after the quota elimination (Chen and Shih 2004; JUST STYLE 2007; XINHUA 2005).

1.3.4 Labor and Management

Every global competitor needs a comparative advantage. In the case of China, the comparative advantage is its specialization in labor-intensive products and its great population of inexpensive and skilled workers (Towers and Peng 2006; Lemoine and Ünal-Kesenci 2004). The managers within the labor force are also low-cost, yet very effective. Prior to the 1990s, Hong Kong, Taiwan, and Macau were the dominant textile producers in the China region. It was in these areas where many current managers in the clothing industry began their careers before migrating to the more productive mainland China for better opportunities and expanding factories (Towers and Peng 2006). Compared to some other developing nations such as Bangladesh, India, and Vietnam which compete in the textile and clothing industry, China's wages are higher, but because of the higher resultant productivity, the actual labor cost is lower when evaluated in terms of cost per unit produced (USITC 2004).

1.3.5 Raw Material Inputs: Access to Quality and Cost-Competitive Fabric Production

China remains the world's largest textile exporter and an attractive leader in textile exports for global retailers as a result of several reasons, including the domestic availability of plentiful raw materials, and a highly supported logistical network of exporters, shippers, administrators, etc (Chan and Au 2007; Spinager 1999). China imports as well as domestically grows a large amount of the cotton which it spins, weaves, and sells as finished fabric and garments to ensure lower production costs with abundant supply and easy accessibility through a vertical supply-chain (Abernathy et al. 1999; Towers and Peng 2006). Without regional accessibility to raw material goods, a country cannot vertically integrate its supply chains or offer competitive delivery schedules.

1.3.6 Vertical Integration of Industry Service: Quality and On-Time Delivery

The final and most critical determining factor for a retailer in seeking a supplier is whether a factory can offer services and products which meet the market requirements (Birnbaum 1993). China benefited from a reorganization of manufacturing throughout in Asia in the 1970s which allowed China to become the production base of Asia by developing an infrastructure familiar with exportation, familiarization with the production of foreign innovations in the technology industries, and rapid growth along the provinces on the southern coast, namely Guangdong province (Lemoine and Ünal-Kesenci 2004). The long-established business networks within China, Hong Kong, Taiwan, and Macau help provide a platform of smooth logistics for development, skills exchanges, shipping, administration, licensing, and banking. This connectedness and vertical integration throughout the industry in China and Chinese areas allow for modern product innovation, knowledge growth, and easier exporting processes which help prevent delivery delays. This vertical ability is a major competitive advantage in supplying both commodity goods and fashion-forward goods for the fast fashion industry because the supply chain from raw materials through to garment production and exporting is integrated for straightforward communication and short cycles capable of modifying product development according to market fluctuations (Towers and Peng 2006; USITC 2001).

1.4 Supplier Management

Upon evaluating and establishing supply chain locations and building a matrix of suppliers, competitive retailers must further improve links in their manufacturing network with QR efficiencies by reducing the inconsistency of production and bringing together the business processes along the supply chain to shorten delivery lead-times and lower costs—both vital in fast fashion businesses (Garg et al. 2004; Perry and Sohal 2000). In textile manufacturing, building a long-term relationship with a retailer through careful management of committed customer service is an effective competitive advantage in an industry challenged to compete for product differentiation and short lead-times (Abratt and Kelly 2002; Helander and Möller 2007; Vargo and Lusch 2004). Customer focused strategies designed for cooperative assessment along the supply-chain help to ensure efficient and effective delivery of correct merchandise by use of IT tools and flexible processes which eliminate wasted resources (Sheridan et al. 2006). The requirement for suppliers to be customer driven is a relatively new change in the industry as retailers demand far more of their suppliers than in previous years and evaluate manufacturers on meticulous sourcing criteria in an effort to achieve "lean retailing and replenishment" objectives which are cost savings, fewer warehouses, lower transport costs, and faster deliveries. Suppliers must handle the burden of added costs and risks of lean retailing through an understanding of their retailers' needs and creation of their own management strategies and systems to accommodate demands for shorter development cycles and more efficient delivery and transport processes (Birtwistle et al. 2003; Abernathy et al. 1999). Fast fashion retailers require rapid replenishment through readily available stocks of fabric and therefore often request suppliers to hold production space in the factory or to begin fabric production before an order confirmation. If the confirmed order is less than anticipated, there is an over-abundance of yardage or unoccupied machines on the factory floor. If the confirmed order is larger than expected, it challenges suppliers to manufacture additional yardage in a shorter length of time. The relationship between the supplier and retailer is critical to ensure that both parties profit and maintain fair expectations (Birtwistle et al. 2003; Burger and Cann 1995).

Once retailers establish a relationship with a fabric supplier, they continue to discuss factors pertaining to each order – reaching new agreements and compromising on terms like price, payment methods, inventory management, order size, lead-times, and logistic parameters such as transportation, inspections, and color breakdowns. The garment manufacturer also becomes involved in the contract process, and all three parties must agree on terms before production will begin (Yu 2008). Although the garment manufacturer becomes involved, the textile and garment industries are not similarly structured. The textile industry heavily depends upon strong capital investment in machinery and relies on efficiency in order to be successful. The overhead is relatively constant, profiting through steady orders and efforts to achieve production close to maximum capacity. Textile mill performance is based on productivity and factory managers seek to maintain a competitive advantage with lower unit production costs by increasing processing volume. A fabric supplier's production management determines its success, as this establishes the quality of goods, speed of delivery, and inspection of the fabrics. Figure 3 illustrates the production and processing operations of a fabric supplier. Careful management of these planning processes is essential for retailers to guarantee there is capacity in the fabric supply factory. Without on-time fabric production, clothing manufacturers cannot begin their design, and cut and sew production, and the merchandise will be late to the store floor. Clothing manufacturing is highly labor intensive and requires less capital investment compared with textile production. In this regard, labor wages are a primary consideration for retailers aiming to keep production costs down and they are likely to shift garment factories into different regions to command lower prices. On the other hand, retailers find it more difficult to establish a long relationship with an efficient textile factory and therefore, buyers and

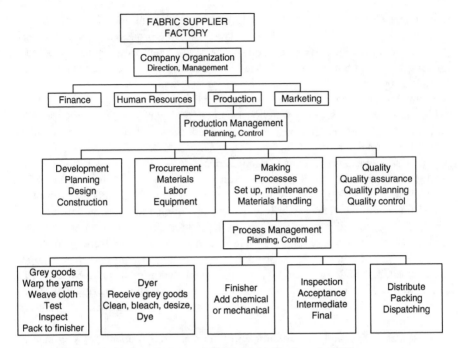

Fig. 3 Factory structure and organization (Modified from Eberle et al. 2004)

clothing manufacturers who source fabric tend not to shift production location due to of a limited fabric supplier base (Jackson and Shaw 2006, Bruce et al. 2004; Eberle et al. 2004; and Yu 2008).

Although the supplier base is more constant, strong local and global competition exists and suppliers face dire competition to out bid one another as retailers reduce clothing prices to consumers by sourcing in low cost countries where new suppliers are emerging (Bruce and Daly 2006; Gereffi 1999). Retail merchandisers aim to establish contracts with the most competitive suppliers with the fastest deliveries and the lowest costs (Bruce and Daly 2006, Hammond 2006; Sheridan et al. 2006; and Sen and Zhang 2009). Suppliers should achieve basic criteria such as successful past sales, similar current customer base, competitive price points, fast delivery speed, and the innovation and aesthetic ability to develop compatible products. Beyond these classic supplier characteristics, suppliers must differentiate with added value factors such as inventory risk management, problem solving skills, fluid communication, knowledge sharing, innovation and product diversity, replenishment flexibility, service, and the application of integrity and protection for their clients (Abernathy 2000; Asanuma 1989; Helander and Möller 2007; Towers and Peng 2006). Factories which are able to offer all of these qualities are employing "dynamic capabilities" and will benefit from developing the best long-term, trust-based relationships with client retailers, which is a critical factor in the supply chain for mutual buyer/supplier benefits of solutions and expertise (Abernathy 2000;

Asanuma 1989; Sheridan et al. 2006). Through the adoption of dynamic capabilities, suppliers may differentiate themselves from their competitors in critical elements such as innovation, service, and quality.

1.5 Supplier Dynamic Capabilities and Innovation

The theory of dynamic capabilities builds upon foundations provided by Schumpeter (1934), Penrose (1959), Williamson (1985), Barney (1986), Nelson and Winter (1982), and Teece and Pisano (1994). Schumpeter's Theory of Economic Development (1934) relies on the belief that successful development involves a process of creating a product and offering its advantages to the customer before anyone else does the same thing. Dynamic capabilities rely on this theory but add that the managerial processes within the firm (supplier) are vital in order to properly exploit and organize the development of change and innovation. In order to connect with fast fashion retailers and meet their expectations, suppliers should adopt dynamic capabilities, influenced by internal learning, organization and ability within a firm, competitor, or customers' influences, and capture new opportunities and markets (Johnsen and Ford 2006; Teece et al. 1997; Teece 1998). Applying this internal learned knowledge of market changes in a valuable way for one's customers will provide a competitive advantage in the level of service and will help build long-term relationships (Johnsen and Ford 2006; Leonard-Barton 1992). Without the ability to effectively harness learned information in tandem with a third party such as a retailer, however, a capability does not truly exist (Johnsen and Ford 2006).

The essence of dynamic capabilities is a firm's behavioral orientation and core capabilities responding to external changes (Wang and Ahmed 2007). These core capabilities are firm-specific assets acquired through development and change, as opposed to resources which are controllable inputs (Johnsen and Ford 2006; Teece et al. 1997; and Teece 1998). Changes in a company model are often expensive and time-consuming (Teece 1998); therefore, fabric suppliers investing in developing dynamic capabilities must be prepared to alter the management to production systems, specialize (in a process, type of fabric, or customer base), understand their strengths and niche in the T + C industry, and build upon their achievements, experiences, and values in order to differentiate from their other suppliers in product innovation, flexibility, cost control, production lead-times, service, quality, etc (Jackson and Shaw 2006; Walter et al. 2001). Those suppliers who adjust their production methods to variations in trends with flexible and responsive efficiency improvements will benefit with a competitive advantage and will be valued, attractive contributors in today's fashion industry (Chesbrough and Teece 1996; Möller and Törrönen 2003). The ability of fabric suppliers to refine their dynamic capabilities to primarily improve time valuable production and processing management (see Fig. 3) will improve attractiveness to retailers – paramount for survival in the modern textile industry (Eberle et al. 2004; Yu 2008).

Three component factors reflect the common features of dynamic capabilities across firms. These are adaptive capability, absorptive capability, and innovative capability. Adaptive capability, for example, is a fabric supplier's ability to identify and capitalize on emerging market opportunities, such as fast fashion. Absorptive capability is the ability of a supplier to recognize the value of new external information, assimilate it, and apply it to commercial end, such as creating on-trend fabrics or improving production lead-times. Firms with a high absorptive capability demonstrate a strong ability of learning from partners, integrating external information, and transforming it into firmly embedded knowledge. The cluster approach and China's vertical strong networks of production will help Chinese suppliers better utilize absorptive capabilities from their manufacturing connections for shared information and resources (Homburg and Kiedaisch 1999; Schiele 2006; Towers and Peng 2006; USITC 2001). Innovative capability would refer to a supplier's ability to develop new products and/or markets, through aligning strategic innovative orientation with innovative behaviours and processes. Conceptually, these three capabilities underpin a firm's ability to integrate, reconfigure, renew, and recreate its resources and capabilities in line with industry changes (Wang and Ahmed 2007).

Innovation is a major economic driver and platform for competition in industrialized economies, pushing companies to create novel information, develop new products, and improve performance in globally changing business environments with new merchandise, ideas, methods, devices, services, technologies, or strategies (Bala Subrahmanya 2003; Foster 1986; Lannes and Logan 2004; Montalvo 2006; Mukherjee et al. 2004; PDMA 2008). Companies face financial challenges to sustain growth in sales and profits, largely determined by whether or not they understand strategies in survival. The S-shaped learning curve for innovative products (see Fig. 4) shows that under continued technology, increased production will bring diminishing returns. In the case of textile suppliers and fabric production, continual innovations through dynamic capabilities can prevent this decrease and ensure increasing profits by resetting the company's position on the curve (Foster 1986; Liao et al. 2008).

Correct direction of knowledge resources such as research and development teams is an important issue for innovation management and maintaining an organization's competitive information technologies needed to prevent reliance upon

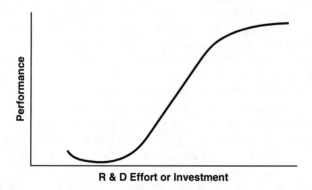

R & D Effort or Investment

Fig. 4 Technology curve for R&D performance (Foster 1986)

outdated experience (Hammond and Kelly 1990; Nonaka 1994). The capability of a fabric supplier to innovate is dependent upon how that factory obtains knowledge resources and the application of the information to create new processes (Aragon-Correa et al. 2007). The innovations within industrial manufacturing must be efficient in order to be successful. Manufacturing and information technologies exist such as CIM, CAD/CAPP/CAM-CAQ to facilitate swift development and production innovation within the textile and clothing industry. Their purpose is to offer advantages in cost reductions, quality improvements, and time efficiencies. Such technology is an example of how textile suppliers may use software and other available resources to contribute toward a competitive advantage (Aragon-Correa et al. 2007; Mukherjee et al. 2004; Yu 2008). Application of new information technologies will likely require a higher standard of employee education in many factories which traditionally employed uneducated workers. In strategically planning to innovate, suppliers must be willing to question and change long-held beliefs about their mission, customers, capabilities, and/or strategy to produce changes in practices, policies, and values (Argyris and Schön 1996; Senge 1990; Shahimpoor and Matt 2007).

2 Methodology

China is currently the number one textile and apparel manufacturer and exporter in the world with predictions that China will account for providing 36% of the world's textiles by 2010 and 50% by 2020 (Appelbaum 2005; Nathan Associates 2002; USITC 2001; Walmsley and Hertel 2000). In addition, it is the most popular outsourcing location for many retailers in developed countries which compete on price because of lower operating costs in production and wages and as a result, China has developed skills and an understanding of technology in order to maintain a stronghold in the global textile and clothing industry (Anson 2005). For these aforementioned reasons, China is the targeted location for researching how and why fabric suppliers in the textile and clothing industry have adjusted their production methods in the face of the new retail business strategies of fast fashion. Fast fashion is changing the systems for sourcing, buying, and distribution management within the T + C industry, so China's textile factories must evaluate their businesses in terms of what dynamic capabilities they may offer to maintain their position as the world's leader in retail exportation through this period of change (Johnsen and Ford 2006). To achieve the aims and objectives of this study, an empirical approach was adopted, which included the following four major stages:

1. A review of literature on the impact of the fast fashion business strategy on competition and innovation in the global textile and clothing industry in general and the Chinese T + C industry in particular.
2. On the basis of the literature, a theoretical framework was devised as a basis to illustrate process planning in conjunction with fast fashion production.

3. An exploratory study through convergent interviews, a questionnaire survey, and a post-hoc study.
4. A qualitative approach of multiple-case research with convergent interviews was conducted in preference to other research methodologies.

2.1 Case Research Design

Justification: Case research is one of the qualitative research methods. It differs from those case studies/stories used as teaching devices in business administration programs, as case research is widely recognized by researchers (Dyer and Wilkins 1991; Eisenhardt 1989; Miles and Huberman 1994; Parkhe 1993; Perry and Coote 1994; Yin 1994) as a method of developing theories (Parkhe 1993; Stokes and Perry 2005; Yin 1993). This research approach is particularly well suited to new research areas or research areas where existing theory seems insufficient (Bonoma 1985; Deshpande 1983; Eisenhardt 1989; Yin 1994). For this work, the research sought to seek answers to "how" and "why" problems that focused on a firm's development of dynamic capabilities in response to the challenges from fast fashion. This is a "contemporary phenomenon within some real-life context" and the investigator has little or no control (Dyer and Wilkins 1991, Patton 1990; Parkhe 1993; Yin 1994); therefore, the case research is the most appropriate methodology to explore at a practical level.

Once the research methodology was established, it was necessary to decide on types of case research, selection of cases, and number of cases to use in the research. There are four types of design for case research (Yin 1994) (see Table 2). This study adopted Type 4 – multiple-case research with embedded sub-cases.

A single-case research has one case to study while multiple-case research consists of over two cases in the same study. Multiple-case research has been strongly advocated by many authors (Deshpande 1983; Bonoma 1985; Gersick 1988; Patton 1990; Parkhe 1993; Romano 1989; Yin 1989) to improve the quality of collected data and research findings. This preference is because multiple-case design presents data that can be used for testing theory, can offer a full variety of evidence, can be used for theory generation, and can be used for investigation of complex social phenomena (Bonoma 1985; Eisenhardt 1989; Gersick 1988; Patton 1990; Parkhe 1993; Yin 1989). The evidence from multiple-case design is more compelling than single-case research and the overall study is regarded as being more compelling. Therefore, multiple-case research was adopted for this study, so that literal and theoretical replication from a range of respondents can be obtained.

Table 2 Basic types of designs for case research (Yin 1994)

Unit of analysis	Number of cases	
	Single-case designs	Multiple-case designs
Holistic (single unit)	Type 1	Type 3
Embedded (multiple units)	Type 2	Type 4

For the unit of analysis, embedded-case analysis is more preferred to holistic-case analysis, as it was anticipated that there would be a number of smaller cases embedded in a bigger case that is the basic unit of analysis for a study. These sub-cases are called "embedded cases" (Yin 1994). The important issue in embedded cases is that each of the embedded cases in each big case must be considered and compared with other embedded parts of the same big case, *before* the big cases can be compared. For example, the strategic business units within each corporation have to be analyzed to find the pattern within each corporation, before several corporations can be compared.

Each case examined consisted of the analysis of one factory to determine whether it had recognized the need for a change in operational management to suit the production needs for fast fashion retail customers. In addition, the actions taken to alter or modify production and management were determined. The work focused on three major departments of each firm as they are directly affected by the fast fashion business model. The development of dynamic capabilities is crucial for them in response to the challenges incurred:

1. Sample and bulk production planning
2. Quality assurance and efficiency of service
3. Marketing/Sales

2.2   Number of Cases

It is often a misleading idea that more cases would always lead to greater validity of a case research because the amount of information in each case is critical (Romano 1989; Dick 1990). However, Patton (1990) stressed that "the validity, meaningfulness, and insight generated from qualitative inquiry have more to do with the information-richness of the cases selected and the observational/analytical capabilities of the researcher than with sample size." In this research, eight cases were appropriate, as this was a pilot project study intended for further follow-up as PhD research. In addition, time constraints of approximately 8 months limited the length of time available to seek additional factories and production professionals.

2.3   Modified Convergent Interview

Convergent interviewing is an in-depth technique with a structured data analysis process – a technique used to collect, analyze, and interpret qualitative information about a person's knowledge, opinions, experiences, attitudes, and beliefs using a number of interviews which converge on important issues (Dick 1990; Nair and Riege 1995). Such a series of in-depth interviews with experts allows the researcher to refine the questions after each interview in order to converge on the issues in a topic area. The questions are inserted into the "conversation" whenever appropriate

(Carson et al. 2001). In this way, interviewees are able to give more freely their own opinions on and insights into the pre-determined topics. This approach is suitable for uncovering underlying beliefs about, attitudes toward, and deeper insights into a topic being researched (Koste et al. 2004) as well as for providing more opportunities to probe beyond the initial responses, resolve ambiguities, and overcome any unwillingness to answer particular questions (Yin 1994).

The convergent interviews, undertaken in order to solicit the needed information, involved a series of in-depth consultations with production professionals who worked with or for fabric supply companies in order to solicit the needed information. Targeted interviewees included retail industry managers, factory managers, and industrialists. The convergent interview was carried out by first gathering information during a topic-centered conversation with industry professionals regarding changes in the production industry since the year 2000. This unstructured interview provided critical information and answered key questions in a relaxed atmosphere. The answers enabled formulation of the specific questions included in the follow-up survey. The flexibility of convergent interviewing arises out of this continuous refinement of content and process. The interviews in this study were concluded after two rounds of interviews: The first was a relaxed conversation with broad consideration on the topic of production. The second was a questionnaire survey which covered fast fashion specific issues relevant to all interviewees.

As the number of cases was settled at eight, the total number of interviews was 14. The study was therefore on a small scale owing to time limitation and should only be considered a pilot study. In a larger study with greater time and resources, the standard convergent interview process would continue until agreement among interviewees was achieved and disagreement among them was explained, for example, by their different industry backgrounds; on all the issues (Nair and Riege 1995).

Convergent interviewing was used for this research for the following main reasons:

First, the nature of the respondent made it impractical to hold group discussions. The respondents sought for this research are top management or functional managers who are unlikely to be readily available; therefore, gathering six to ten executives in one place at the same time for a focus group discussion would have been extremely difficult.

Second, the kind of information needed for this work was considered to be best collected from the in-depth interview instead of focus groups. That is, the researcher did not plan to obtain unexpected findings from a free-flowing group interaction which is the usual outcome from focus group discussions (Bellenger et al. 1976; Lederman 1989; Levy 1979; Malhotra 1993; Morgan 1988). Instead of having an hour and half to 2 h focus group discussions, the in-depth interviews of the same duration for *each* factory/firm was deemed more suitable as the researcher needed to collect proprietary information from each particular respondent.

Third, the convergent interviewing allowed refinement of both questions and responses over a series of two interviews with knowledgeable people in the early stage of the research (Rao and Perry 2003).

The last reason was that the convergent interviews could be organized so that they were spread over the literature review time span of the research project, enabling important information gleaned from the literature at the time to be incorporated into the discussed topics of the interviews, thereby gaining useful feedback from each respondent. This benefit would not be possible if the focus groups approach was to be adopted (Rao and Perry 2003).

2.4 Design of Questionnaire Survey

Following the initial conversation with broad consideration on the topic of production, a structured questionnaire was first distributed via email in order to allow for the interviewee to prepare and allocate time for the interview. The interviews were administered with the help of a Chinese translator within 1 week of sending the questionnaire via email. Interviews were conducted on the telephone and in-person. The survey questions had eight categories:

1. Promotion
2. Price
3. Product development/Innovation
4. Production (Sample)
5. Production (Bulk)
6. Quality control
7. Delivery and logistics
8. Future expectations

Following the research and data analysis, factory managers and textile experts were contacted again for a follow-up, post-hoc study/conversation. Ideas and information generated from the survey were discussed in order to come up with a conclusion and clear analysis of the data.

2.5 Data Analysis and Model Confirmation

The data captured from the interview were analyzed qualitatively using the content analysis technique (Carson et al. 2001), which is defined as "the objective, systematic, and quantitative description of the manifest content of a communication" (Koste et al. 2004). This analytical approach is based on the theory that repeating certain elements of discourse – that is, words, expressions, and similar meanings – reveals the research context (Thietart 2001). In this study, the answers from different informants to common questions were scrutinized to identify, code, and categorize the primary patterns and themes related to the research issues. The professional opinions were accepted as critical indicators of production improvements, implemented in order to meet fast fashion needs, and highlighted inefficiencies which China may still improve in order to maintain a competitive advantage. Finally, the results of the analysis were used to verify the conceptual framework and thereby illustrate the links of various dimensions of the dynamic capabilities, such as the adaptive, absorptive, and innovative capabilities (Wang and Ahmed 2007), with the achievement of a firm's strategic objectives.

3 Theoretical Framework and Research Issues

A conceptual framework is described, which was developed to show how a manufacturing firm in the textile-apparel supply chain might shift to the strategic approach of using dynamic capabilities to establish rent-creation capabilities in response to the dynamic fast fashion marketing environment. Rent-creation capabilities are composed of resource-picking mechanisms and capability-building mechanisms found within strategic management (Makadok 2001). This framework forms the basis for the lines along which the research was conducted. The framework shows six elements that are believed to be directly or indirectly associated with the background and consequence of dynamic capabilities. A series of propositions may be set to illustrate the interrelationships of these stages (see Fig. 5). The key research issues to be studied are described as below.

3.1 Research Issue 1: Dynamic Capabilities

The essence of dynamic capabilities is a firm's behavioral orientation and core capabilities responding to external changes. Wang and Ahmed identify three component

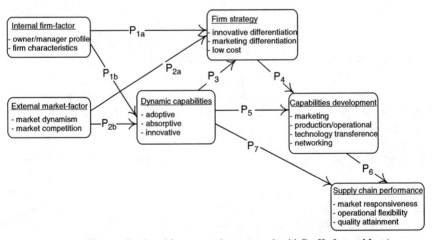

(Source: developed for post graduate research with Dr. Ka-Leung Moon)

Fig. 5 Theoretical framework (Source: developed for post graduate research with Dr. Ka-Leung Moon)

factors which reflect the common features of dynamic capabilities across firms (Wang and Ahmed 2007). These are adaptive capability, absorptive capability, and innovative capability. A firm's dynamic capabilities are believed to be influenced by both internal firm factors, and external market factors. In general, firms with different characteristics may have different motives to acquire dynamic capabilities; while the more dynamic and competitive a market environment is, the stronger is the drive for firms to exhibit dynamic capabilities. Two propositions are set to illustrate these arguments (see Fig. 5):

P_{1b} – *Internal firm factors are the antecedents of a firm's attainment of dynamic capabilities.*

P_{2b} – *External market factors are the antecedents of a firm's attainment of dynamic capabilities.*

3.2 Research Issue 2: Firm Strategy

As stated by Teece et al. (1997), industrial organization theory takes an outside-in approach and considers the essence of strategy formulation as relating a firm to its environment. According to this industrial organization theory, a firm must find itself a favorable position in an industry from which it can best defend itself against competitive forces, or even influence them in its favor by such strategic actions as deterring entry or raising barriers to entrance, etc (Porter 1980). Hence, external market factors may have an impact on a firm's choice of strategies such as innovative differentiation, marketing differentiation, and low cost. Internal firm-related factors, such as organizational, marketing, and technical assets, as well as top management profiles, are also found to have a strong positive effect on a firm's strategy decision. Moreover, the more a firm is equipped with resources and the stronger are its capabilities to use these resources, the more likely it is to develop a more complex and advantageous strategy. Three propositions are set to express these relationships and situations (see Fig. 5):

P_{2a} – *External market factors are the antecedents of the choice of firm strategies.*
P_{1a} – *Internal firm factors are the antecedents of the choice of firm strategies.*
P_3 – *Dynamic capabilities are the antecedents of the choice of firm strategies.*

3.3 Research Issue 3: Capability Development

A fashion supply chain member that attempts to use dynamic capabilities as its strategic approach ought to do the following:

1. Identify latent capabilities within the firm that are widely accepted as valuable and appropriate for advancing supply chain objectives (Pablo et al. 1996).

2. Create opportunities for individuals to take personal initiative for organizational advancement
3. Encourage the development of trusting relationships to support individual initiatives.

Capability development is defined by as "an outcome of a firm's dynamic capabilities over time" (Yin 1993). Measures for such capability development often involve a comparison of the same aspects of certain capabilities of a firm at different points in time. The key to a firm's survival and success lies in its ability to create a set of distinctive capabilities that enable it to stand out in the competition (Dierickx and Cool 1989). Various studies revealed that dynamic capabilities play a substantial part in the accumulation of such rent-creation capabilities as marketing, production/operation, technology, and/or networking by firms of various kinds, for example, technological capability (Figueiredo 2003), new product development capabilities (Clark and Fujimoto 1991), project capability (Brady and Davies 2004), technology adoption and integration capability (technology transference capability) (Woiceshyn and Daellenbach 2005), service capability (Athreye 2005), and networking capability (Lawson and Samson 2001; Weerawardena et al. 2007). A proposition is set to show such relationship (see Fig. 5).

P₅ – The attainment of dynamic capabilities has an influence on a firm's ability of developing needed capabilities.

Firms operating in a certain industry at a certain point of time must choose the right strategy to use or create core capabilities responding to market changes, and hence, the more dynamic a market is, "the 'sooner, more astutely, and more fortuitously' the firm needs to upgrade and recreate its core capabilities, and the higher the level of dynamic capabilities the firm demonstrates." Another proposition is set to illustrate the influence of a firm's strategic decision on its ability to develop rent-creation capabilities (see Fig. 5).

P₄ – A firm's ability of developing needed capabilities is directed by its firm strategy.

3.4 Research Issue 4: Supply Chain Performance

In the competitive market of "fast fashion," the constant ordering process for new development requires that a firm possesses an extremely efficient supply chain performance, such as that in market responsiveness, operational flexibility, and quality assurance. Survival of competition in today's market heavily depends upon the supplier's "ability to integrate, build, and reconfigure internal and external competences to address rapidly changing environments" (Teece et al. 1997). A proposition is established to emphasize this point (see Fig. 5).

P₆ – The development of needed capabilities has an influence on a firm's supply chain performance.

Managers need to be aware of their strengths and weaknesses in acquiring these capabilities, and understand the relevance of these capabilities to their supply chain performance. They should also know how to balance their existing resources, acquire external resources, and combine available resources in new ways (Wilson and Daniel 2007) to maintain their competitiveness in the international arena. Thus, another proposition is set (see Fig. 5).

P_7 – *The attainment of dynamic capabilities has an influence on a firm's supply chain performance.*

4 Case Research Procedure

4.1 Profile of Companies Surveyed

Eight companies that were appropriately related to the fast fashion production life cycle were examined to evaluate how/if the firms had adjusted production and planning control to compete for business in the price-, quality-, and time-competitive clothing industry. Each company represented one case, which was further broken down to analyze differences in material planning and control, production management, marketing, and service. Interviewee Cotton King, for example, is a converter which facilitates and provides trading services among different factories, and as such, offers contrasting, yet insightful information throughout the study. Meanwhile, the other seven firms interviewed are factories with vertical set-ups with yarn spinning, weaving, dyeing or/and finishing processing capabilities with a similar customer base consisting of primarily American, European, and local Chinese end-consumers with a medium price-point. Approximately 30–40% of the factory orders at the time of the study were from fast fashion buyers. The company names have been changed to maintain confidentiality (see Table 3).

4.2 Interview Location and Conduct

In-depth, yet casual conversations with production professionals who worked with or for fabric supply firms helped create a more focused and specific set of survey questions to better tackle the subject of fast fashion. These conversations were the first step in the modified convergent interview process. Through these discussions about the current economic challenges as well as the changing retail business strategies, questions were created to be used on the survey in this study.

Once the survey questions were generated, the format was translated into Chinese characters, as all of the interviewed subjects were Chinese-speaking individuals. Two days prior to interviewing the fabric suppliers in-person and on the telephone, the survey was emailed for a preliminary read-through and preparation for answers

Table 3 Case study profiles

Company	Case 1: cotton king	Case 2: south China yarn-dye	Case 3: Shanghai yarn-dye	Case 4: fine weavers	Case 5: WL peck textiles	Case 6: Jacquard-tex	Case 7: Magic-tex	Case 8: Color-tex
Turnover	$15 Million USD	$30 Million USD	$50 Million USD	$80 Million USD	$100 Million USD	$20 Million USD	$14 Million USD	$25 Million USD
Employees	50	1,500	1,800	2,500	1,000	400	700	700
Operational hours/week	9	24	24	24	16	16	16	24
Function	Converter: woven piece goods	Yarn-dye factory	Yarn-dye factory	Piece-dye weaving factory	Piece-dye weaving and dyeing factory	Jacquard weaving factory	Piece-dyeing finishing factory	Piece-dyeing and finishing factory
Capabilities	Yarn-spinning, Weaving, Piece-dyeing, Yarn-dyeing, Finishing, and printing	Weaving, Yarn-dyeing, and finishing	Yarn-spinning, Weaving, Yarn-dyeing, and finishing	Yarn-spinning, and weaving	Weaving, Piece-dyeing, Finishing, and printing	Weaving and finishing	Piece-dyeing and finishing	Piece-dyeing, Finishing, and printing
Target market	Markets: USA, Europe, China	Markets: USA, Europe, China	Markets: USA, Europe, China	Markets: USA, Europe, China	Markets: USA, Europe, China	Markets: USA, Europe, China	Markets: USA, Europe, China	Markets: USA, Europe, China

Fast fashion customers	Abercrombie and fitch, Armani exchange, Esprit, and zara	Abercrombie and fitch, Armani exchange, Esprit, H& M, Next and zara (Inditex group)	Abercrombie and fitch, American eagle outfitters, H& M, Zara	Abercrombie and fitch, Armani exchange, Esprit, and zara	Armani exchange, Esprit, H& M, Zara	Armani exchange, Esprit, H& M, Mango	Abercrombie, Armani exchange, Esprit, Mango, Top shop	Esprit, H& M, Mango, Zara
Buyer-type	Retailers, Wholesales, Trading companies, Agents, Garment manufacturers	Retailers, Wholesales, Trading companies, Agents, Garment manufacturers	Retailers, Trading Companies, Agents, Garment manufacturers	Wholesales, Trading companies	Retailers, Wholesales, Trading companies, Agents, Garment manufacturers	Retailers, Trading companies, Garment manufacturers	Retailers, Wholesales, Trading companies, Agents, Garment manufacturers	Retailers, Wholesales, Trading companies, Agents, Garment manufacturers

if needed. In addition, most of the conversations with the factory managers and owners were conducted with the aid of a translator who is highly knowledgeable in textile production processes and terminology.

4.3 Interview Observations

Interesting observations during the multiple interview and survey process include the following:

- Most of the interviewees seemed to withhold negative information and provide optimistic responses. For example, one particular factory explained ideas for future growth and progress amidst rumors that the facility was shutting down.
- Interviewees discussed the changing market place since the year 2000 without any mention of the quotas being lifted in recent years.
- A common concern for each respondent was the impending 2008 Beijing Olympic Games due to the increased number of customs inspections, thus slowing logistics. Furthermore, there was a limited supply of dyestuff and chemicals due to North China factories shutting down to help contribute to blue skies for the Beijing 2008 Olympic Games.
- The American economy slow-down had greatly affected production and caused a major slow-down of fabric production.
- The answers from the interviews and surveys indicated that the largest concern was cost. However, 75% of suppliers interviewed said that the most important element for them to control was quality.
- Many fabric manufacturers prefer to say that their largest customers are American and European. Often however, their largest customers are from the rapidly growing Chinese clothing market.

5 Results and Analysis

In this section, the findings from the case studies are assessed to show correlations and significant changes in production or production planning because of the fast fashion business strategy. Emphasis is placed on the suppliers' lead-times for development and production as indications of efficient production planning and control. The data captured from the interviews were analyzed qualitatively using the content analysis technique (Porter 1980) and quantitatively as mentioned in the Methodology. The responses from different interviewees to common or slightly over-lapping questions were examined with the hope of identifying primary concerns relevant to fast fashion production. The survey results interpreted below are categorized into three topics in addition to general company information questions:

1. Sample and bulk production planning
2. Quality Assurance and efficiency of service
3. Marketing/Sales

5.1 Examination of Supplier Dynamic Capabilities

The conceptual developments in this research are on the basis of the premise that by increasing production speed and capacity, a supplier will be able to better provide for fast fashion retailers and compete against other fabric suppliers, globally. In order to achieve faster production and increase production capacity, the management must have adopted certain dynamic capabilities which enable clear understanding of the market direction and, therefore, change. The survey aimed to focus on quantitative information as well as qualitative viewpoints in order to focus on intangible as well as tangible aspects of suppliers' interaction capabilities.

Each of the eight supplier cases in this research seemed to understand the need for change and improvement, but some respondents did not have a plan for change which was focused on or varied from what they had already tried since the year 2000. The most telling answers were from question 44 regarding expansion plans. South China Yarn-dye and Magic Textiles did not have clear visions for the future and throughout the survey, they provided vague answers for improvements and changes. Likewise, their annual sales were not competitive in their operating segment. The factory management for each interviewed company presented strengths and weaknesses. The strongest facility appeared to be Shanghai Yarn-dye, followed by Cotton King. The weakest factory appeared to be Magic Textiles, who subsequently went out of business following the interview portion of this study.

The findings from the case studies illustrate the dynamic capabilities developed by suppliers in relation to the current fast fashion business model. Emphasis is placed on examples of the suppliers' interaction capability developments by drawing on examples from the interviews. Table 4 highlights the dynamic strengths of each factory as it relates to fast fashion production. In many respects, general improvements or seemingly simple changes in factory management have been implemented. However, these small changes still represent that dynamic capabilities are present and that the suppliers are moving forward with changes specifically geared toward fast fashion lead-times, fast fashion technologies, and perhaps most importantly, the idea that fast fashion companies are going directly to their suppliers; therefore, the suppliers and factories must be able to clearly understand their needs through improvements in supplier communication, customer service, and relationship building. As mentioned in the literature review, building trust and relationships through customer service is paramount in the success of modern suppliers. Thus, any improvements toward bridging the gap from the suppliers to the buyers are a clear indicator of dynamic capabilities initiatives, regardless of how profound they might appear.

Table 4 Supplier dynamic capabilities (Source: Modified table from Teece and Pisano 1994)

Definition	Capability king	Case 1: cotton	Case 2: South China yarn-dye	Case 3: Shanghai yarn-dye	Case 4: Fine weavers	Case 5: WL peck textiles	Case 6: Jacquard-tex Ltd.	Case 7: Magic textiles	Case 8: Color-tex
"Knowledge and skills embodied in people" (Leonard-Barton 1992)	Human interaction capability	Yes – Travels to see customers; hires consultants		Yes – wants to directly work with retailers			Uses customer feedback to create new collections		
"Compilations of knowledge from multiple individual sources...results from years of accumulating, codifying and structuring the tacit knowledge in people's heads" (Leonard-Barton 1992)	Technological interaction capability		Hire MIS graduates	Hire MIS graduates	Supports ERP planning	Supports ERP planning			Hire MIS graduates
"Formal and informal ways of creating knowledge and controlling knowledge" (Leonard-Barton 1992).	Managerial systems interaction capability	Material planning and control – Future ideas for change		Vertical capabilities, less costly factory location, design aided tools	Material planning and control – Future ideas for change	Vertical factory abilities, material planning is well controlled	Unique niche market appeal. Focus on developments and fewer buyers		Material planning and control – Future ideas for change

"The value assigned within the company to the content and structure of knowledge' (Leonard-Barton 1992).	Cultural interaction capability	Travels to oversea locations frequently	Hiring mgmt graduates; allows factory visits	Teaching English to staff, hiring new graduates for MIS				Wants to expand and improve	Buy new machines; invest more money
Wang and Ahmed (2007)	Adaptive dimension dynamic capability		Hiring correct people		Vertical operation	Continues vertical set-up; changing production planning			
Wang and Ahmed (2007)	Absorptive dimension dynamic capability		Contracts work			Focuses on many areas	Yes – allows change to affect their business; take cues from market		
Wang and Ahmed (2007)	Innovative dimension dynamic capability	Highly marketable; seeks new angles for success	Resourceful – aggressively seeking new employees and new connections		Buying handloom machines; new production methods				

6 Discussion and Managerial Implications

Although the area of fast fashion is relatively new, companies world-wide are adopting the business strategy in order to further enhance sales by capturing the latest trends and thereby limiting over-stock items and discounted clothing. In turn, textile factories are competing globally for survival. Few published articles exist with information on how Chinese factories are increasing the production capacity and speed necessary to maintain a competitive advantage in the textile industry under the emergence of the fast fashion retail strategy. The textile industry is missing a wealth of information necessary to truly understand the management, marketing, and retailing of clothing if the production dynamics are not investigated. This study explores and highlights the importance of the relationship between supply chain production performance and fast fashion market demand in order to provide insights for planning and executing applicable supply chain strategies for managers both in factories and on the retail side of the textile industry. This information will also be beneficial to research departments in universities, retailers, and other factory managers in better understanding the textile industry.

This study has particularly highlighted the importance for Chinese textile-apparel suppliers to assess their interactions with fast fashion retailers and acquire dynamic capabilities in order to better organize and support their global customers' needs. Dynamic capabilities are critical to the status and success of a supplier in terms of profits, timesaving, efficiencies, and quality control. The framework set for this study evaluates dynamic capabilities on an individual and overall level. This research offers an opportunity for suppliers to use the framework set out in this paper to guide the focus and distribution of their organization's dynamic capabilities in order to improve management and remain competitive.

On the basis of the literature review and the multi-case study, the study provides several significant contributions. The main theoretical contribution is the developed conceptual model which describes the main elements affecting the supplier's production competences and the dynamics between those elements. Additionally, the study offers the management practical insights of the importance of planning and building dynamic capabilities within their organization and suggests sensitivity to changes in the customers' strategy, to maximize success and competitive advantages. Reliable and valid data will be presented for academicians and practitioners to use in future research of supply chain capabilities.

7 Limitations and Future Avenues of Research

The role of the fabric supplier along the fast fashion supply chain has been firmly established, as well as the need for rapid deliveries, low prices, and quality services that match to the needs of retailers. However, some details remain unclear and would benefit from additional research. Future studies must include a larger sample size for testing and more extensive interviewing. This research serves as a pilot study for a follow-up PhD research project and presents opportunities for significant future academic research into the nature and processes of fast fashion productions.

Areas of further research may include the following:

- A closer comparison between converters and factories
- Additional information on profits and costs for production
- Additional information for the processing of batch-orders
- Relationship between sample and bulk capacity per month
- A closer study of commodity fabric usage by fast fashion retailers
- Further study on the relationship between fast fashion retailers and their supplier
- Further analysis of the sourcing process between retailers and suppliers

8 Conclusion

As consumers demand more variety and lower prices for fashion, retailers have to sustain a competitive advantage by ensuring that they have an efficient supply chain. They seek suppliers with dynamic capabilities who can adapt, organize production schedules to meet their delivery demands, and provide consistent services. Implementing new methods to speed production and reduce lead-times is not enough to allow a supplier to be fully efficient at quickly manufacturing fabric. The key to securing orders from customers is to produce the fabrics quickly and be able to apply customer service rational in order to solve problem and respond to customer needs. Suppliers who invest in development to further apply style and trends to their fabrics through new fabric collections each season will reduce the development and design lead-time for retailers and will better serve their designer needs and provide inspiration.

As opposed to the intense pressures retailers currently face, the capable suppliers interviewed for this study indicate that they are all willing to heavily invest in new machinery, information technology, innovative tools, and materials. The one primary concern shared among the suppliers is the uncertainty of the future economy and the rapidly changing retailer strategies. Fortunately, since the year 2000, sample and bulk production lead-times have improved, capacity has increased, marketing techniques have broadened, and new staffs hired are well educated. The factories in China appear to have their finger on the pulse, as if this change in retailing was eminent and they had begun preparations long ago. Suppliers who are capable of meeting the demands are happy to accommodate the rapid developments and buying habits of fast fashion retailers, as opposed to retailers who prolong developments and decision-making. The good factories in China are not adversely affected by fast fashion. They are negatively affected by retailers who do not make fast decisions. This industry seems poised to become supplier-dominated in the coming 10 years, as suppliers and factories that remain standing throughout the economic downturn will be stronger and more able to choose which retailers they seek, rather than vice-versa.

References

Abernathy FH (2000) Retailing and supply chains in the information age. Tech Soc 22:5–31

Abernathy FH, Dunlop JT, Hammond JH, Weil D (1999) a stitch in time: lean retailing and the transformation of manufacturing – lessons from the apparel and textile industry. Oxford University Press, NY

Abratt R, Kelly PM (2002) Customer-supplier partnerships: perceptions of a successful key account management program. Ind Market Manag 31:467–476

Anson R (2005) Editorial: post-quota scenarios – how free is free textile and clothing trader. Textil Outlook Int 115:3–10

Appelbaum R (2003) Assessing the impact of the phasing-out of the agreement on textiles and clothing on apparel exports on the least developed and developing countries. Centre for Global Studies, Institute for Social, Behavioural, and Economic Research, University of California at Santa Barbara, 4 November 2003

Appelbaum R (2005) TNCs and the Removal of Textiles and Clothing Quota. United Nations conference on trade and development, New York

Aragon-Correa JA, Garcia-Morales VJ, Cordon-Pozo E (2007) Leadership and organizational learning's role on innovation and performance: lessons from Spain. Ind Market Manag 36(3):349–359

Argyris C, Schön DA (1996) Organizational learning ii: theory, method and practice. Addison-Wesley, Reading, MA

Asanuma B (1989) Manufacturer-supplier relationships in Japan and the concept of relation-specific skill. J Jpn Int Econ

Athreye SS (2005) The Indian software industry and its evolving service capability. Ind Corp Change 14(3):393–418

Bala Subrahmanya MH (2003) Technological innovations in small enterprises: a comparative perspective of Bangalore (India) and Northeast England (UK). Technovation 23(3):269–280

Barney J (1986) Strategic factor markets: expectations, luck, and business strategy. Manag Sci 4(10):1231–1241

BBC + ETHICAL + FASHION, Nov2007, URL = http://www.bbc.co.uk/blast/art/articles/what_is_ethical_fashion.shtml, 01/11/2007

BBC + FAST + FASHION, November2007, URL = http://www.bbc.co.uk/blast/art/articles/cheap_fashion_fast_fashion.shtm

Bellenger DM, Bernhardt KL, Goldstucker JL (1976) Qualitative Research in Marketing. American Marketing Institute, Chicago, IL

Birnbaum D (1993) Importing garments through Hong Kong. Third Horizon Press, Hong Kong

Birtwistle G, Siddiqui N, Fiorito S (2003) Quick response: perceptions of UK fashion retailers. Int J Retail Distrib Manag 31(2):118–128

Bonoma TV (1985) Case research in marketing: opportunities, problems, and a process. J Market Res 22(2):419–441

Brady T, Davies A (2004) Building project capabilities: from exploratory to exploitative learning. Organ Stud 25(9):1601–1621

Bruce M, Daly L (2006) Buyer behaviour for fast fashion. J Fashion Market Manag 10(3):329–344

Bruce M, Moore C, Birtwistle G (2004) International retail marketing: a case study approach. Butterworth-Heinemann, Oxford

Burger PC, Cann CW (1995) Post-purchase strategy – a key to successful industrial marketing and customer satisfaction. Ind Market Manag 24:91–98

Carson D, Gilmore A, Perry C, Gronhaug K (2001) Qualitative marketing research. Sage Publications, London

Chan E, Au KF (2007) Quick response for Hong Kong clothing suppliers: a total system approach. J Textil Inst 98(5):463–469

Chen C, Shih H (2004) The impact of WTO accession on the Chinese garment industry. J Fashion Market Manag 8(2):221–229

Chesbrough HW, Teece DJ (1996) Organizing for innovation. Harv Bus Rev 65–73

Chi T, Kilduff P (2006) An assessment of trends in China's comparative advantages in textile machinery, man-made fibers, textiles and apparel. J Textile Inst 97(2):173–192

Clark KB, Fujimoto T (1991) Product development performance: Strategy, organization, and management in the world auto industry. Harvard Business School Press, Boston, MA

Deshpande R (1983) Paradigms lost: on theory and method in research marketing. J Market 47:101–110

Dick B (1990) Convergent interviewing, version 3. Interchange, Brisbane

Dierickx I, Cool K (1989) Asset stock accumulation and sustainability of competitive advantage. Manag Sci 35(12):1504–1511

Dyer WG, Wilkins AL (1991) Better stories, not better constructs, to generate better theory: a rejoinder to Eisenhardt. Acad Manag Rev 16(3):613–619

Eberle H, Hermeling H, Hornberger M, Kilgus R, Menzer D, Ring W (2004) Clothing technology, 4th edn. Beuth-Verlag GmbH, Berlin

Eisenhardt KM (1989) Building theories from case study research. Acad Manag Rev 14(4): 532–550

Ferdows K, Lewis MA, Machuca JAD (2004) Zara's secret for fast fashion. Harv Bus Rev 82(11):104–110

Fernie J, Sparks L (1999) Logistics and retail management. Kogan Page Ltd, London

Figueiredo PN (2003) Learning, capability accumulation and firms differences: evidence from latecomer steel. Ind Corp Change 12(3):607–643

Folpe JM (2000) Zara has a made-to-order plan for success. Fortune 142(5):80

Foster RON (1986) Technology in the modern corporation: a strategic perspective, timing technological transition. In: Horwich M (ed) Pergamo, London

Gannaway J (1999) Checkout chic. Grocer, Florida

Garg D, Narahari Y, Viswanadham N (2004) Design of six sigma supply chains. IEEE Trans Autom Sci Eng 1(1):38–57

Gereffi G (1999) International trade and industrial upgrading in the apparel commodity chain. J Int Econ 48(1):37–70

Gersick CJG (1988) Time and transition in work teams: Toward a new model of group development. Acad Manag J 31:9–41

Hammond JH, Kelly M (1990) Quick response in the apparel industry. Harvard Business School Publishing, Harvard, MA

Helander A, Möller K (2007) System supplier's customer strategy. Ind Market Manag 36(6): 719–730

Homburg C, Kiedaisch I (1999) Die Betriebswirtschaft. Ger Bus Econ 59(1):22–43

Jackson T, Shaw D (2006) The fashion handbook. Routledge, New York

Johnsen RE, Ford D (2006) Interaction capability development of smaller suppliers in relationships with larger customers. Ind Market Manag 38(8):1002–1015

JUST + STYLE + FAST + FASHION, November 2007, URL = http://www.just-style.com/article.aspx?ID = 98337, 01/11/2007

Kline B, Wagner J (1994) Information sources and retail buyer decision-making: the effect of product specific buying experience. J Retailing 70(1):75–88

Koste LL, Malhotra MK, Sharma SS (2004) Measuring dimensions of manufacturing flexibility. J Oper Manag 22(2):171–196

Lannes WJ, Logan JW (2004) A technique for assessing an organization's ability to change. IEEE Trans Eng Manag 51(4):483–488

Lawson B, Samson D (2001) Developing innovation capability in organisations: A dynamic capabilities approach. Int J Innovat Manag 5(3):377–400

Lederman LC (1989) Focus group interviews in PR. Teach PR 1–3

Lemoine F, Ünal-Kesenci D (2004) Assembly trade and technology transfer: the case of China. World Dev 32(5):829–850

Leonard-Barton DA (1992) Core capabilities and core rigidities: a paradox in managing new product development. Strat Manag J 13:111–125

Levy SJ (1979) Focus group interviews: a reader. In: Higginbotham JB, Cox KK (eds) Focus group interviews: a reader. American Marketing Association, Chicago, IL, pp 34–42

Liao SH, Fei WC, Liu CT (2008) Relationship between knowledge Inertia, organizational learning, and organizational innovation. Technovation 28(4):183–195

Makadok R (2001) Toward a synthesis of the resource-based and dynamic-capability views of rent creation. Strat Manag J 22(5):387–402

Malhotra NK (1993) Marketing research: An applied orientation. Prentice Hall. Englewood Cliffs, NJ

Menkes S (2002) Is luxury's triangle eternal?. Int Herald Tribune

Miles MB, Huberman MA (1994) Qualitative data analysis: an expanded sourcebook. 2nd edn. Sage Publications, Thousand Oaks, CA

Mintel Group (2002) Mintel Report: Clothing Retailing in the UK, April 2002

Möller K, Törrönen P (2003) Business suppliers' value creation potential: a capability-based analysis. Ind Market Manag 32(2):109–118

Montalvo C (2006) What triggers change and innovation?. Technovation 26(3):312–323

Morgan DL (1988) Focus groups as qualitative research. Sage Publications, London

Mukherjee A, Mitchell W, Talbot B (2004) Adaptation of a focused factory to new objectives: the influence of manufacturing requirements and capabilities. In: Baum JAC, McGahan AM (eds) Business strategy over the industry life cycle – advances in strategic management, vol 21. Elsevier, Oxford, UK, pp 161–198

Nair GS, Riege A (1995) Using convergent interviewing to develop the research problem of a postgraduate thesis. In: Proceedings, Marketing Educators and Researchers International Conference, Griffith University, Gold Coast

Nathan Associates (2002) Recent changes in global trade rules for textiles and apparel: implications for developing countries, Research Report, 2002

Nelson RR, Winter SG (1982) An evolutionary theory of economic change. Belknap Press of Harvard University Press, Cambridge, MA

Nonaka I (1994) A dynamic theory of organizational knowledge creation. Organ Sci 5, 1, 14–37.

Pablo A et al (1996) Acquisition decision-making processes: the central role of risk. J Manag 22(5):723–746

Parkhe A (1993) Messy research, methodological predispositions, and theory development in international joint ventures. Acad Manag Rev 18(2):227–268

Patton MQ (1990) Qualitative evaluation methods. Sage Publications, Thousand Oaks, CA

PDMA:PRODUCT + DEVELOPMENT + MANAGEMENT + ASSOCIATION, February 2008, URL = http://www.pdma.org/

Penrose ET (1959) The theory of the growth of the firm. Blackwell, Oxford

Perry C, Coote L (1994) Processes of case research methodology: tool for management development?. In: Paper presented at the Australia and New Zealand academy of management (ANZAM) conference, Victoria University of Wellington, Wellington, New Zealand

Perry M, Sohal AS (2000) Quick response practices and technologies in developing supply chains. Int J Phy Distrib Logist Manag 30(7–8):627–639

Porter ME (1980) Competitive strategy: techniques for analyzing industries and competitors, Free Press, NY

Rao S, Perry C (2003) Convergent interviewing to build a theory in under-researched areas: principles and an example investigation of internet usage in inter-firm relationships. Qual Market Res Int J 6(4):236–247

Romano CA (1989) Research strategies for small business: a case study approach. Int Small Bus J 7(4):35–43

Ruddock J (2007) About DEFRA: speech to the rite group conference and exhibition 10 October, London, UK

Schiele H (2006) How to distinguish innovative suppliers? Identifying innovative suppliers as new task for purchasing. Ind Market Manag 35(8):925–935

Schumpeter J (1934) The theory of economic development, an inquiry into profits, capital, credit, interest, and the business cycle. Harvard University Press, CA; (Seventh printing, 1961)

Sen A, Zhang AX (2009) Style goods pricing with demand learning. Eur J Oper Res 196(3): 1058–1075

Senge PM (1990) The fifth discipline. Century Business, London

Shahimpoor N, Matt BF (2007) The power of one: dissent and organizational life. J Bus Ethics 74(1):37–48

Sheridan M, Moore C, Nobbs K (2006) Fast fashion requires fast marketing: the role of category management in fast fashion positioning. J Fashion Market Manag 10(3):301–315

Someya M, Shunnar H, Srinivasan TG Textile and clothing exports in MENA: past performance, prospects and policy issues in post mfa context. Middle East and North Africa Region Working Paper, World Bank, Aug 2002

Spinager D (1999) Textiles beyond the MFA phase-out. World Econ 22(4):318–329

Stokes R, Perry C (2005) Chapter 10. Case research about enterprises. In: Hine D, Carson D (eds) Innovative methodologies in enterprise research. Edward Elgar, Northampton, MA

Tait N (2002) Towards 2005: the survival of the fittest. URL = http://www.just–style.com. Accessed April 2002

Teece DJ (1988) Capturing value from technological innovation: integration, stra tegic partnering, and licensing decisions. Interfaces 18(3):46–61

Teece DJ (1998) Capturing value from knowledge assets: the new economy, markets for know-how, and intangible assets. Calif Manag Rev 40(3):55–79

Teece DJ, Pisano G (1994) The dynamic capabilities of firms: an introduction. Ind Corp Change 3(3):537–556

Teece DJ, Pisano G, Shuen A (1997) Dynamic capabilities and strategic management. Strat Manag J 18(7):509–533

(The) Economist (2005) The future of fast fashion: Inditex. Economist 375(8431):57

The World Bank Report (2005) A better investment climate for everyone: Overview 2005. World Development Report, Oxford University Press, Oxford

Thietart RA (2001) Doing management research. Sage Publications, London

Towers N, Peng X (2006) An assessment of international strategic merchandising from China, post quota elimination in January 2005 for the UK apparel market. J Text Inst 97(6):541–548

Tungate M (2005) Fashion brands: branding style from armani to zara. Kogan Page Limited, London

USITC (2001) Official statistics from the Office of Textiles, US Department of Commerce, 2001

USITC (2004) Textile and apparel: assessment of the competitiveness of certain foreign suppliers to the US market. In: USITC Publication no. 3671. Project Leaders: Freund K, Wallace R, Washington, DC, 2004

Vargo SL, Lusch RF (2004) Evolving to a new dominant logic for marketing. J Market 1:1–17

Walmsley T, Hertel T (2000) China's accession to the WTO: timing is everything. In: Global Trade Analysis Project Working Paper No. 13. Purdue University, West Lafayette, IN, 2000

Walter A, Ritter T, Gemünden HG (2001) Value-creation in buyer-seller relationships: theoretical considerations and empirical results from a supplier's perspective. Ind Market Manag 30(4):365–377

Wang CL, Ahmed PK (2007) Dynamic capabilities: a review and research agenda, international journal of management reviews. Int J Manag Rev 9(1):31–51

Weerawardena J, Mort GS, Liesch PW, Knight G (2007) Conceptualizing accelerated internationalization in the born global firm: a dynamic capabilities perspective. J World Bus 42(3):294–306

Williamson OE (1985) The economic institutions of capitalism: firms, markets, relational contracting, 1st edn. The Free Press, New York

Wilson H, Daniel E (2007) The multi-channel challenge: a dynamic capability approach. Ind Market Manag 36(1):10–20

Woiceshyn J, Daellenbach U (2005) Integrative capability and technology adoption: evidence from oil firms. Ind Corp Change 14(2):307–342

XINHUA + NEWS + CHINA + LABOR + BULLETIN, 2005, URL = http://www.china-labour.org.hk

Yin RK (1989) Case study research: design and methods. Sage Publications, Newbury Park, CA
Yin RK (1993) Applications of case study research. Sage Publications, Thousand Oaks, CA
Yin RK (1994) Case study research design and methods, 2nd edn. Sage Publications, Thousand Oaks, CA
Yu CWP (2008) Interview with industry expert and fabric supply company owner in Hong Kong, 2008

Innovative Mass Customization in the Fashion Industry

Ho-Ting Yeung, Tsan-Ming Choi, and Chun-Hung Chiu

Mass customization (MC) is a popular strategy in the fashion industry. MC aims at satisfying individual customer's needs with customized products and at a cost near that of mass production. In this chapter, we first conduct a comprehensive literature review on MC in the fashion industry. We then propose a scheme to classify the MC practices as traditional and innovative. By exploring many real world cases, we compare and develop insights on the applications of different kinds of MC in the fashion industry. Managerial recommendations are generated. We believe that this chapter can lay a good foundation for future studies on MC.

Keywords Customer involvement · Fashion · Mass customization · Modularity · Technology

1 Introduction

Mass customization (MC) is a widely observed practice in logistics and supply chain management. It is especially prominent now (and will probably be even more significant in the future) owing to the advances in information technology and more demanding consumers. The concept of MC was first coined in the book "Future Shock" by Toffler (Toffler 1970). At a later time, Davis described MC as the hybrid system that accommodates mass production and (craft) customization (Davis 1987). Nowadays, MC usually refers to producing customized products or services for satisfying individuals with the efficiency of mass production (MP) (Silveira et al. 2001; Salvador et al. 2004; Chandra and Grabis 2004c; Piller 2007; Gilmore and Pine 1997). Following this modern definition, Silveira et al. argued that "MC is a system that uses information technology, flexible processes, and organizational structures to

C.-H. Chiu (✉)
Institute of Textiles and Clothing, Faculty of Applied Science and Textiles, The Hong Kong Polytechnic University, Hung Hom, Kowloon, Hong Kong
e-mail: chchiu2000@gmail.com

T.C. Edwin Cheng and T.-M. Choi (eds.), *Innovative Quick Response Programs in Logistics and Supply Chain Management*, International Handbooks on Information Systems, DOI 10.1007/978-3-642-04313-0_21,
© Springer-Verlag Berlin Heidelberg 2010

deliver a wide range of products and services that meet specific needs of individual customers, at a cost near that of mass-produced items" (Silveira et al. 2001). All in all, the notions of MC are high responsiveness, low cost, and fulfilling the needs of each customer. MC is even coined as a part of future retailing (Retail Forward Inc 2003).

Short life cycle, economic environment, intense competition (Christopher 2000), changing customer needs, rapid technological innovations (Lee and Chen 2000), globalization (Silveira et al. 2001), and market fragmentation (Svensson and Jensen 2003; Tu et al. 2004a), all lead to market turbulence. Meanwhile, more consumers having great purchasing power express their personality and wealth by means of individualized products (Piller and Muller 2004). In order to deal with market uncertainty and demand, MC has become an imperative measure for the industries as it gives flexibility and quick responsiveness to volatile market demand (Silveira et al. 2001; Peters and Saidin 2000).

MC allows firms to respond promptly to changing customer needs (Chandra and Grabis 2004a). Since firms can learn individual consumer preferences during the MC processes, it is argued that MC improves firms' responsiveness to cope with fashion changes (Sullivan and Kang 1999) and enhances their efficiency. In order to implement MC, the respective supply chain (SC) needs to be changed for accomplishing flexibility and responsiveness (Caddy et al. 2002; Pine et al. 1993; Christopher 2000; Radder and Louw 1999).The traditional lengthy and slow-moving SC becomes unsustainable in this sense. A firm with MC may result in the growth of complexity in its SC (Coronado et al. 2004).The issues in supplier relationship, coordination, inventory management, and postponement are reported to be critical in supply chain management (SCM) for achieving a successful MC strategy.

To implement a successful MC in the fashion industry, information is the most critical factor (Reichwald et al. 2000). MC is characterized as "highly information intensive" because of the close interaction between customers and suppliers. On the other hand, MC usually results in an increased cost (Ahlstrom and Westbrook 1999). Such an increased cost is particularly derived from information cost (Reichwald et al. 2000; Piller 2004); as a result, information management is essential in MC (Silveira et al. 2001). For instance, Brooks Brothers reported that MC program provides vital information, which allows tracking customers' measurements, style preferences, and personal data. With the above information, Brooks Brothers notifies customers the new suit styles and updated merchandises selection by sending automated notices (Stacy 1999). Brooks Brothers can therefore update customers with the latest offerings of the company and improve MC as well as its own MP businesses.

Taking into account the importance of MC in the fashion industry, this chapter contributes in a number of ways. First, we conduct a comprehensive literature review on MC in the fashion industry. Second, we propose a scheme to classify the MC practices as traditional and innovative. Third, by exploring many real world cases, we compare and develop additional insights into the applications of different kinds of MC in the fashion industry. Managerial recommendations are generated. To the best of our knowledge, there is little research to date studying the aforementioned topics. We reckon that this chapter can lay a good foundation for future studies on MC.

2 Literature Review

2.1 Mass Customization: Background

MC is not a new strategy, but its presence in the business world is a well-observed global trend nowadays. Companies in industries, such as automotive (e.g., BMW, Land Rover), computer (e.g., Dell, Fujitsu) (Gunasekaran and Ngai 2005), Hewlett-Packard (Feitzinger and Lee 1997), electronics (e.g., Motorola) and fashion (please see Sect. 3) (Aigbedo 2007; Pine 1993) have all been reported to be MC adopters. For example, in the automotive industry, Land Rover allows customers to discuss their specific needs with the special vehicles team (Alford et al. 2000). This team then collaborates with each customer to develop a customized vehicle which is based on the standard Land Rover (but changing some core elements of design). BMW also offers MC (e.g., changing the color), and it only needs 6 days for final assembly (Gunasekaran and Ngai 2005). Dell is regarded as one of the most successful MC adopters in the computer industry (Gunasekaran and Ngai 2005). Dell offers MC via the Internet, thereby helping customers build their own computers by advising their desired configurations online. Dell would quickly deliver the assembled products to customers in a few days. The success of Dell's MC is based on its close collaboration with suppliers, use of modularity (Gunasekaran and Ngai 2005) and web-based configuration for order processing (Ro et al. 2007).

Ahlstrom and Westbrook found that a lot of companies believe that MC is becoming more and more important and more than half of the respondents are reported with a plan to increase MC in the future so as to accommodate the customer demand for a larger variety of products (Ahlstrom and Westbrook 1999). Essentially, reward is promising (Tu et al. 2001) as MC companies are reported to have double-digit sales growth (Piller 2007). MC is a potential means in achieving cost saving by the economies of MC (EMC) (Piller and Muller 2004). EMC implies low cost with the application of single process to produce a greater product variety in a cheaper and quicker manner (i.e., economies of scope). Economies of integration are also substantial in MC owing to the cost savings connected with better access to customer knowledge (Reichwald et al. 2003).

Development of MC. Piller described the evolution of MC as follows (Piller 2004). In the first generation, MC is mainly implemented in a B2B context. Next, MC companies aim at consumer markets and are eager to interact with customers via the Internet (i.e., to reduce communication cost and reach a large number of customers) in the second generation of MC. However, many players would fail in this generation because they cannot provide a sustainable value of their MC programs to their customers. In the third generation, firms use MC to improve MP. By doing so, firms have better customer knowledge (from MC), and thereby, can improve their businesses on a large scale (i.e., MP).

Benefits of MC. Both companies and their customers can be benefited by the presence of MC. On one hand, customers can enjoy a higher satisfaction level because of the individualized offerings and more unique shopping experiences (Taylor et al. 2003). On the other hand, MC increases customer loyalty towards the companies and reduce their switching to other competitors in the market. Piller and Muller mention that a firm is able to acquire knowledge of customers during product configuration (Piller and Muller 2004). If a customer shifts to other MC firms, he/she will be faced with uncertainty in product quality. Firms hence put up a barrier to retain customers. Customers are willing to pay a premium price for the products that fit them better (Piller 2004). As MC is a pull system, the negative impacts brought by sales forecasting error are reduced. Finished product inventory and markdown are then greatly reduced (Taylor et al. 2003), and these are especially meaningful for the fashion industry. In addition, Kumar also claimed that better quality and service are the consequences of MC (Kumar 2004). For more advantages of MC, we refer readers to (Pine et al. 1993) and (Knolmayer 2002).

2.2 Mass Customization and Supply Chain Management

Enhancing flexibility and responsiveness for MC needs altering SC structure, and MC seems to require a more complex SC (Coronado et al. 2004). Unlike a traditional SC, an MC supply chain should spend extra effort on dealing with the issues associated with supplier relationship, coordination, inventory management, and postponement.

Supplier relationship. The shift to MC not only affects the internal operations of a company but also the relationships between the company and its partners in the SC (Blecker and Abdelkafi 2006). MC requires SC members move to a higher level of trust, integration, and cooperation so as to address problems jointly and in a mutually beneficial manner (Chandra and Grabis 2004c; Gunasekaran and Ngai 2005; Caddy et al. 2002). SC structure would then be changed from the traditional practice into new strategic alliances between the firm and other SC members (Blecker and Abdelkafi 2006; Gunasekaran and Ngai 2005). For this reason, greater care and diligence in identifying potential partners and the endeavor to manage relationships between SC partners are inevitable in running MC (Caddy et al. 2002).

Outsourcing is another way to handle the uncertainty of product flow and customer demand in MC (Gooley 1998). Involving more third parties can potentially lead to a higher level of responsiveness and flexibility as a firm focuses on its own core competencies whereas the other tasks are done by outside parties with the right expertise. However, coordination problem then arises (Caddy et al. 2002) and it is especially prominent when the number of partnering firms increases. On that account, achieving MC objectives under outsourcing requires coordination of all members.

Inventory management. Uncertainty in demand and supply is a big challenge for implementing MC. On the supply side, firms are not sure about the amount of different components and parts to keep in inventory for fulfilling the customers' orders. On the demand side, it is also difficult to estimate the number of customer-orders over a given period of time. In this situation, SCM aims to balance supply and demand and allow the pipeline to adjust with respect to the demands of the consumers (Gunasekaran and Ngai 2005). MC aims at achieving low cost, large variety, and short lead time. These objectives seem to be conflicting with one another and pose new challenges. Chandra and Grabis proposed a solution that designs different inventory management approaches for different modules (Chandra and Grabis 2004c). On the other hand, the synchronization of inventory management for all components under MC should also be well-considered. As a result, precise coordination of both inbound and outbound logistics is essential in MC (Gooley 1998).

Postponement. Postponement is an important tool for enabling MC (Helms et al. 2008). Postponement is a principle of designing products using common platforms, components, or modules and then storing products in the semi-finished state. The final assembly or customization will be postponed and processed only when final customer requirement is known (Christopher 2000; Salvador et al. 2004). Postponement allows firms to outsource materials and production activity, and therefore improving flexibility and responsiveness. The ability to increase variety and customization without parallel increases in costs can also be obtained. However, as what Chandra and Grabis reported, there is a tradeoff between inventory cost and delivery time according to the level of postponement (Chandra and Grabis 2004a). Moreover, pursing postponement should concern the issue of facility location (Chandra and Grabis 2004c). This principle may not be achievable if the production facility is geographically distant. This issue is very important in the fashion industry.

Traditional non-MC supply chain VS MC supply chain. The MC supply chain and the traditional non-MC supply chain (such as the MP supply chain) differ in several aspects such as the flow of information and the roles of customers and suppliers (Chandra and Grabis 2004a). A different level of flexibility and responsiveness to changing market requirements hence results if we compare the MC supply chain with the traditional one (Gunasekaran and Ngai 2005).

A traditional non-MC supply chain is a push system while an MC supply chain is a pull system. The former satisfies customer requirements from stocks. Once production is completed, the finished product is stored in warehouse and waits for customer's orders. For that reason, accurate forecast in production level and inventory is fundamental (Christopher 2000). In other words, less involvement of customers is needed in design and production planning and therefore, customers do not have much contact with the firm. For the MC supply chain, production is based on the received orders according to customers' specifications. The firm should hence have efficient communication with the customers accordingly. A long term relationship with customers is necessary so as to collect and explore customer preferences. Under that condition, the information flows upward in MC supply chain (i.e., from customers to manufacturers) whereas information of traditional SC generally flows downward (i.e., from manufacturers to customers). Instantaneously, MC supply chain requires strategic alliances with suppliers (Chandra and Grabis 2004a). Firms need to have tighter integration and coordination with suppliers in order to deal with the changing markets. The functions of MC firms are usually decentralized with various outsourcing functions while traditional non-MC firms still focus more on centralization. Moreover, traditional SC manages the uncertainty in terms of finished goods inventory. However, MC supply chain focuses on managing the component level inventory (Chandra and Grabis 2004a).

2.3 Modularity

Modularity is one of the key elements in MC (Duray et al. 2000). It describes the degree to which a system's component can be separated and recombined, and it refers both to the tightness of coupling between components and the degree to which the system architecture enables the "mixing and matching of components" (Schilling 2000). Baldwin and Clarks described *modularity as an effective manufacturing strategy that enables firms to cope with rapidly changing customer requirements and increasing technical complexity, thus achieving distinctive MC capability* (Baldwin and Clark 1997). Apparently, modularity is considered as a fundamental method for achieving MC. In this sense, costs can be minimized whereas a wide range of end products can be created (Pine et al. 1993). As a remark, computer and automotive industries have been reported to be the leaders in successful application of modularity (Tu et al. 2004a). Modularity in production allows economies of scale and scope across the production lines (Duray 2002) because standard parts (i.e., modules, Starr 1965) can be produced by mass production (Duray et al. 2000). Right after that, the product differentiation and customization through combination, configuration, and modification of those modules will be postponed until the later stages of the process (Feitzinger and Lee 1997).

Modularity is not only applied in product but also in process. With the application of product modularity, the product can be assembled easily by integrating independent modules together (Lee et al. 1997). Internal manufacturing operations may be simplified by outsourcing the production activities (Salvador et al. 2004). In this manner, the operational challenge raised by MC can be addressed. Ulrich and Tung (1991) showed a typology of product modularity that distinguishes among component-swapping modularity (switching options on a standard product), component-sharing modularity (designing products around a base unit of common components), cut-to-fit modularity (dimensional adjustment of a module before combining with the others), bus modularity (adding a module to an existing series), mix modularity (no unique identity if modules are combined), and sectional modularity (arranging standard modules in a unique pattern). In a later work, Ulrich (1995) modified his typology and proposed slot modularity (each interface is different between components, so components cannot be interchanged), bus modularity (different physical components are connected with common bus), and sectional modularity (same type of interface, no single element for attaching other components). For process modularity, the production process can be separated into different sub-processes (Feitzinger and Lee 1997). Flexibility can hence be obtained as product process is not rigid (i.e., can be done with interruption). Process modularity is generally based on three principles – process postponement (delaying the process for differentiation or customization), process re-sequencing (rearranging the order of process), and process standardization (standardizing earlier portions of process).

Modularity benefits both customers and manufacturers. In the viewpoint of customers, product is easier to be configured and customized by applying modularity, and thereby, greater usability and serviceability are achieved (Tu et al. 2004a). For manufacturers, flexibility is allowed as they can make the modules of the product separately. The components' variety can be reduced, but offering more variety of end products (Duray et al. 2000). In addition, modularity decreases cost due to the economies of scale and scope. McCutcheon et al. (1994) suggested that modularity alleviates the customization responsiveness which occurs when customers want to be offered a larger variety of module choices as well as a short lead time simultaneously. Other benefits of modularity include increasing the feasibility of product or component change, reducing the impact of uncertain demand forecasts, ease of product design, upgrade, maintenance, repair and disposal, and so on (Kumar 2004; Coronado et al. 2004; Mukhopadhyay and Setoputro 2005; Ro et al. 2007). However, modular design also raises costs and introduces problem of warranty, reliability, and complicated system testing (Gershenson et al. 1999).

2.4 Customer Involvement

Apart from modularity, customer involvement is the major factor in the successful implementation of MC (Chandra and Grabis 2004b; Duray et al. 2000; Svensson and Jensen 2003). Duray (2002) found that the level of customer involvement in the SC is important to determine the uniqueness of the product and the type of customization. A product is highly customized if the customers are made to participate in the early design stage of the production cycle (Duray et al. 2000). Therefore, customer involvement in the development of the product is critical for satisfying customers' want. Customers can obtain individualized products and special experiences if they are strongly involved in the design stage (Lee and Chen 2000). At the same time, manufacturers will be greatly benefited from the knowledge and utilization of customer information (Pan and Holland 2006). Zipkin stated that a successful MC firm should have the capabilities of elicitation which is a mechanism for interacting with the customer and obtaining specific information (Zipkin 2001). It is simply because customers sometimes are unsure about what they want and are easily overwhelmed by too many available choices. For that reason, it is important to allow the customers to select and give information about their wants easily in the process of MC (Lee and Chen 2000). Some companies would like to offer "co-design" to the customers in stores or on the website so that they can design the products with the aid of designers, e.g., the Nike Sportwear Bespoke program (Nike's official webpage: sportwear bespoke program 2008). Such direct communication and interaction provides a very reliable and first-hand data about customers' preferences (Kumar 2004). Moreover, CRM (customer-relationship management) scheme helps a lot in MC as it provides detailed customer information and preference.

2.5 Technology

Technology is the prerequisite for pursuing MC (Erens and Hegge 1994; Anderson-Connell et al. 2002). Here, technology includes not only the digital computer based information technology, but also the other scientific advances such as that in materials science. Andel stated that "MC requires mass communication" and communication is mediated by technology (Andel 2002). In essence, technology gives the ability to coordinate among SC partners (i.e., external partners, such as customers and suppliers) effectively (Ghiassi and Spera 2003; Zeleny 1996). Meanwhile, the communication between departments can be improved (i.e., internal partners, such as manufacturing and design) (Silveira et al. 2001).Technology helps information transfer from customers to manufacturers for developing customized products (Anderson-Connell et al. 2002; Christopher 2000). With the efficient information transfer, customers can have what they want (Loker and Oh 2002) in a shorter lead time and at a comparatively lower price (Erens and Hegge 1994). Manufacturers are able to attain flexibility and quick responsiveness to changing market (Schwegmann et al. 2003). This is highly desirable in the fashion industry. Schroeder et al. (1989) reported that the fashion industry has not adopted technology as quickly as other industries. It is argued that the main reason is associated with its labor intensive nature. Moreover, costs, needs for technical support, and worker's technical literacy are the other reasons for non-adoption of technology. Moreover, the adoption of design and production technology in large firms is earlier than in small firms (Sullivan and Kang 1999; Kincade 1995). Interestingly, Loker and Oh (2002) found that small firms are significantly more likely to produce higher levels of customized products than larger firms although they may not fully engage in MC. Development in technology also increases the variability of MC strategy (Helms et al. 2008). The enabling technologies for MC are listed below:

Configuration system. A configuration system is a kind of software tool which guides the customers into a valid solution through the configuration process (Piller et al. 2004). Customers can specify the products and then configure products on their own (Andel 2002). Moreover, a configuration system helps orders to be transmitted for production automatically without intermediaries (Blecker and Abdelkafi 2006). A configuration system also plays an important role in the concept of co-design (Von Hippel 2001).

Internet/Email/E-commerce. The increasing popularity of internet facilitates the emergence of MC (Gunasekaran and Ngai 2005). It allows firms to involve customers in the design of MC products effectively because of rapid communication and ease to learn customer requirements in product features (Helms et al. 2008).

Firms can display their product offerings on their websites (Loker and Oh 2002). Also, customers can view the final prototype product online, like NIKEiD program. E-commerce is a vital means to support MC as buying and selling MC products and transmitting information can be done with the internet. External information, says customer preferences and feedbacks, can then be captured.

CAD/CAM. Computer-aided design (CAD) and computer-aided manufacturing (CAM) systems are considered as the primary tools to support MC (Piller 2007). On one hand, CAD enables the customer's design to be changed and deployed into production instructions quickly. On the other hand, CAM aims to maximize the use of machine with the effective handling in the diversity of parts ordering. In apparel pattern making, CAD/CAM allows the automatic alteration of patterns for individual body measurement specifically (Helms et al. 2008). Those systems alter the patterns automatically according to specific measurement data, without the permanent change in the original garment pattern. Unfortunately, Lee and Chen (2000) manifested that the compatibility between CAD systems and software and hardware systems from different vendors is still a challenging problem in the industry.

Body-scanning technology. With regard to fit customization, body scanning is a critical instrument. Body scanning captures customers with personal and an unlimited number of body measurement for apparel design and pattern drafting (Anderson-Connell et al., 2002). Lee and Chen (2000) claimed that this data collection method gives precise, accurate, and repeatable data in order to create specific garments as different styles of garments need different data points. Customers gain a unique shopping experience in this manner as well. The measurement information of customers can be stored in a central database for many other applications (Helms et al. 2008).

Product data management (PDM). PDM software keeps track of engineering data and documents for managing changes because MC products accelerate the rate of change in product engineering (Zeleny 1996). Hence, it can control the product development and production process in an effective manner as the complexities in managing varieties and volumes of data on MC can be greatly minimized (Pan and Holland 2006). Additionally, it is a common platform for design and production teams to integrate and access the information for MC (Alford et al. 2000).

Apart from the above technologies, other technologies, such as, made to measure software, digital printing (Anderson-Connell et al. 2002), single ply cutters (Lee and Chen 2000), enterprise resource planning (ERP) system (Gunasekaran and Ngai 2005), and electronic data interchange (Silveira et al. 2001), are prominent in the implementation of MC.

2.6 Classifications of Mass Customization

Several authors classified MC with regard to different factors, such as customer involvement, modularity, type of process, and technology. Moreover, some of the scholars identified different levels of MC based on empirical observation. Let us review some of them as follows.

First, Duray (2000) demonstrated an MC typology based on two important identifiers, point of customer involvement in stages (i.e., design, fabrication, assembly, and use) and modularity, and suggested four MC archetypes – fabricators, involver, modularizers, and assemblers — in order to distinguish the level of MC strategies being used by firms. "Fabricator" is similar to pure customization strategy but employing modularity to gain commonality of product as both customer involvement and modularity occur during the design and fabrication stages. Hence, unique products can be created. When customer involvement appears in the design and fabrication stages but uses modularity during the assembly and delivery stages, it is called "involver" as no new modules are made for customers. The third type is "modularizer" which involves customers in assembly and delivery stages but uses modularity in design and fabrication stages. Customers do not specify their requirements until the assembly and use stages. Assembler is found when both customer involvement and modularity occur in the assembly and use stages. In this manner, products have been designed and customers are involved only in specifying the products.

The second classification is suggested by Gilmore and Pine (1997). They identified four customization levels based on empirical observation – collaborative, adaptive, cosmetic, and transparent customization. In collaborative customization, a firm establishes a dialogue with each customer so that his/her respective needs can be identified. Precise and customized products are then offered to customers. Adaptive customizer designs a standard product to customer, but he/she can alter it himself/herself. For cosmetic customization, one standard product is given but presented differently to different customers by methods such as packaging. Transparent customizers offer unique products to individual customers without letting them know explicitly that those products and services have been customized for them.

Lampel and Mintzberg (1996) defined a continuum of five MC strategies based on the configuration of process, product, and customer interaction in the production cycle. The first strategy is "pure standardization" which is similar to mass production due to the use of standard parts and manufacturing procedures without customer involvement in design. "Segmented standardization" offers a few choices on a basic product without customer involvement in design. In "customized standardization," customers can affect the assembly and distribution of product, but not in design and production. Products are manufactured on the basis of standard and mass-produced components. "Tailored customization" is defined as customizing fabrication, assembly, and distribution. Manufacturers still control over design, but may modify the design to meet customers' need. When customization can be found in every design, fabrication, assembly, and distribution step, it is called "pure customization."

Anderson-Connell et al. (1997) created a model for apparel MC specifically. They found that digital information technology applied in the manufacturing process leads to four options of customizing apparels. In "expanded search," each customer is able to access different manufacturers' product lines with intelligent searching capability. The next level is "design option" which means customer designs a garment in the modular selection through CAD. The other level, "co-design" offers fit customization with the help of managers, based on the choices of "design option." Finally, "total custom" enables customers to create a totally customized garment with the use of computer technology.

2.7 Performance Measures

In order to measure the performance of MC, time-based performance measures (e.g., days in inventory, work-in-process, delivery time, order response time), instead of financial measures (e.g., sales volume in dollars or pieces, profitability), are the preferred benchmarks (Loker and Oh 2002; Chandra and Grabis 2004c). The reason is because financial measures are usually biased against the size of firms. In Tu et al. (2004b), the performance in terms of MC capability, which is the ability of a firm to manufacture products that meet a variety of specific customer requirements quickly at a cost that is comparable to MP products, is studied. They stated that customization cost effectiveness (producing customized products without increasing cost significantly), volume effectiveness (enlarging product variety without diminishing production volume), and system responsiveness (reducing the delivery time and reorganizing production processes quickly in response to customization requests) are the major components of MC capability. They further showed that three of the manufacturing practices (re-engineering set-ups, preventive maintenance, and cellular manufacturing) enable firms to increase MC capability. Moreover, these manufacturing practices tend to have a greater impact on MC capability when environmental uncertainty is higher. Tu et al. (2001) also verified that time-based manufacturing practices (including shopfloor employee involvement in problem solving, reengineering setup, cellular manufacturing, preventive maintenance, quality improvement efforts, dependable suppliers, and pull production) have a direct impact on MC capability. Additionally, positive relationships have been found among customer closeness, modularity-based manufacturing practices (dynamic teaming, product modularity, and process modularity), and MC capability (Tu et al. 2004a).

Mchunu et al. (2003) suggested five variables to characterize MC capability. Those variables include effective product variety management, communication and information management efficiency, support from top level management, SCM efficiency, and new product development ability. These measures, though relatively intangible, provide another framework for studying the performance of MC.

2.8 Challenges of Mass Customization

We follow Blecker and Abdelkafi (2006) and discuss the challenges of MC in two dimensions as follows.

2.8.1 External Complexity

Svensson and Jensen (2003) stated that customer is the major, but also the limiting, factor in pursuing MC. As a wide range of product varieties are available in MC, customers are often confused. They are easily overwhelmed by the product selection process. Finally, they may be incapable of deciding what they want (Zipkin 2001). Blecker and Abdelkafi (2006) indicated that limited information processing capacity of humans, lack of customer knowledge about the product, and customer ignorance about his/her real individual needs are the main factors of external complexity. In order to reduce external complexity, firms require a solution to understand the needs of customers. They hence suggested that a configurator (i.e., configuration system) can help in this situation. Nevertheless, Piller (2007) reported that few firms have used configurators in MC in reality.

2.8.2 Internal Complexity

Employee. In the exploitation of MC, trained salesperson is an important issue (Lee and Chen 2000). In the customization process, a salesperson should identify the customers' needs and help them configure their own products. Taylor et al. (2003) indicated that having salespeople equipped with knowledge and skills is a way to gain the customers' trust and confidence to buy an MC product. However, retail industry is always characterized by having a high turnover rate of salespeople. Investment in training salespeople hence becomes a barrier in MC (Svensson and Jensen 2003). MC induces the proliferation of product variety (Aigbedo 2007) and hence, increases the complexity of operational and manufacturing related tasks (Blecker et al. 2005). Ahlstrom and Westbook reported that operational problems such as higher inventories and high manufacturing costs are evoked by MC (Ahlstrom and Westbrook 1999). Instantaneously, MC increases planning and scheduling and SC performance pressures as customers require quick delivery (Aigbedo 2007). It is the reason why effective SCM is needed so as to manage the inventory well. It is a relatively simple concept, but not easy to implement in reality.

Specification. Defining and configuring product variants is a big challenge in MC as different departments may have totally different specifications towards one product (Andel 2002). For example, information for production may be interpreted incorrectly and delivery time may be delayed. Consequently, customers may not be satisfied with the end products (Lee and Chen 2000).

Changes. Broekhuizen and Alsem noted that the requirement for a change in existing business models is the fundamental reason for the low adoption rate of MC (Broekhuizen and Alsem 2002). In particular, MC involves changes in systems, manufacturing processes, organizational structure, and SC structure in order to respond to individual orders (Pine 1996; Caddy et al. 2002). However, the changes can be costly, time consuming, and demanding (Piller and Muller 2004). Meanwhile, MC must be periodically evaluated and amended for the sake of market changes, nature of business, competition, and technology (Pine et al. 1993). More challenges in MC are exhibited in the works of Eastwood (1996), Alford et al. (2000), Knolmayer (2002), and Svensson and Jensen (2003).

3 MC in the Fashion Industry

A recent survey by Fedex Corp. on the apparel industry reported that more than 90% of the respondents had agreed that MC would play a more important role in the near future (Piller and Muller 2004). According to Kurt Salmon Associates Annual Consumer Outlook Survey for $[TC]^2$ (a leading research and development, and education firm for the sewn products industry), there are three varieties in the apparel MC, namely (1) personalization, (2) fit, and (3) design (Ives and Piccoli 2003; Sussman 1998). In apparel MC, customers can order mass-produced products and then customize them based on their own preferences (personalization). They can also provide individual body measurement for creating products that fit them well (fit). Anderson-Connell et al. (1997) noted that "fit" is considered as the most critical issue in apparel MC. Each customer can take part in the design or coloring in the meantime (design). For MC, the fashion industry mainly focuses on dimensional and modular customizations (Lee and Chen 2000). In the dimensional (fit) customization, fit of products can be well-delivered to customers as the products are based on their body measurement. Firms acquire customers' measurement data with various approaches, for instance, by body-scanning the customers (e.g., Brooks Brothers), requiring customers to enter measurement data into website (e.g., Lands' End), or letting customers try on the prototypes and making alteration (e.g., Levi's). The modular customization is also predominantly adopted in the fashion industry (e.g., JC Penney, Ralph Lauren). Customers can pick modules (e.g., components) and then create individualized products. Table 1 shows some MC practices in the fashion industry.

Notwithstanding that MC is not a new strategy in fashion industry, Loker and Oh (2002) argued that most fashion companies are not fully engaged in MC. Some firms have combined MP and MC for their business strategy. Besides, they showed that small firms are more likely to produce a higher percentage of customized products. Lee and Chen (2000) also mentioned that reducing cost is the foremost important objective in apparel MC, instead of fulfilling customers' needs. In the present MC practice, the styles that customers choose are usually limited which are already within a broad style framework prescribed by the firms. In order to reduce costs, the pattern is always based on a "standard size" of the target customers, and hence adjustment of this pattern is required for fitting individual customer specification.

Table 1 Brief descriptions of MC examples in fashion industry

Examples	Brief descriptions
Proper cloth propercloth.com	Proper Cloth was founded in 2008 and its headquarters is located in New York. This company offers high-end customized men's shirts. Customers can first choose fabric pattern, color, collar style, cuff style, and pocket. Next, customers can provide body measurement with three options: (1) Standard sizing (select from S to XXL and type of fit), (2) selecting the similar brand sizing (which is a kind of reverse engineering as customers can specify their shirt's size by selecting another shirt's size they like) (3) entering body measurement into website (e.g., neck around, arm length, shoulder width, chest around). The advanced 3D modeling software allows customers preview their own customized garments. All shirts are manufactured in the US factory.
Beyond clothing beyondclothing.com	Beyond Clothing is a manufacturer of customized outdoor apparels (BeyondFleece.com) and protective combat uniforms (BeyondTactical.com). It offers more than 100 items, for example, pullovers, shorts, vests, pants, and fleece jackets. Customers can order products online or by phone. Beyond Clothing allows customers select fabrics and colors among the preset options. Customers can also add features and components (e.g., pocket, hoods, zippers, and enhanced components) on their own products. In particular, customers can submit sizing information and their own preferences so as to produce best-fit products. The computerized pattern maker software then analyzes the information and changes pattern to accommodate the measurement. The automated cutting system is employed to cut the pattern precisely. Lastly, the garment is hand-sewn by a trained sewing worker. All the products are made in the US. With the help of configurator, customers can preview the final customized product virtually. Tracking order status is also allowed on the website. The lead time is around 6 weeks.
JC Penney jcpenney.com/custom	JC Penney (JCP) currently offers four products – jeans, khakis, dress shirts, and dress trousers for men to customize. Take customized dress shirt as an example, customers can choose one style among several options, for example, collar style, sleeve length and its style, and pleat style, to build their own shirt. JCP's MC is similar to Lands' End – partnering with ASI. Each product will be delivered to customers in approximately 4 weeks.
Zazzle.com	Zazzle gives more than 360 products online for MC, like apparels, accessories, and ties. A wide variety of fabrics, colors, and styles are offered. However, fit customization is not provided, so customers

(Continued)

Table 1 (Continued)

Examples	Brief descriptions
	should choose from the given standard sizes. Customers can upload photos or texts onto website and then create their own products. MC of Zazzle enjoys a high degree of automation. Zazzle has instant communication so order information can be transmitted to the production floor promptly. The data, material, production flow, printing, quality assurance, packaging, and shipping are automated. In the production department, Zazzle uses only direct-to-garment in-jet printers driven by centralized software. This printer is networked and highly automated (Murphy and Shuler 2007). In order to ease the online design process, Zazzle uses the web-based configurator called Ajax. This configurator preloads web content so that users can change text, crop and move pictures, and add multicolored borders immediately (Barret 2006). The final customized products can be previewed. Zazzle is the first company in the industry to offer on-demand embroidery with advanced system. Customers are able to preview the embroidery designs in real-time through 3D Zazzle's innovative Stitch Player (Zazzle's official webpage 2008). To develop MC, Zazzle has more than 250 partners, including Walt Disney Co. Images (DeWeese 2005). Zazzle also partners with technology company called Pitney Bowers in order to manage the information flows, mails, documents, and packages for Zazzle (Zazzle's official webpage 2008). Social networking is important in the success of Zazzle. Zazzle has cooperated with Facebook. Users can design their own products on Zazzle and make them available for sales in Zazzle. Moreover, users can promote them on Facebook (Zazzle's official webpage 2007). Integrated with My Space, a social-networking unit, Zazzle enables musicians with My Space pages to create virtual stores for t-shirts, posters, and other merchandise in Zazzle. With the use of artwork and graphic, their fans can customize them in Zazzle. (Smith 2007).
Ralph Lauren ralphlauren.com	Ralph Lauren (RL) is now offering a wide variety of customized products (e.g., polo tee, tie, dress, and robe) for men, women, boys, girls, and also babies online. Customers can select fabrics and pony-logo colors among the available options. Customers can preview the final products in a real time using an advanced configurator. RL promises customers that their products will be delivered within 1 week. In between, customers can track the orders on the website. Apart from online ordering, RL also gives customer the ability to customize purple label and Polo Ralph Lauren shirt and suit in selected stores. Trained sales associates measure customers manually and customers are able to select from 50 exclusive fabrics (Nygaard 2006), cuff and collar styles for creating personally fitted shirts and suits.

(Continued)

Table 1 (Continued)

Examples	Brief descriptions
Ascot Chang ascotchang.com	Ascot Chang (AS) is a Hong Kong-based high-end tailoring shop and has branch shops in the US, China, and Philippines. AS permits ordering MC shirts by mail, fax, and also in stores. Customers are measured by trained tailors in stores whereas they enter measurement data onto web site for online ordering. Customers create their own shirts from a combination of fabrics, collar and cuff style, pockets, pleats, and monogram. Some pictures of components or styles are not shown as a real product (i.e., computerized drawing only). The final customized product cannot be shown (i.e., can preview separate component or options only). AS takes approximately 3–5 weeks to process customers' orders.
Café press Cafepress.com	Café Press gives more than 50 types of customized apparel products (e.g., tracksuit, hoodies, underwear, and t-shirt) for men, women, kids, as well as babies. Customers are able to choose fabric colour and size (i.e., standard sizing). In addition, photos and images can be uploaded so as to create their own products. The instant preview of final customized products and order tracking service are provided. All the products are produced in the US. The lead time is around 2 days. Similar to Zazzle, customers are able to open virtual shops in Café Press for selling their own designed products.
QVC qvc.com/customfit	QVC is one of the largest multimedia retailers in the world. QVC provides customized jeans and twills online. MC of QVC is done in the same manner as Lands' End and JCP – partnering with ASI. Customers can pick up the choice in fabric type, colors, and features (e.g., rise, fly, back pocket, and leg style) and enter body measurement and ask self-assessment questions for making their own product. However, the virtual preview of final product is not available (customers can preview the choice in text format only). Customer is able to track order status online.
Interactive custom clothes company (IC3D) ic3d.com	Interactive Custom Clothes Company (IC3D) offers customized jeans and pants to both men and women. Customers can select fabric, color, leg style, ankle style, waist style, loops, pocket types, fly, trimmings, label, and thread color. IC3D relied on Genetic Engineered Neural Network (GENN) to make customized patterns in short time. GENN is a neural network which uses genetic algorithms. With the use of non-linear multi-variable solution, searching and sizing algorithm that chooses from and alters pre-existing patterns can run quickly. IC3D enjoys a higher degree of automation in production as the production and inventory replenishment processes are highly automated. All pre-production decisions and marker making are done by computer. However, sewing, finishing and shipping are carried out manually. Besides, customer service is computerized because adaptive behavior over the internet is provided by GENN. All the products are made in the US.

4 Traditional MC and Innovative MC

It is known that different industries would adopt different kinds and levels of innovation in MC (Zipkin 2001). As our focus is on the fashion industry, we will make use of the respective industrial cases for our discussions. In this section, we first define and compare the traditional MC and the innovative MC with four factors – supplier relationship, customer involvement, modularity, and technology. Next, we would discuss five cases of MC in the fashion industry. The five case studies, including Levi's, GS Company, Brooks Brothers, Lands' End, and Nike, illustrate how those companies implement MC in the traditional and innovative ways. Nine MC examples in fashion would also be discussed briefly in this section. All information is collected from primary (interviews and field visits) and secondary data (from published works and the internet) sources. By investigating the above factors in each company, we would then classify the "traditional" and "innovative" MCs.

4.1 Traditional Mass Customization

For traditional MC, it relies on a high degree of manual procedures during the MC process in order to provide a wide range of products to satisfy individual customers. Technology may be less useful in this kind of MC. In the following, Levi's and GS Company are regarded as examples of the traditional MC.

4.1.1 Levi's

In 1994, Levi's introduced "Personal Pair" (PP) program for women to customize their own jeans (Hill 1998). For creating this program, Levi's increased the number of sizes by two orders of magnitude from about 40 to over 4,000 (Pine 1998). The lead time was around 3 weeks (McCann 1996). Jeans under PP just costed customers about $10 more than a pair of off-the-rack jeans (Cuneo 1995). Owing to the success of PP, Levi's then expanded this program for both women and men later, and renamed the program as "Original spin" (Hill 1998). More options were available to the customers (Corcoran 2004). However, these two MC programs were considered as cumbersome, customer-annoying and obsolete in certain extent since customers should visit the store, be measured, and try on several pairs of stock jeans (Zeleny 1996). Later on, Levi's stopped this program. Although Levi's was trying to set up the body scanning in 2005, such data were only used to match customers with the best-fitting jeans in stocks, instead of custom-making any product (Ammenheuser 2008).

Technology. A degree of manual procedure was utilized in Levi's MC. In the PP, customers had to visit the stores for buying customized products, instead of online ordering. In the stores, women would use a kiosk computer system with the help of a trained sales associate to design (i.e., co-design) a pair of jeans (Hill 1998;

Carr et al. 2002). Manual measurement was necessary in this program. The sales associates would take four measurements (i.e., waist, inseam, hips, and rise) from each customer and then enter those data manually into the kiosk (Pine 1996). Next, computers would suggest which of the four prototype jeans would fit best from 400 prototype pairs that were stocked at the kiosk (Ederer 1995; Business Wire 2000). Customers should try on the physical prototypes and then modify the fit based on their preferences (Lee and Chen 2000). In addition, customers were able to decide the color/finish and style of leg cut (Carr et al. 2002). Finally, sales associates would enter the information into the computer and the order would be transmitted by email through modem from the kiosk to Custom Clothing Technology Corp., the software provider of PP, where it would be logged in and transmitted daily to Levi's factory for production (Hawley et al. 1997). In the factory, a pattern would be generated and cut using laser technology. The sewing team would then construct the jeans (Ederer 1995). To facilitate the repurchase, a bar-code label was sewn into the labeling of each personalized pair jeans (Ederer 1995). Simultaneously, those jeans could be tracked through the factory and sent to the correct customers (McCann 1996). Besides, Levi's invested heavily in data warehouses and decision-support technology for the MC program in order to enhance the collection of point of sales (POS) data (Hill 1998).

Supplier Relationship. Levis' did not outsource its own production for MC, but set up own factory in Tennessee (Berman 2002; Carr et al. 2002). Each pair was individually cut, hand-sewn, inspected, and packed for shipment in this factory.

Customer Involvement. According to the classification scheme in Duray (2002), customers were involved in the assembly stage in Levi's MC programs. In PP, customers had five options on colors/finishes and two more on leg cut - boot-cut and tapered legs (Carr et al. 2002). Levi's provided more choices in the "Original Spin". Customers could choose among classic, low cut, or relaxed style, 18 colors and finishes, and leg or fly preference. Fit customization was also allowed. All in all, customers could create own jeans by assembling those components.

4.1.2   GS Company (http://www.blablabra.com/)[1]

Godsend Trading Company (GS) is one of the companies which exercise MC in Hong Kong (in the context of B2B). This company engages in lingerie business. In Hong Kong, GS targets at the young market with the line called "Bla Bla Bra." Apart from trading and retailing, GS also manufactures lingerie with private labels for oversea markets. MP, (craft) customization, and MC are also used in this company. For MC, this company sends lingerie designs to customers and allows them to modify designs, for example, changing the style of shoulder straps or accessories.

---

[1]This company case is based on a personal interview with the company. We are grateful for the information provided by GS.

Technology. GS depends on hand-drawing (no CAD/CAM) for lingerie designs. Physical prototype will be sent to customers for previewing the customized products. Owing to a lack of technological support, virtual prototype cannot be provided. Digitalized information is limited. GS mostly uses technology for communication, instead of the automation of MC process. The order information is entered manually. GS simply transfers data and information by email. Email and face to face discussions are the most important communication means. There is no system linking GS with manufacturers or customers. GS also uses bar-code to track the products. To conclude, email, internet, database (for storing customers' information) and bar-coding are the technologies that GS mostly used.

Supplier relationship. GS outsources most of the production processes, including fabrication, dyeing, finishing. However, long term partnership with suppliers is absent because GS is cost-oriented in supplier selection. No information would be shared between GS and suppliers.

Customer involvement. Apart from craft customization, GS sends its own lingerie designs to customers and allows them to modify designs, like changing the style of shoulder straps or accessories (a kind of MC). Customers can change the components from the given material lists. Therefore, customers are involved in design, fabrication, and assembly stages according to Duray (2002). As GS markets the young lingerie market with the brand called "Bla Bla Bra," it exploits the POS data in order to develop MC and MP.

Modularity. Product modularity and process modularity are employed in GS. The products of GS employ modularized design. Although some technical problems may hinder component sharing (e.g., narrow shoulder straps can't support the bras with large cup size), GS commented that most of the components (like shoulder straps, laces, and accessories) could be shared across the products actually. For the process modularity, the production processes in GS can be rearranged and added easily for changing production needs.

4.2 Innovative Mass Customization

To compare with the traditional MC, some manual operations are replaced by automation in the innovative MC. The contribution of automation is based on partnership, extensive use of technology, modularity, and of course, customer involvement so as to deliver more variety of products to fulfill customers' needs. The idea conforms to Silveira et al. (2001): "MC as a system that uses information technology, flexible processes, and organizational structures to deliver a wide range of products and services that meet specific needs of individual customers, at a cost near that of mass-produced items." The case studies of Brooks Brothers, Lands' End, and Nike show that they pursue MC in an innovative way.

4.2.1 Brooks Brothers

In Brooks Brothers (BB)' MC program, customers can customize their own products (e.g., suit) based on individual fit and preferences (Rabon 2000) both online and in stores. In the beginning, BB had started from the traditional MC that heavily relied on manual operation. As time goes by, the degree of automation in the MC process is enhanced.

Technology. In the initial stage, BB focused on manual process as stores were required to fill out and mail to Pietrafesa Corporation (a Liverpool, NY based manufacturer of private label suits for many leading retail chains) the order forms with alteration information for MC (Rabon 2000). Eventually, data transmission could be done by an automatic computer system which is called "eMeasure." eMeasure has evolved into a kiosk system that allows customers to create and visualize the products. Sales associates assist customers during the process. They validate and enter the measurement information into the system. Following that, the system will suggest try-on prototype from the store's inventory. The orders will be finally sent to Pietrafesa Corp. automatically. The manufacturing process starts when Pietrafesa imports BB's orders from an internet site. After the customers' data have been collected, patterns and markers will be created by Pietrafesa Corp. based on Gerber technology's AccuMark Made to Measure (MTM) system (Stacy 1999) and Pietrafesa Corp. would assign work-in-process number and then allocate or order the necessary fabric. Patterns will be cut from the special ordered fabrics when the fabrics have been sent from suppliers. Simultaneously, the order information is uploaded to Pietrafesa's mainframe. The stock tickets, labels, production coupons, style file, bill of materials, costing information and sales order would automatically be generated. Apart from Gerber's AccuMark system, BB also added cutters, a UPS system, and Made-to-Measure (MTM) software for developing MC (Chelan 2007). The MTM system is a software that allows automatic modification of patterns according to customer's measurement. In other words, a pre-existing set of patterns with standardized alternation can be used. In order to have precise measurement data, BB employed a 3D body scanning tool called "Digital Tailoring" (2008), currently available in its flagship store in New York. The scanning process takes about 12 seconds with the use of white light-based scan (Haisley 2002). More than 200,000 data points will be captured and then created a 3D map of the body. In order to accommodate the individual customers tastes, sales associates can make some adjustments in the program accordingly. The measurement data will be transmitted to factory electronically in order to create patterns in a timely manner. In particular, such data will be stored in the database on a company's server for sharing and facilitating re-ordering processes. Moreover, online ordering of customized product is allowed in BB. With the advanced configurator, customers can create their own products step by step and can preview them virtually.

Supplier relationship. BB's MC relies on long term partnership with Pietrafesa Corp. and Gerber Technology (Rabon 2000; Chelan 2007, Stacy 1999). Essentially, suppliers are long-term partners with BB and Pietrafesa Corp. as the system is integrated between suppliers and them (Stacy 1999).

Customer involvement. Customers can create their own products, such as suits, dress shirts, and dress pants, from the given options. In BB's MC, customers pick up modules, for example, collar style, cuff style, pocket, and fabric types, to build products. For providing best-fit products, customers can enter their own measurement data onto the web site or visit the stores for body scanning. In other words, customers are involved in assembly stage for MC.

Modularity. For obtaining flexibility, process modularity is applied in BB. BB designs the program to be modular, which means the ordering process can be re-sequenced (Haisley 2002), e.g., customers can pick fabric first and then be scanned, or vice versa.

4.2.2 Lands' End

Lands' End (LE) offers shirts and pants (e.g., Chino, Jeans, and Corduroy) which can be customized in LE's website. Fit customization is also given. In order to implement successful MC, automation is found in LE. Ives and Piccoli (2003) reported that 40% of all jeans and chinos sold on the website are custom made in LE case. Essentially, a low return rate of customized products is reported.

Technology. LE provides fit customization with algorithms provided by Archetype solutions, Inc (ASI). As LE gathers the orders entered onto the web site, they will send the information to ASI electronically. Next, ASI software will process those data automatically (Drickhamer 2002). According to the customer's measurement data (weight and body size) and the answers of self-assessment questions (individual fit preferences), an electronic pattern would then be generated with the use of algorithms. After that, the pattern is drafted with the use of Gerber's PDF 2000 and made to measure programs and Nester software (Ives and Piccoli 2003). Software coders have automated all of these decisions. After that, the patterns would be transmitted to a contract factory in Mexico for production, where ASI has already installed its systems (McElwain 2001). Single-ply cutter would be used for cutting patterns (i.e., cutting one layer fabric each time). In the MC program of LE, modular manufacturing is employed (Drickhamer 2002). Bar-code would also be used for tracking products as well.

Supplier relationship. LE partners with ASI to develop MC. ASI can be regarded as a high-tech middleman that uses its MC system to link up retailers and manufacturers/contractors (McElwain 2001). For creating customized products, ASI pattern makers would develop base patterns, including allowances for the various styling alternatives, for each clothing line beforehand (Ives and Piccoli 2003). ASI also partners with the right manufacturers for developing MC (McElwain 2001).

Customer involvement. LE gives ability to customers to select colour, fabric, design, and also fit (Ives and Piccoli 2003) on the basics, instead of the fashionable items (Corcoran 2004). As customers pick up modules to build their own customized products, LE involves customers only in the assembly stage.

Modularity. Corcoran (2004) claimed that LE uses modular manufacturing techniques in MC. LE has modular lines to assemble each item, so the garment products are bundled and moved around the factory together.

4.2.3 Nike

Nike runs its famous MC program, which is known as NIKEiD. This program is popular as Nike's webpage showed that NIKEiD business has grown more than tripled since 2004. More than three million unique visitors are visiting www.Nikeid. com every month. Apart from running shoes, apparels (e.g., performance apparel and graphic tees) and gears (e.g., watches and bags) from two Nike's sub-brands (Nike Sportwear and Nike Pro) can be customized. Customers are able to order customized products online. In addition, design studios are also available in different countries (e.g., UK, USA, and China) so that customers can visit them and thereby design their own products. Besides NIKEiD program, Nike also provides Niketeam.com for providing customizing services on team uniforms and related gears. (PR Newswire 2001).

Technology. To facilitate online ordering, Nike has an advanced web-based configuration system and in-house developed and off-the-shelf software. This configurator and software help to transmit the designs automatically to manufacturing systems at Nike factories (Wilson 1999). In addition, customers are able to track the production status online. It implies that Nike's configuration system is actually linked with the manufacturing partners system. In the Nike design studio, trained sales associates also use this configurator (i.e., laptops are available to access Nike's website) to help customers to design and order customized products. Nike provides a virtual prototype to customers instantly. Nike develops MC using advanced technology. Recently, Nike is working with AKQA (a global interactive marketing agency) to let customers take pictures on their phones and then use multimedia messaging service (MMS) to send them to Nike Photo iD. Next, customers can enter unique design codes at nikeid.com to customize and buy them. In fact, the use of color re-cognition to create the service is claimed to be a world first technological application. As the visibility of information is important in MC, Nike has an ERP system for sharing information with its SC partners (Koch 2004). This application of ERP system is also integrated with supply chain planning software and CRM software. In such a way, Nike can share information up and down the SC with different parties effectively.

Supplier relationship. Nike outsources a large part of production, assembly, finishing, sales and distribution, and packaging to contractors, with only design and marketing kept in Nike (Password and Profile 2005). Although most of the tasks are outsourced, Nike believes in partnership. As mentioned before, Nike's configuration system is linked with their manufacturing partners. Thus, it is believed that Nike's MC program is based on partnership with suppliers. From Nike's webpage, it shows that Nike's business is built upon strong alliance with the SC partners.

Table 2 Traditional MC vs. innovative MC

	Traditional MC	Innovative MC
Supplier relationship	No partnership	Long term partnership
Technology	Limited use, relies on documentation. It results in a low degree of automation in MC process.	Extensive use of technology/advanced technology. It results automation in MC process.
Modularity[a]	Yes	Yes

[a]Here, we mainly focus on whether the company adopts product modularity. Modularity is essential for MC regardless of its innovativeness.

Customer involvement. Nike involves customers in the assembly stage. It is simply because Nike offers opportunity for customers to design own customized products from re-configurating components among the predetermined options, such as fabric color, sleeve style, embellishment, trim style, pants style, logos, and so on. However, fit customization is not provided. It means that customers should select from the standard sizing. In Nike's design studio, co-design is available. Customers can enjoy a 45 min private design section with the help of NIKEiD trained design consultants. The design consultants facilitate customers to design the products.

4.3 Comparison Between Traditional and Innovative Mass Customization

After we have defined the traditional MC and the innovative MC and reviewed some cases, we compare the features of the traditional MC and the innovative MC and summarize the key aspects in Table 2.

After we have described the above MC example cases, we further compare technology, supplier relationship, customer involvement and modularity of each company as follows (see Table 3).

According to our comparison, we then position MC of each company from the most traditional to the most innovative ones as shown in Fig. 1.

4.4 Remarks: New Models

Zafu (http://www.zafu.com/). Although Zafu.com does not allow customers to design their own jeans, it provides an innovative matching service for jeans. Zafu asks women shoppers 11 questions about their preference and then creates a body profile. This profile will be used to find out the best-fit jeans for customers from the database of hundreds of styles. Zafu would then link the customers to a retailer to purchase. Meanwhile, Zafu gets the commissions between 5 and 20% of each sale. Most important, customized jeans, like Indi Jeans, would also be featured in Zafu.

Table 3 Comparison in MC cases covered

Criteria/ examples	Supplier relationship	Level of customer involvement	Modularity	Technology			
				Measurement	Online ordering	Prototype (final customized product)	Information sharing
Levi's	Own factory	Assembly	Yes	Manual	No	Physical	Email
GS	Outsource No Partnership	Design, fabrication and assembly	Yes	No	No	Physical	Email
Nike	Outsource, Partnership	Assembly	Yes	Standard sizes	Yes	Virtual	ERP
BB	Outsource, Partnership	Assembly	Yes	Body scanning	Yes	Physical and virtual	E-measure
LE	Outsource, Partnership	Assembly	Yes	Algorithm calculation	Yes	No	ASI software
JCP	Outsource, Partnership	Assembly	Yes	Algorithm calculation	Yes	No	ASI software
QVC	Outsource, Partnership	Assembly	Yes	Algorithm calculation	Yes	No	ASI software

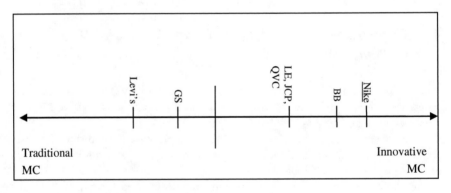

Fig. 1 Positioning of MC examples

My virtual model (MVM). My virtual model (MVM) is considered to help MC potentially (Guay 2003). MVM allows shoppers to create their own 3D virtual model to try on garments. On one hand, each customer can enter personal information, such as body measurements, heights, and weights so as to develop a personal avatar to try on the garment before she/he purchases (Nantel 2004). On the other hand, MVM produces 3D garments based on manufacturer's patterns and specification. In other words, customers can try on garments in a virtual world, instead of in-store fitting. Companies, like Lands' End, adidas, H&M are now employing MVM in their own websites for online shopping.

5 Recommendations and Conclusion

As a result of market turbulence and changing consumer behavior, MC has become a growing trend in the fashion industry. Good MC operations require the support of the whole related supply chain. From our analysis, apart from modularity and customer involvement, technology is a prerequisite for successful MC implementation. Technology, (for instance, configurators, CAD/CAM, Internet, body scanning, and product data management), helps coordination, communication, and information transfer in the MC program. In the fashion industry, MC focuses on dimensional and modular customization. However, most fashion companies have engaged in MC only in a limited extent. Most important, they usually aim at cost reduction, but not fulfilling customers' needs. Several published works in the literature have classified MC with different dimensions, such as customer involvement, modularity, processes, and technology. In order to measure MC performance, a time-based performance measure is one of the benchmarks (Loker and Oh 2002, Chandra and Grabis 2004c).

In this chapter, we have identified the traditional and innovative MCs with respect to supplier relationship, modularity, customer involvement, and technology. These four factors determine the degree of automation in the MC process. We have then revealed some MC practices and classified those cases into either the traditional MC or the innovative MC according to the degree of automation in the MC process. For implementing successful MC, we have the following recommendations:

1. Bar-coding system is employed in either the traditional MC or the innovative MC in the fashion industry. Companies mainly utilize this system for tracking products and storing (limited amount of) customer data. We suggest that MC companies in fashion invest in radio frequency identification (RFID) in order to improve the efficiency during the customization process. RFID helps to track the materials and products in an efficient way. For example, Dell, a pioneer in MC, tracks the processes using RFID and this tracking through the assembly line is linked to customer service systems and order website for tracing orders (Kumar and Craig 2007). Moreover, RFID is able to store a larger amount of customer data, when compared with bar-code. Schenk and Seelmann-Eggebert (2003) also manifested that RFID can contain information about customized working steps and specifications together with delivery date and distribution information. Documentation can also be reduced. It allows the ease of reordering customized products at the same time. In the reality, Ford Motor Co. employs RFID in MC. They use RFID transporters on every vehicle. Such transporters send query to database to find the correct paint code. After that, the system routes the information to a robot and selects the correct paint and sprays the vehicle. In this manner, vehicles can receive the right paint and features automatically on the basis of customers' orders (Greengard 2004). The above successful implementations of RFID are good evidence to support RFID's application for MC in the fashion industry.

2. With the advent of intelligent clothing, MC is not limited only to preference, fit, and design (see Sect. 2.1) but can be extended to functionality in the fashion industry. On one side, smart wearable electronic device (also known as e-apparel) gives a new direction in MC (Langenhove and Hertleer 2004). This type of wearable electronics allows the addition of some electronic components to increase the functionality of garments. For instance, Gap has offered a hooded jacket with built-in FM radio (Langenhove and Hertleer 2004). As the e-clothing is getting its popularity, functionality may emerge as one major issue in MC in the future. Customers can therefore customize the use of technology in their own clothes. On the other side, intelligent clothing is derived from smart materials and textiles. Langenhove and Hertleer (2004) identified that smart textiles are able to sense stimuli from the environment, to reach them and adapt to them by integration of functionalities in the textile structure. Smart textiles include, for example, shape memory materials (materials return to a pre-set shape with the right stimulus), phase change materials (a kind of latent heat-storage materials), thermochromic dyes (color changes with a change in temperature), and photochromic dyes (color changes after activation in visible light and invisible light) (Tang and Stylios 2006). With the use of smart textiles and materials, satisfaction of the changing customers' needs can be achieved to a certain extent; say, garment color changes with customers' moods. It appears to be similar to the MC objective – meeting specific customers' needs with a wide range of products. However, MC is still considered as a vital strategy and will not be replaced by smart technologies. The main reason is that customers can gain unique experience, like knowledge gained from design and configuration processes. Essentially, MC allows customers to satisfy themselves by designing/configuring their own products according their own preferences (i.e., an active way). It is different from smart textiles which accommodate customers' needs by reacting with stimulus (i.e., a passive way). However, if the smart technologies can be combined into MC, MC will become even more interesting (e.g., fit of garment changes with the body shape). We reckon that intelligent clothing (e-clothing or smart textiles) should be regarded as an extension of MC, instead of a replacement.

3. As we mentioned earlier in Sect. 2.2, MC generates outsourcing opportunities. The internet technologies have given possibility of crowdsourcing (Hintikka 2008). Crowdsourcing is an example in the market ideology of web 2.0 (Scholz 2008). Scholz (2008) stated that "Web 2.0 provides continually-updated service that gets better the more people use it, consuming and remixing data from multiple sources, including individual users, while providing their own data and services in a form that allows remixing by others, creating network effects through an architecture of participation, and delivering rich user experiences." For crowdsourcing, it utilizes the talent of the crowd as the job traditionally performed by employees can be outsourced to general public now (Scholz 2008). Innovative MC companies, like Zazzle, Café Press, and Nike, are adopting crowdsourcing principle as they allow customers submit and store the designs in database for selling. In this manner, it provides another way for company to gather customer information and feedback. Customer preferences can be

collected for developing MC program and the related products (Helms et al. 2008). At the same time, customer involvement can be enhanced because of customer participation in content contribution, and thereby, collaboration can be derived. In particular, crowdsourcing leads to a higher level of responsiveness and flexibility as companies focus on their own core competencies. It is one innovative feature of MC.

4. The present configurators, in both the traditional and innovative MCs, seldom give opportunity to customers to verify their own preferences. It has strong product orientation as it only provides components or modules and lets customers choose among them (Blecker et al. 2004). However, most customers are not well-equipped with product knowledge. It is especially true and important for performance and sportswear clothing (e.g., Nike and Beyond Clothing). Customized products may somehow not meet the customers' real expectations. Blecker et al. (2004) noted that "the language in which customers identify and understand their needs is completely different from the language used by engineers and product centered toolkits consisting of modules and components." Customers may find it hard to understand the product specific terms. For example, customers want to stretch easily with an MC product. In product specific term, it means using spandex while most customers do not fully understand its meaning. In order to exactly meet customer's needs, we should start from understanding customers' implicit needs. The system should investigate the customer needs, like asking open ended questions, and then match with the product components so as to create a customized product. To deal with this issue, Blecker et al. (2004) suggested a customer-oriented advisory system that guides customers with their profiles and requirements during the MC process. However, such an advisory system is still rare in practice especially in the fashion industry.

5. Implementing MC would imply changes in the organization (e.g., organizational structure and SC). As mentioned before, a change can be costly and time-consuming. A required big change may lead to employee resistance towards MC. One proposal which reduces the resistance is to implement MC program gradually. In addition, top management's support is important. As MC aims at satisfying customers, MC is regarded as a continual program as customer needs always change. Top management should create a culture that encourages employees to increase their capabilities and skill continually (Pine et al. 1993). Moreover, a diversity of employee capabilities is needed to deal with a greater product variety. In short, a robust change management program is needed for a fashion company to successfully implement MC.

For future studies, it will be interesting to explore how new technologies can further enhance the implementation and applications of MC. Moreover, an exploration on the degree of modularity adoption in both the traditional MC and the innovative MC is another promising extension of this paper.

Acknowledgements This research is partially supported by RGC(HK)-GRF under grant number of PolyU5145/06E.

References

Ahlstrom P, Westbrook R (1999) Implications of mass customization for operations management: an exploratory survey. Int J Oper Prod Manag 19(3):262–274

Aigbedo H (2007) An assessment of the effect of mass customization on suppliers' inventory levels in a JIT supply chain. Eur J Oper Res 181:704–715

Alford D, Sackett P, Nelder G (2000) Mass Customization – an automotive perspective. Int J Prod Econ 65:99–110

Ammenheuser MK (2008) The imperfect fit: apparel chains are wooing shoppers with fitting services, but mixed results. SCT – Shopping Centers Today Online. http://www.icsc.org/srch/sct/sct0308/retailing_made.php. Accessed 19 Jan 2009

Andel T (2002) From common to custom: the case for make-to-order. Mater Handling Manag 57 (12):24–31

Anderson-Connell LJ, Brannon EL, Ulrich PV, Marshall T, Staples N, Grasso M, Butenhoff P, Beninati M (1997) Discovering the process of mass customization: A paradigm shift for competitive manufacturing. http://www.p2pays.org/ref%5C08/07124.pdf. Accessed 31 Dec 2008

Anderson-Connell LJ, Ulrich PV, Brannon EL (2002) A consumer-driven model for mass customization in the apparel market. J Fashion Market Manag 6(3):240–258

Ascot Chan's official webpage (2009) http://www.ascotchang.com. Accessed 19 Jan 2009

Baldwin CY, Clark KB (1997) Managing in an age of modularity. Harv Bus Rev 75(5):84–93

Barret V (2006) Zazzle it. Fobes.com. http://www.forbes.com/entrepreneurs/entretech/free_forbes/2006/0109/050.html. Accessed 19 Jan 2009

Berman B (2002) Should your firm adopt a mass customization strategy? Bus Horiz 45(4):51–60

Beyond Clothing's official webpage (2009) http://www.beyondclothing.com. Accessed 17 Jan 2009

Blecker T, Abdelkafi N (2006) Mass customization: state-of-the-art and challenges. In: Blecker T, Friedrich G (eds) Mass customization: challenges and solutions. Springer, USA

Blecker T, Friedrich G, Kaluza B, Abdelkafi N, Kreutler G (2004) An advisory system for cusomters' objective needs elicitation in mass customization. In: Proceesings of the 4th Workshop on Information System for Mass Cusotmization (ISMC2004) at the fourth International ICSC symposium on engineering of intelligent systems (EIS 2004), pp 1–10

Blecker T, Friedrich G, Kaluza B, Abdelkafi N, Kreutler G (2005) Information and management systems for product customization. Springer, New York

Broekhuizen TLJ, Alsem KJ (2002) Success factors for mass customization: A conceptual model. J Market-Focused Manag 5:309–330

Brooks Brothers' official webpage (2008) http://www.brooksbrothers.com/specialorder/mtm_tailored_info.tem. Accessed 31 Dec 2008

Business Wire (2000) The Levi's brand sews up holiday gifts with Create your own jeans service and seasonal gift certificates. Press release, Internet. Accessed 15 Nov 2000

Caddy I, Helou M, Callan J (2002) From mass production to mass customization: impact on integrated supply chains. In: Rautenstrauch C, Seelmann-Eggebert R, Turowski K (eds) Moving into mass customization. Springer, Heidelberg

Café Press's official webpage (2009) http://www.cafepress.com. Accessed 19 Jan 2009

Carr LP, Lawler WC, Shank JK (2002) Reconfiguring the value Chain: Levi's personal pair. J Cost Manag 16(6):9–17

Chandra C, Grabis J (2004a) Managing logistics for mass customization: the new production frontier. In: Chandra C, Kamrani A (ed) Mass customization: a supply chain approach. Kluwer, New York

Chandra C, Grabis J (2004b). Mass customization: framework and methodologies. In: Chandra C, Kamrani A (eds) Mass customization: a supply chain approach. Kluwer, New York

Chandra C, Grabis J (2004c) Logistics and supply chain management for mass customization. In: Chandra C, Kamrani A (eds) Mass customization: a supply chain approach. Kluwer, New York

Chelan D (2007) Brooks Brothers builds made-to-measure. Apparel Mag 48(10):36–38

Christopher M (2000) The agile supply chain: competing in volatile markets. Ind Market Manag 29:37–44

Corcoran CT (2004) Mass retailers find custom clothing fits them just fine. Women's Wear Daily 188(9):10–12

Coronado AE, Lyons AC, Kehoe DF, Coleman J (2004) Enabling mass customization: extending build-to-order concepts to supply chains. Prod Plann Contr 15(4):398–411

Cuneo A Z (1995) Levi Strauss sizes the retail scene. Advert Age, 66(4):4

Davis SM (1987) Future perfect. Addison Wesley, MA

DeWeese C (2005) Zazzle, a seller of custom goods, gets venture-capital backing. Wall St J (July 18, 2005)

Drickhamer D (2002) A leg up on mass customization. Ind Week 251(8):59

Duray R (2002) Mass customization origins: mass or custom manufacturing? Int J Oper Prod Manag 22(3):314–328

Duray R, Ward PT, Milligan GW, Berry WL (2000) Approaches to mass customization: Configurations and empirical validation. J Oper Manag 18:605–625

Eastwood MA (1996) Implementing mass customization. Comput Ind 30:174–174

Ederer C (1995). Levi Strauss & Co. buys custom clothing technology Corp. PR Newswire

Erens FJ, Hegge HMH (1994). Manufacturing and sales co-ordination for product variety. Int J Prod Econ 37:83–99

Feitzinger E, Lee HL (1997) Mass customization at Hewlett-Packard: the power of postponement. Harv Bus Rev 75(1):116–121

Gershenson JK, Prasad GJ, Allamneni S (1999) Modular product design a life-cycle view. J Integr Design Process Sci 3(4):1–9

Ghiassi M, Spera C (2003) Defining the internet-based supply chain system for mass customized markets. Comput Ind Eng 45:17–41

Gilmore JH, Pine BJ (1997). The four faces of mass customization. Harv Bus Rev 75(1):91–101

Gooley T (1998) How logistics makes it happen. Comput Ind Eng 37(4):49–54

Greengard S (2004) Driving change in the auto industry. RFID J http://www.rfidjournal.com/article/purchase/898; Accessed 5 Feb 2009

Guay L (2003) The configurator: create your identity, create your product. In: Proceedings of the 2nd interdisciplinary World congress on mass customization and personalization

Gunasekaran A, Ngai EWT (2005) Build-to-order supply chain management: a literature review and framework for development. J Oper Manag 23:423–451

Haisley T (2002) Brooks Brothers: digital tailors measure up. Bobbin 43(6):26–30

Hawley M, Poor RD, Tuteja M (1997) Things that think. Pers Tech 1:13–20

Helms MM, Ahmadi M, Jih WJK, Ettkin LP (2008) Technologies in support of mass customization strategy: exploring the linkages between e-commerce and knowledge management. Comput Ind 59:351–363

Hill S (1998) Levi Strauss puts a new spin on brand management. Apparel Ind Mag 59(11):46–47

Hintikka KA (2008) Web 2.0 and the collective intelligence. In: Proceedings of the 12 international conference on entertainment and media in the ubiquitous era

Interactive Custom Clothes Company official webpage (2009) http://www.ic3d.com. Accessed 19 Jan 2009

Ives B, Piccoli G (2003) Custom made apparel and individualized service at Lands' End. Commun Assoc Inform Syst 11:79–93

JC Penney's official webpage (2008) Custom fit program. http://www.jcpenney.com/jcp/customfit.aspx. Accessed 22 Dec 2008

Kincade DH (1995) Quick response management system for the apparel industry: Definition through technologies. Clothing Textiles Res J 13:245–251

Knolmayer GF (2002) On the economics of mass customization. In: Rautenstrauch C, Seelmann-Eggebert R, Turowski K (eds) Moving into mass customization. Springer, Heidelberg

Koch C (2004) Nike rebounds. CIO http://www.cio.com.au/article/166633/nike_rebounds?pp = 1. Accessed 19 Jan 2009

Kumar A (2004) Mass customization: metrics and modularity. Int J Flex Manuf Syst 16:287–311

Kumar S, Craig S (2007) Dell, Inc's closed loop supply chain for computer assembly plants. Inform Knowl Syst Manag 6:197–214

Lampel J, Mintzberg M (1996) Customizing customization. Slogan Manag Rev 38 (1):21–30

Lands' End's official webpage (2008) http://www.landsend.com. Accessed 22 Dec 2008

Langenhove LV, Hertleer C (2004) Smart clothing: a new life. Int J Clothing Sci Tech 16(1–2): 63–72

Lee HL, Feitzinger E, Billington C (1997) Getting ahead of your competition through design for mass customization. Target 13 (2):8–18

Lee SE, Chen JC (2000) Mass customization methodology for an apparel industry with a future. J Ind Tech 16(1):1–8

Loker S, Oh YJ (2002) Technology, customization and time-based performance in the apparel and sewn products industry. J Textile Apparel Tech Manag 2:1–13

McCann S (1996) Business & related services. Comput World 30 (23):96

McCutcheon DM, Raturi AS, Meredith JR (1994) The customization-responsiveness squeeze. Sloan Manag Rev 35 (2):89–99

McElwain J (2001) Archetype Raises the Bar. Bobbin Magazine, December 1, 40–43 http://www.archetypesolutions.com/contentpresentation.cfm?doc=archetype1201.htm&pagetype=news

Mchunu C, Alwis, AD, Efstathiou J (2003) A framework for selecting a best-fit MC strategy. In: Tseng MM, Piller FT (eds) The customer centric enterprise. Springer, Heidelberg

Mukhopadhyay SK, Setoputro R (2005) Optimal return policy and modular design for build-to-order products. J Oper Manag 23:496–506

Murphy T, Shuler H (2007) Online mass customization: This changes everything. Impressions 31(8):20–34

Nantel J (2004) My virtual model: virtual reality comes into fashion. J Interact Market 18(3):73–86

Nike's official webpage: sportwear bespoke program (2008) http://www.nike.com/nikeos/p/sportswear/en_US/view_post?country = US&lang_locale = en_US&blog = en_US&post = en_US/2008/08/18/nike-sportswear-at-21-mercer-street. Accessed 22 Dec 2008

Nygaard S (2006) Ralph expands custom program; designer also gives Rhinelander mansion an update to better spotlight company's label. DNR (New York), 36(41):15

Pan B, Holland R (2006) A mass customized supply chain for the fashion system at the design-production interfaces. J Fashion Market Manag 10(3):345–359

Password FY, Profile M (2005) Nike, IKEA and IBM's outsourcing and business strategies. Hum Resource Manag Int Digest 13(3):15–17

Peters L, Saidin H (2000) IT and the mass customization of services: the challenge of implementation. Int J Inform Manag 20:103–119

Piller FT (2004) Mass customization: Reflections on the state of the concept. Int J Flex Manuf Syst 16:313–334

Piller FT (2007) Observations on the present and future of mass customization. Int J Flex Manuf Syst 19:630–636

Piller F, Ihl C, Huller J, Stotko C (2004) Toolkits for open innovation – the case of mobile phone games. In: Proceedings of the 37th Hawaii international conference on system sciences

Piller FT, Muller M (2004) A new marketing approach to MC. Int Comput Integr Manuf 17(7): 583–593

Pine BJ (1993) Mass customization. Harvard Business School Press, Boston

Pine BJ (1996) Serve each customer efficiently and uniquely. Bus Commun Rev (January 1996): 2–5

Pine BJ (1998) You're only as agile as your customers think. Agility Global Compet 2(2):24–35

Pine BJ, Victor B, Boynton AC (1993) Making mass customization work. Harv Bus Rev 71(5):108–119

PR Newswire (2001) Nike's new web site lets teams design and order uniforms online. Press Release: Internet. Accessed 8 Jan 2001

Proper cloth's official webpage (2008) http://propercloth.com. Accessed 31 Dec 2008

QVC's official webpage (2009) http://www.qvc.com. Accessed 19 Jan 2009

Rabon LC (2000) Mixing the elements of MC. Bobbin 41(5):38–41

Radder L, Louw L (1999) Mass customization and mass production. TQM Mag 11(1):35–40

Ralph Lauren's official webpage (2008) http://www.ralphlauren.com. Accessed 22 Dec 2008

Reichwald R, Piller FT, Moslein K (2000) Information as a critical success factory for mass customization or why even a customized shoe not always fit. ASAC-IFSAM 2000 conference, Montreal, Quebec, Canada

Reichwald R, Piller FT, Jaeger S, Zanner S (2003) Economic evaluation of mini-plants for mass customization. In: Tseng MM, Piller FT (eds) The customer centric enterprise. Springer, Heidelberg

Retail Forward Inc (2003) Twenty trends for 2010. Retailing in an Age of Uncertainty 4:1–3

Ro YK, Liker JK, Fixson SK (2007). Modularity as a strategy for supply chain coordination: The case of US Auto. IEEE Trans Eng Manag 54(1):172–189

Salvador F, Rungtusanatham M, Forza C (2004) Supply chain configurations for MC. Prod Plann Contr 15(4):381–397

Schenk M, Seelmann-Eggebert R (2003) Challenges of mass customization manufacturing. In: Tseng MM, Piller FT (eds) The customer centric enterprise: advances in mass customization and personalization. Springer, Berlin

Schilling M (2000) Towards a general modular systems theory and its application to interfirm product modularity. Academy of Management Review, 25(2): 312–334.

Scholz T (2008) A market ideology and the myths of Web 2.0. First Monday 13(3). http://firstmonday.org/htbin/cgiwrap/bin/ojs/index.php/fm/article/viewArticle/2138/1945

Schroeder DM, Gopinath C, Congden SW (1989) New technology and the small manufacturer: Panacea or plague? J Small Bus Manag 27(7):1–10

Schwegmann V, Strube G, Willats P, Linck J, Boenigk A (2003) Flexible production and supply chain systems: Generating value through effective customization. In: Proceedings of the 2nd interdisciplinary world congress on mass customization and personalization

Silveira GD, Borenstein D, Fogliatto FS (2001) Mass customization: Literature review and research directions. J Prod Econ 72:1–13

Smith E (2007) Virtual art gets body. Wall St J 250(102):B5

Stacy B (1999) Brooks Brothers 2000: repositioned for success. Apparel Ind 60 (12):16–21

Starr MK (1965) Modular-production: a new concept. Harv Bus Rev 43(6):131–142

Sullivan P, Kang J (1999) Quick response adoption in the apparel manufacturing industry: competitive advantage of innovation. J Small Bus Manag 37(1)

Sussman B (1998) Nobody will be wearing the same dress. Discount Merchandiser 38(5):140–141

Svensson C, Jensen T (2003) The customer at the final frontier of mass customization. In: Tseng MM, Piller FT (eds) The customer centric enterprise, Springer, Heidelberg

Tang SLP, Stylios GK (2006) An overview of smart technologies for clothing design and engineering. Int J Clothing Sci Tech 18(2):108–128

Taylor CPA, Harwood RJ, Wyatt JL, Rouse MJ (2003) Implementing a mass customized clothing service. In: Tseng MM, Piller FT (eds) The customer centric enterprise. Springer, Heidelberg

Toffler A (1970) Future shock. Bantam Books, New York

Tu Q, Vonderembse MA, Ragu-Nathan TS (2001) The impact of time-based manufacturing practices on MC and value to customer. J Oper Manag 19:201–217

Tu Q, Vonderembse MA, Ragu-Nathan TS, Ragu-Nathan B (2004a) Measuring modularity-based manufacturing practices and their impact on MC capability: a customer-driven perspective. Decis Sci 35(2):147–168

Tu Q, Vonderembse MA, Ragu-Nathan TS (2004b) Manufacturing practices: antecedents to mass customization. Prod Plann Contr 15(4):373–380

Ulrich K (1995) The role of product architecture in the manufacturing firm. Res Pol 24(3):419–440

Ulrich K, Tung K (1991) Fundamentals of product modularity. In: Proceedings of the 1991 ASME winter annual meeting symposium on issues in design, Manufacturing integration, pp 73–79

Vascellaro JE (2007) Home and family: shopping around/online craft markets. Wall St J (April 5, 2007)

Von Hippel E (2001) Perspective: user toolkits for innovation. J Prod Innovat Manag 18(4):247–257

Wilson T (1999) Custom manufacturing: nike model shows web's limitations. InternetWeek 792:1

Zazzle's official webpage (2007) Zazzle launches on-demand retail application to Facebook. http://www.zazzle.com/mk/welcome/pressreleases/pr110707. Press Release: Internet. Accessed 7 Nov 2007

Zazzle's official webpage (2008) Zazzle® launches embroidery on-demand, an industry first. http://www.zazzle.com/mk/welcome/pressreleases/pr103008. Press Release: Internet. Accessed 30 Oct 2008

Zazzle's official webpage (2009) http://www.zazzle.com. Accessed 19 Jan 2009

Zeleny M (1996) Customer-specific value chain: beyond mass customization? Hum Syst Manag 15(2):93–97

Zipkin P (2001) The limits of MC. MIT Sloan Manag Rev 42(3):81–87

Improving Allocation of Inventory for Quick Response to Customer Orders: A Case Study

Tej S. Dhakar, Charles P. Schmidt, and David M. Miller

Abstract This paper is based on a study of the allocation of available inventory to customer orders at a large apparel manufacturing organization. As a number of items were in short supply at the beginning of each month, few orders were being filled completely. Majority of the orders were being filled at the end of the month when most inventory items become available for shipment. The finished goods distribution center at the company was thus faced with an uneven distribution of workload during the month resulting in reduced labor productivity and significant overtime cost. A new heuristic-based procedure for allocating available inventory to customer orders was developed with a number of unique features. The heuristic was tested against the old allocation procedure as well as against linear and integer programming models of the problem. The heuristic was found to perform much better than the old allocation procedure and almost as well as the mathematical models. The new allocation procedure was implemented and a more even distribution of workload, lower inventories, reduction in labor cost, and quicker response to customer orders were achieved.

Keywords Inventory allocation · Order fulfillment · Order processing

1 Introduction

This study was conducted at a large apparel manufacturing company that produced about 800 different styles of apparel. Each style was produced in many different colors and each style/color in turn in many different construction types and sizes. It all added up to about 12,000 different SKUs. Many of the items were "basic" and available for supply on demand. Other items called "basic fashion" and

T.S. Dhakar (✉)
Department of Quantitative Studies and Operations Management, School of Business
Southern New Hampshire University, Manchester, NH, USA
e-mail: t.dhakar@snhu.edu

T.C. Edwin Cheng and T.-M. Choi (eds.), *Innovative Quick Response Programs in Logistics and Supply Chain Management*, International Handbooks on Information Systems, DOI 10.1007/978-3-642-04313-0_22,

"fashion" were generally not available for immediate supply. These items were assigned promise dates depending on request dates from customers, the inventory-on-hand, and projected inventories based on production schedules.

One of the problems faced by the company was the surge in the volume of work in its distribution center at the end of each month. Only a small proportion of orders were being filled in the first 2 weeks of each month. This was resulting in a very uneven distribution of workload in the distribution center during the month, with not enough work to keep the workers busy in the beginning of the month and more than enough to cause huge amounts of overtime at the end of the month.

Thus, the major objective of this project was to find cost-effective means of leveling the workload in the distribution center by producing more releasable orders during the first 2 weeks of the shipping month. While doing this, it was necessary to ensure that the existing level of customer service in terms of on-time deliveries was maintained or improved and there was no negative impact of the changes on any other functions of the business.

The current case study falls in the general area of order fulfillment process. Waller et al. (1995) examined the topic of reengineering order fulfillment processes and illustrated the role of benchmarking as a tool in the reengineering process. They discussed the tools and techniques that can facilitate reengineering and investigated three firms that manufacture computers to determine what led them to reengineer their order fulfillment processes.

Kritchanchai and MacCarthy (1999) studied evidence from field studies undertaken to investigate the responsiveness of the order fulfillment process in a number of companies. They developed a generic responsiveness framework that incorporated both strategic and operational viewpoints and noted the need for more field studies on responsiveness.

Turner et al. (2002) explained how the customer order fulfillment process in a manufacturing company can be interpreted in terms of reliability engineering concepts. They applied the reliability engineering framework involving the three steps of risk analysis, risk assessment, and risk management to improve the customer order fulfillment process at a label manufacturing firm. They suggested using a similar framework for all key business processes in an organization to improve the overall reliability of the business.

Croxton (2003) described the order fulfillment process in detail to show how it can be implemented within a company and managed across firms in the supply chain. He examined the activities involved in the process; how the interfaces with other functions, processes, and firms can be evaluated; and provided examples of successful implementation.

Pibernik and Yadav (2009) considered a make-to-stock order fulfillment system facing random demand with random due date preferences from two classes of customers. They developed an integrated approach for reserving inventory in anticipation of future order arrivals from high priority customers and for order promising in real-time. They proposed an algorithm that exploited the time structure in order arrivals and time-phased material receipts to determine inventory reservations for high priority orders.

Next section describes the company's existing inventory allocation system used to fill customer orders. This is followed by an analysis of the problems inherent in the existing system. The section-after goes on to propose a new inventory allocation system. This is followed by how the new allocation system was tested by simulation and compared with mathematically optimal solutions. Implementation of the new inventory allocation scheme is discussed next. The last section concludes the paper.

2 Existing Inventory Allocation System

Each customer's order usually contains a large number of different SKUs. Many orders are "at once" orders and can be shipped as soon as they are filled. Other orders are "not before" orders, which can be shipped only after the "request date" specified in the customer's order.

Each order, when it is received, is keyed into the computer. An acknowledgment, which specifies a promise date for each item, is printed out for each order. The promise date for an item on an order is the later of the production availability date for the item and the customer's request date for the order. The customers' orders together with the promise dates for the items on the orders constitute the order file.

The first step in the order-filling process is the prioritization of customer orders. The basic field used is the customer class, determined on the basis of customer's sales volume in the previous year. Dollar value of the orders is used to sort the orders within a particular customer class. Available inventory is allocated to the orders based on their place in the priority sequence.

The second step in the order-filling process is the inventory allocation scheme (program), which allocates available inventory to customer orders. Company's policy is to protect the promise dates assigned to the items on the orders. Protection of the promise dates requires that available inventory not be allocated to an item on an order with a given promise date until inventory has been allocated to all orders with earlier promise dates for the item. This is achieved by allocating the available inventory by item (SKU) by promise date. That is, available inventory of a particular item is first allocated to orders with the earliest promise date for the item. If any inventory remains, it is allocated to the orders with next later promise date for the particular item and so on. When all available inventory of a particular item has been allocated, the same process is repeated for other items until available inventory of all items has been allocated.

After the available inventory of all SKUs has been allocated to the orders, the orders are evaluated for their completion status. All completed orders are sent to the distribution center for picking and shipping to the customers. Orders that are completed 70–99% are reviewed manually for possible partial shipment, if allowed by the customer. All nonreleased orders together with new orders are run through the system the next day.

3 Problems with the Existing Allocation Scheme

In the beginning of the month, a number of items are in short supply, i.e., the available inventory is inadequate to fill the orders on hand. The situation improves progressively during the month and by the end of the month, production managers are able to meet most of the shortages.

In the existing allocation scheme, the high priority orders were able to reserve large quantities of merchandise early in the month, even though their order will not be sufficiently completed to be released for picking until more stock became available later in the month. Meanwhile, lower priority orders that could have been allocated completely earlier in the month would not be allocated because stock was being held for the higher priority orders. As a result, neither high nor lower priority orders would be completed and released for picking until the last week of the month, when more merchandise became available to fill both kinds of orders. This would lead to the month-end rush of orders for picking and shipping in the distribution center.

The fact that production was able to make most items available by the end of the month, made sense that some stock be allocated to smaller orders early in the month while the larger orders are filled towards the end of the month.

4 Analysis of the Problems

We conducted a regression analysis on historical overtime information to determine the relationship between the overtime costs and workload in the distribution center. For this, we used weekly data on total overtime costs, total dozens shipped and total orders shipped for the weeks when the shipping requirements exceeded the distribution center's normal capacity. We were trying to support the assumption that the overtime costs were being caused by the additional shipping requirements and not some other factor.

The regression analysis showed that 82.89% of the variation in overtime costs was accounted for by the total dozens shipped and the total orders shipped. The regression equation indicated that for the weeks when the shipping requirements exceeded capacity, there was a $1.52 increase in overtime cost for every order shipped and a 15 cent increase for each dozen shipped. Given that total orders shipped alone accounted for most of the variation (82.20%) in the overtime costs, regression analysis supported the assumption that the total orders shipped had a greater impact on overtime costs than the dozens shipped.

Thus, the regression analysis proved statistically what was already believed and are enlisted here:

- Above capacity shipping requirements in the last part of the month contributed most of the materials handling overtime cost in the distribution center.

- The number of orders shipped during a week had a bigger impact on the overtime costs than the total dozens shipped.

Thus, increasing the number of orders filled during the earlier part of the month was the key to leveling the workload in the distribution center and reducing the overtime costs. We also believed that increasing the number of orders filled with the given inventories would reduce inventories, lower inventory holding costs, lead to faster inventory turnover, quicker response to customers, and earlier payments from customers as the customers will be getting their merchandise earlier in the month. These side benefits might well dwarf the actual savings in overtime costs.

5 New Allocation Scheme

The new allocation scheme proposed had four key features: prioritization of orders by the promise dates, preallocation of stock to promised dates, horizontal allocation by order, and the unallocation of nonreleasable orders. Orders were sorted by the earliest promise date so that those with earlier promise dates could be processed first. Preallocation of inventory provided protection to the promised availability dates given to the customers. Horizontal allocation by order allowed the system to determine if an order had been filled completely (or met the required fill percent). Unallocarion process prevented nonreleaseable orders from tying up inventory early in the month by releasing the inventory to fill other orders.

The first major change was to prioritize the orders by the promise dates. With input from company personnel, we designed a simple four step priority sequence. First, orders are sorted into three groups based on promise dates: previous month orders, current orders, and future dated orders. This sort ensured that orders eligible for shipping now and therefore, more likely to be filled, were given priority over future dated orders in the allocation process. Next, orders within the three groups were sorted according to pre-determined customer classes (based on previous year's sales volumes). The third sort was based on the dollar value of the orders so that orders with higher dollar volumes had an opportunity to be allocated first within each customer classification. Finally, the order registration number would serve as a tie-breaker, if needed.

The second major change was to allocate available inventory by order instead of by item as done in the existing allocation scheme. One of the main shortcomings of the current system was that high priority orders would tie up stock for several weeks without being completely filled. Allocating inventory by order made it possible to unallocate an order if it could not be filled completely (or did not meet the required fill percent) and to add the inventory back into the pool of available inventory to be made available to the subsequent orders.

At first, we were confident that the new priority scheme together with allocation by order, and unallocation of nonreleasable orders would help accomplish the objectives of the project. But, one major concern still remained. Under the new allocation scheme, the merchandise promised to an order for delivery in a certain

period could be given to an order with a later promised delivery date if the former order was nonreleasable. The priority scheme was designed to minimize this
risk but the possibility still remained. We worked hard to find a way to realize the
benefits of horizontal allocation by order and unallocation of nonreleasable orders
without increasing the potential for missed deliveries. We finally hit upon a solution
to this problem – preallocation of stock to promised delivery periods before actual
allocation to orders.

The preallocation process is relatively simple but important procedure. Before
actual allocation of stock to orders, the total quantity of each SKU required for
each promised availability period for all orders is computed. Available inventory
for the SKU is then reserved for each availability period starting with the earliest.
This process is repeated until all items have been "pre-allocated." This preallocation
procedure prevents stock that is needed for orders with earlier promised delivery
periods from being given to orders with later promised delivery periods during the
actual order allocation process.

When allocating to orders, inventory is drawn from the pool of inventory reserved
for each promise date for each item during the preallocation process. No inventory
is taken away from an earlier promise date and given to a later date. And as we are
still allocating by order, we can unallocate the orders that are not filled completely
and use the inventory for other orders on the order file.

With the preallocation process, the company could now take advantage of horizontal allocation by order and unallocation of nonreleasable orders while still
providing complete protection to the availability dates promised to the customers.
The unallocation of stock assigned to nonreleasable orders was still the key to the
new allocation scheme. This unallocation prevented nonreleasable orders from tying
up inventory early in the shipping month that could be used to completely fill and
ship other orders.

6 Testing of the New Allocation Scheme

We developed a simulation model that closely approximated the existing allocation
scheme in effect at the company and also, developed a model of the new allocation
scheme. Both models included consideration of priorities, the preallocation process, and different levels of availability of inventory. These allocation schemes were
compared with each other and also to an integer programming model and its linear programming relaxation. The integer programming formulation, given below,
was geared to provide the optimal solution. The linear programming formulation
involved relaxing the integer constraints of the integer programming model.

D_{ijt} = Demand for item i in order j for delivery in period t
I_{it} = Inventory of item i allocated to period t through the preallocation process
Y_j = 1 if order j has been filled; 0 otherwise

Maximize $\sum_{j} Y_j$

$$\sum_{j} D_{ijt} Y_j \leq I_{it} \text{for all } i \text{ and } t$$

All the four allocations schemes were tested with one another by generating 100 customer orders with ten inventory items and four promise dates. The procedures were tested in terms of the numbers of orders filled completely at different levels of availability of inventory. (An availability level of 80% implies that the inventory available is 80% of what is required to fill all the orders completely.)

The simulation tests showed that the new allocation scheme provided 6–141% increase in completed orders over the existing allocation scheme depending on the level of inventory. There was also an 8–180% improvement in the quantity allocated to completed orders. It was found that as the availability of inventory went down, the new allocation scheme did considerably better than the existing allocation scheme. The mathematical models provided almost no improvement in allocation over the results provided by the new allocation scheme until inventory availability dropped to under 60% of the required inventory. A test of the prioritization scheme showed that prioritization of orders by the quantity ordered produced less completed orders but allocated greater quantity compared to random prioritization (no prioritization).

7   On-Site Programming, Testing and Implementation

The modified allocation scheme was coded by the MIS staff of the company and then run in parallel with the existing allocation scheme for 5 days. Actual releases and inventory status were still based on the old scheme, so these tests could only provide a daily snapshot evaluation of the two schemes. The performance was monitored each day and the new allocation scheme consistently performed better than the existing scheme. During the 5 days of running the two schemes in parallel, the number of completed orders increased 41–89%, the number of dozens allocated to completed orders increased 36–90% and the dollar value of the completed orders increased 26–85%. There was also a substantial improvement in the number of dozens allocated to near-complete (70–99% complete) orders.

Encouraged by the performance of the new allocation scheme during the parallel run, an actual on-line test, where releases were made using the new allocation scheme, was conducted for 3 days. The on-line test was a great success. The computer program ran smoothly and processed the orders within a reasonable time frame. More importantly, the allocation scheme did what it was designed to do: increase the number of completed orders and release more orders earlier in the month. The test also identified a potential stock mismatch problem – there was stock shortage of 50,950 dozens though there were 245,994 dozens of unusable stock available during the test period. This pointed to the need for better forecasting and scheduling of production.

As the testing of the new allocation scheme yielded very positive results, the management decided to fully implement the new allocation scheme from the first shipping week of the following month. The new program executed well and the results for the first full shipping month under the new allocation scheme were very good. The new scheme generated more completed orders earlier in the month, i.e., 18.9% of the total orders completed during the month were completed during the first shipping week as compared to 11.9% during the same week in the previous year.

Also, for the rest of the month, the order workload was more balanced than the same month of the previous year. We measured the leveling in the workload by the mean of the absolute deviations from the ideal distribution of workload on a weekly basis (25% workload per week). On the basis of this measure, the leveling of workload in the distribution center improved by 41.5% as compared to the same month of the previous year. The proportions of orders shipped on a weekly basis before and after the implementation of the new allocation scheme are shown in Fig. 1.

As a result of leveling of the workload, the total labor cost for the distribution center declined by 22.6%. This was achieved by a decline of 19.7% in the regular labor cost and a decline of 45.8% in the overtime premium. Accordingly, the labor cost per dozen shipped declined 12.5% from $.65 per dozen shipped to $.57 per dozen shipped during the first month.

A comparison of the dozens shipped during the last week of the month highlighted another important aspect of the new scheme. Even though the percentage of orders shipped during the last week was lower than the same period of the previous year, the actual percentage of total dozens shipped was higher under the new allocation scheme. This was another indication that the new scheme was helping to

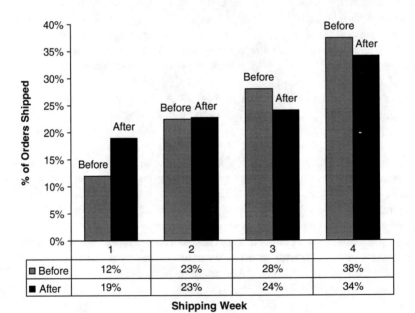

Fig. 1 Percentage of orders shipped by week

clear out many of the smaller orders by filling them completely earlier in the month, leaving the larger orders to be completed and picked in bulk at the end of the month.

Convinced of the results, the new allocation scheme was adopted by the company on a permanent basis. The scheme has been helping the company achieve a more balanced workload in the distribution center by producing more releasable orders earlier in the shipping month.

8   Conclusion

The work reported in this paper was an attempt to improve the allocation of available inventory to customer orders in order to maximize the number of orders filled at a large apparel manufacturing company. The motivation for this effort was to improve the productive use of warehouse manpower as well as the productive use of inventory. This goal was successfully achieved by the development and implementation of a new scheme for allocating inventory to customer orders.

The new scheme allowed the company to lower their overtime labor costs by allowing the distribution center to pick a larger number of the more time consuming (per dozen) smaller orders earlier in the month and avoid the month-end rush to fill both large and small orders. Evaluation of the new scheme was positive at every step, from simulation testing to the partial and full implementation of the scheme.

The resulting leveling in workload in the distribution center led to a 12.5% reduction in labor cost per dozen. More importantly, being able to fill more orders from the available inventory benefited the company in terms of lower inventories, more inventory turns, and a quicker response to customers. However, stock shortages were still limiting the performance of the order filling process and steps needed to be taken to improve the company's production planning and forecasting procedures as the next step.

References

Croxton KL (2003) The order fulfillment process. Int J Logist Manag 14(1):19–32

Kritchanchai D, MacCarthy BL (1999) Responsiveness of the order fulfilment process. Int J Oper Prod Manag 19(8):812–833

Pibernik R, Yadav P (2009) Inventory reservation and real-time order promising in a make-to-stock system. OR Spectrum 31(1):281–307

Turner TJ, Mendibil K, Bititci US, Daisley P, Breen THJ (2002) Improving the reliability of the customer order fullfilment process in a product identification company. Int J Prod Econ 78(1):99–107

Waller MA, Woolsey D, Seaker R (1995) Reengineering order fulfillment. Int J Logist Manag 6(2):1–10

Index